Troubleshooting Microsoft Technologies

The Ultimate Administrator's Repair Manual

Chris Wolf

ADDISON–WESLEY

Boston • San Francisco • New York • Toronto • Montreal
London • Munich • Paris • Madrid
Capetown • Sydney • Tokyo • Singapore • Mexico City

Many of the designations used by manufacturers and sellers to distinguish their products are claimed as trademarks. Where those designations appear in this book, and Addison-Wesley was aware of a trademark claim, the designations have been printed with initial cap letters or in all capitals.

The author and publisher have taken care in the preparation of this book, but make no expressed or implied warranty of any kind and assume no responsibility for errors or omissions. No liability is assumed for incidental or consequential damages in connection with or arising out of the use of the information or programs contained herein.

The publisher offers discounts on this book when ordered in quantity for bulk purchases and special sales. For more information, please contact:

U.S. Corporate and Government Sales
(800) 382-3419
corpsales@pearsontechgroup.com

For sales outside of the U.S., please contact:

International Sales
(317) 581-3793
international@pearsontechgroup.com

Visit Addison-Wesley on the Web: www.awprofessional.com

Library of Congress Cataloging-in-Publication Data
Wolf, Chris
   Troubleshooting Microsoft technologies: the ultimate administrator's repair manual /
   Chris Wolf.
       p. cm.
   ISBN 0-321-13345-5 (alk. paper)
   1. Software maintenance. 2. Microsoft software. I. Title.

QA76.76.S64W64 2003
005.1'6--dc21   2003052157

Copyright © 2003 by Pearson Education, Inc.

All rights reserved. No part of this publication may be reproduced, stored in a retrieval system, or transmitted, in any form, or by any means, electronic, mechanical, photocopying, recording, or otherwise, without the prior consent of the publisher. Printed in the United States of America. Published simultaneously in Canada.

For information on obtaining permission for use of material from this work, please submit a written request to:

Pearson Education, Inc.
Rights and Contracts Department
75 Arlington Street, Suite 300
Boston, MA 02116
Fax: (617) 848-7047

ISBN 0-321-13345-5
Text printed on recycled paper
1 2 3 4 5 6 7 8 9 10—CRS—0706050403
First printing, June 2003

This book is dedicated to Carol Carr, whose impact on my writing cannot be measured by mere words.

"I have come to believe that a great teacher is a great artist and that there are as few as there are any other great artists. Teaching might even be the greatest of the arts since the medium is the human mind and spirit."

—John Steinbeck

Contents

Preface xxix

Chapter 1: Introduction 1
    Chapter 2: Fundamental Networking 2
    Chapter 3: Troubleshooting Techniques 2
    Chapter 4: Monitoring and Diagnostic Tools 3
    Chapter 5: Client-Server Troubleshooting 3
    Chapter 6: Office XP 3
    Chapter 7: Disk Subsystems 4
    Chapter 8: DNS 4
    Chapter 9: WINS 5
    Chapter 10: DHCP 5
    Chapter 11: Network and Application Services 5
    Chapter 12: Routing and Remote Access 6
    Chapter 13: Active Directory 6
    Appendices 7
    Summary 7

Chapter 2: Fundamental Networking 9
    Network Protocols 9
        NetBEUI 10
        NWLink (IPX/SPX) 11
            Frame Type 12
            Internal Network Number 12
            External Network Number 13
        TCP/IP Basics 13
            Binary Conversion 13
            IP Address Structure 14
            TCP/IP in a Routed Environment 17
            NetBIOS Names versus FQDNs 18
            Name Resolution Methods 18

v

Name Resolution with DNS   19
   Resolver Cache   20
   Hosts   21
   DNS Query Types   22
   NetBIOS Cache   22
   WINS/Broadcast/LMHosts   22
WINS   23
DHCP Overview   24
   DHCP Lease   24
   DHCP Scope   25
   Reservation   25
   DHCP Options   26
   DHCP Relay Agent   26
   Automatic Private IP Addressing   26
Need More Knowledge?   27
Summary   28

Chapter 3: Troubleshooting Techniques   29

Optimism versus Pessimism   29
Troubleshooting Process Overview   30
Identifying the Problem   31
Documenting the History of the Problem   31
Analyzing the Current Environment   34
   Operating System State   35
   Latest Virus Scan   35
   Network Configuration   36
   Installed Applications   36
   Firmware   37
   Good Computer, Bad Computer   38
Documenting Processes Involved in the Problem   38
   A Picture's Worth a Thousand Words   38
Eliminating What's Right   40
   Don't Reinvent the Wheel   40
   Document What You Do!   41
   Never Forget the Obvious   41
   Move from the Big Picture to Small Details   41
   If You Pay for Support, Use It!   41
Correcting the Problem   42
   When Speed Is of the Essence   42
   Don't Use Duct Tape   42
   Process-Oriented Corrective Action   43
Testing the Corrective Action   44
Following Up   44
Summary   45

Chapter 4: Monitoring and Diagnostic Tools 47

Operating System Tools 47
Disk Management Tools 51
   Command Line Tools 51
      chkdsk 51
      chkntfs 52
      defrag 54
   GUI Tools 56
      Disk Management 56
      Disk Defragmenter 57
Network Monitoring and Troubleshooting Tools 58
   Command Line Tools 58
      arp 59
      getmac 60
      hostname 60
      nbtstat 61
      netdiag (ST) 62
      Net Services Commands 64
      netstat 67
      pathping 69
      ping 71
      telnet 72
      tracert 73
   GUI Tools 75
      Network Diagnostics 75
      Network Monitor 75
Performance Monitoring Tools 79
   Command Line Tools 79
      memsnap (ST) 79
      pagefileconfig 80
      pfmon (ST) 83
      pmon (ST) 86
      taskkill 86
      tasklist 88
      uptime (RK) 90
   GUI Tools 91
      System Monitor (Perfmon) 92
      Task Manager 94
Security Management Tools 95
   Command Line Tools 95
      cacls 95
      efsinfo (ST) 97
      takeown 98

GUI Tools   99
    Security Configuration and Analysis   99
    Security Templates   101
System Management Tools   101
    Command Line Tools   101
        driverquery   101
        eventquery   102
        eventtriggers   104
        systeminfo   107
        sfc   108
    GUI Tools   109
        Computer Management   110
        Event Viewer   110
        MSinfo32   111
        Windows Update   113
Troubleshooting Wizards   115
Freeware Tools   117
    Subnetting with the IP Subnet Calculator   118
    Testing Throughput with Netperf   119
    Remotely Controlling Systems with TightVNC   121
        Configuring the TightVNC Server   123
        Using TightVNC Viewer   123
Summary   125

Chapter 5: Client-Server Troubleshooting   127

Troubleshooting Tools   127
    Automated System Recovery   127
    driverquery   129
    msconfig (Windows Server 2003)   131
    msicuu (ST)   133
    Online Crash Analysis   134
    Remote Desktop and Remote Assistance   135
        Allowing Remote Desktop Connections   136
        Connecting to a Remote System   137
        Using Remote Assistance   139
    Shadow Copy (Windows Server 2003 Systems Only)   141
        Server-Initiated Recovery   143
        Client-Initiated Recovery   145
    System Restore (XP Clients Only)   145
Troubleshooting System Startup   149
    Last Known Good Configuration   150
    Safe Mode   150
    Safe Mode with Networking   151
    Safe Mode with Command Prompt   151
    Enable Boot Logging   151

Enable VGA Mode   151
Directory Services Restore Mode   152
Debugging Mode   152
Disabling Services and Drivers with the Recovery Console   152
   Recovery Console Diagnostic Commands   152
      listsvc   153
      enable   153
      disable   154
      Additional Commands   155
   Accessing the Recovery Console   155
Repairing the OS Installation   156
Troubleshooting System Shutdown   157
Troubleshooting Devices   159
   Checking Device Status   161
   Rolling Back Device Drivers   162
   Updating Device Drivers   162
   Uninstalling Devices   163
   Disabling Devices   164
Troubleshooting Fax Problems   164
   Diagnosing Fax Problems   164
   Testing the Solution   165
Troubleshooting Display Problems   166
Troubleshooting Internet Connection Sharing   167
Troubleshooting Application Compatibility   169
   Using the Program Compatibility Wizard   170
Summary   171

Chapter 6: Office XP   173

Office Troubleshooting Tools   173
   Application Recovery   173
   Automatic Recovery   174
   Detect and Repair   175
   Document Recovery   176
   Open and Repair   176
   Setup   178
      From Add/Remove Programs   179
      From the Setup CD or the Network   180
Troubleshooting Office Setup   181
   Eliminating the Obvious   181
   Using the Setup Log Files   182
Access Errors and Solutions   183
   Using the Compact and Repair Tool   184
   Manually Repairing a Database   185
      Problems Running Reports   186
      Problems with Macros or Modules   187

Problems with a Database Table   187
Excel Errors and Solutions   188
   Repairing Corrupted Spreadsheets   188
   Isolating and Resolving Formula Errors   191
Outlook Errors and Solutions   192
   Testing Outlook Configuration   192
PowerPoint Errors and Solutions   195
   When the Problem Resulted from a Modification to the Presentation   196
   When the Problem Resulted from a Specific File Being Opened   196
      Open Presentation Version in Temp Folder   196
      Extract Corrupted Slides   197
      Apply Corrupted Presentation as a Template   197
   When the Problem Resulted from Any File Being Opened   198
Word Errors and Solutions   199
   Resolving Problems with the Support.dot Troubleshooting Template   199
      Installing the Troubleshooting Template   200
      Using the Troubleshooting Template   200
   General Word Troubleshooting   206
      Replacing Corrupt User Dictionaries   207
      Replacing Corrupt AutoCorrect Files   207
      Replacing Corrupt Fonts   208
      Replacing Corrupt Spelling and Grammar Files   209
Summary   209

Chapter 7: Disk Subsystems   211

Windows Server 2003/XP Disk Architecture 101   211
   Basic and Dynamic Disks   212
   Master Boot Record   212
   Boot Sector   213
   The boot.ini File   213
   Master File Table   216
   GPT Disks   217
Disk Troubleshooting Tools   217
   bootcfg   217
      bootcfg /addsw   218
      bootcfg /copy   219
      bootcfg /dbg1394   219
      bootcfg /debug   220
      bootcfg /default   221
      bootcfg /delete   222
      bootcfg /ems   222
      bootcfg /query   223
      bootcfg /raw   223
      bootcfg /rmsw   224
      bootcfg /timeout   225

dmdiag (ST)   225
fsutil   226
    fsutil behavior   226
    fsutil dirty   229
    fsutil file   229
    fsutil fsinfo   230
    fsutil hardlink   231
    fsutil objectid   232
    fsutil quota   233
    fsutil reparsepoint   234
    fsutil sparse   235
    fsutil USN   236
    fsutil volume   239
ftonline (ST)   239
recover   240
Diagnosing and Repairing Boot Sector and MBR Problems   241
Repairing Failed Disks with Disk Management   242
    Failed Spanned or Striped Volumes   244
    Failed Mirrored Volumes (RAID 1)   245
    Failed RAID 5 Volumes   246
Common Stop Messages   246
    Stop 0x00000024 (NTFS File System) or Stop 0x00000023
    (FAT File System)   246
    Stop 0x00000050 (Page Fault in Nonpaged Area)   247
    Stop 0x00000077 (Kernel Stack Inpage Error)   248
    Stop 0x0000007A (Kernel Data Inpage Error)   249
    Stop 0x0000007B (Inaccessible Boot Device)   249
Summary   250

Chapter 8: DNS   251

DNS Architecture   251
    Essential Terminology   251
        Dynamic Updates   252
        Recursion and Iteration   252
        Forwarders   253
        Caching-Only Server   254
        Resource Record Types   254
    DNS Hierarchy   255
    Name Resolution Process   256
    DNS Zones   258
        Zone Types   258
        Zone Configurations   258
        Zone Transfers   259
        Zone Delegation   260

Advanced Configuration 260
    Round Robin 261
    Netmask Ordering 262
    BIND Secondaries 262
  Client Considerations 262
    Windows Server 2003 Enhancements 263
DNS Troubleshooting Tools 263
  DNS MMC 263
    Debug Logging 264
    Event Logging 265
    Monitoring 267
  dnscmd (ST) 267
    clearcache 268
    Statistics 269
  dnslint (ST) 270
  nslookup 272
    exit 274
    ls 274
    lserver 276
    server 277
    set 277
    view 282
    Troubleshooting with nslookup 283
Troubleshooting DNS Clients 287
Troubleshooting DNS Servers 289
  Incorrect Query Results 289
  Cannot Access Resources Outside of Domain 290
  Server Not Responding to Requests 290
  Troubleshooting DNS-DHCP Integration 291
  Zone Transfer Problems 292
  DNS Error Events 293
Summary 295

Chapter 9: WINS 297

WINS Architecture 297
  What's New? 298
    Windows 2000 Enhancements 298
    Windows Server 2003 Enhancements 298
  WINS Relationships and Replication 299
  Filling in the Gaps 301
    Static Mapping 302
    WINS Proxy Agent 302
WINS Troubleshooting Tools 303
  WINS MMC 303
    Event Logging 304

netsh wins   305
   dump   306
   check   307
   init   309
   show   311
Troubleshooting WINS Clients   313
Troubleshooting WINS Servers   315
Troubleshooting Replication   317
Troubleshooting WINS-DHCP Integration   317
Recovering a Corrupted WINS Database   319
Summary   322

Chapter 10: DHCP   323

DHCP Architecture   323
  What's New?   324
    Windows 2000 Enhancements   324
    Windows Server 2003 Enhancements   324
  Scopes   325
    Standard   325
    Superscopes   325
    Multicast Scopes   326
  Classes   327
    Vendor Classes   327
    User Classes   328
  Conflict Detection   328
DHCP Troubleshooting Tools   329
  DHCP MMC   330
  Audit Logging   330
  dhcploc (ST)   334
Troubleshooting DHCP Clients   334
Troubleshooting DHCP Servers   336
  Troubleshooting DHCP Scope Migration   338
  Troubleshooting DHCP-RAS Integration   339
    Clients Unable to Access Resources Beyond RAS's Subnet   340
    Clients Unable to Access Resources on RAS's Subnet   341
  Troubleshooting DHCP Relay Agents   342
  Recovering a Corrupted DHCP Database   343
    Recovering from Backup   343
Summary   346

Chapter 11: Network and Application Services   347

The Lay of the Land   348
  Print Services   348
    Advanced Settings   349
    Printer Permissions   350

Terminal Services   350
Distributed File System   351
Remote Installation Services   352
Client and Gateway Services for NetWare   353
Network Service Troubleshooting Tools   355
DFS MMC   355
dfsutil (ST)   355
General dfsutil Switches   356
/clean   356
/export   357
/import   357
/importroot   358
/pktflush   359
/purgemupcache   360
/purgewin2kstaticsitetable   360
/showwin2kstaticsitetable   360
/spcflush   361
/unmapftroot   361
/updatewin2kstaticsitetable   361
health_chk (ST)   362
ipxroute   364
lpq   365
prndrvr.vbs   365
prndrvr.vbs –a (Add Driver)   366
prndrvr.vbs –d (Delete Driver)   367
prndrvr.vbs –l (List Drivers)   368
prndrvr.vbs –x (Remove All Unused Drivers)   369
prnmngr.vbs   369
prnqctl.vbs   370
query   371
query process   371
query session   372
query termserver   373
query user   374
reset session   375
Terminal Services Manager MMC   376
Troubleshooting Printers   376
General Printing Concerns   377
Network Printers   378
Administrator Configures the Share   379
Client Connects to Network Printer   379
Client Application Generates Job   380
Client Sends Job to Print Server   381
Server Spools and Queues Job   381
Server Sends Job to Print Device   382
Print Device Prints Job   383

Troubleshooting Terminal Services   383
   Troubleshooting Server Connection Problems   383
   Troubleshooting Session Problems   385
Troubleshooting DFS   386
   Inaccessible Root   387
   Inaccessible Share Folder   387
   User Permissions   388
Troubleshooting Remote Installation Services   389
     Client Does Not Get Past "DHCP"   390
     Client Does Not Get Past "BINL"   390
     Client Does Not Get Past "TFTP"   390
Troubleshooting NetWare Integration   391
Summary   392

Chapter 12: Routing and Remote Access   393

RRAS Architecture   393
   Remote Access Servers   394
     Multilink   395
     LCP Extensions   395
     Remote Access Policies   395
     Remote Access Profiles   396
     User Dial-in Properties   396
   Virtual Private Networks   396
   Routing Protocols   398
   Network Address Translation   399
RAS Troubleshooting Tools   399
   atmadm   399
   iasparse (ST)   402
   Netsh RAS Diagnostics   403
     dump   403
     show all   404
     show cmtracing   406
     set cmtracing   406
     show configuration   406
     show installation   407
     show logs   408
     show modemtracing   409
     set modemtracing   410
     show rastracing   410
     set rastracing   410
     show securityeventlog   410
     set securityeventlog   410
     show tracefacilities   411
     set tracefacilities   411

netsh routing   411
   netsh routing ip autodhcp   411
   netsh routing ip relay   412
   netsh routing ip dnsproxy   414
   netsh routing ip igmp   414
   netsh routing ip nat   416
   netsh routing ip ospf   416
   netsh routing ip rip   418
   netsh routing ip routerdiscovery   420
portqry (ST)   420
route   422
RRAS MMC   424

Troubleshooting RAS   425
  Troubleshooting RAS Client Connections   426
   Problems with User Systems   426
   Problems with the RAS Server   427
  Troubleshooting the RAS Server Network   428

Troubleshooting Routing   429
  General Routing Problems   429
  Troubleshooting NAT   430
   Problems with NAT Clients   431
   Problems with the NAT Server   431
  Troubleshooting DHCP Relay Agents   432
  Troubleshooting Demand-Dial Routing   433
   Router Not Dialing on Demand   433
   Data Not Reaching Beyond Calling or Answering Router   434
  Troubleshooting RIP   435
  Troubleshooting OSPF   435

Troubleshooting VPN Access   437
  Troubleshooting Remote Access VPNs   438
   Server Connection Problems   438
   Resource Access Problems   440
  Troubleshooting Router-to-Router VPNs   440

Summary   441

Chapter 13: Active Directory   443

AD Architectural Overview   443
  Forests and Domains   444
  Organizational Units   446
  Sites   446
  Domain Controllers   447
  Group Policy Objects   449
  Active Directory Functional Levels   449
   Domain Functional Levels   450
   Forest Functional Levels   451

What's New?   452
AD Troubleshooting Tools   453
   acldiag (ST)   453
   Active Directory MMCs   456
      Active Directory Users and Computers   456
      Active Directory Domains and Trusts   457
      Active Directory Sites and Services   458
      Active Directory Schema   458
   dcdiag (ST)   460
   gpresult   463
   gpupdate   464
   nltest (ST)   465
   ntdsutil   467
      authoritative restore   468
      files   469
      metadata cleanup   472
      roles   474
      semantic database analysis   476
   Replmon (ST)   476
   Resultant Set of Policy   476
Troubleshooting Domain Controllers   480
   Cannot Connect to a Windows 2000 Domain Controller   481
   DCPromo Fails to Promote a New Server to Be a Domain Controller   481
   Receive "Domain Not Found," "Server Not Available," or
      "RPF Server Is Unavailable" Error Message   481
   Unable to Log On Locally   482
   Unable to Uninstall Active Directory   483
   Group Membership Changes Fail   483
   Security Principals Cannot Be Created   483
Troubleshooting Replication   484
   Access Denied Error Occurs When Attempting Manual Replication   485
   Event ID 1265 in the Directory Service Log   485
   Event ID 1311 Appears in Event Log   486
   Slow Replication between Sites   486
Troubleshooting Group Policy Objects   487
   Loopback Processing   488
   Block Inheritance versus No Override   489
   Troubleshooting Considerations   490
Troubleshooting the AD Schema   492
   Cannot Modify or Extend Schema   492
   Cannot Add Attributes to a Class   492
   Cannot Connect to a Windows 2000 Domain Controller   493
Troubleshooting Trusts   493
   Clients Cannot Access Resources in Trusted Domain   493
   Errors Occur After Upgrade from Windows NT   493

AD Backup and Recovery 494
Summary 495

Appendix A: Troubleshooting Command Line Reference 497

acldiag (ST) 497
arp 498
atmadm 499
bootcfg 501
   bootcfg /addsw 501
   bootcfg /copy 502
   bootcfg /dbg1394 503
   bootcfg /debug 503
   bootcfg /default 504
   bootcfg /delete 504
   bootcfg /ems 505
   bootcfg /query 506
   bootcfg /raw 506
   bootcfg /rmsw 506
   bootcfg /timeout 507
cacls 507
chkdsk 509
chkntfs 510
dcdiag (ST) 510
defrag 513
dfsutil (ST) 514
   General dfsutil Switches 514
   /clean 515
   /export 515
   /import 515
   /importroot 516
   /pktflush 517
   /purgemupcache 517
   /purgewin2kstaticsitetable 517
   /showwin2kstaticsitetable 518
   /spcflush 518
   /unmapftroot 518
   /updatewin2kstaticsitetable 518
dhcploc (ST) 519
dmdiag (ST) 519
dnscmd (ST) 520
   clearcache 521
   statistics 521
dnslint (ST) 522
driverquery 523

efsinfo (ST)   524
eventquery   525
eventtriggers /create   526
eventtriggers /delete   528
eventtriggers /query   528
fsutil behavior   529
fsutil dirty   530
fsutil file   531
fsutil fsinfo   532
fsutil hardlink   533
fsutil objectid   533
fsutil quota   534
fsutil reparsepoint   535
fsutil sparse   535
fsutil USN   536
fsutil volume   538
ftonline (ST)   538
getmac   538
gpresult   539
gpupdate   540
health_chk (ST)   541
hostname   543
iasparse (ST)   543
ipxroute   544
lpq   545
memsnap (ST)   545
nbtstat   546
netdiag (ST)   547
net start | stop | pause | continue   548
net statistics   548
net session   549
net view   549
Netsh RAS Diagnostics   550
   dump   550
   show all   550
   show cmtracing   551
   set cmtracing   551
   show configuration   552
   show installation   553
   show logs   554
   show modemtracing   555
   set modemtracing   555
   show rastracing   555
   set rastracing   555

show securityeventlog 555
set securityeventlog 556
show tracefacilities 556
set tracefacilities 556
netsh routing 556
  netsh routing ip autodhcp 556
    show global 557
    show interface 557
  netsh routing ip relay 557
    show interface 557
    show global 558
    show ifstats 558
  netsh routing ip dnsproxy 559
    show global 559
    show interface 559
  netsh routing ip igmp 559
    show interface 559
    show global 560
    show ifstats 560
    show iftable 560
    show grouptable 560
    show rasgrouptable 560
    show proxygrouptable 561
  netsh routing ip nat 561
    show global 561
    show interface 561
  netsh routing ip ospf 562
    show global 562
    show virtif 562
    show interface 562
    show routefilter 563
    show protofilter 563
    show area 563
  netsh routing ip rip 564
    show interface 564
    show flags 564
    show global 564
    show ifstats 564
    show ifbinding 565
  netsh routing ip routerdiscovery 565
netsh wins 566
  dump 566
  check 567
    check database 567

check version   568
init   568
   init backup   568
   init compact   569
   init pull   569
   init push   569
   init replicate   570
   init restore   570
show   570
   show info   570
   show partner   571
   show partnerproperties   571
   show pullpartnerconfig   572
   show pushpartnerconfig   572
   show server   572
netstat   572
nltest (ST)   573
nslookup   574
   exit   575
   ls   575
   lserver   576
   server   576
   set   577
      set all   577
      set class   577
      set d2   578
      set debug   578
      set defname   578
      set domain   578
      set ignore   578
      set port   579
      set querytype   579
      set recurse   579
      set retry   579
      set root   580
      set search   580
      set srchlist   580
      set timeout   580
      set vc   580
   view   581
pagefileconfig /change   581
pagefileconfig /create   582
pagefileconfig /delete   583
pagefileconfig /query   583

pathping 584
pfmon (ST) 585
ping 586
pmon (ST) 588
portqry (ST) 588
prndrvr.vbs 589
   prndrvr.vbs –a (Add Driver) 590
   prndrvr.vbs –d (Delete Driver) 591
   prndrvr.vbs –l (List Drivers) 592
   prndrvr.vbs –x (Remove All Unused Drivers) 593
prnmngr.vbs 593
prnqctl.vbs 594
query 594
   query process 595
   query session 596
   query termserver 596
   query user 597
recover 598
reset session 598
route 599
sfc 600
systeminfo 601
takeown 602
taskkill 602
tasklist 604
telnet 605
tracert 606

Appendix B: Common Error Codes and Messages 607

Device Errors 607
   Code 1—The device is not configured correctly 608
   Code 3—The driver for this device might be corrupted… 608
   Code 10—This device cannot start 609
   Code 12—This device cannot find enough free resources that it can use… 609
   Code 14—This device cannot work properly until you restart your computer 611
   Code 16—Windows cannot identify all the resources this device uses 611
   Code 18—Reinstall the drivers for this device 611
   Code 19—Windows cannot start this hardware device because its configuration… 611
   Code 22—This device is disabled 612
   Code 24—This device is not present, is not working properly… 612
   Code 28—The drivers for this device are not installed 612
   Code 29—This device is disabled because the firmware of the device… 613
   Code 31—This device is not working properly because Windows cannot load the driver… 613

Code 32—A driver (service) for this device has been disabled. An
       alternate driver... 613
Code 33—Windows cannot determine which resources are required for this device 614
Code 34—Windows cannot determine the settings for this device... 614
Code 35—Your computer's system firmware does not include
       enough information... 614
Code 36—This device is requesting a PCI interrupt but is configured for an ISA... 614
Code 37—Windows cannot initialize the device driver for this hardware 615
Code 38—Windows cannot load the device driver for this hardware... 615
Code 39—Windows cannot load the device driver for this hardware... 615
Code 40—Windows cannot access this hardware because its service key... 616
Code 41—Windows successfully loaded the device driver for this hardware... 616
Code 42—Windows cannot load the driver for this hardware... 616
Code 43—Windows has stopped this device because it has reported problems 617
Code 44—An application or service has shut down this hardware device 617
Code 45—Currently this hardware device is not connected to the computer 617
Code 47—Windows cannot use this hardware device... 618
Code 48—The software for this device has been blocked from starting... 618
Code 49—Windows cannot start new hardware devices because the system hive is
       too large 618
Stop Errors 619
    Stop 0x0000000A (IRQL Not Less or Equal) 619
    Stop 0x0000001E (KMode Exception Not Handled) 620
    Stop 0x00000024 (NTFS File System) or Stop 0x00000023
      (FAT File System) 621
    Stop 0x0000002E (Data Bus Error) 621
    Stop 0x0000003F (No More System PTES) 622
    Stop 0x00000050 (Page Fault in Nonpaged Area) 623
    Stop 0x00000077 (Kernel Stack Inpage Error) 624
    Stop 0x00000079 (Mismatched HAL) 625
    Stop 0x0000007A (Kernel Data Inpage Error) 625
    Stop 0x0000007B (Inaccessible Boot Device) 625
    Stop 0x0000007F (Unexpected Kernel Mode Trap) 626
    Stop 0x0000009F (Driver Power State Failure) 627
    Stop 0xBE (Attempted Write to Read Only Memory) 628
    Stop 0xC2 (Bad Pool Caller) 628
    Stop 0x000000CE (Driver Unloaded without Canceling Pending Operations) 629
    Stop 0x000000D1 (Driver IRQL Not Less or Equal) 629
    Stop 0x000000D8 (Driver Used Excessive PTES) 630
    Stop 0x000000EA (Thread Stuck in Device Driver) 631
    Stop 0x000000ED (Unmountable Boot Volume) 631
    Stop 0x000000F2 (Hardware Interrupt Storm) 631
    Stop 0x0000021A (Status System Process Terminated) 632
    Stop 0x00000221 (Status Image Checksum Mismatch) 633

Appendix C: Third-Party Tools   637

Executive Software   637
  Diskeeper   637
    Measuring Fragmentation   638
    Fitting the Pieces Together   638
    Analysis versus Defragmentation   638
    Graphic Analysis Display   639
    Analysis Report   639
    Different Defragmentation Modes   639
    Frag Guard   641
    Getting the Most from Diskeeper   641
  Undelete   642
    Recovery Bin   642
    Undelete From Disk   642
    Emergency Undelete   642
    Using Undelete   642
    Using Undelete From Disk   643
  Sitekeeper   643
    Using Sitekeeper   644
    Using PushInstaller   644
    Checking License Compliance   645
    Checking Hardware Inventory   647
FullArmor—FAZAM 2000   648
  FAZAM 2000 GP Repository   649
  FAZAM 2000 Administrator   649
  FAZAM 2000 Policy and Planning   650
  FAZAM 2000 Auditing and Diagnostics   650
  Installing FAZAM 2000   650
    Opening the FAZAM 2000 Tools   651
SmartLine   652
  Active Network Monitor   652
    Installing Active Network Monitor   653
    Collecting Diagnostic Information   654
  Active Ports   654
    Installing Active Ports   654
    Using Active Ports   655
  Active Server Watcher   656
    Installing Active Server Watcher   656
    Configuring Active Server Watcher   657
  Remote Task Manager   658
    Installing Remote Task Manager   658
    Remotely Installing the RTM Service on Other Systems   659
    Querying the State of a Remote System   660

TechTracker   660
    Installing the TechTracker ITX Demo   661
    Monitoring Systems with TechTracker ITX   662
Tsarfin   664
  IPMonitor   665
    Installing IPMonitor   665
    Using IPMonitor   666
  NetInfo   667
    Installing NetInfo   668
    Using NetInfo   669
Wildpackets—iNetTools   670
    Installing iNetTools   671
    Using iNetTools   671

Index   673

Preface

Many have long considered the act of troubleshooting to be more art than science. However, with the right methodology, one can systematically analyze and repair problems affecting an individual computer or an entire network. Whether you are an end user looking to exert a new level of problem solving independence or are an experienced help desk analyst or systems administrator, this book has something for you. The book not only provides answers to some of the most puzzling Microsoft computer problems, but also presents the answers in the context of the troubleshooting methodology most highly regarded in the computer industry, allowing you to learn and apply a proven troubleshooting technique to any computer problem.

The book begins by presenting the most common approaches for diagnosing and resolving problems, and then moves on to documenting all of the Microsoft troubleshooting tools at your disposal. With a troubleshooting foundation securely in place, the book then focuses exclusively on individual problem sets, including

- Common Windows Server 2003 and Windows XP problems
- Microsoft Office
- Hard disk errors
- DNS and WINS
- DHCP
- Routing and network services
- Active Directory

With chapters organized and dedicated to specific problems, this book is an invaluable tool that you can use in repairing software glitches on all of the computers you manage. Since you cannot solve problems without understanding the underlying fundamentals of the technology involved, you will appreciate the concise technical introductions at the beginning of each chapter. So if you are called on to resolve a DNS problem in which you have little experience, using this reference will allow you to quickly get up to speed with DNS concepts and in turn solve the error.

While one can attempt to solve problems with just the available tools that come with the operating system, troubleshooting is much easier with the help of several tools provided by third-party vendors. When troubleshooting problems such as those that involve network name resolution or group policy objects in the Active Directory, you will be able to find the problem faster with one of the 15 third-party tools that are included with this book's companion CD.

Repairing computer problems requires the right approach, an understanding of the technologies involved, knowledge of the available troubleshooting tools, and insight into the most common operating system and application problem areas. Microsoft networks comprise a vast array of technologies, each of which is covered by its own technical reference. If you need to troubleshoot many of these technologies, you could carry 20 books around with you, which may provide some troubleshooting information on each technology, or you can carry this single reference, which details troubleshooting for nearly all of the software dilemmas you are likely to encounter.

Acknowledgments

Writing a book of this magnitude has certainly been a monumental task, and to that end I owe thanks to many. First, I would like to thank you. Without a reading audience, this book would not exist. Thank you for your support of this and of other books that I have written to date.

Next I would like to thank my wonderful wife, Melissa. Melissa has been by my side throughout many of my writing adventures and is always willing to make the extra cup of coffee or do whatever it takes to lend support.

I must also thank my mother at this time, since she is perhaps my greatest PR person and has always supported my dreams.

In ensuring that this book was at the highest technical level, Addison-Wesley had many highly qualified IT professionals read and critique this book. Among those whose contributions enhanced the finished manuscript are Peter Bruzzese, Michael Kelly, Joel Rosenblatt, Glenn Berry, and David Chunn. I must especially thank James Edelen, who went above and beyond to truly make this manuscript rock.

Several contributors at Addison-Wesley were also extremely dedicated to this book's success. First, I must thank my editor, Karen Gettman, who truly won me over with her commitment to quality. Next, I must thank Emily Frey, whose persistence, dedication, and fortitude elevated the content of this book to levels that I could not have envisioned. Next, I must thank my copy editor, Debby English, whose keen eye for detail truly made this book enjoyable to read. Finally, I must also thank Marcy Barnes-Henrie, Curt Johnson, and the rest of the Addison-Wesley team for their hard work in making this book's publication and success a reality.

One of the true values of this book is the multitude of software that is available on the companion CD. I must thank the following software vendors for so graciously allowing their products to accompany this book: Executive Software, FullArmor Corporation, Hewlett-Packard, SmartLine Incorporated, TechTracker Incorporated, TightVNC, Tsarfin Computing, and Wildpackets Incorporated.

Finally, I must thank several technical associates that also added to the content of this book with their own tips and war stories. Please appreciate the contributions and efforts of the following IT warriors: Mike Dahlmeier, Kevin Low, Tracy Kirsteins, Stacy Nekervis, Jeff Rembish, Pete Gilmore, Mohammad Shanehsaz, Jonathan Cragle, Victor Abyad, Jim Souliotis, Dave Swiatek, Bill Leroy, Jon Randolph, Barry Kaufman, and Paul Mancuso.

1

Introduction

Pause and think for a moment about the perfect network. Imagine an enterprise network that is without failure of any type, and users that never ask for help or have problems with their systems. Now pinch yourself and wake up because you are surely dreaming. No matter how large or small the networks you manage, odds are that some type of failure creeps up on either an hourly, daily, or weekly basis.

For many, troubleshooting has become an art, or even an act of wizardry. Senior wizards roam some networks, magically dispelling problems as they occur, while junior administrators try to learn from their wisdom. While wisdom is certainly beneficial to troubleshooting any environment, and the need for real-world experience is surely helpful, how can one keep up with today's vast interrelationships of network technologies? In trying to merely keep up with technology, many learn enough about a service or technology to implement it, but then sometimes take hours to fix it when it breaks. The purpose of this book is not to tell you everything you need to know to manage network services and clients in a Microsoft network infrastructure. Instead, you will see how to approach, diagnose, and resolve problems on Microsoft networks.

This book starts at the roots of network troubleshooting and grows from there. After being introduced to Microsoft network infrastructure and fundamental troubleshooting methodology, you can then move on to reading about the technology where the problem exists. For example, if you are experiencing a DNS problem, check out the DNS chapter. If a user is having a problem opening a Word document, turn to the Office XP chapter. For each troubleshooting scenario, this book provides you with the tools and know-how to diagnose and quickly resolve a problem.

Since the array of technologies on Microsoft networks is so vast, this book focuses on the foundational technologies that are common to nearly all Microsoft networks. In troubleshooting Microsoft networks, while you could get by with Microsoft tools alone, you can significantly streamline the troubleshooting process by using the many third-party applications available. In addition to documenting the available Microsoft tools, this book includes over 15 third-party tools on the companion CD-ROM. Each of these tools is documented in Appendix C.

So that you can fully understand the flow of this book, the next 14 sections describe the purpose of each chapter as well as provide details on the book's included appendices.

Chapter 2: Fundamental Networking

This chapter is primarily designed for those with little to moderate experience with Microsoft networks. If you are confident in your understanding of network services such as DNS, WINS, and DHCP and have a solid command of TCP/IP networking, you can get by with merely skimming this chapter. Far too often, many technical books jump to assumptions, sometimes at the expense of the reader, which is something that this book avoids.

Too much is often assumed in IT, including an understanding of the fundamentals. Chapter 2 clears the smoke on Microsoft network components, providing quick-to-read and easy-to-understand explanations of Microsoft networking. Topics covered in this chapter include

- An overview of network protocols, including TCP/IP and IPX/SPX
- DNS
- DHCP
- WINS

After a quick review of the fundamentals, you can then move on to reading about the proven troubleshooting techniques that are highlighted throughout this reference.

Chapter 3: Troubleshooting Techniques

Many consider troubleshooting a journey filled with many stops, starts, twists, and turns. As on any journey, whether it's a trip to the grocery store or a vacation to Wally World, you have to take a series of sequential steps to reach your ultimate goal. For most, these steps have been repeated so often that they are now instinctive. When you go to the grocery store, you get in the car, start it, check the gauges, stop for gas along the way if it is needed, make a series of turns that get you to the store, and eventually park the car.

While many would like to jump in the car and drive off in the midst of a troubleshooting dilemma, that's not the point here. When you understand the techniques, troubleshooting can become as logical as driving a car. You need to know where and how to start, what to do in the middle, and what to do when you get there. Think of this chapter as "driver's ed" for troubleshooters.

Chapter 4: Monitoring and Diagnostic Tools

Resolving problems requires knowledge of what tools to use in each unique circumstance. Think of driving a car without having knowledge that the brake pedal helps you stop. Instead, you plan ahead and put the car in neutral about a half mile before each intersection. This approach may get you where you want to go (and maybe a few tickets as well) but will certainly take a lot longer.

The same can be said for troubleshooting. For most situations, there are likely dozens of tools available for use, some that you are aware of and others that you may have never heard of. This chapter begins to build your troubleshooting toolbox, outlining the use of the most frequently used troubleshooting tools for Microsoft networks. The chapter shows you tools that are available with the operating system, the OS support tools, and the OS resource kit. Also, you will see a few popular freeware troubleshooting tools that are included on the companion CD.

In subsequent chapters, additional tools that are specific to the chapter's content will be added to your toolbox. Choosing the right tool for the job will go far in helping you to resolve that 3:00 PM problem so that you're home in time for dinner.

With an understanding of the common troubleshooting tools at your disposal, you can then work through the remaining chapters of this book in any order that is appropriate. Client-server troubleshooting is the first troubleshooting topic covered, primarily because many of the troubleshooting tools in this chapter are useful in many other scenarios. The topics discussed in this chapter are covered next.

Chapter 5: Client-Server Troubleshooting

The majority of the computers on practically all networks are client systems. By simply weighing the odds alone, we can assume that resolving client computer problems is an inevitable part of day-to-day operations for most organizations. This chapter shows you the tools and techniques for quickly isolating and resolving faults on user systems. Since the client tools covered in this chapter are also available on Windows servers, the techniques used in this chapter also complement the troubleshooting techniques found in the server-specific chapters that begin with Chapter 7.

In addition to an explanation of operating system troubleshooting tools and techniques, this chapter presents the most common problems with XP clients and Windows Server 2003, along with their solutions. Regardless of what level of systems you support, this chapter is a "must read."

Chapter 6: Office XP

Office XP problems come in two forms: usability problems and application or file faults. Usability problems are often the result of a lack of user training and thus are not covered in this chapter. Answers to usability problems come merely from experience with the product and not from fault isolation.

While it would be nice if Office were the utopian application that never failed, that is not the case. Many tools have been included in Office XP to allow it to repair itself when application corruption occurs. This chapter describes these tools and explains what to do when these "automatic" tools fail to automatically correct an application problem.

Aside from the application itself failing, users may also experience problems with Word, PowerPoint, Excel, and Access files. Files occasionally become corrupted and oftentimes can be saved, or repaired at the very least. The remainder of this chapter breaks down common Office document faults and explains how to resolve them without having to turn to your trusty backup software to give the user yesterday's version of the needed file.

Chapter 7: Disk Subsystems

Regardless of the arrangement of your storage infrastructure, much of your organization's data will reside on hard disks, whether on IDE drivers on client systems, or on a server's storage array. Disk failures can be catastrophic, and oftentimes your job after a disk failure will be to get the system back to working order as quickly as possible.

This chapter focuses on giving you the tools and techniques for speedily troubleshooting disk-related problems. In addition to learning about the multitude of available diagnostic tools, you will see methods for identifying and resolving problems by using the Disk Management tool. The chapter concludes by showing you the common disk-related stop messages and how to isolate and resolve each of their associated problems.

Chapter 8: DNS

Domain Name Service (DNS) is a key cog in the core of nearly all networks. For many technicians and administrators, spending hours troubleshooting a problem that merely required a one-minute DNS-related fix is something that normally only has to occur once. Countless services rely on DNS for name resolution, so it is not unusual for what appears to be the failure of an application to actually be the lack of the existence of a needed A record in a DNS zone.

The chapter starts from the top, literally, by briefly covering the DNS hierarchy. Understanding the big picture makes it much easier to follow the flow of the DNS name resolution process and thus pinpoint the source of a DNS problem. From there, two additional tools will be added to your virtual toolbox, with the essential DNS tools `nslookup` and `dnscmd` being fully explored.

The remainder of the chapter focuses on troubleshooting both client- and server-side DNS issues, including client configuration, server configuration and replication, zone configuration, and Active Directory integration.

Chapter 9: WINS

While Windows Internet Naming Service (WINS) is dying a slow death, it is still not absent from most Microsoft networks. To that end, problems with WINS are still inevitable, and troubleshooting them should not be ignored. The chapter shows you the common `netsh` (Netshell) commands available for troubleshooting WINS problems and then follows a format similar to Chapter 8. Client and server resolution problems are first explored, and then the chapter finishes up at the heart of WINS troubleshooting: server and database configuration, and WINS database replication problems.

If you have already eradicated WINS from your network and see no hot spots of the disease remaining, consider yourself lucky. For the rest of us that still cannot avoid dealing with WINS problems at the beginning, middle, and end of the day (a slight exaggeration), this chapter is definitely beneficial.

Chapter 10: DHCP

Odds are that DHCP, unlike WINS, is alive and well on your enterprise network. When clients and servers can no longer communicate, and you see Automatic Private IP Addressing (APIPA) popping up on clients around your network, it's time to sound the DHCP problem siren.

This chapter answers the call by first showing you three handy tools for DHCP troubleshooting: the DHCP MMC snap-in, audit logging, and `dhcploc`. Further into the chapter, you will learn how to isolate and correct problems on both DHCP clients and DHCP servers, as well as problems relating to the Active Directory. In the event that you have DHCP relay agents deployed on your network, the chapter also includes a section on identifying problems relating to a relay agent and then provides steps on how to correct this type of problem.

DHCP problems can be localized to a single client computer or can have far-reaching consequences, such as when an entire network segment can no longer communicate with the rest of the network. When the DHCP problem siren rings (if we were only so lucky to have one), this chapter helps you answer the bell and come out punching.

Chapter 11: Network and Application Services

There are many more network services in addition to DNS, WINS, and DHCP, all of which have dedicated chapters. This chapter is the catch-all for the remaining services that are not wide-scale enough to warrant their own troubleshooting chapters. This chapter focuses on isolating and resolving faults for a potpourri of services, including

- Print services
- Terminal services

- Distributed File System (DFS)
- Remote Installation Services (RIS)
- NetWare integration

As with earlier chapters, each topic covered in this chapter begins with a quick refresher on its architecture, followed by descriptions of useful troubleshooting tools, and concludes with details on identifying and resolving the service's related problems.

Chapter 12: Routing and Remote Access

Routing and Remote Access Service (RRAS) has often stirred up more controversy in the certification world than in the real world. Plenty have had to learn to deal with common Windows RRAS troubleshooting issues in order to pass the dreaded network infrastructure administration exam, but few have had to apply these concepts in real life.

Many that work in and around enterprise networks would never build a Windows server and then convert it to a router, when they could simply purchase a router that is likely more efficient for far less money than a server. On the other hand, if you support small businesses, there is a likely chance that they are using at least a portion of Routing and Remote Access Service, such as Network Address Translation (NAT), in order to provide routing services and Internet access while keeping costs down. If you find yourself in this boat, then this chapter will be extremely valuable for you, since Routing and Remote Access Service can be fraught with danger.

If routing is not a concern of yours, then don't forget about the other half of the service: remote access. Maybe routing is not important, but you have remote access configured for dial-up connections to a Windows server. If this is the case, then you will find the remote access troubleshooting portion of the chapter very useful.

In addition to the usual quick architectural and fault resolution explanations, this chapter provides descriptions of some hidden treasures in the troubleshooting world by documenting many unknown tools that you will find invaluable when trying to pinpoint the source of an RRAS problem.

Chapter 13: Active Directory

What a way to end! Some have said that they fear Active Directory (AD) more than public speaking. AD is a vast sea of entwined objects and interrelationships, but with a general understanding of its framework and a troubleshooting game plan in place, you will see that approaching, troubleshooting, and resolving problems with the Active Directory is not much different from approaching any other network service.

Perhaps the key differentiator between AD and the other services mentioned in this book is that it is much newer than they are. This means that there are not many out there that can honestly state that they have years of troubleshooting experience on AD issues. If Cliffs Notes were ever needed for AD troubleshooting, you will find them here.

This chapter outlines the abundance of Microsoft tools available for locating and correcting AD faults and also references the AD tools contained on this book's CD. All aspects of Active Directory fault isolation are covered in this meaty chapter, including

- Group policies
- Domains
- Trusts
- Replication
- The Active Directory schema
- Flexible Single-Master Operations (FSMO) roles
- Security

With the pressure still on AD to prove itself as a reliable directory service, its credibility depends on you. The quicker that you can resolve AD problems as they occur, the sooner your organization will come to accept your Active Directory integrated network infrastructure. This chapter leaves no stone unturned in its pursuit of AD fault detection and correction.

Appendices

The book's three appendices are jammed with valuable troubleshooting information. Appendix A provides an alphabetical list and description of every command line troubleshooting tool referenced in this book. Appendix B lists the most common error and stop messages, along with ways to quickly identify and resolve the cause of their related problem. Appendix C is a troubleshooter's treasure chest. In it you will find documentation on all of the third-party tools included on this book's companion CD as well as documentation on tools available for download over the Internet. With these tools in your toolbox, you will resolve network faults quicker and even know about many faults before anyone else realizes that there's a problem.

Summary

This chapter introduced you to the framework for this reference. These are the key points to remember about navigating through this book.

- Start with Chapters 2 and 3 to build a troubleshooting foundation.
- Continue to Chapter 4 to familiarize yourself with the tools at your disposal.

- Move to Chapter 5 to understand XP client and Windows Server 2003 troubleshooting as well as tools such as Remote Desktop and System Restore that will aid you in resolving many of the server-related problems you may encounter.
- Work through the remaining chapters in any order you desire.

It is recommended that you initially read through the book to familiarize yourself with the many troubleshooting concepts and tools presented, and then keep the book handy so that you can refer to a particular chapter when you find yourself in a bind in any troubleshooting scenario. When you have the proper technique and knowledge of the systems you are troubleshooting, troubleshooting can quickly become one of the most enjoyable and rewarding aspects of your job. Turn to Chapter 2 to let the fun begin.

2
Fundamental Networking

What? Basic networking? In Chapter 1 it was mentioned that this book cannot explain everything about network administration but rather focuses on fault diagnosis and resolution. However, you cannot troubleshoot without fundamental knowledge of the big picture. If you're confident in your knowledge of the fundamental concepts of TCP/IP, DNS, DHCP, and WINS, then move on to Chapter 3; otherwise, take a few minutes to review the basics.

This chapter focuses on reviewing the core components of Microsoft TCP/IP networking as well as some of the other network protocols still commonly found in today's networks. Since many network infrastructures today still incorporate several network protocols, let's begin by looking at the common protocols in a heterogeneous Microsoft environment.

Network Protocols

A lack of knowledge of the most common network protocols can easily turn an easy problem into a tough one. This section briefly discusses the network protocols that you may run into when managing your Microsoft networks. Before we get to the protocols, let's first look at where to find them.

To access the network configuration settings on a Windows Server 2003 (W2K3) system, take these steps.

1. Click Start > Control Panel > Network Connections.

2. Right-click the network interface that you would like to configure, and select Properties. As shown in Figure 2-1, you should now see your installed network services and protocols listed.

3. Click the Install button to install additional services and protocols.

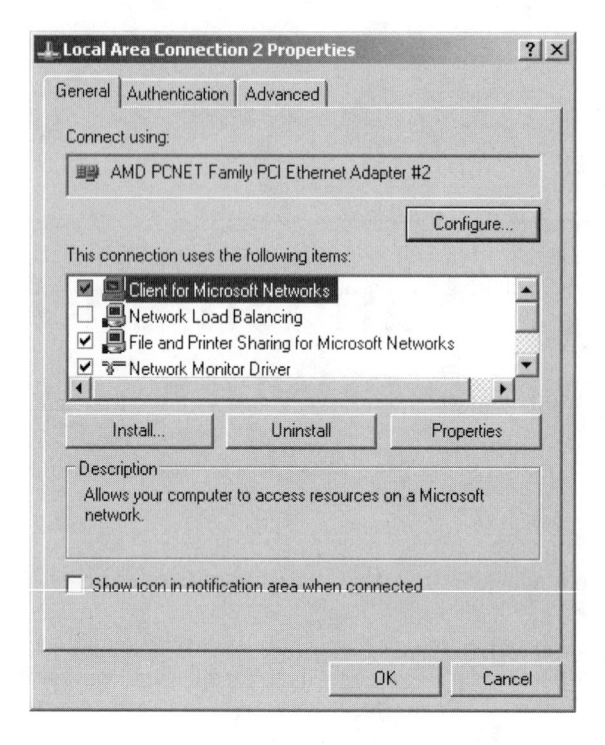

Figure 2-1. Viewing installed network settings

While it would be nice to assume that you are faced with only TCP/IP on a daily basis, that would be naive. The next three sections present the fundamentals of

- NetBEUI
- NWLink (IPX/SPX)
- TCP/IP

NetBEUI

The NetBIOS Enhanced User Interface (NetBEUI) protocol has been commonly used with Windows 95/98 computers configured in workgroups in small office/home office (SOHO) scenarios. The only configuration involved in setting up a NetBEUI network was to simply install and enable the protocol on each network adapter, so it was very easy to use to set up small office computers in a workgroup. NetBEUI's primary flaw is that it is not routable, thus limiting its communication to a single network subnet. With XP and Windows Server 2003, Microsoft has dropped support for NetBEUI, and thus you will not find it used for access to resources on Microsoft Windows servers.

NWLink (IPX/SPX)

NWLink is Microsoft's version of Novell's Internet Packet Exchange/Sequenced Packed Exchange (IPX/SPX) protocol. Although NetWare 5.0 and above servers theoretically can exclusively use TCP/IP for network communications, Microsoft's Client Services for NetWare (CSNW) and Gateway Services for NetWare (GSNW), which are discussed in Chapter 11, require the NWLink IPX/SPX protocol in order to run.

From a troubleshooting standpoint, you need to be aware of some of the basic functionality of IPX/SPX, including the use of the following terms:

- Frame type
- Internal network number
- External network number

These settings can be seen on Windows servers by accessing the NWLink protocol properties, as shown in Figure 2-2.

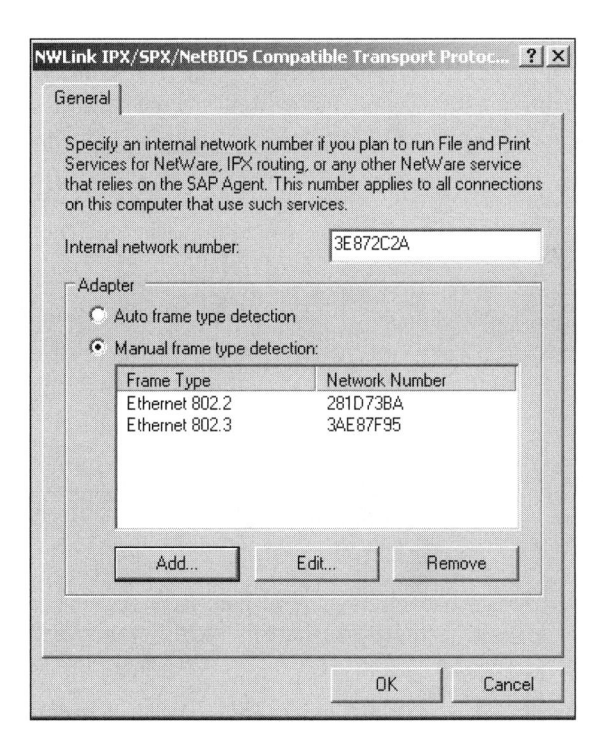

Figure 2-2. NWLink configuration settings on W2K3 servers

Frame Type

Frame types in an IPX network indicate the means by which data is encapsulated in IPX packets. The frame types that you need to be concerned with are

- Ethernet II
- 802.3
- 802.2
- SNAP
- Arcnet

When NWLink is installed on a Windows system, the computer automatically detects a frame type on the IPX network and uses the first frame type that it encounters. The problem with autodetection is that Windows systems can only integrate with one frame type on an IPX network and have problems when the network contains two different frame types. For example, if NetWare 3.11 (802.3 frame type) and NetWare 5.0 (802.2 frame type) systems were on the same network segment as a Windows box running NWLink, by default the Windows system would only be able to communicate with either the NetWare 3.11 systems or the NetWare 5 systems, because they use different frame types in their IPX packets. With autodetection, the first frame type encountered is the one used by Windows, so you cannot just assume that the newer frame type (802.2 in this example) would be the one used. Instead, you would have to manually set the frame types to be used on each Windows system running NWLink.

Aside from problems that can be encountered with incorrect frame types, the other issue of importance with IPX is the use of network numbers, which are discussed next.

> The procedure for manually configuring NWLink frame types for Windows clients and servers can be found in Chapter 11, Network and Application Services.

Internal Network Number

Internal network numbers are unique numbers assigned to all NetWare servers and are required on Windows servers in the following situations:

- Windows servers with two or more network interface cards (NICs)
- Windows servers with a single NIC that has two different IPX frame types bound to it
- If you plan to run File and Print Services for NetWare on the Windows server
- If required by an IPX application on the Windows server

An internal network number is made up of eight hexadecimal characters and can range in value from 00000001 to FFFFFFFE.

External Network Number

While internal network numbers provide a unique ID for each server on a network segment, external network numbers are used to provide a unique logical identifier to represent a single network segment. If you are familiar with TCP/IP concepts (covered next), the internal network number can be equated to the host ID, and the external network number is equivalent to the network ID.

TCP/IP Basics

Later chapters of this book will spend considerable time on the more advanced aspects of the TCP/IP protocol and troubleshooting TCP/IP problems. For now, let's focus only on the very basics of TCP/IP.

Beginning with Windows 2000, Transmission Control Protocol/Internet Protocol (TCP/IP) has been the default Windows network protocol. This section introduces you to the core concepts of TCP/IP, and later sections discuss the other major components of a TCP/IP network infrastructure:

- DNS
- DHCP
- WINS

Let's start with the TCP/IP address structure. An IP address is divided into four parts, which are known as *octets*. Each portion of the address is called an octet because it contains 8 bits, providing a total of 32 bits in an IP address. An example of an IP address is 10.8.32.6. The address has four decimal numbers separated by periods. Each of the numbers represents an octet of 8 bits. Since there can only be 8 bits in an octet, the highest number contained in any octet is 255 (11111111). The address of 10.8.32.6 expressed in decimal actually represents the binary bits 00001010.00001000.00100000.00000110. How did we get that? Let's look at binary conversion.

Binary Conversion

In binary, there are only two numerical possibilities: 0 and 1. Since it is a base 2 numbering system, each position in the binary sequence represents a power of 2. If you relate this to the standard decimal numbering system that you use every day, you'll find that it isn't too bad. Let's take the number 201. When looking at the three-digit number, you would say that there's a 1's, 10's, and 100's place. So the number 201 equals $1 \times 1 + 0 \times 10 + 2 \times 100$. For each position, you started at 1 and multiplied by 10. Since binary is base 2, you start at 1 and multiply by 2 for the weight of each position. To convert decimal numbers to binary, you can simply start at 1 and keep doubling the number until you reach 128. Then use the numbering sequence in a chart for conversion.

In Table 2-1, the IP address 10.8.32.6 is converted to binary.

Table 2-1. Using a Simple Chart to Convert Binary Numbers

Decimal Number	Binary Bit Columns (Powers of 2)							
	128	64	32	16	8	4	2	1
10	0	0	0	0	1	0	1	0
8	0	0	0	0	1	0	0	0
32	0	0	1	0	0	0	0	0
6	0	0	0	0	0	1	1	0

Here is a simple technique to convert decimal numbers to binary.

1. Find the largest number in the conversion chart that is less than or equal to the number you are working with (128, 64, 32, 8, and so on) and place a 1 in its column.

2. Subtract the number from the marked column from the number you started with.

3. Find the largest number in the conversion chart that is less than or equal to the number that you were left with after step 1, and place a 1 in its column.

4. Subtract the number from the marked column from the number you were left with after step 2.

5. Repeat steps 3 and 4 until you reach 0; then place a 0 in all columns that do not have a 1. That is your binary number!

To convert the number 10, you would look in the chart for the highest number that fits into 10, which is 8, so you would place a 1 under the 8 column. Then subtract 8 from 10, which leaves you with 2. Now place a 1 under the 2 column. This leaves you with 0, so to finish the conversion, just place 0s in all other columns.

Using the chart to convert a binary number to decimal is even easier. Simply write out the 8-bit number in the chart, placing a single bit in each column. Then add up the value of each column that is marked with a 1. For example, the binary number 10100001 would be 128 + 32 + 1, which equals 161.

In Chapter 4, you will see how to use a freeware tool on this book's companion CD to convert IP addresses and how to effectively troubleshoot them. So let's not spend any more time on binary, and get to the TCP/IP address structure.

IP Address Structure

IP addresses are divided into these two parts:

- *Host ID*—Identifies the individual system on the network
- *Network ID*—Identifies the network segment containing the systems

The way that you can separate the host portion of an IP address from the network ID is by using the IP address's related *subnet mask*. A subnet mask, like an IP address, consists of 32 bits divided into four octets. Subnet masks are different, however, in that they always contain consecutive binary 1s. For example, the first octet in a subnet mask could look like 11110000 but could not be 11100110.

To demonstrate how a subnet mask determines the network and host IDs, let's assume that the IP address used earlier (10.8.32.6) had a subnet mask of 255.0.0.0. Converting each to binary allows you to quickly see how the subnet mask draws the line between the host ID and the network ID. This is shown in Figure 2-3.

In the illustration, the subnet mask 1s occupy the entire first octet. This means that the entire first octet of the IP address represents the network ID, and the remainder of the IP address determines the host ID. When networks are divided at the octet level, that is known as *classful addressing*. Classful IP addresses are identified by letter, and are shown in Table 2-2.

Table 2-2. A, B, and C IP Address Classes

Class	Number in First Octet	Subnet Mask	Number of Networks	Hosts per Network
A	1–126	255.0.0.0 or /8	126	16,777,214
B	128–191	255.255.0.0 or /16	16,384	65,534
C	192–223	255.255.255.0 or /24	2,097,152	254

As you can see, as the subnet mask gets larger, the number of hosts on a subnet gets smaller; however, the number of possible networks increases. Notice the other notation in the table in the subnet mask column. Since subnet masks are always consecutive 1's, you may see a subnet mask simply listed as /8, meaning that it consists of 8 consecutive 1's. This would equal 255.0.0.0. If you saw an IP address written as 139.42.4.25/16, that would mean that its subnet mask is 255.255.0.0.

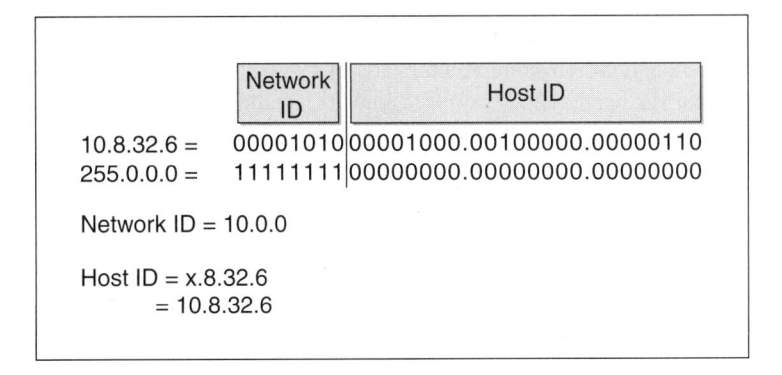

```
                        | Network |
                        |   ID    |            Host ID

10.8.32.6 =   00001010 00001000.00100000.00000110
255.0.0.0 =   11111111 00000000.00000000.00000000

Network ID = 10.0.0

Host ID = x.8.32.6
        = 10.8.32.6
```

Figure 2-3. How the subnet mask divides an IP address

Some IP addresses are viewed as nonroutable by Internet routers, and are exclusively reserved for use on internal networks. For your organization's internal network, any of the following are valid:

- 10.0.0.0 to 10.255.255.255
- 169.254.0.0 to 169.254.255.255
- 172.16.0.0 to 172.31.255.255
- 192.168.0.0 to 192.168.255.255

Keep in mind, however, that these addresses are not routable and thus cannot be accessed from the Internet.

Now let's get to the troubleshooting portion of TCP/IP. For computers on the same physical network segment to communicate, they need to have the same network ID. When one system cannot talk to any others, it is possible that its IP address was entered incorrectly or that it has the wrong subnet mask.

> Systems on different logical networks cannot communicate without the use of a router.

If you have a system with an IP address of 10.0.14.20 and another with 11.0.18.6, each having a subnet mask of 255.0.0.0 and on the same segment, they could not communicate with each other. In this example, one system is on the 10.0.0.0 logical network and the other is on the 11.0.0.0 logical network.

The bottom line is that if the network IDs and subnet masks don't match, the hosts (computers on the network) will not communicate with each other using TCP/IP. After working with IP addresses for a while, you will be able to simply look at two addresses and determine if they are on the same network. When classful subnet masks are used (/8, /16, or /24), network IDs are easy to identify, but this is not the case when you have a classless subnet mask, such as /19. Breaking addresses down to binary and seeing if their network IDs match is still the method for determining like networks with classless addressing. Luckily for you, there are tools that can do this for you. If you're not a subnetting wizard, determining like networks when classless addressing is used may take you 30 minutes to an hour. To spare you the pain of manual calculation, Wildpackets IP Subnet Calculator has been included on this book's CD, and Chapter 4 will show you how to use the tool for IP subnet-related troubleshooting.

> For a great online tutorial on IP subnetting, point your Web browser to www.learntosubnet.com.

TCP/IP in a Routed Environment

In most enterprise-scale networks, or even SOHO networks with an Internet connection, you need to know the basics of TCP/IP routing. Figure 2-4 shows a small office using a router to connect to the Internet.

Each network interface on the router that connects to a network has its own IP address and subnet mask. A router is used to send IP packets to remote networks either directly or by sending the packets to another router. A router uses its routing table to determine where to send a packet based on its destination IP address. A routing table is a cross-reference table that stores information on how to get to IP networks.

We'll be getting heavily into router diagnostics and troubleshooting in Chapter 12, but for now the most important concept to understand about routers is the concept of a *default gateway*. Earlier it was mentioned that computers with the same network ID and subnet mask can communicate with each other. So how does a computer communicate with systems on other networks? That is where the default gateway comes into play. For computers to send data beyond their local subnet, they must have a default gateway specified. For any computer, its default gateway is where it sends all packets that don't have the network ID of their local subnet. The default gateway answers the question "If I don't know where it goes, where do I send it?"

In Figure 2-4, the default gateway address for the computers in the office is 192.168.1.1. Notice that there are two IP addresses for the router: one for its local network connection and one for the connection to the organization's Internet Service

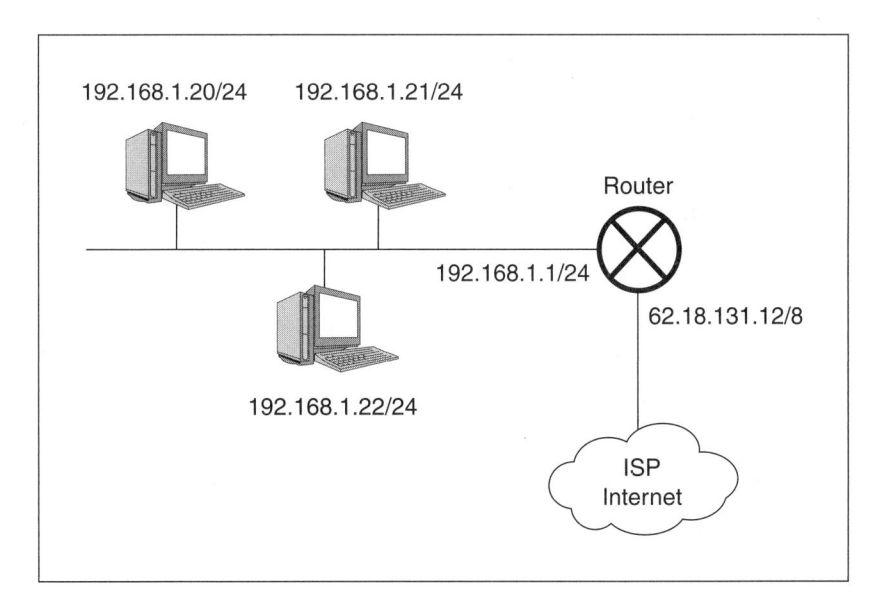

Figure 2-4. Router connecting a small office to the Internet

Provider (ISP). Since the router acts as the way out, and consequently the way back into a network, its configuration is crucial. In Chapter 12, Routing and Remote Access, considerably more time is spent on routing concepts.

NetBIOS Names versus FQDNs

One last aspect of TCP/IP networking that is essential to understand at this point is the concepts of NetBIOS names and fully qualified domain names (FQDNs). With computers running TCP/IP, it is much easier to remember a friendly name than the IP address of a system. NetBIOS naming and FQDNs both give you the ability to associate a friendly name with a network object, but the primary difference between the two is how you see the name written. An FQDN is typically *<computer name>.<domain name>.<domain extension>*, such as www.awl.com. A NetBIOS name is a simple name used to represent a system but is limited in size to 15 characters. For the FQDN www.awl.com, its NetBIOS name equivalent would be www.

Now consider how many www's there are out there. If we used NetBIOS on the Internet, there would be no way to tell systems apart, and that is why the naming convention for any distributed networked environment has to be fully qualified domain names.

Now that you understand the fundamental differences between NetBIOS naming and FQDNs, let's look at the naming rules associated with each.

Here are the rules for NetBIOS naming.

- The names can't begin with a number.
- The name can be no larger than 15 characters.
- The name can use the characters A–Z, a–z, 0–9, hyphens, and is not case sensitive.
- The name can have spaces (a space counts as one character).

These are the rules for FQDNs.

- The name can begin with a number.
- The name can be no larger than 255 characters (domain controllers are limited to 155 characters).
- The name can use the characters A–Z, a–z, 0–9, hyphens, and is not case sensitive.
- The names cannot have spaces.
- Portions of the name are separated by periods (www.microsoft.com).

Name Resolution Methods

So you have seen that we can use NetBIOS names and FQDNs as easier methods to remember computers. While we can remember names, something has to exist to connect the dots. There are several ways on a network for a name to become associated with an IP address. These are the predominant methods.

- *Domain Name Service (DNS)*—The server that resolves FQDNs to IP addresses.
- *Windows Internet Naming Service (WINS)*—The server that resolves NetBIOS names to IP addresses.
- *Hosts file*—The file stored locally on every computer that maps IP addresses to FQDNs.
- *LMHosts file*—The file stored locally on every computer that maps IP addresses to NetBIOS names.
- *Broadcast*—A way for your computer to shout out to the network, "Hey, does anyone know computer X?" (Routers drop broadcast packets, so broadcasts only work on the subnet connected to the system sending the broadcast. Also, broadcasts gobble up network bandwidth.)

In two later sections, DNS and WINS, we'll look at these name resolution techniques in much more depth.

If you're looking for more about TCP/IP than just a basic introduction, pick up a copy of *TCP/IP Illustrated, Volume I*, by W. Richard Stevens (Addison-Wesley, 1994).

Name Resolution with DNS

Domain Name Service (DNS) is a TCP/IP service that is used to map IP addresses to FQDNs or vice versa. Think of a DNS server as nothing more than a TCP/IP phone book. When you need to call someone, you need that person's phone number. When one computer needs to communicate with another, the other computer's IP address is needed. For example, if you were at your home computer and wanted to view books at www.AWL.com, your computer would query its DNS server and ask, "What's the IP address for www.AWL.com?" The DNS server would then respond with 165.193.123.224, and your computer would use that IP address to contact the www.AWL.com Web server. This example is known in the DNS world as a *forward lookup*. If the process were reversed, and you had an IP address and wanted to know the FQDN for the address, a *reverse lookup* would be performed.

Before getting further into DNS terminology, let's first get the complete name resolution process out of the way. Other logical components may be involved in the name resolution process instead of a DNS server. When an FQDN needs to be resolved to an IP address, Windows 2000 and newer systems try to resolve the name to an IP address in the following order:

1. Resolver cache and Hosts file
2. DNS
3. NetBIOS cache
4. WINS
5. Broadcast
6. LMHosts

Resolver Cache

When an IP address needs to be found for a particular FQDN, the first place a system looks is in its own resolver cache. The resolver cache is where the local computer stores its previously queried FQDN to IP address mappings. Having the cache is purely for performance. For example, if you visited www.Microsoft.com 20 times a day, you would not want to wait for your computer to have to find the IP address for www.Microsoft.com every time you attempted to visit the site. Instead, your computer will perform faster when it returns to sites that it has already visited if its FQDN–to–IP address mapping is locally cached on your computer's hard drive in its resolver cache. Since six steps are involved in the name resolution process, Windows also negatively caches FQDNs that do not exist. For example, if you tried to ping Barry Kaufman's favorite site, "freesoftware.Microsoft.com," you would find that it doesn't exist (the result of a Microsoft DNS server saying, "There's no such animal!"), and your system would write a negative entry for the FQDN in its resolver cache. This way, the next time that you try to go to freesoftware.Microsoft.com, your computer will quickly tell you that the site, or page, could not be found.

If you would like to see the contents of the resolver cache on your system, from the command prompt run `ipconfig /displaydns`. On the other hand, if you would like to clear the contents of your local resolver, run `ipconfig /flushdns`. If you're unsure of the complete usage of the `ipconfig` command, don't worry, because it is covered in its entirety in Chapter 4.

By default, Windows systems cache positive entries for the Time to Live (TTL) value provided to them by the authoritative DNS server that answered the request, but never for longer than 86,400 seconds (24 hours). Think of TTL as being an expiration period, measured in seconds, for a DNS record. To prove it, you can repeatedly run the command `ipconfig /displaydns` and watch the TTL values for cached records continually decrease. Negative entries are cached for 300 seconds (5 minutes). Either of these values can be changed by editing the HKEY_LOCAL_MACHINE\SYSTEM\CurrentControlSet\Services\DNSCache\Parameters Registry key. To change the maximum lifetime for positively cached entries, create the DWORD value `MaxCacheEntryTtlLimit` and set its value to the desired maximum in seconds. To change the duration that negatively cached queries are kept in the cache, create the DWORD value `NegativeCacheTime` and set its value to the number of seconds that you would like your system to maintain negative name resolution queries. If you do not want negative responses cached at all, the value can be set to 0.

Hosts

When a system boots, the contents of its Hosts file are automatically loaded into the resolver cache, so you could say that the Hosts file contents and the resolver cache are always checked simultaneously. Also, whenever you alter and save a Hosts file, it is automatically reloaded into the resolver cache.

The easiest way to think of a Hosts file is as a client's own local "mini DNS server." Like a DNS server, a Hosts file resolves FQDNs to IP addresses. One of the primary differences, however, is that the Hosts file is nothing more than a static text file that is locally stored on each computer, meaning that to use Hosts files in an enterprise environment, you would have to manually configure or deploy the Hosts file to every system where you would like to have the FQDN–to–IP address mappings.

If you would like to see a Hosts file, on any system open Windows Explorer and navigate to the %systemroot%\system32\drivers\etc folder (C:\Windows\system32\drivers\etc by default). From the "etc" folder, you can use Notepad to view and edit the Hosts file. An example of a Hosts file is shown in Figure 2-5.

> When a single client has trouble accessing a system by its FQDN and all other systems on your network can access the system without incident, check the Hosts file on the problem system for an incorrect static entry.

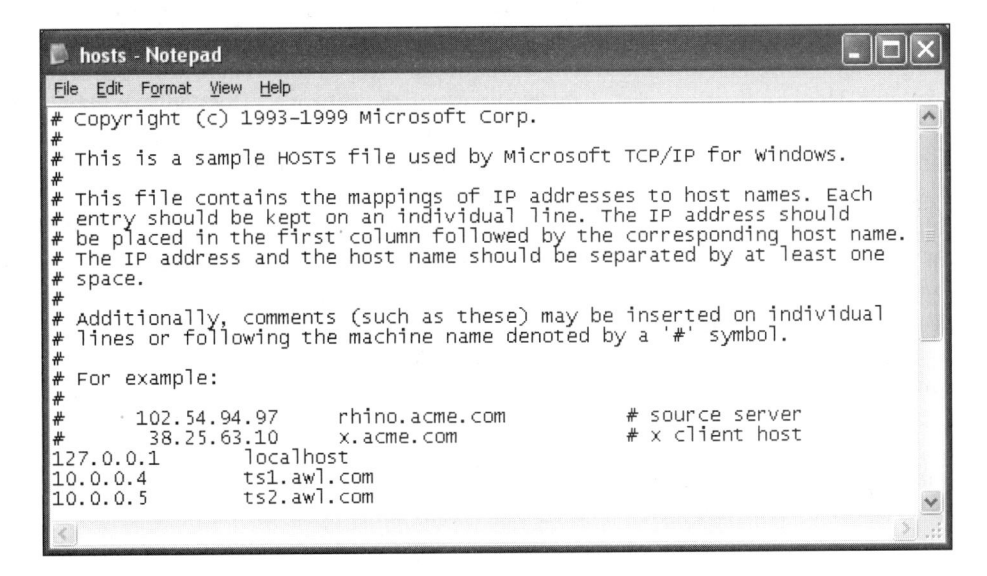

```
# Copyright (c) 1993-1999 Microsoft Corp.
#
# This is a sample HOSTS file used by Microsoft TCP/IP for windows.
#
# This file contains the mappings of IP addresses to host names. Each
# entry should be kept on an individual line. The IP address should
# be placed in the first column followed by the corresponding host name.
# The IP address and the host name should be separated by at least one
# space.
#
# Additionally, comments (such as these) may be inserted on individual
# lines or following the machine name denoted by a '#' symbol.
#
# For example:
#
#      102.54.94.97     rhino.acme.com          # source server
#       38.25.63.10     x.acme.com              # x client host
127.0.0.1        localhost
10.0.0.4         ts1.awl.com
10.0.0.5         ts2.awl.com
```

Figure 2-5. Hosts file

DNS Query Types

If the FQDN queried is not found in the resolver cache or the Hosts file, the client will then perform a *recursive query* to its primary DNS server. A recursive query is a request for IP address resolution of the entire FQDN. If the DNS server has knowledge of the record, it will respond to the client making the request with the answer. If the DNS server does not know the answer, it may make several *iterative queries* to root-level name servers. An iterative query is a request to resolve only a portion of an FQDN. For example, if your system queried its DNS server for the IP address of freesoftware.Microsoft.com and the DNS server didn't know the address, it could first make an iterative query to the .com root-level server asking for the IP address of a Microsoft.com DNS server. Once it had the IP address for the Microsoft.com DNS server, it would then make a second iterative query to the Microsoft.com server asking for the IP address of the host named freesoftware. If you're still a little in the dark on the iterative and recursive query process, don't worry because it will be discussed in more detail in Chapter 8, DNS.

NetBIOS Cache

After all queries to a client's listed DNS servers turn up no results, it will then check its NetBIOS cache for any records that match the host portion of the FQDN, such as freesoftware. The NetBIOS cache is the NetBIOS equivalent of the DNS resolver cache and is only different in that it shows NetBIOS name–to–IP address mappings as opposed to FQDN–to–IP address mappings. To view the contents of the NetBIOS cache on a system, you can run `nbtstat -c` on that system.

WINS/Broadcast/LMHosts

If the NetBIOS name is not located in the NetBIOS cache, the client will next ask its WINS server for the IP address of the host portion of the FQDN. If no WINS server is configured for the client or if the WINS server doesn't respond, the client will then do a broadcast. Think of the broadcast as the client asking the network, "Does anyone know the IP address for freesoftware?" Routers always drop broadcasts, so any broadcast made by a client or a server is heard only on its local subnet. If no answer is found by doing a broadcast, the client will then check its LMHosts file to see if it contains an IP address–to–NetBIOS name mapping for the host in question. The LMHosts file is very similar to the Hosts file in configuration, and both are located in the same folder. The primary difference, however, between a Hosts file and an LMHosts file is that the LMHosts file only resolves NetBIOS names to IP addresses and not FQDNs to IP addresses.

As you can see, name resolution can be quite a lengthy process. That is why when you try to go to a Web site and mistakenly type in the wrong host information (it doesn't exist), you wind up waiting a few seconds before the search for the page times out. To finish filling in the blanks of the "big picture," you should have a basic understanding of DHCP and WINS, so let's take a quick look at these services now.

WINS

WINS is used to resolve NetBIOS names to IP addresses. If you have a pristine W2K/XP/W2K3 environment, there is no reason to even be running WINS. However, if for political reasons or for backward compatibility you do run WINS, then this section is important.

It was mentioned earlier that one method for resolving NetBIOS names to IP addresses was by using broadcasts. Since a bunch of "chatty" computers could significantly slow down a network, WINS was devised as a way to map IP addresses to NetBIOS names, thus minimizing the number of broadcasts on a network segment. Instead of a client asking the entire network for the IP address of a NetBIOS name, the client simply sends the request directly to the WINS server. If the WINS server doesn't have a record of the NetBIOS name, then the client may do a broadcast in an attempt to resolve the name.

The method or order that a client uses to try to resolve a NetBIOS name to an IP address depends on the type of NetBIOS client that the system is configured as. NetBIOS clients can be configured to use any one of the following NetBIOS name resolution modes.

- *B-node (Broadcast node)*—Uses broadcasts to resolve NetBIOS names to IP addresses.

- *P-node (Peer node)*—Uses point-to-point communication with a NetBIOS name server (i.e., WINS server) to resolve IP NetBIOS names to IP addresses.

- *M-node (Mixed node)*—Uses a combination of B- and P-node communications to resolve NetBIOS names to IP addresses. The client first attempts to use a broadcast, and if unsuccessful, queries a NetBIOS name server.

- *H-node (Hybrid node)*—Uses a combination of B- and P-node communications to resolve NetBIOS names to IP addresses. The client first attempts to query a NetBIOS name server, then checks for an entry in its LMHosts file, and then uses a broadcast.

Normally, to minimize network traffic, clients using WINS are configured as H-node clients. This configuration provides the least impact on network performance. Windows clients can get practically every imaginable TCP/IP configuration from a DHCP server, if they're configured to use DHCP (covered next). With that in mind, if NetBIOS name resolution appears to be running below expectations, you may need to consider checking the WINS/NBT Node Type option on the DHCP server.

In the NT days, WINS was thought of as a great service because it was dynamic. This meant that WINS clients could automatically register their NetBIOS names and IP addresses with their WINS servers, meaning that network administrators would not have to manually track client NetBIOS name–to–IP address relationships. The early versions of DNS were not dynamic, so if you wanted dynamic name–to–IP address resolution, WINS was your only answer. Beginning with Windows 2000 DNS, Windows 2000 and above clients could dynamically register their FQDNs and IP addresses with the DNS server. For pre–Windows 2000 clients, a Windows 2000 DHCP server could register their IP and FQDN information with the DNS server for them. With these considerations in mind, with a Windows 2000 or higher network infrastructure, you have very little reason, if any, to use WINS.

> Chapters 8 and 9 spend considerable time on DNS-WINS and DHCP-WINS integration issues.

DHCP Overview

Dynamic Host Configuration Protocol (DHCP) allows clients and servers on your network to automatically obtain an IP address from a DHCP server. When dealing with hundreds or even thousands of computers, DHCP can save you quite a bit of time, considering the alternative of having to manually configure static IP addresses on network interfaces.

To understand the operation of DHCP, you need to be familiar with the following terms:

- DHCP lease
- DHCP scope
- Reservation
- DHCP options
- DHCP relay agent
- Automatic Private IP Addressing

DHCP Lease

In Ethernet networking, hardware components such as network adapters are identified by their 48-bit Media Access Control (MAC) address. MAC addresses are embedded on network cards by their manufacturer, and thus each adapter has its own unique MAC address. Unlike other networking addresses, MAC addresses are expressed in hexadecimal. Since a single hex character represents 4 bits, a typical 48-bit MAC address would be expressed as 00-03-2F-01-D0-1B.

The reason that we're discussing MAC addresses is that they provide a means for a network card to identify itself on the network without any user intervention. When a computer boots up and is configured to obtain an IP address automatically, it broadcasts a DHCP Discover packet. By broadcasting a DHCP Discover, the system is asking the network, "Are there any DHCP servers out there?" The DHCP server or servers that receive the request respond to the MAC address of the requesting computer and offer an IP address. This part of the process is known as DHCP Offer. The client then sends a DHCP Request packet back to the first DHCP server from which it received an offer, requesting use of the offered IP address. Finally, the DHCP server sends the client a DHCP Acknowledge packet, signifying that the IP address has been leased to the client.

DHCP servers only lease IP addresses to DHCP clients. So once a client gets an IP address from a DHCP server, it does not automatically own the IP address for life. For example, if a DHCP server was configured to lease IP addresses for two weeks and the DHCP client was not connected to the network after receiving its lease for the next two weeks, the DHCP server would remove the client's lease and could in turn hand out the IP address to another computer. As long as a client is connected to the network, at the 50% point of its DHCP lease duration it will automatically try to contact the DHCP server and renew its lease.

DHCP Scope

DHCP address allocations and leases are configured in DHCP scopes. In addition to defining a range of IP addresses to hand out to clients and lease duration, a scope also defines many more DHCP settings, including

- Subnet mask
- IP address exclusions
- IP address reservations
- DHCP options

The subnet mask for the IP address range is specified at the time a DHCP scope is created and cannot be changed. The only way to change a scope's subnet mask would be to delete and then re-create the scope. If you have several servers on the network using static IP addresses, you may decide to define a range of *IP address exclusions*. When configured, all IP addresses in the defined exclusion range will not be handed out by the DHCP server.

Reservation

If you have DHCP clients that you want to always have the same IP address, you can configure *DHCP reservations*. When you create reservations, you must know the MAC address of the computer you want to reserve an IP address for. A reservation is nothing more than a mapping on the DHCP server of an IP address to a MAC address. Since a MAC address must be entered for every DHCP reservation, it is much easier to configure static IP addresses on the systems whose IP address can't change, and then simply exclude the range of IP addresses from the DHCP lease. So far, you have seen that the scope defines the IP address range and subnet mask settings that DHCP clients will receive. All other networking settings are configured under DHCP options.

DHCP Options

DHCP options allow you to automatically provide clients with much more than an IP address and a subnet mask. By configuring DHCP options, you can automatically assign the following to DHCP clients:

- Default gateway
- DNS server(s)
- DNS domain name
- WINS server(s)
- WINS node type

With a properly configured DHCP server, you can practically plug your clients into the network, and in terms of networking configuration, the DHCP server can do the rest.

DHCP Relay Agent

It was mentioned in the DHCP Lease section that when a DHCP client boots up, its sends out a broadcast to locate a DHCP server. The problem with broadcasts is that routers will drop them. DHCP broadcasts, however, may be the exception, depending on the router. If the router is RFC 1542 compliant and has BOOTP forwarding enabled, the router will forward DHCP Discover packets. If your routers are not RFC 1542 compliant, and you have a DHCP server on a single subnet and require clients on multiple subnets to obtain IP address leases from the server, you have two options.

- Buy newer RFC 1542–compliant routers.
- Configure a Windows server running Routing and Remote Access Service as a DHCP relay agent.

The concept of the second option is shown in Figure 2-6.

Notice in Figure 2-6 that the DHCP relay agent is placed on the network segment of the clients that are not on the same segment as the DHCP server. In being on the same segment as the clients, the DHCP relay agent will hear their DHCP Discover broadcasts, capture them, and forward them directly to the DHCP server. Since the transmission between the relay agent and the server is directed (it includes the DHCP server's IP address), it is not dropped by the router.

But what if a DHCP relay agent weren't present? ... That's why Microsoft invented APIPA!

Automatic Private IP Addressing

If you have ever wondered what it would be like to use TCP/IP without any effort, the answer has arrived. Out of the box, Microsoft systems are configured to use TCP/IP and obtain an IP address automatically. With Automatic Private IP Addressing (APIPA), a

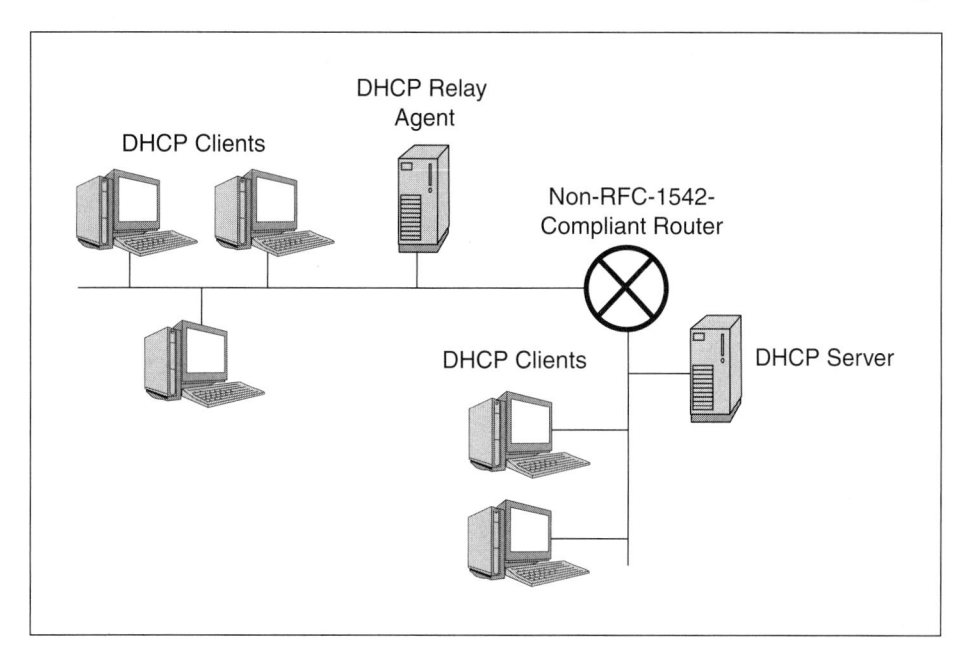

Figure 2-6. Placement of a DHCP relay agent

Windows 2000 or higher client that cannot contact a DHCP server gives itself its own IP address. The address the system gives itself is a Class B address in the 169.254.0.1 to 169.254.255.254 range with a subnet mask of 255.255.0.0. This feature allows you to automatically set up a TCP/IP network by doing nothing more than plugging the computers into a hub or switch.

> APIPA is a DHCP troubleshooter's best friend. Why? If you have a client or clients that cannot talk to any computers on their network, run `ipconfig` on one of them. If it has a 169.254.x.x address, you know that the problem is that the client cannot contact a DHCP server.

Need More Knowledge?

The focus of this book is troubleshooting. If you're unsure of some of the background concepts or terminology for network administration or are looking for additional information on a particular topic, here are some great places to check.

- www.webopedia.com—Simple definitions for most acronyms and concepts.
- www.whatis.com—An IT-specific search engine.

- support.microsoft.com—The official Microsoft support site. Answers to most problems can be found by searching the Knowledge Base at this site.
- www.mcpmag.com—Search and read past articles from *MCP Magazine*.
- www.winnetmag.com—Plenty of troubleshooting-related articles to search for from *Windows and .NET Magazine*.
- www.labmice.net—Tons of NT, 2000, and Windows Server 2003 resources.
- www.microsoft.com/technet—TechNet is a searchable database providing a wealth of troubleshooting and conceptual information.
- www.techrepublic.com—A great source for Windows and IT articles and products.
- www.windows2000faq.com—Have questions? Find answers at the Windows FAQ.

Summary

Having reviewed some of the important foundation terms, concepts, and protocols of networking, you are now in a position to dip into the central topic of this book: troubleshooting. The next chapter gives you a high-level overview of a proven troubleshooting method. Subsequent chapters take up network protocols and their role in troubleshooting in more depth.

3

Troubleshooting Techniques

Is there a magic recipe for troubleshooting? After reading this chapter, will you be a troubleshooting wizard? Well, everyone wishes it were that easy, but unfortunately troubleshooting is half technique and half experience. In this chapter you will be presented with a proven successful methodology for approaching and troubleshooting problems on your Microsoft networks. Since the other half of troubleshooting is experience, the remainder of this book focuses on the experience part. With the right technique and the aid of the technology-specific chapters in this book, you will be able to approach a problem and fix it. Wait a minute! That may mean that you will now be the one getting all the late night calls from the CEO when "The Internet is down," so continue reading at your own risk.

Optimism versus Pessimism

There are two fundamental methods for approaching any network problem: the optimistic way and the pessimistic way. Some try to define what's right, while others try to look for what's wrong. Perhaps this is why so many find troubleshooting to be so difficult. If there were a way to go straight to the problem—consistently—then everyone would do it.

Unfortunately, the pessimists (those who look for what's wrong) can quickly find the problem—sometimes. Those few victories make the pessimists believe that their troubleshooting method is tried and true. Is there a method to the pessimistic approach? The most common thread in pessimistic troubleshooting is pure experience. With experience, anyone can be a master of troubleshooting certain technologies, but try telling your manager, or client (for the brave souls that work at a help desk), to wait ten years for you to solve the problem while you gain experience. While that might be fun to say, most of us don't think that the wait-and-learn strategy will keep you employed for very long. Pessimism generally works very well for hardware troubleshooting.

For example, on a few occasions some technicians have been able to say, "That smells like a bad power supply," and have been right on the money. Unfortunately, software troubleshooting is not as easy as smelling the air, not that hardware is always that easy either, so you cannot always assume that the approach that works for finding bad power supplies will fix your IIS server.

While some pessimists have made a living troubleshooting hardware, so have some optimists. No matter what you troubleshoot, the optimistic approach is always predictably the same—methodical but successful. Stepping through a process of finding what's right may seem tedious at first, but with practice it becomes very elementary. To illustrate the optimistic approach, consider a common example of lost network connectivity. Suppose that Max, a user on your network, cannot connect to the company intranet server to view his employee handbook. Here's the optimist's way of resolving the problem.

1. Can I ping the intranet server by its host name from my system? Yes? Great—I have name resolution, so DNS works; and since I can ping, that means that network connectivity from my system to the server is good.

2. Since I already found that inbound network connectivity to the intranet server was good in step 1, I look for a network problem associated with Max's computer. A quick look at his network interface card's (NIC) patch cord reveals that it's unplugged from his workstation. Problem solved!

While substantially more difficult problems than this one are addressed in this book, the methodology to diagnose the problems does not change. The remainder of this chapter focuses on the troubleshooting process itself, further examining the sequence and logic behind a successful troubleshooting strategy.

Troubleshooting Process Overview

For many, the art of troubleshooting is self-taught. Some senior engineers have a process in their head for resolving problems that has become instinctive over time. For example, you may have encountered some IT folks that when presented with a problem respond, "I can't tell you, but I'll show you." For some problems, instincts can kick in, and all you need to do is react. Unfortunately, we are not born with computer troubleshooting instincts, so it is an art that must be learned and practiced.

The complete troubleshooting process can be summarized as involving eight steps, which are

1. Identifying the problem

2. Documenting the history of the problem

3. Analyzing the current environment

4. Documenting processes involved in the problem
5. Eliminating what's right
6. Correcting the problem
7. Testing the corrective action
8. Following up

In the next eight main sections of this chapter, each of these steps is specifically addressed. In reading the remainder of this chapter, you will experience a tested troubleshooting methodology that has proven itself in the field. While eight steps may at first seem overwhelming, you will see that many are very quick to get through. Although you sometimes can take shortcuts and succeed in resolving a problem, taking shortcuts often equates only to patching a problem, and a patched problem often returns at a time when network performance is most critical.

Let's get to the process itself, beginning with the identification of the problem.

Identifying the Problem

Problem reporting usually begins at the user level. The trouble call could begin with "The printer doesn't work," or "E-mail is down," and usually ends with "I didn't change anything on my computer." On many occasions, the end user may be the least helpful in aiding you to arrive at the cause of the problem. If the problem is server or network related, then most likely the user will not be able to offer too many clues, except that many users likely will report the same problem.

In this stage of the troubleshooting process, you are only looking to identify the "what" of the problem. Later in the troubleshooting process, you will look at the question "Why?" For now, all that needs to be documented is the problem itself, such as "Max cannot connect to the company intranet server by using its host name." Once you have the problem documented, the next step is to look at the computer's, network's, and application's history.

Don't forget to "Read what you click." Too many of us have made the mistake of clicking OK as soon as an error message pops up, without even allowing time to read it. If the computer is trying to give you clues about the problem, take a moment to read them.

Documenting the History of the Problem

Many problems are fixed by simply undoing something that was done earlier. Perhaps the installation of a new driver is causing the network card to no longer function. In this case, you could simply roll back to the previous driver or reinstall the correct driver. While this example may seem elementary, problems such as this one have the potential to turn in to multihour adventures simply because the technician failed to ask the user a few questions.

Once a problem is reported, ask the user what, if anything, was recently done to the computer. Good questions to ask include these.

1. Have you recently installed anything (hardware or software) on the computer?
2. Did you receive any error messages? If so, what did they say?
3. Does a single user or all users on the system experience the problem?
4. When was the last time the system was backed up?
5. Is the problem related to certain software you run or something you do?

For company-wide problems, your best course of action is to check with the IS department manager. If your Exchange server, for example, had to be taken down for a reboot when an application was installed and you were unaware of the issue, you may wind up wasting time troubleshooting a user's Outlook client configuration, when all that was needed was to tell the user to wait a few minutes. This will save you the embarrassment of saying, after looking at the user's Outlook setup, "I don't know what I did, but I must have fixed it!"

> On more than one occasion, many of us have witnessed users that obediently followed their computer's command as it booted, by "Pressing F2 to Enter Setup." After they inadvertently changed several BIOS settings in their attempt to start their system from the BIOS Setup, their systems would not start, ran extremely slow, or had a host of other problems. Problems like this stress the importance of learning what the user did prior to beginning any further problem analysis or troubleshooting. In situations where BIOS settings were changed on a user's workstation, in most instances simply resetting the BIOS settings to the system defaults would solve the problem.

Aside from arriving at system history from interviewing the users, don't forget that many operating system occurrences are automatically recorded in the event log, which is a great place to find information on a computer's history. To access the Event Viewer, click Start > Administrative Tools > Event Viewer.

Two event logs that consistently provide system history information are the system log and the application log.

An example of good information being provided by an event in the system log is shown in Figure 3-1. Figure 3-2 shows an application error reported in the application log.

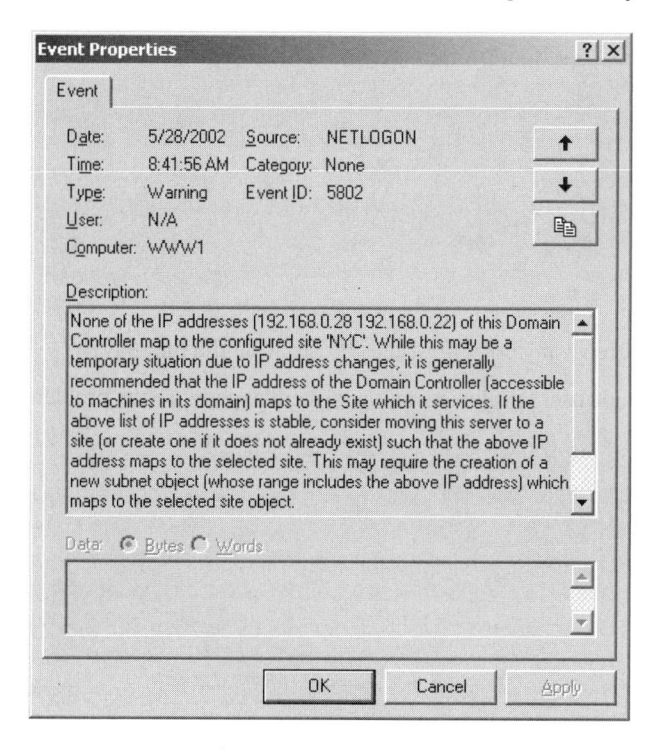

Figure 3-1. System log warning event

Depending on the type of system and the problem, you may also find these logs helpful in checking system history:

- Directory service
- DNS server
- File Replication Service
- Security

Chapter 4 discusses the use of the event logs for troubleshooting in much more detail.

Documenting system and network history is often useful in identifying the problem, if not the solution as well. If further investigation is required, the next step is to analyze the current environment. For remote users that don't understand an error message, consider having them e-mail you a screenshot of the problem. To do this, have the user press the Print Screen key and then open Paint and press Ctrl-V to paste the desktop image. From Paint the user can save the image and then attach the saved file to an e-mail message.

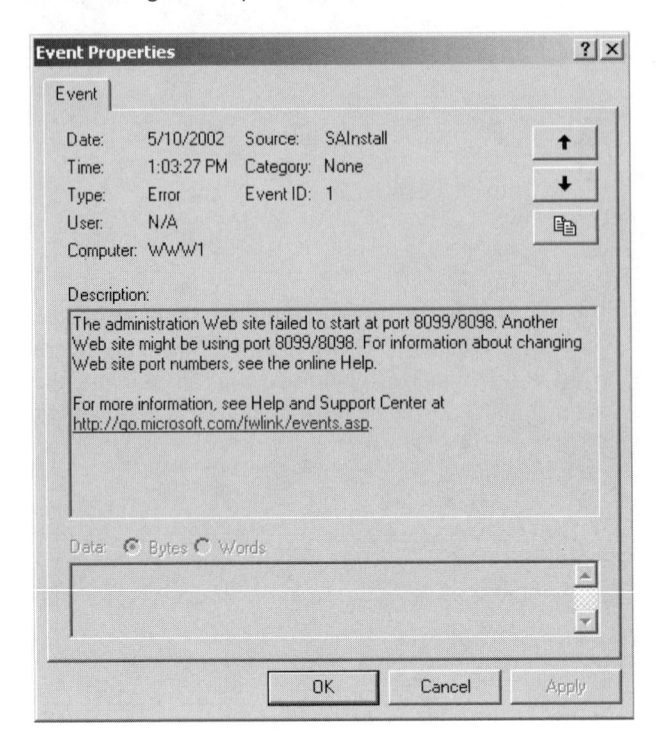

Figure 3-2. Application log error event

Analyzing the Current Environment

With history documented, you should next turn your attention to analyzing the current network and local system environment. The type of problem, whether it is local or network related, determines your course of action in this phase. When you examine the environment, attention should primarily be focused on the following areas:

- Operating system state
- Latest virus scan
- Network configuration
- Installed applications
- Firmware

If time and resources permit, another aspect of analysis is to compare the problem system with a known good system. Each of these facets of the environment analysis is described in the next six sections.

Operating System State

Several problems occur that are simply bugs in the operating system and can often be solved by upgrading the operating system to the latest service pack or by installing a hotfix. *Service packs* are tested improvements to the OS that normally fix up to hundreds of small problems and sometimes add additional features to the operating system. On the other hand, *hotfixes* are used to fix a single problem that requires immediate attention. Since hotfixes are not as thoroughly tested as service packs, you should only install a hotfix when it is needed.

You can determine if an operating system is at its current required service pack/hotfix state by running Windows Update, provided that the system has Internet connectivity. Beginning with the XP/W2K3 Windows platforms, you can configure the Windows Update service to automatically download critical updates, thus automatically keeping your systems current. This is especially useful with your IIS servers, when security vulnerabilities are found on nearly a monthly basis. In Chapter 4, you will see how to configure the Windows Update service on XP workstations and W2K3 servers in your enterprise to automatically load updates for you.

Beginning with Windows 98 and Windows 2000 workstations, and with Windows 2000 servers, you can install the Critical Update service, which automatically checks Microsoft.com for critical OS updates. To install the service, point your Web browser to windowsupdate.microsoft.com. From there, just click the Product Updates icon and then select "Windows Critical Update Notification."

Latest Virus Scan

Many unusual workstation or server problems can be attributed to a virus. Even if your network is not connected to the Internet, you may want to install antivirus software, since many viruses enter enterprise-scale corporate networks by being brought in on a user's floppy disk. On the other hand, if your network is connected to the Internet, antivirus software can give you a false sense of security. No amount of it on your Exchange or Lotus Domino mail server will prevent backdoor mail viruses from attacking your network via users reading their Web-based Hotmail at work. To prevent this, many organizations today are blocking outbound access to most Hotmail sites, thus not even giving the users the opportunity to bring viruses into the network via their personal mail. No one can place a firm argument that accessing personal mail from the desks at work is a business necessity, so if you do plan to block outbound access to these sites, you shouldn't get much of an argument. Oftentimes, problems that appear to be an operating system or application failure are the result of an undetected virus. Failure to first rule out the possibility of a virus (by running a virus scan using up-to-date antivirus software) may cause you to waste hours of unnecessary troubleshooting time. Some technicians have gone so far as to waste hours reinstalling an entire operating system, only to have the problem return, which would be the case if a boot sector virus was never properly removed.

Antivirus software can go a long way toward eliminating what's right when you are faced with diagnosing operating system and application faults.

Now let's suppose that you have the latest and greatest antivirus software installed on all your workstations and servers. To be protected against viruses, you should be able to answer "Yes" to each of these questions.

- Are periodic virus scans scheduled so that they run automatically on each system?

- Is each system configured so that it will automatically download the latest virus signatures?

If you answered "No" to one of these questions, then your network is not as safe as it should be. In many situations, a company's data is its value, so not having a budget to purchase and implement an enterprise-class antivirus solution is simply an excuse for the misinformed. Unfortunately, some organizations don't learn the value of antivirus software until its stops business production for one or several days.

Remember that even if your antivirus software runs regular scans, monitors both inbound and outbound traffic, and automatically updates the latest signatures, it does not mean that the network is invincible to a virus outbreak. Some organizations have the misfortune of being the first to be hit with a new virus, before virus signatures have even been made available. I was with an organization that was hit hard by a particular strain of the Nimda virus, in spite of its excellent antivirus practices, so never simply rule out a virus as possibly being the source of a problem.

Network Configuration

The next environment and local computer settings to examine should be the network configuration. The fastest means to find the network configuration settings on a computer is to run the `ipconfig /all` command from the command prompt. The command's output is shown in Figure 3-3.

Information on each network interface is displayed in the command output, including all the important TCP/IP configuration information. For network-wide problems affecting many or all users, you will see the specific methods for identifying and resolving problems on DNS, DHCP, WINS, and RRAS servers in Chapters 8–12.

Installed Applications

Next, note the applications installed on the system. Does the problem occur when an application executes? Was a new application recently installed, and has its installation resulted in the reported problem? Does the problem only occur when a particular application is printing? If you can get a "Yes" answer to any of these questions, then you are in luck since these types of application-related problems can be reproduced, and thus you can duplicate the fault yourself.

If the application has services that run on startup, a quick check is to note the application's related services and their dependencies. There may be a hung service that is at

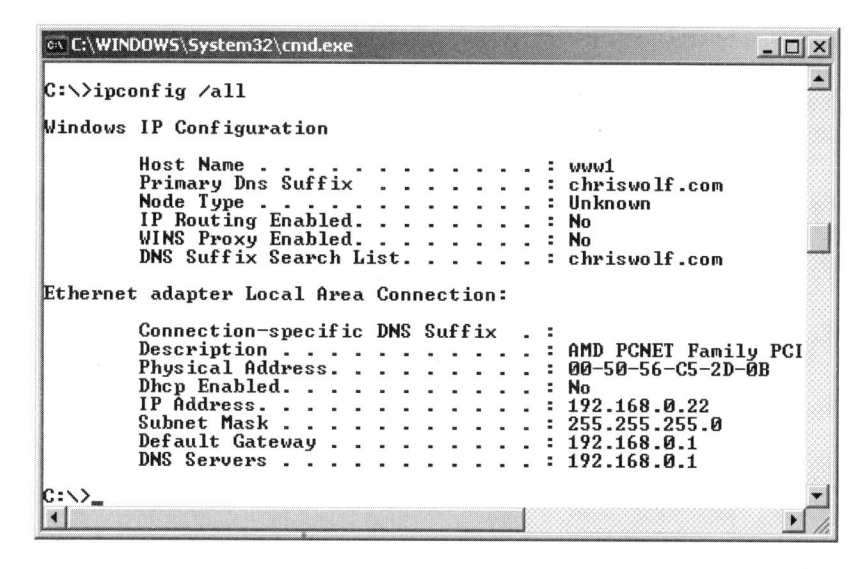

```
C:\>ipconfig /all

Windows IP Configuration

        Host Name . . . . . . . . . . . . : www1
        Primary Dns Suffix  . . . . . . . : chriswolf.com
        Node Type . . . . . . . . . . . . : Unknown
        IP Routing Enabled. . . . . . . . : No
        WINS Proxy Enabled. . . . . . . . : No
        DNS Suffix Search List. . . . . . : chriswolf.com

Ethernet adapter Local Area Connection:

        Connection-specific DNS Suffix  . :
        Description . . . . . . . . . . . : AMD PCNET Family PCI
        Physical Address. . . . . . . . . : 00-50-56-C5-2D-0B
        Dhcp Enabled. . . . . . . . . . . : No
        IP Address. . . . . . . . . . . . : 192.168.0.22
        Subnet Mask . . . . . . . . . . . : 255.255.255.0
        Default Gateway . . . . . . . . . : 192.168.0.1
        DNS Servers . . . . . . . . . . . : 192.168.0.1

C:\>
```

Figure 3-3. ipconfig /all output

the root of the problem. Most likely, as mentioned earlier in the Documenting the History of the Problem section, you will find evidence of this type of problem in the application log in the Event Viewer.

Remember, each of these checks is nothing more than clues to help you solve the mystery of the reported fault. In noting the installed applications and their relevance to the fault, you are collecting evidence that may aid in the eventual problem resolution. For software-related problems that integrate with hardware, another fault possibility to closely scrutinize is firmware, which is covered next.

Firmware

Not too long ago, I was attempting to upgrade the video driver on my laptop and was surprised to find that after the driver upgrade completed, my display looked worse than it did with the old driver. The problem wasn't that I had installed the wrong driver, but it was incompatible with the outdated firmware in the computer's Basic Input Output System (BIOS). After I downloaded the most recent firmware from the laptop manufacturer, the video display looked great.

Firmware problems are often found when you are attempting to install new software or use hardware that has been idle for an extended period of time. With storage libraries and RAID controllers, validating that firmware is the most recent version has become an automatic consideration for many who see it as preventative maintenance, allowing them to preempt the inevitable problem that would occur during a software installation that expected the new firmware.

You can check the firmware version for hardware when its related system first boots. For SCSI controllers, for example, you are prompted to press a key to enter the

SCSI BIOS during bootup. Once in the BIOS, you can see the current firmware version. On Intel Itanium-based computers, the firmware version is checked by accessing the Extensible Firmware Interface (EFI), which you access as you would the BIOS on an x86-class computer. In Chapter 4, you will see how to use the operating system tool MSinfo32 to check hardware settings such as the BIOS firmware version.

Once you have the current firmware version documented for the hardware in question, you should then go to the hardware manufacturer's Web site, where you can find information on the most recent firmware revisions available for download for their products. Some firmware upgrades can be downloaded directly to the device, as is the case with routers. Other upgrades, such as those that involve upgrading the BIOS on a computer's motherboard, may require you to place the firmware update on a floppy disk and then boot the computer from the floppy disk.

Good Computer, Bad Computer

If resources and time permit, another proven method for isolating faults on a system is to compare it with a known good reference. If you have two identical workstations, for example, you could compare the settings of each. If one system is not able to access the network, moving it to another desk with a known good connection allows you to eliminate or confirm that the network is the problem.

For software-related faults, you could compare network settings, such as DNS or WINS server addresses, or subnet masks. For troubleshooting a network with which you are not familiar, comparing the settings of two computers is often an easy way for you to quickly learn the software configuration on the network. Otherwise, if it is a network that you have been managing for some time, you probably already know the correct configuration information, and this would be an unnecessary step.

Documenting Processes Involved in the Problem

For any faults whose scope extends beyond the local computer, documentation of the big picture can be invaluable. Listing the processes involved in the problem not only allows you to build a list of possible faults, but also allows you to have a checklist of network objects to eliminate as possible faults during the troubleshooting process. In this section, you will see the power of diagramming the processes involved in a problem, and where to find information to help you list all involved processes.

A Picture's Worth a Thousand Words

When the reported problem's scope extends beyond a single localized system, a map can be your best friend. Take a blank paper, or if a whiteboard is available, use it to draw a map of the problem's related processes. For a site-level problem, you may need to include the site's DNS server, domain controller(s), global catalog server(s), WINS servers, and IIS servers. All potential problem pieces should be listed in your diagram. Once all the parts are listed, use simple lines to illustrate their dependencies. With dependencies listed, confirming one network object as running properly will allow you to eliminate its dependent objects as possible problems as well.

The faster that you can eliminate multiple potential problems, the faster you will narrow your search down to the actual problem. This approach is illustrated in Figure 3-4. In the illustration, the TCP/IP network is shown as a single object. Keep in mind that a TCP/IP network itself is full of relationships. In the diagram, the TCP/IP network encompasses the proper IP addresses and subnet mask for all dependent network components. Knowledge of the hardware involved on the network segment in question, including switches and routers, could also be documented.

Figure 3-4 is being used to troubleshoot a suspected network problem in which a client cannot access the company's intranet Web server. The server requires Integrated Windows authentication, and the client may need appropriate share or NTFS permissions, so objects for domain controllers (DC1, DC2) are listed as well. The client tries to contact the intranet server by its FQDN, so only it is dependent on the DNS servers. Note that everything depends on the TCP/IP network. With the optimist troubleshooting approach, you would first check the TCP/IP network by pinging the systems involved in the problem. If a problem is found, such as an improper static IP address, your work is finished. Since all other objects involved in the suspected problem depend on TCP/IP, checking it first is the quickest way to successfully identify the problem (as opposed to checking DNS1, DNS2, DC1, and DC2).

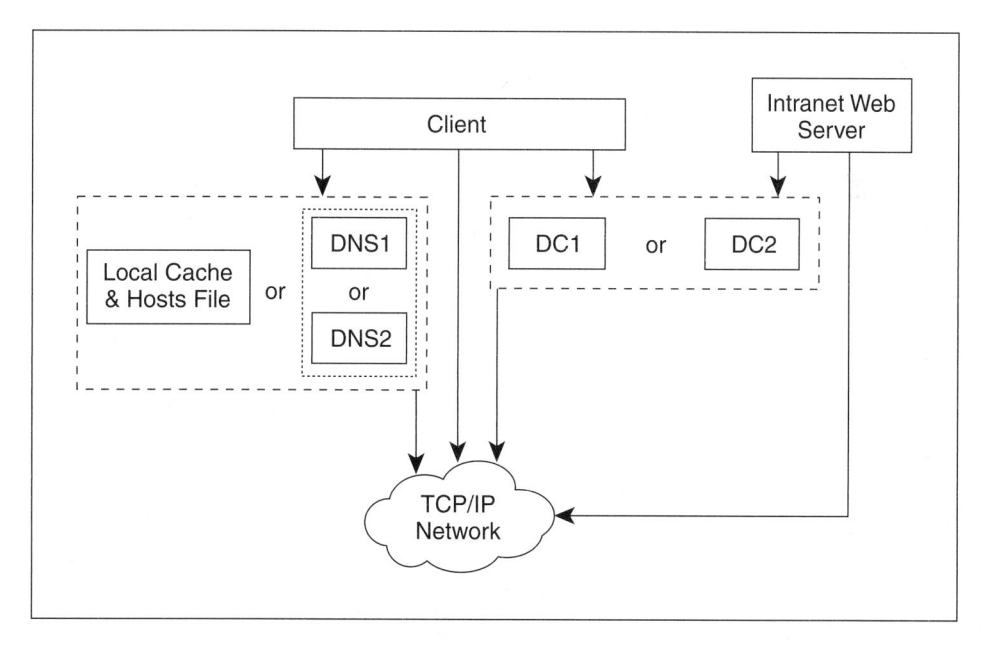

Figure 3-4. Troubleshooting dependency diagram

Eliminating What's Right

Now that you have all the evidence collected, it's time to process it. The quickest way to get to the cause of the fault is to start eliminating the processes involved in the problem that are working correctly. This section focuses on doing the little things in the troubleshooting process that almost always save you and others from circular troubleshooting.

Don't Reinvent the Wheel

If "Don't reinvent the wheel" isn't the most overused phrase in the IT community, it's right up there. Perhaps this phrase is uttered so much because we never seem to learn and have been doomed to continually repeat history. In troubleshooting, history is often repeated when network administrators respond to reported problems like firefighters running off to fight a fire. Sometimes, the best way to troubleshoot when a problem is first reported is to not even leave your seat. "Why?" you ask. The answer is simple. For most problems, an answer already exists, and someone has been kind enough to place the solution on the Internet.

Here are some places to find already documented solutions for the problem you are faced with.

- support.microsoft.com—From here, enter keywords for the error you are receiving, or enter the particular error code. If Microsoft has discovered your problem, you'll find the answer here.

- Application manufacturer's site—Most software vendors have their own public knowledge base for customers to find answers to common application problems.

- Readme files that came with the application—Here you can find information that may have been discovered just prior to the software release and thus will not be present in the product's documentation.

- Internet newsgroups—Newsgroups exemplify the true power of teamwork and are usually where you can find answers to very pointed and serious questions. You can also search newsgroup postings from www.google.com.

Aside from spending a few minutes looking for an already existing solution, don't neglect to check with your coworkers. They may have already seen the ghost you're chasing.

Microsoft has several excellent newsgroups for both troubleshooting and product information. Links to and information for accessing Microsoft newsgroups can be found at www.microsoft.com/technet/newsgroups.

Document What You Do!

What is *circular troubleshooting*? Circular troubleshooting occurs when several members of the same team find themselves repeatedly rechecking the same things. If you have already determined that something is functioning correctly, make a note of what you checked and how you confirmed that it was good. If you have been searching for a reason to justify billing the company for a new iPac or Palm Pilot, you have found it here. As you go through the process of eliminating the possible problems on the network, having a handheld or notepad handy will allow you to track what you do, thus preventing others from wasting their time repeating steps that you have already taken. Ever lose your keys and search the same drawer for them about ten times? Most of us have. Do we ever find them in that drawer? Nope! You probably have a similar story. Whether it's searching for keys or testing the same network components over and over again, repeating steps is simply wasting time.

Never Forget the Obvious

For most of us, at least one time in our troubleshooting lives we have made the mistake of spending minutes or hours troubleshooting a problem while ignoring the obvious. If you have troubleshot network connectivity problems for an hour only to find that the computer with the problem was not plugged into the network, you are not alone.

You may have had a user report to you that his or her monitor didn't work, only to later find that it wasn't plugged in. While we can go on and on with examples of overlooking the obvious, it is not necessary to make the point. Remember the Keep It Simple Stupid (KISS) rule. In your excitement to finally justify the use of your fancy network monitoring application, don't neglect to walk over to the computer with the network connectivity problem and see if its patch cable is even plugged in.

Move from the Big Picture to Small Details

Don't focus on the small details first. Top-down troubleshooting, where you focus on verifying the successful operation of parent services or processes, is generally the most efficient means to arrive at the source of a fault. Start at top-level services involved in the fault process, such as DNS, and work your way down to smaller, more specific possibilities that could be potential problems. Think of troubleshooting as a big game of Minesweeper. The more network objects (Minesweeper cells) that you can eliminate in one shot, the faster you will only have a handful of potential problems to check.

If You Pay for Support, Use It!

Let's face it—when you're dealing with hardware or software, odds are that you're not the first one to experience a particular problem. If the product you are having a problem with has a support contract, use it. The people that work with the product every day might be able to provide you with a quick resolution for your problem, instead of you having to spend hours trying on your own to solve the problem.

Prior to calling a support hot line, you may want to first check the vendor's Web site for a searchable knowledge base. Most of the problems the help desk staff solves on a daily basis are listed in the knowledge base. Do a search of your problem's description at the vendor's Web site, and you might be surprised to find the solution to your problem just a click away.

Anticipation can also save you time when you are at your wit's end with a problem. For hardware problems, the support staff will most likely ask you if you have the most recent driver installed or if you have downloaded the latest firmware revision. Before you pick up the phone, make sure that the software that relates to the hardware is current, because odds are that updating your driver may be the first thing the support staff has you do anyway. If, after you update the driver or firmware, the product still does not function properly, then it's time to call the support hot line.

Correcting the Problem

Once you have identified the problem, you will be faced with choices on how to correct it. While an optimal fix for any problem normally exists, several workarounds probably do as well. The way you go about correcting a problem can be just as important as the process of identifying the problem in the first place. This section addresses how to approach correcting problems once you have found them and looks at the consequences to the many workaround solutions.

When Speed Is of the Essence

Your time is valuable, just as it is for the network users, so if you can fix a problem in minutes, then do so. When a server or system needs to be brought up as quickly as possible, performing a restore from backup might be the fastest approach. Of course, if your problem is with a high-gigabyte or -terabyte file or a database server, then restoring from backup will most likely be the last resort.

For workstations, if you have a clone image from imaging software such as Ghost, or from Microsoft's Remote Installation Service (RIS), then you could perhaps consider reimaging the machine. If all of the user's business-related files are stored on a server, then reimaging the user's system should be your first course of action. The user, on the other hand, may not like losing all of his or her MP3s and other personal files stored on the workstation, but downloading some non-business-related application may have been what caused the problem in the first place.

Unfortunately for you, the decision to reimage or not to reimage might be driven by politics. If the CEO's laptop is having problems, odds are that you will be tasked with fixing the system at all costs, and reimaging would become the absolute last resort.

Don't Use Duct Tape

Duct tape troubleshooting methodology is commonly employed in many circumstances at home. If you have a leaky hose, just duct tape it. Have a tear in your awning? Duct tape! Have a broken car window? Duct tape! Believe it or not, one summer I was on a fishing trip, and one of the fishermen sustained a severe cut on his hand after a nasty encounter with a large bluefish. What did the deckhands use to stop the bleeding? You guessed it. Duct tape! The worst part of the story is not the fact that duct tape was used, but that it was actually stored in the first aid kit! OK, I know, you get the idea. With network troubleshooting, it's not the use of duct tape that will get you in trouble; instead, it's the use of "duct tape mentality."

What is duct tape mentality? Consider it to be the process of always looking for the quick fix. After all, it's faster to duct tape some plastic around a window instead of replacing the window. Sometimes a quick fix is only temporary, as in a broken window. However, oftentimes in the corporate world, a "temporary" fix might last for years.

If a user or group of users is experiencing a problem, look to fix the process causing the problem and not always the problem directly. For name resolution problems, it is usually easier to simply edit a Hosts file on a computer than it is to address the underlying problem with the DNS server. In time, changes in network naming or IP addresses may change, and as a result you would have to reconfigure the Hosts file everywhere that it was deployed, instead of making a single change to a now properly running DNS server. Duct taping a network problem will impress your peers, as they see how quickly you resolved the trouble, but will almost always cause problems down the road if the underlying process causing the problem is not addressed.

Process-Oriented Corrective Action

The more you correct the underlying processes that caused a problem, the easier your job will get. In the last section, you read an example of working around a DNS problem to arrive at a quick fix instead of taking the time to resolve the problem with the DNS server itself. Sometimes fixing a problem requires initially taking a step backward. For example, you may decide that several application problems are a result of users performing their own installations instead of the network administrators because there simply isn't enough time. If you have an Active Directory infrastructure in place, group policies can be used to distribute applications and application updates throughout your enterprise.

> Chapter 13 includes a section dedicated to the use of Active Directory group policies as a means to distribute and maintain applications.

Another example of process-related corrective action deals with NTFS and share-level permissions. Many administrators have on numerous occasions worked to correct a problem where a single user needed to access a particular shared folder, and granted the user's account access permissions directly to the share, instead of placing the user in a group with appropriate permissions. In other circumstances, some have applied the "fail proof" practice of placing a user with access problems in the Domain Administrator's user group. The immediate problem was solved, but the opportunity for additional problems down the road would increase significantly.

Always address the big picture whenever possible. Whether you need to reconfigure your DNS infrastructure, change your DHCP scope configuration, or even look at solutions involving distributed load balancing when issues are caused by congestion, you are always better off taking the time to correct the cause of the problem and not just the resultant problem itself.

Testing the Corrective Action

Now that you have corrected the problem, make sure that you test your corrective action first before sending out an e-mail alerting the company that you have triumphantly conquered the problem. Just because your system can connect to a server that was down, or you can now run a problematic application on a terminal server, don't assume that everyone can. On several workstations, including the workstation from where the problem was originally reported, verify that your solution has successfully resolved the problem.

Many troubleshooters, myself included, have made the mistake of proclaiming victory too soon, only to realize that what works on one system, still fails on all others. If you had to update software on several terminal servers, Internet servers, on intranet servers, test connectivity to all servers that were updated, and not just a select few to ensure that the update completed successfully.

Following Up

It was mentioned earlier in this chapter that many troubleshooting problems are simply duct taped. If you cannot permanently resolve a problem and you simply institute a hack to work around the true problem, don't forget to follow up and budget time to fix the real problem. If you use Outlook, you may consider placing a follow-up event at a later date in your calendar with a reminder for the event. This way, you can ensure that you will not forget to follow up your corrective action with any additional work.

If user error was the source of the problem, you may need to train the user on his or her mistake. If multiple users are making the same mistake (I'll refrain from making any user jokes here), then scheduling instructor-led group training may be the best course of action, to prevent the fault from reoccurring in the future.

Aside from users, also make sure to check at periodic intervals that your corrective action has improved performance on the systems and network components themselves. The application and system event logs should be periodically scanned on the problem systems in the weeks that follow the corrective action, to verify that no residual problems remain.

Summary

At this point, it probably is useful to briefly review the major steps of the troubleshooting method discussed in this chapter:

1. Identifying the problem
2. Documenting the history of the problem
3. Analyzing the current environment
4. Documenting processes involved in the problem
5. Eliminating what's right
6. Correcting the problem
7. Testing the corrective action

Don't get ahead of yourself or skip steps in troubleshooting if you want to identify the optimal solution. A merely patched problem will only crop up again, often at an inopportune time. The pessimistic approach may solve a network problem faster, but the optimistic approach—identifying what's working correctly as well as what's broken—usually solves it better.

In this chapter, you were exposed to the method behind the madness of troubleshooting. Now the fun is just beginning. Next, you will look at the abundance of operating system, resource kit, and freeware tools available for diagnosing and monitoring network performance and problems.

4

Monitoring and Diagnostic Tools

Many problems often overlap, especially when network troubleshooting is involved. This chapter outlines over 100 monitoring and troubleshooting tools available for Windows Server 2003 and XP systems. If you're wondering about the countless other troubleshooting and monitoring tools available for Windows enterprise networks, don't worry, because they are covered in later chapters. This chapter focuses exclusively on general troubleshooting and monitoring tools. Each remaining chapter in this book includes information on additional troubleshooting and monitoring tools that are relevant to its topic.

Operating System Tools

Many valuable tools with Microsoft operating systems go unnoticed because they are not installed by default. While installation of the operating system does provide you with a multitude of tools, many advanced tools can by found in the System Tools folder on the Windows OS installation CD, and others exist in Windows resource kits. This chapter shows you how to use all tools, not just those installed with the OS. For tools included in the Support Tools folder, you will see (ST) next to the tool's name. Resource kit tools are identified in this book with (RK) adjacent to them.

To install the support tools on a server or workstation, follow these steps.

1. Log on to the system using an account with local administrative privileges, and insert the Windows installation CD into the CD-ROM drive.

2. Click Start > Run, and then click the Browse button.

3. Navigate to the <CD drive letter>\SUPPORT\Tools folder.

4. In the Files of Type drop-down menu, select All Files.

5. Now click the SUPTOOLS.msi file in the Browse dialog box and click Open.

6. Verify that the path to the SUPTOOLS.msi file is listed in the Run dialog box and click OK.

7. Once the wizard welcome window opens, click Next.

8. Click I Agree to accept the terms of the license agreement and then click Next.

9. Enter your name and organization in their associated fields and click Next.

10. Select Complete to install all support tools and click Next.

11. Enter the path for where you wish to install the tools and click Install Now.

12. Once the installation completes, click Finish.

> You may want to consider publishing the Support Tools installation MSI file in a domain or organizational unit (OU) group policy that only applies to administrators or help desk personnel. This way, if you need to perform advanced tests on a user's workstation, you will have the ability to install the Support Tools once you log on to the workstation. More information on group policy management can be found in Chapter 13, Active Directory.

Resource kit tools differ from support tools primarily in two ways.

- To get all resource kit tools, you have to purchase the resource kit (a few sample resource kit tools are available for download from Microsoft).

- Resource kit tools are not supported by Microsoft, so you cannot get technical assistance if you have trouble running one of them.

Microsoft's resource kits for their products are usually very inexpensive, generally priced less than a few hundred dollars. Considering the wealth of knowledge and additional tools that you get when purchasing a resource kit, they are well worth their price. All Microsoft operating systems have resource kits associated with them for purchase, and nearly all Microsoft .NET Enterprise Servers (Exchange, SQL, and so on) do as well. Resource kit tools do not undergo the same extensive testing as operating system and support tools, and thus are not supported. Do not worry too much about the support issue. Resource kit tools are always well documented and are very reliable.

Often, a tool appears for one release in a resource kit and by the next release graduates to the Support Tools folder. This was the case with many Windows 2000 resource kit tools, since most became Windows Server 2003 and Windows XP support tools.

To install a Microsoft resource kit on a system, follow these steps.

1. Log on to the system using an account with local administrative privileges, and insert the Windows installation CD into the CD-ROM drive.
2. Click Start > Run, and then click the Browse button.
3. Navigate to the CD drive letter, and then double-click the Resource Kit folder (if present).
4. Then click the Setup file and click Open.
5. In the Run dialog box, click OK.
6. At the resource kit setup welcome window, click Next.
7. Click I Agree to accept the terms of the license agreement and click Next.
8. Enter your name and organization in their associated fields and click Next.
9. Select Typical for the installation type and click Next.
10. Click Next to begin the installation.
11. When the installation completes, click Finish.

This chapter assumes some use of the Microsoft Management Console (MMC). The MMC is not a tool in itself, but rather a single interface, or shell, that can contain numerous tools, which are known as snap-ins. If you work with six tools on a daily basis, you can load their equivalent snap-ins into a single MMC for convenience of monitoring. All of your management tools will be present in a single window. Nearly all Microsoft tools have MMC snap-ins, and any third-party application that claims to be Windows certified will have a snap-in for their product as well.

Follow these steps to configure an MMC.

1. Click Start > Run, enter MMC in the Run dialog box, and click OK.
2. Now click the Console menu and choose Add/Remove Snap-in, or press Ctrl-M on your keyboard.
3. Click the Add button and select the MMC snap-ins to add to the console by double-clicking each snap-in that you wish to add.
4. When finished selecting snap-ins, click the Close button in the Add Standalone Snap-in dialog box.
5. Click OK to close the Add/Remove Snap-in dialog box.
6. You should now see the snap-ins displayed in the console. You can save the console by clicking Save As from the Console menu. By default, all MMC consoles are saved to the Administrative Tools folder.

One other invaluable tool for troubleshooting XP workstations and W2K3 servers is the Help and Support Center. If you have had poor experiences with online Help in the

Chapter 4 Monitoring and Diagnostic Tools

past, don't let it discourage you. With Windows NT, online Help had little value. With Windows 2000, Help had some value. With XP/W2K3, navigating to the Help and Support Center is well worth your time. To access the online Help, simply click Start and then Help and Support.

Figure 4-1 shows the Help and Support Center home window on a W2K3 server. From this interface, you can do the following:

- Find information on OS tools, support tools, and resource kit tools
- Launch one of the several troubleshooting wizards
- Find information about a particular error message
- Check for hardware or software incompatibilities
- Run or configure the Windows Update service
- Read the online documentation

Although many would never recommend using online Help with previous Windows versions, with XP/W2K3 it's much more than a development afterthought and is something that even most experienced network administrators will find useful.

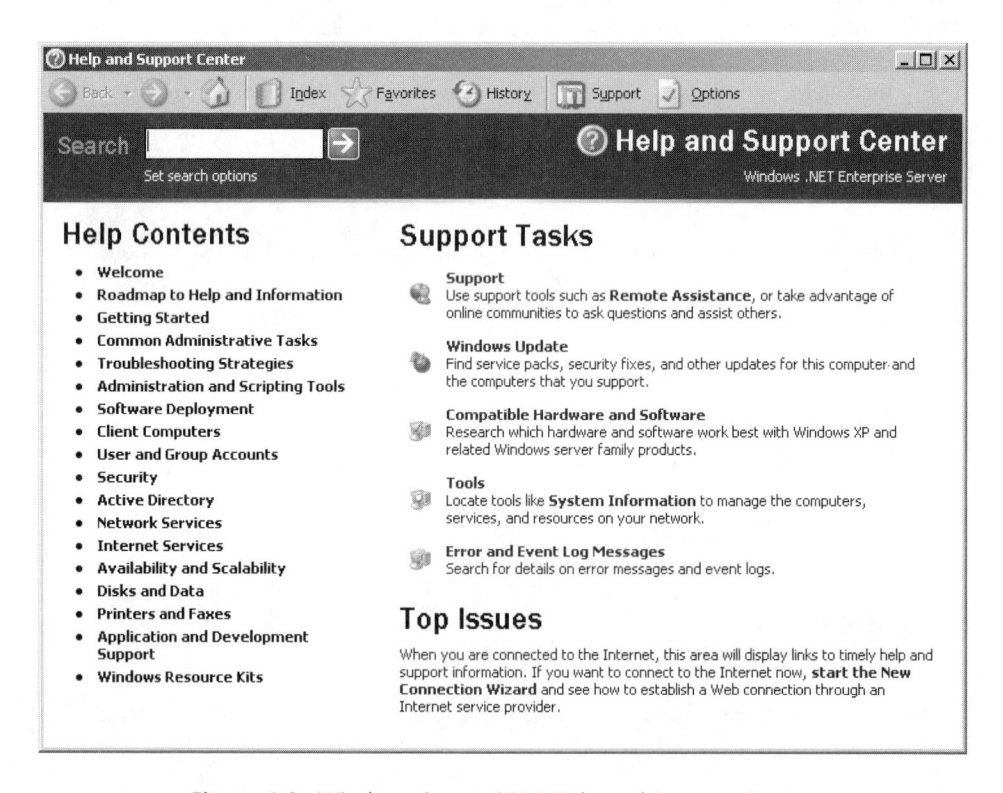

Figure 4-1. Windows Server 2003 Help and Support Center

Before we look at specific tools, you need to understand the way syntax is described in this chapter. It is a standard notation.

- [ ] = Optional parameter
- <> = Required parameter
- | (pipe symbol) = OR function; so if you saw <a|b> you would include a or b in the syntax, but not both.

Now that you know where to find the tools discussed in this chapter and how they are defined, let's get to using them. The following sections focus on the common Microsoft troubleshooting and monitoring tools. Each section is organized by subsections called Command Line Tools and GUI Tools so that you can easily find the tool you're looking for.

Disk Management Tools

In Chapter 7, Disk Subsystems, you will examine the more advanced disk troubleshooting and monitoring tools. Since faulty hard disks can cause so many problems with other W2K3 services, it is important to have a solid understanding of Microsoft's core disk testing and monitoring tools. This section examines three command line tools available to aid you in disk management, as well as two handy GUI tools.

Command Line Tools

The most common disk management command line tools are

- chkdsk
- chkntfs
- defrag

The syntax and usage for each of these tools are explained in the next three sections.

chkdsk

Suspect that a faulty hard disk is at the root of a problem? Then running chkdsk may allow you to verify your suspicions. When run, chkdsk, short for *check disk*, performs a check of a hard disk and alerts you of any problems with the disk. You can also use the command to fix any errors that it finds on the specified disk. The syntax for the command is:

```
chkdsk [volume | [[path] filename]]] [/c] [/f] [/i] [/l:[size]] [/r] [/v] [/x]
```

The command parameters are explained in Table 4-1.

Chapter 4 Monitoring and Diagnostic Tools

Table 4-1. chkdsk Command Options

Option	Use
volume	Indicates the drive letter (followed by a :), mount point, or volume name on which the chkdsk command should be run.
filename	Only for FAT or FAT32 volumes; lists the file(s) to check for fragmentation.
/c	On NTFS volumes only; causes the command to skip checking cycles within the folder structure, thus reducing the amount of time needed for the command to complete.
/f	Causes the command to fix any errors it finds on the disk.
/i	On NTFS volumes only; causes a less detailed check of the volume's indexes to be performed, thus shortening the amount of time required for the command to complete.
/l:size	On NTFS volumes only; when used, can either display the log file or change its size. The log file is used if the system crashes while chkdsk is running, allowing the chkdsk command to complete from where it left off once the computer restarts.
/r	Recovers readable information found on bad disk sectors (implies /f).
/v	Verbose mode—for NTFS, cleanup messages are displayed; for FAT or FAT32 file systems, the full path and name of every file on the disk that is checked is displayed.
/x	Forces the volume to dismount before chkdsk is run, invalidating all open handles on the volume.

The most common use of the chkdsk command is to check and fix disk problems. For example, to check and repair bad sectors on the E drive, you would run chkdsk e: /f.

The execution and output from running chkdsk is shown in Figure 4-2.

chkntfs

By default, when Windows restarts after an improper shutdown, chkdsk runs automatically. For large gigabyte or even terabyte file systems, chkdsk could take hours to complete. Since it is run during startup after a system crash, you may decide that it is better to have the system restart automatically, without running chkdsk on certain volumes. This is where chkntfs comes into the picture. With chkntfs, you can disable chkdsk from automatically running on certain volumes, thus preventing a slow system restart after a failure.

Here is the syntax for chkntfs:

```
chkntfs [/C] [/X] volume
chkntfs /D
chkntfs /T:time
```

The command options are explained in Table 4-2.

Table 4-2. chkntfs Command Options

Option	Use
volume	Indicates the drive letter (followed by a :), mount point, or volume name on which the chkntfs command should be run.
/C	Schedules chkntfs to run on the drive at the next reboot.
/X	Causes the command to skip checking cycles within the folder structure, thus reducing the amount of time needed for the command to complete.
chkntfs /D	Resets the autochk (chkdsk) settings to the system defaults.
chkntfs /T:<time>	Used to show or set the autochk initiation countdown time, which is the time the system pauses before running chkdsk when a "dirty" volume is detected at startup.

You could use chkntfs to disable chkdsk from automatically running if it thought the E drive was dirty by typing the command chkntfs /X E:. If you wanted to set chkdsk to run on the F drive the next time the system booted, you would enter chkntfs /C F:.

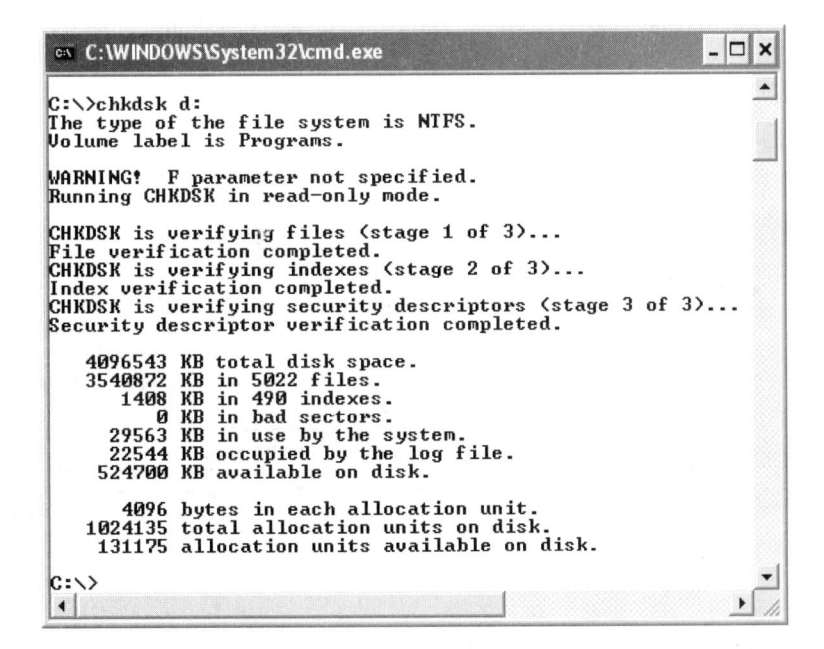

```
C:\>chkdsk d:
The type of the file system is NTFS.
Volume label is Programs.

WARNING!  F parameter not specified.
Running CHKDSK in read-only mode.

CHKDSK is verifying files (stage 1 of 3)...
File verification completed.
CHKDSK is verifying indexes (stage 2 of 3)...
Index verification completed.
CHKDSK is verifying security descriptors (stage 3 of 3)...
Security descriptor verification completed.

   4096543 KB total disk space.
   3540872 KB in 5022 files.
      1408 KB in 490 indexes.
         0 KB in bad sectors.
     29563 KB in use by the system.
     22544 KB occupied by the log file.
    524700 KB available on disk.

      4096 bytes in each allocation unit.
   1024135 total allocation units on disk.
    131175 allocation units available on disk.

C:\>
```

Figure 4-2. Using chkdsk to check the status of the D drive

defrag

In the early days of NTFS volumes at the time of Windows NT's birth, Microsoft insisted that NTFS volumes do not fragment, and thus a defragmenting tool was not needed. After a few third-party tools proved this to be wrong, Microsoft backtracked and included its own defragmenting tool with the OS, beginning with Windows 2000.

Since files are continually written to and deleted from hard drives, parts of a single file may become spread across a hard drive (fragmented), making it time consuming for the OS to retrieve the file when needed.

> When nothing has changed on a system for several months, and it progressively runs slower and slower, odds are that its hard disk is fragmented.

With Windows 2000, administrators and users can use a GUI tool (explained in the next section) to analyze suspected fragmented drives and defragment them. Beginning with Windows XP/W2K3, administrators also have a command line tool at their disposal in `defrag`. While this may not seem so exciting (why do at the command line what I can do with a GUI?), being able to defragment a disk with a command line utility opens up numerous scripting possibilities that previously were not possible. For example, `defrag` could be included with other commands in a batch file that is scheduled to run once a month. Having this run on the first Sunday of every month, at 3:00 AM, for example, allows you to repair disk performance problems on users' systems before they even occur.

Here is the syntax for `defrag`:

```
defrag <volume> [-a] [-f] [-v]
```

Table 4-3 describes the command options.

Table 4-3. defrag Command Options

Option	Use
volume	Indicates the drive letter (followed by a :), mount point, or volume name on which the `defrag` command should be run.
-a	Analyze only—displays a report on disk fragmentation status.
-f	Forces defragmentation to run even if defragmentation is not necessary.
-v	Verbose mode—causes detailed information about the defragmentation analysis to be displayed.

The result of running `defrag` to analyze a hard disk is shown in Figure 4-3.

Disk Management Tools

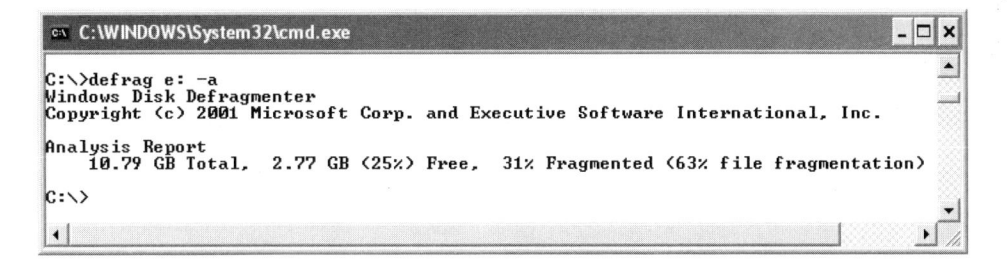

```
C:\>defrag e: -a
Windows Disk Defragmenter
Copyright (c) 2001 Microsoft Corp. and Executive Software International, Inc.

Analysis Report
    10.79 GB Total,  2.77 GB (25%) Free,  31% Fragmented (63% file fragmentation)
C:\>
```

Figure 4-3. Using defrag to analyze fragmentation status on the E drive

Now that you've seen how the `defrag` command works, let's quickly look at using it to perform some preventative maintenance. Windows Task Scheduler provides a simple interface to schedule commands to run at regular intervals. These are the steps to set up Task Scheduler to run a monthly defragmentation of a system's D drive.

1. Open Task Scheduler by clicking Start > All Programs > Accessories > System Tools > Scheduled Tasks.

2. In the Scheduled Tasks window, click the File menu, select New, and then click Scheduled Task.

3. When an icon for the new task appears, name the task "MonthlyDefrag."

4. Now right-click the task icon, and select Properties.

5. As shown in Figure 4-4, enter `defrag d:` in the Run field.

6. Now click the Schedule tab to set the day and time for the job to run.

7. In the Schedule Task drop-down menu, select Monthly.

8. For the Start Time, select 1:00AM.

9. In the Schedule Task Monthly portion of the window, click the radio button, select First and then Saturday.

10. Click OK.

11. The scheduled task can be tested by right-clicking the task icon in the Scheduled Tasks window and selecting Run.

Scheduled tasks can also be configured from the command prompt by using the command `schtasks`. For more information on how to use this command, at a command prompt type `schtasks /?`.

Figure 4-4. Scheduling regular defragmentation using Task Scheduler and the defrag command

GUI Tools

Two common Windows GUI disk maintenance tools are Disk Management and Disk Defragmenter. These tools are essential components for both server and workstation management and are included with the operating system.

Disk Management

Disk Management is a GUI tool that allows you to configure and check the status of hard disks on a computer. The tool is located in the Computer Management MMC, so to access it, follow these steps.

1. Click Start > All Programs > Administrative Tools > Computer Management.

2. In Computer Management, expand the Storage object and click Disk Management (see Figure 4-5).

Some common troubleshooting scenarios for using Disk Management are shown in Table 4-4.

Chapter 7 covers troubleshooting fault-tolerant disks, such as RAID 1 and RAID 5 volumes.

Disk Management Tools   57

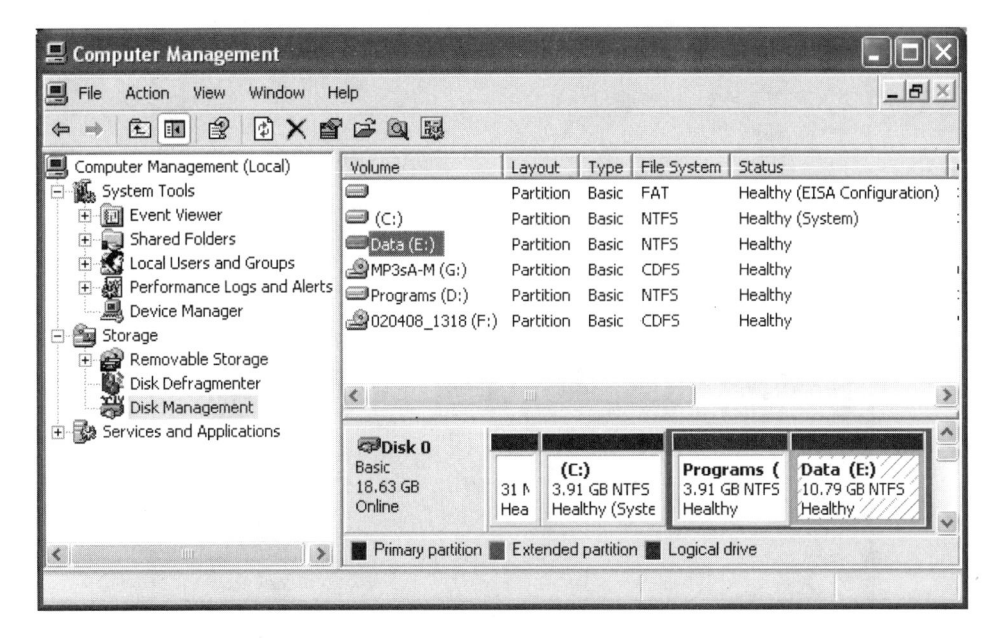

Figure 4-5. Accessing Disk Management in the Computer Management MMC

Table 4-4. Disk Management Troubleshooting

Problem	Solution
Hot-swappable replacement disk added to array—disk not shown in disk management	Right-click the Disk Management icon and select Rescan Disks.
Volume listed as Failed or Offline	Right-click the failed volume and select Reactivate Disk. If the disk still does not come online, replace the disk.

Disk Defragmenter

When you suspect that fragmentation is at the root of a system's performance problems, it's time to open Disk Defragmenter. Disk Defragmenter is located in the System Tools folder and is accessed by clicking Start > All Programs > Accessories > System Tools > Disk Defragmenter.

Once you have opened it (see Figure 4-6), you should first perform an analysis of the suspected drive by selecting a drive and then clicking the Analyze button.

If the disk is more than 15% fragmented, you will be prompted by the OS that it needs to be defragmented. At that point, you can select whether to defragment the drive, view the defragmentation report, or simply close the window. Remember that defragmentation is very disk and CPU intensive, so make sure that when you elect to defragment a disk, it is during a period when access to the system's resources is not necessary.

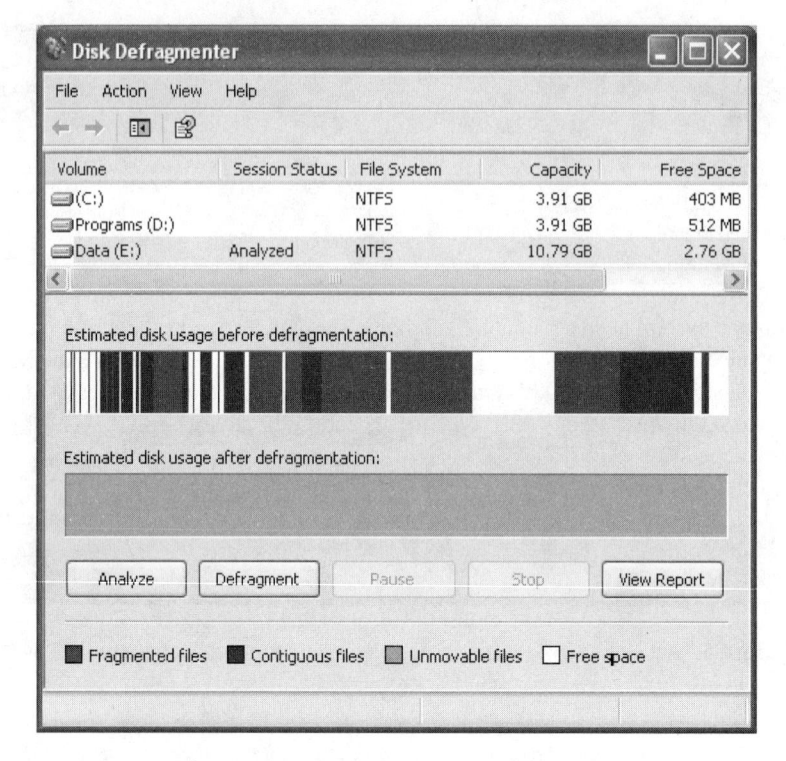

Figure 4-6. Disk Defragmenter

Now that you've seen some of the basic disk management tools, let's get to the many indispensable operating system tools for monitoring and troubleshooting network-related problems.

Network Monitoring and Troubleshooting Tools

When troubleshooting is considered in the enterprise, the network is most often looked at when a problem arises. While sometimes the network is indeed the source of a problem, on other occasions it is merely the scapegoat. When you are troubleshooting, there are several tools that will allow you to quickly determine whether or not the network is the source of a problem. In this section, we'll look at the countless command line network troubleshooting tools and then move on to the many GUI tools.

Command Line Tools

Numerous command line tools exist for managing Microsoft networks. In this section, we look at each tool and its syntax, as well as outline the situations where each command is most useful. We begin with the command with the funny name: `arp`.

arp

Usually when I speak about `arp`, at least one person in the audience acts like a seal and shouts, "Arp, arp, arp!" Aside from bringing a smile to us computer geeks, `arp` does have other uses.

The `arp` command is derived from Address Resolution Protocol (ARP), which is a required TCP/IP standard. Every piece of hardware connected to a network has a unique 48-bit Media Access Control (MAC) address, which is normally expressed in hexadecimal. ARP is used to associate a network interface's MAC address, such as 00-50-56-40-1E-BE, to its IP address, such as 10.0.0.100.

When one system needs to contact another system on its local subnet, it broadcasts an ARP request on the local subnet, which is its way of saying, "Hey, what's the MAC address for system 10.10.29.108?" Once the MAC address for that IP address is discovered, it is stored in the system's ARP cache. By caching IP address–to–MAC address associations, the system will not have to broadcast an ARP request the next time a computer needs to send a packet to the same system on its local subnet.

The `arp` command can be handy for troubleshooting when one system cannot contact another system on the same subnet. An example of when you would run into an improper ARP cache entry could be when two systems on the same subnet were accidentally assigned the same IP address. When this happens, a computer could have the wrong MAC address cached for a particular IP address. This is where the `arp` command is useful. Here's its syntax:

```
arp -a [IP address] [-N <Interface_address>]
arp -d <IP address> [Interface address]
arp -s <IP address> <MAC address> [Interface address]
```

The `arp` command options are explained in Table 4-5.

Table 4-5. arp Command Options

Option	Use
`-a`	Displays IP address–to–MAC address mappings stored in a system's ARP cache.
`-d`	Deletes the ARP cache entry for the IP address specified.
`-s`	Adds a static (permanent) IP address–to–MAC address mapping to the ARP cache.
`<IP address>`	Causes information to be displayed only for the IP address entered.
`<Interface address>`	For systems with multiple NICs, this is used to specify the MAC address of the local NIC that you wish to run the `arp` command on; otherwise, the command is always run on the first bound NIC in the network binding order.
`<MAC address>`	Used to specify a MAC address on which to create a static ARP cache entry.

Here are some examples of using `arp` for troubleshooting.

- Display the entire ARP cache on a computer with a single NIC: `arp -a`
- Delete an invalid entry in the ARP cache: `arp -d 10.98.7.205`
- Add a static entry to the ARP cache: `arp -s 10.98.7.205 00-aa-73-51-b8-4e`

While `arp` is a great tool, notice that in some situations, you will need to know the MAC address of a remote system, and that's where `getmac` is valuable.

getmac

With `getmac`, you can determine the MAC address of a remote system without having to leave your desk. Here is the syntax for `getmac`:

```
getmac [/s <system> [/u <username> [/p <password>]]] [/fo <format>]
[/nh] [/v]
```

The `getmac` parameters are explained in Table 4-6.

Table 4-6. getmac Command Options

Option	Use
/s <system>	Used to specify the name or IP address of the remote system for which you need the MAC address(es).
/u <username>	Specifies the name of the domain user under which the command should run.
/p <password>	When /u is used, specifies the password for the domain user.
/fo <format>	Specifies the format for the output data; valid choices are table (default), list, or csv.
/nh	For table and csv output formats, causes the column header not to be displayed.
/v	Verbose mode—causes more detailed information to be displayed.

Figure 4-7 shows the execution of `getmac`.

hostname

The `hostname` command provides a quick way to determine the host name of a local system. This command cannot be run remotely. The command syntax is `hostname`. Once the command is executed, the host name of the system is displayed.

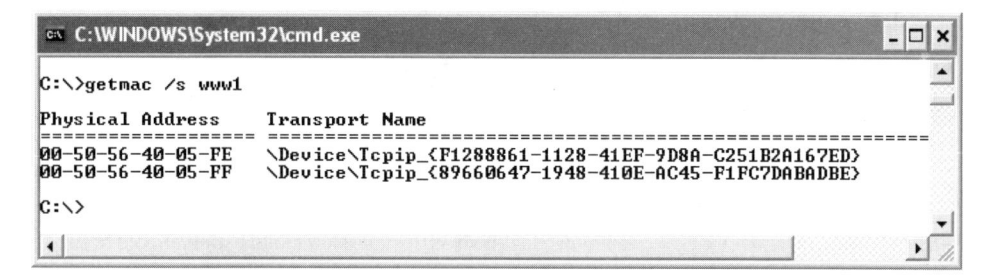

Network Monitoring and Troubleshooting Tools 61

```
C:\>getmac /s www1

Physical Address    Transport Name
=================   ===========================================================
00-50-56-40-05-FE   \Device\Tcpip_{F1288861-1128-41EF-9D8A-C251B2A167ED}
00-50-56-40-05-FF   \Device\Tcpip_{89660647-1948-410E-AC45-F1FC7DABADBE}

C:\>
```

Figure 4-7. Using getmac to find MAC addresses for a remote system

nbtstat

While `hostname` is the simplest command line tool you'll see in this section, `nbtstat` is one of the more advanced commands. It is useful for displaying NetBIOS over TCP/IP (NetBT) information and is primarily useful when you are troubleshooting older systems (pre–Windows 2000) on your network. Beginning with Windows 2000, NetBT is no longer a Windows TCP/IP requirement, so you will find this tool helpful mainly when you are working with Windows NT workstations.

Here is the syntax for `nbtstat`:

```
nbtstat [-a <computer name>] [-A <IP address>] [-c] [-n] [-r] [-R]
[-RR] [-s] [-S][Refresh interval]
```

The `nbtstat` parameters are explained in Table 4-7.

Table 4-7. nbtstat Command Options

Option	Use
-a <computer name>	Used to display the NetBIOS name table of the remote computer specified.
-A <IP address>	Used to display the NetBIOS name table for the remote computer with the IP address specified.
-c	Displays the NetBIOS cache table.
-n	Displays the NetBIOS name table of the local computer.
-r	Used to display NetBIOS name resolution statistics, including name resolution performed by broadcast and by a WINS server.
-R	Purges the contents of the NetBIOS cache. Any static NetBIOS name–to–IP address mappings with the "#PRE" designation in the LMHosts file are then added to the NetBIOS cache.

continues

Table 4-7. nbtstat Command Options, continued

Option	Use
`-RR`	Used to release the client's NetBIOS names from its associated WINS server(s) and then refresh the client's NetBIOS names with its WINS server(s). This command is useful for updating a WINS server after a client's IP address has changed.
`-s`	Used to display the NetBIOS session table, listing remote hosts by NetBIOS names.
`-S`	Used to display the NetBIOS session table, listing remote hosts by IP addresses.
`Refresh interval`	If a refresh interval is specified (number of seconds), the command will continually loop and refresh its output until it is manually terminated by pressing Ctrl-C.

> Notice that many of the command switches are case sensitive. Be careful not to use `-r` when you meant to use `-R`.

Here are some common uses for `nbtstat` when you are troubleshooting NetBIOS name resolution.

- To purge and then reregister a client's dynamic WINS registration: `nbtstat -RR`
- After changing a server's IP address, use this if a client is still trying to connect to the server using its old IP address: `nbtstat -R`

netdiag (ST)

The `netdiag` command is a great tool for troubleshooting networking-related issues on workstations. When run from the command prompt, this tool performs a series of tests on the client's TCP/IP network configuration and reports any errors that it finds. When it is run without parameters, all possible tests are run; otherwise, you can run one or more tests. The tests that the command performs are

- `Autonet`—Automatic Private IP Addressing (APIPA)
- `Bindings`—Network bindings
- `Browser`—Browser and Redirector
- `DCList`—Domain controller list

Network Monitoring and Troubleshooting Tools 63

- `DefGW`—Default gateway
- `DNS`—DNS recursive query
- `DsGetDC`—Domain controller discovery
- `IPConfig`—IP address configuration
- `IPLoopBk`—IP address loopback ping
- `IPX`—IPX networking
- `Kerberos`—Kerberos security
- `Ldap`—Lightweight Directory Access Protocol (LDAP)
- `Member`—Domain membership
- `Modem`—Modem diagnostics
- `NbtNm`—NetBT name
- `Ndis`—Netcard queries
- `NetBTTransports`—NetBT transports
- `Netstat`—Network statistical information
- `NetWare`—NetWare server
- `Route`—Routing table
- `Trust`—Trust relationships
- `WAN`—WAN configuration
- `WINS`—WINS service
- `Winsock`—Winsock test

As you can see, the utility performs several tests. What makes this utility so useful is that many of the tests performed are tests that you would manually do during the troubleshooting process. With `netdiag`, you can run all these tests simultaneously and have the command just tell you which tests have failed, thus allowing you to quickly nail down a problem with a client computer.

Here's the syntax for `netdiag`:

```
netdiag [/q] [/v] [/l] [/debug] [/d:<domain name>] [/fix]
[/dcaccountenum] [/test:<test name>] [/skip:<test name>]
```

The `netdiag` options are described in Table 4-8.

Chapter 4 Monitoring and Diagnostic Tools

Table 4-8. netdiag Command Options

Option	Use
/q	Quiet output—only reports errors (normally the results of all tests are displayed).
/v	Verbose output—detailed information is shown.
/l	Log output—output data is sent to the Netdiag.log file stored in the same directory where the command was run.
/debug	Even more verbose output than with the /v switch (the command takes longer to complete).
/d:<domain name>	Locates a domain controller in the specified domain.
/fix	Repairs minor problems.
/dcaccountenum	Enumerates domain controller computer accounts.
/test:<test name>	Performs only the test listed (except for basic tests that cannot be skipped).
/skip:<test name>	Used to release the client's NetBIOS names from its associated WINS server(s) and then refresh the client's NetBIOS names with its WINS server(s). This command is useful for updating a WINS server after a client's IP address has changed.

One of the most popular ways to run the `netdiag` command is with the `/q` switch. This way, you only see the potential problems displayed.

Figure 4-8 shows a portion of the `netdiag` test results, indicating a problem with DNS server connectivity.

Net Services Commands

There are several Net Services commands at your disposal for managing a network. In this section, you will see the most useful Net Services commands for troubleshooting Windows workstations and servers. Let's start with the four basic Net Services commands for starting, stopping, pausing, and resuming Windows services.

net start | stop | pause | continue
The `net start`, `stop`, `pause`, and `continue` commands are used to administer services from the command line. The syntax for these commands is:

```
net <start | stop | pause | continue> <service name>
```

These commands can be run locally or through a Telnet session to another computer. For example, if you wanted to start the DNS Server service on a local system, from the command prompt you would type `net start DNS`. To stop the DNS Server service, you would enter `net stop DNS`.

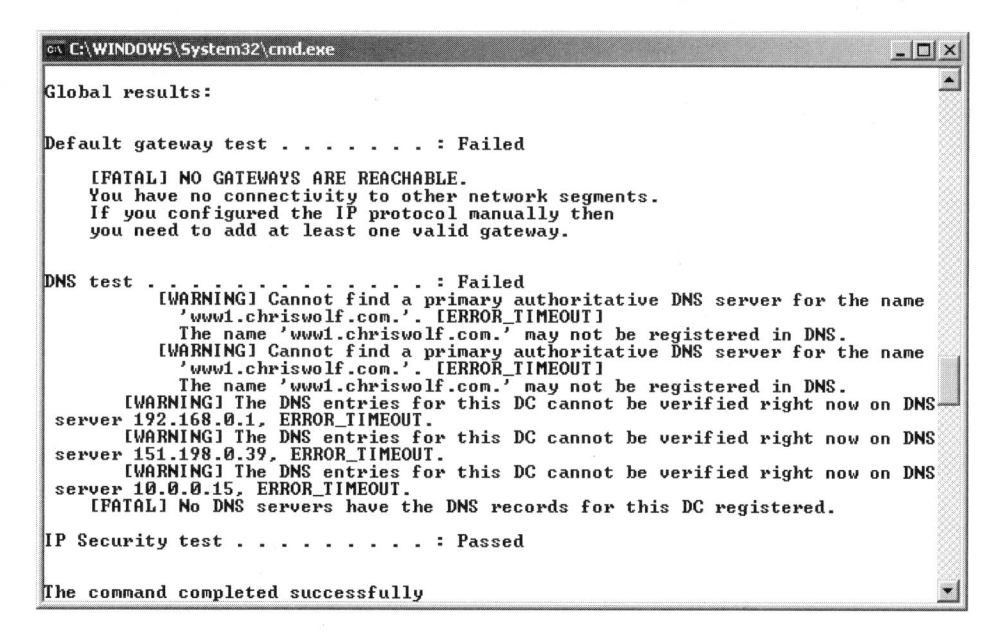

Network Monitoring and Troubleshooting Tools   65

```
Global results:

Default gateway test . . . . . . . : Failed
        [FATAL] NO GATEWAYS ARE REACHABLE.
        You have no connectivity to other network segments.
        If you configured the IP protocol manually then
        you need to add at least one valid gateway.

DNS test . . . . . . . . . . . . . : Failed
        [WARNING] Cannot find a primary authoritative DNS server for the name
                'www1.chriswolf.com.'. [ERROR_TIMEOUT]
        The name 'www1.chriswolf.com.' may not be registered in DNS.
        [WARNING] Cannot find a primary authoritative DNS server for the name
                'www1.chriswolf.com.'. [ERROR_TIMEOUT]
        The name 'www1.chriswolf.com.' may not be registered in DNS.
        [WARNING] The DNS entries for this DC cannot be verified right now on DNS
 server 192.168.0.1, ERROR_TIMEOUT.
        [WARNING] The DNS entries for this DC cannot be verified right now on DNS
 server 151.198.0.39, ERROR_TIMEOUT.
        [WARNING] The DNS entries for this DC cannot be verified right now on DNS
 server 10.0.0.15, ERROR_TIMEOUT.
        [FATAL] No DNS servers have the DNS records for this DC registered.

IP Security test . . . . . . . . . : Passed

The command completed successfully
```

Figure 4-8. Identifying a DNS error by running netdiag

net statistics

The net statistics command is useful for identifying operational networking statistics for both the Server and Workstation services. This command is useful for identifying TCP/IP networking problems such as

- Network errors
- Hung sessions
- Failed sessions
- Failed operations

While the command only reports on errors, it does allow you to confirm or deny your suspicions about a suspected problem. Here is the syntax for the net statistics command:

```
net statistics [server | workstation]
```

When used without parameters, net statistics reports on whatever statistics are available. Otherwise, you can examine statistics particular to either the Server service or the Workstation service. Using net statistics to view workstation statistics is shown in Figure 4-9.

```
C:\>net statistics workstation
Workstation Statistics for \\WOLF-LP

Statistics since 4/23/2002 5:53 PM

  Bytes received                               159210
  Server Message Blocks (SMBs) received        975
  Bytes transmitted                            212372
  Server Message Blocks (SMBs) transmitted     973
  Read operations                              0
  Write operations                             0
  Raw reads denied                             0
  Raw writes denied                            0

  Network errors                               0
  Connections made                             14
  Reconnections made                           0
  Server disconnects                           0

  Sessions started                             0
  Hung sessions                                0
  Failed sessions                              0
  Failed operations                            13
  Use count                                    60
  Failed use count                             0

The command completed successfully.

C:\>_
```

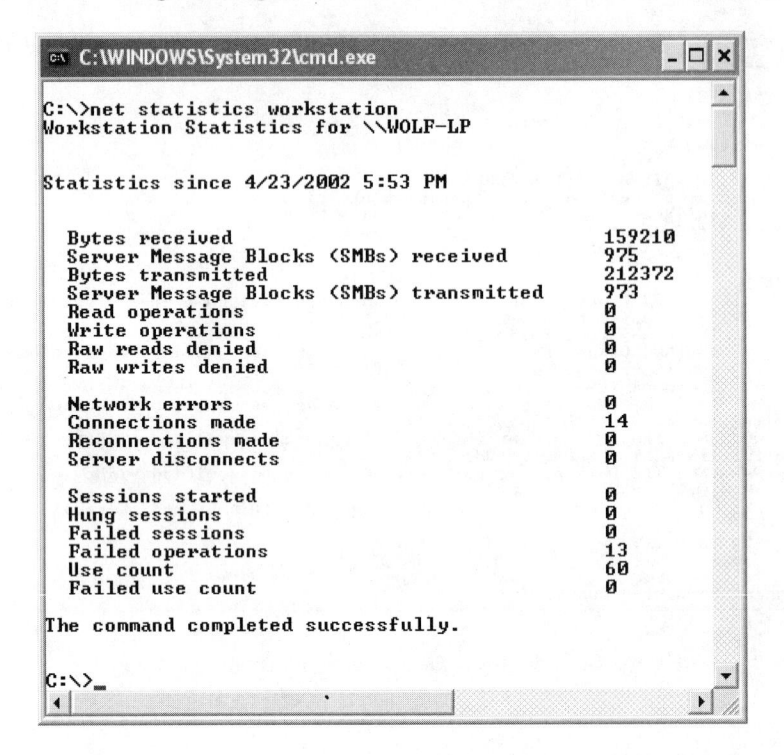

Figure 4-9. Checking for workstation session failures with net statistics

net session

Suppose with `net statistics` you were able to identify a hung session. How do you terminate it? For that, Microsoft gives you `net session`. This command, which only works on servers, allows you to view active sessions and to disconnect sessions. The syntax for `net session` is:

```
net session [\\computer name] [/delete]
```

The command options are explained in Table 4-9.

Table 4-9. net session Command Options

Option	Use
\\computer name	Displays session information for the named computer.
/delete	When this option is used by itself, all sessions with the server are terminated and all open files are closed. When a computer name is specified, only the sessions with the selected computer are terminated.

Network Monitoring and Troubleshooting Tools

If the command is used without parameters, information on all sessions with the server is displayed. Here are a couple of ways to use `net session`:

- View information on all sessions: `net session`
- Terminate all sessions with the computer Leatherneck: `net session \\leatherneck /delete`

net view

The last Net Services command that is helpful for troubleshooting is `net view`. With NetBIOS over TCP/IP enabled, many use Windows Explorer as a means to browse resources on the network. The `net view` command provides the same functionality from the command line. If you want to see a list of shared resources on a particular server, `net view` provides a quick way to view the system's shared folders and printers. The syntax for `net view` is:

```
net view [\\computer name] [/domain:<name>]
net view /Network:NW [\\computer name]
```

Table 4-10 describes the command options.

Table 4-10. net view Command Options

Option	Use
`\\computer name`	The name of the computer whose shared resources you want to view.
`/domain:<name>`	Used to view a list of computers in the specified domain.
`/Network:NW`	Used to display all available servers in a NetWare network.

An example of using `net view` would be to verify that a user is attempting to access a share using the proper name or path. To see a list of all shared resources on a system called Dempsey, you would enter the command `net view \\Dempsey`.

netstat

A useful command called `netstat` allows you to view information on the TCP and UDP port connections to a system. The command can be executed so that it runs every *n* number of seconds and allows you to see the following in a table format:

- The protocol (TCP or UDP)
- The local IP address and port number used by the socket connection
- The foreign (destination) IP address and port number used by the socket connection
- The status of the connection (Listening, Established, and so on)

Examining the port connection status between two systems may allow you to rule out TCP/IP connectivity as the source of a potential problem. In order to fully understand what this command is telling you, you must first understand the TCP/IP connection (handshake) process. Here are the fundamental steps to a TCP/IP handshake.

1. When attempting to connect, the client sends a SYN message to the server.
2. The server responds with its own SYN and an acknowledgment (ACK).
3. The client then sends an ACK back to the server, completing the connection.

These are the steps that occur when a connection is terminated.

1. The client says "I'm done" by sending a FIN message to the server. At this point, the client will only receive data from the server and will not send any data.
2. The server then sends the client an ACK and sends its own FIN to the client.
3. The client then sends an ACK back to the server, acknowledging the server's FIN request.
4. Upon receiving the ACK from the client, the server closes the connection.

With an understanding of the connection and disconnection process, you can now more easily interpret the connection states displayed by `netstat`. You may see a connection listed as being in one of several possible states.

- CLOSE_WAIT—Indicates passive close, meaning that the server has received the FIN from the client.
- CLOSED—The connection has been terminated and closed by the server.
- ESTABLISHED—The client established a connection with the server, receiving the server's SYN message.
- FIN_WAIT_1—The client initiated the closure (sent the FIN message) of the session with the server.
- FIN_WAIT_2—The client has received the ACK and the FIN from the server.
- LAST_ACK—The server has sent the FIN message to the client.
- LISTEN—A server is ready to accept connections.
- SYN_RECEIVED—The server has received the SYN from a client and has responded.

Network Monitoring and Troubleshooting Tools   69

- TIMED_WAIT—The client has sent its FIN message to the server and is awaiting a response.

- YN_SEND—The listed session is active and open.

Now that you have all you need to know about netstat, let's look at its syntax:

netstat [-a] [-e] [-n] [-o] [-p <protocol>] [-r] [-s] [interval]

The netstat options are listed in Table 4-11.

Table 4-11. netstat Command Options

Option	Use
-a	Displays all connections and listening ports.
-e	Shows Ethernet statistics.
-n	Shows addresses and ports in numerical format (IP address instead of interface name).
-o	Displays the owning process ID for each connection.
-p <protocol>	Shows connections for the protocol specified. Protocol choices are TCP, TCPv6, UDP, and UDPv6. When used in conjunction with -s, this may also include IP, IPv6, ICMP, and ICMPv6.
-r	Displays the system's routing table.
-s	Displays statistics on a per-protocol basis; by default, statistics are shown for TCP, TCPv6, UDP, UDPv6, IP, IPv6, ICMP, and ICMPv6. A small subset of protocols can be specified using the -p switch.
interval	The interval in seconds in which the command output data refreshes. When an interval is specified, press Ctrl-C to terminate the command.

Figure 4-10 shows the use of netstat to monitor port usage on a system.

pathping

The pathping command allows you to isolate the location of a problem a packet is having when traveling between two routed networks. To test the routers between two communication points, pathping sends multiple Echo Request messages to each router and displays the percentage of packets that were lost when sent to each router in the path. A high value of lost packets may indicate a faulty router or a saturated network segment and thus the source of your WAN connectivity problems.

The syntax for pathping is:

pathping <destination name or IP> [-n] [-h <max hops>] [-g <host list>] [-p <period>] [-q <number of queries>] [-w <timeout>] [-T] [-R]

Table 4-12 describes the pathping command options.

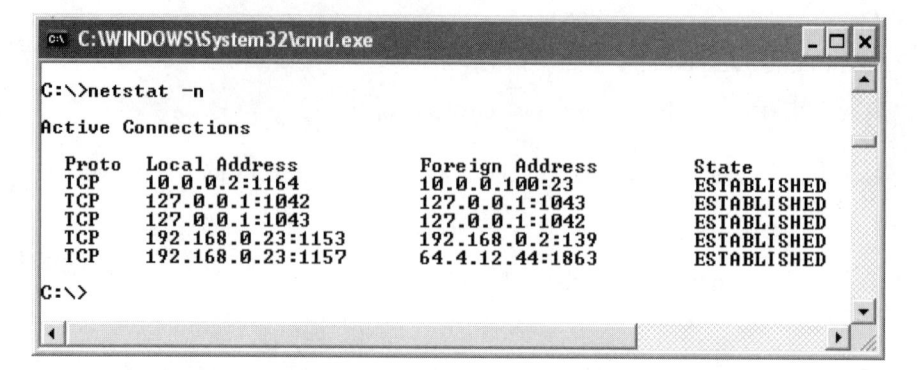

```
C:\>netstat -n

Active Connections

   Proto  Local Address          Foreign Address        State
   TCP    10.0.0.2:1164          10.0.0.100:23          ESTABLISHED
   TCP    127.0.0.1:1042         127.0.0.1:1043         ESTABLISHED
   TCP    127.0.0.1:1043         127.0.0.1:1042         ESTABLISHED
   TCP    192.168.0.23:1153      192.168.0.2:139        ESTABLISHED
   TCP    192.168.0.23:1157      64.4.12.44:1863        ESTABLISHED

C:\>
```

Figure 4-10. Monitoring port usage with netstat

Table 4-12. pathping Command Options

Option	Use
<destination name or IP>	Specifies the destination FQDN or IP address.
-n	Speeds up the command execution by preventing pathping from trying to resolve the IP addresses of intermediate routers.
-h <max hops>	Specifies the maximum hops to travel to search for the destination (default maximum = 30).
-g <host list>	Causes the Echo Request messages to use the Loose Source Router option in the IP header.
-p <period>	Lets you specify the time in milliseconds (ms) that the command will wait between consecutive pings (default = 250ms). Too frequent consecutive pings may inaccurately result in network congestion being reported.
-q <number of queries>	Lets you set the number of Echo Requests to be sent to each router in the path (default = 100).
-w <timeout>	Lets you set the time (in milliseconds) to wait for a reply from each router (default = 3000ms, or 3 seconds).
-T	Used to test for Quality of Service (QoS) connectivity by checking for devices that do not have layer 2 priority capability.
-R	Also used for QoS; determines if each network device along the route supports Resource Reservation Protocol (RSVP).

Suppose you believe that there are WAN connectivity problems between your New York and Los Angeles sites. You could use pathping in this circumstance to verify your suspicions. To check for congestion or a problem at a router along the path, from New York you could run the command pathping docshare.la.awl.com. If a router has a high lost-packet percentage, you have found the source of the routing problem on the WAN.

ping

The `ping` command has long been a trusted friend of many network administrators. With `ping`, you can quickly verify

- Network connectivity between two systems
- Name resolution

The `ping` command also allows you to perform additional tests on the network between two systems, as you will see in its syntax.

```
ping <destination name or IP> [-a] [-f] [-i <TTL>] [-j <host list>]
[-k <host list>] [-l <size>] [-n <count>] [-r <count>] [-s <count>]
[-t] [-v <TOS>]
```

The options for the `ping` command are described in Table 4-13.

Table 4-13. ping Command Options

Option	Use
`<destination name or IP>`	Specifies the destination FQDN or IP address.
`-a`	Performs reverse name resolution on the destination IP address, causing the destination's FQDN to be displayed in the command output.
`-f`	Helpful when troubleshooting Maximum Transmission Unit (MTU) problems; `ping` Echo Request messages are sent with the "Don't Fragment" flag in the IP header set to 1, preventing the Echo Request message from being fragmented by routers on its path to its destination.
`-i <TTL>`	Specifies a Time to Live (TTL) value for the Echo Request messages; the default value is 128; with this option, you can set the value as high as 255, meaning that the Echo Request message sent by the `ping` command will travel a maximum of 255 hops before being discarded by the 256th router.
`-j <host list>`	Allows you to list intermediate destinations by IP addresses separated by spaces (the `host list` portion of the switch). This option specifies Loose Source Routing, meaning that the intermediate destinations specified can be separated by one or more routers. With this command, you can list up to nine hosts.
`-k <host list>`	Allows you to list intermediate destinations by IP addresses separated by spaces (the `host list` portion of the switch). This option specifies Strict Source Routing, meaning that the intermediate destinations specified cannot be separated by one or more routers (they must be adjacent). With this command, you can list up to nine hosts.

continues

Table 4-13. ping Command Options, continued

Option	Use
-l <size>	Allows you to specify the size of the payload in bytes of the Data field in the Echo Request messages sent by ping. The default size is 32, but you can specify a maximum payload up to 65,527 bytes. This is a good way to test whether limited bandwidth or congestion is the source of networking problems.
-n <count>	Used to specify the number of Echo Requests sent by ping. The default value is 4.
-r <count>	Allows you to specify a count (1–9) of hops recorded in the Echo Request and Echo Reply messages. The count specified must be greater than or equal to the number of routers in the path.
-s <count>	Allows you to specify a hop count (1–4), where the time of arrival for each Echo Request and Echo Reply message is recorded. This is possible when the routers in the path support the Internet Timestamp option in the IP header.
-t	Forces ping to continually send Echo Request messages until the command is interrupted when Ctrl-C is pressed.
-v <TOS>	Lets you specify the Type of Service (TOS) value in the IP header for the ping Echo Request message. The default value is 0. You can specify any value between 1 and 255.

Here are a couple examples of common uses for ping:

- Verify name resolution and connectivity to a system named www2.awl.com:
  ping www2.awl.com

- Verify IP connectivity to a remote host:
  ping 183.52.9.73

- Test network bandwidth-related connectivity issues by sending a 32KB payload with each Echo Request:
  ping 10.23.8.5 -l 32768

telnet

Telnet has long roamed the UNIX world as a means to remotely administer servers, and beginning with Windows 2000 Server, the OS had its own Telnet Server service. With telnet, you can quickly access the command line interface of a remote system and perform tasks such as

- Starting and stopping services
- Managing files and directories
- Running scripts

Network Monitoring and Troubleshooting Tools

While there are variations of how to Telnet to another system, the following basic syntax allows you to connect to and manage a remote system.

```
telnet <remote host> [port:<port number>]
```

The two options for the `telnet` command are described in Table 4-14.

Table 4-14. telnet Command Options

Option	Use
`remote host`	The host name or IP address of the remote server running the Telnet Server service.
`port: <port number>`	The port to use for the Telnet session. The default port is 23. Specifying a port number allows you to test connectivity over a range of ports, such as seeing if you can negotiate a session over a particular port for a service you are having trouble with between two WAN sites.

To Telnet to a server called Docshare in the awl.com domain, you would run `telnet docshare.awl.com`. Once you have finished performing the remote administration, you can end the Telnet session by typing `exit` from within the Telnet session command window.

> For security reasons, the Telnet service is stopped and set to manual by default on Windows 2000 and higher servers. For more secure remote administration, you should consider using Terminal Services instead.

tracert

The `tracert` command is somewhat similar to `pathping` in usage, allowing you to check the path between two routed networks, but it does not check each router in the path as thoroughly as `pathping`. Like `pathping` and `ping`, `tracert` uses ICMP Echo Requests to check for network connectivity. Like `pathping`, `tracert` displays each hop (or router) between the source where the command is run from and the destination entered, but it does not display the statistical information, such as the percentage of lost packets, that you see with `pathping`.

Here's the syntax for `tracert`:

```
tracert <destination name or IP> [-d] [-h <maximum hops>] [-j <host list>] [-w <timeout>]
```

The `tracert` command options are explained in Table 4-15.

The command output from using `tracert` to check the route to the Web site www.verizon.net is shown in Figure 4-11.

74 Chapter 4 Monitoring and Diagnostic Tools

Table 4-15. tracert Command Options

Option	Use
<destination name or IP>	Specifies the destination FQDN or IP address.
-d	Speeds up the execution of tracert by preventing the command from attempting to resolve the IP addresses of intermediate routers to their respective host names.
-h <maximum hops>	Used to specify the maximum number of hops in the path to the destination. The default value is 30.
-j <host list>	Allows you to list intermediate destinations by IP addresses separated by spaces (the host list portion of the switch). This option specifies Loose Source Routing, meaning that the intermediate destinations specified can be separated by one or more routers. With this command, you can list up to nine hosts.
-w <timeout>	Used to specify the time (in milliseconds) to wait for an ICMP Time Exceeded or Echo Reply message from an Echo Request. If a reply is not received within the time represented by the timeout parameter value, an asterisk (*) is displayed. The default value is 4000 (4 seconds).

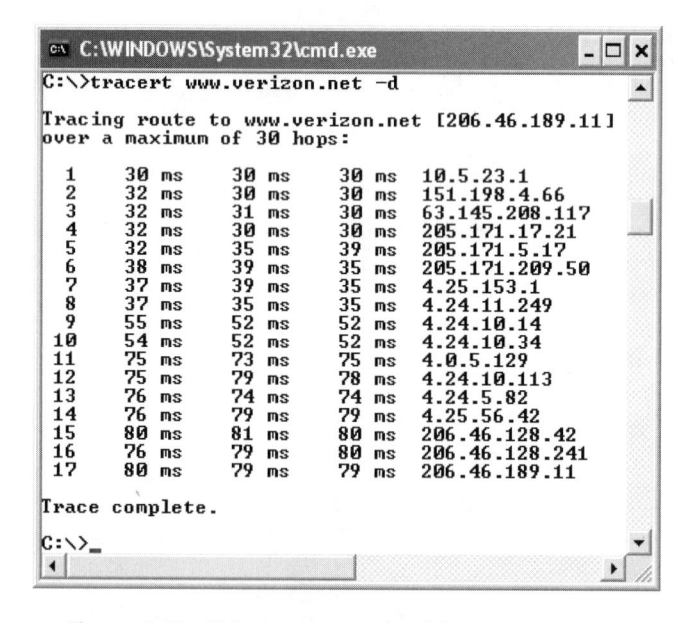

```
C:\>tracert www.verizon.net -d

Tracing route to www.verizon.net [206.46.189.11]
over a maximum of 30 hops:

  1    30 ms    30 ms    30 ms  10.5.23.1
  2    32 ms    30 ms    30 ms  151.198.4.66
  3    32 ms    31 ms    30 ms  63.145.208.117
  4    32 ms    30 ms    30 ms  205.171.17.21
  5    32 ms    35 ms    39 ms  205.171.5.17
  6    38 ms    39 ms    35 ms  205.171.209.50
  7    37 ms    39 ms    35 ms  4.25.153.1
  8    37 ms    35 ms    35 ms  4.24.11.249
  9    55 ms    52 ms    52 ms  4.24.10.14
 10    54 ms    52 ms    52 ms  4.24.10.34
 11    75 ms    73 ms    75 ms  4.0.5.129
 12    75 ms    79 ms    78 ms  4.24.10.113
 13    76 ms    74 ms    74 ms  4.24.5.82
 14    76 ms    79 ms    79 ms  4.25.56.42
 15    80 ms    81 ms    80 ms  206.46.128.42
 16    76 ms    79 ms    80 ms  206.46.128.241
 17    80 ms    79 ms    79 ms  206.46.189.11

Trace complete.

C:\>
```

Figure 4-11. Using tracert to check WAN connectivity

GUI Tools

Now that we have conquered the vast world of network troubleshooting command line tools, this section serves as a cooldown for you. Here you will see a few GUI tools that are helpful when attempting to resolve network-related issues.

Network Diagnostics

Network Diagnostics is an easy-to-use tool that can be run from the Help and Support Center or can be executed manually by running the command `netsh diag gui`. The command output displays an abundance of information on the many network configuration tests that it performs. Help desk technicians and systems administrators can have users run this utility on their systems and then save the command output to a file. This is all done by the click of a button right from the command window. Even your most hopeless users will be able to successfully provide you with important troubleshooting information by running this command.

When the command executes (see Figure 4-12), users have the option to set the command's options to specify which tests are to be performed. Among the many network objects checked by the command for connectivity are

- DHCP, DNS, and WINS servers
- Mail server
- Proxy server
- Default gateways
- Modems
- Network adapters

In addition to testing for configuration, the command displays an abundance of information, such as the OS version and IP settings. Consider Network Diagnostics to be the answer to all of the questions that you would previously have to struggle with users to get. Now you can just have them run the command and click the Save button. The results of the command are then saved in an HTML file to the user's desktop. Instruct the user to e-mail you the file, and you are on your way toward identifying the problem.

Network Monitor

While Network Diagnostics is a tool that you can instruct end users to run, Network Monitor, on the other hand, is primarily a tool for administrators. Network Monitor allows you to capture and analyze network packets and view statistics on network data on the local subnet of the system running the Network Monitor Tools. One of the primary reasons that in most enterprise environments administrators use tools such as Network Associates Sniffer Pro, is that Network Monitor is limited in its functionality. For example, a system running the Network Monitor Tools can only capture and analyze packets on its local subnet. Hey, what do you want for free?

Chapter 4 Monitoring and Diagnostic Tools

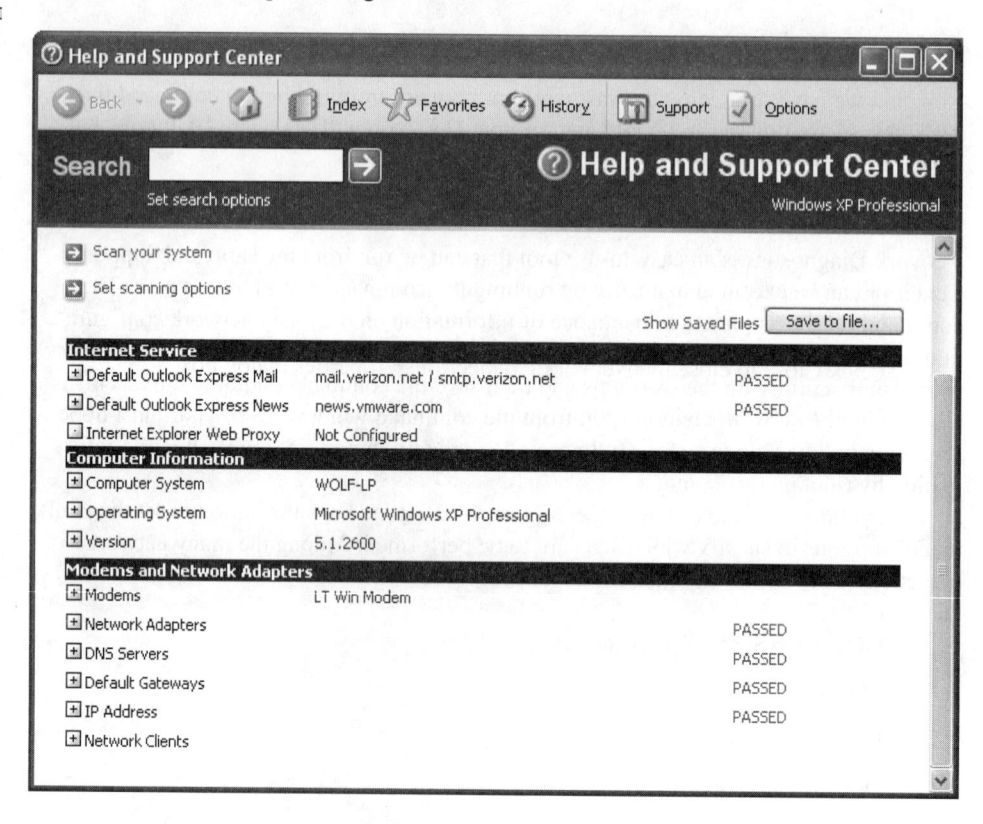

Figure 4-12. Checking network settings with Network Diagnostics

In particular, this is what you can capture with Network Monitor:

- Unicast packets to or from the server running Network Monitor
- Multicast packets on the local subnet
- Broadcast packets on the local subnet

Network Monitor is nothing more than a light version of Microsoft's Systems Management Server (SMS), which is much more robust and does allow the capture and analysis of packets bound for remote systems.

To monitor a system with Network Monitor, you must have the Network Monitor Driver installed and enabled on it. The driver is installed and enabled on W2K3 servers by default, but for XP workstations and earlier versions of Windows, you need to manually install the driver.

To install the Network Monitor Driver, follow these steps.

Network Monitoring and Troubleshooting Tools

1. From the Control Panel, double-click the Network Connections icon.
2. Right-click the connection you wish to monitor, and select Properties.
3. Now click the Install button.
4. Click Protocol and then click Add.
5. Click Network Monitor Driver and then click OK.
6. You should now see the Network Monitor Driver listed under the General tab of the Connection Properties dialog box.
7. Click Close to close the Network Connections Properties dialog box.
8. Close the Network Connections window.

By itself, the Network Monitor Driver does nothing. To monitor network traffic, you need the Network Monitor Tools. The tools are not available for installation on XP workstations, so you can only install them on and monitor the network from W2K3 and earlier Windows servers. Here are the steps to install the Network Monitor Tools.

1. Click Start > Control Panel.
2. Double-click the Add/Remove Programs icon.
3. Click Add/Remove Windows Components.
4. Double-click Management and Monitoring Tools.
5. Select the Network Monitor Tools checkbox and click OK.
6. In the Windows Components Wizard dialog box, click Next.
7. If prompted, insert the Windows Server 2003 CD and click OK.
8. When the wizard completes, click Finish.
9. Close the Add/Remove Programs window.
10. Close the Control Panel.

You can now open the Network Monitor Tools by clicking Start > Administrative Tools > Network Monitor Tools. Once the tools open, select the network connection that you wish to monitor, and you are ready to go.

Understanding Network Monitor is much easier with a basic grasp of its terminology. Here are the core concepts.

- *Capture*—Using Network Monitor to listen for and save network traffic to and from the specified network interface.
- *Capture Buffer*—RAM used to temporarily store captured data before it is written to disk.

- *Capture Buffer size*—Size in megabytes of the Capture Buffer. By default, the size is 1MB. To maximize the amount of data captured by Network Monitor, Microsoft recommends setting the Capture Buffer size to as high as 16MB less than the amount of physical RAM in the system.

- *Capture Trigger*—A means to configure Network Monitor to start capturing data when a specific type of traffic is encountered.

- *Capture Filter*—Used to limit the data that is captured. Network monitor still has to examine every network packet to see if it meets the filter requirements, so filtering is CPU intensive.

- *Display Filter*—Display Filters allow you to filter the captured packets that are displayed by Network Monitor. Capturing everything and then using Display Filters to pinpoint what you are looking for places less of a burden on the CPU but in turn consumes more disk space.

With the lingo out of the way, let's look at using Network Monitor to capture network traffic. After opening Network Monitor, click the Capture menu and select Start to begin capturing data. When finished, again click the Capture menu and select Stop and View. In the Capture Summary window, you can see additional details of captured frames by double-clicking any of the captured frames listed. An HTTP capture is shown in Figure 4-13.

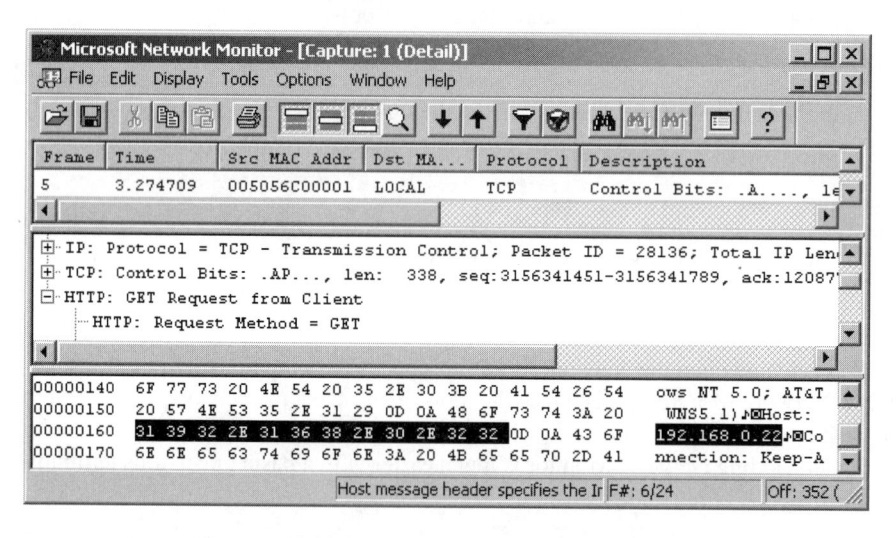

Figure 4-13. Monitoring IIS server traffic with Network Monitor

Performance Monitoring Tools

As with networking monitoring, there are several performance monitoring tools available that are very useful both for preventing faults and for diagnosing them. In this section, I show you the countless tools at your disposal, again organizing the tools by command line and then GUI.

Command Line Tools

For Windows XP/W2K3 networks, there are countless command line tools available for performance monitoring and diagnosis. Since many of the tools described in this section are found in either the support tools or resource kit, they often go unnoticed, until now. Let's get started with `memsnap`.

memsnap (ST)

If you need documentation of memory consumption on a particular server or would like to prove the existence of a memory leak, you can do so by using the support tool `memsnap`. It takes a snapshot of all running processes and their associated resource consumption and dumps the snapshot to a log file. The default name for the file is Memsnap.log, but the name can be specified in the command syntax, which is shown next.

```
memsnap [/t] [/g] [file name]
```

Table 4-16 details the options for the `memsnap` command.

Table 4-16. memsnap Command Options

Option	Use
/t	Tagging information—causes the time (GMT), date, and computer name to be included in the output log file.
/g	Adds user and graphical device interface (GDI) information to the command output log file.
file name	Used to specify the name of the output log file. If this option is not used, the output file will be named Memsnap.log.

To use `memsnap` to dump a snapshot of memory consumption to the file D:\Snaps\Leakcheck.log, you would run `memsnap D:\Snaps\Leakcheck.log`.

As with many of the tools in this section, `memsnap` serves a small but targeted purpose. The same can be said for the command `pagefileconfig`, which is discussed next.

pagefileconfig

The `pagefileconfig` command gives you the ability to remotely configure and manage the pagefile on remote systems from the command line. If you are one that likes to do everything from the command line to display your mastery of Windows commands, then this tool is for you. For most, however, it is easier to remotely control a workstation using Remote Assistance or VNC Viewer and simply reconfigure the pagefile that way than to dabble with command line syntax.

If you're wondering where this command reaches its true value, it is actually in the fact that it can be included in a script. This way, to change the pagefile configuration on 100 workstations, for example, you can implement a version of the `pagefileconfig` command in a startup script in a group policy object (GPO) associated with the workstations in question. Now you have unleashed the true power of scripting!

To call `pagefileconfig` a single command doesn't do it justice. It is actually a Visual Basic Script that can be run in four different ways. Each of the different methods for running `pagefileconfig` is described in the next four sections.

> The `pagefileconfig` command must be executed using the cscript version of Windows Scripting Host and must be run in the directory where it resides (System32). To do this, navigate to the Windows\System32 folder, and when you enter the `pagefileconfig` command, precede it with the syntax `cscript`.

pagefileconfig /change

The `/change` version of the `pagefileconfig` command allows you to modify the configuration of the pagefile on a system. Its syntax is:

```
pagefileconfig.vbs /change [/s <computer> [/u <domain\user>
[/p <password]]] [/i <initial size>] [/m <maximum size>]
[/vo <volume letter> | *>]
```

The `pagefileconfig /change` options are described in Table 4-17.

Table 4-17. pagefileconfig /change Command Options

Option	Use
/s <computer>	Used to specify the IP address or FQDN of the remote computer on which to run the command.
/u <domain\user>	Executes the command using the domain and user account specified. By default, the credentials for the user issuing the command are used.
/p <password>	When a domain and user are specified, this switch allows you to include a password for the user account.
/i <initial size>	Used to specify a new initial size (in megabytes) for the pagefile on the system.

Performance Monitoring Tools   81

Table 4-17. pagefileconfig /change Command Options, continued

Option	Use
/m <max size>	Used to specify a new maximum size (in megabytes) for the pagefile on the system.
/vo <volume letter | *>	If the pagefile is distributed across multiple logical volumes, this option allows you to select the volume you would like the change in configuration specified in the command to apply to. When used with the * parameter, the command modifies all volumes.

Here are two examples of using `pagefileconfig` to modify pagefile settings:

- To change the initial pagefile size to 256MB and the maximum size to 512MB on the local system's C drive:
  `cscript pagefileconfig.vbs /change /i 256 /m 512 /vo c:`

- To make the same configuration changes on the remote system Mercury:
  `cscript pagefileconfig.vbs /change /s mercury /i 256 /m 512 /vo c:`

pagefileconfig /create

The `/create` option allows you to add an additional paging file to a system. Here is its syntax:

`pagefileconfig.vbs /create [/s <computer> [/u <domain\user> [/p <password>]]] [/i <initial pagefile size>] [/m <maximum pagefile size>] [/vo <volume letter>]`

The command options are explained in Table 4-18.

Table 4-18. pagefileconfig /create Command Options

Option	Use
/s <computer>	Used to specify the IP address or FQDN of the remote computer on which to run the command.
/u <domain\user>	Executes the command using the domain and user account specified. By default, the credentials for the user issuing the command are used.
/p <password>	When a domain and user are specified, this switch allows you to include a password for the user account.
/i <initial size>	Used to specify the initial size (in megabytes) for the new pagefile on the system.

continued

Table 4-18. pagefileconfig /create Command Options, continued

Option	Use
/m <max size>	Used to specify the maximum size (in megabytes) for the new pagefile on the system.
/vo <volume letter>	Used to specify the volume on which to create the new pagefile.

Here are two examples of using `pagefileconfig` to create new pagefiles:

- To create a pagefile on the D drive with an initial size of 256MB and a maximum size of 512MB:
  `cscript pagefileconfig.vbs /create /i 256 /m 512 /vo d:`
- To make the same configuration changes on the remote system Venus:
  `cscript pagefileconfig.vbs /create /s venus /i 256 /m 512 /vo d:`

pagefileconfig /delete

Now that you have seen how to create and modify pagefile settings, it is also important to understand how to delete the pagefile on drives where it hinders performance. For example, suppose you have a SCSI drive on each system with the drive letter E that you would like to be used exclusively by the pagefile. You begin by using `pagefileconfig /create` to add a new pagefile to the E drive. Now you must remove the pagefile from the C drive. This is where `pagefileconfig /delete` is needed. This is its syntax:

```
pagefileconfig.vbs /delete [/s <computer> [/u <domain\user> [/p <password>]]] [vo <volume letter>]
```

The command options are described in Table 4-19.

Table 4-19. pagefileconfig /delete Command Options

Option	Use
/s <computer>	Used to specify the IP address or FQDN of the remote computer on which to run the command.
/u <domain\user>	Executes the command using the domain and user account specified. By default, the credentials for the user issuing the command are used.
/p <password>	When a domain and user are specified, this switch allows you to include a password for the user account.
/vo <volume letter>	Used to specify the volume from which to delete the pagefile.

Here are two examples of using `pagefileconfig` to delete the pagefile from the C drive:

- To delete the pagefile on the C drive of the local system:
  `cscript pagefileconfig.vbs /delete /vo c:`
- To delete the pagefile from the C drive on the remote system Mars:
  `cscript pagefileconfig.vbs /delete /s mars /vo c:`

pagefileconfig /query

If you are unsure of the pagefile configuration on a remote system, the `/query` option can be quite handy. If you are an administrator tasked with remotely troubleshooting a user's system on the LAN, running this command from your desktop is much easier than stepping the user through the process of determining his or her pagefile configuration.

Here is the syntax for `pagefileconfig /query`:

```
pagefileconfig.vbs /query [/s <computer> [/u <domain\user>
[/p <password>]] [/fo <table|list|csv>]
```

The options for `pagefileconfig /query` are detailed in Table 4-20.

Table 4-20. pagefileconfig /query Command Options

Option	Use
`/s <computer>`	Used to specify the IP address or FQDN of the remote computer on which to run the command.
`/u <domain\user>`	Executes the command using the domain and user account specified. By default, the credentials for the user issuing the command are used.
`/p <password>`	When a domain and user are specified, this switch allows you to include a password for the user account.
`/fo <table|list|csv>`	Used to specify the format for the script's output (the default is `list`).

Figure 4-14 shows using `pagefileconfig /query` to check the pagefile configuration of the remote system Wolf-lp.

pfmon (ST)

When a system is short on RAM, increased paging occurs to the hard disk. Normally when a disk bottleneck occurs, the result is an increase in hard page faults. Many troubleshooters take an educated guess at RAM being the answer to a suspected paging-related performance problem. When you suspect that a disk bottleneck resulting from

Chapter 4 Monitoring and Diagnostic Tools

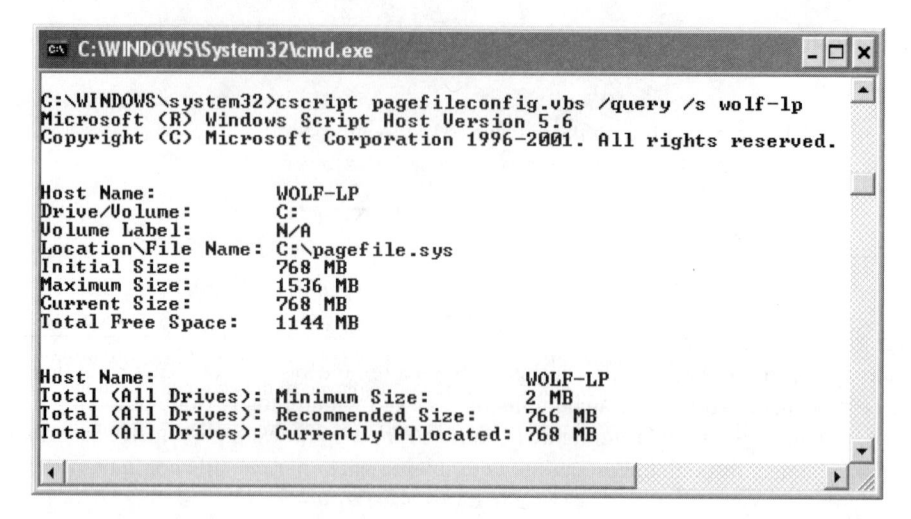

```
C:\WINDOWS\system32>cscript pagefileconfig.vbs /query /s wolf-lp
Microsoft (R) Windows Script Host Version 5.6
Copyright (C) Microsoft Corporation 1996-2001. All rights reserved.

Host Name:                  WOLF-LP
Drive/Volume:               C:
Volume Label:               N/A
Location\File Name:         C:\pagefile.sys
Initial Size:               768 MB
Maximum Size:               1536 MB
Current Size:               768 MB
Total Free Space:           1144 MB

Host Name:                                    WOLF-LP
Total (All Drives): Minimum Size:             2 MB
Total (All Drives): Recommended Size:         766 MB
Total (All Drives): Currently Allocated:      768 MB
```

Figure 4-14. Checking the pagefile configuration of a remote system with pagefileconfig

hard page faults is occurring, you can verify your suspicions by running `pfmon`. The `pfmon` command allows you to

- Identify the number of page faults for a process
- Identify the source of page faults in a process

In addition to checking for hard page faults, `pfmon` monitors for soft page faults. Hard page faults occur when a program looks for a page in memory, only to find that the page must be retrieved from the hard disk. Soft page faults, on the other hand, occur when a program attempts to retrieve a page from virtual memory that is not in the working set but is still in memory (not on disk). Soft page faults are generally not as much of a concern for an administrator trying to troubleshoot performance programs. When using this command, focus on hard page faults as a clear indication that additional RAM is needed.

When run, `pfmon` attaches itself to a process and displays any page faults resulting from the process until the command is manually terminated when Ctrl-C is pressed. Instead of having the output displayed on the screen, you can have the command's output dumped to a file for later analysis.

Here is the syntax for `pfmon`:

```
pfmon <[/p <PID>] | [Application Command]> [/n] [/c] [/h] [/k]
[/K] [/d]
```

The `pfmon` command options are described in Table 4-21.

Table 4-21. pfmon Command Options

Option	Use
/p <PID>	Specifies the process ID (PID) to monitor (the currently running process). You can find a process's PID by accessing a list of the currently running processes under the Processes tab in Task Manager. When you terminate pfmon, the process that you have the command attach to also terminates.
Application Command	Used to list the full path of the process to invoke and monitor (for example: D:\Program Files\Doom\Doom.exe). If you specify an application command to run, you cannot use the /p switch to specify a process ID.
/n	Faults are written to the pfmon.log file (written in the directory where pfmon is executed) and are not displayed in the command window.
/l	Faults are written to the pfmon.log file and are displayed in the command window as well.
/c	Displays soft page faults and summary information. Hard page faults are not displayed.
/h	Displays hard page faults and summary information. Soft page faults are not displayed.
/k	Displays both kernel mode and user mode page faults.
/K	Displays only kernel mode page faults.
/d	Causes the following tab-delineated information to be displayed in the command output: • Page fault number • Fault type (hard or soft) • Program counter's module, symbol, and decimal value • Decimal value for the program counter of the virtual address accessed • Virtual address's symbol and value

Here are two examples of using pfmon to identify hard page faults:

- To check for faults associated with the current process with a PID of 2348 and write the results to the pfmon.log file:
  `pfmon /p 2348 /h /l`

- To invoke the command mspaint.exe and monitor for hard page faults:
  `pfmon mspaint /h`

> You may find that pfmon tells you more than you ever cared to know about page faults. If you're looking to determine the frequency of hard page faults for a particular system, your best bet is to use System Monitor, which is covered later in this chapter.

pmon (ST)

The pmon command closely simulates the output you see under the Processes tab in the Task Manager. The primary difference, however, is that it is run from the command line, and its output is displayed in tabular format in the command window, periodically refreshing every few seconds. Since it is a command line utility, this is something you could consider running when remotely troubleshooting through a Telnet session.

There is no syntax for pmon, so to execute it, you just type pmon from the command prompt. The output from running pmon is shown in Figure 4-15.

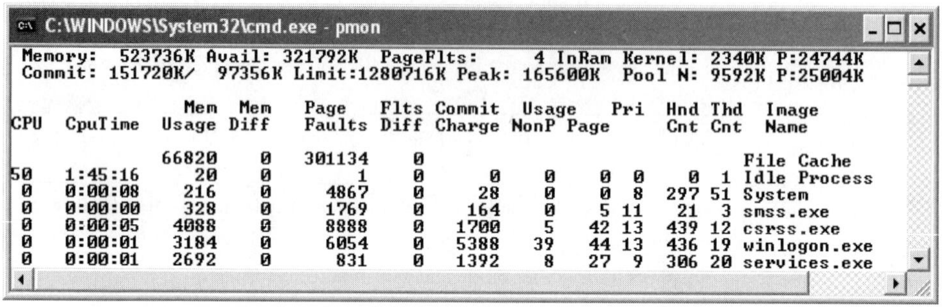

Figure 4-15. Checking process activity with pmon

taskkill

The taskkill command allows you to terminate processes on a local or remote system from the command line. Its syntax is:

```
taskkill [/s <computer>] [/u <domain\user>] [/p <password>] [/fi
<filter name>] [ /pid <Process ID>] [/im <image name>] [/f] [/t]
```

The taskkill command options are described in Table 4-22.

Table 4-22. taskkill Command Options

Option	Use
/s <computer>	Specifies the name or IP address of the remote computer.
/u <domain\user>	Specifies the name of the user under which to execute the command.
/p <password>	Used with the /u switch to specify the user's password.
/fi <filter name>	Allows you to filter processes to include in or exclude from termination. Valid filter names and operators are shown in Table 4-23.

Table 4-22. taskkill Command Options, continued

Option	Use
/pid <Process ID>	Specifies the process ID of the process to be terminated.
/im <image name>	Used to specify an image name of the process(es) to terminate. It can be used with the * wildcard for multiple processes.
/f	Forcefully terminates the process. This is done automatically when the command is run on a remote system.
/t	Terminates the entire process tree, terminating all child processes for the process specified.

Table 4-23. Valid taskkill Filters and Operators

Filter	Operator	Allowable Values
CPUTime	eq, ne, gt, lt, ge, le	Valid time expressed in hh:mm:ss
Hostname	eq, ne	Any string of characters
Imagename	eq, ne	Any string of characters
Memusage	eq, ne, gt, lt, ge, le	Any positive integer
PID	eq, ne, gt, lt, ge, le	Any positive integer
Services	eq, ne	Any string of characters
Session	eq, ne, gt, lt, ge, le	Any active session number
Status	eq, ne	Running | Not Responding
Username	eq, ne	Any user name
Windowtitle	eq, ne	Any string of characters

The meanings of the operators shown in Table 4-23 are listed in Table 4-24.

Table 4-24. Common Command Operators

Operator	Meaning
eq	Filter processes equal to the specified value
ne	Filter processes not equal to the specified value
gt	Greater than the specified number
lt	Less than the specified number
ge	Greater than or equal to the specified number
le	Less than or equal to the specified number

Here are two examples of using `taskkill`:

- To forcibly terminate the process minesweeper on the remote system named slacker:
  `taskkill /s slacker /f /im winmine.exe`

- To terminate all processes initiated by the user jteti on the local system named boss:
  `taskkill /fi "Username eq boss\jteti" /fi "Imagename eq *"`

tasklist

While you may agree that `taskkill` is quite a useful program, especially since it allows you to terminate hung processes without a reboot, the command still requires knowledge of a particular task's name or its PID, which is exactly what you can find by running `tasklist`. If you're at a corporate help desk, try asking a user to locate a process ID. Now clear that thought from your mind, wipe the smirk off your face, and get back to business. With `tasklist`, you can remove the user from the equation, since the command can be run remotely.

Now that you have seen its value, here's its syntax:

```
tasklist [/s <computer name> [/u <domain\user>] [/p <password>]
[/fo <table | list | csv>] [/nh] [/fi <filter name>] [/m [module name]
| /svc | /v]
```

Each of the command options is explained in Table 4-25.

Table 4-25. tasklist Command Options

Option	Use
/s <computer name>	Specifies the name or IP address of the remote computer.
/u <domain\user>	Specifies the name of the user under which to execute the command.
/p <password>	Used with the /u switch to specify the user's password.
/fo <table | list | csv>	Allows you to specify how the command output is displayed. When the switch is not used, the output is in `table` format.
/nh	When the /fo switch is used to set the output to tabular or `csv` format, this switch causes the column headers to not be displayed in the output.
/fi <filter name>	Allows you to filter processes to include in or exclude from the list. Valid filter names and operators are shown in Table 4-26.

Table 4-25. tasklist Command Options, continued

Option	Use
/m [module name]	Displays the modules associated with each process, which allows you to see all the .dlls associated with the processes on a system. If a module name is included with the switch, all processes associated with the module are displayed. This switch cannot be used in conjunction with /svc or /v.
/svc	When the /fo switch is set to table, it allows you to see service information for each process. This switch cannot be used with /m or /v.
/v	Verbose output—highly detailed output information is displayed. This switch cannot be used with /m or /svc.

Table 4-26. Valid tasklist Filters and Operators

Filter	Operator	Allowable Values
CPUTime	eq, ne, gt, lt, ge, le	Valid time expressed in hh:mm:ss
Imagename	eq, ne	Any string of characters
Memusage	eq, ne, gt, lt, ge, le	Any positive integer
Modules	eq, ne	Any string of characters
PID	eq, ne, gt, lt, ge, le	Any positive integer
Services	eq, ne	Any string of characters
Session	eq, ne, gt, lt, ge, le	Any active session number
SessionName	eq, ne	Any string of characters
Status	eq, ne	Running	Not Responding
Username	eq, ne	Any user name
Windowtitle	eq, ne	Any string of characters

Here are some examples of using tasklist for troubleshooting:

- To see a list of running processes on the computer Pinball:
  tasklist /s pinball
- To see all processes on the system Pinball initiated by the user ghartigan:
  tasklist /s pinball /fi "Username eq training\ghartigan"

uptime (RK)

The `uptime` tool allows you to collect statistical information on system availability. This command is ideal for tracking historical problems with server crashes and provides

- Current uptime (time since the last shutdown or reboot)
- Stop errors (blue screens)
- Application failures
- Date and time of shutdowns or restarts
- Service pack installations

> The `uptime` command should be run under an account with administrative privileges.

As the note indicates, the command should be run under an administrative account. After all, `uptime` does not hop in a time machine and go on a magical journey back in time on a server. Instead, it gathers information from reading the event logs. In addition, it accesses a remote computer's system time to make time zone adjustments, if necessary, and works with the System Performance Counter.

One other consideration with `uptime` is that it only provides accurate output when its target system's heartbeat is active. By default, the heartbeat is active on all Windows 2000 and higher servers. The heartbeat is nothing more than a date/time stamp that is recorded in the Registry at regular periods. Since it causes the system to dump the Registry to the hard disk at regular intervals, the heartbeat should not be enabled on systems running power management, such as laptops. To enable the heartbeat on a remote system, you would run this command:

```
uptime <remote server name> /heartbeat
```

Here is the complete syntax for `uptime`:

```
uptime [server name] [/s] [/a] [</d:mm/dd/yyyy> | </p:n>] [/heartbeat]
```

The `uptime` command options are detailed in Table 4-27.

An example of running `uptime` to determine system uptime and failure information is shown in Figure 4-16.

> For system monitoring, a common use of `uptime` is to configure the command in a batch file that redirects its output to a text file by following the command syntax with `> computername.log`. This way, you can schedule the command to run at regular intervals with the Task Scheduler and periodically check the generated log files.

Table 4-27. uptime Command Options

Option	Use
`server name`	Name or IP address of the remote server to check.
`/s`	Displays statistics and important system information.
`/a`	Displays application failure events.
`/d:mm/dd/yyyy`	Displays statistics information for only the time after the date specified.
`/p:n`	Displays statistics and information for only the previous number of days specified.
`/heartbeat`	Toggles heartbeat off or on.

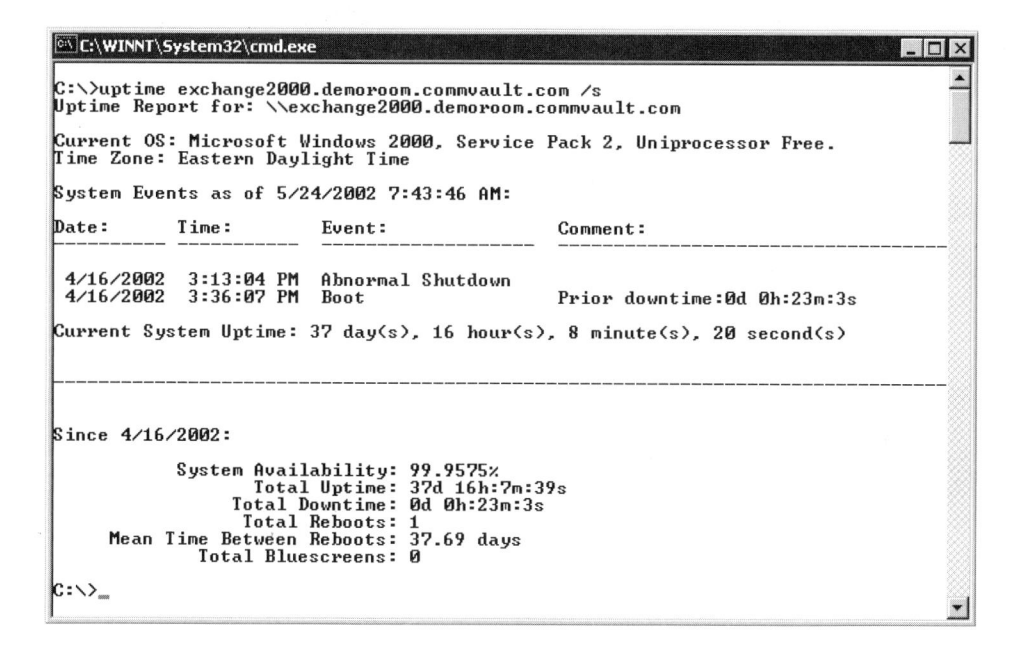

```
C:\>uptime exchange2000.demoroom.commvault.com /s
Uptime Report for: \\exchange2000.demoroom.commvault.com

Current OS: Microsoft Windows 2000, Service Pack 2, Uniprocessor Free.
Time Zone: Eastern Daylight Time

System Events as of 5/24/2002 7:43:46 AM:

Date:        Time:          Event:              Comment:
----------   ----------     ---------------     -----------------------------------
4/16/2002    3:13:04 PM     Abnormal Shutdown
4/16/2002    3:36:07 PM     Boot                Prior downtime:0d 0h:23m:3s

Current System Uptime: 37 day(s), 16 hour(s), 8 minute(s), 20 second(s)

Since 4/16/2002:
             System Availability: 99.9575%
                    Total Uptime: 37d 16h:7m:39s
                  Total Downtime: 0d 0h:23m:3s
                    Total Reboots: 1
          Mean Time Between Reboots: 37.69 days
                Total Bluescreens: 0
C:\>
```

Figure 4-16. Determining system availability statistics on a remote system with uptime

GUI Tools

The two predominant performance troubleshooting and monitoring GUI tools are System Monitor and Task Manager. Both of these tools are very complex and offer an abundance of performance monitoring options. In this section, however, only the troubleshooting aspects of each tool are examined. Additional information on using these tools for simple monitoring can be found in the Windows Help and Support Center.

System Monitor (Perfmon)

System Monitor allows you to confirm suspected problems on a user's system or a network server. For example, you may suspect that reported performance problems are the result of not enough RAM being in the system. To confirm this, you can use System Monitor to examine the number of pages (to the hard disk) per second. Too many pages per second indicates that the system is having to use the pagefile on the hard disk much more than it should and is indicative of not enough physical RAM being in the system.

The most common performance bottlenecks are listed in Table 4-28. The table lists the most common System Monitor counters to use in identifying faults on system resources along with the threshold recommended by Microsoft. If a memory threshold is passed, it may indicate that more RAM is needed in the system. If the network threshold is surpassed, you should consider further segmenting the system's associated network subnet. The fact of physical disk thresholds being exceeded usually points to the need for a faster disk. For these problems, you could consider replacing the IDE disk with a faster SCSI disk or look to implement a hardware-based RAID solution, such as RAID 0 (striped volume). Normally when processor thresholds are exceeded, it is time for a faster processor. If the system is running many multithreaded applications, you could also consider adding a second processor if the second CPU is supported by the system board.

Table 4-28. Common Performance Bottlenecks

Resource	Counters	Threshold
Memory	Committed Bytes	Less than the physical amount of RAM
	Pages/sec	20
Network	Bytes Total/sec	Sum for all systems involved in the problem should be less than the available network bandwidth (example: 100Mbps)
Physical disk	Average Disk Transfer/sec	0.3
	Disk Queue Length	2
	% Disk Time	90%
Processor	% Processor Time	80%
	Processor Queue Length	2

You can open System Monitor by clicking Start > All Programs > Administrative Tools > Performance. Another way to open System Monitor is to click Start > Run, type `Perfmon` in the Run dialog box, and click OK.

Once System Monitor opens, you will notice that the three most popular counters (Pages/sec, Disk Queue Length, and % Processor Time) are automatically loaded. In the example shown in Figure 4-17, notice the average number of Pages/sec shown, which is 49.593 (way over the threshold of 20)! This performance bottleneck is the result of running a W2K3 server with 128MB of RAM.

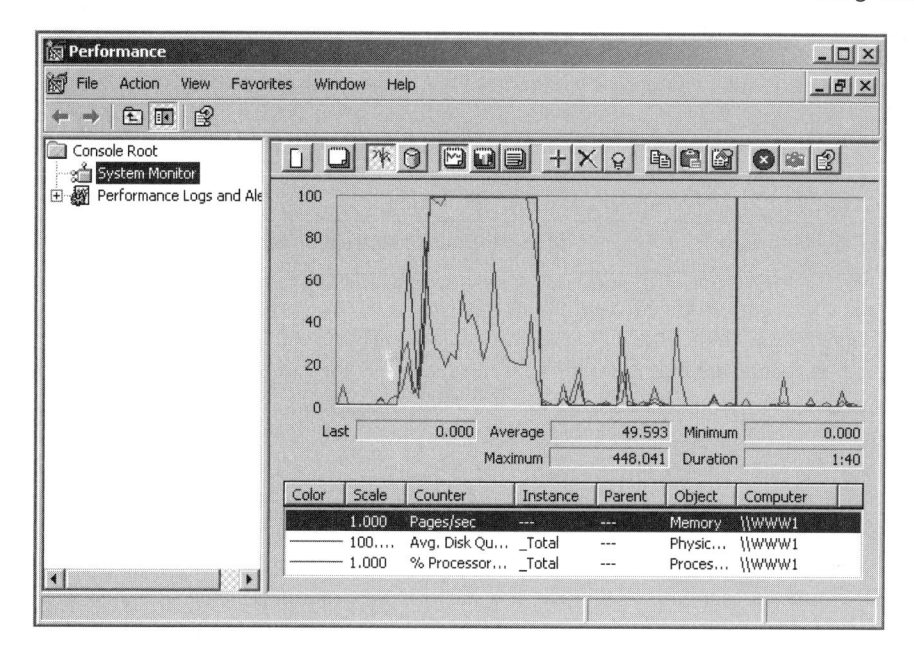

Figure 4-17. Monitoring for performance bottlenecks with System Monitor

To add additional counters, follow these steps.

1. Right-click anywhere in the System Monitor output display and select Add Counters (or click the + icon on the toolbar).

2. Select an object to monitor in the Performance Object menu, such as Network Interface.

3. Select the counters for the object to use, or choose All Counters.

4. Select any additional parameters required by the performance object. For example, when using the Network Interface object, you must select which network interface instances to monitor.

5. Click Close to close the Add Counters dialog box.

Now that you have seen the fundamental methods for troubleshooting with System Monitor, let's take a look at troubleshooting performance with Task Manager.

Task Manager

When you need immediate information about the status of a system, Task Manager is often the answer. You can access Task Manager by pressing Ctrl-Alt-Del and then clicking the Task Manger button or by right-clicking the taskbar at the bottom of the desktop and selecting Task Manger. The troubleshooting uses for Task Manager are outlined in Table 4-29.

Table 4-29. Troubleshooting Uses for Task Manager

Task Manager Tab	Actions to Correct Problems
Application	• Check status of open applications. • Terminate hung applications by clicking the application and then clicking the End Task button.
Processes	• Check CPU and memory consumption for running processes. • Terminate processes by right-clicking the process and selecting End Process.
Performance	• Monitor CPU, pagefile, and physical memory usage.
Networking	• Monitor network utilization for each active network adapter.
Users	• Check logged-on users. • Log off users. • Disconnect users (session and applications remain open).

Oftentimes a user can experience slow performance on his or her system due to a hung application. With Task Manger, you can quickly end a hung application and allow the user to continue working without having to reboot the system. For quick system status checks and for terminating hung applications and processes, Task Manager is the right tool for the job. An example of using Task Manager to check network utilization statistics is shown in Figure 4-18.

Now that you have seen the many performance monitoring tools at your disposal, let's take a look at the many security management tools.

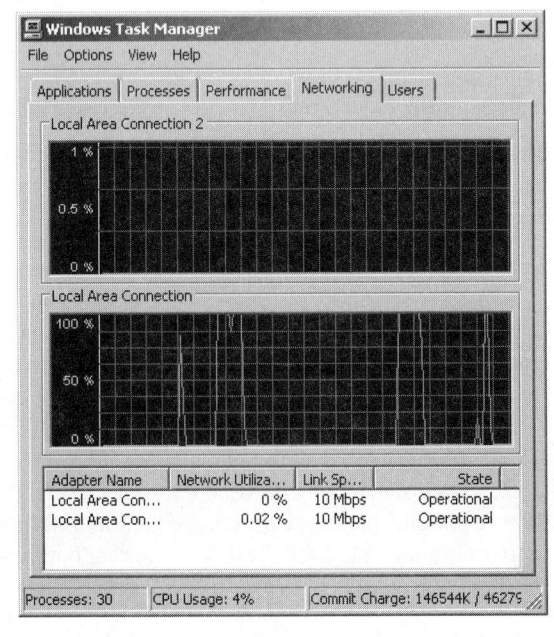

Figure 4-18. Checking network utilization with Task Manager

Security Management Tools

Security problems often mask themselves as other faults and thus can lead to prolonged fault resolution if you don't know what to look for. It is not uncommon for what is initially believed to be a network problem to actually be an NTFS permissions problem.

In this section, you will see the countless command line and GUI tools (mainly MMC snap-ins) that allow you to quickly isolate security faults on your network.

Command Line Tools

The command line tools described in this section cover the vast areas of security, including tools to troubleshoot access control lists, Encrypting File System (EFS), and security policies.

cacls

The `cacls` command allows you to display or modify the discretionary access control list (DACL) for a file or files. If you suspect that failure of a user to access a particular file is related to permissions, you can use `cacls` to confirm your suspicions. If you notice a problem with the access control list for a folder or file after running `cacls`, you can also use the command to modify the access control list.

Here is the syntax for `cacls`:

```
cacls <filename> [/t] [/e] [/c] [/g <user|group:permission>]
[/r <user|group>] [/p <user|group:permission>] [/d <user|group>]
```

The `cacls` command options are shown in Table 4-30.

Table 4-30. cacls Command Options

Option	Use
<filename>	Specifies the folder or file whose DACL you wish to manage. The * and ? wildcards can be used to specify multiple files.
/t	Causes the command to apply to the specified folders and files in the current directory and all subdirectories.
/e	Edits the DACL for the file or folder specified.
/c	Causes the command to continue changing DACLs, even if errors are encountered.
/g <user|group:permission>	Grants permission to the user or group specified. Valid permissions are shown in Table 4-31.
/r <user|group>	Revokes access rights for the specified user.
/p <user|group:permission>	Replaces the access rights for the user or group specified. Valid permission choices are shown in Table 4-31.
/d <user|group>	Denies access for the user or group specified.

Chapter 4 Monitoring and Diagnostic Tools

Table 4-31. Valid cacls Permission Values

Permission Value	Description
F	Full Control
C	Change (write)
W	Write
R	Read
N	None

When the DACL is displayed in the command output, in addition to permissions displayed for specific users and user groups, you will see whether the permissions apply to the current folder, subfolders, and/or files for each access control entry (ACE) listed. The output codes for the "where" portion of the output are displayed in Table 4-32.

Table 4-32. cacls Output Codes

Output Code	User/Group Permissions Apply To
No code displayed	Target folder only
CI	Target folder and subfolders
IO	ACE does not apply to the current file or folder.
OI	Target folder and files
(CI)(IO)	Subfolders of target folder only
(OI)(CI)	Target folder, subfolders, and files
(OI)(IO)	Target's files only
(OI)(CI)(IO)	Target's subfolders and files only

Figure 4-19 shows the use of `cacls` to check the DACL for the E:\Collateral folder. In this example, the Administrators group has Full Control permissions, while Marketing has Read, and Sales has Change. For all three user groups, the command output shows that the permissions apply to the target folder and its subfolders and files.

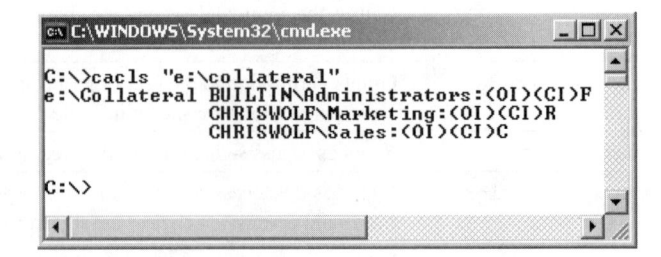

```
C:\>cacls "e:\collateral"
e:\Collateral BUILTIN\Administrators:(OI)(CI)F
              CHRISWOLF\Marketing:(OI)(CI)R
              CHRISWOLF\Sales:(OI)(CI)C

C:\>
```

Figure 4-19. Using cacls to display the DACL of a folder

Suppose that members of Marketing also needed to modify documents in the Collateral folder. To grant the Marketing group Change permission using `cacls`, you would execute this command:

```
cacls "e:\collateral" /p ChrisWolf\marketing:c /e
```

> When using `cacls` to modify an existing DACL, be sure to use the /e switch in conjunction with the command. Otherwise, the DACL will be replaced by what was specified in the command instead of simply being edited. If ten other groups were listed in the DACL, and only one group was specified in the command, without the /e switch the new DACL would only list the one group.

efsinfo (ST)

Encrypting File System (EFS) information (`efsinfo`) provides an easy way to list files and folders encrypted with Encrypting File System on NTFS partitions. Users sometimes may not understand why they cannot access a file or folder created by another user that is stored locally or on a network share, when the reason may be that the file or target folder was encrypted by its creator. In this situation, users not having the proper key or certificate cannot open the file.

When you suspect encrypted files may be the cause of access problems to files or shared folders, `efsinfo` will provide you with everything you need, not only telling you if a folder has the encrypted attribute, for example, but also telling you who can decrypt the folder or its contents.

Here is the syntax for `efsinfo`:

```
efsinfo [/u] [/r] [/c] [/i] [/y] [/s:<directory>] [path]
```

The command options are described in Table 4-33.

Table 4-33. efsinfo Command Options

Option	Use
/u	Displays encryption information about files and folders in the current folder from where the command is executed (the default).
/r	Displays EFS recovery agent information.
/c	Displays certificate thumbprint information.
/i	Continues execution of the command, even if errors are encountered.
/y	Displays the digest (thumbprint) of the certificate data.
/s:<directory>	Used to specify a path in which to check the target directories and all subdirectories for encrypted files.
path	Used to provide a path (local or Universal Naming Convention, UNC) in which to check for encrypted files. If no path is specified, `efsinfo` checks for encrypted files in the current directory.

Here is an example of using `efsinfo` to check for encrypted folders and files on the network share \\neutron\docshare:

```
efsinfo /s:\\neutron\docshare
```

> Encrypted file and folder names are displayed in green text in Windows Explorer, making them easy to spot.

takeown

Suppose that you have a renegade user that, before leaving the company, decides to make your life more difficult by denying everyone in the organization access to his files. The solution for this type of problem is for you, as an administrator, to take ownership of the affected files and then modify their DACL. One easy way to perform this task is to use the `takeown` command line utility.

The `takeown` syntax is:

```
takeown /f <file> [/s <system>] [/u <domain\user>] [/p <password>]
```

The `takeown` command options are described in Table 4-34.

Table 4-34. takeown Command Options

Option	Use
/f <file>	Used to indicate the file of which to take ownership. The * wildcard can be used to indicate multiple files.
/s <system>	Used to provide the name or IP address of a remote computer on which to run the command. By default, the command will run on the local system where it is executed.
/u <domain\user>	Used to execute the command with the credentials of another user. This may be needed if you need to take ownership of files on a standalone system using its local administrator account.
/p <password>	Used to specify a password for the user account specified with the /u switch.

Here are some examples of using the `takeown` command:

- To take ownership of all files in the E:\Personal folder:
  ```
  takeown /f "E:\Personal"
  ```
- To take ownership of the resume.doc file on the remote system CrocHunter.awl.com:
  ```
  takeown /f "C:\resume.doc" /s CrocHunter.awl.com
  ```

Once you have taken ownership of a file or the contents of a folder, as the administrator you have ownership and thus can access the file. It the folder needs to be accessed by many users, don't forget to update the folder's DACL by using the `cacls` command or Windows Explorer.

GUI Tools

As with the command line tools outlined in the Security Management Tools section, the GUI tools available for security troubleshooting range from being simple and used in broad situations to being complex and used in limited scenarios. This section focuses on two widely used Microsoft security analysis and troubleshooting tools: Security Configuration and Analysis, and Security Templates.

Security Configuration and Analysis

Security Configuration and Analysis is a tool that is useful in examining the local security settings on a computer. If a user is unable to perform specific local or network tasks, it may be because the user inadvertently applied a strict security policy. While this is unlikely, you should never underestimate the power of a user. Not to mention, it is possible that a wily administrator who just learned about security just locked down a server and now no one can access it. This is where Security Configuration and Analysis can be very useful.

Security Configuration and Analysis is an MMC snap-in, so to open it, you need to load the snap-in into an MMC console. To do this, follow these steps.

1. Click Start > Run, type MMC in the Run dialog box, and click OK.

2. In the MMC console, press Ctrl-M to add a new snap-in.

3. Click the Add button.

4. Select Security Configuration and Analysis from the list and click Add. At this time, you can also add the Security Templates snap-in, which is addressed in the next section.

5. Now click the Close button in the Add Standalone Snap-in dialog box, and then click OK in the Add/Remove Snap-in dialog box.

At this point, you are ready to analyze the system. Analysis does require that you check the system against a known security template. For troubleshooting purposes, it is easiest to use the default template in your analysis. With XP/W2K3, the default template is stored as "setup security.inf" (or "DC Security.inf" for domain controllers) and represents the security settings that you would have after initially installing the operating system. The Setup Security template is the equivalent to the Basic templates that were used in Windows 2000 and earlier operating systems.

To analyze the security settings on a system, follow these steps.

Chapter 4 Monitoring and Diagnostic Tools

1. Right-click the Security Configuration and Analysis Snap-in and select Open Database.

2. For testing purposes, you can create a new database, so in the File Name field in the Open Database dialog box, type `test` and click Open.

3. Now, in the Import Template dialog box, click the "setup security.inf" file and click Open.

4. With the template imported, the system security settings can now be analyzed. To do this, right-click the Security Configuration and Analysis Snap-in and select Analyze Computer Now.

5. Leave the default error log file path intact or enter a new error log file path in the Perform Analysis dialog box and click OK.

The analysis will take a couple of minutes to run on the system. Once it is complete, you can browse the security configuration settings that are listed under the snap-in. It is easy to spot differences in a system's configuration when compared with a security template, because differences are noted by a red X that appears next to the setting. This is shown in Figure 4-20, where it is noted that there is a difference in the digital signing configuration between a system and the default template.

Especially when you are working with a foreign network, you never know what you may run into. On one occasion, I could not connect to a particular server, even though the folders I needed to access were shared by everyone. As it turned out, the server was requiring that secure channel data always be encrypted, and clients were not configured to encrypt data, even if asked. In other words, the client tried to start a session with the server, and the server said, "We can talk, but only if you agree to encrypt." The client

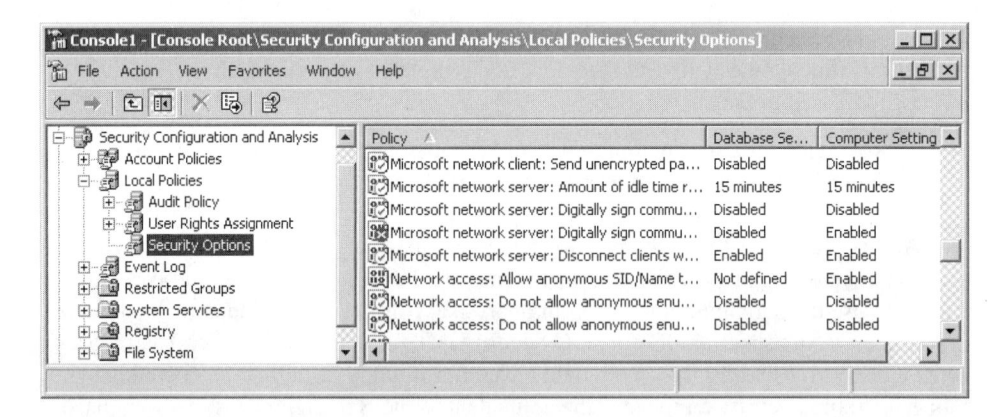

Figure 4-20. Finding security configuration variations with Security Configuration and Analysis

then said, "Nope, I don't agree to that," and in response the server said, "Talk to the hand!" While the analogy may seem silly, don't lose focus on the point that this problem was quickly identified by seeing with Security Configuration and Analysis that the server was requiring secure communication, and this was not configured on the client as well. Sometimes just having an awareness of a tool is sufficient. Many rarely, if ever, use Security Configuration and Analysis, but remembering what it can be used for may help to quickly make you the hero of the day.

Security Templates

In the last section when Security Configuration and Analysis was run, a security template was required in order to compare system settings to those that existed in a known template. If you would like to view and configure template settings prior to analyzing a system, this can be done with the Security Templates snap-in. You can follow the same procedure outlined in the last section to load the snap-in, if you have not done so already.

Once the snap-in is loaded, you can then browse and analyze the settings of each security template.

System Management Tools

There are several system management tools at your disposal that are extremely useful in isolating system faults. In this section, you will see numerous command line tools and GUI tools that not only allow you to quickly find system configuration problems, but also set up alerts so that a system can tell you when something is wrong.

Command Line Tools

The command line tools described in this section are among the most useful tools in this chapter. As you will see, they are very targeted in their troubleshooting purpose and allow you to quickly find answers to questions you have listed as possible faults.

driverquery

If you suspect that the cause of a problem may be related to the wrong device driver being installed, you can confirm your suspicion by running `driverquery`. When executed, `driverquery` lists all installed device drivers and information on their properties. For example, you can run `driverquery` to retrieve a list of all device drivers installed on the system that are not digitally signed.

Here is the syntax for `driverquery`:

```
driverquery [/s <remote system>] [/u <domain\user>] [/p <password>]
[/fo <table|list|csv>] [/nh] [/v] [/si]
```

The options for `driverquery` are described in Table 4-35.

Table 4-35. driverquery Command Options

Option	Use
`/s <remote system>`	Specifies the name or IP address of the remote system on which to query drivers.
`/u <domain\user>`	Allows you to run the command under the context of a different account.
`/p <password>`	When the /u switch is used, this option allows you to specify the password associated with the user account.
`/fo <table|list|csv>`	Used to specify the format for the command's output (the default is `table`).
`/nh`	When the output is set to `table` or `csv`, this option suppresses the table header information from the command output.
`/v`	Verbose output—highly detailed driver information is displayed in the output.
`/si`	Displays digital signature and manufacturer information for each installed driver.

To check the signature status and manufacturer of each driver on a system, you run `driverquery /si`. Another example of using `driverquery` would be to compare all of the installed drivers on two different workstations. If you are having problems with one system, you could print its `driverquery` output and compare it with the `driverquery` output on a known good system.

eventquery

The `eventquery` command allows you to retrieve event information from the event logs on local or remote systems. With this tool, you can search events based on their

- Date and time
- Event ID
- Type
- User
- Computer

If you are not running any event monitoring tools, you could, for example, configure a batch file that runs `eventquery` at regular intervals to report any critical system events on remote systems. If you redirect the command output to a text or log file, you could check the files every week or every other week to look for early signs of trouble. Now that you have seen where `eventquery` can be used, let's look at its syntax.

```
eventquery.vbs [/s <remote system>] [/u <domain\user>] [/p <password>]
[/fi <filter>] [/fo <table|list|csv>] [/r <range>] [/l <log name>]
```

The many options for `eventquery` are described in Table 4-36.

Table 4-36. eventquery Command Options

Option	Use
`/s <remote system>`	Specifies the name or IP address of the remote system to query.
`/u <domain\user>`	Specifies the user account under which to execute the script.
`/p <password>`	When a user account is specified with the `/u` switch, this option is used to provide a password.
`/fi <filter>`	Allows you to use one of the filters listed in Table 4-37 in the query to find specific event types.
`/fo <table|list|csv>`	Used to specify the format for the script's output (default is `table`).
`/r <range>`	Allows you to set the number of events to display. Use a positive integer to signify the most recent and a negative integer to show the oldest. For example, a `range` value of 15 would return the 15 most recent events, whereas a `range` value of –8 would return the 8 oldest events.
`/l <log name>`	Allows you to specify the name of the log to query (application, security, system, and so on). The * wildcard can be used to indicate multiple logs.

Table 4-37. Valid eventquery Filters and Operators

Filter	Operator	Allowable Values
`Category`	`eq, ne`	Any string of characters
`Computer`	`eq, ne`	Any string of characters
`Datetime`	`eq, ne, ge, le, gt, lt`	`mm/dd/yyyy, hh:mm:ss (AM|PM)`
`ID`	`eq, ne, gt, lt, ge, le, or`	Any positive integer
`Source`	`eq, ne`	Any string of characters
`Type`	`eq, ne`	`Error	Information	Warning	SuccessAudit	FailureAudit`
`User`	`eq, ne`	Any string of characters

All of the operators except for `or` were described in Table 4-24 earlier. The `or` operator is used to signify an OR logic function. For example, to filter for event IDs 5719 or 2506, you would use the switch `/fi "ID eq 5719 or ID eq 2506"` when you execute the command. Remember that since `eventquery` is a Visual Basic Script, you need to precede the command with `cscript` and run the command in the directory where it resides (i.e., System32).

Here are two examples of querying events with `eventquery`:

- To check for critical (error) system events on the computer www2.awl.com:
  `eventquery.vbs /s www2.awl.com /l system /fi "type eq error"`

- To query all events in the local security log:
  `eventquery.vbs /l security`

Now that you have seen how to check for event types that have already happened, next you'll see how to have the system alert you when a particular type of event occurs.

eventtriggers

One of the easiest ways to arrive at optimum system uptime is to have systems tell you when they have something wrong, instead of you continually polling and monitoring network servers. With `eventtriggers`, you can have systems send alerts or execute a program (.bat, .exe, .vbs, and so on) when a particular type of event is encountered.

The `eventtriggers` command can be run to create, delete, or query triggers. Here is the syntax for `eventtriggers /create`:

```
eventtriggers /create [/s <system>] [/u <domain\user>]  [/p <password>]
[/tr <trigger>] [/l <log name>] {[/eid <ID>] | [/t <type>] | [/so
<source>]} [/d <description>] [/tk <task>] [/ru <domain\user>] [/rp
<password>]
```

The command parameters are described in Table 4-38.

Table 4-38. eventtriggers /create Command Options

Option	Use
/s <system>	Specifies the name or IP address of the remote system to set up an event trigger for.
/u <domain\user>	Specifies the user account under which to execute the command.
/p <password>	When a user account is specified with the /u switch, this option is used to provide a password.
/tr <trigger>	Allows you to specify a friendly name to associate with the event trigger.
/l <log name>	Allows you to specify the name of the log to monitor (application, security, system, and so on). The * wildcard can be used to indicate multiple logs. All logs are monitored by default.

System Management Tools

Table 4-38. eventtriggers /create Command Options, continued

Option	Use
/eid <ID>	Specifies the event ID number type that eventtriggers should monitor.
/t <type>	Used to have eventtriggers monitor a specific event type. Valid type values are error, warning, information, successaudit, or failureaudit. This parameter cannot be used in conjunction with either /eid or /so.
/so <source>	Used to specify an event source for the trigger to monitor. The source value can be represented by any string. This parameter cannot be used in conjunction with either /eid or /t.
/d <description>	Allows you to specify a description for the trigger.
/tk <task>	Allows you to specify a command to execute when the trigger conditions are satisfied.
/ru <domain\user | system>	When a task is run, this parameter allows you to specify the account that the task will run under. You can specify a user name or enter system to have the task run under the local system account.
/rp <password>	When user information is entered with /ru, /rp is used to specify a password for the user account. When the system account is specified with /ru, no password is required.

Here is an example of creating an event trigger. Suppose you wanted to know every time the DNS service stopped on the server DNS1. The first thing to do is create the task to run when the trigger event occurs. To do this, create a batch file called DNSAlert.bat and add this line to its content:

```
Net Send Administrator "The DNS Service is down on the system that
sent this message."
```

In the command syntax, you just need to replace the name Administrator with your own user name. Once you have the batch file saved, you next need to know the event ID associated with the DNS Server service stopping. You can find this by manually stopping the service and then checking the DNS Server event log to see the event's associated event ID. You can use the same practice to identify any event IDs in the other event logs. With the event ID identified, you are now ready to configure the event trigger.

If the batch file was saved in the C:\Alerts folder on DNS1, you could run the following command at DNS1 to set up the event trigger:

```
eventtriggers /create /tr "DNSDown" /l "DNS Server" /eid 3 /tk
"C:\Alerts\DNSAlert.bat"
```

Chapter 4 Monitoring and Diagnostic Tools

To verify that the alert works, just stop the DNS Server service on DNS1, and within seconds you should see the alert. While creating triggers is relatively easy, it is still important to be able to track them. This can be done with `eventtriggers /query`.

The `eventtriggers /query` command allows you to identify all of the event triggers configured on a system. To run the command, you would use the following syntax:

```
eventtriggers /query [/s <system>] [/u <domain\user>] [/p <password>]
[/fo <table|list|csv>] [/nh] [/v]
```

The options for this `eventtriggers` command version are described in Table 4-39.

Table 4-39. eventtriggers /query Command Options

Option	Use
/s <system>	Specifies the name or IP address of the remote system to check for a list of event triggers.
/u <domain\user>	Specifies the user account under which to execute the command.
/p <password>	When a user account is specified with the /u switch, this parameter is used to provide a password.
/fo <table|list|csv>	Used to specify the format for the command's output (the default is `table`).
/nh	When the output is set to `table` or `csv`, this parameter suppresses the table header information from the command output.
/v	Verbose mode—output displays specific information about each event trigger, including the parameters of the event associated with the trigger. Normally, only the trigger name, trigger ID, and trigger task are displayed.

If you wanted to see the event triggers created on the server DNS1, you could run `eventtriggers /query /s DNS1`. Getting a list of configured event triggers for a system is important in the event that you wanted to delete a trigger. To delete a trigger, you need its trigger ID, which is displayed in the output of `eventtriggers /query`. Once you have the trigger ID, you are ready to delete the event trigger. Here is the syntax to do so:

```
eventtriggers /delete [/s <system>] [/u <domain\user>] [/p <password>]
[/tid <trigger ID>]
```

The `eventtriggers /delete` options are explained in Table 4-40.

Table 4-40. eventtriggers /delete Command Options

Option	Use
/s <system>	Specifies the name or IP address of the remote system in which to delete event triggers.
/u <domain\user>	Specifies the user account under which to execute the command.
/p <password>	When a user account is specified with the /u switch, this parameter is used to provide a password.
/tid <trigger ID>	Used to specify the trigger ID of the event trigger to be deleted. The * wildcard can be used in place of the trigger ID value to delete all event triggers.

If you wanted to delete all event triggers on the server DNS1, you would run eventtriggers /delete /s DNS1 /tid *.

As you can see, eventtriggers is a very robust and useful program for identifying system problems at the time they occur. Another useful, but underrated, tool is systeminfo, which is covered next.

systeminfo

The systeminfo command can almost be thought of as a trimmed-down command line version of the GUI tool MSinfo32, which is described in the upcoming GUI Tools section. The systeminfo command provides general system information on either a local or remote system, and from a troubleshooting perspective provides the following useful information:

- The operating system version and service pack level
- The product ID (if you need to call support)
- Processor type(s)
- The BIOS version
- Windows and system directory locations
- Physical and virtual memory
- A list of each installed hotfix

To run systeminfo, you would use the following syntax:

```
systeminfo [/s <system>] [/u <domain\user>] [/p <password>]
[/fo <table|list|csv>] [/nh]
```

Table 4-41 describes the available command options.

Chapter 4 Monitoring and Diagnostic Tools

Table 4-41. systeminfo Command Options

Option	Use
/s <system>	Specifies the name or IP address of the remote system in which to acquire system information.
/u <domain\user>	Specifies the user account under which to execute the command.
/p <password>	When a user account is specified with the /u switch, this parameter is used to provide a password.
/fo <table|list|csv>	Used to specify the format for the command's output (the default is table).
/nh	When the output is set to table or csv, this parameter suppresses the table header information from the command output.

Suppose a user reports a problem to you, and you believe that a resolution already exists in a particular Microsoft hotfix. To check to see if the hotfix is installed on the system (suppose it's named "2boxers"), you would run systeminfo /s 2boxers.

sfc

Back in the days when Windows NT was the predominant Windows-based networking OS, oftentimes performing a task such as installing a new application would cause several other applications to no longer work or even to crash the system. This instability was often the result of the new application modifying a system .dll file that was shared by other applications.

This problem was remedied beginning with Windows 2000, with the operating system no longer allowing applications to modify or overwrite critical system files. These files were designated as protected files by the OS and are mainly .dlls and .exe files in the System32 folder. If an application does overwrite a protected file, the operating system should automatically replace the overwritten file with a copy of the original, which is stored locally in the Windows\system32\dllcache folder. If the original version of the protected file is not in the dllcache folder, then the user will be prompted for the Windows installation CD, and the protected file will be replaced with the original version on the CD.

Now that you've had a quick history of protected files, let's get to sfc. The name sfc is short for System File Checker, and the command is primarily used to scan your system and verify the authenticity of all protected files. If a user is complaining about system instability, there is a chance that the problem is the result of a protected file that has been altered. To eliminate this as a possible problem, you could run sfc on the system.

Here is the syntax for sfc:

```
sfc [/scannow] [/scanonce] [/scanboot] [/revert] [/purgecache]
[/cachsize=<size>]
```

The `sfc` command options are explained in Table 4-42.

Table 4-42. sfc Command Options

Option	Use
`/scannow`	System protected files are scanned immediately.
`/scanonce`	System protected files are scanned once at the next reboot.
`/scanboot`	System protected files are scanned each time the system boots.
`/revert`	Reverts the System File Checker to its default setting (does not scan at startup).
`/purgecache`	Purges the contents of the dllcache folder and runs an immediate scan of protected files. Files in the dllcache folder are replaced by their original versions on the installation CD.
`/cachesize=<size>`	Sets a maximum size (in megabytes) for the dllcache folder.

Here are two examples of checking protected files with `sfc`:

- To scan protected files immediately: `sfc /scannow`
- To scan protected files each time the system boots: `sfc /scanboot`

The `sfc` command takes some time (up to 30 minutes) to complete and is CPU and disk intensive, so only run this tool during periods of low system activity. Once `sfc` finishes checking protected files, you can look in the system event log to see which files, if any, were replaced. Events related to files being replaced by `sfc` are identified by Event ID 64020.

GUI Tools

This section addresses four prominent system management GUI tools:

- Computer Management
- Event Viewer
- MSinfo32
- Windows Update

As you will see, this collection of tools is helpful not only in diagnosing problems, but in preventing them as well.

Computer Management

Computer Management is a single console that provides a collection of nearly all the tools needed to visually inspect the status of a system. When you open Computer Management, you have access to these tools.

- *Event Viewer*—Check recent system events (covered in the next section).
- *Shared Folders*—View and manage all shared folders on the system.
- *Performance Logs and Alerts*—Check and configure performance logs and alerts (based on system performance thresholds).
- *Device Manager*—Manage system hardware. Install and update drivers.
- *Removable Storage*—Configure and manage removable storage (libraries, tape drives, Zip drives).
- *Disk Defragmenter*—Defragment system hard disks.
- *Disk Management*—Manage and configure hard disks.
- *Services*—Manage all installed system services.

A nice feature about Computer Management is that it can be run remotely. If you support 20 systems, for example, you can configure a custom MMC console that has the Computer Management snap-in loaded for each system. To configure this type of console, perform these steps.

1. Click Start > Run, type MMC in the Run dialog box, and click OK.
2. Now press Ctrl-M to add new snap-ins.
3. In the Add/Remove Snap-in dialog box, click the Add button.
4. Click Computer Management and then click the Add button.
5. In the Computer Management dialog box, click the Another Computer radio button, and manually enter the name of the remote computer or use the Browse button to select the remote computer to manage.
6. Once you have selected the computer, click Finish in the Computer Management dialog box.
7. Repeat steps 4–6 to add additional computers to the console.

Once the console is complete with the systems you need to manage, click the Console menu and select Save As to save the console. By default, it will be saved in your Administrative Tools folder, so you can access the console by clicking Start > All Programs > Administrative Tools, and then selecting the name you specified for the console.

Event Viewer

It was mentioned in Chapter 3 that troubleshooting often involves a good deal of detective work. No matter how honest the users you support are, odds are that they will not know all of the events leading up to a particular problem or failure. That is where the Event Viewer comes in handy. As incidents occur on a system, they are logged in the event logs, which can be viewed using the Event Viewer.

The primary logs with which to concern yourself with when troubleshooting are

- *Application log*—Displays application-related events
- *Security log*—Displays security-related audit events
- *System log*—Displays operating system–specific events

On W2K3 servers, depending on how the server is configured, you may find other specific logs that record events for specific services installed on the system, such as Directory Service, DNS Server, or File Replication Service. To access the Event Viewer, click Start > All Programs > Administrative Tools > Event Viewer. An example of using the Event Viewer to observe system-related events is shown in Figure 4-21.

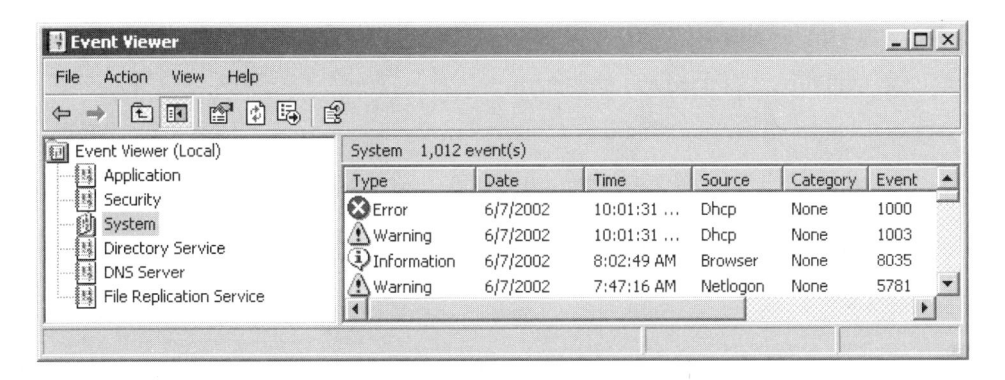

Figure 4-21. Checking system events in the Event Viewer

MSinfo32

MSinfo32 is the command that in the NT days was known as WinMSD. In fact, many have trouble remembering "MSinfo32" and instead launch MSinfo32 by running WinMSD. Regardless of whether you run MSinfo32 or WinMSD, the resultant program that is launched is the same.

Have you ever wanted proof of what is on a system, instead of taking a user's word for it? Then MSinfo32 is the answer. With MSinfo32, you can have a user save his or her system configuration to a file and e-mail it to you. This command is especially useful for systems engineers (SEs) who often have to perform software installations at remote sites. Prior to arriving at a site, many SEs check with the site's local administrators to verify that the systems involved in the installation meet the minimum requirements. The answer is almost always "Yes."

112 Chapter 4 Monitoring and Diagnostic Tools

When performing work in an unknown environment, many have come to expect the worst, and this way they are pleasantly surprised if the site's systems are configured as they were described. With MSinfo32, an SE can request that a sample of system information files (these are the files generated by MSinfo32) be sent to her at a predetermined time before she arrives at a site. This way, the SE can visually verify the system configuration of the remote systems and be prepared for what she will have to face at the remote site.

Now that you have seen the many uses for MSinfo32, let's look at the information provided by the command. From a computer's system information file, you will be able to see the following:

- OS version, service pack level, and installed hotfixes
- System hardware, including the amount of RAM installed and the CPU
- System BIOS version
- Hardware conflicts
- Hardware devices installed
- Software installed
- System drivers (signed and unsigned)
- System services configuration
- Internet Explorer configuration information

As you can see, this file tells you practically anything you could possibly want to know about the configuration of a system. A sample system information file is displayed in Figure 4-22.

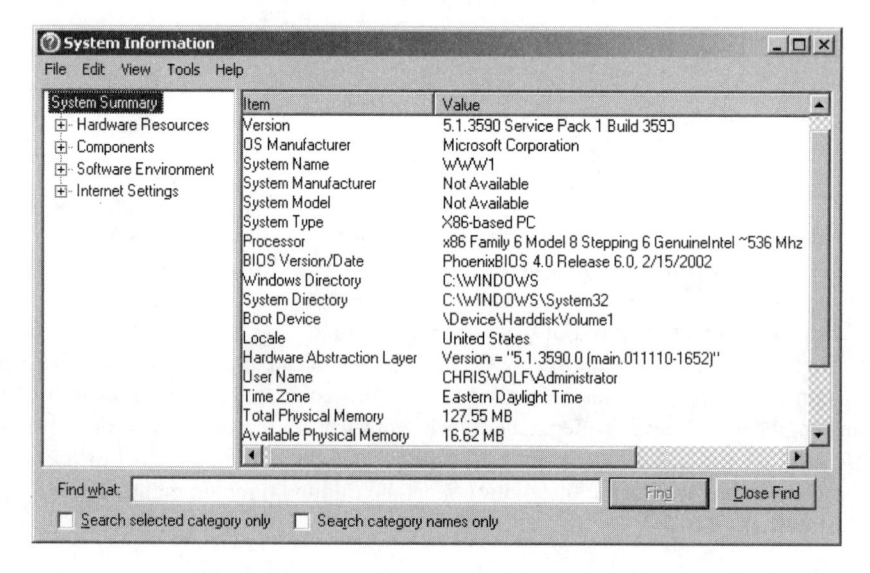

Figure 4-22. System information file from Windows Server 2003 Enterprise Edition

To view the system information for a computer, click Start > Run, enter `MSinfo32`, and click OK.

To save the save the system information file, follow these steps.

1. In the System Information dialog box, click the File menu and select Save.

2. In the Save As dialog box, enter a name for the file and click OK. Note that it is saved as an .nfo file.

Once a system information file has been saved, it can be checked by opening the file in the System Information dialog box. To do this, perform these steps.

1. Open the System Information dialog box by running MSinfo32.

2. Click the File menu and select Open.

3. Browse to and select the appropriate .nfo file in the Open dialog box and click the Open button.

Now you can view the configuration of the remote system. As you can see, this is a very useful tool for concise summarization of a system's configuration. Another indispensable tool for not only resolving faults but also preventing them is Windows Update. That's what we'll look at next.

Windows Update

When you hear of Microsoft security vulnerabilities being exploited, sometimes you have to consider how hackers discover the vulnerabilities in the first place. Oftentimes, especially with IIS, hackers can find security holes right from Windows Update. With Windows 2000 and earlier Microsoft OS versions, users were not automatically notified of new available updates for their systems, and instead would have to periodically check with the Microsoft Windows Update Web site to see if their systems were current.

The fact that vulnerabilities were made public, in spite of their published fixes, allowed hackers to exploit these public holes, because most users either did not even know about Windows Update, or did and simply did not use it. With IIS Web servers, there have been success and failure stories stemming from Windows Update. The failures were the administrators that did not update their systems and consequently were hit by viruses exploiting known security holes. Those that were prepared installed and ran the Windows Critical Update Notification Service on their systems, which alerted them of new critical updates automatically. Those that were not prepared either suffered the misery of rebuilding or restoring systems, or were lucky enough to be missed in the attack. Needless to say, Microsoft learned its lesson with critical updates with Windows 2000 and has made them automatic with XP/W2K3.

With Windows Update on XP/W2K3 systems, you have three configuration options:

- Download updates automatically
- Notify before downloading
- Turn off automatic updating

Downloading updates automatically is the default on Windows XP systems. With this selection, critical updates are automatically checked for and subsequently downloaded. Users are then prompted to follow a wizard to complete the installation of the updates and most likely will need to reboot their systems. If the "Notify before downloading" option is selected, users are notified when updates are available and at that point can elect to download them. This setting is most ideal for mobile users who often connect to the Internet using a dial-up modem. The last choice is to turn off automatic updates entirely. Unless you have a system in place to roll out updates as software installation packages in group policy objects, this is not a wise choice. While not having automatic updating on does save you a small degree of network bandwidth utilization, it does so at the expense of leaving open potential security vulnerabilities.

Windows Update can be configured by performing these steps.

1. Click Start > Control Panel.

2. Double-click the System icon.

3. Click the Automatic Updates tab.

4. Select the desired automatic update setting and click OK.

The available automatic update settings are shown in Figure 4-23.

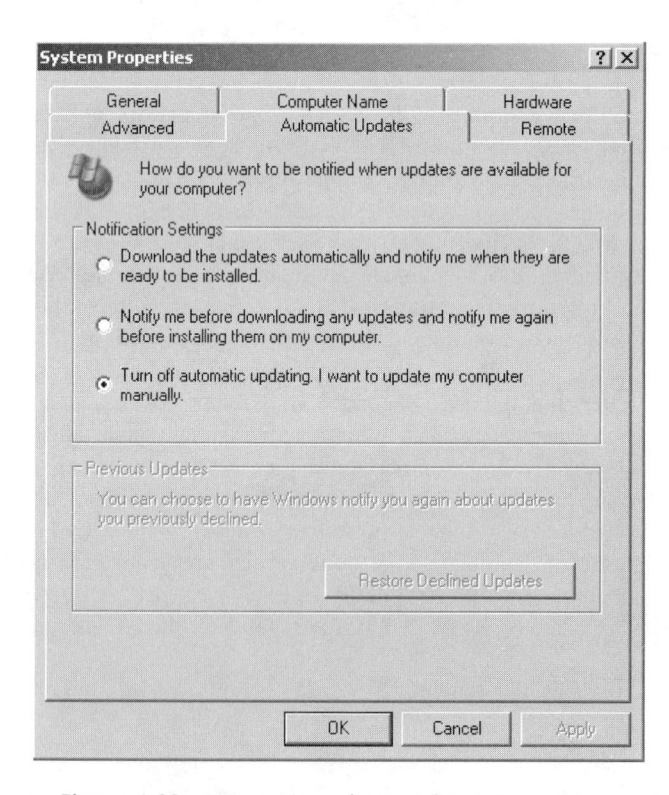

Figure 4-23. Automatic update configuration settings

Now that you have seen a great tool for staying out of trouble, next you'll see some excellent tools for getting out of trouble, which are the new and improved troubleshooting wizards.

Troubleshooting Wizards

If this book were about Windows 2000, I would not even be wasting precious ink describing the troubleshooting wizards, because they generally provided relatively useless information. In the past, Microsoft's troubleshooting wizards did little more than point out the painfully obvious and rarely helped to solve problems. However, with XP/W2K3 Microsoft took troubleshooting wizards to a new level, and users and administrators alike will find some value in them. If you are still in a state of doubt, read on and give me about two minutes to convince you otherwise.

Table 4-43 lists the troubleshooting wizards along with the command to execute them. Each of the wizards can be started by clicking Start > Run, and then entering the wizard's related command in the dialog box. Otherwise, links to the troubleshooting wizards can also be found in the Help and Support Center.

Table 4-43. Troubleshooting Wizards

Wizard	Command	Use
Digital Video Disks (DVDs)	hcp://help/tshoot/ts_dvd.htm	Troubleshoot DVD drives and decoders.
Display	hcp://help/tshoot/tsdisp.htm	Troubleshoot video adapters, monitor settings, and video drivers.
Drives and Network Adapters	hcp://help/tshoot/tsdrive.htm	Troubleshoot hard disks, removable storage (CD-ROMs, DVD drives, floppy drives, tape drives, Zip and Jaz drives), and network cards.
File and Print Sharing	hcp://help/tshoot/tsnetwrk.htm	Troubleshoot security-related sharing problems and network connection problems to remote resources.
Hardware	hcp://help/tshoot/tshardw.htm	Troubleshoot all system hardware and drivers (drives, sound cards, NICs, mice, keyboards, USB, and so on).
Home Networking	hcp://help/tshoot/tshomenet.htm	Troubleshoot Internet connection settings, and file and print sharing configuration.

continues

Table 4-43. Troubleshooting Wizards, continued

Wizard	Command	Use
Input Devices	hcp://help/tshoot/tsinputdev.htm	Troubleshoot mice, keyboards, cameras, scanners, and infrared devices.
Internet Connection Sharing	hcp://help/tshoot/tsics.htm	Troubleshoot Internet connection setup (ISP connection settings), and network and modem settings.
Internet Explorer	hcp://help/tshoot/tsie.htm	Troubleshoot browsing, download, and Web printing problems.
Modem	hcp://help/tshoot/tsmodem.htm	Troubleshoot modem configuration, detection, and setup.
Multimedia and Games	hcp://help/tshoot/tsgame.htm	Troubleshoot gaming- and multimedia-related hardware and drivers (game cards, sound cards, DVD, joysticks, and USB).
Outlook Express (Messaging)	hcp://help/tshoot/tsmessaging.htm	Troubleshoot Outlook Express and the Windows Messenger Service.
Printing	hcp://help/tshoot/tsprint.htm	Troubleshoot printer installation, connection, and quality, and check for proper print drivers.
Sound	hcp://help/tshoot/tssound.htm	Troubleshoot sound input, output, and sound card hardware and driver settings.
Startup/Shutdown	hcp://help/tshoot/tsstartup.htm	Troubleshoot problems that occur during startup or shutdown.
System Setup	hcp://help/tshoot/tssetup.htm	Troubleshoot Windows setup and installation problems.
USB	hcp://help/tshoot/tsusb.htm	Troubleshoot USB connectors and attached peripherals.

Using the Startup/Shutdown Troubleshooting Wizard to resolve a startup problem is shown in Figure 4-24.

If you are still not convinced that these wizards are worthy of your attention, try running a few of them. The XP/W2K3 troubleshooting wizards seriously take on real-world problems and often require system reboots during the troubleshooting process. These tools are now very aggressive in their fault resolution tactics and often result in solved

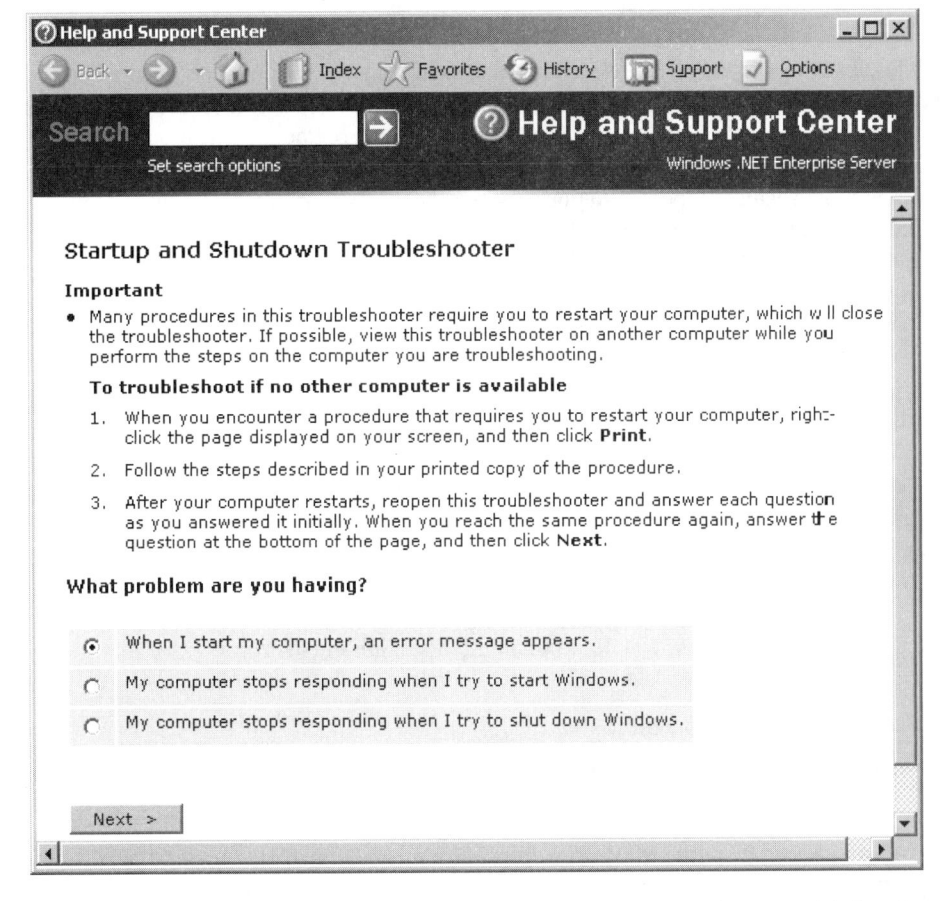

Figure 4-24. Troubleshooting startup problems with the Startup/Shutdown Troubleshooting Wizard

problems. Now that you have seen most of what Microsoft has to offer in terms of troubleshooting tools, in the next section you'll see tools available from other vendors that will make your troubleshooting experience easier and more efficient.

Freeware Tools

While you may be able to solve all your network problems exclusively with Microsoft tools, your life can be made much easier with the support of the thousands of companies whose products support Microsoft networks. Although most of the free tools included with this book are described in Appendix C, in this section you will see three freeware tools that are useful in many situations.

Subnetting with the IP Subnet Calculator

While subnetting is generally a design issue and subnetting-related problems generally occur during new network implementations, it would be naive to say that these types of troubles do not occur. Perhaps you support a small office that has network communication problems, or maybe you are even faced with dealing with a user who is adamant that his network configuration is valid. In these situations, Wildpackets (www.wildpackets.com) IP Subnet Calculator can be your best friend. Consider these two IP addresses: 194.19.43.62/27 and 192.19.43.66/27. At first glance, you may believe that these two IP addresses are on the same subnet and thus should have no problem communicating with each other. However, closer examination will reveal that these two addresses are on different subnets.

While subnetting by hand is a valuable skill (especially on Microsoft exams), the IP Subnet Calculator can allow you to quickly discover the range of subnets associated with a particular IP address and subnet mask.

To get started, you first need to install the IP Subnet Calculator. To do this, run `Wildpackets\IPSubCalc\SetupIPCalc3.exe` from the companion CD. Once the program is installed, launch it by selecting WildPackets IP Subnet Calculator from the All Programs menu. Now that the program is open, here is the procedure to check the relationship between the two IP addresses listed earlier to see if they are on the same subnet.

1. Enter the IP address 194.19.43.62 in the IP Address field. You will see that it is identified as a Class C address.

2. Now click the Subnet Info tab.

3. Check the Allow 1 Subnet Bit checkbox (valid for Microsoft W2K and higher TCP/IP networks).

4. Now select 27 in the Mask Bits drop-down menu. Note that you could also have selected a mask expressed in dotted decimal notation. At this point, you will see information on the maximum number of subnets as well as the maximum number of hosts that can exist on each subnet.

5. Finally, click the Subnets/Hosts tab to see the valid IP address range for each subnet. This is shown in Figure 4-25.

As you can see in the illustration, 194.19.43.62/27 and 192.19.43.66/27 are in different ranges and thus represent hosts on different subnets. If the hosts are on the same physical network segment without a router, you have found the problem. Most organizations try to use classful addressing on their internal networks to avoid such problems, but IP addresses spanning different logical subnets is a probable fault that you should not rule out, especially on networks that you are not familiar with.

Now that you have seen the value in the IP Subnet Calculator, which is useful for quick IP subnetting-related troubleshooting as well as planning, let's dig a little deeper in the weeds and look at Netperf.

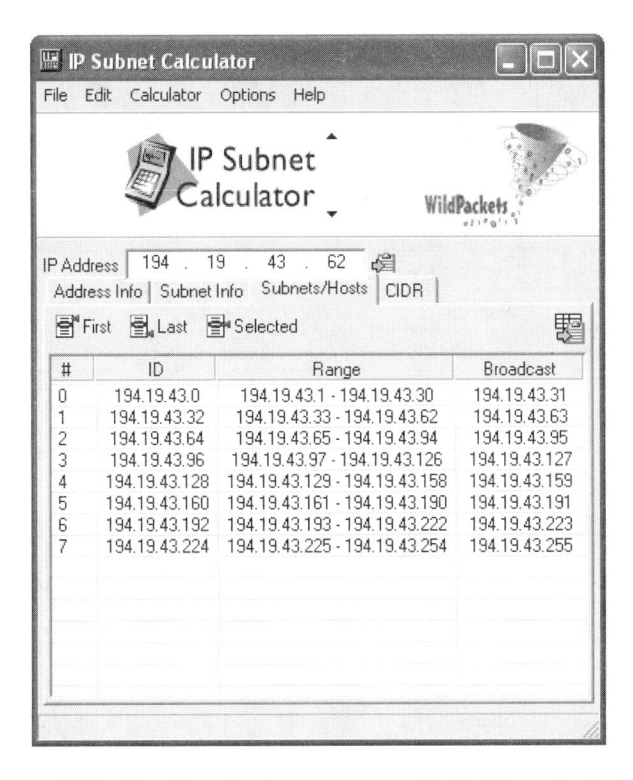

Figure 4-25. Checking IP subnet ranges with IP Subnet Calculator

Testing Throughput with Netperf

Netperf is a free tool developed by Hewlett-Packard that allows you to get an instantaneous glimpse of network throughput. Updated information on Netperf can be found at its official Web site, www.netperf.org.

Sometimes when you are troubleshooting a new software installation, a debate over the software's performance arises. Some network administrators are quick to blame the software, while others point their finger toward the network. If you would like a quick-to-execute tool for giving you a definitive answer on available network throughput between two points, then Netperf is your answer. Not only is it easy to use, but it is also small enough to fit on a floppy disk, allowing you to take it along with you to customer sites.

The tool consists of two executables: `Netserver` and `Netclient`. To perform a throughput test, you need to run `Netserver` on one system and `Netclient` on another. The `Netclient` program offers many options when it is executed. Here is its syntax:

```
Netclient -H <remote host> [-a <send,recv>] [-A <send,recv>] [-c]
[-C] [-d] [-f <G | M | K | g | m | k>] [-F <fill file>] [-i <max,min>]
[-I <lvl>] [-l <seconds>] [-o <send,recv>] [-O <send,recv>] [-n
<numcpu>] [-p <port>] [-P <0 | 1>] [-t <testname>] [-v <verbosity
level>] [-W <send,recv>]
```

Chapter 4 Monitoring and Diagnostic Tools

The usage for each `Netclient` switch is shown Table 4-44.

Table 4-44. Netclient Command Options

Option	Use
`-H <remote host>`	Name or IP address of the system running `Netserver`.
`-a <send,recv>`	Sets the local send/receive buffer alignment.
`-A <send,recv>`	Sets the remote send/receive buffer alignment.
`-c`	Reports local CPU usage statistics.
`-C`	Reports remote CPU usage statistics.
`-d`	Increases debugging output information.
`-f <G|M|K|g|m|k>`	Sets the output unit of measure for the displayed bandwidth. The default is M (megahertz).
`-F <fill file>`	Prefills buffers with data from the specified fill file.
`-i <max,min>`	Specifies the maximum and minimum number of command iterations to perform. The default values are 15 and 1.
`-I <lvl>`	Specifies the command confidence level. Acceptable `lvl` values are 95 or 99 (99 is the default).
`-l <seconds>`	Specifies the duration of the Netperf test (in seconds)
`-o <send,recv>`	Sets the local send/receive buffer offsets.
`-O <send,recv>`	Sets the remote send/receive buffer offsets.
`-n <numcpu>`	Sets the number of processors for CPU utilization.
`-p <port>`	When the `Netserver` application runs with a port other than the default (12865), this switch is required to specify the port to use and must match the port provided when the `Netserver` command was executed.
`-P <0|1>`	Displays (1) or suppresses (0) command output headers.
`-t <testname>`	Specifies the custom test to perform.
`-v <verbosity level>`	Specifies the verbosity level (1-3) for command output.
`-W <send,recv>`	Sets the number of send/receive buffers.

`Netserver` has fewer options and only includes one switch. Here is the syntax for `Netserver`:

```
Netserver [-p <port number>]
```

By default, when you run `Netserver`, it uses port 12865. With the `-p` switch, you can specify a different port for the command to use. Once executed, `Netserver` will continue to run until a client connects to it.

While admittedly there are numerous options that accompany the `Netclient` command, for performing throughput tests, you only need to be concerned with -H and possibly -p if testing throughput between two remote sites through a firewall. Before running the programs, copy the Netclient.exe and Netserver.exe files from the Netperf folder on the companion CD to each system.

With the files copied, here are the steps to perform a throughput test.

1. On one remote system, access the command prompt and run `Netserver` (you must run the command from the folder where it resides).

2. From the second system, run `Netclient -H <remote server name>` from the command prompt.

3. Wait a few seconds and you will see the throughput information displayed on the system that ran `Netclient` (see Figure 4-26). You will also see the `Netserver` command execution automatically terminate on the first system.

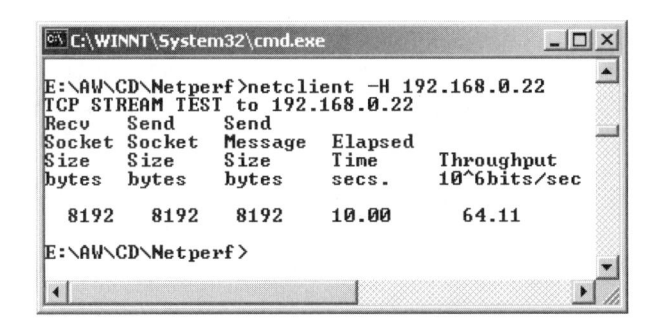

```
C:\WINNT\System32\cmd.exe

E:\AW\CD\Netperf>netclient -H 192.168.0.22
TCP STREAM TEST to 192.168.0.22
Recv   Send    Send
Socket Socket  Message  Elapsed
Size   Size    Size     Time       Throughput
bytes  bytes   bytes    secs.      10^6bits/sec

 8192   8192    8192    10.00       64.11

E:\AW\CD\Netperf>
```

Figure 4-26. Netclient command output

Remotely Controlling Systems with TightVNC

TightVNC (www.tightvnc.com) is an improved version of AT&T's Virtual Network Computing (VNC) Viewer that was spearheaded by Constantin Kaplinsky. The idea behind virtual network computing is to allow you to remotely control another desktop, independent of its platform.

AT&T's VNC Viewer has long been used by help desk technicians to troubleshoot user systems in corporate networks. With it, you can take control of a user's desktop, and the user can watch everything you do. This way, time is saved in not having to explain processes for users to perform, and in addition they can watch what you are doing so that possibly the next time the same problem arises, they will know what to do. Of course, some users, on the other hand, will not like the idea of help desk personnel controlling their systems. For this, a password is required in order to open a VNC session, and

TightVNC can be configured to simply run as an application (default configuration), meaning that a system can only be remotely controlled if the application is running.

Aside from corporate environments, consider that distant relative that is always calling you with questions about his or her computer problems. As long as the relative can connect to the Internet, even with a dial-up modem, you can take over the relative's system and diagnose the problem.

Now that you have seen the merit of TightVNC, let's quickly look at what differentiates it from the original AT&T VNC Viewer. Think of TightVNC as being VNC on speed. Many of the original complaints with VNC Viewer were related to performance, especially over slow dial-up connections. You can also configure compression levels for the session, as well as image resolution quality, in order to achieve faster performance of the session.

In order to control a desktop, two applications are involved:

- TightVNC Server—Run on the system you want to remotely control
- TightVNC Viewer—Run on your local system

TightVNC Viewer is run as an application and can be run from any 32-bit Windows system to control any 32-bit Windows, UNIX, or Linux system running the TightVNC Server software. The TightVNC Server software, in addition to being able to be run as an application, can be configured to run as a service. This way, you can configure the TightVNC Server service to start automatically when a system boots, allowing you to remotely connect to a system whenever needed without having to worry about the state of the TightVNC Server application.

Now that you have the TightVNC basics under your belt, let's look at how to install and use the program. Here are the steps to install TightVNC on 32-bit Windows platforms.

1. On the companion CD, run TightVNC\tightvnc-1.2.4-setup.exe.
2. When the Setup Wizard opens, click Next.
3. Click Yes to accept the terms of the GNU General Public License Agreement.
4. Select the installation directory and click Next.
5. Select the Start menu folder in which the program will reside, and click Next.
6. Leave the File Associations checkbox selected and click Next.
7. Click the Install button to install the application.
8. Once the installation completes, click Finish.

With the software installed, you are ready to remotely control systems. To do this, you need to configure the TightVNC Server and then connect to it with a client running TightVNC Viewer.

Configuring the TightVNC Server

As was previously mentioned, with TightVNC Server, you can run the program as an application or as a service. To start the server as an application, click Start > All Programs > TightVNC > Launch TightVNC Server. The first time you start the server, you will be prompted to enter a password. Users attempting to connect to your system with TightVNC Viewer will need to provide the password. Any other time the server is started, you will not be prompted for a password. You can change the password by double-clicking the VNC icon on the system tray once the server is started and entering a new password.

The TightVNC Server application can be run on any 32-bit Windows operating system, including Windows 95/98/ME. For NT, 2000, and XP systems, you can also configure it to run as a service. To configure TightVNC Server to run as a service, follow these steps.

1. Click Start > All Programs > TightVNC > Administration > Install VNC Service.

2. To start the service, from the command prompt type the command `Net Start winvnc` and press Enter.

3. If no password has been set, you will be prompted to set a default password. Click OK.

4. In the Default Local System Properties dialog box, enter a password and click OK.

At this point, the server is up and running. Now let's look at how to connect with the client software.

Using TightVNC Viewer

The TightVNC Viewer software allows you to connect to any system running the TightVNC Server software, regardless of its platform (Windows, UNIX, or Linux). A key differentiation with TightVNC Viewer compared with AT&T's VNC Viewer is its built-in compression. When you launch TightVNC Viewer, you have three options to start it:

- *Fast compression*—Used for LAN and broadband connections to TightVNC servers

- *Best compression*—Used for dial-up and low-bandwidth connections to VNC servers

- *Listen mode*—Standby state where the connection is initiated by the server

Fast compression provides the best graphical reproduction of the remote desktop but at the cost of bandwidth. Best compression is ideal for dial-up connections. It is more bandwidth-friendly, but the graphical display of the remote desktop is not as crisp. With listen mode, the TightVNC Viewer application starts on the client, with no server connection specified. To connect the client to a system running TightVNC Server, you would perform these steps on the server.

1. Right-click the VNC icon on the system tray and select Add New Client (notice that here you can also terminate all client connections or prevent any new connections).

2. Enter the host name or IP address of the remote client and click OK.

3. On the remote client, a dialog box will appear displaying the desktop of the TightVNC Server.

To connect to a system running TightVNC Server, follow these steps.

1. Click Start > All Programs > TightVNC > Tight VNC Viewer (Fast Compression | Best Compression).

2. In the Connection Details dialog box, enter the host name or IP address of the TightVNC Server and click OK.

If you were planning on using TightVNC to remotely control another user's system over the Internet, you would need to perform these steps.

1. Have the user run `ipconfig` (or `winipconfig` for Windows 95/98/ME) from the command prompt to obtain the IP address of his or her Internet connection.

2. Have the user start the TightVNC Server application and tell you the connection password.

3. Run TightVNC Viewer on your computer, specifying the IP address of the remote system in the Connection Details dialog box.

At this point, we are just scratching the surface of TightVNC's power. If you take the time to explore the advanced connection options, you will see that there is even much more that you can do with this application. Since TightVNC is still in its infancy stage and has little available documentation, the AT&T VNC documentation has been included on the companion CD.

If you're wondering why TightVNC is even mentioned when Remote Desktop is included with XP/W2K3 operating systems, it is because TightVNC is platform independent. You can run TightVNC on Windows 98, Linux, and Solaris systems, for example, thereby allowing you to control several servers from a single desktop.

Summary

You now have dozens of tools under your belt—some ideal for isolating faults, others well suited for collecting information. This is just the beginning. The tools covered in this chapter will continue to be mentioned in later chapters, where appropriate, and you will see additional tools in the coming chapters as well.

For all problems, the solution is eventually found. Often the speed with which a problem is resolved is directly related to the tools used. A good carpenter knows where and when to use a particular tool. The same can be said for a good network troubleshooter. While it would make all of our lives easier, there is no "supertool" that can be used for all situations. Take the time to look back over your toolbox and make note of the new tools that you will add to it in coming chapters. Knowing your tools will not only make you a better troubleshooter, but may also get you home a little earlier at night.

5

Client-Server Troubleshooting

As Microsoft operating systems have evolved, they have not only become more usable, but have also become much more "troubleshooting friendly." In this chapter, you will see the new tools at your disposal that will help you aid users in peril and also help them to quickly recover from problems when they occur. Since many of these tools and problems transcend both client and server operating systems, this chapter addresses issues common to both XP clients and Windows Server 2003 systems.

Before getting to conquering specific problems, let's begin with a look at the troubleshooting tools at your disposal for diagnosing and resolving operating system ills.

Troubleshooting Tools

In this section, we'll look at the useful OS tools that will aid you in locating and fixing client and server problems. Many of these tools are new with Windows XP and Windows Server 2003, and reflect Microsoft's commitment to helping you fix problems when they arise. The tools in this section are arranged alphabetically so that you can easily find the tool you're looking for.

> Don't forget about the numerous troubleshooting wizards that were described in Chapter 4. For nearly all client and server problems, there is a troubleshooting wizard available to guide you through the repair process.

Automated System Recovery

Perhaps a system is corrupt to the point that it cannot even be booted to attempt to perform a system restore, or even using the Last Known Good Configuration feature (discussed later in this chapter) does not help. In these instances, Automated System Recovery (ASR) is the tool of choice, since it provides a means to recover a system when it is not bootable. In order to use this feature, you need to first create an ASR backup using the Windows Backup program. ASR allows you to perform a *bare metal restore* of the operating system. Bare metal restores imply taking a repaired system and recovering it fully from backup without having to reinstall the OS. The difference between an ASR restore and a true bare metal restore is that with ASR, only the contents of the boot and system partitions are recovered. Any applications or data on any other drives are not recovered. Since during the ASR restore process, the boot and system partitions are reformatted, any user data stored on those partitions is lost.

While ASR lets you recover the operating system, you still need to perform regular backups of other partitions, if necessary, to secure data on those partitions as well. While for enterprise-scale disaster recovery you should strongly consider acquiring a single-console enterprise storage management platform, such as CommVault QiNetix or Veritas NetBackup, ASR is ideal for providing limited bare metal recovery for systems in small office environments. Since ASR recovers a system to its exact state at the time the ASR data was created, you should consider updating the ASR backup data at regular intervals or frequently back up each system you manage. This way, if a failure does occur, ASR can return the system to operation, and then you can restore any additional data that was backed up after the last ASR was performed.

To recover with ASR, all you need to do is boot the system from the Windows installation CD and then press F2 when prompted to perform an ASR restore.

Of course, to be able to perform an ASR restore, you will need an ASR backup. To create an ASR backup, follow these steps.

1. Format a floppy disk (it will store ASR configuration data).
2. Click Start > All Programs > Accessories > System Tools > Backup, to open Windows Backup.
3. Click the Tools menu and select ASR Wizard.
4. Follow the prompts to complete the backup.

When you perform the ASR backup, you need free media equal to the size of consumed data on the system's boot and system disks (by default, both are the C drive). The backup data can be written to a separate physical hard disk or external storage such as a tape or Jaz disk. You also need to have a blank floppy disk available. This disk is used when an ASR restore is run, and contains pointers and metadata about the ASR backup file.

ASR has replaced Emergency Repair Disks (ERDs) for system recovery, so there is no automated method for creating an ERD with Windows XP/Server 2003. Although ASR disks have replaced ERDs, they don't contain the same information. ERDs were loaded with valuable data, including the important boot.ini file. With the absence of ERDs, you should still consider backing up core OS files such as the boot.ini file to a floppy disk, just in case a system's primary disk fails and you need the system to boot from a volume mirrored to the primary with a software RAID solution.

> If you're wondering about using the Rdisk utility (NT) or the Emergency Repair Disk (Windows 2000), they have been replaced by ASR and thus are no longer available. ASR does much more than simply back up some basic configuration settings such as the boot.ini file and the Registry.

driverquery

Running `driverquery` allows you to quickly obtain a list of all drivers installed on a system. In addition to running it locally, you can execute this command to query the drivers installed on a remote system. The syntax for `driverquery` is:

    driverquery [/s <computer>] [/u <domain\user>] [/p <password>] [/fo
    <table|list|csv>] [/nh] [/v] [/si]

The `driverquery` options are described in Table 5-1.

Table 5-1. driverquery Command Options

Option	Use
/s <computer>	Used to specify the name or IP address of the remote computer on which to query installed drivers. When this option is not used, the command returns a list of installed drivers on the local system.
/u <domain\user>	Allows you to run the command under the context of a different user.
/p <password>	When the /u switch is used, this switch allows you to specify a password for the user account.
/fo <table|list|csv>	Allows you to specify how the command output is displayed. When the switch is not used, the output is in table format.
/nh	When the /fo switch is used to set the output to tabular or csv format, this switch causes the column headers to not be displayed in the output.
/v	Verbose output—adds information on driver description, startup type, state (running, stopped), and driver installation path to the command output. When using this switch, you should strongly consider redirecting the command output to a text file (> *path and filename*) for easier viewing.
/si	Shows the digital signature information for both signed and unsigned drivers.

To get the most bang for your buck, you should strongly consider using the /v switch. While verbose output oftentimes tells you more than you ever cared to know

Chapter 5   Client-Server Troubleshooting

about a system, `driverquery`'s verbose output is loaded with useful information, including the state of each driver installed on a system, along with its installation path.

Here is a sample output from running `driverquery` on a Windows Server 2003 system.

```
C:\>driverquery

Module Name   Display Name          Driver Type   Link Date
============  ====================  ============  ======================
AFD           AFD Networking Support Kernel       7/16/2002 2:33:12 PM
AsyncMac      RAS Asynchronous Media Kernel       7/15/2002 8:41:52 PM
atapi         Standard IDE/ESDI Hard Kernel       7/15/2002 8:36:32 PM
Atmarpc       ATM ARP Client Protoco Kernel       7/15/2002 8:34:18 PM
audstub       Audio Stub Driver     Kernel        7/15/2002 8:43:54 PM
Beep          Beep                  Kernel        7/15/2002 8:34:34 PM
cbidf2k       cbidf2k               Kernel        7/15/2002 8:36:41 PM
Cdfs          Cdfs                  File System   7/15/2002 8:36:46 PM
Cdrom         CD-ROM Driver         Kernel        7/15/2002 8:36:54 PM
ClusDisk      Cluster Disk Driver   Kernel        7/15/2002 8:45:28 PM
crcdisk       CRC Disk Filter Driver Kernel       7/15/2002 8:38:52 PM
DfsDriver     DfsDriver             File System   7/15/2002 8:37:55 PM
Disk          Disk Driver           Kernel        7/15/2002 8:36:54 PM
dmboot        dmboot                Kernel        7/15/2002 8:43:03 PM
dmio          Logical Disk Manager D Kernel       7/15/2002 8:42:59 PM
dmload        dmload                Kernel        7/15/2002 8:42:57 PM
Fastfat       Fastfat               File System   7/16/2002 2:17:49 PM
Fdc           Floppy Disk Controller Kernel       7/15/2002 8:36:19 PM
Fips          Fips                  Kernel        7/16/2002 2:09:49 PM
Flpydisk      Floppy Disk Driver    Kernel        7/15/2002 8:36:20 PM
Ftdisk        Volume Manager Driver Kernel        7/15/2002 8:37:04 PM
Gpc           Generic Packet Classif Kernel       7/15/2002 8:40:46 PM
HTTP          HTTP                  Kernel        7/16/2002 2:33:07 PM
i8042prt      i8042 Keyboard and PS/ Kernel       7/16/2002 2:18:42 PM
imapi         CD-Burning Filter Driv Kernel       7/15/2002 8:37:19 PM
IntelIde      IntelIde              Kernel        7/15/2002 8:36:30 PM
IpFilterDriv  IP Traffic Filter Driv Kernel       7/15/2002 8:41:25 PM
IpNat         IP Network Address Tra Kernel       7/15/2002 8:41:29 PM
IPSec         IPSEC driver          Kernel        7/16/2002 2:09:47 PM
isapnp        PnP ISA/EISA Bus Drive Kernel       7/15/2002 8:44:04 PM
Kbdclass      Keyboard Class Driver Kernel        7/15/2002 8:34:38 PM
KSecDD        KSecDD                Kernel        7/15/2002 8:36:42 PM
mnmdd         mnmdd                 Kernel        7/15/2002 8:42:39 PM
Modem         Modem                 Kernel        7/15/2002 8:44:47 PM
Mouclass      Mouse Class Driver    Kernel        7/15/2002 8:34:39 PM
MountMgr      Mount Point Manager   Kernel        7/15/2002 8:34:36 PM
MRxDAV        WebDav Client Redirect File System  7/15/2002 8:37:20 PM
MRxSmb        MRXSMB                File System   7/16/2002 2:16:42 PM
Msfs          Msfs                  File System   7/15/2002 8:37:06 PM
Mup           Mup                   File System   7/16/2002 2:13:26 PM
NDIS          NDIS System Driver    Kernel        7/16/2002 3:24:14 PM
NdisTapi      Remote Access NDIS TAP Kernel       7/15/2002 8:41:51 PM
Ndisuio       NDIS Usermode I/O Prot Kernel       7/15/2002 8:40:20 PM
NdisWan       Remote Access NDIS WAN Kernel       7/16/2002 2:09:45 PM
```

```
NDProxy         NDIS Proxy              Kernel       7/15/2002 8:41:55 PM
NetBIOS         NetBIOS Interface       File System  7/15/2002 8:40:28 PM
NetBT           NetBios over Tcpip      Kernel       7/16/2002 2:39:02 PM
nm              Network Monitor Driver  Kernel       7/15/2002 8:36:38 PM
Npfs            Npfs                    File System  7/15/2002 8:37:07 PM
Ntfs            Ntfs                    File System  7/16/2002 2:39:11 PM
Null            Null                    Kernel       7/15/2002 8:34:36 PM
Parport         Parport                 Kernel       7/15/2002 8:35:50 PM
PartMgr         Partition Manager       Kernel       7/16/2002 2:39:14 PM
ParVdm          ParVdm                  Kernel       7/15/2002 8:35:45 PM
PCI             PCI Bus Driver          Kernel       7/15/2002 8:44:09 PM
Pcmcia          Pcmcia                  Kernel       7/15/2002 8:44:06 PM
PCnet           AMD PCNET Compatable A  Kernel       6/5/2001 3:54:43 PM
PptpMiniport    WAN Miniport (PPTP)     Kernel       7/16/2002 2:09:43 PM
Ptilink         Direct Parallel Link D  Kernel       7/15/2002 8:35:45 PM
RasAcd          Remote Access Auto Con  Kernel       7/15/2002 8:42:15 PM
Rasl2tp         WAN Miniport (L2TP)     Kernel       7/16/2002 2:09:41 PM
RasPppoe        Remote Access PPPOE Dr  Kernel       7/15/2002 8:42:04 PM
Raspti          Direct Parallel         Kernel       7/15/2002 8:42:03 PM
Rdbss           Rdbss                   File System  7/16/2002 2:17:56 PM
RDPCDD          RDPCDD                  Kernel       7/15/2002 8:34:31 PM
rdpdr           Terminal Server Device  Kernel       7/15/2002 8:37:38 PM
RDPWD           RDPWD                   Kernel       7/15/2002 8:34:27 PM
redbook         Digital CD Audio Playb  Kernel       7/15/2002 8:36:27 PM
Secdrv          Secdrv                  Kernel       2/9/2001 11:51:30 AM
Serenum         Serenum Filter Driver   Kernel       7/15/2002 8:35:52 PM
Serial          Serial port driver      Kernel       7/16/2002 2:14:11 PM
Sfloppy         Sfloppy                 Kernel       7/15/2002 8:36:57 PM
Srv             Srv                     File System  7/16/2002 2:39:22 PM
swenum          Software Bus Driver     Kernel       7/15/2002 8:35:15 PM
Tcpip           TCP/IP Protocol Driver  Kernel       7/16/2002 3:24:08 PM
TDPIPE          TDPIPE                  Kernel       7/15/2002 8:34:22 PM
TDTCP           TDTCP                   Kernel       7/15/2002 8:34:19 PM
TermDD          Terminal Device Driver  Kernel       7/15/2002 8:34:19 PM
Udfs            Udfs                    File System  7/15/2002 8:37:02 PM
Update          Microcode Update Drive  Kernel       7/16/2002 2:19:23 PM
usbhub          USB2 Enabled Hub        Kernel       7/15/2002 8:44:54 PM
usbuhci         Microsoft USB Universa  Kernel       7/15/2002 8:44:52 PM
vga             vga                     Kernel       7/15/2002 8:42:50 PM
VgaSave         VGA Display Controller  Kernel       7/15/2002 8:42:49 PM
vmscsi          vmscsi                  Kernel       6/4/2002 6:03:21 PM
vmx_svga        vmx_svga                Kernel       9/9/2002 10:15:24 PM
VolSnap         VolSnap                 Kernel       7/15/2002 8:37:21 PM
Wanarp          Remote Access IP ARP D  Kernel       7/15/2002 8:41:46 PM
WLBS            Network Load Balancing  Kernel       7/16/2002 3:23:57 PM
```

msconfig (Windows Server 2003)

The `msconfig` server troubleshooting tool is commonly used by Microsoft support personnel to resolve problems. This tool can be launched by clicking Start > Run, typing `msconfig`, and then clicking OK. The GUI for this utility is shown in Figure 5-1.

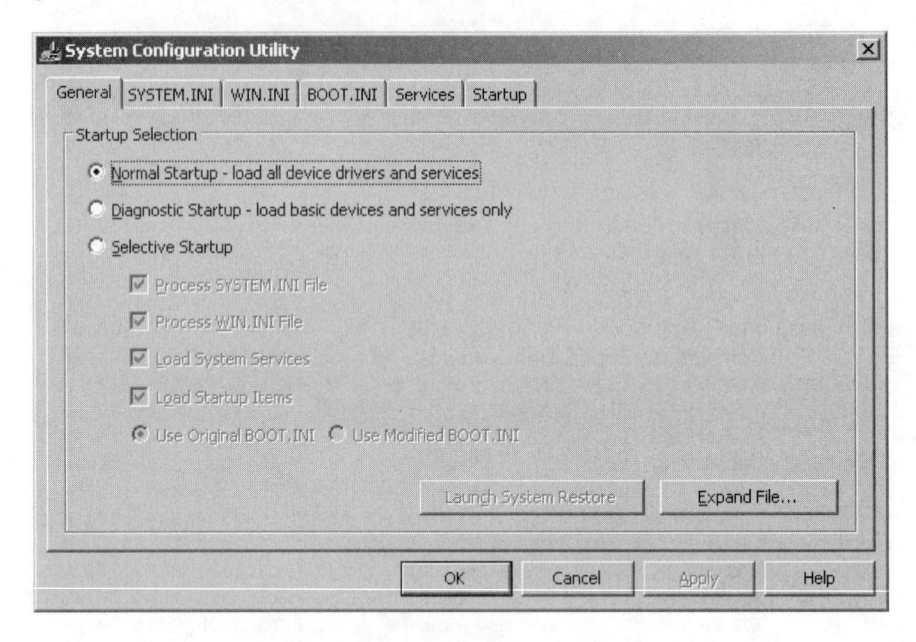

Figure 5-1. System configuration utility

Since the tool is a GUI tool, the operating system must be started in at least Safe Mode in order for it to execute. When you run this utility, you can perform the following troubleshooting tasks:

- Configure system startup in one of the following ways:
    - *Normal*—Load all drivers and services
    - *Diagnostic*—Load basic drivers and services (Safe Mode)
    - *Selective*—Choose startup options from itemized list
- Enable or disable portions of the System.ini file
- Enable, disable, or edit portions of the following startup files:
    - System.ini
    - Win.ini
    - Boot.ini
- Enable or disable system services
- Disable applications from running during system startup

As you can see, this tool provides you with many ways to go about resolving system startup problems. If you believe that a service or application running at startup may be the source of a problem, you can use this utility to disable it. While there are other tools that allow you to perform the same tasks, this tool may allow you to find and make changes faster.

msicuu (ST)

If you have ever found yourself in a software installation quagmire, then you will likely love `msicuu`. If you are wondering what a software installation quagmire is, think of an application that started to install on a system but aborted. Unfortunately, no information on the application is listed in Add/Remove Programs, so it cannot be uninstalled, but when you try to reinstall the application, you get a prompt that the application is already installed.

When you find yourself in this predicament, typically your only option is to manually locate and delete the installation files and then to search for and remove any Registry keys that are related to the application. An alternative and much easier method is to first try to run `msicuu`. One caveat to this tool, however, is that it only works with Microsoft Software Installation (MSI)–based installation packages.

To use `msicuu` to remove an installation package, perform these steps.

1. Click Start > Run, type `msicuu` in the Run dialog box, and press Enter.

2. In the Windows Installer Clean Up dialog box, select the program to remove, and then click the Remove button (see Figure 5-2).

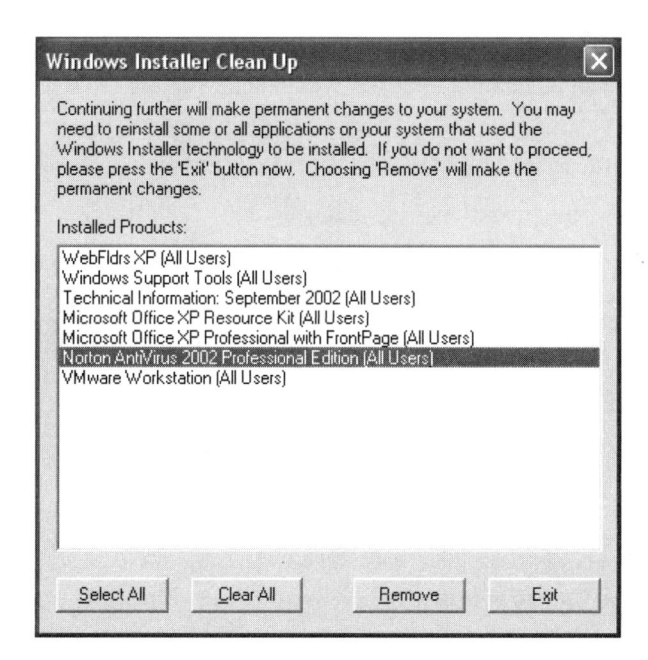

Figure 5-2. Selecting an MSI installation to remove

Once you are finished, the selected MSI installation is permanently removed. This allows you to restart the program installation without errors.

> You should exercise caution when running `msicuu`. When run, this utility makes permanent system changes and may require you to reinstall any or all other applications that were installed using MSI technology.

Online Crash Analysis

Online Crash Analysis can often provide all the information that you need to resolve a problem, especially for problems that generate stop error messages (also known as "blue screens of death"). If you think about the logic behind online analysis of errors, it is definitely a great idea. Your system blows up, it reboots and asks if you want to report the error to Microsoft, you click Send Error Report to report the error, and you're done! If you think about all the possible problems that can happen to a system and the volume of users that are out there, odds are that someone has already experienced your pain. This means that when you submit an error to Microsoft, an answer may be waiting for you at the Online Crash Analysis Web site. In other words, the OS literally collects the crash information, analyzes it, and tells you what to fix.

Of course, to use this feature, you need to ensure it is enabled. While the feature is enabled by default, it is always good to verify that the Error Reporting service is actively looking for problems to report. To verify that Error Reporting is enabled, follow these steps.

1. Click Start, and then right-click the My Computer object and select Properties.
2. Click the Advanced tab and then click the Error Reporting button.
3. Click the Enable Error Reporting radio button.
4. Now select the reporting options. You can select to report on Windows errors, program errors, or both (see Figure 5-3).
5. If you're looking for more granular control of the programs that are to report errors, you can click the Choose Programs button and then select the appropriate programs.
6. When you are finished configuring Error Reporting, click OK.
7. Now from the System Properties window, click OK.

Once Error Reporting is enabled, you will receive a prompt when an error is encountered, asking if you want to upload the error information to Microsoft. If the "Big

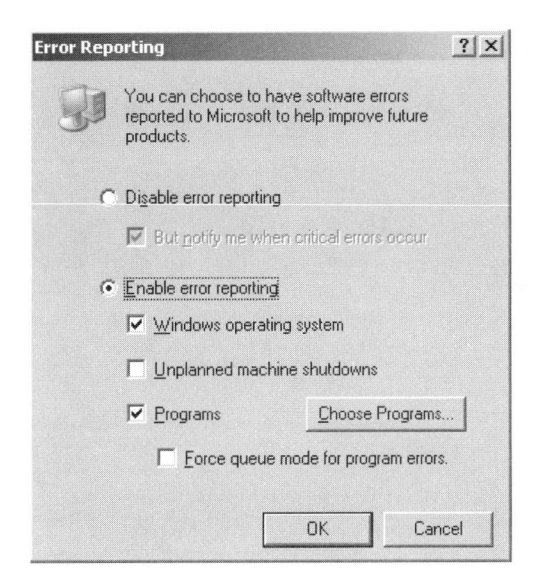

Figure 5-3. Enabling Error Reporting

Brother" fear in you is starting to make you nervous, don't worry. You have the option of not sending any personal information. If you decide to send private information, you can log on with your Microsoft .NET Passport and check the status of the error at a later time.

Whenever you want to check the status of previous error events, point your Web browser to http://oca.microsoft.com/en. This will take you to Microsoft's Online Crash Analysis Web site. By default, you are automatically brought to this site after selecting to send an error report. Once at the site, you can click the Status link to view a status of all error reports that were submitted with your Microsoft Passport. A sample report status is shown in Figure 5-4. This report was from an error that occurred after a laptop returned from standby mode and immediately locked up. From the error report, it was determined that the cause of the error was a faulty NIC driver for the laptop's wireless NIC. Once the driver was updated, the problem was solved. This is a perfect example of the value of Online Crash Analysis. This problem was corrected within minutes, while normal troubleshooting practices may have taken hours.

Remote Desktop and Remote Assistance

When your explanations to a user are going nowhere and you would like to show the user yourself how to correct a problem, you can use Remote Assistance and Remote Desktop. With Remote Assistance, one user can invite another user to share his or her desktop, while the Remote Desktop tool allows you to directly connect to and remotely manage user desktops.

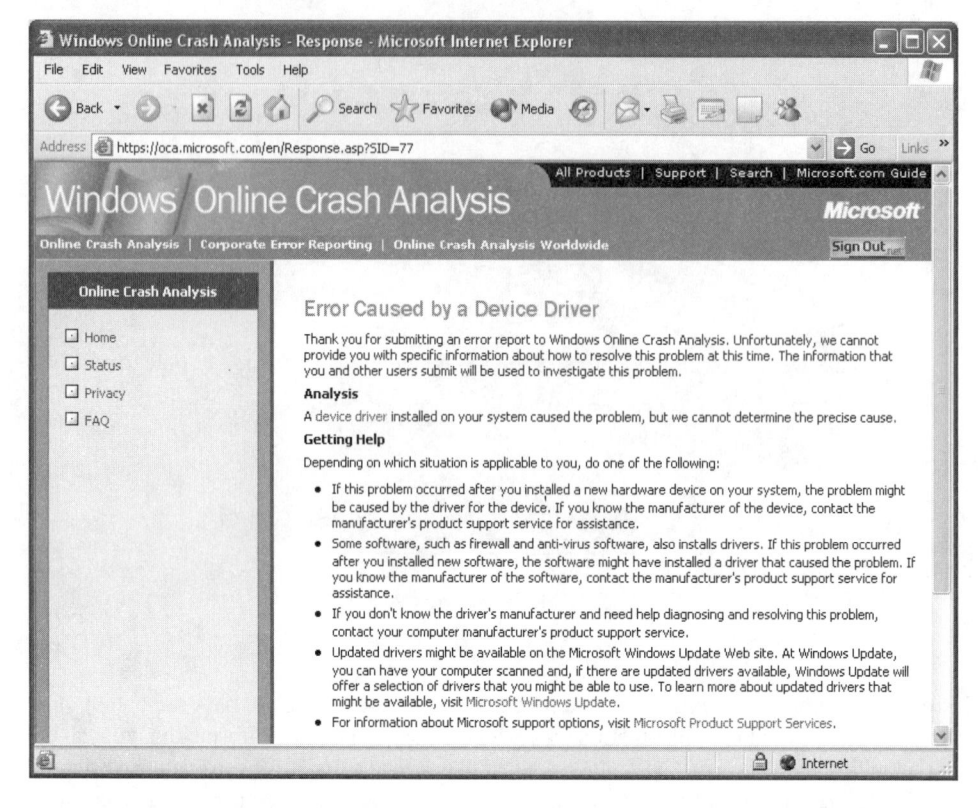

Figure 5-4. Checking an error status

> When you need to remotely control users running diverse platforms, don't forget about TightVNC, which is included on the companion CD and described in Chapter 4.

Allowing Remote Desktop Connections

Enabling Remote Desktop connections on a user's XP workstation is similar to running Terminal Services on a Windows server. However, Remote Desktop is installed by default, so all that you need to do is enable the feature. Remote Desktop should only be enabled for systems that you plan to regularly connect to and administer remotely. Otherwise, for on-demand remote connections when requested by a user, Remote Assistance provides a one-time remote connection without sacrificing security.

To enable Remote Desktop connections, follow these steps.

1. Click Start, and then right-click the My Computer object and select Properties.

2. Click the Remote tab.

3. Now click the Allow Users to Connect Remotely to this Computer checkbox (see Figure 5-5).

4. For Windows XP systems, you can grant specific users the ability to connect to a system, by clicking the Select Remote Users button. For Windows Server 2003 systems, you are essentially enabling the server as a terminal server and thus do not have to manually specify user accounts.

5. Once you have enabled Remote Desktop connections, click OK to close the System Properties dialog box.

Now that we have enabled Remote Desktop connections, let's look at how to connect to a remote system.

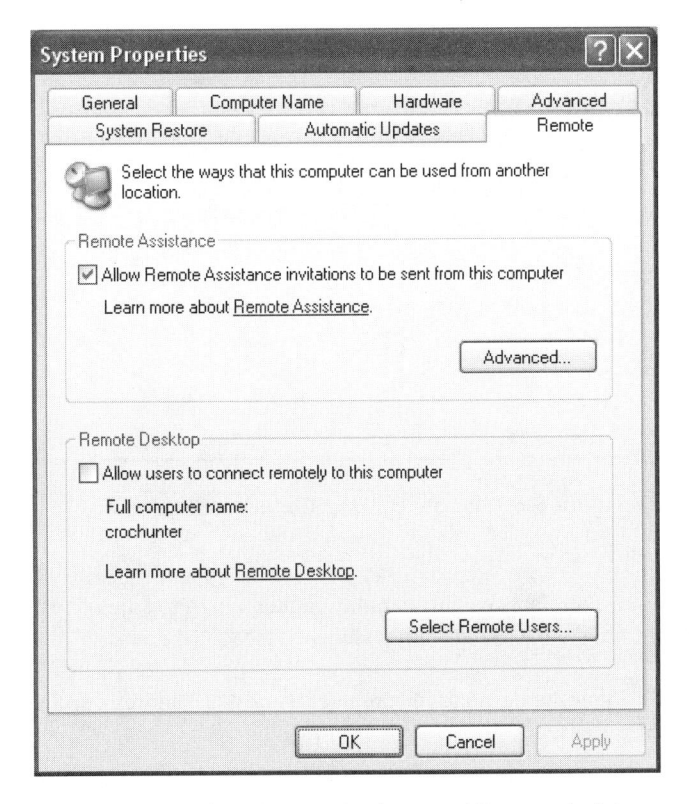

Figure 5-5. Enabling Remote Desktop and Remote Assistance

Connecting to a Remote System

When you plan to connect to a remote system using the Remote Desktop Connection application, it is important to first be aware of the available connection options prior to connecting to a remote system. When you first start a Remote Desktop connection, you

138 Chapter 5 Client-Server Troubleshooting

will have the chance to configure your logon for the connection, as well as numerous settings that affect the performance and environment of the connection. The Remote Desktop Connection dialog box is shown in Figure 5-6.

Figure 5-6. Remote Desktop Connection dialog box

As you can see, there are five different tabs under which to adjust the remote configuration settings. Here's what you can do under each tab.

- *General*—Enter the destination computer name or IP address, and a user name and password.

- *Display*—Set the remote desktop size (800 by 600, and so on) and color resolution (256, 16-bit, and so on). Note that the higher the color resolution, the slower the performance.

- *Local Resources*—Select to bring the remote system's sound to your computer, apply local keyboard hotkeys (such as Alt-Tab) to the remote system, and link local devices (printers, disk drives, or serial ports) to the remote system.

- *Programs*—Configure an application on the remote system, such as Word or PowerPoint, to automatically launch when you connect.

- *Experience*—Select a connection speed (which optimizes performance), and select to allow remote desktop settings such as a custom background and menu, and window animations.

Normally, the default settings are ideal for providing a nice user experience and not sacrificing performance. If you would like to open remote documents and print them to your printer, for example, you should enable your printer for the connection under the Local Resources tab. Also, you can save a particular set of configuration settings under the General tab so that you can quickly reconnect to a remote system without having to reenter the connection parameters.

To connect to a remote desktop, follow these steps.

1. Click Start > All Programs > Accessories > Communications > Remote Desktop Connection.

2. For additional connection settings, click the Options button once the Remote Desktop Connection window appears.

3. Enter the system name or IP address that you would like to connect to.

4. Provide a user name, password, and domain information to use when connecting to the system.

5. Click OK.

With a Remote Desktop connection, you are performing a separate logon to a system, so a user that is already logged on to the system will not see your actions while you are logged on. If you want to have a user watch as you perform specific actions on a system, you should use Remote Assistance instead. With Remote Assistance, you will share the logon session with the active user.

Unlike W2K3 Terminal Servers, Windows XP does not support simultaneous logons of a single user account. This means that you should open Remote Desktop connections using an account that is not actively logged on to the target XP workstation.

Using Remote Assistance

To use Remote Assistance, a user must invite another user to share his session, but prior to sharing, the Remote Assistance feature must be enabled (see Figure 5-5 earlier). Once it is enabled, you can invite another user to share your desktop by a few different methods. The most popular methods for initiating Remote Assistance connections are by e-mailing Remote Assistance invitations and by using MSN Messenger. E-mail is the most commonly used method of initiating Remote Assistance, so let's look at how it's done.

To send a Remote Assistance invitation, follow these steps.

1. Click Start > Help and Support.

2. Under Ask for Assistance, click "Invite a friend to connect to your computer with Remote Assistance."

3. Now click Invite Someone to Help You.

4. At this point, you can either proceed with Windows Messenger or send an e-mail assistance request. To use e-mail, enter the e-mail address of the user that you want to control your system, and then click Invite this Person.

5. Enter your name (which will appear on the invitation) and a message to the recipient, and click Continue.

6. Specify a duration for the invitation to remain valid (default duration is one hour), and then enter and confirm a password for the connection. Finally, click Send Invitation. The password is not sent with the invitation, so you need to communicate this with the recipient by some other means, such as over the telephone.

7. When you have been notified that the request was sent successfully, close the Help and Support window.

Once the recipient receives the e-mail, she sees a file attachment. To initiate the Remote Assistance connection, the recipient needs to double-click the attachment. This opens the Remote Assistance dialog box. From here, the recipient needs to enter the password for the Remote Assistance connection and click Yes.

Now you see a prompt advising you of the Remote Assistance connection. To allow the connection, click Yes. At this point, the user is connected to your system. The default connection setting is Screen View Only, which means that the remote user can only view your screen; she has no control over it. The remote user can take control of your screen by clicking the Take Control button on her desktop. When the remote user selects to take control, you receive a prompt in which you need to grant the user control. Once you click Yes, you can watch the remote user manipulate your desktop. The remote user receives a prompt that she has control and will retain control until either user presses the Escape key on the keyboard.

To end the Remote Assistance session, click the Disconnect button in the Remote Assistance window. This tool is especially useful for trying to remotely manage and repair a relative's computer over the Internet. In using Remote Assistance, your family and friends can easily ask for your help and allow others to connect to their system over the Internet, or any network, without having to worry about leaving their system wide open to attack.

Remote Assistance establishes connections using the same port as Terminal Services (3389), so if a firewall exists between the connection points, you need to ensure that this port is not being blocked by the firewall.

Shadow Copy (Windows Server 2003 Systems Only)

While Windows Server 2003 systems do not offer System Restore, primarily because of the complexity of the server platform, they do give you something better. Many hardware and software vendors have touted the use of snapshot technology to allow you to quickly back up and recover data stored on servers. Now with Windows Server 2003, Shadow Copy allows you to create snapshots of stored data on shared folders on a server. In addition to providing you with the ability to manually create and manage snapshots, enterprise software vendors such as CommVault (www.commvault.com) are building their architectures to integrate with Shadow Copy, allowing you to manage it along with your other backups.

Being free, Shadow Copy does have its limitations. It can only be configured at the volume level, meaning that if you only needed to secure data on two shared folders on the D drive, you would be forced to have snapshots of all shared folders. With this in mind, you should configure your drives and shares so that all shares needing regular snaps can be grouped together. The easiest way to think of snaps is as quick incrementals, with the exception that they read data at the block level instead of at the file level. Their primary advantage is that they allow you to index multiple versions of a volume. For example, you may have hourly versions of shared data on the D drive. If a file became corrupt at 3:20, for example, you could recover the 3 o'clock version, thus losing only 20 minutes' worth of new data. Backups are often run on a nightly basis, meaning that in normal instances of corruption, a full day's worth of data would be lost without the implementation of some type of snap technology. While this is primarily a storage concern, also consider this from a troubleshooting perspective when having to deal with users losing or corrupting data. From a troubleshooting perspective, setting up Shadow Copy will give you a safety net that will likely allow you to recover corrupted data within minutes.

From a user perspective, users running the Shadow Copy Client software can do the following:

- View available versions of a file
- Recover a deleted file from an earlier version
- Recover a replaced file from an earlier version
- Compare the contents of one file version to another

Many help desks are often tasked with restoring single files on behalf of users. By enabling and using Shadow Copy on server volumes that contain user data, you can empower the users to recover their own files, thus freeing the help desk to perform other tasks (if you like being the hero and restoring files yourself, don't tell anyone about this feature!).

To set up Shadow Copy for a volume, follow these steps.

1. Open Computer Management and expand the System Tools object.
2. Right-click Shared Folders, select All Tasks, and then click Configure Shadow Copies.

142 Chapter 5 Client-Server Troubleshooting

3. Select the volume you would like to configure for shadow copies (see Figure 5-7), and then click Settings.

4. In the Storage Area field (see Figure 5-8), select the drive where you would like the snap images stored. If you would like to change the default snap schedule (Monday–Friday at 7:00 AM), click the Schedule button and do so.

5. Once you are satisfied with the settings, click OK.

6. Now with the drive selected in the Shadow Copies dialog box, click the Enable button.

7. When prompted, if you want to enable Shadow Copy, click Yes.

8. Once the copy completes, click OK to close the Shadow Copy dialog box.

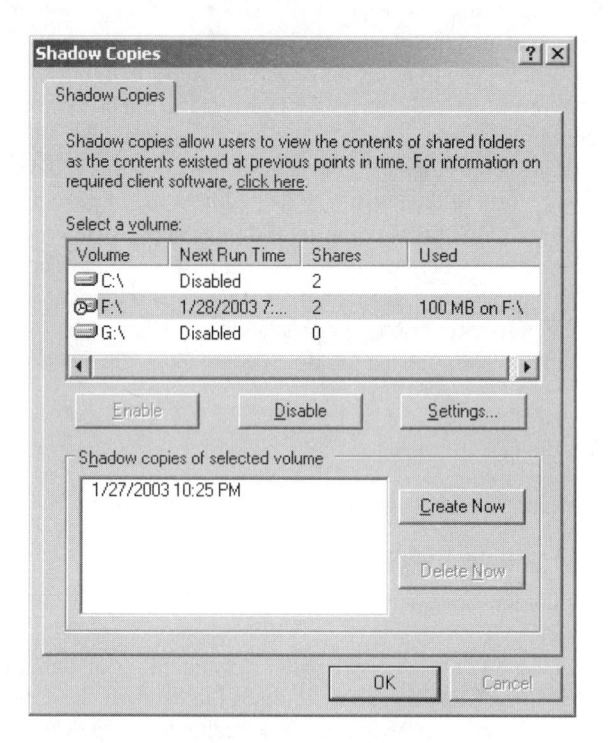

Figure 5-7. Selecting a drive to shadow copy

Windows Server 2003 supports up to 64 shadow copies per volume, so you should schedule shadow copies frequently enough to provide enough protection of user data, but not so frequently as to only allow for a user to roll back a file from two days ago. Suppose you do one shadow copy per hour, from 9:00 AM to 5:00 PM each day. That would

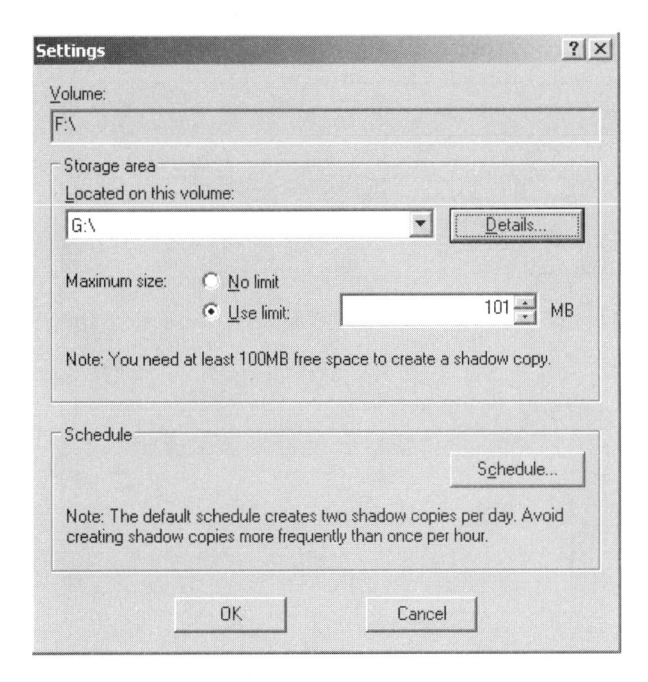

Figure 5-8. Configuring Shadow Copy parameters

give you a total of nine shadow copies each day and would allow users to roll back or recover files that are several days old. If you perform the copy every two hours, then your span of copies could range even further in time. Keep in mind, however, the more copies that you plan for, the more storage you will need to store them. Also, shadow copies are not a replacement for backups. If the server or copy volume fails, you could lose all data. In addition to having shadow copies, you should still perform regular backups of your servers for disaster recovery purposes. When you back up a volume with Windows Backup, keep in mind that the backup application only backs up the current file version of each file. Windows Backup has no means to secure Shadow Copy data.

Server-Initiated Recovery

When you or a user wants to recover an earlier version of a file stored on a volume with Shadow Copy enabled, the easiest way to bring back the file is to access it over the network. To do this, just follow these steps.

1. Click Start > Run, enter the UNC path to the network share in the Run dialog box, and click OK.

2. Browse and locate the needed file.

3. Right-click the file and select Properties.

4. Now click the Previous Versions tab (see Figure 5-9).

5. All previous versions of the file are listed. From here, you can select and recover the needed version.

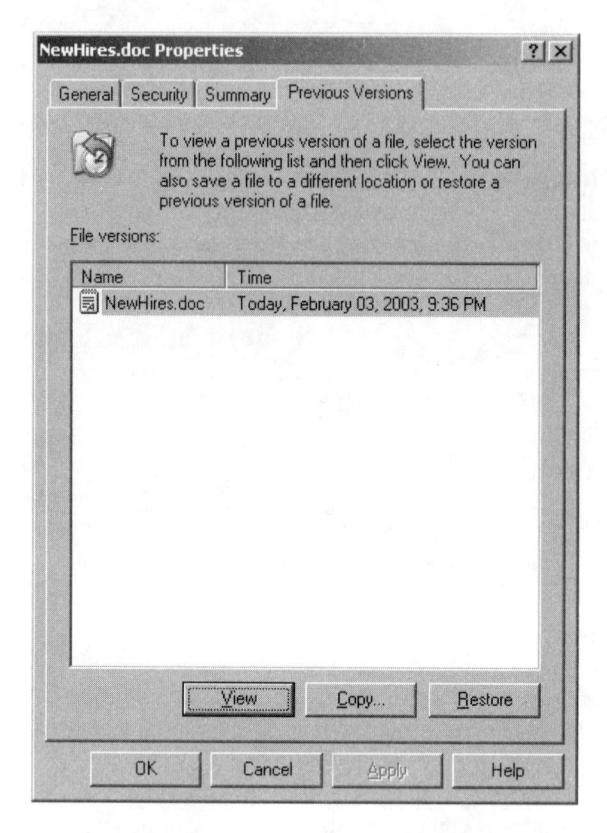

Figure 5-9. Recovering an earlier version of a file

When you select a version, you have three recovery choices:

- *View*—Opens the file
- *Copy*—Copies the selected version to a new location
- *Restore*—Restores the selected version over the current version (overwriting it!)

The most reliable means to recover previous versions of a file is to use the Copy function, since it causes the least damage. By selecting to copy an earlier version to a new location, you are in essence restoring a version without impacting the current version. This way, if the user changes his mind, no harm is done.

> One of the biggest mistakes administrators make when trying to recover earlier versions of a file is to try to view the file using Windows Explorer. Since shadow copied files are designed to be accessed by the CIFS file system, the only way to check for previous versions is to connect to the network share hosting the file. If you are at the server itself, you can connect to the share by entering \\localhost in the Run dialog box.

Client-Initiated Recovery

Since shadow copies are a new feature of Windows Server 2003, users at XP clients cannot restore previous file versions simply by accessing the network share hosting a shadow copied file; instead, they need the Shadow Copy Client software. The Shadow Copy Client installation (.msi) packages are located in the %systemroot%\system32\clients\twclient folder on Windows Server 2003 systems. To make this installation accessible to client systems, either you can copy the needed installation file to a network share and instruct clients on the use of the file and how to install it, or since it is packaged as an MSI file, you can deploy it with a group policy object to users or computers.

Once your XP systems have the client software installed, users can browse and recover previous file versions by following these steps.

1. Browse the network and locate the file to be restored. (This may even be their My Documents folder if it was redirected to a network server.)
2. Right-click the file to recover and select Properties.
3. Click the Previous Versions tab.
4. Select the version to recover, and click the View, Copy, or Restore buttons (discussed earlier).

With this software deployed and a little training, users will be empowered to recover more quickly from their mistakes and free help desk personnel to perform other troubleshooting tasks.

System Restore (XP Clients Only)

Have you ever installed an application on a system and immediately after stated, "I wish I hadn't done that!" If you have, you're not alone. Sometimes installing new applications on a system leads to system corruption, which also may make it difficult to manually undo your changes. For most of us, we've had a time in our lives when we wished that we could just turn back the clock to "happier times." While you cannot turn back the clock of life yet, you can do it with Windows XP by using System Restore.

System Restore is a new feature that allows you to roll back a system to an earlier state, undoing any changes that applications may have made to the system, while not harming any new user data such as document files or e-mail. To provide this ability, XP systems by default automatically create System Restore points. Restore points are created approximately every 24 hours and are also created whenever a new application is installed. You also have the opportunity to manually create a restore point any time you wish. When you wish to roll back a system, it must be to an earlier marked restore point, so you can't arbitrarily pick a date and time and say, "Go there," although you probably wish that you could say that phrase to the user that has you performing the rollback in the first place.

At each recovery checkpoint, the status of the system is recorded. You can think of this as almost being a "mini-image." The state of installed applications is noted, as well as the Registry. With this information, System Restore can effectively roll back a system. There are several instances when restore points are created.

- *System checkpoints*—These occur approximately once every 24 hours. If the computer is turned off when a checkpoint should run, the checkpoint is created the next time the computer starts.

- *Program name installation*—When an application is installed using a standard installer such as InstallShield or Windows XP Professional Installer, a restore point is created.

- *Windows Update*—When the Windows Update service updates the system, a checkpoint is created prior to the installation of the update.

- *Unsigned device driver installation*—This one is a real lifesaver! This checkpoint is created before an unsigned driver is installed, allowing you to quickly and easily remove the driver if problems follow its installation.

- *Restore operation*—Prior to a restore operation, the operating system automatically creates a restore point. This allows you to undo the restore if necessary.

As you can see, there are several occasions when recovery checkpoints are created. If you're now wondering about filling up hard disks with checkpoint data, you're not alone. Microsoft thought of this too. Windows XP only allocates a percentage of disks for System Restore. As your disks get full, you have fewer rollback options. Selecting the amount of disk size to dedicate for System Restore backup data allows you to balance between using too much disk space and not having enough restore choices. To configure System Restore settings, follow these steps.

1. From the Control Panel, click the System icon.

2. Now click the System Restore tab, as shown in Figure 5-10.

3. By default, 12% of the space of each configured drive is allocated for System Restore. To change this setting for any drive, click the drive letter and then click the Settings button.

4. Select the amount of disk space to use, which will range from 5% to 12% of the volume or partition size. When finished, click OK.

5. Once you have finished configuring the System Restore settings, click OK.

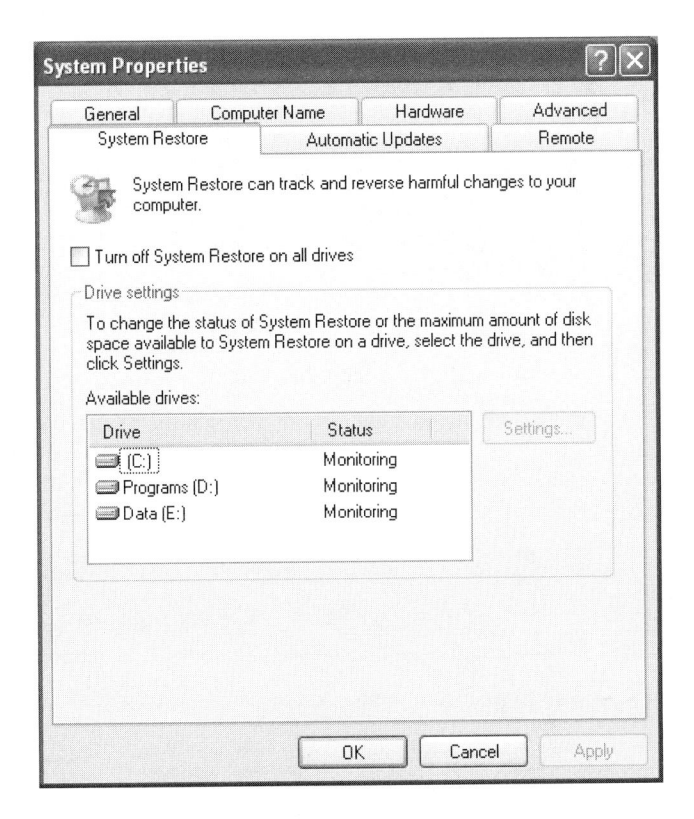

Figure 5-10. Configuring System Restore settings

The amount of disk space that you allocate determines how far back you can roll back a system. The default setting of 12% will give you about three weeks' worth of recovery checkpoints (21). Setting the minimum value of 5% will allow you to roll back the system just over one week. Since most of the time you need to roll back a system right after a failure occurs, allocating 5% for System Restore should be sufficient.

Now that you have seen how to configure System Restore, let's look at how to use it. To create a new restore point, follow these steps.

1. Click Start > All Programs > Accessories > System Tools > System Restore.

2. Click the Create a Restore Point radio button and click Next.

3. Enter a name for the new restore point and click Create.
4. When shown that the new restore point was created, click Close.

To roll the system back to an earlier restore point, follow these steps.

1. Close all open applications on the system, saving all open files.
2. Click Start > All Programs > Accessories > System Tools > System Restore.
3. Click the Restore My Computer to an Earlier Time radio button and click Next.
4. As shown in Figure 5-11, select the restore point to return the system to and click Next.
5. Verify that the selected restore point is correct and click Next.
6. System Restore will run and then reboot the system.
7. Once the system reboots, log on. When prompted that the restore completed successfully, click OK.

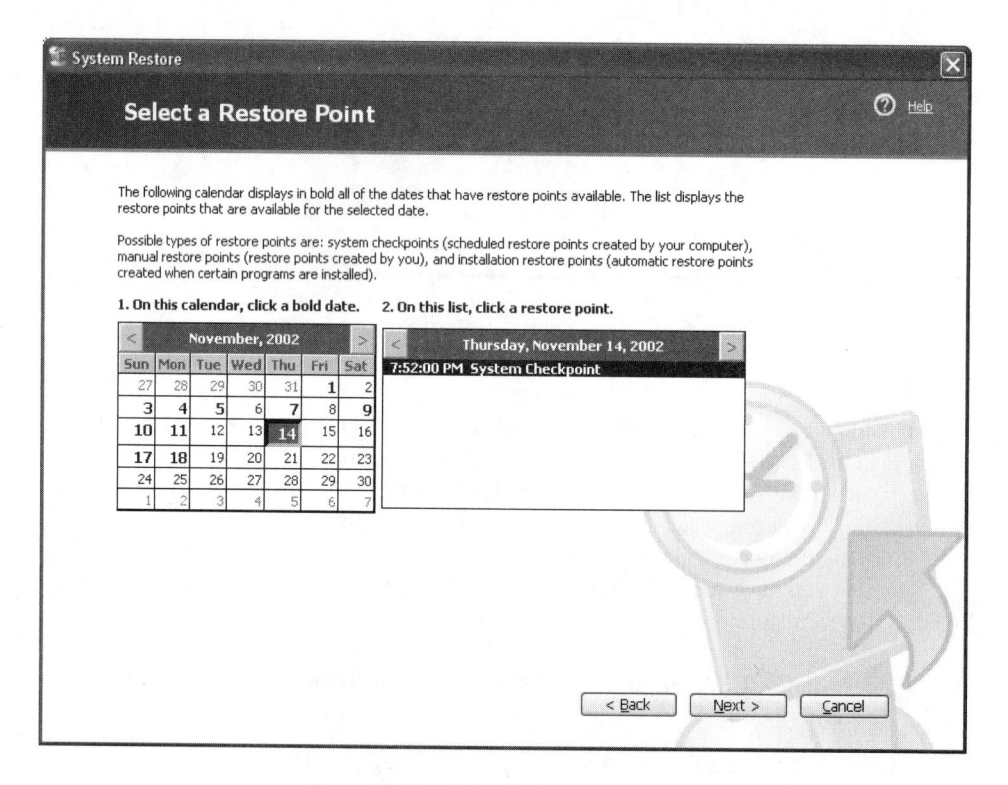

Figure 5-11. Selecting a restore point

If the system is not in the state that you were hoping for after the system restore, you can undo the operation by following these steps.

1. Close all open applications on the system, saving all open files.
2. Click Start > All Programs > Accessories > System Tools > System Restore.
3. Select Undo My Last Restoration and click Next.
4. Verify that you want the listed system restore reversed and click Next.
5. The previous system restore will be removed, and the system will be returned to its previous state following a reboot.
6. Once the system starts, log on to the computer. When prompted that the Undo restore operation completed successfully, click OK.

As you can see, System Restore provides a seamless method for quickly undoing system changes and recovering from mistakes. If a user reports that "Everything was fine yesterday, but I don't know what happened today," you can put your detective skills aside and just use System Restore to quickly resolve the problem. Since System Restore recovers application data, user data is not affected by rolling back a system, so you should strongly consider performing system restores as your first course of action when dealing with problems on user workstations.

> System Restore is only available on XP systems and thus cannot be used to roll back Windows servers.

Now that we have looked at some of the common tools for quickly analyzing and recovering client and server data, the remainder of this chapter focuses on specific troubleshooting scenarios. For many of the situations discussed throughout the remainder of this chapter, keep tools such as System Restore in mind. Remember, if you can get an XP system started, then you can use System Restore to roll it back.

Troubleshooting System Startup

When a system crashes, whether as a result of an application error, a driver error, or a user error, you are faced with recovering the system as quickly as possible. Oftentimes, if you can get the system started, you can manually undo the error (application or driver) that caused the problem in the first place. There are several methods to go about getting a system started when startup fails. Each of these methods is explained in the next several sections.

To start the system in a special startup mode, you must press F8 during startup when you first see the message "Starting Windows" at the bottom of the screen. This allows you to select a startup method from the Windows Advanced Options menu, as shown in Figure 5-12.

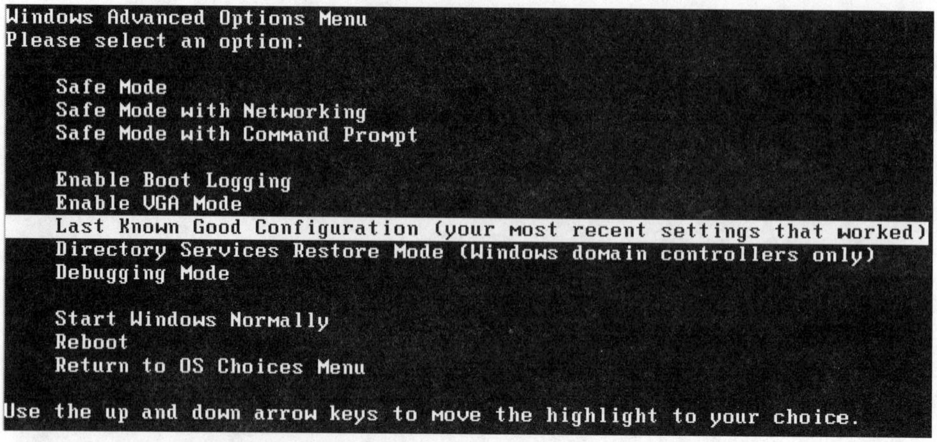

```
Windows Advanced Options Menu
Please select an option:

    Safe Mode
    Safe Mode with Networking
    Safe Mode with Command Prompt

    Enable Boot Logging
    Enable VGA Mode
    Last Known Good Configuration (your most recent settings that worked)
    Directory Services Restore Mode (Windows domain controllers only)
    Debugging Mode

    Start Windows Normally
    Reboot
    Return to OS Choices Menu

Use the up and down arrow keys to move the highlight to your choice.
```

Figure 5-12. Windows startup Advanced Options menu

Last Known Good Configuration

Selecting the Last Known Good Configuration (LKGC) should always be your first choice when trying to recover from a startup failure. However, this option is only valid if a user has not logged on normally since the problem was encountered. If a user logs on in Safe Mode, Last Known Good Configuration is still a viable recovery option.

LKGC works by restoring the previously used drivers and Registry settings in the HKEY_LOCAL_MACHINE\SYSTEM\CurrentControlSet Registry subkey. This can basically return your system to where it was as of the last successful bootup, as far as the OS configuration is concerned. If users saved files during the last session, they will still be intact. LKGC is most useful after installing a bad driver that is preventing the system from starting up successfully. When this occurs, if you can start the system with LKGC, the problem will be resolved. If LKGC does not work, or if a user rebooted and logged on since the failure was noticed, then you should try booting into Safe Mode as your next recovery option.

Safe Mode

When you boot a system into Safe Mode, only the hardware drivers that may be needed for system recovery are loaded. This does include storage devices, since Windows assumes that you may need them available in order to restore from backup. Oftentimes, when faulty drivers are installed (for devices other than storage devices), you can boot into Safe Mode and uninstall the bad driver. After you uninstall the driver and correct the problem, the system should boot normally. If you are in Safe Mode because you recently attempted to update a device driver, you can use Device Manager to roll back the driver to an earlier version. For more information on rolling back drivers, see the Troubleshooting Devices section later in this chapter.

Another common use for Safe Mode is for recovering a system where a user configured video settings that are incompatible with the user's monitor. When this happens, you can boot into Safe Mode, double-click the Display applet in the Control Panel, and adjust the display settings accordingly.

If you would like to simply roll back a failing XP system to an earlier time, you can run System Restore while booted into Safe Mode to do so. Remember, however, that the System Restore feature is not available with Windows servers, so on a server, you manually have to correct the problem or restore from an earlier backup.

Safe Mode with Networking

Normally, Safe Mode loads a limited set of drivers so as to start the operating system with as little overhead and as few problems as possible. If you need access to the network in order to repair a system, then you should choose Safe Mode with Networking instead of Safe Mode in the Advanced Options startup menu. Safe Mode with Networking is often used when a system needs to restore data from another backup server on the network.

Safe Mode with Command Prompt

Safe Mode with Command Prompt allows you to boot to a command prompt, allowing you to run any command line diagnostic tools desired. This is an alternative to booting into the Recovery Console, since the Recovery Console does not provide a true command shell environment and thus only supports a limited number of commands.

Enable Boot Logging

When you select this startup mode, Windows logs the success or failure of each device or service that is loaded during startup and saves this information to the Ntbtlog.txt file, which is located in the Windows directory. This option is useful when you are unsure of exactly which device is causing the startup problem. After unsuccessfully booting using the Enable Boot Logging option, you can boot into the Recovery Console and read the Ntbtlog.txt file to determine the source of the startup problem.

Enable VGA Mode

This option is often best when you are trying to repair video problems. For example, suppose that you accidentally installed the incorrect video driver for a video display adapter. You can boot into VGA Mode, which causes the operating system to load its generic VGA driver (as was used during the initial OS installation), so that you can at least make sense of what is on your monitor. With an incorrect video driver, you may wind up seeing a scrambled picture or nothing at all. Once you boot into VGA Mode, you can either uninstall the incorrect video driver or roll back to a previous version using the Device Manager.

Directory Services Restore Mode

Directory Services Restore Mode is only available for Windows servers that are domain controllers (the option is listed for Windows servers that are not domain controllers, but it just boots them into Safe Mode). This startup mode is used when you need to perform maintenance on the Active Directory database or when you have to restore the Active Directory database. When you boot a domain controller into this mode, the Active Directory database is offline, and thus you cannot log on with a domain user name and password. Instead, you need to use the special Directory Services Restore Mode password that was entered when the server was first promoted to be a domain controller. For more information on Active Directory database maintenance and recovery, turn to Chapter 13, Active Directory.

Debugging Mode

This mode of operation allows you to boot the operating system while debugging information is sent to another system via a serial cable.

Disabling Services and Drivers with the Recovery Console

If a particular service or driver is preventing you from even starting a system in Safe Mode, you can use the Recovery Console to disable the driver or service, and then restart the system into Safe Mode. For example, the installation of some video drivers can corrupt a system to the point that it cannot even start in Enable VGA Mode. When this happens, you can use the Recovery Console to disable the faulty video driver, which forces the OS to use its generic VGA driver.

While the Recovery Console does provide a command shell environment, its available commands are not the same as those that are available at the standard operating system command prompt. Before getting to using the Recovery Console, let's look at some of its most valuable troubleshooting commands.

Recovery Console Diagnostic Commands

Since Recovery Console commands have limited syntax and behave differently from many of their command line counterparts, they are covered in this section instead of with the commands mentioned earlier in this chapter. The most useful troubleshooting and recovery-related Recovery Console commands are

- `listsvc`
- `enable`
- `disable`

Now let's look at the usage and syntax for each command.

listsvc

The `listsvc` command is used to list all installed system services and device drivers on a system. In order to disable a service or driver, you need to know its name. You can determine its name by running this command. There is no optional syntax for this command, so to see a list of all installed drivers and system services, you would just type `listsvc`. The output for this command is displayed one screen at a time. You can scroll the output data by hitting the Enter key, and when you find the driver name you're looking for, you can return to the Recovery Console command prompt by hitting the Escape key. In a few moments, we'll look at using `listsvc` in a troubleshooting scenario, but first let's examine the `enable` and `disable` commands.

enable

The `enable` command allows you to enable a particular system service or device driver. The syntax for this command is:

```
enable <service> [StartType]
```

The `enable` command options are described in Table 5-2.

Table 5-2. enable Command Options

Option	Use
service	Used to specify the name of the service or driver to enable.
StartType	Allows you to set the service or driver startup type. These are the valid values for this parameter. • SERVICE_BOOT_START—Driver or service loaded into memory during initial system boot (required to start the operating system). • SERVICE_SYSTEM_START—Driver or service loaded during normal operating system startup. • SERVICE_AUTO_START—Driver or service configured to Auto-Start. Starts when the operating system starts up. • SERVICE_DEMAND_START—Driver or service configured to Manual Start. Starts as a result of action taken by a user or an application.

When a service or driver is enabled, if no `StartType` is specified, its previously assigned startup type is applied. As an example of using the `enable` command, suppose that you want to enable a SCSI driver (named vmscsi) that will connect a recovered disk that you wish to boot the system from. If you wanted to determine the driver startup type, you could find it by running the `listsvc` command. Otherwise, if you just wanted to ensure that the driver loads as soon as the system boots, you would enter the command `enable vmscsi service_boot_start`.

disable

This is one of the most frequently used Recovery Console commands. With the `disable` command, you can disable a faulty driver or service that is preventing the system from starting. If a failure is happening immediately following a new service or device installation, you will already be aware of the driver or service to disable. If you are not sure of the faulty service, you can first try to start the system with boot logging enabled (Enable Boot Logging option) and then read the contents of the bootlog.txt file while logged on to the Recovery Console. The commands available for displaying the contents of text files will be described shortly.

When you run the `disable` command, you need to use the following command syntax:

```
disable <service>
```

So as with `enable`, you need to provide the name of the service or driver in the command syntax. Let's look at an example of first determining the name of a driver and then disabling it. In the example, the system is having trouble with a display driver provided by VMware.

```
C:\WINDOWS>listsvc

vds               Manual
   Virtual Disk Service
vga               Manual

VgaSave           System
   VGA Display Controller
ViaIDE            Disabled

vmx_svga          Manual
   VMware Display Driver

VolSnap           Boot
   Storage volumes

VSS               Manual
   Volume Shadow Copy Service

C:\WINDOWS>
```

Now that you have the name of the driver (vmx_svga), you can use the `disable` command to prevent it from starting. Here is the syntax you use to disable the driver and then exit the Recovery Console.

```
C:\WINDOWS>disable vmx_svga

The registry entry for the vmx_svga service was found.
The service currently has start_type SERVICE_DEMAND_START
Please record this value.

The new start_type for this service has been set to SERVICE_DISABLED.
```

```
The computer must be restarted for the changes to take effect.
Type EXIT if you want to restart the computer now.

C:\WINDOWS>exit
```

Now that the driver is disabled, you can uninstall it once the system starts.

Additional Commands

The standard DOS directory navigation commands are valid as well. So you can use `cd` to change to a directory, `rd` to remove a directory, and `md` to make a directory. Other general commands that can be used are

- `copy`—Copies a file from a source to a destination location (useful for replacing a corrupted file with a known good version)
- `delete`—Deletes the specified file(s)
- `dir`—Lists the contents of a directory
- `more`—Displays the contents of a file, one page at a time
- `type`—Displays the contents of a complete file

For a complete list of available commands, type `help` at the Recovery Console command prompt.

Accessing the Recovery Console

Of course, in order to use the Recovery Console, you need to get to it first. To boot your system into the Recovery Console, follow these steps.

1. Boot the system off the Windows Setup CD. During startup, you will be prompted to press a key to boot off the CD. When prompted, hit a key on the keyboard.

2. Wait a few moments for Windows Setup to load. When you see the Setup Notification screen, press Enter.

3. Now press R to repair the system with the Recovery Console.

4. You will now see a list of detected Windows installations. Input the number associated with the installation you wish to repair and press Enter.

5. Next, you need to log on to the OS using its local Administrator password. Enter the Administrator password and press Enter.

6. You should now be at the Recovery Console command prompt. When finished performing Recovery Console operations, type Exit to restart the system.

You can also install the Recovery Console so that you will not need a CD to access it in the future. When the Recovery Console is installed, it will appear as a boot option when the system first starts. This is similar to configuring a system to dual boot—as at initial startup, you can choose the operating system (or Recovery Console) that is loaded. To install the Recovery Console, you need to run the Windows Setup application with the /cmdcons switch. To do this, follow these steps.

1. Boot the operating system normally and log on.
2. Insert the Windows Setup CD in the CD-ROM drive.
3. If Autorun starts the Windows Setup application, close the Setup window.
4. Now click Start > Run, and then click the Browse button to locate the winnt32.exe file on the Windows Setup CD. This file is stored in the i386 directory. Once you find the winnt32.exe file, click Open.
5. You should now see the full path to the file shown in the Run dialog box. At the end of the path (but before the final quotation mark, if present), leave a space and then add the text /cmdcons.
6. Now click OK in the Run dialog box.
7. Wait while the Recovery Console is installed. When the installation is finished, you will see the Recovery Console boot option listed when you restart your computer.

In most instances, disabling faulty services in the Recovery Console allows you to get an operating system started and thus repair the problem found. If you get a message on startup that the NTOSKRNL is missing or corrupt, for example, you could copy a known good version of the file from the installation CD to the boot partition using the Recovery Console. More information on this error is located in Appendix B.

Now suppose that you have exhausted all of your repair efforts and there is no end in sight. Instead of spending additional hours trying to track down the problem, you have another alternative: repair the operating system installation.

Repairing the OS Installation

To repair the operating system installation, you essentially rerun the Setup program and reinstall the operating system over what is already in place. This approach does have its disadvantages. For starters, the repaired OS will not have any knowledge of previously installed applications, so you need to manually remove and then reinstall them, unless you plan to restore the original OS configuration from backup. In that case, repairing the OS can just be considered a step in the overall recovery process. Another problem with repairing standalone systems in a workgroup is that if you repair an OU installation, knowledge of local user accounts and user certificates is lost. This can be a major problem if local users are encrypting their files, since the certificate needed to decrypt the files is lost during the OS repair.

While performing a repair of the installation does have its drawbacks, it sometimes is the only way to regain access to valuable data. Since the operating system is simply reinstalled over itself, no other files or folders on the system are affected by the repair process.

To perform a repair of the OS installation, follow these steps.

1. Boot the system off the Windows Setup CD. During startup, you will be prompted to press a key to boot off the CD. When prompted, hit a key on the keyboard.

2. Wait a few moments for Windows Setup to load. When you see the Setup Notification screen, press Enter.

3. Now press Enter to set up Windows.

4. Read the Windows Licensing Agreement and press F8 to accept its terms.

5. Select the damaged Windows installation and press R to repair the installation.

6. Follow the installation prompts to complete the repair process.

If you prefer to make a system bootable and then work to repair the damaged OS at a later time, another option is to perform a parallel installation of Windows. This entails booting off the Windows CD and running setup, but instead of selecting to repair an existing installation, you can press the Escape key and then select a destination for a new OS installation. You should install Windows to a separate partition, if one is available. Otherwise, you need to install the OS to an alternate folder on the same partition as the original OS.

Now that we have tackled methods for resolving the most common startup problems, let's look at what to do if a system will not shut down.

If a system is bootable, you can repair the OS installation by running Setup from within the Windows GUI. To do this, select "upgrade" in the Installation Type dialog box once the Setup program runs.

Troubleshooting System Shutdown

On one hand, if a system wants to stay on all the time, you should count your blessings (tell your fellow UNIX administrators, "Don't talk to me about reboots! My Windows system absolutely refuses to shut down!"). However, odds are that if your system hangs during shutdown, its resources will not be available anyway, and thus troubleshooting is definitely warranted.

The most likely causes of system shutdown failures are

- Faulty device driver
- Faulty service or application
- Hardware failure
- Firmware incompatibility
- BIOS/CMOS incompatibility
- Hard disk failure

If maintenance was recently performed on the system, then that's where you should start to look for the cause of the problem. If a driver was recently updated, it may not be compatible with the device and is thus the cause of instability. For this type of problem, the quickest way to return the system to normal is to roll back the driver to its earlier version. The process of rolling back drivers is discussed in the Troubleshooting Devices section later in this chapter. If the driver cannot be rolled back, you could also upgrade the driver to the correct version.

Similarly, a problematic application that is failing to close could also be the cause of the shutdown problem. If an application was recently installed, you should uninstall the application and then check with the application vendor to ensure that its product (or product version) is compatible with your operating system. Later in this chapter in the Troubleshooting Application Compatibility section, we'll examine how to overcome application compatibility issues. Remember, if you cannot uninstall the application, you can remove it using the `msicuu` utility. Another alternative, if the problem is occurring on an XP system, is to use System Restore to roll back the system to an earlier date and time. Still one other alternative to resolving the problem could be to reboot and select the LKGC startup option. If the shutdown problem occurred immediately after upgrading a device driver, booting into the last known good configuration should restore the previous driver and thus correct the problem.

Hardware issues can also cause a system to hang while shutting down. Sometimes when you upgrade a driver, the new driver is fully compatible with the hardware, but not with the hardware's firmware version. To obtain the most recent firmware for your installed devices, visit each device manufacturer's Web site. On the site, you can download firmware upgrades as well as access instructions on how to install the upgrades. Also, you cannot overlook failing hardware. If you are convinced that the driver and firmware for a failing device are up to date, the problem could be with the device itself. You can check a device's status by locating it in Device Manager. We'll be getting to Device Manager shortly.

While all of the previous suggestions are fine if you have a hunch as to the source of the problem, they are not of much value if you are completely stumped. When this happens, you need a way to log the failure as it happens. That's where booting a system with the Enable Boot Logging option enters this troubleshooting picture. As mentioned earlier, with boot logging enabled, the success or failure of each service and driver as it loads is logged to the ntbtlog.txt file. After the system boots, you can examine this file for startup-related errors. If you notice a failure message for a particular service or device, then you have found the problem. If after a failed shutdown you cannot restart the system, you should still attempt a boot with boot logging enabled (updates bootlg.txt) and then boot into the Recovery Console. From the Recovery Console, you can use the `type` or `more` commands to view the contents of the file. Once you spot the faulty service or driver, you can use the `disable` command to prevent the service from starting. If you notice from the bootlg.txt file that the failing device is critical to the startup of the system (such as a SCSI controller), then you will likely need to replace the device in order to start the system.

Finally, one other source of the shutdown problem could be a failing hard disk. One of the best commands for detecting and repairing disk errors is `chkdsk` (covered in Chapter 4). Before taking action on the disk, you should try to run `chkdsk` first. If `chkdsk` identifies errors but cannot repair them, or if the disk is so badly corrupted that it cannot be accessed, then you will likely need to replace the disk.

Troubleshooting Devices

When hardware problems arise, your first troubleshooting stop should be at the Device Manager. Oftentimes, the information provided from the Device Manager GUI is all that you need to arrive at the source of the problem. Of course, to use Device Manager for troubleshooting, you need to get there first. Here's how to access Device Manager.

1. Click Start > All Programs > Administrative Tools > Computer Management.

2. Under the System Tools parent snap-in, click Device Manager.

3. If there any failing devices or devices with conflicting settings, the device tree will be automatically expanded to display the devices. The Device Manager illustration in Figure 5-13 displays a failing device.

When you open Device Manager, there are several visible clues that will allow you to quickly determine the status of a device. These are some of the clues you may encounter.

- Black exclamation point next to device—A black exclamation point inside a yellow circle adjacent to a device means that the device is currently in a problem state. There are several possible causes for device problems, which we will examine shortly.

- Red X next to device—This indicates that the device has been disabled. If you need to use the device, you can enable it by right-clicking the device object and selecting Enable.

- Blue "i" next to device—A blue "i" next to a device alerts you that the Use Automatic Settings feature was disabled. This means that a user has statically assigned resources to the device and thus overwritten its plug-and-play functionality. Manually configuring device resources can cause conflicts with other hardware devices installed in the system.

- Ghost—If the object has a grayed-out or ghostly appearance, there is no reason to get scared. Instead, just understand that Device Manager is telling you that it realizes that the object at one time was installed but at the moment is not attached to the system. Device Manager considers these devices to be hidden.

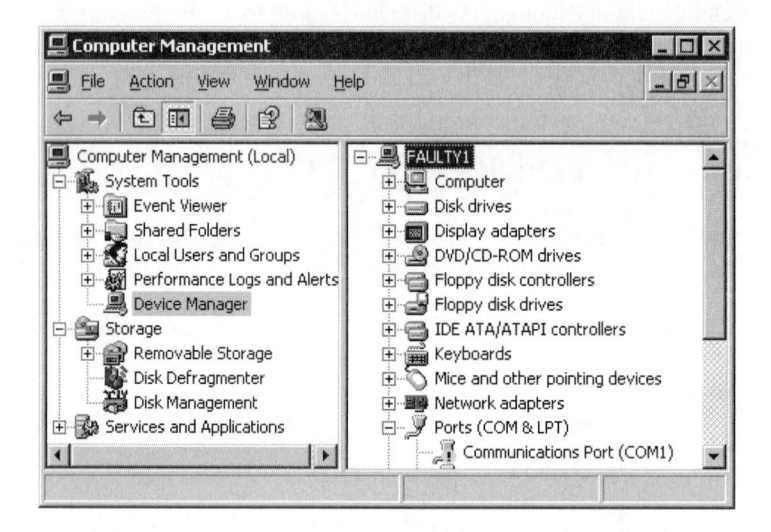

Figure 5-13. Locating failing devices with Device Manager

By default, removed devices are not shown in the Device Manager. If you would like to see a list of all installed devices, regardless of whether or not they are currently physically attached to the system, you need to change the Device Manager View settings to show hidden devices. To do this, while in the Device manager click the View menu and select "Show hidden devices." Now you can see all devices that have been installed in the system. Seeing these devices is useful because there may be some devices, such as network adapters, that were once installed in the system but were upgraded to newer versions. When this happens, Device Manager retains the configuration of the older card. If the card will never be installed back into the system, you can uninstall the device.

Normally, the devices that you should be most concerned with when troubleshooting are devices that are listed as being in a problem state. For these device types, there are several possible failures that could generate an error display. These are some of the most common problems that cause these errors.

Troubleshooting Devices 161

- No driver is installed.
- An incorrect driver is installed.
- A hardware failure occurs.
- There is a conflict with another device.
- A firmware problem exists.

To determine the probable cause of a device problem, you first need to examine the device's status.

Checking Device Status

When a device is showing that it is in a problem state, you should begin the fault diagnosis process by checking the status of the device. To do this, follow these steps.

1. From Device Manager, right-click the device and select Properties.
2. Under the General tab, you will see a description of the device's status (see Figure 5-14).

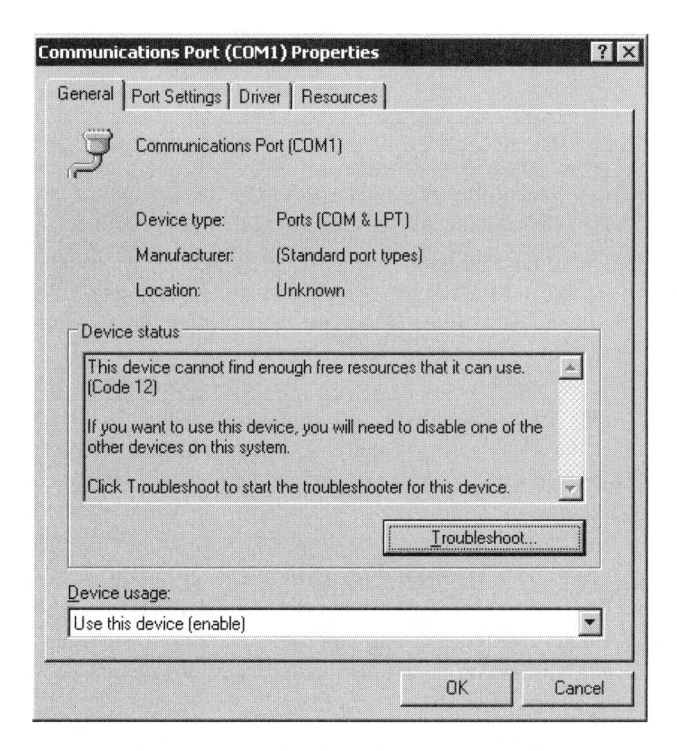

Figure 5-14. Checking device error codes

If a problem is displayed, you will see an error code listed in the Device Status field. With the error code in hand, you can turn to Appendix B of this book for an explanation of the error, along with steps to resolve the problem that generated the error.

Rolling Back Device Drivers

If a device problem began after you upgraded a device driver, Device Manager provides a way to "undo" your previous action. This is known as Driver Rollback. With this feature, a device uses its previously installed driver and discards its current driver. Since a previous driver had to exist in order to roll back, you cannot roll back a device that has only had one driver installed in its history.

To roll back a device driver, follow these steps.

1. From Device Manager, right-click the device and select Properties.
2. Now click the Driver tab.
3. Under the Driver tab, click the Roll Back Driver button.
4. When prompted to confirm your action, click Yes.

When a driver has been rolled back to its previous version, you should have a functioning device. If you are certain that the proper upgrade driver was installed for the device, you should report the problem to the device manufacturer and wait for a new updated driver to be produced before attempting to upgrade the device driver again.

Updating Device Drivers

Updating device drivers oftentimes provides better device performance and reliability. Other times, updating a driver is necessary for getting a system to function properly. For example, if you upgrade a system from an earlier OS version to Windows XP, you may find that the previous device driver is not compatible with the OS, and thus after the upgrade completes, the device will not start. This is a problem that can be quickly corrected by updating the device driver.

Before updating a driver, you need to obtain the most recent driver from the device manufacturer. This can almost always be accomplished by connecting to the manufacturer's Web site and then downloading the driver. Some manufacturers provide drivers as information (.inf) files, zipped collections of .inf files, or installation executable (.exe) files. If the driver update is in the form of an executable file, then you need to follow the manufacturer's instructions for installing the device. It is important to note the installation instructions, since to install some device drivers, it is required that the device be disconnected from the system. This is often the case with some USB and IEEE 1394 devices. If you were able to download a zipped file containing the driver's information file, then you have everything you need to manually install the device.

To update a device driver, follow these steps.

1. Locate the device in Device Manager to be updated, right-click the device, and select Update Driver.
2. When the Hardware Update Wizard opens, click the Install from a List or Specific Location radio button and click Next.
3. Click the "Don't search. I will choose the driver to install" button and click Next. If you have Windows search for a driver, it will only return a list of signed drivers. Many manufacturers put out drivers that do not go through the costly Microsoft certification process but still work perfectly fine. On the other hand, Microsoft tends to not support unsigned drivers, so it is always best to use signed drivers if available.
4. Select the type of device to install and then click the Have Disk button.
5. Now click the Browse button to locate and select the downloaded .inf file. When you locate the file, click it and then click the Open button.
6. In the Install from Disk dialog box, click OK.
7. The appropriate driver will now be listed under the Model field in the Hardware Update Wizard window. Click Next.
8. If prompted that the device is not digitally signed, click Continue Anyway (if you are certain that the driver is appropriate for the device).
9. When the installation completes, click Finish.

If the correct driver has been installed, the device will start after the completion of the driver installation. For some devices, you need to reboot in order to complete the driver update process.

> Sometimes mistakes are made when upgrading drivers because the administrator performing the upgrade assumes an incorrect model number for the device. If there is any doubt as to a device's model number, you should always physically examine the hardware and read the model number directly from it.

Uninstalling Devices

Sometimes, even installing the correct driver for a failed device does not allow it to start. For example, you may run into this problem when performing a full system restore of an operating system. Following the restore, you may find that a NIC driver will not start. If its Registry information is corrupted to the point that even reinstalling its driver does not help, then you need to uninstall the device to remove the corrupted information. To uninstall a device, perform these actions.

1. From Device Manager, locate the device to be uninstalled, right-click its associated icon, and select Uninstall.

2. When warned that you are about to uninstall a device, click OK.

3. Wait while the device information is removed from the operating system.

Once a device has been uninstalled, you can reinstall it by right-clicking the computer object at the top of the device tree and selecting "Scan for hardware changes." If new devices are found, you will be prompted to select the appropriate driver for each device.

Disabling Devices

One other consideration in the troubleshooting process, when you are unsure of the source of a failure, is to disable the suspected device. To disable a device, right-click the device in Device Manager and select Disable. When prompted to confirm your choice, click Yes. The disabled device will now have a red X adjacent to it in the Device Manager MMC snap-in.

If the system can start up and shutdown normally with a particular device disabled, then you have located the source of the problem. To correct the device problem, you could look for a firmware update or a new driver. If applying software updates or attempting to update firmware fails, then you may need to replace the device. You could also check with the device manufacturer for any diagnostic utilities to test the device. Many disk controllers have diagnostic tools built into their BIOS. For these devices, you can access their BIOS while the system boots by pressing a particular hotkey, such as F2.

With device troubleshooting, you can usually systematically determine the cause of the problem within a few steps. When troubleshooting a device, don't forget to start by opening Device Manager and then checking the device's reported error code against the codes provided in Appendix B.

Troubleshooting Fax Problems

Fax modems and the handy all-in-one printers (print, copy, and fax) have allowed nearly anyone to send and receive faxes from his or her desktop. However, the user's experience is not always what he or she might expect. As with other hardware devices, you can usually pinpoint the problem by following a systematic process of eliminating what's right.

Diagnosing Fax Problems

Determining the source of the fax problem should start with the fax device itself. If the device was recently installed and this is the first time an attempt was made to use the device, you should ensure that it is compatible with the operating system. If the user received a great price on the fax modem, for example, it may be because the product only supports NT or Windows 95 operating systems, and no degree of troubleshooting wizardry will help. To be sure that the device is certified to work with Windows, you should navigate to Microsoft.com and check the Hardware Compatibility List (HCL). To access the HCL, just go to www.microsoft.com/hcl. If the device is on the HCL, then you have eliminated the possibility of the device not being supported. However, if you do not see the device on the HCL, you should follow up with the device manufacturer to obtain the proper driver for the device and to verify that it does work with an XP or W2K3 operating system.

Now, if you have determined that the device is supported, you should next look to see if the device problem is due to having an incorrect driver installed. You can open Device Manager to check the device to see if a problem state is indicated with the fax device. If a problem is indicated, check the Device Manager error code and cross-reference it in Appendix B for an appropriate solution. Also, you should verify on the device manufacturer's Web site if there is a newer driver available for your operating system.

Once you have determined that the device is supported and has the correct driver, it's time to see if the problem is hardware related. If the fax device is a fax modem, you should perform a test of the modem by accessing the modem's properties in Device Manager. To test a modem, follow these steps.

1. From the Device Manager, right-click the modem object and select Properties.

2. In the Modem Properties dialog box, click the Diagnostics tab.

3. Now click the Query Modem button.

4. After a moment, the results of the query will be displayed (see Figure 5-15).

If you do not receive any Fail responses in the query output, then the modem itself is probably working properly, so you should check the phone line that the modem is connected to (some even check this first). If the phone line is good, then you should confirm that the modem hardware has failed by connecting a known good modem to the system. If the new modem works, then you have found the problem.

Testing the Solution

Finally, once the problem has been corrected, you need to send a test fax to verify proper operation of the fax device. This can be done from the Fax Console. You can access the Fax Console by clicking Start > All Programs > Accessories > Communications > Fax Console. From the File menu, select Send a Fax, and the New Fax Wizard guides you through the process.

> Do not forget the obvious when troubleshooting fax problems. If a user is complaining that he cannot receive a fax, you should make sure that Receive is enabled in the user's Fax Console. To do this, click the Tools menu and then select Configure Fax.

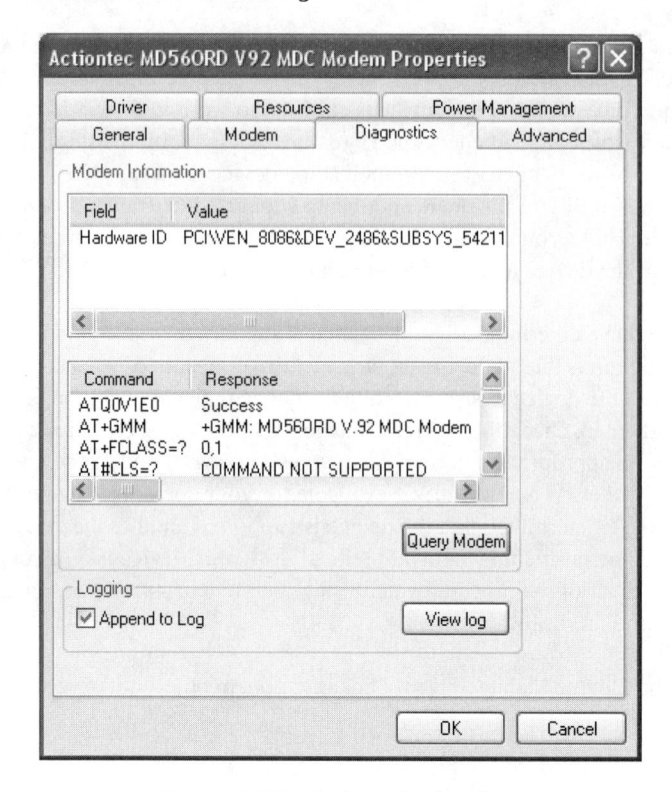

Figure 5-15. Testing a fax modem

Troubleshooting Display Problems

Display problems can often quickly become a source of irritation for users and administrators. Fortunately, the operating system does provide a good deal of help to resolve display problems. Here are some common faults that you may encounter with displays.

- The video resolution cannot be set higher than 640 by 480 and 16 colors.
- The display is garbled.
- The screen flickers.
- You receive this error message: "Display problems. This program can't continue."
- The multiple-monitor feature is not working.
- Videos are not displaying properly.

For these types of problems, you can often find the exact cause by running the Video Troubleshooter. To launch this troubleshooter, perform the following steps.

1. Click Start > Run, enter `hcp://help/tshoot/tsdisp.htm`, and click OK.

2. When the Video Troubleshooter starts, select your problem and click Next to start the troubleshooting process.

The other most common display-related problem arises from using the wrong display adapter driver. There are numerous available versions for each display adapter type, so it is easy to accidentally choose to install the wrong driver. If the manufacturer's Web site has several drivers listed for your operating system, you should start by installing the most recent posted driver version and then work backward until you have found a driver that is acceptable. If the driver does not allow the display to appear at all, then you could reboot the system and first try to use the Last Known Good Configuration startup option. If that does not work, then the next best bet is to boot into Safe Mode and uninstall the faulty driver. Finally, if all else fails, you can boot into the Recovery Console and disable the faulty driver, forcing the operating system to use its generic VGA adapter.

> Users manually changing display settings such as Refresh Rate can cause physical damage to a monitor. So do not rule out hardware failure as a possible cause of the display problems. Also, never set display settings to anything higher than what is allowed by the specific monitor attached to the display adapter.

Troubleshooting Internet Connection Sharing

Internet Connection Sharing (ICS) is often the ideal solution for providing shared Internet connectivity in a small office/home office (SOHO) environment. To share a broadband connection, many individuals and business are purchasing inexpensive routers (under $100) to satisfy their needs. The use of a hardware router maintains the Internet connection, regardless of whether or not any computers are online. With ICS, the ICS host system has to be online in order for the Internet connection to be accessible.

When you have a few computers sharing a hub or switch, and one of the systems has an Internet connection (dial-up, cable, DSL, and so on), they can all share the connection if ICS is enabled. The process for setting up ICS is relatively straightforward and rarely causes problems, but on occasion troubles do pop up. In this section, we look at how to resolve ICS problems and look at the common trouble spots behind ICS failures.

As with display problems, ICS also has a troubleshooting wizard. You can launch the ICS Troubleshooting Wizard by running the command `hcp://help/tshoot/tsics.htm`.

Chapter 5 Client-Server Troubleshooting

If you prefer to tackle the problem on your own without the help of the wizard, here are some common configuration issues that are sometimes overlooked.

- The system running ICS will provide DHCP services to the LAN, so no other DHCP server should be on the same network.
- Clients should be configured to use TCP/IP and have their IP address and DNS server assigned automatically.
- If you assign static IP addresses to clients, they must be on the 192.168.0.0/24 subnet and use 192.168.0.1 as their DNS server and default gateway (being configured for automatic IP assignment is strongly recommended).
- Ensure that the ICS system can access the Internet.

To double-check the ICS connection settings, you need to perform these steps.

1. Click Start > Control Panel > Network Connections, and then double-click the Internet connection (modem, cable modem, LAN adapter).
2. Now click the connection's Properties button.
3. Now click the Advanced tab.
4. Verify that the "Allow other users to connect through this computer's Internet connection" box is checked and the network interface that is available to other systems on the network is selected as the Home Networking Connection (see Figure 5-16).

If the ICS host settings are correct and the ICS host has no problem accessing sites on the Internet, you should then verify the Internet connectivity of the ICS clients. To do this, go to a client system and access the command prompt (Click Start > Run, then enter `cmd` in the Run dialog box, and click OK). From the command prompt, verify that the client can ping the ICS host. The ICS host always has an IP address of 192.168.0.1. To do this, you would run `ping 192.168.0.1`. If the ping fails, then you need to verify network connectivity between the systems or verify that the client is using the proper TCP/IP configuration. To verify the client's IP configuration, run `ipconfig /all` from the command prompt. The client's IP address should be between 192.168.0.2 and 192.168.0.254. You will also see the client's DNS server and default gateway listed. Both of these addresses should be 192.168.0.1. If any of this information is incorrect, configure the client to receive its IP address and DNS server address automatically. If another DHCP server was previously on the network, run the following two commands on the client so that it obtains a new IP address from the ICS host: `ipconfig /release` and then `ipconfig /renew`.

Once you have gotten to the bottom of the ICS problem, and Internet connectivity is restored, office productivity should skyrocket!

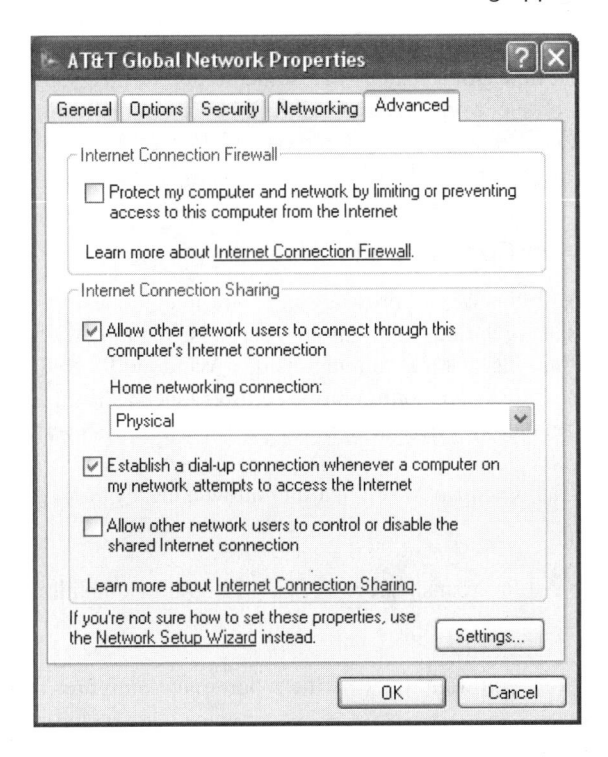

Figure 5-16. Verifying ICS settings

Troubleshooting Application Compatibility

While upgrading often provides users with many new features and a better operating system experience, it may do this at the expense of older applications. One of the primary problems with upgrading operating systems is that applications designed to work on earlier OS versions may not function properly or not even function at all.

Whenever possible, you should try to preempt these problems by checking with application manufacturers to verify that their programs are compatible with your new operating system. You may find that you need to purchase an upgrade of the application or a different version altogether. If the current application can be used, you may need to download updates that must be applied after each system is upgraded.

If there are no updates available, you can try to uninstall and then reinstall the application. Also, it is best to install the application using an account that is a member of the Domain Admins group or a member of a system's local Administrators group. One other consideration may be that the application is not compatible with the Fast User Switching feature of Windows XP. To prevent this problem from popping up, make sure that all users are logged off of a system before attempting to reinstall the application.

While you can always hope that all of your applications' related software vendors have updates for your new OS, it may be that some do not. In fact, some vendors may not even be in business, but your organization still relies on their applications. When you need to find a way to get an application to run on an XP/W2K3 system, you can start with the Program Compatibility Wizard.

Using the Program Compatibility Wizard

The Program Compatibility Wizard provides an environment to test an application in several different modes using various configuration settings. With the wizard, you can trick an application into thinking that it is running inside a Windows 98 environment, for example, or you can alter system configuration settings (such as using a 256-color display) to change automatically when the application is started and revert to normal when the application closes.

To use the Program Compatibility Wizard to allow a legacy application to run on the OS, follow these steps.

1. Click Start > All Programs > Accessories > Program Compatibility Wizard.

2. When the wizard opens, click Next.

3. Next, select how you want to locate the program to configure. You can choose from

    - Selecting the program from a list of installed programs
    - Using the program in the CD-ROM drive
    - Manually locating and selecting the program

4. Next, you can select the recommended operating system for the program. The operating system choices available are

    - Windows 95
    - Windows NT 4.0 (Service Pack 5)
    - Windows 98/ME
    - Windows 2000

5. Next, you need to choose the suggested display settings for the application, if needed. You can choose to configure the display for the application as the following:

    - 256 colors
    - 640-by-480 resolution
    - Visual themes disabled

6. Next, the wizard tests the application and prompts you with "Did the program work correctly?" Here, you just answer the question. These are the choices.

   - Yes, set this program to always use these compatibility settings.
   - No, try different compatibility settings.
   - No, I am finished trying compatibility settings.

7. If you select the last choice (I give up!), the operating system will prompt you to click Yes to send the results from the wizard to Microsoft. This is used to help improve the wizard, to better support legacy applications.

In most circumstances, you should find that the settings provided by the wizard will allow the application to run. If you are still having trouble, you should consult the application vendor for a specific patch for the application.

Summary

This chapter tackled the assortment of general problems that you may encounter on either an XP client or a W2K3 server. For many of the problems that you might run into, as a good start consult one of the troubleshooting wizards described in Chapter 4. This will often point you toward the source of the problem. For hardware device problems, remember that when Device Manager finds a problem with a particular device, it displays an error code. All Device Manager error codes are described in Appendix B, so this appendix is a great place to check when you are having a device-related problem. With all devices, correct drivers are the most important component of their success. You will find that some Windows-certified drivers can be downloaded automatically from Windows Update, while others need to be obtained from their related manufacturer's Web site. When a driver or service is wreaking havoc on the OS, making it nearly impossible to start, remember that you can disable it by using the Recovery Console.

Although in this chapter we went in several directions in an attempt to touch on the tools and techniques for overcoming the most common operating system problems, each of the remaining chapters in this book focuses exclusively on a single topic. Next we'll look at troubleshooting the failures and file corruption issues that are sometimes difficult to overcome with Microsoft Office.

6

Office XP

Microsoft Office applications are utilized by millions of people each day. With this type of usage, the amount of problems that may be encountered is limitless. Countless errors are often the result of users being unaware of how to perform a specific task with Microsoft Office. This chapter focuses not on usage issues or problems that result from a lack of training, but instead concentrates on problems that go beyond what is expected of the typical user, such as how to recover corrupted Office files.

Instead of attempting the impossible and indexing every Office error, this chapter focuses on the tools at your disposal for diagnosing MS Office problems. After examining the many available tools, the chapter then turns to detailing the most common Office application problems, along with their related solutions.

Office Troubleshooting Tools

There are several troubleshooting tools available for Microsoft Office that often go unnoticed. When a user experiences an application failure or corruption in an Office file, your job is to get the user back to productivity as soon as possible. Many of these tools allow you to do just that.

> While many of the tools in this section show you ways to repair Microsoft Office, don't forget about System Restore (see Chapter 5) as an option. With System Restore, you can roll back the user's XP system to an earlier point in time before the application corruption occurred.

Application Recovery

In pre-XP Office versions, a hung Office application meant that the user had to either terminate the program using Task Manager or reboot the computer. Either way, the possibility of corruption in the open Office document existed. Oftentimes, these files can be saved by Document Recovery, which is covered shortly. However, if you want a greater guarantee that a document will be recovered when an Office application stops responding, Application Recovery is the tool for you.

When an Office application stops responding, Application Recovery forces the hung application to fail and then restart. By Application Recovery initiating the failure, Office's Document Recovery feature can save a recovery version of the file, which will be available the next time the Office application starts.

When Office stops responding, follow these steps to recover documents opened in the failed application.

1. Click Start > All Programs > Microsoft Office Tools > Microsoft Office Application Recovery.

2. In the Microsoft Office Application Recovery dialog box, click the hung Office application to recover and then click the Recover Application button.

3. When recovery completes, the recovered documents are displayed in the Document Recovery task pane. From there, you can select the needed document and then save it.

Knowledge of this tool alone could save several Office documents. When Office stops responding, you often immediately either terminate the application using Task Manager or even go as far as rebooting the system. In any instance of a hung Office application, Application Recovery should be the first step taken in recovering a failed Office document. Using Task Manager or rebooting the system should always be your last resort.

Automatic Recovery

Beginning with Office 2000, the Office application was installed using Microsoft Software Installation (MSI) packages. One of the primary reasons for organizations deploying applications with the use of MSI files is that they can be programmed to have the ability to "self-heal." This means that if a user accidentally deleted a file needed by the application, or if a file was overwritten by an older version, the application could automatically repair itself.

Sometimes users that have used Office for years are suddenly surprised when prompted for the Office installation CD when they try to open Outlook. This is a typical example of an application file becoming corrupted, being recognized by the application, and automatically repaired.

The ability to self-heal in Office is known as Automatic Recovery. With this feature, if Office was installed from a network share, recovery will occur transparent to the user as long as the share is accessible. Otherwise, the installation CD will be needed to recover the damaged file. What Automatic Recovery means to you is fewer calls for support. Automatic Recovery will save you time even when dealing with home users who have become adept at following instructions given to them by their computer. If the computer says, "Put in the Office installation CD," the user more often than not will obey the command. The problem is fixed, and the user didn't even realize that a problem ever existed!

Like any automatic tool, Automatic Recovery is not perfect. After all, that's why airplanes have manual overrides. If a hydraulic system fails, a pilot can manually take control of the airplane by shutting down the automatic system. Sometimes Office application problems exist that are not automatically detected and corrected by Automatic Recovery. When this occurs, you can manually perform a "Detect and Repair," which is your way to manually take control of Office troubleshooting when Automatic Recovery fails.

Detect and Repair

Detect and Repair is a tool that is found in the Help menu of every Office application. By default, Office automatically attempts to repair a damaged installation using Application Recovery. When Application Recovery does not do the job and you suspect a problem with a particular Office application, it can be corrected with Detect and Repair.

To start the Detect and Repair process, follow these steps.

1. Open any Office application.
2. Click the Help menu and then select Detect and Repair.

As shown in Figure 6-1, the Detect and Repair dialog box presents you with two repair options.

- Restore my shortcuts while repairing—The default option, it repairs Office and recovers user custom settings (shortcuts, recently accessed files, user name).

- Discard my customized settings and restore default settings—Custom user settings are discarded and replaced with default settings (requires you to reconfigure user's Office settings after the repair completes, such as Outlook information).

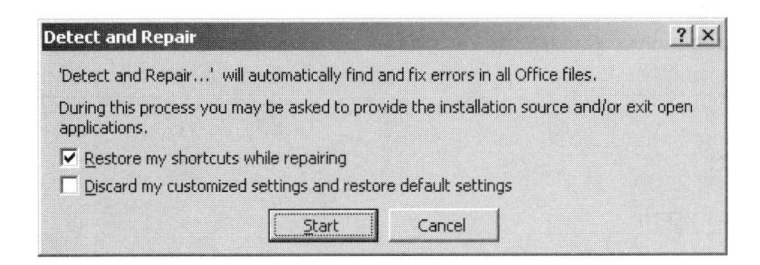

Figure 6-1. Repairing an Office installation with Detect and Repair

Once you choose the repair option in the Detect and Repair dialog box, follow these steps to complete the repair process.

1. Click the Start button, and Office scans and replaces any corrupt or missing files as well as reverts Office-related Registry settings to the installation defaults.
2. If prompted, insert the Office installation CD or browse to the path of the Office installation files.
3. When the repair completes, click OK.

When Office is corrupted to the point that an application cannot be opened in order to perform Detect and Repair, you need to repair the installation using Office Setup. Use of this method is covered later in this chapter.

> In order for Detect and Repair to successfully repair an Office application, all installed Office applications should be at the same version and service pack level; otherwise, the repair process may fail. For example, if you are running Word and PowerPoint XP but also have Outlook 2000 installed, you likely will not be able to repair the older Outlook version and if trouble is encountered, you should instead install Outlook XP.

Document Recovery

Document Recovery has been substantially improved with Office XP. In previous Office versions, a lost document resulting from a user's workstation locking up could quickly add up to an hour or longer of troubleshooting. With Office XP, the application itself does the troubleshooting for you. After a system crash, the next time you start the Office application, such as Word, your previous file versions that were saved by the application will appear in the Document Recovery task pane in the application window. Figure 6-2 shows Document Recovery displaying two versions of the Word file CorruptMe.doc. With Document Recovery, the user just selects the needed version of the file, and it opens. Once the file opens, the user can then save it, overwriting the file's original version, or save it with a new filename.

If any recovered files were not viewed by the user, the user is asked by Office how to treat the unexamined files when the Office application is closed or when the user clicks the Close button in the Document Recovery pane. When prompted, the user has the choice to view the files the next time the Office application is opened or to have the files removed. These options are shown in Figure 6-3.

Open and Repair

When Word or Excel files are opened, if Office detects corruption in the file, it automatically tries to repair the file. Sometimes corrupted files are not noticed by Office, and you may wish to manually initiate a document-level repair. While some files may be corrupted

Office Troubleshooting Tools   **177**

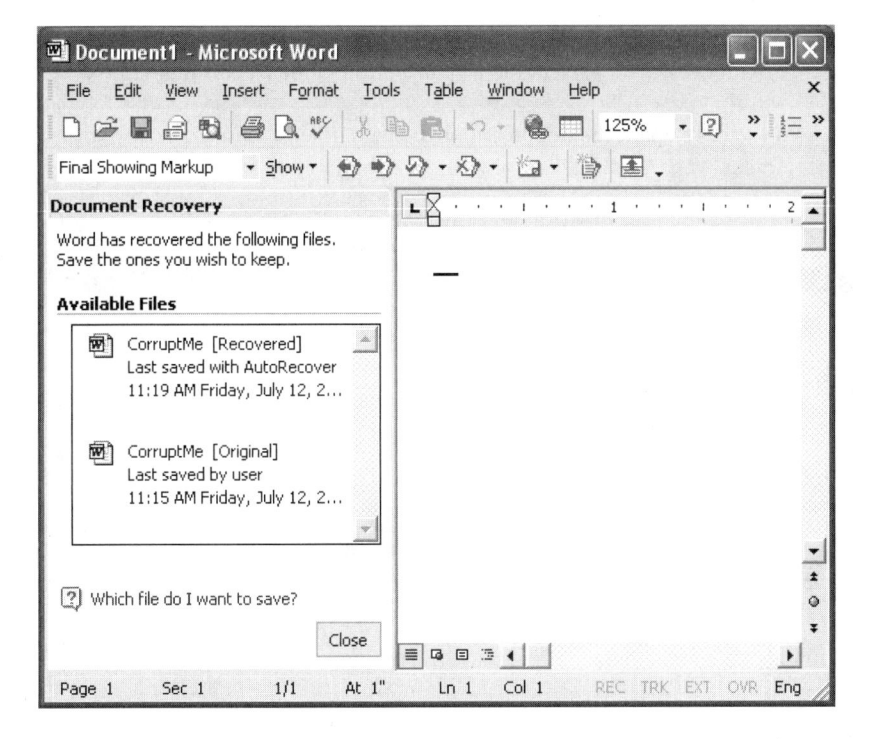

Figure 6-2. Recovering Word documents with Document Recovery

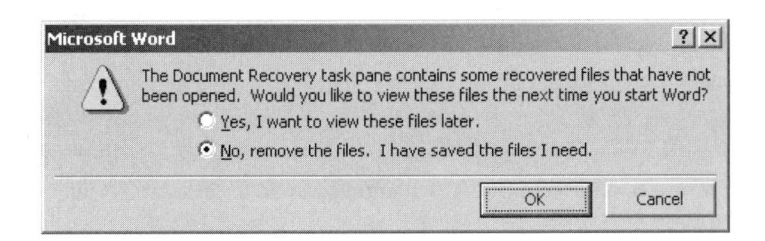

Figure 6-3. Document Recovery prompt

to a point where repair is not possible, for others, however, Open and Repair provides you with a way to recover valuable information.

To use the Open and Repair feature to repair a corrupted Word or Excel file, follow these steps.

1. Open the Office application (Word or Excel).

2. Click the File menu and then select Open.

3. Browse to and select the corrupted file, then click the Open drop-down menu (see Figure 6-4) and select Open and Repair.

4. If a Word file is being repaired, it automatically opens in Word. If you are repairing an Excel file, select the Repair option in the Repair dialog box.

Once you select Repair, the document opens with at least some, if not all, of its original content intact.

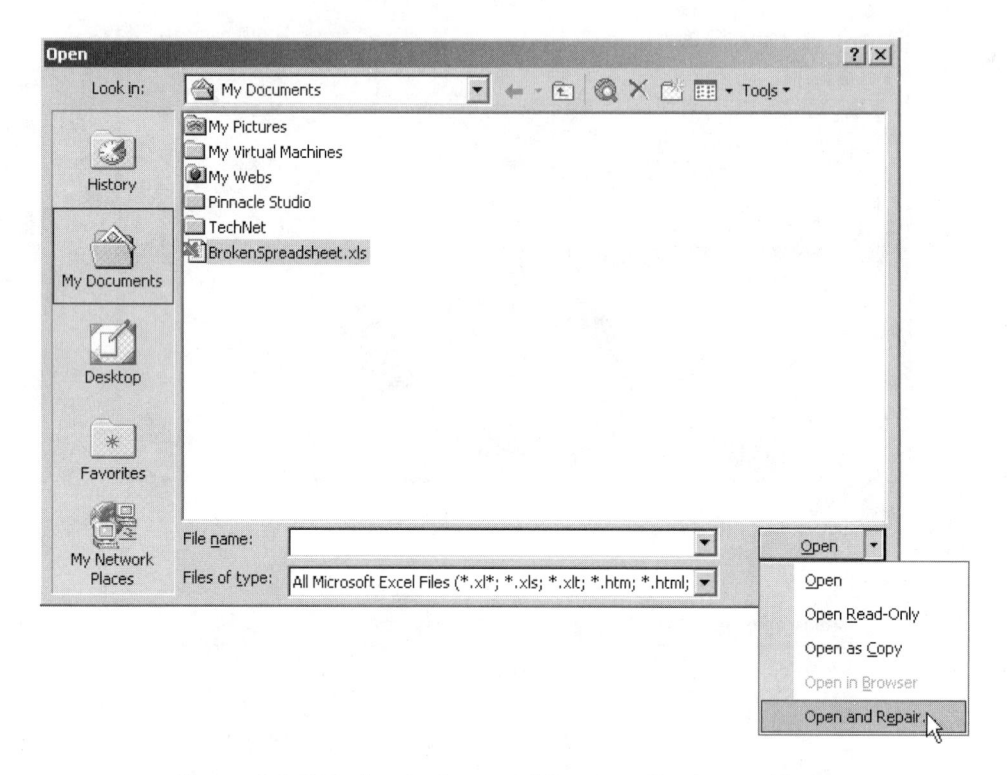

Figure 6-4. Selecting to Open and Repair an Excel spreadsheet

---

One other means of recovering data in a corrupted file is with the use of the `recover` command line utility. Since `recover` is not just limited to Office files, it is described in Chapter 7, Disk Subsystems.

Setup

When Office is inaccessible and the problem has not been corrected by Application Recovery, you can repair the Office installation with Setup. This section shows you the two primary ways to repair Office using Setup.

From Add/Remove Programs

This method is easy for any user to follow, since the user does not need to know the physical location of the Office Setup files. Of course, this assumes that the Setup files exist in the original location from where they were installed, whether on a network or CD.

To repair an Office installation from Add/Remove Programs, follow these steps.

1. From the Control Panel, double-click the Add/Remove Programs icon.

2. Select the Microsoft Office installation and then click the Change button.

3. Select the Repair Office option and click the Next button.

4. To repair the installation, select Detect and Repair. If you want to preserve user shortcuts, select the Restore my Start Menu Shortcuts checkbox and then click Install (see Figure 6-5).

5. Once the repair process completes, you will be prompted that Office Setup has repaired your installation. Click OK.

6. Click Close to close the Add/Remove Programs dialog box.

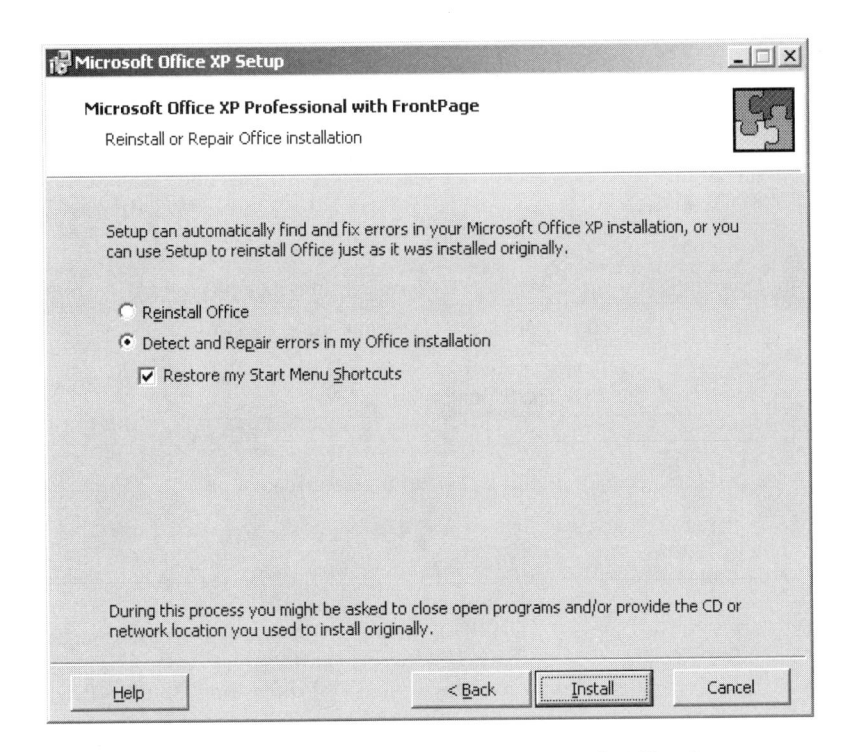

Figure 6-5. Repairing an Office installation with Office Setup

From the Setup CD or the Network

This repair method requires knowledge of the location of the Office Setup files, and for this method to work, you must know the location of both the Setup executable and the installation .msi file. There are several switches available for the Office `setup` command, but only one pertains to repairing an Office installation.

The syntax for using `setup` to repair an Office installation is:

```
setup /f<options> <.msi file path>
```

The `.msi file path` parameter points to the installation's associated .msi file. For a default Office XP Professional installation, the file is named ProPlus.msi. Table 6-1 describes the options associated with the `/f` switch.

Table 6-1. setup /f Command Options

Option	Use
a	Causes all Office Setup files to be reinstalled, regardless of the checksum value or version.
c	Causes corrupted or missing Setup files to be reinstalled.
d	Causes missing files or files with a version other than the Setup version to be reinstalled.
e	Causes missing files or files with a version equal to or less than the Setup version to be reinstalled.
m	Causes all Office-related system Registry values to be rewritten.
o	Causes missing files or files with a version older than the Office Setup version to be reinstalled.
p	Causes missing files to be reinstalled.
s	Causes all shortcuts to be reinstalled, with existing shortcuts being overwritten.
u	Causes all user-specific Office Registry values to be overwritten.
v	Causes Office Setup to run from the Setup package specified (.msi file) and recache it as the local installation package.

There are two predominant methods for running `setup` with the `/f` switch, which are as follows:

- To repair an Office installation: `setup /focums ProPlus.msi`
- To reinstall Office: `setup /fecum ProPlus.msi`

Each of these examples assumes that the Office XP Professional Setup is used and that the installation .msi file resides in the same directory as the Setup executable. Now that you have seen the troubleshooting tools at your disposal, the remainder of this chapter focuses on specific Office troubleshooting scenarios.

> Don't forget about booting the system into Safe Mode at startup as a viable troubleshooting test. If a document or presentation file does not open normally but opens when the system is booted into Safe Mode, check for faulty or outdated drivers on the system. If the document or presentation has sound integrated into it, a likely place to check is a nonexistent or improper driver for the sound card.

Troubleshooting Office Setup

Office Setup is generally very reliable, installing well both through local installations and from software installation packages via a group policy object (GPO). However, Setup is not perfect, and there are several errors that may contribute to its failure. As with troubleshooting other failures, start with the obvious first, eliminating what's right, and then move on to more granular troubleshooting.

Eliminating the Obvious

Table 6-2 lists some quick checks you can perform that allow you to quickly narrow your list of potential causes for the problem.

Table 6-2. Office Setup Failure Quick Checks

Problem	Solution
Setup running slow	If hard disk activity is indicated by the system's hard disk LED, Setup may just be running slower than you anticipate. The solution in this scenario is to apply patience to the problem.
Virus	Viruses can cause countless problems and certainly don't spare program installations. Verify that the system's antivirus software has the most current virus signatures and that a virus scan was run recently.
Dirty or damaged CD	If the CD drive's LED remains on, and Setup is not progressing, try removing, cleaning, and then reinserting the installation CD. If prompted that a file was not copied, click the Retry button.
User permissions	If the installation can be run by an Administrator but cannot be run when the user is logged on with his or her own account, then the user does not have adequate permissions to install the program.
Corrupt profile	Corrupt user profiles can cause a whole assortment of problems with Microsoft Office, and Setup is not excluded. To see if this is the problem, log off the user, and rename the user's profile folder (located by default in C:\Documents and Settings\<username>). Then have the user log back on. The user will get the default system profile. If installation runs successfully, the profile was the problem. Once installation is complete, you can make the user very happy by copying the contents of his original Favorites and My Documents folders in his corrupted profile to his new profile.

If after each of these checks Setup still does not respond, first pat the user on the back and let him know that his system is in overall good shape, and then take a look at the Setup log files.

Using the Setup Log Files

At this point, you have found out quite a bit about what is running right on the system but have still not found the problem. The next ideal place to pinpoint the source of the problem is to look in the Setup log files. Often, they will lead you right to the encountered problem. When Setup is executed, three log files are generated:

- Setup.exe log—saved as "Office XP <Version> Setup(####).txt"

- Windows Installer Office Installation log—saved as "Office XP <Version> Setup(####)_Task(####).txt"

- Windows Installer System Files Update log—saved as "Office XP <Version> Setup(####)_Task(####).txt"

Normally, the System Files Update installation is not required, so it is likely that you will see only two pertinent log files. For example, for an Office XP Professional with FrontPage installation, these two log files would be created in the user's Temp folder (Documents and Settings\<username>\Local Settings\Temp): "Office XP Professional with FrontPage Setup(0001).txt" and "Office XP Professional with FrontPage Setup(0001)_Task(0001).txt".

The generic Setup log file normally does not contain much useful information, since it outlines the install options selected. When an installation problem is encountered, the Task logs are the best places to check. In Figure 6-6, an Office Installation Task log is

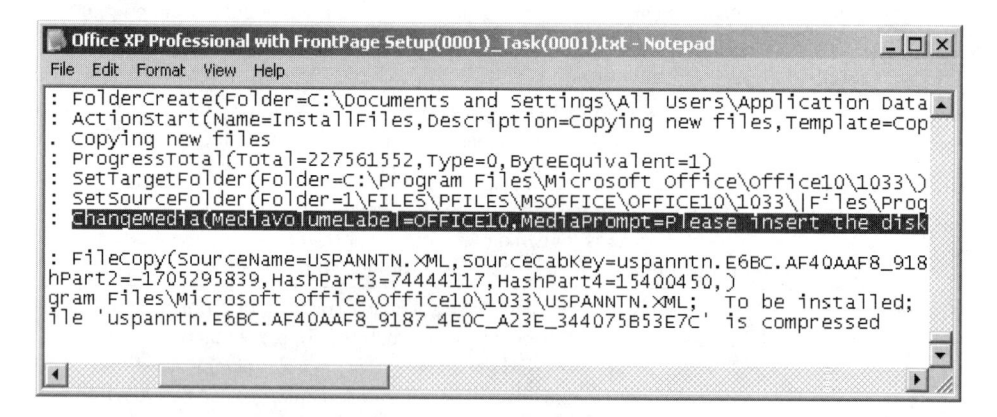

Figure 6-6. Office Installation Windows Installer log

shown. This log file was examined after an Office installation failed while it was beginning to copy files. Note that the highlighted message indicates that the installation no longer believes that the Setup CD is in the CD-ROM drive. It was later determined that the CD-ROM drive had failed. The lesson learned here is that with the help of the Setup logs, you can quickly get pointed toward the direction of the actual problem.

> When reading log files to find the source of a failure, don't read them like a story, starting at the top and working your way to the bottom. Since the logs are written chronologically, start at the bottom to read the most recent information and then work your way to the top. Information regarding the Setup failure is most likely going to be recorded at the end of the log file. If an error code is displayed when Setup terminated, you can find information related to the error by searching the log file for the error code. Events immediately before the code should contain useful information on the problem.

Access Errors and Solutions

When Access databases become corrupted, you have several methods to consider when attempting to recover their data. If the data is not very dynamic, the fastest approach is likely to restore the database from the most recent backup. On the other hand, if quite a bit of new data exists for the database, or if no recent backup exists, you have no alternative but to try to recover its data.

In your moment of misery, having to recover a damaged database under pressure, you can at least take satisfaction in the fact the Access is a very polite application, typically telling you the following before it crashes: "Microsoft Access has encountered a problem and needs to close. We are sorry for the inconvenience." To many, this is probably much more than a mere inconvenience, but at least Access is not laughing at you.

When an error is encountered, normally Access stops responding, and you may or may not receive an error message as a result. Regardless of the error you receive, you should first determine whether the problem is related to the Access application or to the database itself. The easiest way to do this is to restart Access and then open another database. If the problem is only associated with the single database, then you have a corrupted database to deal with, which requires a little more work. On the other hand, if the problem is happening with any database that is opened, consider it your lucky day, since all it means is that the Access installation is damaged. To repair a damaged Access installation, here are your alternatives.

- Open Access and use the Detect and Repair tool.
- Repair the Access installation by running Setup as was described earlier.
- Remove and then completely reinstall Office.

In addition to completing hanging the Access application, corrupted databases often exhibit the following behavior.

- Objects in the database cannot be accessed.
- Some records display *#Deleted*.

Most Access database corruption problems stem from its architecture. As a Microsoft Jet database, it does not use transaction logs, such as are used by enterprise-class databases such as SQL, Exchange, and Oracle.

The main reason for the lack of reliability stems from the fact that when logging is used, database writes can be temporarily stored in a transaction log file and later committed to the database during a period of less database activity. Without the transaction log, having multiple clients read and write data to and from the same database can lead to data corruption. For local databases that are only accessed by a single client, nonlogged databases have proven to be very reliable and thus still are used today for databases such as the DHCP and WINS databases on Windows servers.

If you lost your spot while reading this page, it is probably because the last paragraph put you to sleep. Let's not spend any more time discussing transaction logging and get to troubleshooting. When dealing with recovering a corrupted database, here are your alternatives to fix it.

- Use the Compact and Repair tool.
- Manually repair the corrupted portion of the database.

The next two sections address these recovery techniques.

> Before attempting any recovery method, always make a backup copy of a corrupted database. This way, if one repair method fails, you still have another version of the original database to work with.

Using the Compact and Repair Tool

The quickest means to fix corruption in any Jet database is to compact it, and this rule is no exception with Access databases. When dealing with a corrupted database, you must first verify that it no longer has an .ldb file associated with it.

Consider the .ldb file to be the "hall monitor" for the database. For example, if a user named Juan was currently accessing the "water fountain" record, and another user attempted to write to the same record, Access would check the .ldb file and see that it is Juan's turn, and would politely tell the other user to wait a moment.

With the .ldb issue in mind, here is the general procedure for compacting a database.

Access Errors and Solutions   **185**

1. Make a backup copy of the database.
2. Use Windows Explorer to locate the database file, and delete the associated .ldb version of the file, if it exists.
3. Open Access to compact and repair the database.

For example, if you had an Access database named FixMe.mdb, its .ldb partner would be named FixMe.ldb. Before compacting the database, you would delete FixMe.ldb.

With the preliminary steps out of the way, you can now get to the specifics of using Compact and Repair. To use this utility, follow these steps:

1. Open Access.
2. Click the Tools menu, select Database Utilities, and then click Compact and Repair Database.
3. In the Database to Compact From window, browse to and select the corrupted database file. Then click the Compact button.
4. In the Compact Database Into window, enter a new name for the compacted database and click Save.
5. Try to open the compacted database in Access. If the database corruption is no longer present, rename the compact file to the original database name.

Compact and Repair is generally the most reliable means to eliminate database corruption. If this tool was not successful, avoid playing the lottery today, and instead attempt one of the methods described next.

Manually Repairing a Database

At this point, you are at your last resort in dealing with the corrupted database. This section assumes that the database can at least be opened in Access and that a portion of the database is accessible. If not, your other option is to restore from the most recent backup version of the database file.

The manual repair process differs with the type of problem that needs to be fixed. In this section, you will see how to manually repair these three areas of database corruption:

- Problems running reports
- Problems with macros or modules
- Problems with a database table

Steps to resolve each of these three problem types are listed in the next three sections.

Problems Running Reports

If the problem is associated with a particular report or with one of its controls, the easiest resolution is to take these steps.

1. Delete the report.
2. Restore an earlier version of the database to an alternate location.
3. In Access, open the corrupted database.
4. Click the File menu, select Get External Data, and then click Import.
5. In the Import dialog box, locate and select the restored good database, and then click the Import button.
6. Click the Reports tab in the Import Objects dialog box. Then click the Options button.
7. Select a report and then choose the options needed to ensure that all aspects of the imported report apply to the corrupted database (selecting all options for a particular report is the safest).
8. When finished selecting the report import options (see Figure 6-7), click OK.
9. You should now see the report listed in the corrupted database.
10. Save the database as a new version. If the report functions properly, you have succeeded.

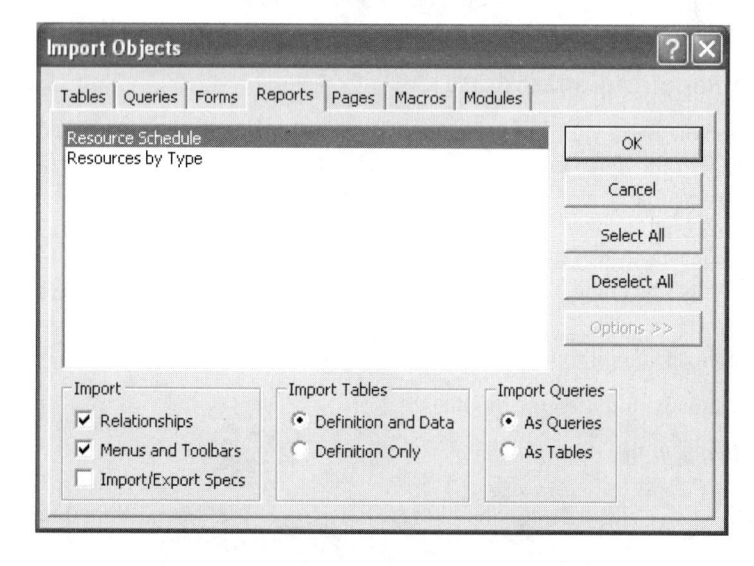

Figure 6-7. Selecting report import options

At this point, your database should be back to normal. If not, as a final alternative, you could start from scratch and re-create the corrupted report.

Problems with Macros or Modules

When the problem is with a macro or module associated with the database, you again have the option of deleting the corrupted macro and importing an earlier version of it from a restored version of the database. These are the steps to perform this process.

1. Delete the macro.
2. Restore an earlier version of the database to an alternate location.
3. In Access, open the corrupted database.
4. Click the File menu, select Get External Data, and then click Import.
5. In the Import dialog box, locate and select the restored good database, and then click the Import button.
6. Click the Macros tab in the Import Objects dialog box. Then click the Options button.
7. Select a macro and then choose the options needed to ensure that all aspects of the imported macro apply to the corrupted database (selecting all options for a particular report is the safest).
8. When finished selecting the macro import options, click OK.
9. You should now see the macro listed in the corrupted database.
10. Save the corrupted database as a new version. If the macro runs normally, your work is finished.

If importing the macro from a backup version of the database failed, or if a backup is not available, then also consider performing one of these actions.

- Create a new macro, and then copy the contents of the corrupted macro to the new one.
- Re-create a new macro from scratch.

Of course, re-creating anything from scratch is never the answer anyone is looking for, but it may be the only answer. Even if importing fails, remember that as long as some backup version exists for the original macro, then you have at the very least a baseline for creating the new macro.

Problems with a Database Table

If a particular database table is not acting as it should, or database corruption resulted from the creation of a new table, you may be able to repair the individual table to restore the database to working order. This is the general procedure for repairing a database containing a corrupted table.

1. Open the database in Access and export the corrupted table to an ASCII (delimited text) file.
2. Delete any relationships associated with the table.
3. Delete the table.
4. Save the database, and then save a copy of the database to an alternate location (backup).
5. Compact and repair the database.
6. Re-create the table as well as any relationships that it had.
7. Open the exported table in Notepad.
8. Remove any out-of-place data from the file, and then resave the file. Note the data that had to be removed, since you will have to manually reenter it later.
9. Import the data from the text file to the new table.
10. Reenter any records that were removed from the exported text file.
11. Save the database.

With this approach, you have systematically removed the corrupt table and replaced it with a new version. Exporting and then reimporting the table's data allowed you to remove the table corruption without losing any of its data.

Excel Errors and Solutions

As with Access databases, Excel spreadsheets sometimes fall victim to data corruption. In addition to recovering from corruption, Excel-related troubleshooting often revolves around locating the source of an errant calculation. This section addresses two common Excel troubleshooting and fault resolution methods:

- Repairing corrupted spreadsheets
- Isolating and correcting formula errors

Repairing Corrupted Spreadsheets

When a user cannot open a spreadsheet, there are three paths that you can take to resolve the problem.

- Restore from backup.
- Repair the spreadsheet.
- Export the contents of the spreadsheet, and then manually re-create it.

Damaged spreadsheets can be repaired using the Excel Open and Repair feature. When you cannot access a spreadsheet, this should be your first course of action in the repair process. To repair the spreadsheet, you need to use the Office Open and Repair feature that was documented earlier in this chapter. With Excel, Open and Repair offers more options than when used in Word, allowing you the choice of repairing a damaged spreadsheet or extracting the data from the spreadsheet. When using Open and Repair, always try the Repair option first. If that option fails, then try to extract the data from the spreadsheet.

To repair a damaged spreadsheet, follow these steps:

1. Open Excel.
2. Click the File menu and then select Open.
3. Browse to and select the corrupted file, then click the Open drop-down menu, and select Open and Repair.
4. When prompted, click the Repair button (see Figure 6-8).

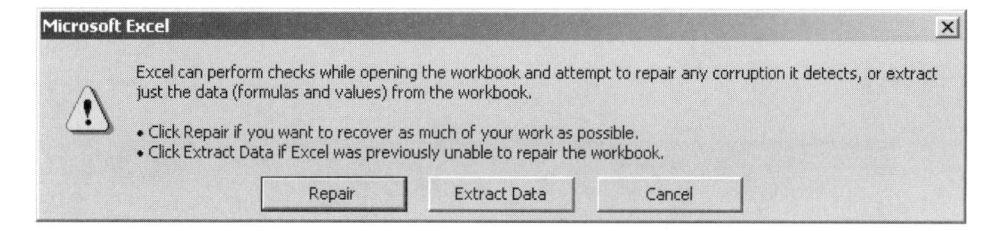

Figure 6-8. Excel Open and Repair options

The repaired spreadsheet should now open in Excel. If it did not open, your final choice is to try to extract the data from the spreadsheet. To do this, follow these steps.

1. Open Excel.
2. Click the File menu and then select Open.
3. Browse to and select the corrupted file, then click the Open drop-down menu, and select Open and Repair.
4. When prompted, click the Extract Data button.

5. You now have two choices (see Figure 6-9), which are to either convert irrecoverable formulas to values or recover as many formulas as possible. If the formulas contained in the spreadsheet are of the most importance, select Recover Formulas; otherwise, select Convert to Values.

6. Excel should now open with some data recovered from the spreadsheet. At this time you will also be prompted with a hyperlink to the repair log file, as shown in Figure 6-10. Click the hyperlink to view the log file, and then close the Repair dialog box.

Unfortunately, when extracting data, you are only left with a plain spreadsheet containing the extracted data. Any graphics or formatting that was used in the original spreadsheet is lost.

Now that you have seen the ways to recover from corruption in Excel spreadsheets, next you will see how to overcome errors when using and manipulating formulas.

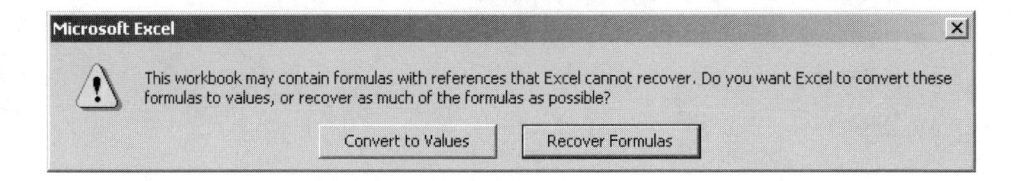

Figure 6-9. Open and Repair Extract Data options

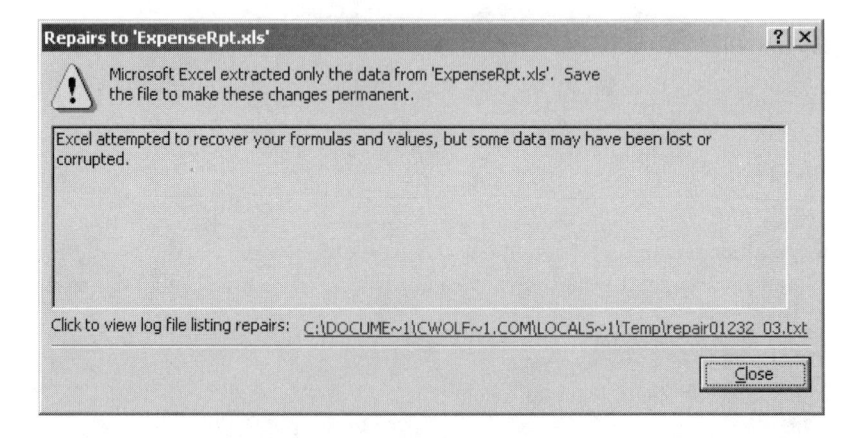

Figure 6-10. Repair log prompt

Isolating and Resolving Formula Errors

There are several available auditing tools that allow you to diagnose the cause of a problematic formula. Invalid formulas are generally easy to spot, since an error code is displayed in the formula's cell. The common Excel error codes are described in Table 6-3.

Table 6-3. Excel Cell Error Codes

Error	Related Problem(s)
#####	• Column is not wide enough.
	• Time or date has a negative value.
#DIV/0!	• Number is divided by zero.
	• Formula references a blank cell.
#N/A	• Value referenced by the formula is not available.
	• Data is missing.
	• Argument in an array formula is used that does not have the same amount of rows and columns as the range that contains the array formula.
#NAME?	• Text used in the formula is unrecognized.
	• Name is misspelled.
	• Another sheet is referenced that is not in quotes.
	• Colon in a range reference is missing.
	• Function that is part of the Analysis Toolpak (add-in) is used without the add-in loaded.
#NULL!	• Incorrect range operator is used.
	• Ranges specified in a range operator do not intersect.
#NUM!	• Invalid numeric values are used in a formula or function.
#REF!	• Formula or function references an invalid cell.
	• Cell referenced by other formulas was deleted.
	• Link exists to a system or program that is not available.
#VALUE!	Incorrect argument or operand used (number expected, letter provided).

Sometimes, the source of an error is very obvious. For example, a column may be too small to represent a numerical value, or you may quickly spot a typographical error in a formula. Other times, however, finding the source of an error may be a bit more challenging. When you are stumped as to the source of an error, Excel provides the following tools to assist you:

- *Trace Precedents*—Shows formulas referenced by the selected formula
- *Trace Dependents*—Shows formulas that require the output of the selected formula

- *Trace Error*—Allows you to step through cell relationships to find the source of an error

- *Evaluate Formula*—Shows the progress of the outcome of a formula as it is calculated, allowing you to see the point in a formula where the error begins (like step-by-step confirmation at startup)

Each of these troubleshooting tools can be accessed by clicking the Tools menu and then selecting Formula Auditing and the desired tool. Each of these tools allows you to visually detect the source of a formula problem, letting you quickly get to its source.

Outlook Errors and Solutions

Once configured properly, Outlook is generally maintenance free. During the initial configuration or after a reinstallation, Outlook problems are most frequently reported. Unlike other Office applications, many external factors—such as network configuration, mail server configuration, and security configuration—can all contribute to the inability of a user to access his or her mailbox. In this section, you will see how to check for a correct Outlook configuration and how to diagnose a problem when one is encountered.

Testing Outlook Configuration

Outlook e-mail configuration can be tested during the initial mailbox setup (the first time Outlook is run) or from within Outlook. You can test the mail configuration during setup by clicking the Test Account Settings button in the E-mail Accounts dialog box (see Figure 6-11). You will then see the test results in the Test Account Settings dialog box, as shown in Figure 6-12. If all tests pass, you will see a green check next to each test. Failed tests are marked by a red X, and their related error messages are displayed under the Errors tab.

For accounts that are already created, you can access the mail account test from within Outlook. To do this, follow these steps.

1. From Outlook, click the Tools menu and select E-mail Accounts.

2. Select View or Change Existing E-mail Accounts and click Next.

3. Select the mail account to test, and click the Change button.

4. Now click the Test Account Settings button.

5. If all tests pass, close the E-mail Accounts dialog box; otherwise, resolve the configuration problem and then click the Test Account Settings button to verify that the configuration change resolved the problem.

The account settings test tells you that there is a problem but does not offer any advice on resolving it. If you're familiar with the typical department meeting environment,

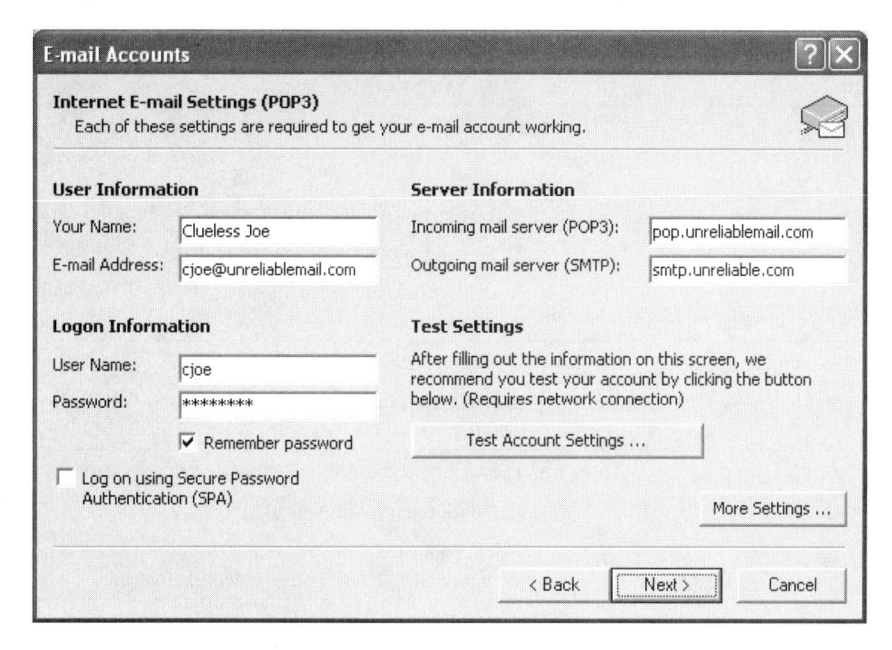

Figure 6-11. Testing e-mail account settings

Figure 6-12. E-mail account test results

this is not much different from the average employee issuing a complaint but providing no alternative. If you don't get upset with your coworkers for acting this way, then don't get mad at Outlook either! At least it's telling you something.

Now that you know a problem exists, you need to identify it in order to correct it. Table 6-4 lists components to check based on the test that failed.

Table 6-4. Typical Problems for Failed Mail Setup Tests

Failed Test	Possible Problem(s)
Establish network connection	• TCP/IP is not installed or is improperly configured. • An Internet connection is not present. • TCP/IP is not listed first in the network binding order.
Find outgoing mail server	• The wrong server name was provided. • A name resolution problem exists (DNS, WINS, Hosts, LMHosts).
Find incoming mail server	• The wrong server name was provided. • A name resolution problem exists (DNS, WINS, Hosts, LMHosts).
Log on to incoming mail server	• The wrong account was provided or does not exist. • The wrong password was used. • The account was entered wrong (you may need to use the entire SMTP address: user@domain.com).
Send test e-mail message	The mail server requires user authentication to send the message, and user credentials were not provided. Provide credentials for the outgoing server by following these steps. 1. In the E-mail Accounts dialog box, click the More Settings button. 2. Click the Outgoing Server tab in the Internet E-mail Settings dialog box. 3. Check the My Outgoing Sever Requires Authentication box, and then elect to use the same settings as the incoming server or manually enter the account information.

As you can see, several different failures can interrupt mail service. Always remember to start from the top and work to the bottom. So, if both the "Find outgoing..." and "Find incoming mail server" tests fail, verify that name resolution is working by pinging the POP and SMTP (or Exchange) servers by fully qualified domain name. If the ping fails, then try to ping by IP address. If pinging by IP address fails, then you have a network connectivity or TCP/IP configuration (subnet) problem. If the IP address ping passed, then the problem is with the name resolution used. Name resolution can be fixed by verifying that the user has the proper name servers listed in her system's TCP/IP properties. After correcting any DNS issue, remember to run `ipconfig /flushdns` on the user's system to clear the contents of its DNS resolver cache; otherwise, the problem will persist.

> Some mail servers may be configured to ignore the Outlook test message, so if all other tests pass and the "Send test e-mail message" test fails, there may be nothing wrong with the mail configuration. Save the configuration, and then send a message from the account to itself. If the mail is sent and received, the account is set up properly.

PowerPoint Errors and Solutions

Corrupted PowerPoint presentations are the most common problem encountered by users running PowerPoint. When corruption is encountered, the user is presented with one of the following symptoms or error messages:

- "Part of the file is missing"
- "PowerPoint cannot open the type of file represented by ..."
- "This is not a PowerPoint presentation"

These errors all point directly to the PowerPoint presentation being accessed by the user, but some error messages may not be as obvious, including:

- General Protection Fault
- Illegal instruction
- Invalid page fault
- Low system resources
- Out of memory

As you can see, many PowerPoint presentation errors may be masked as other errors, which is again why the user interview is so important. If the problem occurred when a presentation file was being opened, you can try to duplicate the error by having the user open the same and subsequently different presentation files. If the errors are only displayed when a particular file is opened, then you can assume that the cause of the error is file corruption. When this occurs, the easiest solution is often to restore the file from a known good backup. If a backup does not exist, or if the backup version is corrupted as well, then you will have a little more work to do.

First, you need to determine the cause of the problem before weighing other solutions. To arrive at the cause, ask the user each of the following questions, until you get a "Yes" answer.

- Did the problem occur during or after the time something was added to the presentation?
- Does the problem occur when a specific file is opened?
- Does the problem occur when any file is opened?

When the Problem Resulted from a Modification to the Presentation

The type of problem may be the result of the user attempting to copy and paste a new page or object into the presentation. If the problem only exists when accessing a particular slide, you have several choices.

- Delete and then manually re-create the slide.
- Copy all slides in the presentation, and paste them into a new presentation.
- Copy portions of the corrupted slide to a new slide, and then delete the corrupted slide.

Regardless of which action you take to resolve the corruption problem, you should also consider saving the presentation file as a new version, just in case the existing version is on the brink of corruption. When an entire presentation file becomes corrupted, the corrective action involved in resolving the problem is much more detailed than corruption in a single slide and is discussed next.

When the Problem Resulted from a Specific File Being Opened

Problems associated with a single file are easily identified, since you can quickly open a different file with the PowerPoint application to verify the limitation of the problem. As long as all other files open without incident, you are only concerned with repairing a single file, as opposed to correcting a corrupt PowerPoint installation.

There are several ways to go about extracting useful data from a corrupt presentation file, each of which is described in the next three sections. If none of these solutions can save the corrupted presentation, then your last alternative is to restore an earlier version of the presentation from the most recent backup.

Open Presentation Version in Temp Folder

AutoRecover versions are saved in the Temp folder located with the user's profile. By default, the Temp folder resides in the Documents and Settings\<Username>\Local Settings directory. Presentation files saved in this folder begin with the characters PPT followed by four numbers and have the .tmp extension.

The easiest way to locate these files on a user's XP system is to follow these steps.

1. Click Start and then select Search.
2. Select All Files and Folders.
3. Now click More Advanced Options and select the Search Hidden Files and Folders checkbox.
4. In the All or Part of the File Name field, enter `PPT*.tmp` as the search criteria, select to look in the C drive, and then click the Search button.

5. All autosaved PowerPoint files should now appear in the right pane of the Search Results window. Click the Date Modified column to sort the files by date, which should make it easier for you to spot the needed file.

6. Once you locate a file, click its name once, and then click it again. You should now be able to rename the file. Rename the file anything you want, but make sure to change its extension to .ppt.

7. Double-click the file to attempt to open it.

Even after you locate the autosaved file, there are no guarantees that PowerPoint can even open it. If the file opens and its data is intact, your work is finished. Otherwise, you can either throw in the towel here and restore from backup or attempt one of the next two methods shown in this section to recover data from the original file.

Extract Corrupted Slides

Another method for recovering data from a corrupted PowerPoint presentation file is to open a new blank presentation and attempt to extract the slides from the corrupted presentation file. This can be done by performing these steps.

1. Open PowerPoint, click the Insert menu, and then select Slides from Files.

2. In the Slide Finder dialog box, click the Browse button and locate the corrupted file. Then click Open in the Browse window.

3. You should now see the presentation file displayed in the File field and its slides displayed in the Select Slides portion of the window. If no slides are displayed, this method will not work for you, and you should move on to the third method, described in the next section.

4. Click the Select All button to import all slides, or use the Ctrl key and your mouse to select the slides that you would like to import. If work on the last slide is the suspected cause of the corruption, then select all slides but the last. When finished selecting the slides to import, check the Keep Source Formatting checkbox, and then click the Insert button (see Figure 6-13).

5. With the slides imported into the new presentation, you can now delete the first slide (which should be blank) and then save the new presentation.

With your extraction operation complete, you can now exhale, especially if you were working without a safety net and had no available backup to fall back on.

Apply Corrupted Presentation as a Template

If both the first two methods failed, your last hope is to recover the slide master. If the corrupted presentation was the only file that used an original important master slide

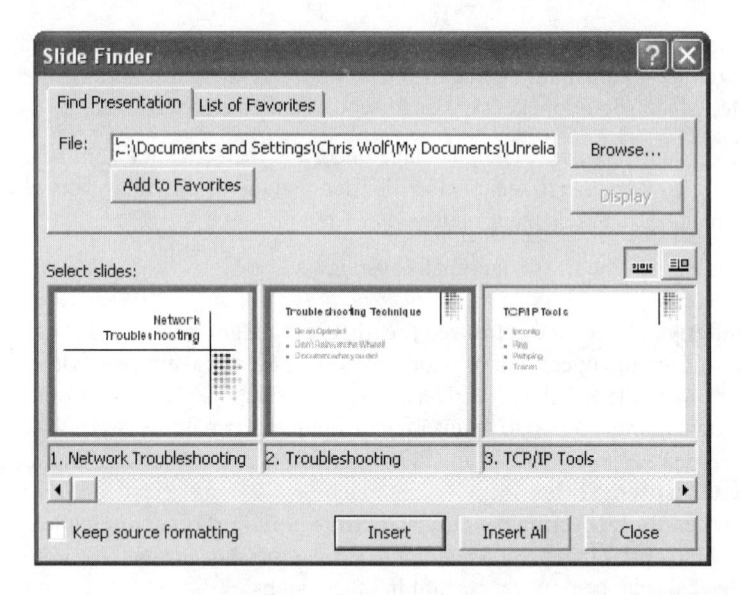

Figure 6-13. Importing slides using the Slide Finder dialog box

template, then you can use this method to attempt to recover the master. To do this, follow these steps.

1. Open PowerPoint, click the Format menu, and then select Slide Design.
2. You should now see the Slide Design window displayed on the right side of the PowerPoint window. At the bottom of the Slide Design window, click Browse.
3. Browse to and select the corrupted presentation file and then click Apply.
4. The slide master from the corrupted presentation replaces the slide master for the new presentation.

If you could not recover any potion of the corrupted file, then your last choice is to turn to your trusty backup and restore the last backed-up version of the file, or you can kindly instruct the user to start all over, declaring the corrupted presentation file deceased and alerting the user that it will be given a proper burial.

When the Problem Resulted from Any File Being Opened

If you cannot open any PowerPoint files, then pump your fist in victory because this is the easiest PowerPoint problem to correct. After all, the worst scenario that you are faced with when no files can open in PowerPoint is to reinstall Office from scratch.

When the PowerPoint installation is damaged, you can manually initiate a Detect and Repair process to correct the problem, or you can rerun Setup to repair the application. Regardless of how you perform the repair or reinstallation, the user's Office application will be restored and no presentation data will be lost.

Word Errors and Solutions

Word is arguably the most powerful and certainly the most diverse Office application. Due to its diversity, however, it is also the most problematic. This is not because of poor design or even a lack of reliability but because of the fact that so many other Office components can be integrated into it, including spreadsheets, graphics, and voice. Some compare the architecture of Word to how newer expensive cars are built. When you buy a new car with "power everything," you are buying a lot more items that have the potential to break. The same can be said of Word, with the only difference being that your "options" were already chosen for you.

This portion of the chapter is divided into two sections:

- Resolving Problems with the Support.dot Troubleshooting Template
- General Word Troubleshooting

Due to the frequent necessity for support personnel to troubleshoot Word problems, Microsoft created a troubleshooting template for it. This first part of this section shows you how to install and use the template. Following the template section, you will then see how to approach and resolve the most common Word problems.

Resolving Problems with the Support.dot Troubleshooting Template

Sometimes problems can be quickly spotted and resolved, while others are more complex. To aid in solving Word problems, Microsoft has included several macros in the Support.dot template. There are three macros included with the template, which are described in Table 6-5.

Table 6-5. Troubleshooting Template Macros

Macro	Use
AutoCorrect Backup	Allows you to back up the AutoCorrect list on one system and then use the macro on another system to restore it.
Registry Options	Provides an easy means to modify Word Registry settings.
Troubleshoot Utility	Provides a means to troubleshoot and repair Word startup problems.

If you performed a complete installation of Microsoft Word, the template is already installed on the user's system. If not, you need to manually install the template.

Installing the Troubleshooting Template

Since the template is not installed by default, odds are that you will have to manually install it on most systems. For mass deployment, the best choice is to deploy the Office update using a group policy. Regardless of how you deploy the template, the method for installing it on a user's system or test system is still the same.

To install the troubleshooting template, follow these steps.

1. Close Microsoft Word and all Office applications.

2. From the Control Panel, double-click the Add/Remove Programs icon.

3. Select the Microsoft Office installation and then click the Change button.

4. Select Add or Remove Features and click Next.

5. In the Features to Install field, expand the Microsoft Word for Windows object and then expand the Wizards and Templates object.

6. Now select the More Templates and Macros icon and select Run All from My Computer.

7. Finally, click the Update button to revise the Microsoft Word installation.

Once the template is installed, you can put it to use.

Using the Troubleshooting Template

To use the troubleshooting template, you must first open Word in Safe Mode. To do this, click Start > Run, type `winword.exe /a`, and press Enter. Once Word has started, follow these steps to open the template.

1. Click the File menu and select Open.

2. In the Open dialog box, click the Files of Type field and select Document Templates.

3. Now click the Look In field and browse to the following folder: <Office installation drive>\Program Files\Microsoft Office\Office 10\Macros.

4. You should now see the Support.dot template file. Click the file and then click Open.

5. If you receive a security warning, click the "Always trust macros from this source" checkbox and then click Enable Macros.

Once the template has opened, you are ready to troubleshoot.

Using the Troubleshoot Utility

The Troubleshoot Utility is used to solve Word startup problems. This macro accomplishes this by allowing you to revert particular files and startup settings to their default values. One of the problems with restoring settings to their default values is that any custom configuration data set up by the user is lost. With this template, only damaged data is lost. For example, if you thought that the default startup template, Normal.dot, was the source of the problem, you could test your theory by replacing this file with the default. If your repair did not help, then you could restore the previous version of the template, taking the Word installation right back to the point where it was when you first started troubleshooting.

With this utility, you can systematically replace Word startup files one at a time until you find which one is bad. At the end, only the problem files will be replaced and all others will be in their user-specific configuration. If you're still a little confused about how and when to use this tool, you must first understand the files that are loaded when Word starts, which are

1. Data Registry key
2. Normal.dot global template
3. Add-ins and templates
4. COM add-ins
5. Options Registry key

If any of these components are corrupted, Word is not likely to start. When you run `winword.exe /a`, none of these files are loaded. If Word starts with the `/a` switch but doesn't start without it, then the problem is definitely in one of the five configuration files, and you should resolve the problem by running the Troubleshoot Utility. If Word still does not start with the `/a` switch, then you should repair the Word installation using Detect and Repair or by running Office Setup.

Determining the startup file that is the cause of the corruption requires a systematic approach. The easiest way to find the problem is to disable one startup file at a time until the problem does not return. To incorporate this process to find a faulty startup file, follow these steps.

1. As was described earlier in this section, start Word in Safe Mode (`winword.exe /a`) and open the Support.dot template.
2. In the Support.dot template, click the Troubleshoot Utility button.
3. As shown in Figure 6-14, select Data Registry Key in the Select an Item field and then click Delete.
4. When prompted about the location of the backup Registry key, click OK.
5. Click Close to exit the Troubleshoot Utility.
6. Close Word.
7. Start Word normally

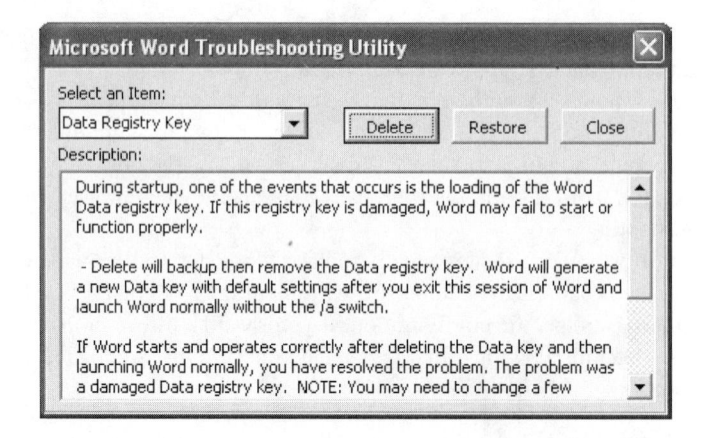

Figure 6-14. Using the Troubleshoot Utility to repair Word

If Word starts normally, the problem is fixed. If not, you need to restore the old Registry settings and then check to see if the Normal.dot template is causing the problem. This involves performing the following steps.

1. Close Word.

2. Run `winword.exe /a` to start Word in Safe Mode. Then open the Support.dot template.

3. In the Support.dot template, click the Troubleshoot Utility button.

4. Select Data Registry Key in the Select an Item field and click the Restore button.

5. When prompted that the Registry key restoration was successful, click OK.

6. Now select Normal.dot Global Template in the Select an Item field and click Rename. When prompted with the new name for the template, click OK.

7. Click Close to exit the Troubleshoot Utility.

8. Close Word.

9. Start Word normally.

If Word starts normally, your work is now finished; if not, you now know that the Normal.dot template file is fine, and it's on to check number 3.

1. Close Word.

2. Run `winword.exe /a` to start Word in Safe Mode. Then open the Support.dot template.

3. In the Support.dot template, click the Troubleshoot Utility button.

4. Select Normal.dot Global Template in the Select an Item field and click the Restore button.

5. When prompted that the backup template was copied over the default template, click OK.

6. Now select Word Startup Folder Add-ins in the Select an Item field and click Rename. When prompted with the new name for the Add-ins, click OK.

7. Click Close to exit the Troubleshoot Utility.

8. Close Word.

Start Word normally. If Word does not start, you can conclude that the Add-ins were not corrupt and can proceed to the fourth check.

1. Close Word.

2. Run `winword.exe /a` to start Word in Safe Mode. Then open the Support.dot template.

3. In the Support.dot template, click the Troubleshoot Utility button.

4. Select Word Startup Folder Add-ins in the Select an Item field and click the Restore button.

5. When prompted that the Add-ins were restored successfully, click OK.

6. Now select COM Add-ins Registry Key in the Select an Item field and click Delete. When prompted that the Registry key has been deleted, click OK.

7. Click Close to exit the Troubleshoot Utility.

8. Close Word.

Again you need to attempt to start Word normally. If Word does not start, and you are sure that it would initially start with the /a switch, then there is only one other potential problem. To rid yourself of this problem, follow these steps.

1. Close Word.

2. Run `winword.exe /a` to start Word in Safe Mode. Then open the Support.dot template.

3. In the Support.dot template, click the Troubleshoot Utility button.

4. Select COM Add-ins Registry Key in the Select an Item field and click the Restore button.

5. When prompted that the Registry key restoration was successful, click OK.

6. Now select Options Registry Key in the Select an Item field and click Delete. When prompted that the Registry key has been deleted, click OK.

7. Click Close to exit the Troubleshoot Utility.

8. Close Word.

For the last time, start Word normally. You should see that at this point Word starts without incident. As you have witnessed, not only is this tool terrific in isolating and fixing a Word problem, but it also employs a systematic "textbook" approach to troubleshooting.

Using Registry Options

Suppose that a Registry problem has caused Word to stop responding, but you don't want to completely delete the Word Registry keys, leaving you with the default settings. If you want to manually attempt to patch the Word Registry values, you can do so with the Registry Options tool. Not only does this tool make modifying the Word Registry parameters easy, but it also explains the purpose of each Registry value to you, making it difficult to make an editing mistake.

To use this tool, follow these steps.

1. Start Word normally and then open the Support.dot template.

2. In the Support.dot template, click the Registry Options button.

3. Now you can select the option you plan to modify and view a description of it at the bottom of the Set Registry Options dialog box.

4. If needed, change the data for the option in the Setting field and click Change (see Figure 6-15).

5. When finished modifying the Word Registry settings, click close and exit the Registry Options tool.

When you want to quickly modify a user's custom Word settings, nothing is faster than the Registry Options tool. The last tool offered by the Support.dot template is AutoCorrect Backup.

Using AutoCorrect Backup

If you would like to take a user's custom AutoCorrect settings and apply them to another user's profile, then the AutoCorrect Backup utility is the perfect tool for the job. Due to its limited role, this is the least frequently used of the Support.dot tools, but is nonetheless valuable.

To export AutoCorrect settings with this tool, follow these steps.

1. Start Word normally and then open the Support.dot template.

2. In the Support.dot template, click the AutoCorrect Backup button.

3. In the AutoCorrect Utility dialog box, click the Backup button.

4. Select a name and location for the backup file in the Save As dialog box and click Save.

5. Click Cancel to close the AutoCorrect Utility dialog box.

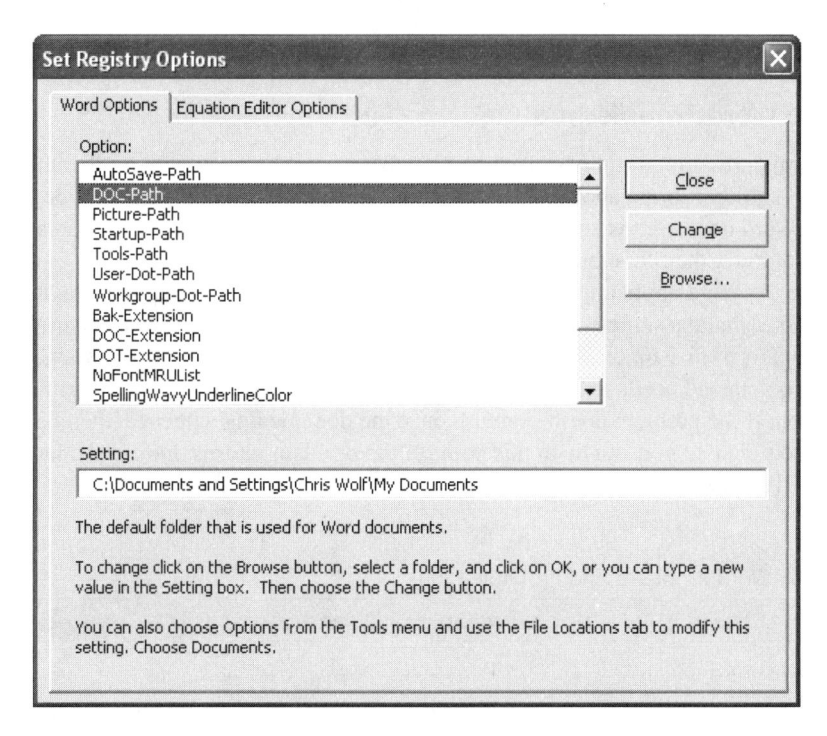

Figure 6-15. Modifying Word Registry values with the Registry Options tool

Once the AutoCorrect configuration has been saved to the network or to portable media, you can import the configuration for another user's profile. Have the user log on, and then follow these steps.

1. Start Word normally and then open the Support.dot template.

2. In the Support.dot template, click the AutoCorrect Backup button.

3. In the AutoCorrect Utility dialog box, click the Restore button.

4. When prompted that this will replace the current AutoCorrect entries, click Yes.

5. Browse to and select the AutoCorrect backup file to import and click Open.

6. When prompted that the restore is complete, click OK.

7. Click Cancel to close the AutoCorrect Utility dialog box.

8. Close the Support.dot template.

Now that you have seen the value of Support.dot, the all-around troubleshooting tool, let's look at how to solve other Word problems that cannot be corrected with Support.dot.

General Word Troubleshooting

For general corruption of the Word application that cannot be fixed with the Troubleshoot Utility, don't forget about using Detect and Repair to correct the application problem. If a Word document is corrupted and will not open, then try to use the Open and Repair tool to fix the file; otherwise, you need to restore it from backup.

Since the Word application's scope extends far beyond the Word application itself, you may find that the source of a Word problem has little to do with Word. When Word fails and starts to give up on you, or you receive the error "Microsoft Word has encountered a problem and needs to close," you should first close Word and then restart the application. If the problem does not return once the document is reopened, there is little troubleshooting that you can do at this point. If the problem returns, look to the faults and related problems listed in Table 6-6 as your means to resuscitate Word.

Table 6-6. Word Problems and Probable Faults

Problem (Error)	Probable Faults and Solutions
Error occurs when printing.	• Bad printer driver.
	• Download an updated or correct printer driver from the printer manufacturer. If one does not exist, it's time to upgrade the printer.
Error occurs while typing or moving the mouse (mouse pointer skips across the screen).	• Bad video driver.
	• Download an updated or correct video driver.
	• Not enough memory—add RAM.
Error occurs while typing text into a document.	• Corrupt user dictionary.
	• Corrupt AutoCorrect file.
	• Corrupt fonts.
	• Corrupt spelling and grammar files.

For problems occurring while the user is typing text, you have to determine which of four likely faults is the source. Remember that Word checks your work as you're typing, so when errors occur at this time, the cause of the problem is usually related to one of the files used while Word autochecks your work. When these types of errors occur, the easiest approach to resolving them is to systematically replace the files involved until the problem disappears. In the next four sections, we begin with replacing the dictionary and finish with replacing the spelling and grammar files.

Replacing Corrupt User Dictionaries

When Word stops responding while the user is editing a document, begin by closing Word and all other Office programs, and then follow these steps to replace the dictionary.

1. Click Start and then select Search.

2. Select All Files and Folders, then scroll down, and select More Advanced Options.

3. Check the Search Hidden Files and Folders box.

4. Scroll back up and enter `*.dic` in the All or Part of the File Name field, make sure that Local Hard Drives is selected in the Look In field, and then click Search.

5. The search should return a list of Custom.dic files. Locate the file that resides in the profile folder for the user having the problem, right-click the file, and select Rename.

6. Enter a new name for the file, such as Custombak.dic, and press Enter.

7. Restart Word and try to edit the document. If the problem disappears, your work is finished. If not, the custom dictionary file was not corrupted, so you can repeat steps 1–5 to find the .dic files. This time, delete the new Custom.dic file in the user's profile and rename the backup version back to Custom.dic.

If replacing the user's custom dictionary file did not solve the problem, your next option is to try to replace the AutoCorrect file.

Replacing Corrupt AutoCorrect Files

To replace a user's AutoCorrect file, close Word and all Office applications, and then follow these steps.

1. Click Start and then select Search.

2. Select All Files and Folders, then scroll down, and select More Advanced Options.

3. Check the Search Hidden Files and Folders box.

4. Scroll back up and enter `*.acl` in the All or Part of the File Name field, make sure that Local Hard Drives is selected in the Look In field, and then click Search.

5. The search should return a list of MSO###.acl files (for example, MSO1033.acl). Locate the file that resides in the profile folder for the user having the problem, right-click the file, and select Rename.

6. Enter a new name for the file, such as MSO1033bak.acl, and press Enter.

7. Restart Word and try to edit the document. If the problem disappears, your work is finished. If not, the AutoCorrect file was not corrupted, so you can repeat steps 1–5 to find the .acl files. This time, delete the new MSO####.acl file in the user's profile and rename the backup version back to its original name, such as MSO1033.acl. If you did not try to access the AutoCorrect Options from the Word Tools menu, a new .acl file might not have been created. If this is the case, just rename the .bak version of the file back to its original name.

Some Microsoft documentation states that you should not rename any MSO####.acl files. This is incorrect. In fact, there is normally only one MSO####.acl file in each user's profile, so it is the only .acl file that you would have a choice to rename to replace a corrupt AutoCorrect file.

Replacing Corrupt Fonts

If the AutoCorrect file was not the source of the Word problem, then your next option is to assume that the font being used is corrupt and replace it. Unlike the previous two problems, a corrupt font affects all users running Word on the system, not just a single user. Fonts are installed on computers and are not unique to users using the computer. When a font is suspected as the fault, you should first make a list of the fonts used in the document and then replace the fonts one at a time until the problem disappears. To replace a corrupt font, follow these steps.

1. Open the Control Panel and double-click the Fonts icon.

2. Find the suspect font, and then drag and drop it onto the Desktop. This removes it from the installed fonts without deleting it.

3. Open Word. Since the font is no longer installed, it is replaced in the document with another font. If the problem is resolved, then run Detect and Repair to repair the Office installation. The font will be replaced during this process, and you can delete the instance of the font that appears on the desktop.

4. If the problem still exists, then reopen the Fonts folder in the Control Panel and drag the font that was moved to the Desktop back to the Fonts folder. Next, move another font contained in the document to the Desktop, and repeat step 3 to see if the problem is resolved.

If replacing the suspected corrupted font did not resolve the problem, your last option is to replace corrupt spelling or grammar files, since by default they are also queried while a user is editing a document.

Replacing Corrupt Spelling and Grammar Files

To replace corrupt spelling and grammar files, follow these steps.

1. Open Word, click the Tools menu, and select Options.

2. Click the Spelling and Grammar tab in the Options dialog box.

3. Now clear the Check Spelling as You Type and Check Grammar as You Type checkboxes and click OK.

If the problem goes away after you disable the spelling and grammar checking tools, then you can fix the corruption by running Detect and Repair.

Summary

As you have witnessed, manually diagnosing and repairing Office corruption problems is a lengthy process. When the problem is associated with a single user, you may want to simply rename the user's profile folder. To do this, log the user off, rename the user's folder in the Documents and Settings folder, and then have the user log back on. If the problem disappears, then it was embedded in the user's profile. To make the user happy, you can copy his Favorites and My Documents folder contents into his new profile and copy his Outlook.pst file into his new profile, if e-mail is stored locally. While there is always a way to identify the exact cause of a problem, it doesn't always make the most business sense.

Detect and Repair often allows you to quickly repair Office application problems, and when document corruption rears its ugly head, don't forget about the Open and Repair tools available in Word and Excel. When diagnosing and repairing Office problems, remember to use the right tool for the job and use the right process when troubleshooting. You cannot go wrong with the systematic "checklist" approach for eliminating what's right. Eventually, you will find the fault. When dealing with Office corruption, always remember to refrain from wanting to flex your troubleshooting muscle when diagnosing a problem. All too often, the 30 minutes of work lost by the user results in two or more hours of diagnosis and repair. If a backup exists for a corrupted file, and only noncritical data that can easily be replaced will be lost, use the backup. If you really want to practice troubleshooting in a non-mission-critical situation, remember "That's what friends and family are for!"

> A great way to prevent corruption problems with Office documents from ruining everyone's day is to educate users to get in the habit of saving documents daily using the Save As feature instead of simply using Save. For daily versions, the user could use Save As, then enter the regular name of the file, followed by a hyphen and then the name of the day. This way, the most work that will ever be lost due to corruption will be that of a single day.

7
Disk Subsystems

With disks and memory, quite a bit can go wrong, but the good news is that normally a problem can be pinpointed very quickly. Aside from hardware failures and disk corruption giving you headaches, the threat of a virus must always be considered as well. The core of system operation revolves around its data, which normally resides on a hard disk. Whether or not you have fault-tolerant disks in place on your servers, odds are that you cannot afford to have such protection on all of your managed workstations. Disk failures are inevitable. This chapter will help you to quickly diagnose the source of a disk failure and in turn repair the problem.

In addition to describing the multitude of disk management and diagnostic tools at your disposal, this chapter also shows you the most common disk errors and faults, and proven procedures for resolving them.

Windows Server 2003/XP Disk Architecture 101

Before jumping headfirst into the pool of disk troubleshooting, let's first test the water. Resolving faults and repairing disk-related problems does require some knowledge of the basics. In this section, you will not read the dry information on the guts of hard disks (a proven tranquilizer for IT professionals). Instead, this section quickly reviews Microsoft disk terminology, including

- Basic and dynamic disks
- Master Boot Record
- Boot sector
- boot.ini file
- Master File Table
- GPT disks

Basic and Dynamic Disks

Basic disks are the disk type that you have come to know and love when working with Microsoft products. Basic disks are compatible with all Microsoft operating systems and are divided into logical partitions. Dynamic disks, on the other hand, are only compatible with post–Windows 2000 operating systems and are divided into volumes.

While basic disks are limited in functionality, dynamic disks offer a great deal of flexibility in their configuration options. With dynamic disks, you can configure the following software-based disk solutions.

- *Spanned volume*—A single volume that spans two or more physical disks, with data written to the first disk until it is full and then written to the next disk.

- *Striped volume (RAID 0)*—Data stored on two or more physical disks, with data reads and writes going to all disks simultaneously.

- *Mirrored volume (RAID 1)*—Data stored on two or more disks that mirror each other for fault tolerance. If one disk fails, all data can be recovered from the second disk.

- *Striped volume with parity (RAID 5)*—Data stored on three or more physical disks, with data reads and writes going to all disks simultaneously. Unlike RAID 0, RAID 5 volumes can withstand the loss of a single disk.

Whenever possible, you should elect to invest in a hardware RAID solution, which offers better performance and recoverability. Since this reference is dedicated to software troubleshooting, this chapter addresses diagnosing and recovering basic and dynamic disks. As far as RAID configurations are concerned, you will see in this chapter how to recover failed dynamic disks. For hardware RAID troubleshooting and recovery procedures, you should be able to find plenty of information from your systems' RAID controller vendors.

While you can convert a basic disk to a dynamic disk, you cannot convert dynamic disks to basic disks. Once you make a disk dynamic, reverting it to a basic disk requires you to back up its data, delete the disk's volumes, convert it to a basic disk, and then restore the original data.

Master Boot Record

The Master Boot Record (MBR) is an entry located on the first sector on the first partition of a hard disk that contains information on its partition structure and a small amount of executable code that is loaded into RAM at startup. A portion of the executable code contained in the MBR is the location of the boot sector. The fact that the MBR contains the initial information for your system to start makes it a very vulnerable target. A corrupt MBR can easily shut down a system, and thus diagnosing it and repairing the MBR is an important aspect of disk subsystem troubleshooting.

Boot Sector

The boot sector is located on the next sector in the first partition, or on the first sector of subsequent disk partitions. The boot sector contains information on how the computer can "boot" the operating system, and thus is just as critical as the MBR in terms of system vulnerability. On Windows systems, the boot sector locates information on operating systems by reading the boot.ini file, which is covered next.

The boot.ini File

The boot.ini file is a file located on a computer's system partition that contains information on where to find operating systems on the boot partitions. If you're scratching your head and wondering about a boot file on a system partition, you're not alone. Believe it or not, this really is not analogous to cars driving on parkways and parking on driveways.

Here's why. Your computer starts by reading data on its system partition because it is looking for information on where to find operating systems. The boot.ini file that is on the system partition contains that information. When your computer boots up, it is loading an operating system. Since operating systems are needed to boot, they are found on the boot partition. Of course, if your operating system is installed on the C drive, then your boot and system partitions are actually on the same partition, and thus you have absolutely nothing to ponder!

The most important information found in boot.ini files are Advanced RISC (Reduced Instruction Set) Computing (ARC) paths. The ARC paths tell your system where to find operating systems. ARC paths only cause confusion when they need to be manually edited, and unfortunately these times are often when a system has crashed and you need to recover as quickly as possible. One of the most frequent needs to edit an ARC path comes when the primary drive in a software mirror fails. When this happens, the ARC path in the boot.ini must be edited to tell the computer that the operating system must be loaded from the second disk in the mirror and not the first. With hardware mirroring, this problem does not occur, because both disks in the mirror are seen by the system software as a single physical disk.

Figure 7-1 shows a typical boot.ini file. In this example, the file references two operating systems, one for test and the other for production. What is not indicated in the file is that the second OS, "Windows Server 2003 Enterprise Edition (production)," is mirrored with a second physical disk for fault tolerance. If the disk containing the second OS fails, you need a way to tell the system to boot from the disk that the second operating system is mirrored with. This means that you have to edit the boot.ini file.

In the example, assume that the system contains four SCSI disks, with OS 1 on disk 1 (SCSI ID 0), and OS 2 mirrored on disk 2 (SCSI ID 1) and disk 3 (SCSI ID 2). If OS 2

Chapter 7 Disk Subsystems

```
[boot loader]
timeout=30
default=multi(0)disk(0)rdisk(0)partition(1)\WINDOWS
[operating systems]
multi(0)disk(0)rdisk(0)partition(1)\WINDOWS="windows Server 2003 Enterprise Edition (test)" /fast
multi(1)disk(0)rdisk(1)partition(1)\WINDOWS="windows Server 2003 Enterprise Edition (production)"
```

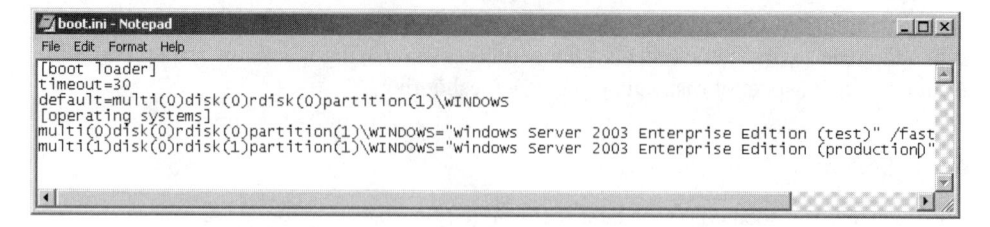

Figure 7-1. Sample boot.ini file showing two operating systems

failed, you would need to end the second line in the [operating systems] portion of the boot.ini file to read as follows:

```
multi(1)disk(0)rdisk(2)partition(1)\WINDOWS="Windows Server 2003
Enterprise Edition (production)" /fastdetect
```

If you notice, the only item that was changed was the `rdisk` value. This told the system that the operating system could be found on the third disk in the SCSI chain. While having the answer to the solution is fine, it is more important to understand how the answer was reached.

For starters, all ARC path entries begin with either `multi` or `scsi`. Notice in the example that even though SCSI disks were installed on the system, `multi` was used. This is because you only use `scsi` in place of `multi` when the system boots from SCSI disks whose associated SCSI controller's BIOS is disabled. If the SCSI BIOS is enabled, you always use `multi`. To summarize:

- Use `multi` for all IDE disks and SCSI disks when their controller's SCSI BIOS is enabled.
- Use `scsi` for SCSI disks whose controller's SCSI BIOS is disabled.

Now that `multi` and `scsi` are out of the way, let's focus on the next two entries: `disk` and `rdisk`. The easiest way to remember the usage of these two entries is with the "4-5 Rule." There are four letters in `scsi` and `disk` and five letters in `multi` and `rdisk`. This means that whenever `scsi` is the first term in an ARC path, you edit the `disk` parameter, and when `multi` is listed, then you edit the `rdisk` value. Values for `rdisk` begin with 0 and go up based on physical disk location. Keep in mind that this may not have any relation to SCSI IDs—for example, if you have four disks with IDs 0, 2, 4, and 6. The disk with SCSI ID 6 (logically the fourth disk) would have an `rdisk` value of 3 (the fourth logical value). If you had operating systems on three IDE disks (primary master, primary slave, secondary master), you would use `rdisk` values of 0, 1, and 2, respectively.

The first three entries get the system to a physical disk. The last entry, `partition`, simply tells the system the logical partition on the disk where the OS resides. Unlike the other values, partition values begin at 1 instead of 0. So an OS on the second physical disk on the second partition would have these values: `rdisk(1)partition(2)`. Several switches may accompany operating system entries in the boot.ini file; while not completely relevant from a troubleshooting perspective, they are listed in Table 7-1 to satisfy your curiosity. Relevant switches for troubleshooting purposes are explained in the `bootcfg` command section of this chapter.

Table 7-1. ARC Path Operating System Switches

Switch	Purpose
`/3GB`	For applications designed to take advantage of additional address space, this option is used to tell x86-based systems to allocate 3GB of virtual address space for applications and 1GB for OS kernel and executive components.
`/basevideo`	Tells the OS to boot using standard VGA colors (640 by 480, 16 color), which is useful if the system hangs or the screen locks after you install a new video driver.
`/baudrate=<value>`	Allows you to specify a baud rate to be used for kernel debugging. The default is 9600, but you can change the rate up to 115200. This switch is used in conjunction with the `/debug` switch.
`/bootlog`	This switch enables bootup events to be written to the %systemroot%\bootlog.txt file, which may be helpful for troubleshooting startup problems.
`/bummemory=<value>`	This option is used to specify a value of memory (in megabytes) that cannot be used by the OS. This option is normally used to test for problems caused by a lack of available memory.
`/crashdebug`	This switch is useful if you experience continual stop errors on a system. With this switch, the kernel debugger is loaded with the OS and activates when a stop event is encountered.
`/debug`	This switch loads and activates the kernel debugger as soon as the OS starts.
`/debugport=<port>`	This switch is used to indicate the COM port to be used for kernel-level debugging. The default value is `COM1`, but you can specify other ports, such as COM2 or 1394.
`/fastdetect[=<port>]`	This default switch turns off serial and bus mouse detection in the Ntdetect.com file. If you specify an optional port, such as COM1 or COM2, the system will detect components attached to that port during startup.

continued

Table 7-1. ARC Path Operating System Switches, continued

Switch	Purpose
/maxmem=<value>	Allows you to specify a maximum value of memory for use by the OS. While the /bummemory switch takes a specific amount of memory away, this switch lets you indicate exactly how much physical memory can be seen and used by the OS and is generally used to diagnose memory-related performance problems.
/noguiboot	This option disables the Windows bitmap from appearing while the OS is loading.
/nodebug	Disables kernel debugging.
/numproc=<value>	Allows you to force a multi-CPU computer to only use the number of CPUs that you specify.
/pcilock	On x86 systems, this switch prevents the OS from dynamically assigning IRQs and I/O addresses to PCI devices, leaving that job up to the system BIOS instead.
/safeboot:<value>	Makes the system start in Safe Mode. The version of Safe Mode the system starts in is determined by the value specified, which may be minimal or network.
/sos	Causes the name of each device driver to be displayed as it loads, allowing you to clearly see whether a faulty driver is causing a system to not respond or is failing to load.

This section has shown you all you need to properly edit the boot.ini file. In Chapter 5, you learned how to boot the system to the Recovery Console. When you need to edit the boot.ini file after a failure, the easiest method to modify the file is to run the bootcfg command from the console. With bootcfg, you can modify an OS entry so that its rdisk value points to the proper physical disk, for example.

Master File Table

The Master File Table (MFT) is a database that stores attribute information for each file and folder on a disk. Since this database is continually written to and read from, it is extremely important that the file reside on contiguous disk space. Otherwise, performance would significantly suffer. To prevent MFT fragmentation, NFTS automatically reserves 12.5% of the total disk space for the MFT. This space is known as the MFT Zone. Still, if the MFT grows beyond this allocation, which is extremely rare, the MFT can become fragmented, and disk performance will suffer. If you have a volume that consists mainly of very small files, then MFT fragmentation is a real possibility, and you should consider expanding the allocated size of the MFT Zone. Information on how to increase the size of the MFT Zone is found in the section on fsutil behavior later in this chapter.

GPT Disks

With Itanium-based systems, a new partition style exists that replaces the MBR format. On Itanium systems, a Globally Unique Identifier (GUID) Partition Table (GPT) format can be employed, which offers support for much larger partition sizes (128 partitions per disk, 18 exabytes per partition). With MBR disks, the maximum supported volume size is 2 terabytes.

While these numbers may initially seem extreme, they are certainly very realistic considering the exponential growth of storage requirements. Think back to the days when the 100MB storage plateau was surpassed for hard disks. We were all naive to think that you can never fill up a 100MB disk. From a troubleshooting perspective, you do not need to worry about how GPT disks operate under the hood. However, when you view them in Disk Management, they are indexed as GPT disks, and traditional disks are displayed as MBR disks.

Be careful not to use traditional MBR disk tools on GPT disks, such as running `fdisk /mbr`. Doing so may damage the file system to the point that the system will not start.

Disk Troubleshooting Tools

In this section, you will be shown additional tools to add to your toolbox. As was the case with earlier chapters, the tools presented in this section are primarily for advanced troubleshooting and go above and beyond the fundamental disk troubleshooting tools presented in Chapter 4. Following this section, the remainder of the chapter focuses on additional fault isolation methods in disk subsystem troubleshooting as well as how to fix disk problems once they're discovered.

bootcfg

Oftentimes when a disk fails and a system will not boot, technicians realize that they need to edit the boot.ini file to resolve the problem. However, editing the boot.ini file has been a lesson in patience for many, and others look at this task as more of a craft that is learned through years of pain and experience. Regardless of how you look at boot.ini file editing, Microsoft has decided to make your life much easier with `bootcfg`.

The `bootcfg` tool automates editing the boot.ini file, eliminating much of the guesswork that is normally associated with editing the file. There are 11 different ways to run `bootcfg`, each of which will be addressed shortly. Before we get to each command version, first note the switches that each command option has in common. The common command switches are for executing the command to manage a remote system and are shown in Table 7-2.

Table 7-2. bootcfg Common Command Options

Option	Use
/s <system>	Used to specify the name or IP address of the remote system you wish to manage.
/u <user>	Specifies the name of the domain user under which the command should run.
/p <password>	When /u is used, specifies the password for the domain user.

The next 11 sections describe the usage of each bootcfg version.

> The boot.ini file is loaded at startup, so to apply any changes to the boot.ini file, you must restart the system.

bootcfg /addsw

The bootcfg /addsw command allows you to configure loading options, such as maximum allowable RAM for a specific operating system entry in the boot.ini file. The syntax for bootcfg /addsw is:

```
bootcfg /addsw /id <OSNumber> [/s <system>] [/u <domain\user>]
[/p <password>] [/mm <MaxRAM>] [/bv] [/so] [/ng]
```

The bootcfg /addsw options are described in Table 7-3.

Table 7-3. bootcfg /addsw Command Options

Option	Use
/id <OSNumber>	This switch is required to tell the command which OS reference in the boot.ini file to apply to. Numbering for this switch begins at 1, so to apply the command to the second OS listed in the [operating systems] portion of the boot.ini file, you would enter /id 2. You can determine the OS–line number relationship by running bootcfg /query.
/mm <MaxRAM>	Adds the /maxmem switch along with the amount of memory specified (in megabytes) to the OS line number specified with the /id switch.
/bv	Adds the /basevideo switch to the OS line number specified with the /id switch. Adding /basevideo to an OS entry in the boot.ini file causes the operating system to boot using a standard VGA video driver.
/so	Adds the /sos switch to the OS line number specified with the /id switch. Adding this switch causes the OS to display device driver names as they are loaded when the system boots.
/ng	Adds the /noguiboot switch to the OS line number specified with the /id switch. This switch hides the Windows progress bar that appears while the system boots.

Here are two examples of using `bootcfg /addsw`:

- To configure the second OS referenced in the boot.ini file to use 128MB of the available 512MB of RAM for testing purposes:
  `bootcfg /addsw /id 2 /mm 128`

- To set the first OS in the boot.ini file to boot using standard VGA video:
  `bootcfg /addsw /id 1 /bv`

bootcfg /copy

The `bootcfg /copy` command is used to duplicate an operating system reference line in the boot.ini file. For example, if only one OS was referenced, you could use `bootcfg /copy` to duplicate the reference and cause the boot.ini file to list two operating systems. Once the line is duplicated, you can then use other `bootcfg` commands to edit the OS entry; otherwise, the new entry will point to the same operating system as the original entry, leaving you with two entries that reference the same operating system.

Here is the syntax for `bootcfg /copy`:

```
bootcfg /copy /id <OSNumber> [/s <system>] [/u <domain\user>]
[/p <password>] [/d <description>]
```

Table 7-4 describes the command options for `bootcfg /copy`.

Table 7-4. bootcfg /copy Command Options

Option	Use
/id <OSNumber>	This switch is required to tell the command which OS reference in the boot.ini file to apply to. Numbering for this switch begins at 1, so to apply the command to the second OS listed in the [operating systems] portion of the boot.ini file, you would enter /id 2. You can determine the OS–line number relationship by running `bootcfg /query`.
/d <description>	Provides a description for the new operating system entry in the boot.ini file.

Since all this command does is duplicate a boot.ini OS entry, there are not many options. To duplicate the first OS reference in the boot.ini file and have users see it referenced as "Test OS" in the boot menu, you would run this command:

`bootcfg /copy /id 1 /d "Test OS"`

bootcfg /dbg1394

This option is primarily a concern of developers and not for systems administrators and help desk staff. With `boofcfg /dbg1394`, 1394 port debugging is configured for the operating system specified. The primary advantage of 1394 port debugging is that it offers a substantial performance advantage of using debugging tools through a standard serial port.

The syntax for `boofcfg /dbg1394` is:

```
bootcfg /dbg1394 <on|off|edit> /id <OSNumber> [/s <system>]
[/u <domain\user>] [/p <password>] [/ch <channel>]
```

The `boofcfg /dbg1394` options are explained in Table 7-5.

Table 7-5. bootcfg /dbg1394 Command Options

Option	Use
on	Adds the `/dbg1394` switch to the OS line number specified with the `/id` switch. Adding `/dbg1394` to an OS entry in the boot.ini file enables 1394 remote debugging support for that OS.
off	Removes the `/dbg1394` switch from the OS line number specified with the `/id` switch, thus disabling 1394 remote debugging support.
edit	Allows you to change the port and baud rate settings for the specified OS entry based on the values provided in the `/ch` switch.
/id <OSNumber>	This switch is required to tell the command which OS reference in the boot.ini file to apply to. Numbering for this switch begins at 1, so to apply the command to the second OS listed in the [operating systems] portion of the boot.ini file, you would enter `/id 2`. You can determine the OS–line number relationship by running `bootcfg /query`.
/ch <channel>	Allows you to specify the channel to use for debugging. Allowable values are any integer between 1 and 64. This switch cannot be used in conjunction with the `off` option.

To turn on IEEE 1394 port debugging on the first operating system referenced in a system's boot.ini file, you would run this command:

```
bootcfg /dbg 1394 on /id 1
```

bootcfg /debug

This command is used to configure standard debugging (via serial port) to an OS entry in the boot.ini file. With serial communications, unlike with IEEE 1394, you need to specify a baud rate and a COM port for the system to use for communication. This syntax for `bootcfg /debug` is:

```
bootcfg /debug <on|off|edit> /id <OSNumber> [/s <system>] [/u
<domain\user>] [/p <password>] [/port <COM Port>] [/baud <baud rate>]
```

The command options are described in Table 7-6.

Table 7-6. bootcfg /debug Command Options

Option	Use
on	Adds the /debug switch to the OS line number specified with the /id switch. Adding /debug to an OS entry in the boot.ini file enables standard remote debugging support for that OS.
off	Removes the /debug switch from the OS line number specified with the /id switch, thus disabling standard remote debugging support.
edit	Allows you to change the port and baud rate settings for the specified OS entry based on the values provided in the /port and /baud switches.
/id <OSNumber>	This switch is required to tell the command which OS reference in the boot.ini file to apply to. Numbering for this switch begins at 1, so to apply the command to the second OS listed in the [operating systems] portion of the boot.ini file, you would enter /id 2. You can determine the OS–line number relationship by running bootcfg /query.
/port <COM Port>	Adds the /port switch to the OS line number specified with the /id switch. This is used to indicate which COM port should be used for remote debugging. Valid COM Port values are COM1, COM2, COM3, or COM4.
/baud <baud rate>	Adds the /baud switch to the OS line number specified in the /id switch. This is used to indicate the baud rate to be used for debugging. Valid baud rate values are 9600, 19200, 38400, 57600, or 115200.

Here is an example of removing debugging information from the boot.ini file on the remote system BigBox:

```
bootcfg /debug off /id 1 /s BigBox /u awl\administrator /p password
```

bootcfg /default

The `bootcfg /default` command is used to specify an operating system listed in the boot.ini file as the default OS. The syntax for this command is:

```
bootcfg /default /id <OSNumber> [/s <system>] [/u <domain\user>]
[/p <password>]
```

As with other `bootcfg` command versions, the /id switch is used to specify the operating system line in the boot.ini file to designate as the default. So to make the third OS listed in a local system's boot.ini file the default OS, you would run `bootcfg /default /id 3`.

bootcfg /delete

This command is used to delete an operating system reference in the boot.ini file by removing its associated entry in the [operating systems] portion of the file. The syntax for `bootcfg /delete` is:

```
bootcfg /delete /id <OSNumber> [/s <system>] [/u <domain\user>]
[/p <password>]
```

When you run the command, you use the `/id` switch to indicate the OS reference line to delete, so to delete the second OS reference, you would run `bootcfg /delete /id 2`.

bootcfg /ems

This command allows you to change the redirection configuration of the Emergency Management Services (EMS) console (W2K3 servers) to a remote computer. When you run this command, a `redirect-Port#` entry is added to the [boot loader] section of the boot.ini file, and a `/redirect` switch to the specified operating system in the [operating systems] portion of the file.

Here is the syntax for `bootcfg /ems`:

```
bootcfg /ems <on|off|edit> /id <OSNumber> [/s <system>] [/u
<domain\user>] [/p <password>] [/port <COM Port>] [/baud <baud rate>]
```

The command options are described in Table 7-7.

Table 7-7. bootcfg /ems Command Options

Option	Use
on	Enables remote output for the OS line number specified with the `/id` switch. When this parameter is used, the `/redirect` switch is added to the OS number specified, and redirect settings are added to the [boot loader] file section based on the value you specify with the `/port` switch.
off	Disables EMS remote output on the OS specified.
edit	Allows you to change current EMS port settings (set with the `/port` switch) for an OS you specify.
/id <OSNumber>	This switch is required to tell the command which OS reference in the boot.ini file to apply to. Numbering for this switch begins at 1, so to apply the command to the second OS listed in the [operating systems] portion of the boot.ini file, you would enter `/id 2`. You can determine the OS–line number relationship by running `bootcfg /query`.
/port <COM Port>	Indicates which COM port should be used for redirection. Valid `COM Port` values are `COM1`, `COM2`, `COM3`, `COM4`, or `BIOSSET`. When `BIOSSET` is used as the `COM Port` value, EMS gets the valid COM port to use from the system BIOS.
/baud <baud rate>	Indicates the baud rate to be used for redirection. Valid `baud rate` values are 9600, 19200, 38400, 57600, or 115200.

To use `bootcfg` to turn on and configure EMS (using COM1 at 115200 baud) on a W2K3 Server (first OS), you would run this command:

```
bootcfg /ems on /id 1 /port COM1 /baud 115200
```

bootcfg /query

The `bootcfg /query` command allows you to see the [boot loader] and [operating systems] configuration settings in the boot.ini file of a local or remote system. The syntax for this command is:

```
bootcfg /query [/s <system>] [/u <domain\user>] [/p <password>]
```

This is especially useful for troubleshooting since you can quickly check the boot.ini file settings on a remote system. An example of using `bootcfg /query` to check local boot.ini file settings is shown in Figure 7-2.

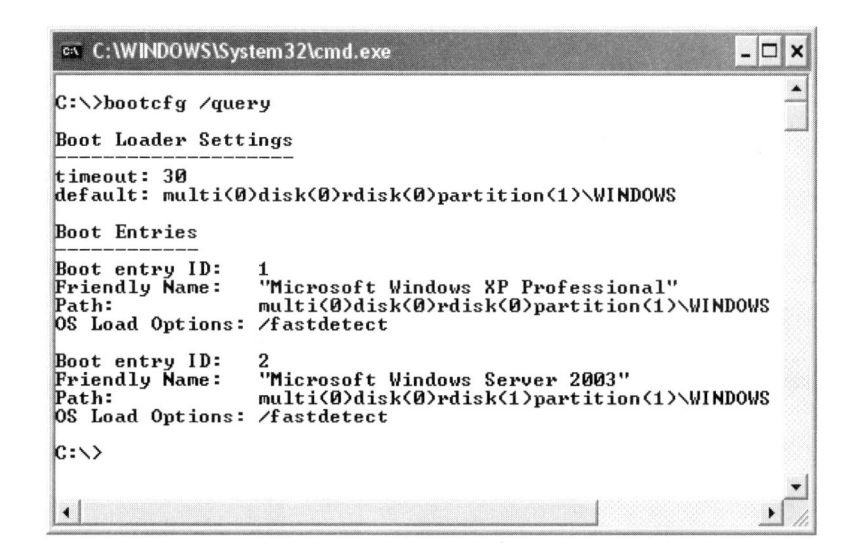

```
C:\WINDOWS\System32\cmd.exe

C:\>bootcfg /query

Boot Loader Settings
--------------------
timeout: 30
default: multi(0)disk(0)rdisk(0)partition(1)\WINDOWS

Boot Entries
------------
Boot entry ID:     1
Friendly Name:     "Microsoft Windows XP Professional"
Path:              multi(0)disk(0)rdisk(0)partition(1)\WINDOWS
OS Load Options:   /fastdetect

Boot entry ID:     2
Friendly Name:     "Microsoft Windows Server 2003"
Path:              multi(0)disk(0)rdisk(1)partition(1)\WINDOWS
OS Load Options:   /fastdetect

C:\>
```

Figure 7-2. Checking local boot.ini settings with bootcfg /query

bootcfg /raw

This command is used to add text to the end of an operating system entry in the boot.ini file and replaces any text that had previously existed at the end of the entry. Think of the `/raw` switch as the "catchall" option, allowing you to add any other valid switches to the boot.ini file (shown in Table 7-1) that are not natively supported in the other `bootcfg` commands.

The syntax for `bootcfg /raw` is:

```
bootcfg /raw "<OptionString>" /id <OSNumber> [/s <system>]
[/u <domain\user>] [/p <password>]
```

The command options are described in Table 7-8.

Table 7-8. bootcfg /raw Command Options

Option	Use
`OptionString`	Specifies a string of options, in quotes, to list at the end of the operating system reference line.
`/id <OSNumber>`	This switch is required to tell the command which OS reference in the boot.ini file to apply to. Numbering for this switch begins at 1, so to apply the command to the second OS listed in the [operating systems] portion of the boot.ini file, you would enter `/id 2`. You can determine the OS–line number relationship by running `bootcfg /query`.

Here is an example of using `bootcfg /raw` to turn off serial port mouse detection (`fastdetect`) and enable boot logging on a system:

```
bootcfg /raw "/fastdetect /bootlog" /id 1
```

These options can be removed with the `bootcfg /rmsw` command, which we'll look at next.

bootcfg /rmsw

The `bootcfg /rmsw` command allows you to remove options associated with operating system entries in the boot.ini file. Here is the syntax for `bootcfg /rmsw`:

```
bootcfg /rmsw /id <OSNumber> [/s <system>] [/u <domain\user>]
[/p <password>] [/mm] [/bv] [/ng]
```

The `bootcfg /rmsw` options are described in Table 7-9.

Table 7-9. bootcfg /rmsw Command Options

Option	Use
`/id <OSNumber>`	This switch is required to tell the command which OS reference in the boot.ini file to apply to. Numbering for this switch begins at 1, so to apply the command to the second OS listed in the [operating systems] portion of the boot.ini file, you would enter `/id 2`. You can determine the OS–line number relationship by running `bootcfg /query`.
`/mm`	Removes the `/maxmem` switch from the specified OS reference.
`/bv`	Removes the `/basevideo` switch from the specified OS reference.
`/so`	Removes the `/sos` switch from the specified OS reference.
`/ng`	Removes the `/noguiboot` switch from the specified OS reference.

Disk Troubleshooting Tools

For an example of using this command, consider a scenario in which you have configured the boot.ini file to display device drivers as a system boots. After watching the system boot and verifying the problem, you replace the faulty driver and do not want all device drivers to be displayed as they load during startup. To stop driver names from appearing during startup, you run the command `bootcfg /rmsw /id 1 /so`.

bootcfg /timeout

When a system is dual booted, the user has a configured amount of seconds to choose an OS before the default OS is loaded. The waiting period is known as the timeout value, which can be modified with `bootcfg /timeout`.

The syntax for `bootcfg /timeout` is:

```
bootcfg /timeout <time> [/s <system>] [/u <domain\user>]
[/p <password>]
```

In the command syntax, `time` is the amount of seconds that you would like the boot menu to appear before the default OS is loaded. The default `time` value is 30 seconds. To change the value to 10 seconds, for example, you would run `bootcfg /timeout 10`.

dmdiag (ST)

The `dmdiag` command is used to quickly retrieve configuration information on a system's hard disks. You can run the command and have its output dumped to a file or displayed on the screen. One of the most useful features of this command is that it displays all the configured mount points on a system as well as any symbolic links on the system. If a computer's storage configuration is unknown to you, running `dmdiag` is a quick way to get brought up to speed.

Here is the complete list of what you will learn after running `dmdiag`:

- Drive letter usage
- A kernel list
- Logical Disk Manager (LDM) file versions
- The LDM size
- A listing of all physical disks and their disk type (basic or dynamic)
- The mount points on the system
- Partition configuration information
- Symbolic links
- The system name and OS version

Tracking down symbolic links can be a tricky process. With `dmdiag`, you can allow you coworkers to believe that you will endure a great deal of stress in locating all the links on a system, while in reality you can have the list dumped to a text file in seconds.

Here is the syntax for `dmdiag`:

```
dmdiag [/v] [/f <filename>]
```

The `dmdiag` command options are described in Table 7-10.

Table 7-10. dmdiag Command Options

Option	Use
/v	Used to provide verbose output, which displays all of the configuration data mentioned earlier in this section. Without this switch, very little information is displayed in the output.
/f	Causes command output to be dumped to a text file named by the `filename` parameter. If no filename is specified, the file will be called dmdiag.txt and will be placed in the folder from where the command was run.
filename	Used with the /f switch to provide a path and a filename for the `dmdiag` output file.

To use `dmdiag` to display detailed disk information for a system, you would run `dmdiag /v`. While `dmdiag` is relatively simple in its use and functionality, next you'll see a much more complex series of commands in `fsutil`.

fsutil

The File System Utility (FSutil) command, `fsutil`, is available in several different forms, all of which are covered in this section. This utility allows you to perform a multitude of troubleshooting and administrative tasks on volumes and storage devices. While some `fsutil` commands are very useful, others are specific in their purpose, but knowledge of them may allow you to quickly get out of a troubleshooting jam down the road. Each of the `fsutil` commands is fully explained in the next 11 sections.

> Most of the system configuration modifications made by `fsutil` are changes to the Registry. In order for the changes to be applied, you need to reboot the system after running the `fsutil` command.

fsutil behavior

The `fsutil behavior` command allows you to check several FAT and NTFS volume configuration characteristics as well as modify them. Among the configuration settings that you can modify with `fsutil behavior` are

- Support of 8.3 filename conversion
- The last access timestamp for a volume

- Disk quota notification
- Paged pool memory
- The Master File Table size

From a troubleshooting and fault resolution perspective, the last two configuration options listed are the most important. When additional physical RAM is added to a system, Windows does not automatically increase the amount of paged pool memory available. For systems having performance lags resulting from the opening and closing of many files, using `fsutil behavior` to extend the operating system's amount of paged pool memory allocation may improve system performance.

The use of the MFT was explained earlier, in the section on Disk Architecture 101. With NTFS file systems, disk space is automatically allocated for future MFT growth, which is known as the MFT Zone. If the MFT Zone is not large enough, the MFT can grow beyond the disk space reserved for it in the MFT Zone, which would result in a fragmented Master File Table, thus hindering disk performance. This performance problem can be corrected by using `fsutil behavior` to modify a volume's MFT Zone allocation setting.

Now that you have seen some of the most important uses for `fsutil behavior`, let's look at its syntax.

```
fsutil behavior query <disable8dot3 | allowextchar | disablelastaccess
 | quotanotify | memoryusage | mftzone>
fsutil behavior set {disable8dot3 <1 | 0> | allowextchar <1 | 0> |
disablelastaccess <1 | 0> | quotanotify <frequency> | memoryusage
<memvalue> | mftzone <zonevalue>}
```

The `query` command option allows you to check the setting of one of the available parameters, while you can use the `set` option to modify an existing setting. With the `set` command option, a value of 1 turns on the option, while a value of 0 turns it off. All other available command parameters and options are described in Table 7-11.

Table 7-11. fsutil behavior Command Options

Option	Use
`disable8dot3`	Disables (1) or enables (0) creation of 8.3 character length filenames on FAT and NTFS volumes.
`allowextchar`	Enables (1) or disables (0) the use of characters from the extended character set in short file names on NTFS volumes.
`disablelastaccess`	Disables (1) or enables (0) the use of the last access timestamp for NTFS folders.
`quotanotify`	Allows you to set the frequency in which disk quota violations are written to the system event log.

continues

Table 7-11. fsutil behavior Command Options, continued

Option	Use
<frequency>	Used with the `quotanotify` parameter to set the time period in seconds (values of 0 to 4294967295 are valid) in which quotanotify events are written to the system event log. The default is 3600 (one hour).
memoryusage	Used to modify the internal cache settings for NTFS paged pool and non–paged pool memory, which may improve disk performance by changing the `memvalue` parameter to 2.
<memvalue>	This parameter has two allowable values: 1 (the default) and 2. When the parameter is set to 2, the size of NTFS memory thresholds and lookaside lists is expanded, and additional memory cache is available for file system read operations, thus improving disk performance at the expense of storage space.
mftzone	Used to change the volume's MFT Zone setting, which may prevent Master File Table fragmentation that would diminish disk performance. This parameter requires that a `zonevalue` be specified.
<zonevalue>	Used with the `mftzone` parameter to specify new MFT Zone configuration settings. Allowable values are 1 (the default) to 4. Each value increment represents one-eighth of the volume's allocated space, so by default, 12.5% of the volume is automatically allocated to the MFT Zone. Changing `zonevalue` to 4 would offer the best read performance, but at the cost of 50% of the available storage space.

When you suspect that MFT fragmentation is the source of a problem, don't just blindly increase the size of the MFT Zone. The easiest way to determine the true size of the MFT, see if it is fragmented, and determine if more disk space must be allocated, is to run the `defrag` command line utility (see Chapter 4) to analyze the volume. To see the MFT portion of the analysis, you must use the verbose (-v) switch in the command syntax. So to use `defrag` to check the MFT consumption and fragmentation information on the C drive, you would run `defrag -a -v c:`. The MFT portion of the command output is shown in Figure 7-3.

```
C:\WINDOWS\System32\cmd.exe

Master File Table (MFT) fragmentation
    Total MFT size                    = 16 MB
    MFT record count                  = 16,138
    Percent MFT in use                = 99
    Total MFT fragments               = 2
```

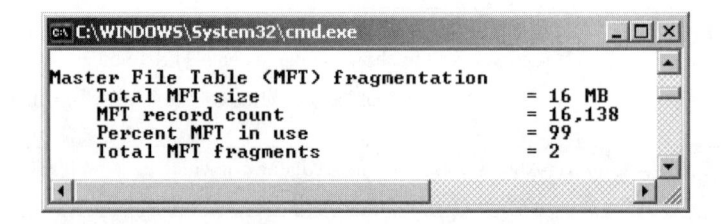

Figure 7-3. Using defrag to check for MFT defragmention

The command output shown in Figure 7-3 shows that the MFT is only consuming 16MB of space on the volume, so in this situation you could eliminate something that is right (MFT fragmentation) in a search for a disk performance problem.

fsutil dirty

With `fsutil dirty`, you can query or set a volume's dirty bit. In Chapter 4 in the section on `chkdsk`, it was mentioned that when a volume's dirty bit is set, `chkdsk` automatically runs the next time the system is restarted.

With `fsutil dirty`, you can query the status of or set the dirty bit for a volume. Here is its syntax:

```
fsutil dirty <query | set> <volumepath>
```

Here are two examples of using `fsutil dirty`:

- To check the dirty bit status on the D drive:
  ```
  fsutil dirty query d:
  ```
- To set the dirty bit and cause `chkdsk /f` to run at the next boot on the E drive:
  ```
  fsutil dirty set e:
  ```

fsutil file

The `fsutil file` command is a very versatile tool that allows you to

- List files by user name (if disk quotas are enabled).
- Create new files of any size for testing purposes (ideal for testing backup performance).
- Set a file's short name.
- Check allocated ranges for a file.

The command syntax for `fsutil file` is:

```
fsutil file createnew <filepath> <size>
fsutil file findbysid <username> <filepath>
fsutil file queryallocranges offset=<offset> length=<length>
<filepath>
fsutil file setshortname <filepath> <shortname>
fsutil file setvaliddata <filepath> <datalength>
fsutil file setzerodata offset=<offset> length=<length> <filepath>
```

As you can see, this command comes in several different versions. The options for each version are described in Table 7-12.

Table 7-12. fsutil file Command Options

Option	Use
createnew	Creates a new file (the contents consist of all 0s) with the name and size specified.
filepath	Used to specify the complete path to a file, folder, or volume.
size	Specifies the size of a file in kilobytes.
findbysid	Used to locate files owned by a specific user (only works on volumes with disk quotas enabled).
username	Used with the findbysid option to specify a user name.
queryallocranges	Reports the allocated ranges a file consumes on a volume. This is ideal for determining if a file has sparse regions.
offset	Used to indicate the start of the range to set to 0s.
length	Specifies the length of the range (in bytes).
setshortname	Used to set the short name (8.3) for a file.
shortname	Used to specify a file's short name for the setshortname parameter. It must follow the 8.3 standard.
setvaliddata	Used to configure the valid data length for a file on an NTFS volume.
datalength	Specifies the length of data (in bytes) for use with the setvaliddata parameter.
setzerodata	Used to fill a portion of a file with 0s.

For an example of using `fsutil file`, consider dealing with a user (suppose his name is Chong, who is a member of the Seventies domain) that saved an important file to the network share where disk quotas are enabled. The user needs to locate the file but does not remember what it was named. All that he remembers is that it was saved in the Docshare folder. To quickly locate the file, you can run this command:

```
fsutil file findbysid chong E:\Docshare
```

fsutil fsinfo

The `fsutil fsinfo` command allows you to quickly retrieve information on a system's drives. In particular, you can find out the following information by executing this command:

- A list of drives on the system
- The type of drives on a system (fixed disk, CD-ROM, and so on)
- Disk configuration information (sectors, clusters, MFT Zone parameters)

Disk Troubleshooting Tools

- Statistical data for a drive (metadata, MFT reads/writes)
- Volume-related information (file system type, disk quotas, Unicode support, case-sensitive filename support)

As with other `fsutil` commands, the `fsinfo` option allows you to quickly retrieve very specific information on a particular volume. The `fsutil fsinfo` syntax is:

```
fsutil fsinfo drives
fsutil fsinfo drivetype <volumepath>
fsutil fsinfo ntfsinfo <rootpath>
fsutil fsinfo statistics <volumepath>
fsutil fsinfo volumeinfo <rootpath>
```

The command parameters are described in Table 7-13.

Table 7-13. fsutil fsinfo Command Options

Option	Use
drives	Displays all drives on the system by their access path (drive letter or mount path).
drivetype	Displays the type of the drive for the drive specified (CD-ROM, fixed disk, and so on).
ntfsinfo	Displays NTFS configuration information (total sectors, total clusters, bytes per sector, bytes per cluster, and MFT Zone configuration).
statistics	Lists statistics on read and write data for the specified volume.
volumeinfo	Displays configuration information for the specified volume (see Figure 7-4).
volumepath	Used with the `drivetype` and `statistics` parameters to specify the path to a logical volume (drive letter, mount path, volume name).
rootpath	Used to specify the drive letter (followed by a colon) of a root drive.

The `fsutil fsinfo` command is a valuable tool for gathering information. Next, you will see an `fsutil` tool that may serve as the perfect Band-Aid in a tough situation.

fsutil hardlink

Suppose that after you have moved files from one volume to another, an application that is hard-coded to find a file in a single location no longer works properly. This is where `fsutil hardlink` is handy. With this tool, you can create multiple logical files in different locations that all reference the same physical file. With hard links, users and applications accessing a particular file in one location can be transparently redirected to another location, where the actual file data is stored.

To create a hard link using `fsutil hardlink`, you would use the following syntax:

```
fsutil hardlink create <newpath> <existingpath>
```

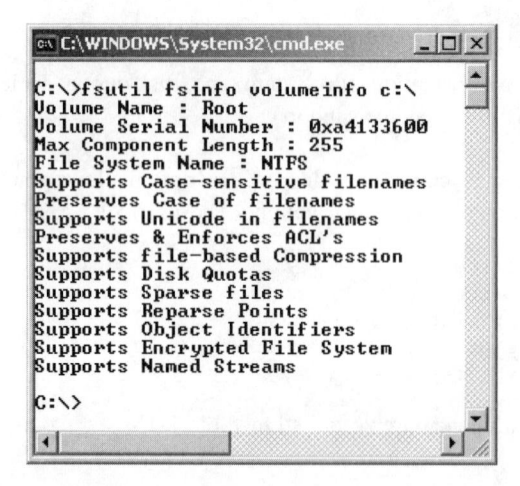

Figure 7-4. Querying volume information with fsutil fsinfo volumeinfo

When you run this command, you must specify the path and a name for the new file that will link to the original file, along with the complete path and name of the original file. For example, suppose an application is looking for a file called payroll.dat that was originally located in the C:\data folder but was moved to the E:\accounting\data folder. The quickest was to resolve this problem would be to re-create the payroll.dat file in the C:\data folder as a hard link. This operation would require that you run the following command:

```
fsutil hardlink create C:\data\payroll.dat
E:\accounting\data\payroll.dat
```

fsutil objectid

The `fsutil objectid` command allows you to manage Object Identifiers (OIDs) associated with files, folders, and links. Both the Distributed Link Tracking (DLT) Client service and File Replication Service (FRS) track objects (files, folders, and links) by their associated OIDs, which are 16-byte (32-character) hexadecimal codes that uniquely identify an object on a volume. With `fsutil objectid`, you can create, delete, query, and set OID parameters. Since there is rarely ever an instance where you would need to modify an OID (Microsoft even recommends only doing so at your own risk!), simply keep the usage of this tool in the back of your mind.

Here is the command syntax:

```
fsutil objectid <create | delete | query> <volumepath>
fsutil objectid set <ObjectID> <BirthVolumeID> <BirthObjectID>
<DomainID> <volumepath>
```

These command options are fully described in Table 7-14.

Table 7-14. fsutil objectid Command Options

Option	Use
`create`	Creates an OID for the file or folder specified. If one already exists, then this command acts like the `query` command.
`delete`	Deletes a file or folder's OID.
`query`	Displays a file or folder's OID.
`set`	Modifies a file or folder's OID.
`volumepath`	Specifies the complete path to a file, folder, or link.
`ObjectID`	Used with the `set` parameter to provide a specific 32-hex-character OID.
`BirthVolumeID`	Used with the `set` parameter to provide the OID for the volume where the object originally resided.
`BirthObjectID`	Used with the `set` parameter to provide the original OID for the object.
`DomainID`	Used with the `set` parameter to provide the domain OID for the object. This should be 32 0s.

Here is an example of checking the OID for the Windows folder on the C drive:

```
fsutil objectid query C:\Windows
```

> Microsoft strongly warns against deleting or modifying Object IDs. Doing so may result in the loss of file data or an entire volume. Modifying an Object ID may also cause problems with the DLT Client service and FRS.

fsutil quota

The `fsutil quota` command allows you to manage disk quota configuration from the command line, as opposed to using Windows Explorer. Suppose that a user is unable to save documents to his home folder, which gets backed up nightly on a network server. You suspect that the user's problem may be the result of his exceeding his quota limit. You can quickly verify your suspicions by running `fsutil quota`.

The syntax for `fsutil quota` is:

```
fsutil quota disable <volume>
fsutil quota enforce <volume>
fsutil quota modify <volume> <threshold> <limit> <domain\user>
fsutil quota query <volume>
fsutil quota track <volume>
fsutil quota violations
```

The options and usage for each `fsutil quota` command version are described in Table 7-15.

Table 7-15. fsutil quota Command Options

Option	Use
`disable`	Disables disk quotas on the specified volume.
`enforce`	Enforces disk quota limits on the specified volume.
`modify`	Changes an existing disk quota or creates a new quota for the specified volume.
`query`	Displays disk quota information for the specified volume.
`track`	Tracks disk usage on the specified volume.
`violations`	Checks the local system and application logs, and displays a list of users that have exceeded quota limits or have reached their quota threshold.
`volume`	Used to indicate the volume to manage.
`threshold`	Used with the `modify` parameter to set a limit (in bytes) at which a user is warned that he or she is approaching the quota limit.
`limit`	Used with the `modify` parameter to set a maximum amount of disk space (in bytes) that can be used by the user.
`domain\user`	Used with the `modify` parameter to specify a user account to which the quota entry applies.

In the example mentioned earlier, you can check for quota violations with `fsutil quota` by running `fsutil quota violations`. If the user had exceeded the quota limit, you could either tell the user to remove some files from the share to free up space, or you could create a custom quota entry for the individual user by running `fsutil quota modify`.

fsutil reparsepoint

The easiest way to think of reparse points is to compare them to shortcuts on your desktop. A shortcut is not a true executable file but is a pointer to one. The same could be said for reparse points, since they provide shortcuts to objects stored at other locations. When you click on a shortcut link, you are transparently redirected to wherever the shortcut points. This is also true with reparse points. A file that contains a reparse point may redirect users and applications to another file or directory without their knowledge.

Reparse points can be tricky in terms of getting rid of them. The mistake that some users make is to delete them right from Windows Explorer. When this is done, sometimes not only is the reparse point deleted, but the actual file or folder that is referenced by the reparse point is deleted as well. This is why `fsutil reparsepoint` is so useful. This tool allows you to query reparse points, letting you determine what true object they reference, and also allows you to cleanly delete reparse points.

The syntax for `fsutil reparsepoint` is:

```
fsutil reparsepoint <query | delete> <filepath>
```

The three options for this command are described in Table 7-16.

Table 7-16. fsutil reparsepoint Command Options

Option	Use
query	If a reparse point exists for the file or folder in the specified path, information on its data length, tag value, and GUID is displayed.
delete	Deletes a reparse point associated with the file or folder in the specified path.
filepath	Used to specify the path to a file or folder containing a reparse point.

The most common use of `fsutil reparsepoint` is to delete reparse point references from files. This may be needed for applications that leave behind reparse points or even from Windows services such as Remote Storage Service (RSS) or Distributed File System (DFS) that may also not cleanly remove reparse point references if they become corrupt. For example, after disabling DFS on a member server in your domain that previously had the role of a standalone DFS root, you notice that when accessing a folder, you are still being redirected to another system. To remove the reparse point from the folder, you run this command:

```
fsutil reparsepoint delete D:\public\sales
```

fsutil sparse

Sparse files are a file system improvement that first appeared in Windows 2000. The idea of sparse files is to save some of the disk space consumed by very large files. Imagine if you had to read a book to someone that contained only 1s and 0s, much as a computer reads data off a hard drive. Suppose that the data in the file being read consisted of a single 1 followed by one million 0s. Instead of writing 100000000 (to spare you the pain of reading many more pages of 0s, we'll stop here), wouldn't it be much easier to simply write 1 [one million more 0s]? This is what sparse files do. Nonmeaningful data (large strings of consecutive 0s) is not allocated as disk space and instead is simply referenced. With sparse file support, not only is disk space saved, but read and write operations run faster as a result.

With `fsutil sparse`, you can

- Identify sparse files.
- Mark a file as a sparse file.
- Scan a file, looking for its ranges of nonzero data.
- Fill a portion of a file with 0s.

The `fsutil sparse` syntax is:

```
fsutil sparse <queryflag | queryrange | setflag | setrange> <path>
[offset] [length]
```

The `fsutil sparse` options are explained in Table 7-17.

Table 7-17. fsutil sparse Command Options

Option	Use
queryflag	Determines if a file is set as a sparse file.
queryrange	Displays ranges in sparse file that contain nonzero data.
setflag	Sets a file to be a sparse file.
setrange	Fills the designated sparse file with a range (specified with the `offset` and `length` parameters) with 0s.
path	Specifies the complete path to the sparse file. If the path contains spaces, include the path in quotes.
offset	Specifies the point within the file to mark as sparse (the beginning of a continuous string of 0s).
length	Specifies the length (in bytes) of the region to be marked as sparse.

To set the file E:\Data\Records.dat as a sparse file, you would run the following command:

```
fsutil sparse setflag e:\data\records.dat
```

To then view the file's ranges of nonzero data, you could run this command:

```
fsutil sparse queryrange e:\data\records.dat
```

fsutil USN

The `fsutil USN` command is used to query and manage the NTFS Change Journal on a volume. If you are unaware of the Change Journal, it may be because it is a relatively new (W2K and above) and underpublicized Windows feature. Primarily, the Change Journal is most useful to backup applications mainly because it can streamline the incremental backup process. In the pre–Windows 2000 days, when an incremental backup was performed, the entire volume was scanned, and a list of files that had changed since the last backup was accumulated. This list was the result of either checking the archive bit on each file or checking a file's date-time stamp and comparing it with the time of the last backup. Regardless of how the list was obtained by the application, the problem with this process was that it was both resource intensive and time consuming, neither of which

Disk Troubleshooting Tools

are conditions you wish to see on any application running on your IIS Web server, for example. The other problem with archive bit and date-time stamp scanning was that when a file was renamed or had its access control list (ACL) modified, neither would flip the archive bit or change its date-time stamp. This meant that it would not get backed up with an incremental backup.

All of these problems were remedied with the Change Journal. With the Change Journal, the operating system maintains its own file index and records when changes are made to a file through the use of update sequence numbers (USNs). Even changes to a file's name or ACL are noted in the Change Journal. Backup applications that are truly W2K or higher compliant can interface with the Change Journal. This means that on incremental backups, they do not need to scan the entire volume and instead can simply formulate a list of what needs to be backed up by reading the Change Journal, saving both time and resources. Also, in being able to note changes in filenames and ACLs, incremental backups from Change Journal–aware applications are more accurate.

Besides backup applications, the following Windows services also interact with the Change Journal:

- File Replication Service
- Indexing Service
- Remote Installation Service
- Remote Storage Service

In particular, `fsutil USN` allows you to perform the following administrative tasks on a volume's Change Journal:

- Create a new Change Journal
- Modify an existing Change Journal
- List Change Journal entries between a low and high USN value
- Query general Change Journal information (capacity, record information)
- Display USN data for a given file

These tasks can be performed using the following syntax:

```
fsutil USN createjournal <MaxSize> <AllocationDelta> <VolumePath>
fsutil USN deletejournal <flags> <VolumePath>
fsutil USN enumdata <FileRef> <LowUSN> <HighUSN> <VolumePath>
fsutil USN queryjournal <VolumePath>
fsutil USN readdata <FilePath>
```

As you can see, there are several variations of this command. The options for each command version are explained in Table 7-18.

Chapter 7 Disk Subsystems

Table 7-18. fsutil USN Command Options

Option	Use
`createjournal`	Creates a new Change Journal on the volume specified. If one already exists, the Change Journal is modified with the parameters specified in the command.
`Maxsize`	Used to indicate the maximum size (in bytes) to allocate on the volume for the Change Journal.
`AllocationDelta`	Used to specify the amount of data (in bytes) to be removed from the beginning and added to the end of the Change Journal. In other words, once the Change Journal reaches its maximum size, how much of the oldest data should be purged to make room for new data.
`VolumePath`	Used to specify the drive letter or mount path to a particular volume.
`deletejournal`	Used to disable an active Change Journal.
`flags`	Two flag options are available for the `fsutil USN deletejournal` command. • `/d`—Disables the active Change Journal, with I/O control returned to the system before the operation completes. • `/n`—Disables the active Change Journal, with I/O control returned to the system after the operation completes.
`enumdata`	Itemizes and lists Change Journal data between two specified points.
`FileRef`	Specifies the ordinal file position at which itemization is to begin.
`LowUSN`	Specifies the lower boundary of USN records in the Change Journal that are returned in the command output.
`HighUSN`	Specifies the upper boundary of USN records in the Change Journal that are returned in the command output. Files with USNs equal to or between the `LowUSN` and `HighUSN` values are returned by the command.
`queryjournal`	Used to display Change Journal configuration information, including the first USN, the maximum journal size, and the allocation delta.
`readdata`	Used to display the USN data for a single file.
`Filepath`	Used to specify the complete path to a file to be checked with the `fsutil USN readdata` command.

While this command certainly is complex, there are still troubleshooting purposes for it. Suppose that you do not feel that all of your changed files on a system's D drive are being backed up with an incremental backup. It is possible that the maximum size allocated for the Change Journal is not large enough. In this event, you would either run incremental backups more frequently or increase the size of the Change Journal. Suppose that you wanted to increase the size of the Change Journal to 500MB, to ensure that it will not run out of space, and reallocate old space in increments of 5MB. Before running the command, you would first need to convert both values from megabytes to bytes, which are 524,288,000 and 5,242,880, respectively (1MB = 1,048,576 bytes). You would use these values in the following command:

```
fsutil USN createjournal 524288000 5242880 D:
```

fsutil volume

The `fsutil volume` command allows you to dismount a volume or to check the amount of free space on the volume. The syntax for `fsutil volume` is:

```
fsutil volume <diskfree | dismount> <drivename | volumepath>
```

The command syntax requires that either `diskfree` or `dismount` be specified, along with a drive name or a volume path. These options are further explained in Table 7-19.

Table 7-19. fsutil volume Command Options

Option	Use
diskfree	Used to query the amount of free space on the drive or volume specified.
dismount	Used to dismount the drive or volume specified.
drivename	Used to specify the logical drive on which to run the command.
volumepath	Used to specify the logical path to a mount point or volume name representing a logical volume.

The `diskfree` option is ideal for checking for space on a volume when you suspect that it may be out of space. The `dismount` option provides a way to quickly terminate any open processes or user sessions currently accessing the volume. Dismounting a volume may be necessary if you are attempting to run a maintenance application on the volume, and the application cannot continue due to a conflicting process accessing the volume. Dismounting the volume should correct the problem, and the application should execute cleanly the next time you attempt to start it. For example, to dismount the logical volume E, you would run this command:

```
fsutil volume dismount e:
```

ftonline (ST)

While Windows 2000 supported fault-tolerant volumes on basic disks for backward compatibility with Windows NT, Windows XP/W2K3 does not. Prior to upgrading a system to XP/W2K3, you should upgrade any fault-tolerant basic disks to dynamic disks or perform a backup so that you can restore the data to another volume. If a user does not perform either of these tasks and simply upgrades his or her system, then the user will be in a bit of trouble, since the fault-tolerant volume will no longer be accessible. That's where `ftonline` comes into play.

When an upgraded system first boots into an XP/W2K3 OS, fault-tolerant basic disks appear in the Disk Management UI as failed and are not accessible. With `ftonline`, you can temporarily mount and bring the failed fault-tolerant basic disks online so that you can copy or back up their data. Once you reboot the system, the fault-tolerant basic disks will again show a failed status and should be deleted and reconfigured.

Here is `ftonline`'s syntax:

```
ftonline <Driveletter>
```

To see an example of `ftonline` in use, consider an example of a user upgrading his system to Windows XP Professional. The system was upgraded a few years ago from Windows NT to Windows 2000 and contained a fault-tolerant basic disk. When the user complains about lost data access to his E drive after the upgrade, you perform these steps:

1. Run `ftonline E:` on the user's system.
2. Back up the data on the online E drive.
3. Reboot the system.
4. Use Disk Management to delete the fault-tolerant basic disk.
5. Re-create the disk as either a new basic or dynamic disk.
6. Restore the backup data to the new volume.

recover

In Chapter 4, it was mentioned that `chkdsk` can be used to spot and repair bad sectors on a disk. Sometimes sectors cannot be repaired, which often results in a file spanning those sectors being considered lost as well. However, with the `recover` command you can get back the portions of a file that remain on the good sectors of a disk. If the file is an important document and no good backup exists, this command provides you with an alternative with which you can save at least a portion of the lost data.

The `recover` command only works at the filename level and does not support the use of wildcards, so this command can only be executed on a single file at a time. The syntax for `recover` is:

```
recover [drive:] [path] filename
```

When the command is run in the directory in which the corrupted file resides, only the filename needs to be included in the command syntax. Otherwise, you can list the complete path to the filename in the command syntax. For example, if the Word document D:\Free Software\Penguin.doc mysteriously became corrupted on your Windows system, you could run the following command:

```
recover "C:\Free Software\Penguin.doc"
```

to try to get back at least portions of the document. When a large document is lost, most users will agree that anything is better than nothing. After running `recover` on a corrupted file, you many not have much, but at least to the user's delight, you will not have "nothing" either.

Diagnosing and Repairing Boot Sector and MBR Problems

Earlier in this chapter, you learned of the differences between the boot sector and the MBR. On most occasions, it is very easy to spot an MBR problem or a boot sector problem. When there is a problem with the MBR, you will see one of the following messages at startup:

- "Error loading operating system"
- "Invalid partition table"
- "Missing operating system"

If the MBR is good, it will point to the boot sector at startup. If it cannot find the boot sector, one of the following error messages will be displayed:

- "A disk read error occurred"
- "NTLDR is compressed"
- "NTLDR is missing"

Before attempting to repair either an MBR or a boot sector error, first attempt to boot the system with a recent scan disk from your antivirus software. With some MBR and boot sector viruses, the Windows repair tools that will be discussed shortly may cause more harm to the partition tables, so checking for viruses should always be your first course of action.

To resolve an MBR error, the quickest course of action is to follow these steps.

1. Boot the system into the Recovery Console and run `fixmbr` from the command prompt.
2. When warned, press Y to continue.
3. Restart the system.

To repair the boot sector, you would take the following steps.

1. Boot the system into the Recovery Console and run `fixboot <drive letter>:` from the command prompt, specifying the drive letter that contains the system volume.
2. Restart the computer.

Chapter 7 Disk Subsystems

While under nearly all circumstances `fixboot` and `fixmbr` will resolve a startup problem, they are not guaranteed. If your startup problem cannot be repaired with `fixboot` or `fixmbr`, then you should do the following.

1. Repartition and format the affected drive.
2. Reinstall Windows (if your backup software does not support bare metal restores).
3. Restore necessary data from backup.

This section has shown you a systematic approach for resolving startup problems with the MBR or boot sector. Next you will see how to fix storage problems using the Disk Management tool.

> When you see disk errors at startup, always make sure that there isn't a floppy in the disk drive before spending minutes or even hours troubleshooting a startup problem. This problem runs rampant among users, and the solution to "Remove the floppy from your drive and hit the reset button" has been uttered millions of times by help desk professionals.

Repairing Failed Disks with Disk Management

Disk Management allows you to not only spot disk problems on a system, but repair them as well. In Figure 7-5, the Disk Management display for a system with two disk errors is shown. In the illustration, you can see that Disk Management has placed warning symbols

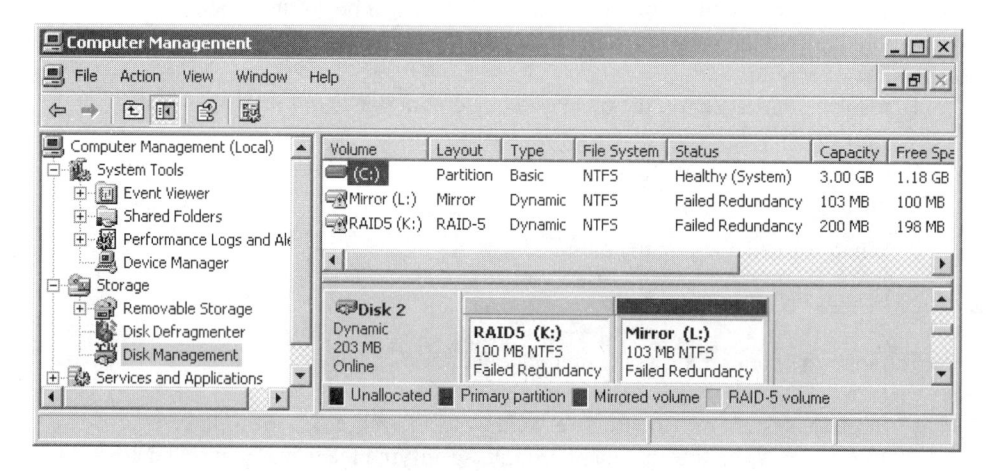

Figure 7-5. Troubleshooting disk faults with Disk Management

next to the two disks that have been labeled as having "failed redundancy," allowing you to quickly spot the faulty disks. In the lower right corner of the display, you can see that the failed redundancy problems with the L and K volumes are both associated with Disk 2, which allows you to quickly diagnose Disk 2 failure as being the likely source of the problem.

Aside from failed redundancy, you may see several other disk status indications listed in Disk Management. Each status is described in Table 7-20.

Table 7-20. Disk Status Indications

Status	Cause	Corrective Action(s)
Foreign	A dynamic disk from one system has been added to another. The OS recognized that a signature resides on the disk, but has no record of it.	Right-click the disk and select Import Foreign Disks.
Missing	A dynamic disk is disconnected, not powered, or corrupted.	1. Repair the hardware or communication problem. 2. Right-click the disk and select Reactivate Disk.
Not Initialized	A disk does not have a valid signature in the MBR or GUID in the GPT.	Right-click the disk and select Initialize Disk.
Offline	A disk is inaccessible due to loss of power, communication, or corruption.	1. Repair the hardware or communication problem. 2. Right-click the disk and select Reactivate Disk.
Online	Normal operation.	None
Online (Errors)	The OS has detected I/O errors with the disk.	1. Run `chkdsk /f` to repair any physical errors to the disk. 2. Check for communication or power problems. 3. Right-click the disk and select Reactivate Disk.
Unreadable	• A dynamic disk's Dynamic Disk Database is corrupted. • A disk is spinning up. • Corruption, hardware failure, or I/O errors have occurred.	1. Repair the problem (if necessary). 2. Right-click the Disk Management icon and select Rescan Disks.

When dynamic disks are configured in a software RAID-based solution, you may encounter other errors. These errors are listed in Table 7-21.

Table 7-21. Dynamic Disk with RAID Configuration Errors

Status	Cause	Corrective Action(s)
Failed	A disk is damaged or corrupted.	1. Repair the hardware or communication problem. 2. Right-click the disk and select Reactivate Disk. 3. If the volume is not listed as healthy, right-click the volume and select Reactivate Volume.
Healthy	Normal operation.	Nothing.
Healthy (At Risk)	I/O errors are continually occurring.	1. Run `chkdsk /f` to repair any physical errors to the disk. 2. Check for communication or power problems. 3. Right-click the disk and select Reactivate Disk.
Healthy (Unknown Partition)	The OS cannot recognize the System ID (if MBR disk) or GUID (if GPT disk).	1. Delete the partition. 2. Re-create the unused space as a new volume. 3. Format the volume.
Unknown	A corrupted boot sector exists.	1. Scan for viruses. 2. Run fixboot from the Recovery Console. 3. If steps 1 or 2 do not fix the problem, repartition and format the disk, and restore lost data from backup.

Now that you have seen how to repair the immediate errors, let's not lose sight of the big picture. With fault-tolerant dynamic disk configurations, the loss of one disk might affect several disks. The remainder of this section focuses on the steps necessary to repair dynamic volumes spanning two or more physical disks.

Failed Spanned or Striped Volumes

Neither spanned volumes nor striped volumes are fault tolerant. If a disk in one of these logical volumes fails, then you are faced with re-creating the volume from scratch and restoring its most recent data from backup. From Disk Management, you need to right-click the failed volume and select Delete Volume. From that point, you can replace the failed disk, and re-create the new volume and restore from backup. So that lightning does not strike twice, you may want to consider creating the new volume using a fault-tolerant configuration such as RAID 0 or RAID 5.

Failed Mirrored Volumes (RAID 1)

If a disk in a mirrored volume must be replaced, you need to follow these steps

1. Power down the system (if necessary) and replace the failed disk. Then power up the system (if the disk was not hot-swappable).
2. Right-click the failed mirrored volume and select Remove Mirror.
3. When prompted that the volume will no longer contain redundant data, select the missing disk, as shown in Figure 7-6, and click Remove Mirror.
4. When asked if you are sure you want to remove the mirror, click Yes.
5. Right-click the working disk from the original mirrored volume and select Add Mirror.
6. Select the newly installed disk (or an existing disk with equal or more free space) to add to the new mirror and click Add Mirror.

At this point, data from the original disk will be copied to the new disk in the mirrored volume. When the copy is finished, the mirrored volume will show a status of Healthy.

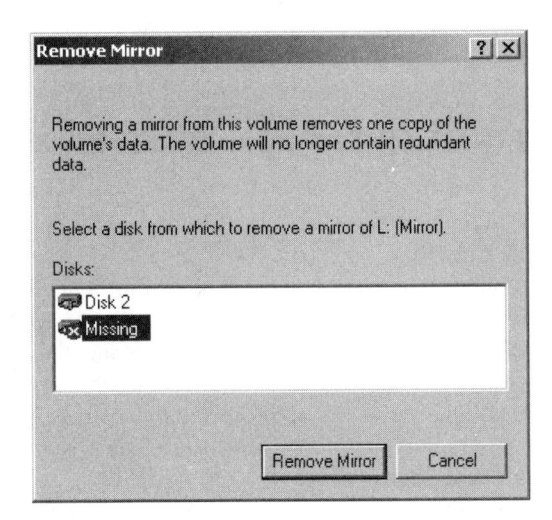

Figure 7-6. Removing the mirror from a failed RAID 1 volume

Failed RAID 5 Volumes

If a disk in a RAID 5 volume must be replaced, you need to take these steps.

1. Power down the system (if necessary) and replace the failed disk. Then power up the system (if the disk was not hot-swappable).

2. Right-click the failed RAID 5 volume and select Repair Volume.

3. Select an available disk as the replacement for the failed disk and click OK.

Windows at this point will regenerate the failed volume. Once it completes, the RAID 5 volume will return to a healthy status.

If you're looking for more disk management and troubleshooting tools, check on the suite of products from Executive Software that are located on the companion CD and documented in Appendix C.

Common Stop Messages

This section shows you the most common disk-related stop messages. Although the notorious blue screen of death (BSOD) certainly makes far fewer appearances on XP/W2K3 systems, it does not disappear altogether. Actually, from a troubleshooting perspective, a BSOD can be your best friend. That is because the stop error that appears on the screen may lead you directly to the problem. The five most common XP/W2K3 disk-related stop error messages are examined in the next five subsections.

Stop 0x00000024 (NTFS File System) or Stop 0x00000023 (FAT File System)

This error tells you that a problem was encountered with the Ntfs.sys file for NTFS file systems or with the File Allocation Table on a FAT file system. This normally indicates that some type of corruption has occurred on the disk. At this point, you should first run `chkdsk <driveletter:> /f` on the system volume. If you are unable to start Windows in order to access the command prompt, then boot into the Recovery Console by booting the system on the Windows installation CD, and run `chkdsk` from there. If physical corruption was found on the disk and resolved by `chkdsk`, your troubles may be over. However, if this is not the first time that the system has experienced this problem, you need to dig a little deeper.

If the problem is repetitive, failing or malfunctioning hardware should be the next components to check. The most common hardware issues related to this type of error are

- A malfunctioning IDE controller
- A bad IDE cable

- A malfunctioning SCSI controller
- A bad SCSI cable
- Improper SCSI termination

Also, don't automatically rule out software as possibly causing the corruption. If software was recently installed on the system, that should be the first place you look. If the following application types are not compatible with the Windows OS version, disk corruption may result:

- Disk defragmenters
- Virus scanners
- Backup utilities

Stop 0x00000050 (Page Fault in Nonpaged Area)

The stop error occurs when requested data cannot be found in memory. This type of page fault is caused by a problem with system memory and is not directly related to a hard disk fault. If RAM was recently added, then that is the likely problem. If this is not the case, then you need to isolate the physical memory that is the cause of the problem. Don't limit the possible faults to this problem to only system RAM. This paging error can also be caused by any of the following being bad:

- Main memory
- L2 cache
- Video RAM

The easiest way to isolate the problem is to replace what is suspected to be bad with a known good component. To eliminate bad video RAM as the cause, replace the video card with a known good card and see if the error no longer occurs. A problem with onboard cache can be isolated by disabling the cache in the system BIOS. After you do this, the system will run noticeably slower, which is normal for a system operating without the use of onboard cache. If the stop error disappears, you will most likely need to replace the motherboard to resolve the problem. Since most organizations have plenty of RAM on hand, whether stored or in other systems, you can quickly replace RAM chips to see if the problem is corrected. If several sticks of RAM are in the system, replace one stick at a time and then reboot the system to see if the problem disappears. With a little patience, you can easily pinpoint the failed hardware that caused this problem.

As with other memory problems, you should not give software a free pass on this problem either. If the hardware checks out OK, or if a new application was recently installed, you should first look at the software. Besides applications, check system services and drivers. This stop error has also been known to appear as a result of the wrong driver being used. For example, an incorrect video driver may cause a video RAM–related paging error. The driver can be updated by running Windows Update, or you can check with the hardware manufacturer for the latest driver.

Stop 0x00000077 (Kernel Stack Inpage Error)

This error message alerts you that a page of kernel data requested from virtual memory could not be found. Since virtual memory is stored on the hard disk, the disks that store virtual memory are where you should focus your troubleshooting efforts. These are the main culprits for this failure.

- Disk corruption—Fix by running `chkdsk /f`.
- Disk hardware failure—Check all of the disk hardware that was mentioned in the section on stop 0x00000024.
- Virus infection—Download the latest virus signatures and run a virus scan on the volume.

Oftentimes, the status code that is listed in the stop error message points you directly to the problem. Table 7-22 lists the most common status codes along with their related problem.

Table 7-22. Stop 0x00000077 Status Codes

Code	Related Problem
0xC000009A (Status Insufficient Resources)	Depleted nonpaged pool resources (very rare).
0xC000009C (Status Device Data Error)	Bad sectors on hard disk.
0xC000009D (Status Device Not Connected)	Loose or disconnected power or data cables, controller or disk configuration problem, or SCSI termination problem.
0xC000016A (Status Disk Operation Failed)	Bad sectors on hard disk.
0xC0000185 (Status IO Device Error)	Loose or disconnected power or data cables, controller or disk configuration problem, SCSI termination, or multiple devices are attempting to access the same resources.

For hardware-related problems, you again need to test and replace the defective component. If disk corruption is indicated, first attempt to fix the problem by running `chkdsk /f` on the bad volume. If disk corruption is excessive, you then need to replace the defective disk.

Stop 0x0000007A (Kernel Data Inpage Error)

This error code indicates that a page of kernel data could not be located in virtual memory (the pagefile). The problems that cause this error are very similar to the ones associated with the previous stop error (0x00000077). With this stop error, you will see the same status codes that were previously listed in Table 7-22. These status codes will give you the information you need to quickly isolate the problem.

The primary culprits behind this error are

- Bad sectors on disk
- Memory hardware (RAM, L2 cache, video RAM)
- Disk cables
- SCSI termination
- A disk controller
- Virus infection

As was mentioned earlier, the easiest way to isolate memory hardware problems is to replace what is suspected to be bad with a known good card or chip from another system. With onboard cache, simply disable it in the BIOS and see if the problem returns.

Stop 0x0000007B (Inaccessible Boot Device)

This error indicates that the operating system has lost access to either the system or boot partition during system startup. This stop error is generally the result of an incorrect storage device driver being installed. For example, after you upgrade the driver for a system's SCSI host bus adapter (HBA) card, this error may appear when the system restarts. If you added new storage devices, such as additional SCSI hard disks to a SCSI bus, the SCSI IDs assigned to the new disks may conflict with existing settings in the boot.ini file. For example, assume that a system's boot partition was located on a SCSI disk with SCSI ID 3, with no other disks attached to the SCSI adapter with BIOS enabled. The operating system's entry in the boot.ini file would look similar to `multi(0)disk(0)rdisk(0)partition(1)`. If the new SCSI disk's SCSI ID was lower than 3, then you would get an Inaccessible Boot Device error. To correct the problem, you could take these actions.

- Edit the operating system entry in the boot.ini file to read `multi(0)disk(0)rdisk(1)partition(1)` (the `rdisk` value is incremented to signify the second logical SCSI disk in the chain).
- Change the SCSI ID of the new disk to a value higher than that of the original disk (ideally 4–6 in this situation, since 7 is normally reserved for the SCSI adapter).

When a boot device is inaccessible, don't rule out taking the error literally. Perhaps a cable is loose or disconnected, the disk's controller is bad, or the disk is corrupted. As always, a virus may be lurking and causing the problem as well. For hardware connection–related troubleshooting, a quick check to see if a physical connection exists is to use the BIOS menu. Use the system BIOS to autodetect IDE drives, and access the SCSI adapter's BIOS to detect the presence of SCSI drives.

You have just seen the most common disk-related stop error messages. Remember, BSODs are not bad by any stretch. In fact, get excited when you see them. They have just made it much easier for you to solve a problem. As always, *never* just turn off the system in disgust when you see the BSOD on your way out the door on a Friday night. Instead, always remember to jot down the stop error message first.

Summary

In this chapter, you were exposed to the tools and techniques for troubleshooting and repairing Windows disk problems. While some of the problems ranged from obvious to obscure, one theme was consistent throughout many of the problem resolution steps. That theme was to restore from backup. This step assumes that the system in question actually was backed up. If a system stores important data, it should be backed up frequently (at least nightly). Sometimes, rebuilding a disk from scratch and restoring data from a backup copy is your only option in correcting a problem. Don't take this option out of the equation when trying to fix a problem. With today's backup networks and Storage Area Networks (SANs), sometimes performing a restore to a previous point in time may be faster than the entire troubleshooting process. Since the mission of the company is the primary motivation for resolving the problem, always go with the resolution that will get the system back up and running the fastest. Also, when time permits, test your backup data by restoring it to a test system. Your job may depend on that backup data, and too many administrators (yours truly, included) have learned the hard way not to instinctively trust backups. Don't make this mistake too.

In the next chapter, you will begin a march through troubleshooting core Microsoft network infrastructure services, starting with DNS.

8
DNS

While Chapter 2 got you started with understanding how DNS fits into a network infrastructure, there is much more to understand about this essential and complex service in order to successfully diagnose and resolve its problems. In Chapter 2, you learned primarily about the client-side architecture of the DNS hierarchy. In addition to understanding the client considerations in a DNS hierarchy, you also need to be familiar with the architecture of DNS servers in an enterprise environment.

To troubleshoot your DNS infrastructure, you must have knowledge of its architecture so that you can fully document the processes involved in a suspected problem. To that end, this chapter starts by looking at how DNS works. To troubleshoot DNS, you don't need to know everything about how to administer the service, but you do need to understand how it works. After being presented with an architectural overview, you will then see how to use four essential tools for DNS troubleshooting: the DNS MMC snap-in, `dnslint`, `nslookup`, and `dnscmd`. With architecture and tools covered, the remainder of this chapter is dedicated to the nuts and bolts of DNS troubleshooting, examining how to diagnose and resolve both client- and server-related problems.

DNS Architecture

This section shows you the complete DNS landscape, starting with its hierarchical arrangement and then moving on to the specific details that are unique to Windows Server 2003 and Windows 2000 DNS.

Essential Terminology

Many of the processes described in this section assume knowledge of several DNS-specific terms. Before proceeding, make sure that you are familiar with all of the terms listed in the next five sections.

Dynamic Updates

Dynamic updates refer to a system's ability to automatically register its IP address and host name with its primary DNS server. By default, dynamic registration occurs when a system first starts up. Beginning with Windows 2000, Windows servers began to support dynamic updates. Before Windows 2000, WINS servers supported dynamic updates and thus were well suited for providing name resolution services for Microsoft clients. Today, WINS servers are still around mainly for backward compatibility. If you have a pristine Windows 2000 or XP network that you manage and are still running WINS, it's time to give it a burial.

Now back to dynamic updates. Dynamic updates can come from two sources: Windows 2000 and higher computers or Windows 2000 and higher DHCP servers. By default, Windows 2000 clients automatically register their own host records with their DNS server. When DHCP is used, clients still register their host names, and the DHCP server registers the clients' pointer records. For pre–Windows 2000 clients, you can have the DHCP server dynamically register client host names and IP addresses on their behalf. More information on the DHCP-DNS relationship can be found in the Troubleshooting DNS-DHCP Integration section later in this chapter.

Dynamic updates made by clients and DHCP servers are meaningless if they are not accepted by the DNS server. Dynamic updates are enabled or disabled under the General tab of a zone's Properties dialog box, as is shown in Figure 8-1. These are the three choices for dynamic update configuration.

- No—Dynamic updates are not allowed.

- Yes—All dynamic updates are allowed (the least secure choice).

- Only secure updates—This is available only on Active Directory integrated zones. Only systems whose computer accounts reside in the Active Directory can update the DNS zone data (the most secure choice).

If you want clients and other services to connect to a multihomed server by a single IP address, you should disable dynamic update on the network interfaces that you don't want to dynamically register their IP addresses. This is especially important if each network interface is on a different logical network, since clients on one subnet may receive from the DNS server the IP address for the interface on a different subnet. If routing is not properly configured, clients would intermittently be unable to access the multihomed server. An alternative to disabling dynamic update is to enable netmask ordering on the DNS server, which is described later.

Recursion and Iteration

Name resolution requests come in two forms: recursive queries and iterative queries. Recursive queries are requests for complete resolution of an FQDN, such as asking for the IP address of bigbadserver.marketing.awl.com. Iterative queries, on the other hand, are requests for the resolution of a portion of a name. For example, a DNS server may

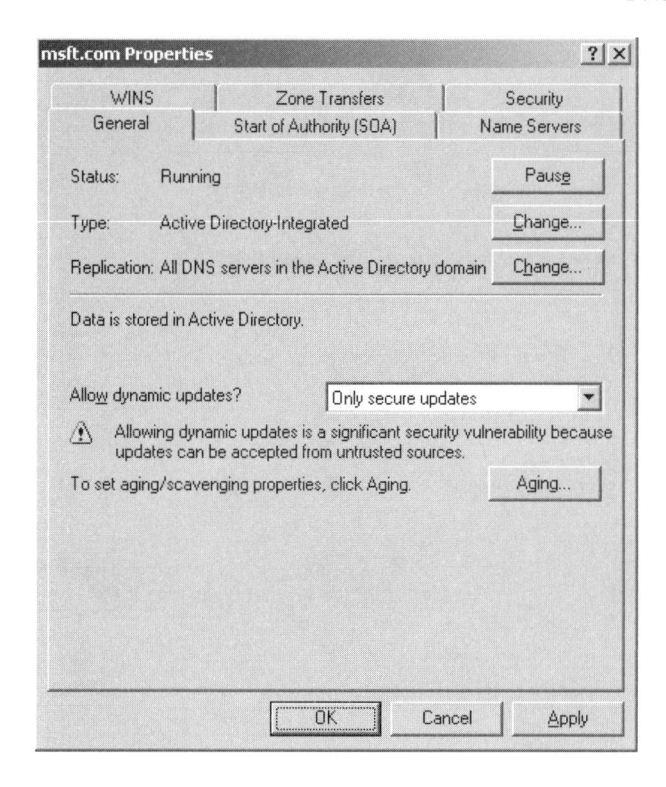

Figure 8-1. Setting zone dynamic update configuration

need to find an IP address for the name bigbadserver.marketing.awl.com, and it may first just get the IP address for a name server in the awl.com domain. This would be an iterative query, since only a portion of the address is resolved. After getting the address of a name server for the awl.com domain, the DNS server would then make a second iterative query, this time asking the awl.com name server for the address of a name server in the marketing.awl.com domain. Finally, with an address for a name server in marketing.awl.com, the DNS server can make a recursive query for the address of bigbadserver.marketing.awl.com. Recursive queries are always made by clients making requests to DNS servers and also by DNS servers that forward requests. We'll look at the role of forwarders in the name resolution process next.

Forwarders

If you're familiar with the game show "Who Wants to Be a Millionaire?" you already know the rules about forwarders. When a DNS server doesn't know the answer for a particular name resolution request, it can "phone a friend," or, in other words, ask a forwarder. Forwarders are configured at the DNS server level in the DNS MMC snap-in, which is shown in Figure 8-2. Forwarders are queried in the order that they're listed in, with the DNS server waiting a default timeout period of five seconds for each forwarder to respond. Requests are made serially, so once a request is made to forwarder 1, the DNS server will wait for five seconds before sending a request to forwarder 2.

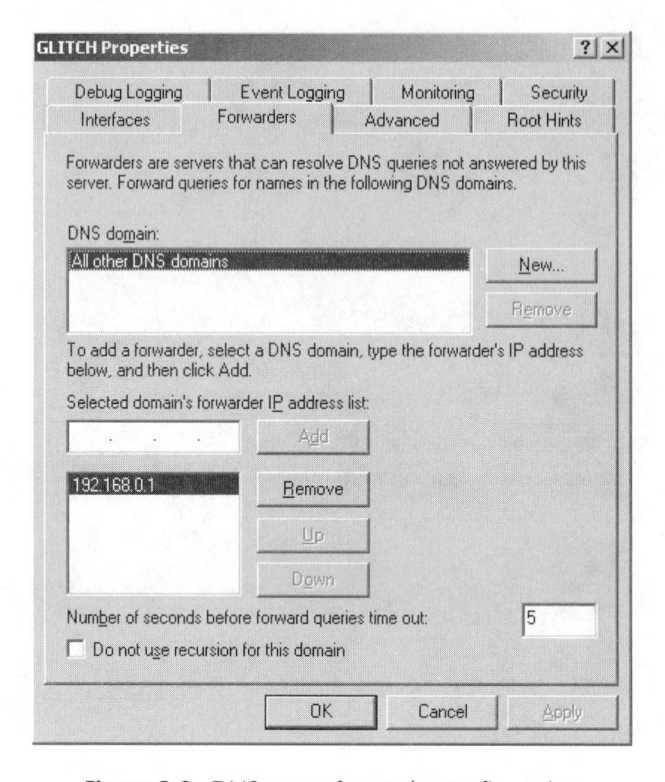

Figure 8-2. DNS server forwarder configuration

Caching-Only Server

A caching-only server refers to a DNS server with no configured zones. This type of server forwards client requests to any forwarders that it has listed or uses its root hints file (cache.dns) to query root-level DNS servers to resolve a name resolution query. All resolved queries are then locally cached by the server (hence its name) so that the server will not have to repeat the same query within a short period of time. The concepts behind root-level servers and forwarding are explained shortly.

Resource Record Types

Names and addresses are referenced in DNS zones as resource records. Records are organized by type, and there are a few record types that you should be aware of when managing and troubleshooting DNS. Here are the most frequently used record types.

- *Host (A)*—Matches a host name to an IP address (like a phone book).

- *Pointer (PTR)*—Matches an IP address to a host name (have number, don't know name).

- *Canonical Name (CNAME)*—Provides an alias for a host (also known as…).

- *Mail Exchange (MX)*—Used to identify a mail exchange server for a domain. This allows you to identify the SMTP server(s) responsible for routing mail within a domain.

- *Name Server (NS)*—Identifies a name server for a domain.

- *Start of Authority (SOA)*—Indicates specific information about a DNS zone, including the authoritative name server for the zone.

- *Service (SRV) Records*—Identifies specific servers in a domain, such as domain controllers.

- *WINS*—Identifies a WINS server to be used for forward lookups (If I don't have an IP address for a host in this zone, I'll ask the WINS server listed in the WINS record).

- *WINSR*—Identifies a WINS server to be used for reverse lookups.

The WINS record types are only supported by Microsoft DNS servers and thus are not compatible with UNIX BIND servers. Now that the terms are out of the way, let's move on to the DNS hierarchy.

DNS Hierarchy

The DNS hierarchy transcends both public and private networks. This arrangement is illustrated in Figure 8-3.

Everything in the DNS hierarchy begins at the top, or root level, and is signified by a "." By default, when DNS is installed on a new domain controller as part of a Windows 2000 Active Directory deployment, a root zone is automatically added to the DNS zone configuration. What this means is that the domain controller believes that it is the root and essentially has all the answers. If the DNS server does not have knowledge of a particular host, it replies to the requester, "The host does not exist," instead of saying, "I don't know." In several instances, an administrator sets up a DNS server and configures clients to use the internal name server as their primary server and the organization's Internet Service Provider's (ISP) name server for Internet name resolution. In this configuration, it is typically quickly discovered that clients cannot access resources on the Internet using their fully qualified domain names, but have no problems accessing internal network resources. Normally, all that is needed to remedy this type of problem is to delete the "." root zone on the internal DNS server. With W2K3 servers, this automatic feature has been removed, so if you want to have a root zone on a W2K3 DNS server, you have to manually create it.

Now that we have established that the root is the source of all knowledge and of the DNS hierarchy, the next tier represents the uppermost-level domains, such as .com, .edu, and .gov. After the upper-level domains, the privately managed DNS namespace resides. Here you see the remainder of the namespace for a particular host. Consider the host freesoftware.Microsoft.com. The system freesoftware is part of the Microsoft domain, which is a child of the .com domain.

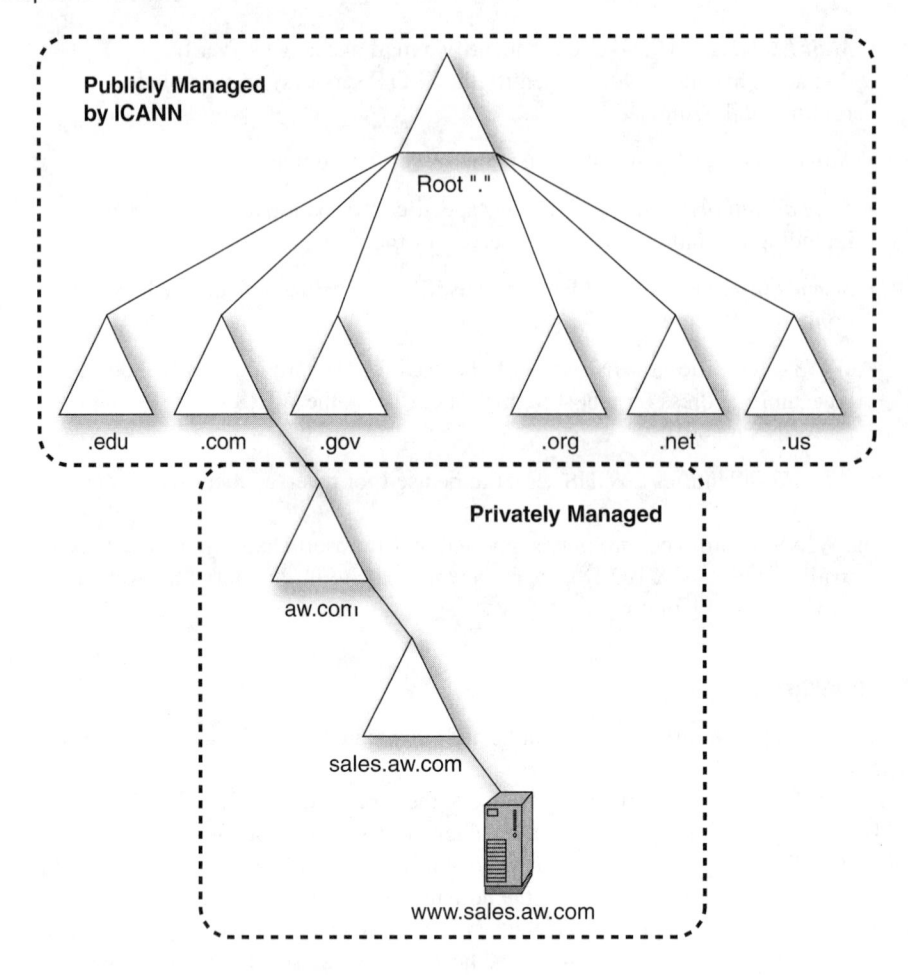

Figure 8-3. DNS hierarchy

Name Resolution Process

To understand this hierarchy a little further, consider the example of the host www.sales.aw.com in Figure 8-3. The system www resides in the sales domain, which is a child domain of the aw domain.

Now suppose that you tried to access the site www.sales.aw.com from your system. First, your system would check its DNS resolver cache for the record. If no record for the host was cached locally, it would send a recursive query to its primary DNS server and await the response. When the DNS server received the request, it would first check its local cache for the record, and then check its zone data. If it had the record or had a root-level zone configured, it would send a reply to the client that made the request. If the DNS server had other DNS servers listed as forwarders, it would then send recursive queries to each forwarder sequentially and await their response, forwarding it to the requesting client and caching the record locally. Finally, if no forwarders were listed, or if no definitive reply was received, the DNS server would then send a series of iterative queries to the root-level servers. First, it would ask a .com root-level server (iterative request) for the IP address of a DNS server authoritative for the aw.com domain. If a server address was returned, the DNS server would then make a second iterative query, this time to an aw.com name server, asking for the address of a name server in the sales.aw.com domain. Upon receiving the address of a sales.aw.com domain, the DNS sever would complete the query process by making a recursive query to the sales.aw.com domain for the host record for www.sales.aw.com. Once the DNS server received the IP address for the host, it would locally cache the address in case another client made the same request and would then reply to the client that initially made the request. As you can see, there are several variables involved in the name resolution process, which sometimes makes it difficult to fully trace the flow of DNS queries involved to locate a host record. To better grasp the processes involved in a name resolution query, take a look at the flow chart shown in Figure 8-4.

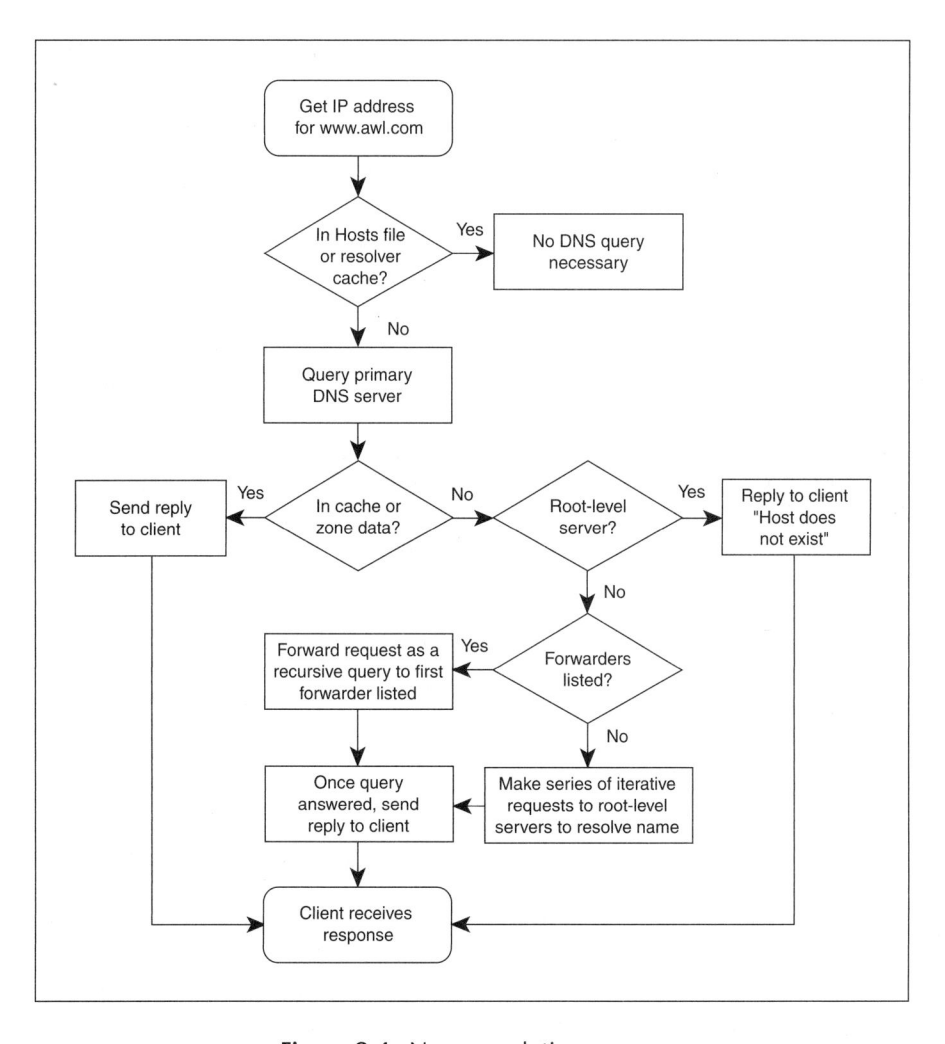

Figure 8-4. Name resolution process

In the previous example, it was noted that if no forwarders existed for a DNS server and it did not have knowledge of a particular record, it would forward the request to the root-level servers. While some would argue that knowledge of root-level servers is something that all DNS servers are born with (natural instinct), this knowledge actually resides in the cache.dns file, which is located in the %systemroot%\system32\dns folder. This file contains the IP addresses for root-level servers, and queries the file when attempting to resolve the name of a remote host. Later, we'll look at what to do if this file becomes corrupted.

DNS Zones

Much of the configuration (and problems) relating to a DNS implementation revolves around DNS zone configuration. In this section, you will quickly review the core concepts of Windows DNS zones, including

- Zone types
- Zone configurations
- Zone transfers
- Zone delegation

Zone Types

There are two types of DNS zones: forward lookup zones and reverse lookup zones. Forward lookup zones resolve host names to IP addresses, and reverse lookup zones match IP addresses to host names. Forward lookup zones contain A records, and reverse lookup zones contain PTR records. Other popular records included in forward lookup zones are CNAME, MX, NS, SOA, SRV, and WINS. In addition to PTR records, you may see WINSR records in reverse lookup zones. While you may see other record types in these zones, the most frequently used records have been listed.

Zone Configurations

Both forward and reverse lookup zones can be configured in one of three different ways:

- Standard primary
- Standard secondary
- Active Directory integrated

Standard primary and standard secondary make up the traditional DNS hierarchy. In this approach, only one writable copy of the DNS zone data exists and is located on the server hosting the standard primary zone. Standard secondary zones update their zone data via zone transfers from a standard primary zone on another DNS server. The standard primary-secondary model can provide fault tolerance of name resolution, but does not provide fault tolerance for name registration. This is because zone updates and dynamic registrations can only be made to the standard primary zone. In addition to being able to receive zone updates from standard primary zones, standard secondary zones can also be configured as secondaries to Active Directory integrated zones.

The primary disadvantage to Active Directory integrated zones is that they must reside on domain controllers. This is because their zone data is stored in the Active Directory database. Because of this relationship, you can configure AD integrated zone replication in one of four different ways:

- To all DNS servers in the Active Directory forest
- To all DNS servers in the Active Directory domain
- To all domain controllers in the Active Directory domain
- To all domain controllers specified in the replication scope of the application directory partition

Replicating zone data to all domain controllers in the domain provides the highest degree of fault tolerance while not impacting replication performance throughout the forest. With DNS zone data automatically replicated to all domain controllers in the domain, if a domain controller acting as a DNS server fails, you can simply install DNS on another domain controller, and the DNS zone configuration and zone data for all Active Directory integrated zones will automatically appear. Active Directory integrated zones also provide fault tolerance for both name registration and name resolution, because with multimaster replication, DNS zone data can be updated on any DNS server.

Another advantage of Active Directory integrated zones is that since their zone data is stored in the Active Directory database, it is more secure, and data moved during zone transfers is secured as well by Kerberos at a minimum. Active Directory integrated zones can be configured to transfer data to other Active Directory integrated zones or to secondary zones but cannot share data with standard primary zones.

Zone Transfers

Standard primary and standard secondary zones store their zone data in the form of a text file, while Active Directory integrated zone information is stored in the Active Directory database. This means that zone transfers between AD integrated zones occur during normal domain controller replication and thus do not fall under the DNS configuration.

When an AD integrated zone transfers data to a standard secondary zone, the DNS server stores the data in a text file in the %systemroot%\system32\dns directory, titled <zone name>.dns, so a secondary zone for the aw.com domain would be stored as aw.com.dns. This configuration is also the same with a primary-secondary zone relationship. The major difference here is that is that when primary and secondary zones are employed, the zone data on all servers involved is stored in a text file.

When an AD integrated—secondary or primary—secondary relationship exists between DNS servers, the frequency of replication of zone data is set by the Refresh Interval setting found under the Start of Authority (SOA) tab of the zone properties on the master server. The default value is 15 minutes. While you may initially think that this is very frequent, you may even decide to lower the interval when using Windows 2000 or higher DNS servers. The reason for this is that beginning with Windows 2000, Incremental Zone Transfer (IXFR) is supported as a means to transfer DNS zone data. With IXFR, only changed records are replicated instead of the entire zone data file. For optimal replication, you could elect to enable DNS Notify by clicking the Notify button under the Zone Transfers tab of a DNS zone's Properties dialog box. When Notify is configured, secondary servers are automatically notified of changes to a primary zone's data. This way, you can configure a higher Refresh Interval, if desired, and still not worry about primary and secondary zones being out of sync. Since AD integrated–to–AD integrated zone replication occurs during normal AD database replication, DNS Notify and Refresh Interval settings have no bearing on Active Directory replication.

> By default, DNS zones are configured to only allow zone transfers to servers listed under the Name Servers tab of the zone's Properties dialog box. If you configure a secondary zone and its first zone transfer fails, check to see that it is listed as a server to which the master will transfer zone data.

Zone Delegation

Zone delegation is a technique used to minimize the amount of data stored on DNS servers dispersed throughout an enterprise. To understand this concept, consider an enterprise consisting of three domains: company.com, east.company.com, and west.company.com. For the most part, users in each domain access local resources, but occasionally access resources on systems in other domains. In this environment, delegation can be used so that the DNS infrastructure models the Active Directory infrastructure. With delegation, DNS servers in west.company.com do not need to contain host records for systems in east.company.com but could instead just contain stub zones.

Stub zones are zones that do not contain data about hosts but instead contain information about name servers for that zone. Think of them as "who to ask" lists. When a system in west.company.com asks for the address of superserver.east.company.com, it queries its local DNS server. With delegation configured, the west.company.com DNS server queries the DNS server listed in its east.company.com stub zone. Once the west server receives a reply, it caches it to speed up performance if it is queried again.

Advanced Configuration

There are a few other options with Windows Server 2003 DNS configuration that you should also be aware of when troubleshooting DNS infrastructure. While not all DNS implementations take advantage of these features, they still cannot be omitted. This section addresses three advanced configuration issues that sometimes lead to DNS implementation problems. Each of the features detailed in this section can be checked and modified by accessing the Advanced tab of the DNS server Properties dialog box in the DNS MMC snap-in, which is shown in Figure 8-5.

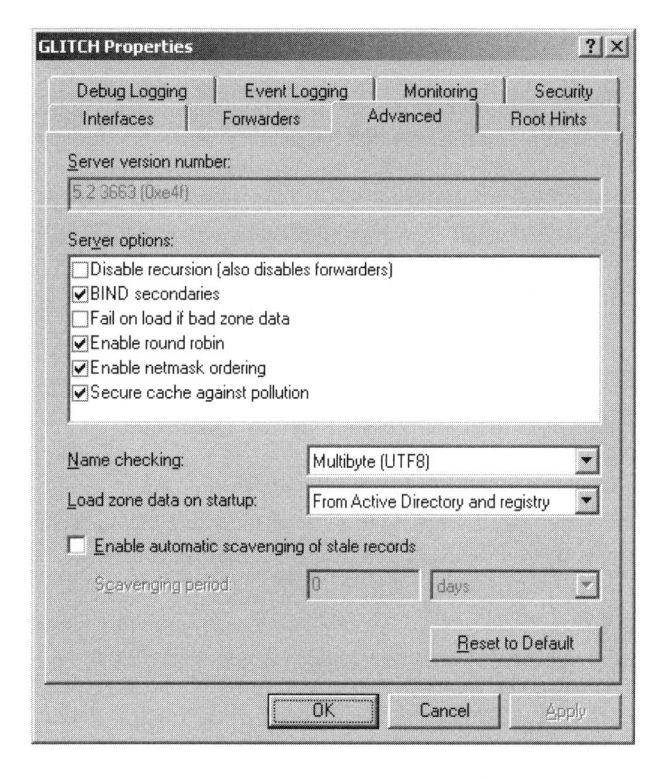

Figure 8-5. DNS advanced features

Round Robin

With the rise of Network Load Balanced (NLB) clusters, round robin is not as popular as it used to be but is still implemented as a means to provide static load balancing, sometimes between two identically configured clusters. Static load balancing using DNS is a relatively easy configuration to set up and literally just requires that you enter multiple A records for the same host, each with a different IP address, and then enable round robin. With multiple A records configured in the zone, each time a clients asks the DNS server for the IP address of that record, it provides a different answer, alternating between available choices. Suppose that four IP addresses existed for the host www.awl.com. The first client that requested its IP address may receive 10.0.0.10, the second would receive 10.0.0.11, followed by 10.0.0.12, and 10.0.0.13. On the fifth request, the DNS server would then reply with 10.0.0.10, starting back at the beginning.

Sometimes round robin implementations fail because they are only halfway configured. Administrators provide multiple A records for the same host but forget to enable round robin. When this happens, the IP address contained in the first listed record for the host is always what is used by the DNS server to answer requests. Round robin can be enabled by checking the Enable Round Robin box under the Advanced tab of the DNS server Properties dialog box.

Remember that even with round robin properly implemented, its static nature can still cause problems. For example, if the host that one of the A records referenced failed, the DNS server would have no way of detecting this and would continue to send some clients to the server. The biggest symptom for this type of problem is that some clients will have no problems accessing the "virtual" server, while others will not be able to connect.

Netmask Ordering

When round robin is enabled, you may also wish to enable netmask ordering. The feature works in conjunction with round robin and adds a level of intelligence to the DNS server. If multiple A records exist for the same host and list IP addresses on different subnets, the DNS server will provide the IP address for the host that resides on the requesting client's local subnet whenever possible. If the requesting client is not on the local subnet of any of the addresses listed for the host, then the DNS server will round robin the response as normal. When you are trying to performance tune local access to a Web server, for example, you should ensure that netmask ordering is enabled.

BIND Secondaries

If your environment consists of UNIX BIND servers that are acting as secondary servers, you should at the very least be aware of this option. UNIX DNS servers running pre-4.9.4 BIND do not support compressed zone transfer data, which is native to Windows DNS zone transfers. If you have a BIND secondary server that is running a pre-4.9.4 version, you need to make sure that the BIND Secondaries advanced option is selected in order for zone transfers to complete successfully. For newer BIND servers, there is no need to select this option.

Now that you have seen the most important DNS server configuration points, let's quickly take a look at a few client issues.

Client Considerations

While you have already been exposed to the general approach to troubleshooting client-side name resolution problems, there are still additional considerations to ponder specifically when troubleshooting DNS name resolution. Here are a few rules to remember about DNS clients when troubleshooting name resolution on the network.

- Alternate DNS servers are only queried if no authoritative response is received from the primary DNS server.

- Clients that cannot connect to a host by its NetBIOS name should have domains added to append to host names (configure the Append These DNS Suffixes option under the DNS tab of the client's advanced TCP/IP settings).

- When clients still cannot connect to a host after an address problem has been corrected on a DNS server, run `ipconfig /flushdns` to clear the client's DNS resolver cache.
- If client host records are not dynamically registering in their DNS server's zone, make sure that dynamic registration is enabled on the clients (register this connection's address in DNS) and also on the DNS server.

Windows Server 2003 Enhancements

There were several DNS enhancements with the Windows Server 2003 operating system, some of which have already been mentioned. These are the most prominent DNS improvements with W2K3 servers.

- *Stub zones*—They provide a simple means to maintain DNS efficiency throughout an enterprise.
- *DNS zone replication in AD*—As previously mentioned, you now have control over how AD integrated DNS zones are replicated.
- *Conditional forwarders*—You can now configure forwarders by domain name, so requests for addresses in a particular domain can be directed to a specific DNS server, regardless of its position as a forwarder (by default, all queries are sent to the first forwarder listed).
- *DNSSEC supported*—DNS Security Extensions protocol is supported.
- *Improved round robin support*—Round robin can be employed to statically load balance all record types, as opposed to the previous standard of just supporting A records.
- *Enhanced debug logging*—More logging makes it easier to pinpoint DNS problems.

Now that you have a solid dose of DNS theory under your belt, let's take a look at the tools of the trade.

DNS Troubleshooting Tools

The Windows operating system makes you well equipped to diagnose and resolve DNS problems by providing you with four excellent tools. This section shows you the tools that make resolving DNS problems a snap. Many DNS problems can be quickly pinpointed if you use the appropriate tool when troubleshooting. Three command line tools—`dnscmd`, `dnslint`, and `nslookup`—will quickly become your best friends while you are attempting to resolve DNS problems. Because of their importance, this

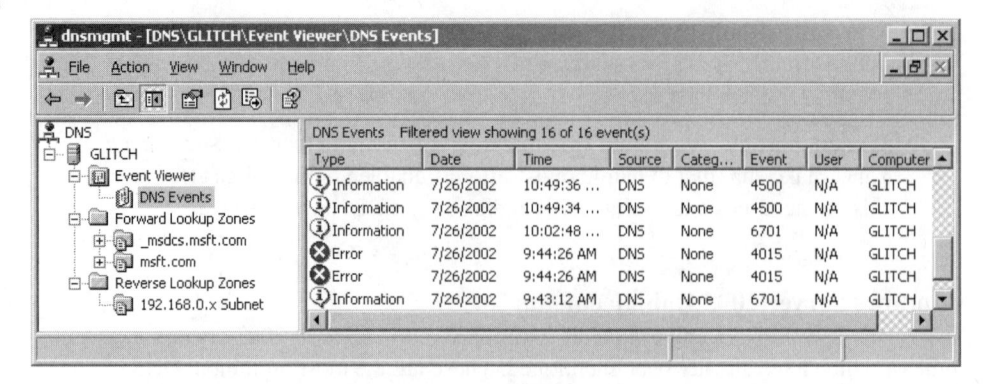

Figure 8-6. DNS MMC snap-in

section spends a good deal of time introducing you to them. The tools are presented in order from the most simplistic to the most advanced.

DNS MMC

The DNS MMC is the standard DNS management tool on Windows 2000 and W2K3 servers. While mainly a pure administrative tool, it does have its uses for troubleshooting too, especially when you are trying to locate problems with a new DNS infrastructure implementation. To access the tool, just click Start > Administrative Tools > DNS. Once the DNS MMC has opened, you can examine the events, properties, and zone configurations of a DNS server. The DNS MMC snap-in is shown in Figure 8-6.

There are three troubleshooting tools located in the DNS MMC:

- Debug logging
- Event logging
- Monitoring

Each of these tools is explained in the next three sections.

Debug Logging

Debug logging is disabled by default. When problems are encountered with a particular DNS server, and the fault doesn't just jump right out at you, you should enable debug logging. To enable this feature, follow these steps.

1. Open the DNS MMC.
2. Right-click the DNS server object and select Properties.

3. In the DNS server Properties dialog box, click the Debug Logging tab.

4. As shown in Figure 8-7, select the Log Packets for Debugging checkbox and click OK.

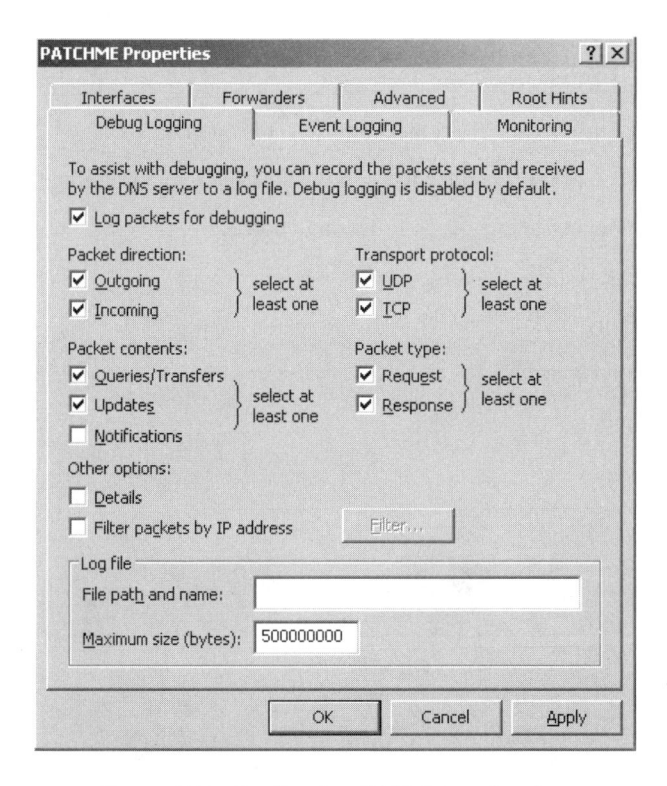

Figure 8-7. Configuring DNS debug logging

As you can see in the illustration, you can be broad or granular in how you decide to log DNS data. While some may try to select just what is needed to "catch" the problem, it is often best to log everything. This way you are sure not to miss information that would actually have helped you resolve the problem. Once you have enabled logging, you can then look for errors in the %systemroot%\system32\dns\dns.log file. Once you have resolved the problem, make sure to disable logging on the server, since it will degrade system performance.

Event Logging

Unlike debug logging, event logging is enabled by default. With event logging, all DNS-related events are written to the DNS log and can be accessed from the DNS MMC. DNS events are often very descriptive in reporting problems and usually allow you to quickly pinpoint the source of a failure. Figure 8-8 shows a typical example of a critical DNS event. As you can see, the event practically points right at the problem, informing you that zone transfer for the DNS server is not enabled on the master server.

If you need to update or change the event logging configuration for a DNS server, follow these steps.

1. Open the DNS MMC.
2. Right-click the DNS server object and select Properties.
3. In the DNS server Properties dialog box, click the Event Logging tab.
4. Set event logging to one of the following choices:
   - No events
   - Errors only
   - Errors and warnings
   - All events
5. Click OK.

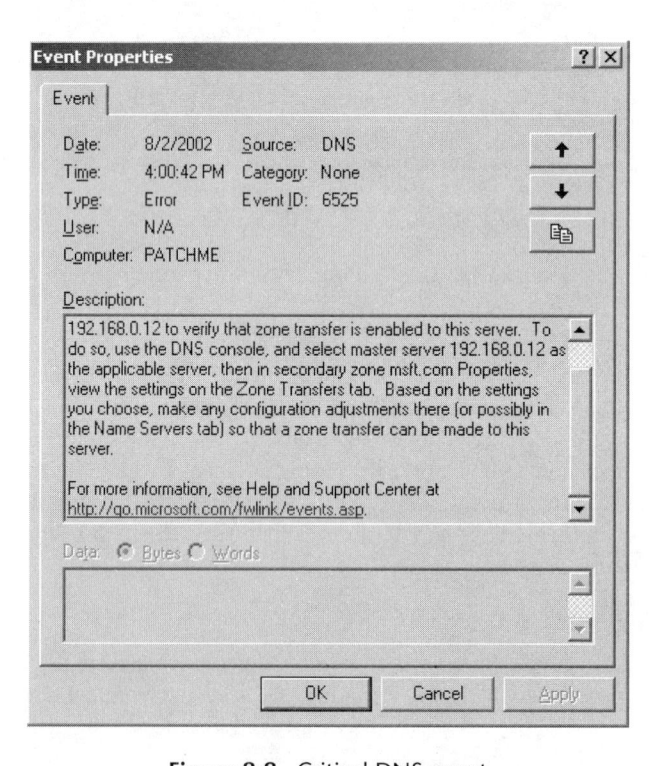

Figure 8-8. Critical DNS event

Monitoring

Monitoring is another tool that is accessed through the DNS MMC snap-in. It performs two tests:

- Simple query to this DNS server
- Recursive query to other DNS servers

When the simple test is run, it queries the local DNS database. More specifically, the simple test

- Performs an iterative test to the local DNS database.
- Tests the A record of the DNS server itself.

The recursive test attempts to connect to a root-level server. The recursive test

- Checks the connection to the root-level server.
- Fails if the local root or the external (Internet) root is unavailable.
- Fails if the cache.dns file is corrupt or missing.

If the DNS server has a root zone configured, it passes the recursive test; otherwise, if this test fails, you should check the DNS server's outbound WAN network configuration. If you suspect a corrupt cache.dns file may be the cause of the problem (after verifying that outbound connectivity is good), then copy the %systemroot%\system32\dns\samples\cache.dns file to the %systemroot%\system32\dns folder. This overwrites the existing cache.dns file with the default installation version.

To test DNS zone data access with monitoring, follow these steps:

1. Open the DNS MMC.
2. Right-click the DNS server object and select Properties.
3. In the DNS server Properties dialog box, click the Monitoring tab.
4. Select the Simple and Recursive query boxes and click Test Now (see Figure 8-9).

The test results are displayed at the bottom of the dialog box.

dnscmd (ST)

The `dnscmd` support tool is the first of the two very popular DNS troubleshooting command line tools covered in this section. The `nslookup` command, which is covered next, generally is used for performing queries and testing DNS server responses, while `dnscmd` allows you to diagnose and resolve configuration issues as well as perform an abundance of administrative tasks on a DNS server.

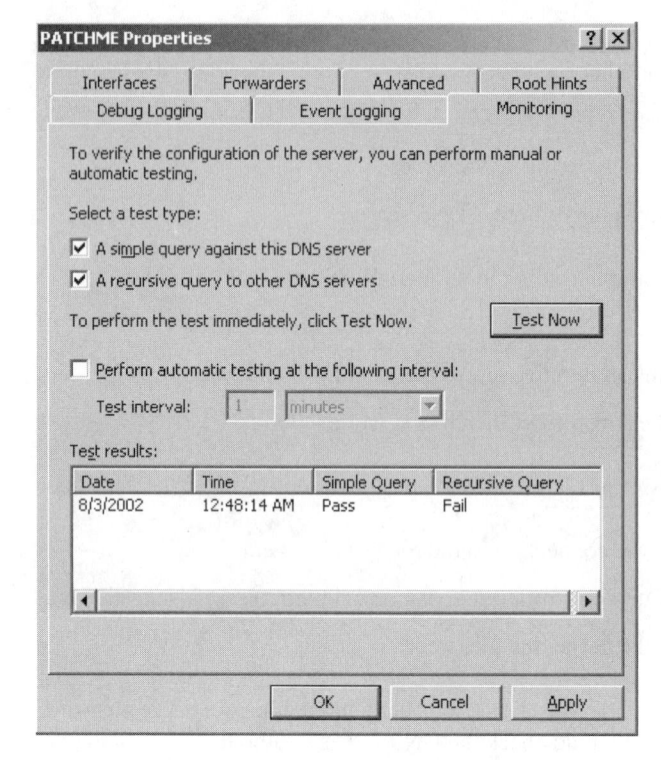

Figure 8-9. Testing DNS zone access

The general syntax for `dnscmd` is:

```
dnscmd [server] <operation> [Parameters] [Arguments]
```

In the syntax, you need to specify the name of the DNS server to administer, or the command executes on the local system. There are countless different operation values that can be used with `dnscmd`. The operations that are relevant to DNS troubleshooting are discussed in the next two sections.

clearcache

The `clearcache` operation allows you to remove all cached resource records in a DNS server's cache. This is useful, for example, when a DNS server forwards a query to another DNS server that responds with the wrong answer. Even if you correct the address on the DNS server hosting the queried zone, other DNS servers may have the address cached. To correct the problem, you can run `clearcache` on each DNS server in your enterprise that may have cached the entry. Any new queries to the DNS server will cause it to forward the request to the server with the proper record and then will cache the correct record.

Now that you have seen why to use it, this is how to use it.

```
dnscmd [server] /clearcache
```

So, to clear the cache of the name server ns1.aw.com, you would run the following command:

```
dnscmd ns1.aw.com /clearcache
```

Statistics

The `statistics` operation allows you to see an abundance of information about a DNS server, including

- Queries received and sent
- Query types received (A, NS, MX, PTR)
- Zone transfer attempts and success rate
- WINS referrals
- Dynamic update statistics (secure updates, record types)
- Write performance statistics

The command outputs an abundance of information, some of which is more useful for development purposes than for troubleshooting. Normally, concentrate on checking the command output for recorded errors and then work to isolate the problem based on the errors that are reported.

The command syntax for the `statistics` operation is:

```
dnscmd [server] /statistics [id] [/clear]
```

The options for the `statistics` operation are described in Table 8-1.

Table 8-1. dnscmd /statistics Command Options

Option	Use
server	Used to specify the name or IP address of the remote DNS server on which to report statistics.
id	When you do not want to report on all DNS server statistical categories, this option allows you to specify the categories to return in the command output. Valid `id` values are listed in Table 8-2.
/clear	Resets the target DNS server's statistics counter to 0. Counters automatically clear and start once the DNS server is started or resumed.

Table 8-2. dnscmd /statistics id Parameter Values

Value	Associated Statistics
1	Time
2	Query
4	Query2
8	Recurse
10	Master
20	Secondary
40	WINS
100	Update
200	SkwanSec
400	DS
10000	Memory
40000	Database
80000	Records
100000	Packet Memory
200000	NBTStat Memory

Although the statistical ID categories are not the most intuitive in name, you should focus more on their related records. The first time that you run this command, specify no `id` parameter, and note the categories that are of most relevance to you. This way, on subsequent attempts the command output will be much smaller. Since so many DNS server statistics are reported by the command, you should consider redirecting the command output to another source, such as a text file. For example, to report on all statistics for the server dns1.aw.com and have its output stored in the D:\Logs\dns1stats.txt file, you would run the following command:

```
dnscmd dns1.aw.com /statistics > "d:\logs\dns1stats.txt"
```

Once the command completes, you can then view its output by opening the file in Notepad.

While some administrators resolve problems using `dnscmd`, others ignore this command completely. One command that also reports on DNS statistics but is much easier to use is `dnslint`. We'll look at it next.

dnslint (ST)

The `dnslint` command is a tool that lets you check and verify DNS records for a particular domain. The most common use for `dnslint` is troubleshooting problems in a multidomain enterprise DNS infrastructure utilizing stub zones and delegation. This tool is very quick, traversing a network and reporting in under a minute, and generates its output as an HTML page. The command does the following:

- Verifies all A, NS, MX, and glue records associated with delegation
- Checks that all authoritative DNS servers are responding to queries
- Verifies that data on all DNS servers is synchronized

In addition to testing name servers, you can also use `dnslint` to test mail servers on the network. The `dnslint` command identifies mail servers by locating MX records on DNS servers, and then tests the following e-mail-related ports on each mail server:

- Internet Mail Access Protocol (IMAP) version 4 (TCP port 143)
- Post Office Protocol (POP) version 3 (TCP port 110)
- Simple Mail Transfer Protocol (SMTP) (TCP port 25)

When run to check the status of mail servers (shortly you will see that this is done with the `/c` switch), `dnslint` reports on the status of each mail port. The status can be listening, not listening, or no response.

Now let's look at its syntax:

```
dnslint /d <domain> [/r <report name>] [/s <alternate DNS server>]
[/y] [/v]
```

The command options are described in Table 8-3.

Table 8-3. dnslint Command Options

Option	Use
`/d <domain>`	Required parameter; specifies the domain to test.
`/r <report name>`	Used to specify a custom name for the report file. By default, the file is named Dnslint.htm and is stored in the folder from which the command was executed.
`/s <alternate DNS server>`	Used to specify an alternate DNS server address, bypassing the InterNIC servers, which is ideal for testing nonregistered domains.
`/y`	Causes the existing report file to be overwritten without prompting the user.
`/v`	Verbose output—highly detailed output data is returned.

To test the DNS infrastructure of the domain company.com, you would run `dnslint /d company.com`. If you needed to test the infrastructure of an unregistered internal test domain, you would include the `/s` switch and specify the IP address of an internal name server. When the output report is generated, any reported errors are displayed in red. A portion of a `dnslint` output report is shown in Figure 8-10.

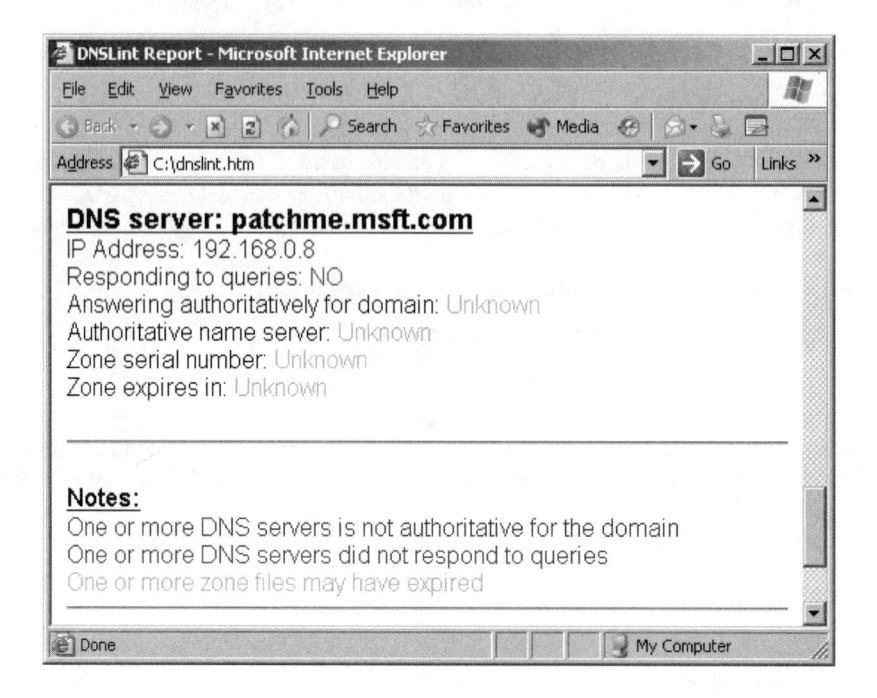

Figure 8-10. dnslint output report

In the report shown in Figure 8-10, you can see that `dnslint` has found that the name server patchme.msft.com is not responding to queries. With this information, you can then turn your troubleshooting attention to this system. In particular, you may want to ping it to see if it is responding to any network traffic. While `dnslint` is certainly valuable, it is still limited in its capabilities. The next tool, `nslookup`, on the other hand offers you a great deal of freedom when you are troubleshooting name resolution problems and thus is the most frequently used.

nslookup

The `nslookup` command is the most powerful of all the available DNS troubleshooting tools. With a little practice, use of this tool to locate the source of any DNS problem will become instinctive. With `nslookup`, you can directly make name queries to a DNS server, thus simulating the actions taken by a DNS client computer. To use this command to query DNS servers, you can simply run `nslookup`, or you can extend the command's capabilities by including any one of its several subcommands. The syntax for the core `nslookup` command is:

```
nslookup [-<subcommand>] [host] [-<nameserver>]
```

By just providing a host name, FQDN, or IP address with the `nslookup` command, you can test a system's ability to resolve names. Often, before you install any network agents for products such as backup software, it is a good idea to make sure that each system used by the software can communicate with the others. If DNS is not properly configured, you can find out by running `nslookup`. Suppose you wanted to see if a system could resolve the IP address for the host beavis.cartoons.com. To check name resolution, you would run `nslookup beavis.cartoons.com`. The command would return the name and IP address of the name server that was queried, along with the name and IP address for the queried host (beavis). This type of test would verify the proper configuration of the forward lookup zone on the DNS server. You could similarly test the reverse lookup zone by substituting the system's name with its IP address. So, for example, you could run `nslookup 10.1.1.82`. Again, the command would return the queried DNS server's name and IP address, along with the name and IP address of the particular host. When records are returned, you receive one of the two response types from the name server.

- Authoritative answer—The DNS server had the record itself. ("I have that one, here you go!")

- Nonauthoritative answer—The DNS server queried and received information about the record from another name server ("I had to ask someone else, but I think it's correct.").

While in a perfect world, the results just mentioned would always be the case, unfortunately sometimes DNS servers are not properly configured or are missing records. In these instances, `nslookup` fails to resolve a particular query. The errors returned by `nslookup` when a query cannot be resolved are shown in Table 8-4.

Table 8-4. nslookup Errors

Error Message	Cause
Connection refused	No connection could be made with the DNS server. This error is common with the `ls` subcommand when you connect to a server that only allows zone transfers to specific servers.
Format error	The DNS server found an error in the `nslookup` request packet. Run `nslookup` again to reconnect to the name server.
Network is unreachable	No connection could be made with the DNS server. Look for a network routing problem by seeing if you can ping other hosts on the DNS server's subnet.

continues

Table 8-4. nslookup Errors, continued

Error Message	Cause
No records	No records exist for the query type specified by the `querytype` subcommand (shown later).
No response from server	DNS is not running on the specified name server (either in the command syntax or in the system's TCP/IP properties).
Nonexistent domain	No record of the requested domain name could be located.
Refused	The `nslookup` request was refused by the name server. This error is common with the `ls` subcommand when you connect to a server that only allows zone transfers to specific servers.
Server failure	There is a problem or inconsistency in the DNS server's zone data file. Restore the zone file from an earlier backup.
Timed out	The DNS server did not respond after a given timeout and Retry Interval. The default timeout value is 5 seconds, and the Retry Interval is 4, meaning that the command will wait 20 seconds for a response before timing out.

Much of `nslookup`'s functionality is derived from its multitude of subcommands. The easiest way to reach any subcommand menu is to first type `nslookup` and press Enter. This brings you to interactive mode, from where you can directly enter any of the `nslookup` subcommands. The next several sections introduce you to each of the available troubleshooting-related `nslookup` subcommands. Once all the subcommands are covered, you will then see examples of how to use `nslookup` in various troubleshooting scenarios.

exit

The `exit` command is used to return you to the command prompt when you are running `nslookup` in interactive mode. You know when you are in interactive mode because the prompt appears as just > with a flashing cursor.

ls

The `ls` subcommand is used to display the contents of a particular zone on the DNS server. If the zone is not configured to allow zone transfers to the system where you are running the `nslookup` command, you will get a Refused error. Since zone data can be very large, you also have the option with the `ls` subcommand to redirect the command output to a file.

The syntax for `ls` is:

```
ls [option] <domain> [> <filename>]
```

The `domain` parameter in the `ls` syntax is used to specify the zone whose contents you would like to view. If the > redirector is used, you can specify the filename where you would like the command output directed to. The `option` parameter has five possible values, which are listed in Table 8-5.

Table 8-5. ls Command Options

Option	Use
-a	Returns the aliases (CNAME records) of computers in the specified domain.
-d	Returns all records in the specified domain.
-h	Returns CPU and operating system information for the specified domain, if HINFO (host information) records are present in the zone.
-t <querytype>	Returns all records of the type specified with the `querytype` parameter. Valid `querytype` values are listed in Table 8-6.
-s	Returns well-known services of systems in the specified domain.

Table 8-6 lists the valid query types that can be performed with the `-t` option. Some queries may return no data if no records of the query type exist in the target domain.

Table 8-6. Valid querytype Values

Value	Records Returned
a	Host records (names and IP addresses)
any	All records
cname	Aliases
gid	Group identifier number (used by NFS in UNIX applications)
hinfo	Host information records (specify the CPU and OS type for systems)
mb	Mailbox domain names
mg	Master group members
minfo	Mailbox information
mr	Mail rename domain names
mx	Mail exchangers
ns	Name servers
ptr	All pointer records
soa	Start of authority records
txt	Text information records
uid	User ID (used by NFS in UNIX applications)
uinfo	User information records
wks	Well-known service records

276 Chapter 8 DNS

While there are countless record types that you can query, the most popular query types are

- A
- Any
- CNAME
- MX
- NS
- PTR
- SOA

Although at first glance the `ls` subcommand does look a little tricky, it really isn't that bad. Figure 8-11 shows the `nslookup` command sequence to locate name servers in the msft.com domain.

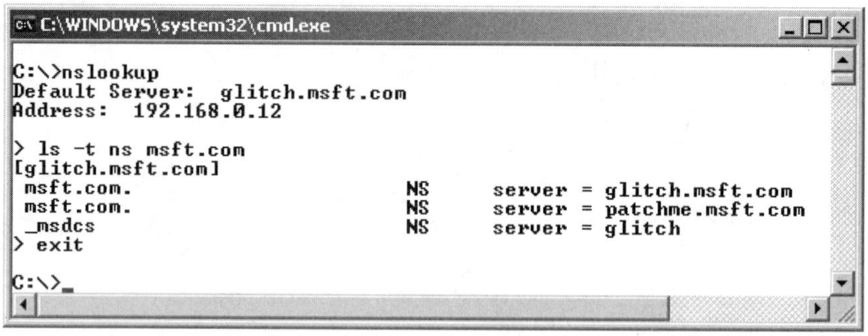

Figure 8-11. Listing all name servers for a domain with nslookup

Suppose that you wanted to see all records in the msft.com domain and have the information stored in the msftzonedata.txt file. To do this, you would run the following command:

```
ls -t any msft.com > msftzonedata.txt
```

lserver
When you run `nslookup` in interactive mode, you are connected to either your local system's default name server or a server that you specified at the time you executed the command. If you want to change the server you're connected to, that's what `lserver` is for.

The syntax for `lserver` is:

```
lserver <server | domain>
```

When a server name is specified, `nslookup` connects directly to the server. When you specify a domain, `nslookup` connects to the first name server listed in the domain's associated DNS zone.

server

The `server` subcommand works exactly like `lserver`, with the exception that the system's current default DNS server is used to resolve the name of the new name server to connect to, as opposed to resolving the name through the context of the current `nslookup` connection.

Take away the L from the `lserver` syntax, and you have the syntax for this command, which is:

```
server <server | domain>
```

Again, you need to specify either a server or a domain in which to connect.

set

The `set` subcommand is used to configure how the currently running `nslookup` command shell queries and retrieves records. There are several versions of `set`, and each is described in the next several sections.

set all

This command displays the current configuration settings for the name server that you're connected to with `nslookup`. The syntax for `set all` is:

```
set all
```

Once the command has executed, configuration information about the DNS server in context is displayed.

set class

This is a setting that you will likely never have to change, since practically every name server today is using the Internet class of resource records. However, before the growth of the Internet class well over a decade ago, there were two other popular classes for DNS records: Chaos and MIT Athena Hesiod. The Chaos class supported Chaosnet networks and is likely of value to you only if you appear on computer "Jeopardy" one day. The same can probably be said for the Hesiod class, since you are unlikely to run into it as well. Rather than bore you with any more history, let's just get to the `set class` syntax.

```
set cl[ass]=<class>
```

For this command, you do not need to enter the three letters that follow `cl`, but feel free to if you feel your fingers need the exercise. The default class for `nslookup` is Internet, but this can be modified by specifying one of the classes listed in Table 8-7.

Table 8-7. Valid class Values

Class	Description
`in`	Internet class
`chaos`	Chaos class
`hesiod`	MIT Athena Hesiod class

So, to change the current `nslookup` interaction to use the Hesiod class, you would type `set cl=hesiod` and press Enter.

set d2

This subcommand allows you to turn on exhaustive debugging (debugging^2). When exhaustive debugging is enabled, not only does your computer get pretty tired, but also you will see all fields of every `nslookup` packet displayed in the command output. When this feature is enabled, each `nslookup` query result displays the information that was sent, the answer that was received, and the system that provided the answer. For difficult-to-solve problems where you are looking for every bit of information that you can collect to analyze, you may want to turn on exhaustive debugging; otherwise, you can leave it off.

The syntax for this command is:

`set [no]d2`

To turn on exhaustive debugging, you would run `set d2`, and to turn it off, you would run `set nod2`.

set debug

The `set debug` subcommand allows you turn debugging on and off for `nslookup` queries. With debugging mode enabled, you will see detailed information about the question-and-answer packets involved in `nslookup` queries, but not to the detail of the information provided when exhaustive debugging is enabled.

The `set debug` syntax is:

`set [no]deb[ug]`

To use this command to enable debugging, you would enter `set deb`, and to disable debugging, you would type `set nodeb`. When `nslookup` is initially launched, no form of debugging is enabled.

set defname

This command is used to append the local system's default domain name to `nslookup` queries (which is the system default). This way, if you are looking up IP addresses for hosts in the computers.com domain, you can just enter the system name in the query instead of having to type its fully qualified domain name.

The syntax for `set defname` is:

```
set [no]def[name]
```

To configure `nslookup` to automatically append the local system's default domain name, you would enter `set def`. When you are performing multiple queries for the same local domain, using this subcommand can save you quite a bit of time.

set domain

The `set domain` subcommand allows you to append a domain name other than the default domain name to lookup requests. The syntax for this command is:

```
set do[main]=<domain>
```

Here's an example of using `set domain` to change the default domain for queries to reliablesoftware.net:

```
set do=reliablesoftware.net
```

set ignore

This subcommand allows you to configure `nslookup` to ignore packet truncation errors, which result from name servers truncating host record names longer than 28 characters, as may be the case with Windows 9x clients. By default, `nslookup` does not ignore these errors, so if you wanted them to be ignored, you would run the `set ignore` command.

The syntax for this command is:

```
set [no]ig[nore]
```

To configure `nslookup` to ignore packet truncation errors, you would run `set ig`. To return `nslookup` to its default and have it no longer ignore truncation errors, you would then run `set noig`. The other option for returning `nslookup` to normal is to exit out of interactive mode and then run `nslookup` again.

set port

By default, DNS servers use TCP/UDP port 53. If you are using `nslookup` to connect to a DNS server not using port 53, this command allows you to change the port number used by `nslookup` for communications with the DNS server. Here's `set port`'s syntax:

```
set po[rt]=<port>
```

For an example, assume that you are connecting to a DNS server using port 8408. To have `nslookup` use this port, you would run `set port=8408`.

set querytype

The `set querytype` subcommand is used to configure `nslookup` to look up a particular type of resource record. The syntax for this command is:

```
set q[uerytype]=<record type>
```

The possible record type values are the same as those with the `nslookup ls` command described earlier and are listed in Table 8-6. This command is very handy when you are trying to quickly locate specific record types. For example, to locate mail server records for a particular domain, you could run `set q=mx`. The complete command sequence for finding mail servers in the msft.com domain is shown in Figure 8-12.

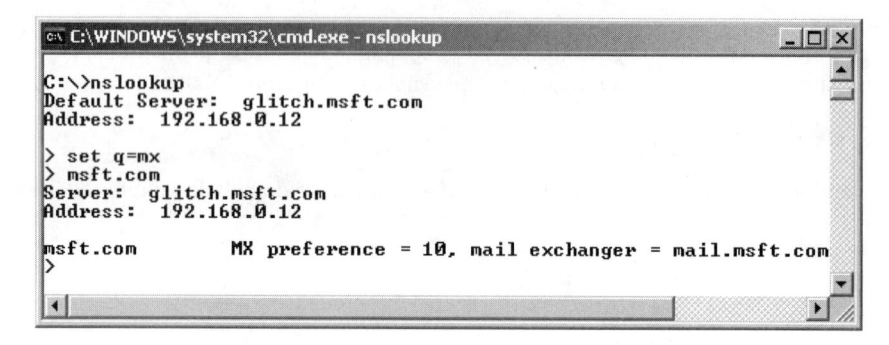

Figure 8-12. Locating mail servers with nslookup

> You can also run `set type` instead of `set querytype`. Both perform the same function.

set recurse

Recursion is set by default with `nslookup`. This means that if the target name server does not have knowledge of the record you are requesting, it automatically queries other name servers. The `set recurse` command allows you to change this default behavior by turning off recursion or by turning it back on. The command syntax is:

```
set [no]rec[urse]
```

To disable recursion, you would run `set norec`. If you then wanted to enable recursion, you could run `set rec`.

set retry

When a request is made with `nslookup`, the command waits a predetermined amount of time for a response before timing out. Two factors that determine the amount of elapsed time before a timeout are the Retry Interval and the timeout period. The default value for retries is 4, and the default timeout is 5 seconds. The `set retry` command, as you might have guessed, allows you to change the Retry Interval. The syntax for `set retry` is:

```
set ret[ry]=<value>
```

In the command syntax, the `value` parameter represents an integer value for the new Retry Interval. In a few moments, you will see the other half of configuring the timeout setting for `nslookup`.

set root

This command allows you to specify a root name server other than the default (ns.nic.ddn.mil) to be used by `nslookup`. You may decide to use this option when running `nslookup` to find names on an internal network that has a root name server configured. The syntax for `set root` is:

```
set ro[ot]=<rootserver>
```

For example, if an internal domain's root server is ns1.admin.aw.com, you would run this command:

```
set ro=ns1.admin.aw.com
```

set search

By default, when a name is queried with `nslookup`, any DNS suffixes listed to be appended in the local system's advanced TCP/IP properties are appended to the name until a match is found. If you want to turn off this default behavior and have no DNS suffixes appended to the name, you can use `set search` to turn off automatic DNS suffix appending in `nslookup`. The syntax for this command is:

```
set [no]sea[rch]
```

To stop `nslookup` from appending DNS suffixes while searching for a record, you would run `set nosea`.

set srchlist

If you want to specify a custom domain suffix search list to be used by `nslookup`, you can run `set srchlist`. The syntax for this command is:

```
set srchl[ist]=<domain>[/<domain2>...]
```

If you want to specify multiple domains to be searched, each domain must be separated by a /. For example, if you wanted `nslookup` to search the domains sales.aw.com and marketing.aw.com, you would run this command:

```
set srchl=sales.aw.com/marketing.aw.com
```

set timeout

Aside from the Retry Interval, the timeout period is the other parameter in an `nslookup` timeout. The default timeout value is 5 seconds. To change the timeout value, you would use the following command syntax:

```
set ti[meout]=<seconds>
```

Remember that the timeout period is multiplied by the Retry Interval to give you the total query timeout value. So if you used `set timeout` to change the timeout period to 10 seconds, assuming that the Retry Interval was still set to its default value of 4, queries would wait up to 40 seconds for a response.

set vc

The `set vc` command is used to tell `nslookup` whether or not to use a virtual circuit when querying a DNS server. The syntax for `set vc` is:

```
set [no]v[c]
```

By default, `nslookup` does not use virtual circuits. To allow `nslookup` to use a virtual circuit when querying a name server, you would run `set v`.

You have seen an abundance of parameters that can be set to customize how `nslookup` responds. Some of the most frequently used versions of the `set` command are

- `all`
- `debug`
- `domain`
- `querytype`
- `recurse`
- `srchlist`

Of this list, `querytype` is the most common. You will see some of these options used later in the Troubleshooting with nslookup section.

view

When the output of the `nslookup ls` command is redirected to a text file, you can use the `view` `nslookup` subcommand to see the file's contents. The syntax for this command is:

```
view <filename>
```

Now that you have probably had more than your fill of the ins and outs of `nslookup`, let's put that knowledge to work.

Troubleshooting with nslookup

In a few of the examples in the preceding subsections, you were able to see how to methodically use `nslookup` to retrieve information about a particular host or domain. In this section, we'll go from basic examples to those that are a little more advanced. This should give you a good feel for how, when, and why to use `nslookup` for diagnosing and resolving name resolution problems on your network.

Verifying Forward and Reverse Lookup Zones

Oftentimes, forward lookup zones are configured properly, but reverse lookup zones are not. Sometimes, reverse lookup zones are not created at all, which may cause problems if applications running on your network rely on reverse lookups. Here is a series of commands that you can use to test for the presence of both forward and reverse lookup zones for the host king.company.net.

```
C:\>nslookup
Default server: NS1.company.net
Address: 10.1.1.9

>king.company.net
Server: NS1.company.net
Address: 10.1.1.9

Name: king.company.net
Address: 10.1.2.203

>10.1.2.203
Server: NS1.company.net
Address: 10.1.1.9

Name: king.company.net
Address: 10.1.2.203

>exit
```

Verifying SRV Resource Record Presence

If clients are unable to log on to the domain, it may mean that the domain's associated SRV records are not present in the domain's forward lookup zone on the clients' primary DNS server. To test for the presence of SRV records for the domain company.net, you would perform the following commands using `nslookup`.

```
C:\>nslookup
Default server: NS1.company.net
Address: 10.1.1.9

>set q=srv
>_ldap._tcp.dc._msdcs.company.net
Server: NS1.company.net
```

```
Address: 10.1.1.9

_ldap._tcp.dc._dsdcs.company.net   SRV service location:
        priority                = 0
        weight                  = 100
        port                    = 389
        svr hostname            = dc1.company.net
dc1.company.net internet address = 10.1.1.14

>exit
```

In the company syntax, you would substitute company.net with the name for the domain that you are attempting to query. If no SRV records were located, you would receive the following error message:

```
*** Can't find _ldap._tcp.dc._msdcs.company.net: Non-existent domain
```

If the domain controller is running, take these actions.

1. Make sure that dynamic updates are enabled on the domain's associated zone on the DNS server.

2. Make sure that the domain controller has the correct primary DNS server listed in its TCP/IP properties.

3. Stop and restart the NetLogon service on the domain controller.

Once NetLogon restarts, it will attempt to dynamically register its SRV records with the DNS server.

Verifying Zone Delegation

Assume that you've just set up zone delegation so that your corporate domain will refer requests for hosts in the eur.company.net domain to name servers in the eur domain. After setting up a stub zone and configuring glue records for the domain, you want to verify that delegation is working. To verify delegation, you would run the following commands with `nslookup`.

```
C:\>nslookup
Default server: NS1.company.net
Address: 10.1.1.9

>set norecurse
>set q=ns
>zeus.east.company.net
Server: NS1.company.net
Address: 10.1.1.9

east.company.net
        primary name server = dns3.east.company.net
```

```
              responsible mail addr = hostmaster.east.company.net
              serial = 20
              refresh = 900 (15 mins)
              retry = 600 (10 mins)
              expire = 86400 (1 day)
              default TTL = 3600 (1 hour)

    >exit
```

Since you were querying for name server records, note that when you entered a host in the query, the records for name servers that can provide an authoritative response were returned. In this example, the domain had only one name server that could respond to the query, which was dns3.east.company.net. If you wanted to see the IP address for the host Zeus, you could now change the query type to A and then rerun the query. This time, `nslookup` would provide the IP address for Zeus as a nonauthoritative answer, because the record did not reside on the name server that you are connected to.

Verifying WINS Lookup

To finish off this section, let's quickly look at one more example of using `nslookup`. This time, we'll use `nslookup` to verify that the name server in company.net is querying the WINS server WINS1.company.net for records. In the example provided, assume that no record for the host upgrademe.company.net exists in the server DNS1's forward lookup zone for the company.net domain. This sequence of commands allows you to verify that DNS1 was able to successfully pass the query to WINS1 and provide a response to the request.

```
    C:\>nslookup
    Default server: NS1.company.net
    Address: 10.1.1.9

    >set debug
    >set q=a
    >upgrademe.company.net
    Server: NS1.company.net
    Address: 10.1.1.9
    _____

    Got answer:
        HEADER:
            Opcode = QUERY, id = 8, rcode = NOERROR
            Header flags: response, auth.answer, want recursion, available
            Questions = 1, answers = 1, authority records = 0, additional= 0

        QUESTIONS:
            upgrademe.company.net, type = A, class = IN
        ANSWERS:
        -> upgrademe.company.net
            internet address = 10.1.5.198
            ttl = 886 (14 mins 46 secs)
```

```
Name: upgrademe.company.net
Address: 10.1.5.198

>upgrademe.company.net
Server: NS1.company.net
Address: 10.1.1.9


Got answer:
   HEADER:
      Opcode = QUERY, id = 8, rcode = NOERROR
      Header flags: response, auth.answer, want recursion, available
      Questions = 1, answers = 1, authority records = 0, additional= 0

   QUESTIONS:
      upgrademe.company.net, type = A, class = IN
   ANSWERS:
   -> upgrademe.company.net
      internet address = 10.1.5.198
      ttl = 886 (13 mins 28 secs)


Name: upgrademe.company.net
Address: 10.1.5.198

>exit
```

Note the fact that two identical queries were performed and the TTL value of the record decreased. This is your confirmation that the record was retrieved from a WINS server. If you had just wanted to check the presence of WINS lookup configuration on the DNS server, you could have run the following commands.

```
C:\>nslookup
Default server: NS1.company.net
Address: 10.1.1.9

>set q=wins
>company.net
Server: NS1.company.net
Address: 10.1.1.9

company.net
        WINS lookup
            Flags = 10000 (local)
            Lookup timeout = 2
            Cache TTL = 900
            Server count = 1
            WINS server = (10.1.1.19)
>exit
```

With a WINS server record returned, you have verified that WINS lookup is configured in the DNS zone. If you had wanted to check for WINS reverse lookup, you would have set the query type to WINSR.

So far, you have seen many general methods to resolve problems in your DNS infrastructure. The remaining sections in this chapter provide guidance on locating and correcting specific DNS-related problems.

Troubleshooting DNS Clients

When clients are having problems accessing network resources by their host or fully qualified domain name, the cause for the problem usually stems from one of these faults.

- A negatively cached entry exists in the local resolver cache.
- An incorrect name server address was provided by the DHCP server.
- Incorrect static TCP/IP settings exist.
- Incorrect static entries exist in the client's Hosts file.
- Names for other domains to access are not listed as suffixes to append in the DNS suffix search order (advanced TCP/IP properties).
- A network hardware failure (NIC, cable, switch, router, and so on) occurred.

When clients cannot access a system by its fully qualified domain name, you should first try to determine whether the problem is related to name resolution or the network itself. The easiest way to do this is to ping the remote system by its IP address. If the remote system successfully responds to the ping request, then you have verified that the problem is with name resolution (if not, check for network hardware issues). Next, you can attempt to ping the same system by its fully qualified domain name. If the wrong IP address appears in the ping request, then you should check for the source of the invalid address, which is likely either from the DNS server or stored in the client's Hosts file (found in the %systemroot%\system32\drivers\etc folder). If no static entries exist in the Hosts file, then you can locate the source of the errant record by running `nslookup`.

Now let's suppose that the right IP address appeared when you pinged by FQDN. Now see if you can ping the remote system from the client computer by using just the remote system's host name. If the ping fails, then you have found that your problem is that no other DNS suffixes are appended to name resolution requests. This is corrected by adding DNS suffixes to append in the DNS suffix search order, which is located under the DNS tab of a client's network interface's TCP/IP properties.

Table 8-8 describes the most common DNS client problems along with their likely causes.

Table 8-8. Common DNS Client Problems

Symptom	Probable Faults
After a host's record is modified on the DNS server, clients cannot access the host.	• The original IP address for the host is cached locally on the client. On the client system, run `ipconfig /flushdns` to clear the contents of the resolver cache. • An improperly configured local Hosts file.
The user receives a "Network Path Not Found" error when trying to access a resource on the network.	• Improperly configured TCP/IP settings or a lease was not obtained from the DHCP server. • The DNS server is unavailable. • Incorrect static entries exist in the system's local Hosts file. • The user is trying to access resources in a different domain. Add appended DNS suffixes to the DNS suffix search order under the DNS tab on the system's Advanced TCP/IP settings window.
The client receives an incorrect response from the DNS server.	• The queried system's host (A) record has the wrong IP address. Modify the IP address for the host on the DNS server, clear the client's resolver cache, and have the client run the query again. • The client's requests are being resolved by a secondary DNS server whose zone is out of date. To correct this, decrease the Refresh Interval for the primary zone or add the secondary server to the primary zone's Notify List. To immediately update the secondary, you can right-click the zone on the secondary server and select Transfer from Master.
New clients' host names and IP addresses are not dynamically registering with their primary DNS server.	• Dynamic updates are disabled in the clients' TCP/IP properties. Check to see that the "Register this connection's addresses in DNS" box is selected. • The DNS zone is configured to not allow dynamic updates. • No zone exists for the clients' domain on their primary DNS server. • The DNS zone is configured to only allow secure dynamic updates, and the computers having the registration problem are not members of the domain.

Client issues are normally small in scale and with the right technique can usually be solved very quickly. On the other hand, server problems sometimes take a little more time to isolate. We'll look at them next.

Troubleshooting DNS Servers

DNS servers have much more to worry about than just registering client names and responding to client queries. In addition to client-related troubleshooting issues, you also have to deal with DHCP integration and zone transfer problems on DNS servers. Due to the range of DNS server problems you may encounter, they are described in the next six sections, as opposed to being summarized in a table.

Incorrect Query Results

Here's the scenario: A client asks a question and a DNS server gives the wrong answer. Odds are that the DNS server is not a compulsive liar but is just misinformed. The fact that a client is receiving incorrect query results means that the resource records on the DNS server are not current. This type of problem is the result of the following faults.

- Outdated zone information exists.
- A zone was not configured to allow dynamic updates.
- A record was manually configured incorrectly.
- A subdomain delegation problem exists.

Zones often can become outdated and thus provide wrong information as a result of replication not happening frequently enough. To keep DNS zone data up to date, perform one or all of the following tasks.

- Decrease the Refresh Interval on the primary server's zone's SOA.
- Add secondary servers to the primary server's zone's Notify List.
- Use the DNS MMC snap-in to manually force a zone transfer.

In environments where mobile users often receive different IP assignments from a DHCP server, the use of dynamic updates to keep zone data current is extremely important. If the DNS zone does not allow dynamic updates, its zone data can quickly become outdated. The easiest correction that you can perform without sacrificing security is to configure the zone to allow Secure Dynamic Updates. This way, only systems with valid computer accounts in the domain can update their information on the DNS server. This problem may also be the result of improper configuration on the DHCP server. We'll look at DHCP-related problems shortly.

Earlier, in the `nslookup` section, you saw how to test for the proper operation of delegated subdomains. Subdomain delegation problems occur when a subdomain's name servers are replaced or their IP addresses change. When this happens, administrators often forget to change the NS and A records for the name servers in any created stub domains. To repair problems with referrals to delegated subdomains, you should take these actions.

1. Use `nslookup` to retrieve a list of NS records for the subdomain by querying a known name server in the subdomain.

2. Modify the existing records in the name server's stub zone so that they match the results for the name server query in `nslookup`.

Once the name server list for the subdomain has been updated, clients should not have any problems accessing resources in the subdomain.

Cannot Access Resources outside of Domain

In instances where name resolution within the domain works normally, but external name resolution is failing, you should check the following for the problem.

- The root-level (.) zone resides on the DNS server.
- The root-level zone resides on a DNS server listed as a forwarder.
- The root hints file (cache.dns) is missing or corrupt.
- External network problems exist.

If the "." root zone exists on a system involved in the name resolution process, then the client will receive an authoritative answer that the host does not exist for hosts located in domains that have no configured zones on the DNS server. When a DNS server does not contain a root-level zone, it forwards requests as a series of iterative queries to Internet root-level servers. The locations (IP addresses) for these servers are stored in the cache.dns file, which is located in the %systemroot%\system32\dns folder. If you suspect that the cache.dns file is corrupt, take these steps to replace it with its original version.

1. Open Windows Explorer and navigate to the %systemroot%\system32\dns\samples folder.

2. In the samples folder, right-click the cache.dns file and select Copy.

3. Now right-click the dns folder and select Paste.

4. When prompted if you want to overwrite the existing file, click Yes.

Remember that for external resource access, external network access needs to be present as well. While, to many, the last sentence may be nothing more than stating the obvious, it still shouldn't be ignored. Too many have made this mistake in the past.

Server Not Responding to Requests

When client queries are going unanswered from the DNS server, odds are that the server didn't just develop an attitude and is responding to clients, "Talk to the hand!" Most likely, one of these problems is causing the lack of response.

- The DNS service is not running.
- A network problem (NIC, patch cable, switch, router) exists.

If the source of the DNS problem still is not obvious, don't forget to check the DNS event log in the DNS MMC snap-in. Look for error (critical) events, and read their related description. The event descriptions will point you in the right direction on most occasions.

Troubleshooting DNS-DHCP Integration

Normally, DNS-DHCP integration issues involve dynamic update parameter configuration. For example, you may see that Windows 2000 and higher systems' host records are being dynamically added to the DNS zone, but dynamic updates are not occurring for legacy clients. This problem is solved by enabling the "Dynamically update DNS A and PTR records for DHCP clients that do not request updates" checkbox under the DNS tab in the DHCP server Properties dialog box. This configuration option is shown in Figure 8-13. A common error with dynamic update configuration on DHCP servers is that administrators select the "Always dynamically update DNS A and PTR records" option. This setting only applies to Windows 2000 and higher clients, but that is not explicitly

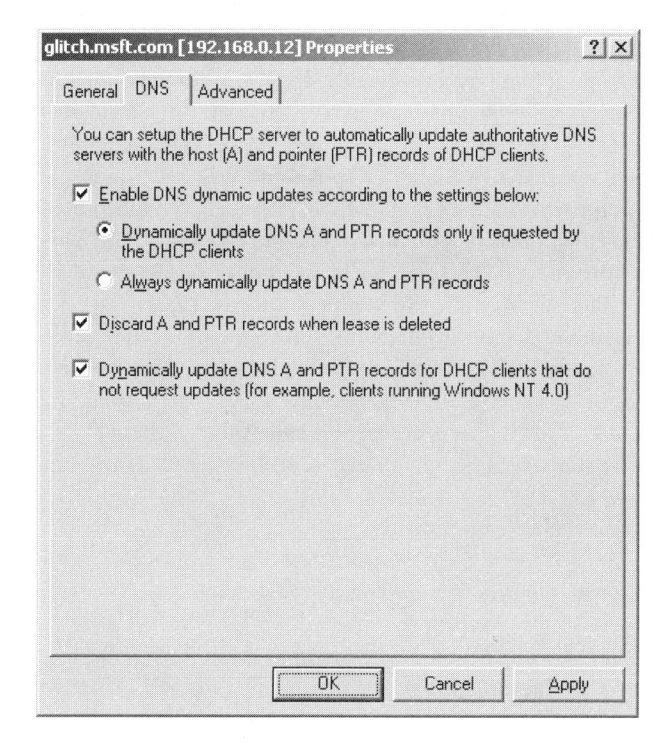

Figure 8-13. DHCP options for DNS dynamic update

noted. For environments where two or more DHCP servers are trying to perform dynamic updates to the same DNS server, you may find that only one DHCP server is able to perform updates for a particular client. The methods for resolving this problem are described in Chapter 10.

Zone Transfer Problems

Depending on the layout of your network, there may be several possible faults that are preventing the successful completion of zone transfers between DNS servers. Here are some common hot spots to look at when zone transfers are failing.

- A network failure (cables, switches, NICs, routers, and so on) has occurred.
- A DNS service has stopped on one server.
- A transfer is occurring between a Windows Server 2003 system and a legacy BIND (pre-4.9.4) server.
- A DNS port used for replication is blocked by a firewall.
- DNS servers are configured to use different static ports.

Networking-related problems can normally be quickly solved using one of the many tools presented in Chapter 4, such as `ping`. If network connectivity exists between the two servers, you should then check the status of the DNS service on each server.

Another potential problem may involve the BIND server that you are working with. If the BIND version is pre-4.9.4, you need to select the BIND Secondaries advanced option on the primary zone's Properties dialog box. Also, don't forget that BIND servers do not support the native Microsoft records WINS and WINSR.

For security purposes, you may find that DNS servers positioned between multiple sites replicate data using a port other than the default DNS port (53). While there is nothing wrong with modifying the DNS port for security purposes, sometimes this configuration results in problems when a new site is added or a new DNS server is installed. If the new DNS server is set up with its default settings, it will try to replicate zone data using port 53, and the zone transfer will in turn fail. If you did not do the initial DNS implementation, or other hands are involved in managing your network infrastructure, you should check the following Registry key on one of the working DNS servers: HKEY_LOCAL_MACHINE\System\CurrentControlSet\Services\DNS\Parameters. If a `SendOnNonDnsPort` DWORD value is shown, then you have found the problem. These are the possible values you may see.

- Value not listed—Server uses default port (53).
- 0—Server uses default port (53).
- 1—Servers negotiate an arbitrary port.

- Any value higher than 1024—Value listed is the port used for communication.

The key to resolving this type of conflict is to have the `SendOnNonDnsPort` values match on all DNS servers. As long as the values are equal and the assigned port is not blocked by the firewall, there will not be any port conflict–related replication problems.

If you are experiencing slower than expected zone transfers or too much zone transfer traffic, you may consider one of the following strategies to optimize zone transfer performance.

- If zone transfers are occurring with pre–BIND 8.2 UNIX servers, upgrade the BIND version to 8.2 or higher so that incremental zone transfers occur (only what's changed is replicated).

- Increase the Refresh Interval on the SOA of the primary zone.

- Convert the zones to Active Directory integrated.

DNS Error Events

It was mentioned earlier that scanning the DNS event logs is an easy way to identify problems. Table 8-9 provides a quick reference for problems that relate to the most common DNS error events.

Table 8-9. Common DNS Error Events

Event ID	Error Message	Probable Faults and Corrective Action
408	The DNS server could not open socket for address *IP address*. Verify that this is a valid IP address for the server computer.	• If the IP address is valid, check to see if another application is trying to use the DNS service's port (53 by default). Reconfigure application or DNS port usage. • The specified IP address is no longer valid. Remove it from the list of restricted interfaces under the Interfaces tab of the DNS server Properties dialog box in the DNS MMC snap-in. • The IP address is no longer valid but originally was the only available address at the time of the DNS service installation. To correct this, delete the following Registry key: HKEY_LOCAL_MACHINE\System\CurrentControlSet\Services\DNS\Parameters\ListenAddress. Then restart the server.

continues

Table 8-9. Common DNS Error Events, continued

Event ID	Error Message	Probable Faults and Corrective Action
413	The DNS server will send requests to other DNS servers on a port other than its default port (TCP port 53).	This problem occurs when the server is multihomed, and DNS has been configured to use only some of the system's available IP addresses. Also, you may find that responses from other DNS servers could wind up trying to use a port other than the port the DNS server is configured to use and thus cause problems transferring zone data over WAN links (through firewalls). To ensure the DNS server uses its configured port for all DNS communications, change the server's IP interfaces configuration so that one of these occurs. • All IP addresses are used. • Only a single IP address is used.
414	The server computer currently has no primary DNS suffix configured.	The server's name is dns1, for example, instead of dns1.company.net. This configuration can lead to incorrect or failed referrals. To correct this problem, join the DNS server to a domain, or provide a full DNS name that is appropriate for its workgroup.
708	The DNS server did not detect any zones of either primary or secondary type. It will run as a caching-only server but will not be authoritative for any zones.	If your intent was to build a caching-only server, then you should do nothing here. Otherwise, this message tells you that you need to configure zones on the server.
3150	The DNS server wrote a new version of zone *zonename* to file *filename*. You can view the new version by clicking the Record Data tab.	This event occurs when a DNS server is configured as a root server. If this is unintentional, you should delete the root (.) zone to eliminate the event message.

6527	Zone *zonename* expired before it could obtain a successful zone transfer or update from a master server acting as its source for the zone. The zone has been shut down.	• The secondary DNS server lost network connectivity to its primary server, so replication was unable to occur.
		  • Resolve the network failure.
		  • On the secondary server, delete and re-create the zone, specifying the proper IP address for the same or a new master server.
		• Poor SOA configuration existed on the primary zone. Correct it by performing one or more of the following actions.
		  • Verify that the Refresh Interval is shorter than the Expires After period.
		  • Decrease the Retry Interval.
		  • Increase the Expires After period.
		  • Add the secondary server to the Notify List.

Summary

This chapter has given you plenty to chew on in regards to troubleshooting a DNS infrastructure. While it is impossible to identify every possible DNS problem that may be encountered in the real world, the methodology behind isolating and resolving DNS issues is still the same. To fully prepare yourself for a DNS failure, take time to practice using `nslookup`, since it is the most thorough DNS testing tool at your disposal. Also, don't forget about the DNS event log, as well as DNS monitoring and debug logging. When combined, all of these tools more often than not will help you to quickly spot the source of a problem. Much time in this chapter was spent reviewing the core components of the DNS infrastructure. Without knowledge of the hierarchical nature of DNS in your environment, it is difficult to truly "climb the ladder" with tools such as `nslookup` to reach the source of a fault.

This chapter categorized and listed the most common DNS problems, so at least you have a head start; however, don't forget the methodology, since it is always more valuable than any provided answer. While problems may change, the techniques used to locate them do not.

9
WINS

In Chapter 2, you were introduced to the fundamentals of WINS architecture. Understanding the processes involved when WINS is used for NetBIOS name resolution will go far in helping you to quickly resolve a problem. This way, instead of making an educated statement like "WINS is broken," you can instead observe, "There is a replication problem between WINS1 and WINS2, and I'm all over it!"

This chapter begins with a more detailed look at WINS architecture, extending beyond the fundamental concepts explained in Chapter 2, and then moves on to examining WINS diagnostic tools. Following the introductory concepts and tools are sections that detail troubleshooting techniques and potential faults for each component in a WINS infrastructure. The WINS components outlined in this chapter are

- WINS clients
- WINS servers
- Replication
- DHCP-WINS integration
- WINS databases

Before jumping headfirst into troubleshooting, let's take a couple of minutes to examine WINS architecture in more detail.

WINS Architecture

While WINS architecture has not changed much over the years, it has gotten better and become more reliable with age. In Windows 2000, and continuing with Windows Server 2003, Microsoft made several improvements to the WINS service. In this section, you will see the improvements that have been made to make WINS more reliable, followed by descriptions of the operation of the components in the WINS infrastructure.

What's New?

Realizing that WINS is still alive and breathing and likely to remain around for several more years, Microsoft invested time to make a couple of improvements to WINS with the release of Windows 2000 and the subsequent release of Windows Server 2003.

Windows 2000 Enhancements

In Windows 2000, several improvements were made to the WINS service, making it much more reliable and manageable than it was with Windows NT. These are the major WINS improvements that were included with Windows 2000.

- *Database engine*—The WINS database was upgraded to use the same engine as the AD database, making it more robust and reliable.

- *Fault tolerance*—WINS clients can list up to 12 WINS servers.

- *Filter and record searching*—Records are much easier to locate in large WINS databases.

- *Manual tombstoning*—Records can be manually flagged for deletion.

- *MMC console*—WINS is more easily managed as an MMC snap-in.

- `netsh` *(Netshell) commands*—Additional WINS administration flexibility is available from the command line (explained later in the chapter).

- *Persistent connections*—Replication partners can maintain an open session, improving replication speed.

- *Record deletion*—Dynamic entries and static mappings can quickly be deleted in the WINS MMC snap-in.

With most of the holes in the WINS architecture repaired in Windows 2000, few improvements were needed with the rollout of Windows Server 2003.

Windows Server 2003 Enhancements

In Windows Server 2003, two improvements were made to WINS.

- *Advanced search capabilities*—It is much easier now to find exactly what you are looking for in a search with the improvement of search filters. You can now use all of the following as search criteria when trying to locate a WINS record: IP address, NetBIOS name, record owner, and record type.

- *Better replication control*—WINS servers can now block name records from particular WINS servers during pull replication, preventing the server's database from having unnecessary data and thus keeping its size to a minimum.

Chapter 2 introduced you to the fundamental client architecture of WINS but did not go into detail on WINS replication or some of the other terms mentioned in this chapter. If some of the concepts touched on in this chapter are new to you, then you will find the next two sections very useful. Otherwise, jump ahead to WINS Troubleshooting Tools.

WINS Relationships and Replication

There are two primary relationships in any WINS network infrastructure: client-server and server-server. WINS clients query WINS servers to query the IP addresses of NetBIOS names, and WINS servers work with other WINS servers to share WINS database data through replication.

In the client-server paradigm, WINS clients dynamically register their NetBIOS names and IP addresses with a WINS server, and also query the WINS server when they need an IP address for a particular host.

With WINS servers, on the other hand, their relationship is determined by the type of replication that you configure. There are three ways in which you can configure replication between WINS servers:

- Push
- Pull
- Push/pull

Push replication is primarily employed when WINS servers reside on the same LAN. The reason for this is that replication will likely occur frequently and at unregulated intervals. With push replication, you configure a WINS server to initiate replication with a replication partner after a specific number of changes are made to the WINS database. The default setting for the number of changes that trigger replication is 0, which means that every change to the WINS database would be pushed to the WINS server's push replication partners.

While push replication is ideal for keeping local WINS servers synchronized, it does so at the expense of network overhead. When WINS servers are positioned at multiple sites and separated by WAN links, pull replication is often used instead. With pull replication, the replication interval is determined by time instead of a number of changes. For example, you could configure pull replication to run every 12 hours, where WINS server 1 would pull the changes from WINS server 2 twice daily.

The last replication type that can be configured is push/pull. This configuration gives you the best of both worlds. You can arrange regular pull replication intervals while also setting up replication to happen after every so many changes. For example, you may configure pull replication for every 12 hours and push replication for every 25 changes. This way, bandwidth is minimized, and you are guaranteed that the WINS servers will not fall too far out of sync.

Knowing the replication configuration between multiple sites will aid in resolving suspected replication problems. For example, suppose that you changed the IP address of a system at site A two hours ago, but clients at site B still cannot connect to it using its NetBIOS name. The problem may result from only pull replication being set up between the two WINS servers or from having too high a change interval for push replication. Correcting the problem may require a change in the replication configuration between the two systems. Or to immediately solve the problem, you could right-click the Replication Partners folder in the WINS MMC on the WINS server and select Replicate Now, forcing an immediate replication. WINS replication settings are shown in Figure 9-1.

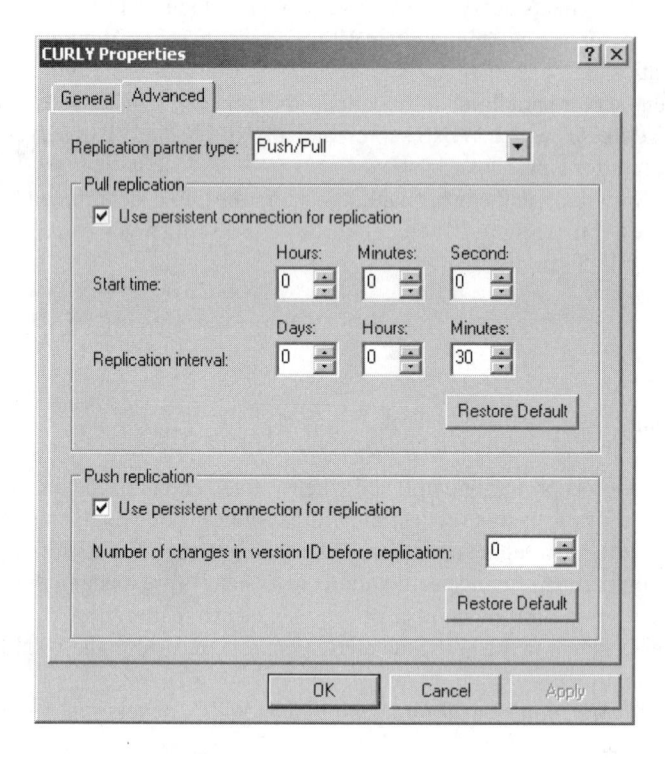

Figure 9-1. WINS server replication configuration

When multiple sites are involved in a WINS infrastructure, the hub-and-spoke replication topology is most often employed. This topology is shown in Figure 9-2. The primary reason for this structure is that it minimizes convergence time, which is the maximum amount of time required for a change in one site to be replicated to all other sites. In the illustration, the total convergence time is two hours. The WINS server at the Chicago site acts as the central replication hub for all other sites. Since replication occurs every 60 minutes, you could assume that the longest amount of time for a change in New York, for example, to reach Los Angeles would be 120 minutes. That assumes a 60-minute wait, then a jump to Chicago, followed by another 60-minute wait, and then a jump to Los Angeles. If the same replication intervals were used and a ring topology was employed, New York–to–Los Angeles replication could take three hours. When troubleshooting replication, remember these two concepts about the hub-and-spoke replication topology.

- When convergence time is too slow, configure the replication topology as hub and spoke, or if it already is that topology, lower the replication interval.
- The hub represents a single point of failure. When replication is not occurring between remote sites, check the WINS server at the hub first.

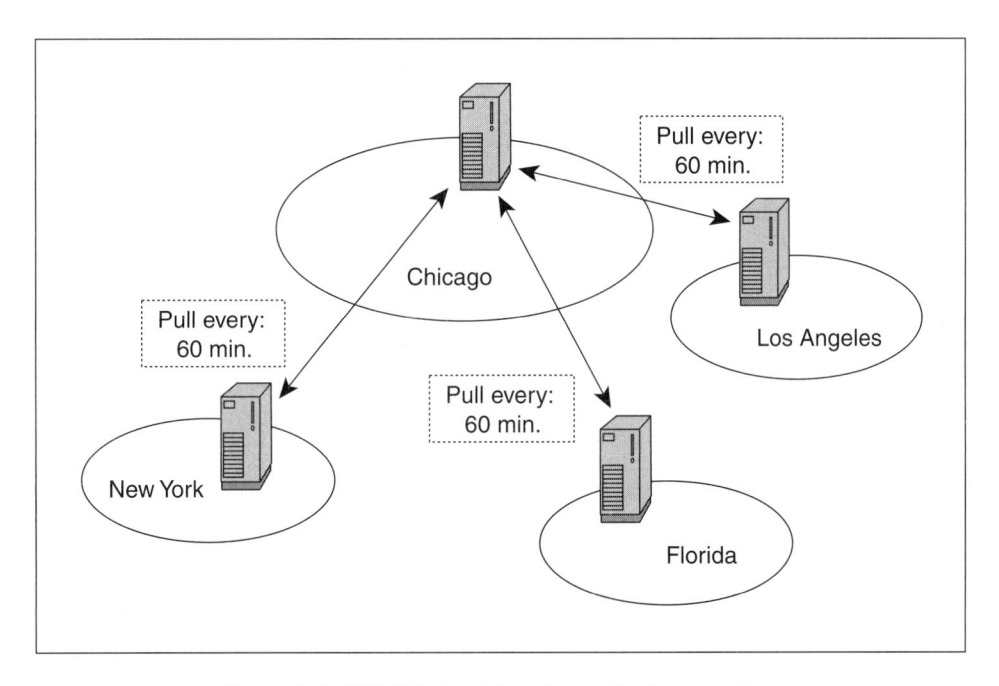

Figure 9-2. WINS hub-and-spoke replication topology

WINS replication is always incremental. This means that only the changes to the WINS database are replicated between partners.

Filling in the Gaps

The remaining sections in this chapter also throw some additional terminology at you. In order to effectively "speak" WINS and diagnose WINS-related network issues, make sure you are familiar with the two concepts presented in this section.

Static Mapping

WINS servers operate today much like many fast-food restaurants. They want their clients to do as much work as possible (fill your drink and in some places even put your burger together), but they do not go out of their way to solicit clients for anything. WINS clients willingly provide their names and IP addresses to WINS servers without even being asked. The problem with WINS servers' fast-food approach to name registration is that the non-WINS clients are left out of the loop. That's what static mappings are for.

Static mappings allow you to provide NetBIOS names and IP addresses in the WINS database for non-WINS clients. This way, WINS clients can connect to non-WINS clients using NetBIOS names. Without static mappings, WINS clients would need to know the IP address of non-WINS clients in order to talk to them, assuming that no other name resolution source existed, such as DNS or configured Hosts or LMHosts files.

The lone problem with static mappings, however, is that they're static. This means that if a non-WINS client's IP address changes, you have to manually make the update at the WINS server. Otherwise, clients will eventually experience connectivity problems with the system whose IP address has changed.

WINS Proxy Agent

WINS Proxies are the "Good Samaritans" on a WINS network. If a non-WINS client supports NetBIOS broadcasts for resolution but cannot work with WINS servers, it is limited to communication on its local subnet (assuming DNS, Hosts, or LMHosts are not used). So if a non-WINS client needs the IP address for the system Curly, it will shout out (broadcast) to the network, "Anyone know Curly's number?" If a Windows system on the local subnet is configured as a WINS Proxy, it will hear the broadcast and use the information to query the WINS server, asking, "Hey, WINS, what's Curly's number?" Once the WINS server replies to the WINS Proxy, the Proxy will in turn relay the information (IP address) back to the client that originally made the request.

In order to be Good Samaritans, Windows systems have to be configured to be WINS Proxies (many would step in and say that they are intentionally "not good" by default). Making a Windows workstation or server a WINS Proxy requires a modification to the Registry and necessitates these steps.

1. Click Start > Run, enter `Regedt32` in the Run dialog box, and click OK to open the Registry Editor.

2. Browse to the HKEY_LOCAL_MACHINE\SYSTEM\CurrentControlSet\Services\Netbt\Parameters subkey.

3. To enable the system as a WINS Proxy, change the EnableProxy (REG_DWORD) value from 0 to 1.

4. Close the Registry Editor.

5. Reboot the system.

Now that the essential lingo is out of the way, let's move on to the required tools.

WINS Troubleshooting Tools

For troubleshooting client configuration issues, two tools that were documented in Chapter 4 are predominantly used: `nbtstat` and `ipconfig`. Uses for both of these tools are shown later, but their syntax is not repeated in this section. Instead, here you will see how to use the WINS MMC snap-in, WINS event logging, and the `netsh` (Netshell) WINS commands. Each of these tools is invaluable in identifying and resolving WINS problems. The WINS MMC is the most frequently used of the tools, so let's start with it.

WINS MMC

The WINS MMC snap-in can be loaded into any MMC console or can be opened directly by clicking Start > Administrative Tools > WINS on any WINS server. The MMC snap-in is shown in Figure 9-3.

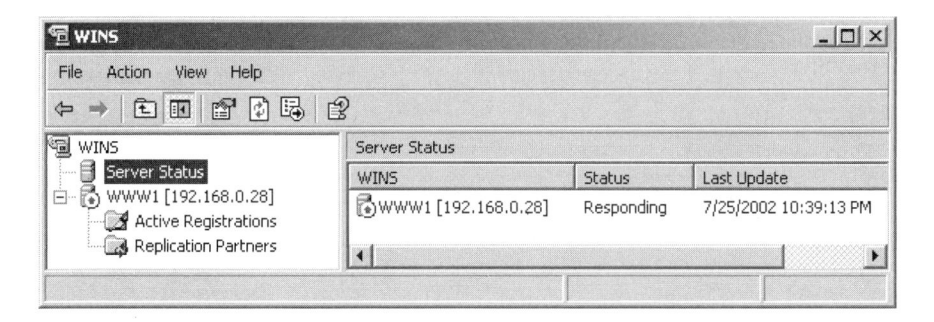

Figure 9-3. WINS MMC snap-in

As is shown in Figure 9-3, one of the nice features of this tool is that by clicking the Server Status object, you can quickly check the server status as well as see the last time the database was updated. At the WINS server icon, you can edit the server properties to configure backups for the WINS database and configure burst handling, which is explained in the Troubleshooting WINS Servers section later in this chapter. Other important tasks that can be performed at the server object include running backups on demand, verifying database consistency, and initiating immediate replication.

By clicking the Active Registrations folder, you can search for and view all or a particular subset of the records currently in the WINS database. The last folder in the WINS MMC snap-in is the Replication Partners folder. Clicking this folder allows you to see a list of all replication partners of the WINS server as well as the type of replication that is configured. When you are attempting to document or modify the WINS replication topology, this feature is very useful.

While the WINS MMC by itself is very powerful, your troubleshooting work will be much easier with the aid of WINS event logging, which we'll look at next.

Event Logging

If you are getting stumped while troubleshooting a WINS server, you can ask it for clues by enabling event logging. When enabled, this feature causes WINS startup, error, and database change events to be recorded in the system event log. When using this feature, you can confirm the startup of processes as well as see any possible WINS errors recorded.

To enable WINS event logging, follow these steps.

1. Click Start > Administrative Tools > WINS to open the WINS MMC.
2. Right-click the WINS server object and select Properties.
3. Click the Advanced tab in the WINS server Properties dialog box.
4. Now click the Log Detailed Events to Windows Event Log checkbox and click OK (see Figure 9-4).

Once event logging has been enabled, you can check the WINS server's system log for WINS-related events. When looking at the system log, click the Source field to sort events by their source. Then locate the events whose source is WINS. In particular, look

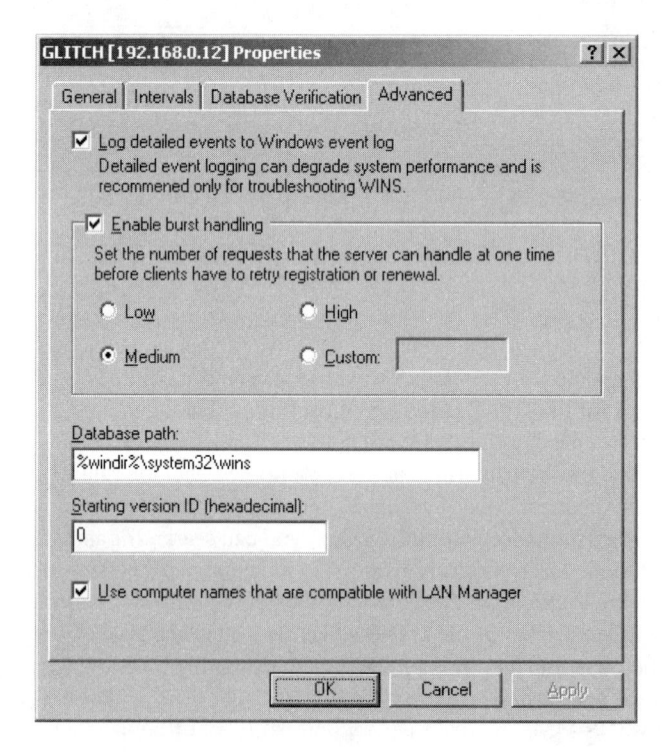

Figure 9-4. Enabling WINS event logging

for critical events. An example of an event you may see is shown in Figure 9-5, where an event was recorded indicating that the WINS server was unable to connect to one of its replication partners.

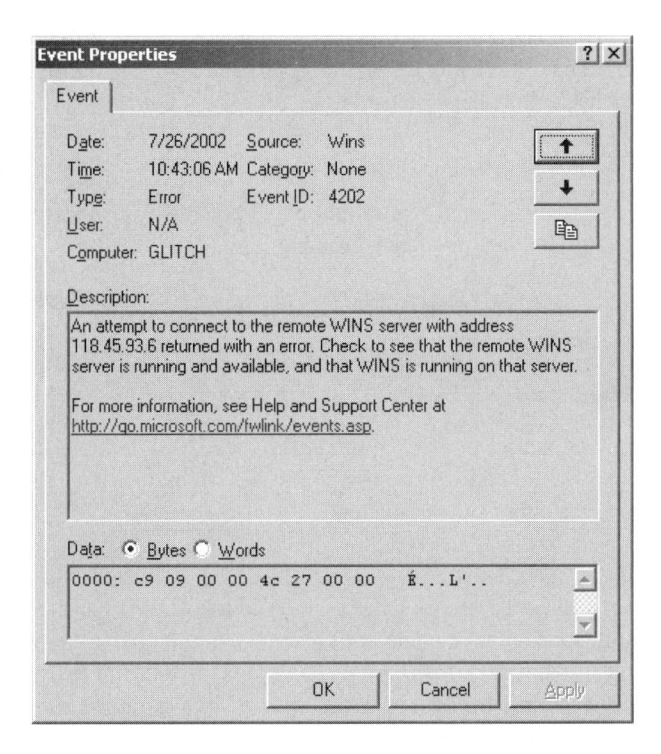

Figure 9-5. Finding a WINS replication error by checking the system event log

> Enabling WINS event logging significantly increases the size of the system event log. Use this feature only when troubleshooting a WINS problem, and then disable it once the problem has been found. When you enable it, consider increasing the size of the system event log or enabling wrapping for the log (older events are overwritten as needed).

netsh wins

With `netsh wins`, you can both troubleshoot and administer local and remote WINS servers. Some of the `netsh wins` commands are useful in troubleshooting, while others are provided exclusively to allow you to perform the same administrative tasks from the command line that you could in the WINS MMC. Since there are over 50 versions of this command, this section documents only the versions of the command that are valuable when you are troubleshooting a suspected WINS problem. If you would like information on all WINS `netsh` commands, open Windows Help and perform a search using the keywords "netsh wins."

The first version of the command that you need to understand is `netsh wins server`. All other commands presented in this section are run under the `netsh wins server` command. The easiest way to run this command is to first access the `netsh wins` shell. To do this, follow these steps.

1. From the command prompt, type `netsh` and press Enter.

2. Type `wins` and press Enter. You should now be in the `netsh wins` shell, as indicated by the `netsh wins>` prompt.

The `netsh wins server` command is used to specify a local or remote WINS server to manage. The syntax for this command is:

```
server [\\servername | ipaddress]
```

When run without parameters, the command connects you to the local system, assuming that WINS is installed. To manage a remote system, provide either the server's name or IP address as a command parameter.

Once you connect to a WINS server, the command outputs the access rights that you have to the server. As an administrator, you should see that you have read and write access to the server you connected to. Once connected to a server, you can type `help` to see a list of available management commands, or you can run one of the two diagnostic commands discussed in this section. The four most popular Netshell WINS server troubleshooting tools are `dump`, `check`, `init`, and `show`. Each of these commands is described in more detail in the following subsections.

dump

This command allows you to quickly review basic configuration information for a WINS server. This command's output includes information about

- The WINS database backup path
- Name record renewal, extinction, extinction timeout, and verification intervals
- Push and pull replication parameters
- Replication partners
- Burst handling parameters

To view this information, from the `netsh wins server>` menu, type `dump` and press Enter. While `dump` is relatively simple in scope, you will find the next two commands much more powerful.

check

The following two versions of the `check` command are useful for troubleshooting:

- `check database`—Checks and reports on WINS database consistency
- `check version`—Checks for consistency of version ID numbers for WINS record owners in the WINS database

check database

The `check database` command triggers a database consistency check to run on a WINS server. When the command is run, you can execute a single consistency check on the local WINS database or have the command check consistency on all replicas of the database. If you elect to check consistency on all database replicas, a significant load will be placed on all WINS servers and on the network. By default, the command is not executed immediately on any WINS server that is currently overloaded. In these situations, the command is queued until some of the WINS server's resources are free, and then it is executed.

Once the command completes, you need to check the system event log on each WINS server to verify that the consistency check was successful. The syntax for `check database` is:

```
check database [all=<1|0>] [force=<1|0>]
```

The command's optional parameters are described in Table 9-1.

Table 9-1. check database Command Options

Option	Use
all=<1|0>	When this option is used with a value of 1, a consistency check is performed on the database of the target WINS server and all of its replication partners. With a value of 0 specified, the consistency check runs on the WINS server and its partners only if their consistency check verification interval has expired. This interval is disabled by default. When the interval is enabled, the default verification interval is 24 hours.
force=<1|0>	When used with a value of 1, this option overrides the WINS overload condition check, forcing a database consistency check to run regardless of how busy the system is. Using this option with a value of 0 is the same as not using it at all, meaning that when an overload condition is detected, the consistency check operation is delayed.

For an example of using this command, suppose that you fear corruption exists on one of the databases on your WINS servers. To check for consistency, you enter the following `check database` command:

```
check database all=1 force=1
```

The entire sequence of commands used in this example is shown in Figure 9-6.

```
C:\>netsh
netsh>wins
netsh wins>server
***You have Read and Write access to the server glitch.msft.com***
netsh wins server>check database all=1 force=1
Operation has been queued. Check Event log for start and completion information.
netsh wins server>
```

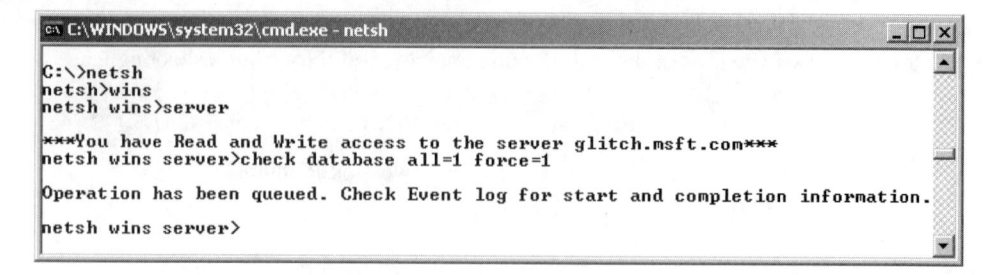

Figure 9-6. Checking database consistency with check database

check version
This command allows you to verify the version number consistency of a WINS server's records with those of its replication partners. If version number inconsistency is found, you should use the WINS MMC to force replication between the WINS servers. The replication and subsequent record updates should correct any inconsistencies between WINS records. When executed, the command checks for and reports on any version inconsistencies found and displays a mapping table of WINS records found in the server's database. For the table to display properly, you should widen the size of the command window so that it is much larger than its default size. If the output does not display properly, it is also written to a text file, so you can read it from there as well. By default, the text output file is named wins.rec and is stored in the directory from where the `netsh` command was run.

Here is the syntax for `check version`:

```
check version server=<ipaddress> [file=<filename>]
```

The `check version` command options are described in Table 9-2.

Table 9-2. check version Command Options

Option	Use
`server=<ipaddress>`	This required parameter specifies the IP address of the WINS server where version checking should begin.
`file=<filename>`	If you would like the command output stored as a different filename in a different location, you can use this parameter to do so.

Here is an example of using this command to verify WINS record version information on a WINS server with an IP address of 192.168.0.22 and on its replication partners, with the output written to the file versioncheck.log:

```
check version server=192.168.0.22
    file=d:\troubleshooting\versioncheck.log.
```

init

The `netsh wins server init` command is primarily used for database maintenance operations, including backups, restores, database compaction, and initiating replication. In previous versions of Windows, the Jetpack utility was used to perform compaction of the WINS database. With Windows Server 2003, this utility is no longer available and thus the `netsh wins server init` command is the only method for performing database compaction. Compaction is often the best method for recovering from database corruption and often salvages the WINS database so that you do not have to restore the database from backup. The six versions of this powerful command are invaluable for troubleshooting WINS server problems. Each version is explained next.

init backup

Once you specify a database backup path for the WINS database in the WINS MMC (see the Recovering a Corrupted WINS Database section later in this chapter), online backups of the WINS database will run every three hours. If you would like to manually perform a backup or perform the backup as part of a script, you can do so by running `netsh wins init backup`.

The syntax for this command is:

```
init backup [dir=<backupdir>] [type=<0|1>]
```

The options for this command are described in Table 9-3.

Table 9-3. init backup Command Options

Option	Use
`dir=<backupdir>`	Used to specify the directory in which the backup should be stored. If this option is not used, the database will be backed up to the default directory that is specified in the WINS MMC.
`type=<0|1>`	Used to specify the type of backup: 0 = full, and 1 = incremental. If no type is specified, a full backup will run.

This command is useful for securing a full backup of the database as a part of a backup script, or for backing up the database prior to compacting it. An example of using this command to create an alternate backup is to enter `init backup dir=d:\winsbak type=0` from the `netsh wins server>` command prompt.

init compact

The `init compact` command is used to compact the WINS database. Database compaction is normally the first resolution step taken to repair a corrupted WINS database. There are no options for this command, so to compact a WINS database, you would run `init compact` from the `netsh wins server>` command prompt. You will see a complete example of this utility in action in the Recovering a Corrupted WINS Database section later in this chapter.

init pull

Suppose that you are aware that a remote WINS server was just updated, and you want to manually initiate a pull replication so that your local WINS server will be updated by the new data on the remote WINS server. This may be needed to prevent name resolution problems. To perform this task, you can use the `init pull` command. The syntax for this command is:

```
init pull server=<remoteserver>
```

When you run this command from the `netsh wins server>` command prompt, you need to specify the name or IP address of the remote server that you wish to pull the data to your server from, so to pull data from the remote server wins1.west.aw.com, you would run this command:

```
init pull server=wins1.aw.com
```

init push

This command allows you to initiate a push replication of data from a local WINS server to its remote replication partners. A good time to run this command is after updating a WINS record on a WINS server. This ensures that the WINS server's replication partner(s) receive the new updates. Here is the syntax to use this command to initiate push replication:

```
init push server=<remoteserver> [propreq=<0|1>]
```

As with `init pull`, you use the `remoteserver` parameter to specify the name or IP address of your WINS server's remote replication partner. If you want to initiate a push replication to all replication partners, you can use the `propreq` parameter. When this parameter is set to 0, the push only propagates to the specified server in the command syntax. When `propreq` is set to 1, the push propagates data to all replication partners.

init replicate

The `init replicate` command is the most popular method for forcing WINS replication, because it initiates both push and pull replication with all of the WINS server's replication partners. The syntax for this command is `init replicate`, so to initiate replication on your local WINS server, you would enter `init replicate` from the `netsh wins server>` prompt.

init restore

When you need to recover a WINS database from an earlier backup, you use the `init restore` command. The backup you use for the restore could be located in the default WINS backup directory, which is specified under the WINS server properties in the WINS MMC. You could also restore data from an alternate backup path that may have been created when using the `init backup` command to manually perform a backup.

The syntax for `init restore` is:

```
init restore [dir=<backupdir>]
```

If the `dir` parameter is not specified, the restore data will come from the default backup directory. Otherwise, you can specify a particular backup directory by entering a path to directory with the `dir` parameter. Here is an example of using this command to restore data located in the D:\winsbak folder:

```
init restore dir=d:\winsbak
```

show

As with `init`, there are several versions of `show` that are useful for troubleshooting purposes. As was the case with the section on `init`, this section details the versions of the `show` command that are most relevant to troubleshooting and resolving WINS-related problems. Many of the `show` commands are most useful for resolving replication-related problems, where improper configuration is the overriding source of the problem.

show info
The output for `show info` is very similar to that of `dump`, but the output is presented in a format that is much easier to read and interpret. The `show info` command provides the following information about a WINS server:

- The database backup path
- Name record settings (refresh interval, extinction interval, extinction timeout, and verification interval)
- Database consistency check parameters
- WINS logging parameters
- Burst handling configuration

When you are trying to quickly get a glimpse of a WINS server's configuration, this command is ideal. The syntax for the command is:

```
show info
```

There are no optional parameters. To get information on a WINS server, you would run `show info` from the `netsh wins server>` prompt.

show partner
The `show partner` command allows you to quickly acquire a list of a WINS server's replication partners. The syntax for this command is:

```
show partner [type=<0|1|2|3>]
```

When you run the command without the `type` parameter, all replication partnerships are shown. If you were looking for a particular list of partners, such as only push partners, then you would use the `type` parameter. These are the valid values that can be entered with the `type` parameter.

- 0—All (the same as not using the `type` parameter)
- 1—Pull
- 2—Push
- 3—Push/pull

If you were looking specifically for the remote pull partners of a WINS server, you would run the command `show partner type=1` from the `netsh wins server>` prompt. Now that you have seen how to get a list of servers by replication type, next you'll see how to list the properties for each of those servers.

show partnerproperties
Once you have identified all of a WINS server's replication partners, you can use `show partnerproperties` to view their configurations. The syntax for the command is `show partnerproperties`. There are no parameters for this command. If you are just looking to list the configuration for a single replication partner, you can use either the `show pullpartnerconfig` or `show pushpartnerconfig` commands, which are described next.

show pullpartnerconfig
The `show pullpartnerconfig` command is used to display the configuration information of a single pull partner of a WINS server. The syntax for this command is:

```
show pullpartnerconfig server=<servername|ipaddress>
```

The required parameter for this command is the name or IP address of the remote server whose configuration you wish to view. For example, to view the WINS configuration of the pull replication partner PatchMe, you would run `pullparnterconfig server=patchme` from the `netsh wins server>` prompt.

show pushpartnerconfig
The `show pushpartnerconfig` command works just like `show pullpartnerconfig`, except that it is for checking the configuration of a WINS server's push replication partners. The syntax for this command is:

```
show pushpartnerconfig server=<servername|ipaddress>
```

As you can see, the syntax and options are virtually the same.

show server
If you forget which server you are currently administering in the `netsh wins server>` context, you can use this command to remind you. The syntax is simply `show server`, and when the command is executed, you will see the name and IP address of the WINS server that you are currently connected to.

Once you are finished running commands from within the `netsh wins` shell, type `quit` to exit the shell. Now that you have seen all of the commands at your disposal, let's put them to use and start troubleshooting.

Troubleshooting WINS Clients

Most of your troubleshooting dilemmas will inevitably come from WINS clients. This is not because the clients aren't very reliable but is more of a testament to the hands that touch them. Servers, for the most part, are set up and then left alone. The same cannot be said for clients. You may have deployed the operating system and all configuration data automatically to clients so as to eliminate the chance of an error during the installation and to save you an abundance of time.

Normally, client problems are not the result of the initial installation or configuration, but instead normally result from a user inadvertently changing a setting. When a client cannot connect to a remote system by its NetBIOS name, one of the quickest ways to identify the potential problem is to run `ipconfig /all` on the system. This command outputs the complete TCP/IP configuration of the client, allowing you to quickly spot a configuration error.

Table 9-4 references the most common WINS client errors.

Table 9-4. Common WINS Client Problems

Symptom	Probable Faults
WINS clients cannot connect to non-WINS systems (UNIX, NetWare servers) by their short name.	• No static mappings for non-WINS clients exist on the WINS server. Create a static mapping for each non-WINS-supported system, providing its host name and IP address. • The local Hosts file is improperly configured.
Clients cannot browse the network.	NetBIOS is not enabled under the WINS tab of the Advanced TCP/IP properties.
The user receives a "Network Path Not Found" error when trying to access a resource on the network.	• TCP/IP settings are improperly configured, or a lease was not obtained from the DHCP server. • The WINS (or DNS) server is unavailable. • The resource's IP address has changed and has not yet replicated to the user's local WINS server. • WINS is not employed on the network. Add appended DNS suffixes to the DNS suffix search order under the DNS tab on the system's Advanced TCP/IP settings window.
After the IP address of a WINS client was changed, the client is no longer accessible to other clients.	Its old IP address still resides in the WINS database. Run nbtstat –RR on the client system to release and renew its client registration with the WINS server.

The solutions shown in Table 9-4 reference both the DNS and WINS advanced TCP/IP settings. Both of these configuration areas are shown in Figures 9-7 and 9-8.

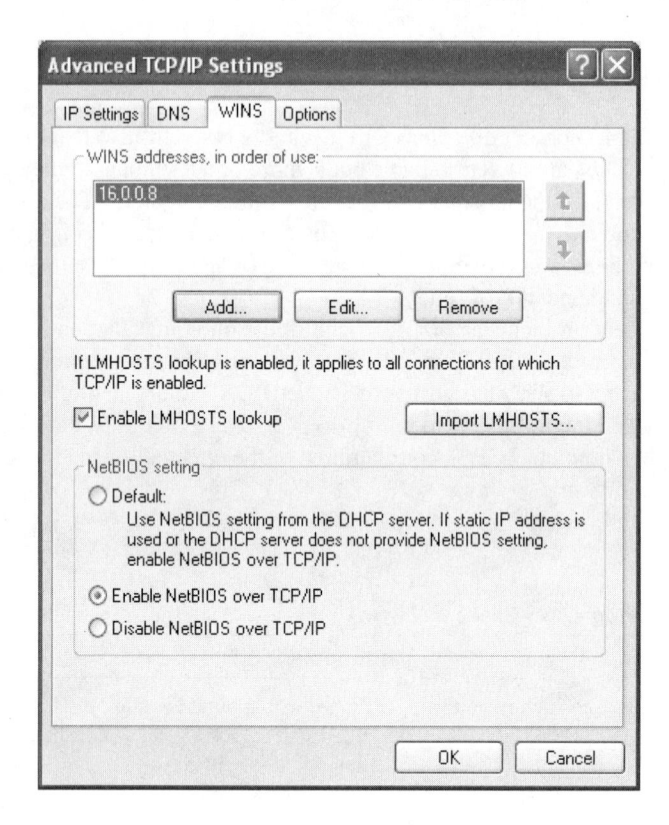

Figure 9-7. Advanced TCP/IP WINS settings

Remember not to overlook the obvious when troubleshooting "Network Path Not Found" errors. Too many times technicians tear systems apart to later realize that the system's network path cable is not plugged in or the switch that it connects to is powered off.

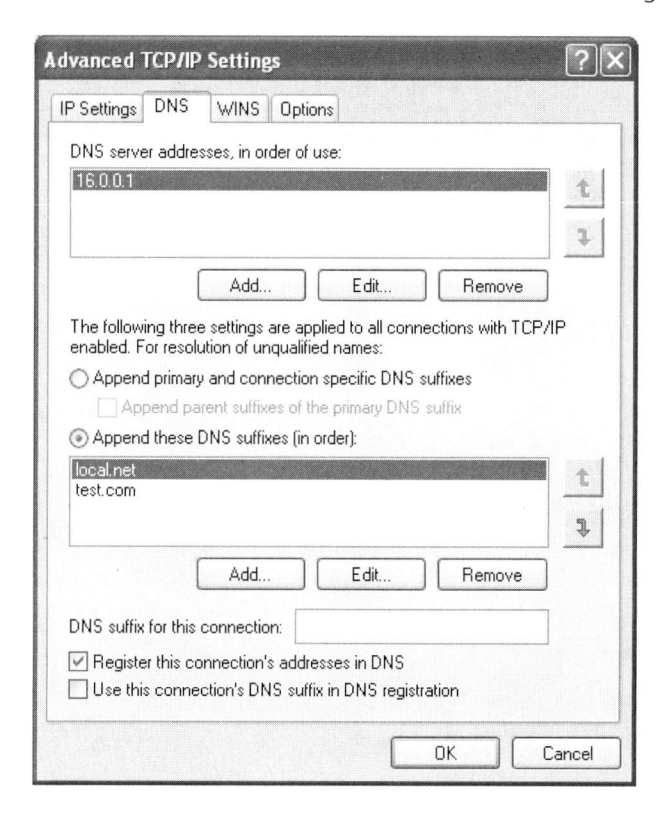

Figure 9-8. Advanced TCP/IP DNS settings

Troubleshooting WINS Servers

Most WINS server problems result from actual system failure, since they are normally tested at the time of implementation. You will see how to recover from database failure or corruption later in this chapter in the Recovering a Corrupted WINS Database section, so this section just focuses on the server-specific configuration issues that you may run into. Table 9-5 describes the most common WINS server problems along with the probable causes of them.

Table 9-5. Common WINS Server Problems

Symptom	Probable Faults
Clients can connect to all systems on the network by their NetBIOS names, except for the WINS server.	The WINS server needs to be a client of itself. Enter its IP address as its primary WINS server under the WINS tab of its TCP/IP properties.

continues

Table 9-5. Common WINS Server Problems, continued

Symptom	Probable Faults
Clients are receiving the wrong IP address for a system. The system is configured to dynamically provide its name and IP address to the WINS server.	• A static mapping already exists for the system. To fix this, you should delete the static mapping and then run `nbtstat -RR` on the client so that it registers its correct information with the WINS server. By default, static mappings are not overwritten by dynamic client registrations. • To prevent a reoccurrence of this problem, check the migrate-on box (see Figure 9-9) in the WINS Replication Partners Properties dialog box. This will allow future dynamic updates to overwrite static records, if they exist.
No clients can resolve NetBIOS names with the WINS server.	• The WINS service has not started. • The server is not connected to the network. • The WINS database is corrupted.

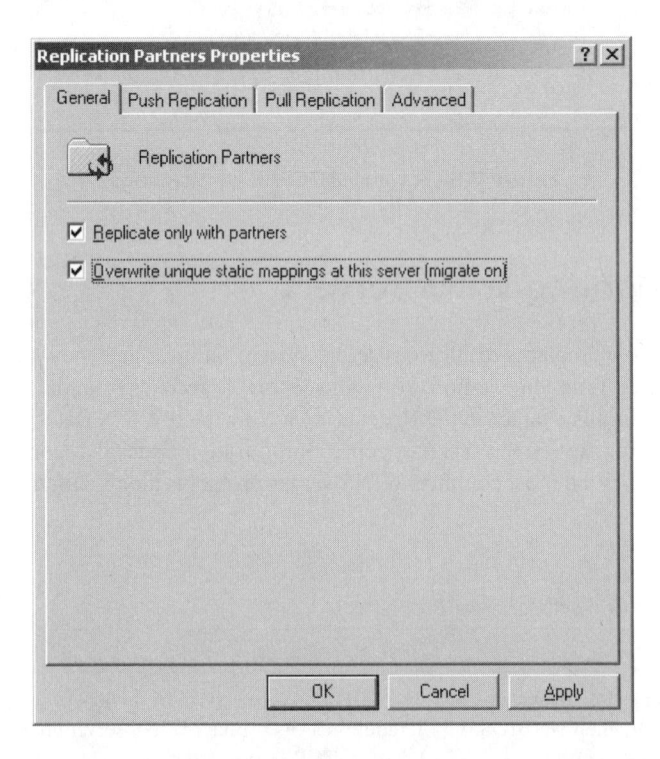

Figure 9-9. Setting migrate-on to allow static entry overwrites

When collecting information to diagnose WINS server problems, you should begin by using the `netsh wins dump` command, which will give you a quick glimpse of how the WINS server is configured. Now that you have seen the fundamental server troubleshooting concerns, many of which revolve around configuration issues, next you will see additional server-related troubleshooting concerns by looking at how to diagnose replication problems.

Troubleshooting Replication

WINS replication failure is generally caused by a network failure or an improper WINS replication topology. The most common WINS replication problems are shown in Table 9-6.

Table 9-6. Common WINS Replication Problems

Symptom	Probable Faults
Push or pull replication fails between two WINS servers.	• Network connectivity between two servers is unavailable (cables, switches, routers, and so on). • TCP/IP is configured incorrectly.
Replication fails intermittently.	• The WINS replication topology is improperly configured. • A hub-and-spoke replication topology is not configured. • Too many WINS servers (more than 20) are in the WINS topology.

When you are troubleshooting network connection problems between two WINS servers, the easiest tool to use is `ping`. When routers are between the two WINS servers, you may need to use `pathping` to determine where the problem begins. If you are unaware of the replication topology configuration, the `netsh wins show` command, which was described earlier, allows you to fully document the servers involved in replicating the WINS database.

For problems associated with replication, check to see if a hub-and-spoke topology is in place. If not, you should reconfigure the WINS replication settings on each WINS server. If more than 20 WINS servers are configured, then you may also see latency-related WINS replication problems. Microsoft recommends that you employ one WINS server for every 10,000 WINS clients. Even when adding an additional WINS server for fault tolerance, you will only need three WINS servers to service 20,000 clients.

Troubleshooting WINS-DHCP Integration

If clients on your network are receiving their configuration information from a DHCP server, improperly configuring the WINS options in the DHCP scope may lead to poor performance for the clients on the network. If DHCP-enabled clients are experiencing poor performance when attempting to connect to other systems on the network, it may be for one of these reasons.

- They are not receiving WINS options in their DHCP lease.
- The IP address of the WINS server has changed, and they are receiving an incorrect WINS server IP address.
- They are configured as B-nodes and thus only broadcast to resolve NetBIOS names.

The two most commonly configured DHCP WINS options are

- 044—WINS server IP address(es)
- 046—WINS/NBT node type

When you configure the 044 DHCP option, you enter the WINS servers (up to 12) to assign to clients. Depending on the node type that you want to assign to DHCP clients, you enter one of the following parameters for DHCP option 046:

- 0x1—B-node
- 0x2—P-node
- 0x4—M-node
- 0x8—H-node (most common)

WINS configuration options are set at either the server or scope options level. These options are shown in Figure 9-10.

Problems related to DHCP configuration options are usually easy to spot, since they occur after the implementation of a new DHCP server or a new DHCP scope. The most common DHCP configuration–related WINS faults, along with their solutions, are listed in Table 9-7.

Table 9-7. Common DHCP-Related WINS Problems

Symptom	Probable Faults
Network performance is slow.	• Clients are not getting any WINS options (they are not configured) and are using broadcasts for NetBIOS name resolution.
	• The WINS server is unavailable.
Clients are getting WINS options, but performance is still slow.	• Clients are getting the wrong WINS server address.
	• Clients are configured as B-node or M-node; change to H-node.

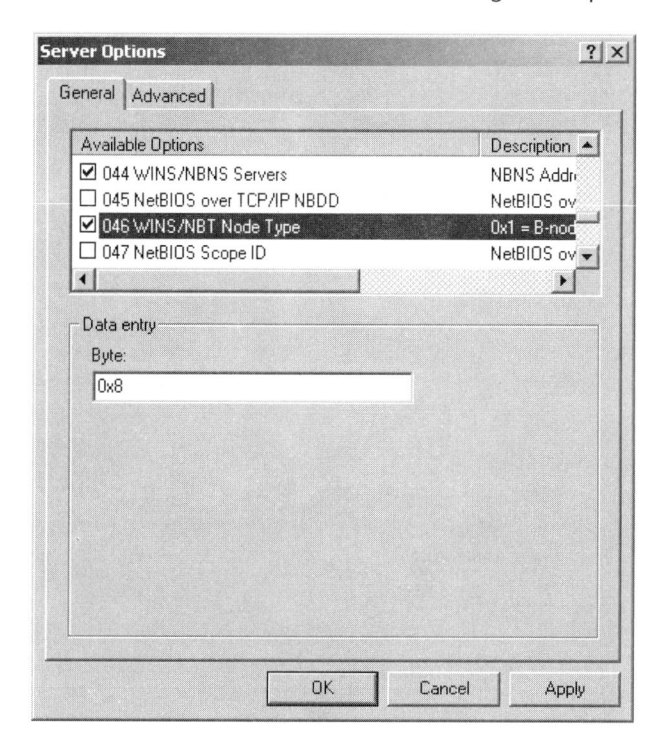

Figure 9-10. WINS-specific DHCP scope options

Now that you have seen how to troubleshoot and resolve general WINS server- and client-related faults, next you will see how to respond to a WINS server disaster.

Recovering a Corrupted WINS Database

If the WINS database becomes corrupted, or if the WINS server fails entirely, you may need to recover the WINS database from a backup. Before resorting to the backup, you should first try to detect and resolve inconsistencies in the WINS database by using the `netsh init compact` command, described earlier. If this fails, you should check to see that you have a reliable backup.

When a WINS server is initially set up, you should configure a WINS database backup path at that time. Once a database backup path is specified and you manually run a backup, WINS will automatically back up its database every three hours.

To configure the WINS server for automatic online backups, follow these steps.

1. On the WINS server, open the WINS MMC snap-in.
2. Right-click the WINS server object and select Properties.

3. As shown in Figure 9-11, enter a backup path for the WINS database and then click OK.

4. Now that a backup path is specified, right-click the WINS server object and select Back Up Database.

5. When prompted that the database backup completed successfully, click OK.

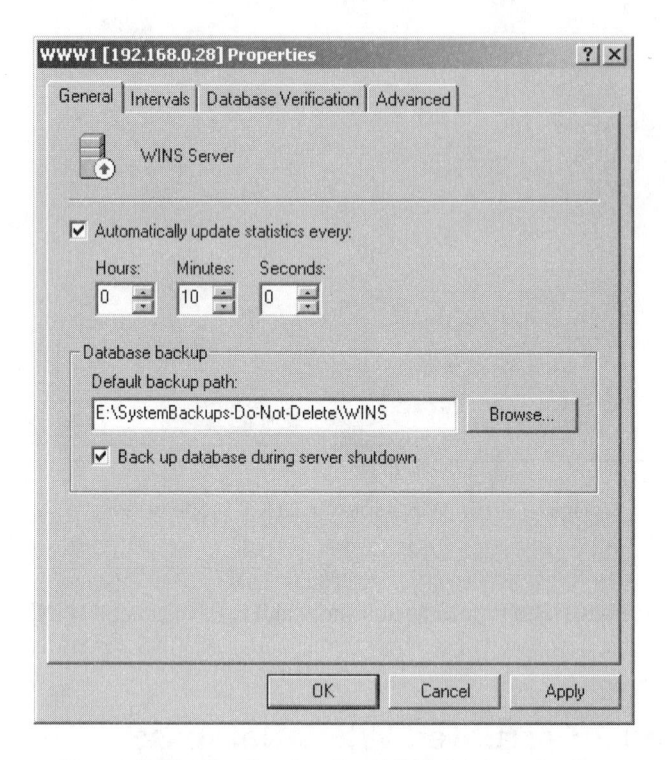

Figure 9-11. Configuring the WINS database backup

With automatic online backups of the WINS database now set up, you are fully prepared if the WINS service fails to start, or if the server itself crashes. In the event of a crash or database corruption, you should first try to recover the WINS database via compaction, which sometimes is all you need to do to repair a corrupted Jet database.

Perform these steps to compact the WINS database.

1. Click Start > Run, enter cmd in the Run dialog box, and click OK to access the command prompt.

2. Type net stop wins and press Enter to stop the WINS service.

3. Copy the %systemroot%\system32\wins\wins.mdb file to an alternate location so that you have a backup in case the compact job fails.

4. Type `netsh wins server init compact` and press Enter to compact the database.

5. Start the WINS service by typing `net start wins` and pressing Enter.

6. If the service starts, you should be good to go. Open the WINS MMC to verify that the WINS data is intact.

If, after you run compaction, the database still remains corrupted and the WINS service will not start, your final alternative is to restore the database from a backup. If the database was backed up with your backup software, you can use it to restore the wins.mdb file. If you used the WINS backup feature for automatic online backups, then you can recover the database using the backup file. To restore the WINS database from the WINS MMC, follow these steps.

1. Stop the WINS service if it is running.

2. Using Windows Explorer, navigate to the %systemroot%\system32\wins folder and delete the wins.mdb file.

3. In the WINS MMC, right-click the WINS server object and select Restore Database.

4. Browse to and select the WINS backup folder that you originally configured for WINS backups and click OK. Do not browse to any subfolders created by the WINS service.

5. When prompted that the restore completed successfully, click OK.

Once the restore completes, the WINS service should automatically start. Remember that if the backup is hours or even days old, some client registrations may not be in the WINS database. The easiest way to cure this problem, especially in environments containing hundreds or thousands of systems, is to wait. The database will be back up to date within 24 hours. Otherwise, you could run `nbtstat -RR` on every client so that they release and renew their WINS registration with the WINS server.

If another WINS server is already configured on the network for fault tolerance, you can repair the corrupted WINS database from the database of the second WINS server. To do this, follow these steps.

1. Stop the WINS service on the server containing the corrupted WINS database.

2. Delete the corrupted database.

3. Restart the WINS service. The service will start and WINS will have its default configuration.

4. Configure replication between the WINS server and the secondary WINS server.

There are several ways to recover a WINS database in the event of corruption. Remember, though, that nearly all of these recovery steps are not possible unless the WINS backup is configured. One of the most important aspects of troubleshooting is giving yourself options when a problem occurs. Planning for failure and allowing yourself options for recovery by having a valid backup will go far toward making your job much easier.

> The WINS automatic backup feature can only back up the WINS database to a local drive. If WINS backups are failing, check to make sure that the local drive that WINS is configured to back up to is available.

Summary

This section provided you with more tools to aid in your search for WINS problems, but don't lose sight of the basics. Pinging a system by IP address, for example, allows you to rule out TCP/IP and the entire network as the cause for a problem. Using tools like `ping` let you eliminate quite a bit of "what's right" right off the bat. Once you have established what is working, then start to examine the root of the problem. Simply running `ipconfig /all` on a user's system will most likely point you right at a configuration problem, if one exists.

Also, don't forget to get yourself in a DNS state of mind. With many organizations slowly phasing out WINS and keeping it around primarily for backward compatibility, WINS should normally be the last place you look for a name resolution problem on your network. Instead, focus on DNS and especially the DNS suffix search order configuration on a client's system. After all, the suffix search order is what, in a sense, allows DNS servers to act like WINS servers, as far as the clients are concerned.

This chapter got you started on thinking about how DHCP integrates into your network troubleshooting methodology. In the next chapter, you'll see the complete DHCP picture, which will complete the core network service troubleshooting landscape that you have been painting beginning with Chapter 8.

10
DHCP

In Chapter 2, you were introduced to the core concepts of a DHCP implementation. Understanding the data flow and relationships existing on a DHCP infrastructure, as with all network services, will go far in allowing you to quickly find the source of a problem. DHCP is significantly different in architecture from the services examined in the previous two chapters. Primarily, each DHCP server maintains its own local data and does not replicate information with other DHCP servers. Looking at this concept from the positive side, you can say that no replication means one less thing that can break. While this is true, don't forget that no replication may also mean that you have a single point of failure. To eliminate this, most organizations incorporate at least two DHCP servers with scopes using the "80-20 Rule" to provide for fault tolerance.

Since we need to stay focused on troubleshooting, this chapter does not contain information on fault-tolerant DHCP planning. If you need a refresher on this, consider picking up a copy of *The Ultimate Windows Server 2003 System Administrator's Guide*, by Robert Williams and Mark Walla (Addison-Wesley, 2003). Like previous chapters, this chapter starts with a quick review of core DHCP architectural components and terminology and then transitions to showing you the useful available tools for DHCP troubleshooting. We finish this chapter by looking at how to approach and resolve DHCP client and server issues and DHCP-RAS integration, and finally how to recover a corrupted DHCP database file.

DHCP Architecture

Without replication in the DHCP landscape, DHCP architecture is much easier to grasp than the configuration of DNS or WINS. Essentially, the DHCP infrastructure consists of a client-server network. Clients request addresses, and DHCP servers answer the requests. When no DHCP server resides on a client's local subnet, client requests for an IP address are forwarded to a DHCP server by a DHCP relay agent or a BOOTP-enabled (RFC 1542–compliant) router.

Even though the general structure of the DHCP architecture is relatively simple, don't underestimate the complexity of the DHCP service. This section will help you to see some of the intricate details that sometimes lead to confusion with a DHCP implementation. In this section, we look at the newest features of DHCP, the types of DHCP scopes, and vendor and user classes, and we conclude with a look at conflict detection.

What's New?

The birth of Active Directory (AD) with Windows 2000 brought about several improvements to the DHCP service. With Windows Server 2003, additional usability and reliability improvements were added, making a good service even better. The next two sections briefly outline these improvements.

Windows 2000 Enhancements

Here are the improvements that came about with Windows 2000.

- *Automatic Private IP Addressing (APIPA)*—If no DHCP server is available, clients will give themselves an IP address in the 169.254 subnet.

- *Enhanced performance monitoring*—Many DHCP counters in System Monitor allow you to quickly locate DHCP performance bottlenecks.

- *Support for user and vendor classes*—DHCP servers provide a custom group of options to a select group of systems.

- *DNS integration*—Windows 2000 DHCP servers can dynamically register client lease information with a DNS server that supports dynamic updates.

- *Unauthorized server detection (AD integration)*—Windows 2000 DHCP servers that are joined to a Windows 2000/W2K3 domain must be authorized by a member of the Enterprise Administrators group prior to being able to actively respond to client lease requests.

Windows Server 2003 Enhancements

There were two significant DHCP improvements with Windows Server 2003.

- *Backup and restore*—DHCP backups and restores can now be automatically run from the DHCP MMC. With Windows 2000 and earlier, restoring the DHCP database required several manual steps.

- *Client alternate configuration*—Clients configured to obtain an IP address automatically can be also configured with a static IP address. This way, if no DHCP server is discovered, the alternate address is used. This option is very useful when a user moves between multiple offices.

Scopes

Three types of scopes may exist on DHCP servers. While the Standard scope is the most common, you may also run into Superscopes and Multicast scopes. Each of these types of scopes is examined in the next three sections.

Standard

Standard scopes are the scope type that many administrators have come to know and love. They solve the problem of dynamically allocating IP addresses to network clients and may also deliver DNS and WINS server addresses to clients, among other options. You will find the following in a Standard scope:

- *Range of IP addresses*—Addresses to be given out
- *Subnet mask*—The subnet mask to be used by the addresses
- *Lease duration*—The length of the IP address lease, measured in days
- *Exclusions*—The range of IP addresses within the scope not to be leased (used to prevent the DHCP server from leasing static addresses used by servers on the subnet)
- *Reservations*—A listing of address leases reserved for a particular MAC address (one MAC address gets one IP address reservation)
- *DHCP options*—Additional TCP/IP configuration information, including the DNS server IP address, the WINS server IP address, and default gateway IP addresses

While Standard scopes are the most common, sometimes you will see Standard scopes combined to form Superscopes.

Superscopes

A Superscope is a grouping of Standard scopes created for the purpose of supporting a *multinet*. A multinet is nothing more than a grouping of several logical subnets on a single physical subnet. Sometimes multinets are created to support large groupings of clients on a single physical network while using a Class C IP addressing scheme, while other times they are created as a temporary bridge to dynamically change the IP addresses on a physical subnet from one range to another. Regardless of the reason behind their creation, the implementation process for a Superscope is relatively straightforward.

Suppose that you wanted two logical subnets to reside on a single physical network, with the network's associated router interface configured to use two IP addresses. Let's say that we'll use the following two network IDs: 172.16.2.0 and 172.16.3.0. The IP addresses for the physical network's router interface would be 172.16.2.1 and 172.16.3.1. These are the basic steps to create this Superscope.

1. Configure a Standard scope for the 172.16.2.0 subnet.
2. Configure a Standard scope for the 172.16.3.0 subnet.
3. Create the Superscope and select for the Superscope to contain the two previously created subnets.

This configuration is shown in Figure 10-1.

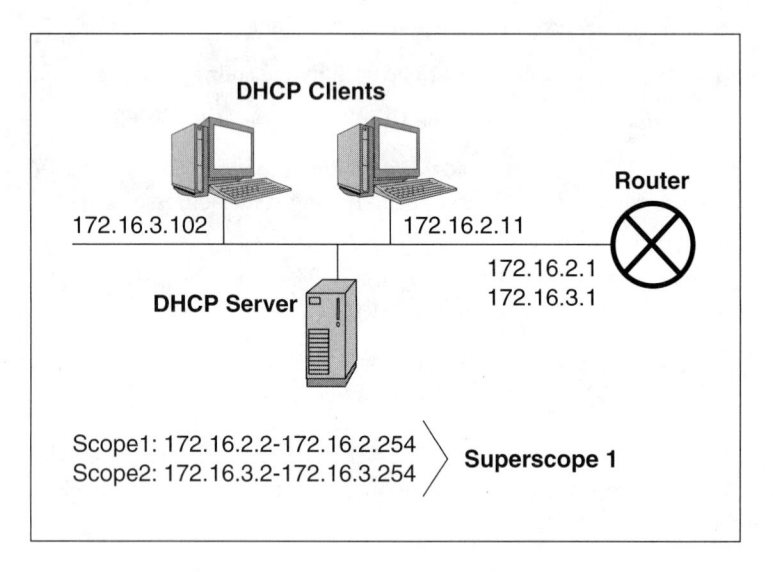

Figure 10-1. Superscope configuration

Multicast Scopes

With Standard scopes and Superscopes, the DHCP server leases *unicast* addresses to clients. This means that a one-to-one relationship between an address lease and a client exists (one address goes to one client). With Multicast scopes, *multicast* addresses are leased to clients, meaning that one IP address may be shared by multiple clients for the purpose of obtaining shared information over the network. To further understand the usage of multicast addresses, first think about the use of disk imaging software. Often a single system image exists that is sent over the network and is copied to multiple systems simultaneously. With several systems over the network downloading the same data via a multicast session, significant bandwidth is saved. For example, if you were trying to send a 1GB disk image to ten systems, doing so with a multicast session would mean that

1GB of data would traverse the network. On the other hand, if the same data was sent to ten systems, with each using a separate unicast session, 10GB of data would traverse the network.

Now consider the use of streaming media presentations over a network. It is not practical to stream the same data to 200 systems using individual unicast sessions, so multicast is almost always used in this type of situation. In fact, this is one of the most popular uses for dynamic allocation of multicast addresses from a DHCP server. Multicast scopes allow DHCP clients using Multicast Address Dynamic Client Allocation Protocol (MADCAP) to lease a multicast IP address. When working with Multicast scopes, remember these important considerations.

- The valid IP address range for Multicast scopes is 224.0.0.0 to 239.255.255.255.

- A Time to Live (TTL) value is used to specify the number of routers that multicast traffic can traverse on your network.

- Multicast address leases (30 days by default) are generally longer than standard leases (8 days by default) because the lease should be longer than the amount of time the lease is expected to be in continuous use on the network.

- A lifetime value can be configured under the scope's properties, causing the entire scope to expire on a selected date and time.

While scopes have been a part of DHCP configuration from its onset, classes were first introduced with Windows 2000. We'll examine them next.

Classes

DHCP classes allow you to set up customized DHCP options for a particular group of systems. This allows you to have a shorter lease duration for laptop users, for example, and a longer duration for all other users. There are two types of DHCP classes: vendor classes and user classes. Each of these two types is described in the next two sections.

Vendor Classes

Vendor classes are used to identify DHCP clients by their operating systems and to assign specific DHCP options to those clients. The two most common vendor class options are

- 001—Microsoft Disable NetBIOS over TCP/IP

- 002—Microsoft Release DHCP Lease on Shutdown

By configuring vendor class options, you could disable NetBIOS over TCP/IP, for example, for all clients running the Windows 2000 or XP/W2K3 OS.

User Classes

User classes are far more robust than vendor classes, allowing you to configure custom options for very specific groups of systems. For example, you may have a group of users in the sales department that are almost always on the road. For these users, you could then elect for them to get a shorter lease duration or even have their systems automatically release their DHCP lease when they are shut down. With any defined or manually created user class, you can customize any assignable DHCP option, including DNS servers and gateway addresses. By default, two predefined user classes exist:

- BOOTP.Microsoft—Used for BOOTP clients
- RRAS.Microsoft—Used for RRAS clients

You can also manually create a user class by right-clicking the DHCP server object in the DHCP MMC and selecting Define User Classes.

One of the most common mistakes made with the use of user classes is that administrators don't enable the use of the class on all DHCP client computers that they wish to have the user class options. This can be done by running the following command:

```
ipconfig /setclassid <network connection name> <class name>
```

To set a system to use the user class SalesClass on the default network interface, you would run this command:

```
ipconfig /setclassid "Local Area Connection" SalesClass
```

Conflict Detection

Before we get to troubleshooting tools, there is one more aspect of DHCP configuration that you should be aware of, which is conflict detection. Conflict detection is normally configured after a DHCP database has been restored from a backup and should never be enabled for normal day-to-day operation. After a restore, it is possible that leases were assigned that the DHCP server is unaware of, since the restore may be based on a backup of the DHCP database that is hours or even days old. To prevent the leasing of duplicate IP addresses, Microsoft recommends that, following a restore, you set the conflict detection attempts to 1 for a period equal to half the longest lease duration. You can check and configure conflict detection attempts under the General tab of the DHCP server Properties dialog box (see Figure 10-2). When the number of attempts is set to 1, the DHCP server pings an IP address and waits one second to hear a response before leasing it. If the value is set to 2, the server waits two seconds. As you can imagine, leaving conflict detection enabled significantly degrades DHCP server performance, so you should have this feature enabled only as long as it is necessary to ensure that duplicate IP addresses do not exist on the network.

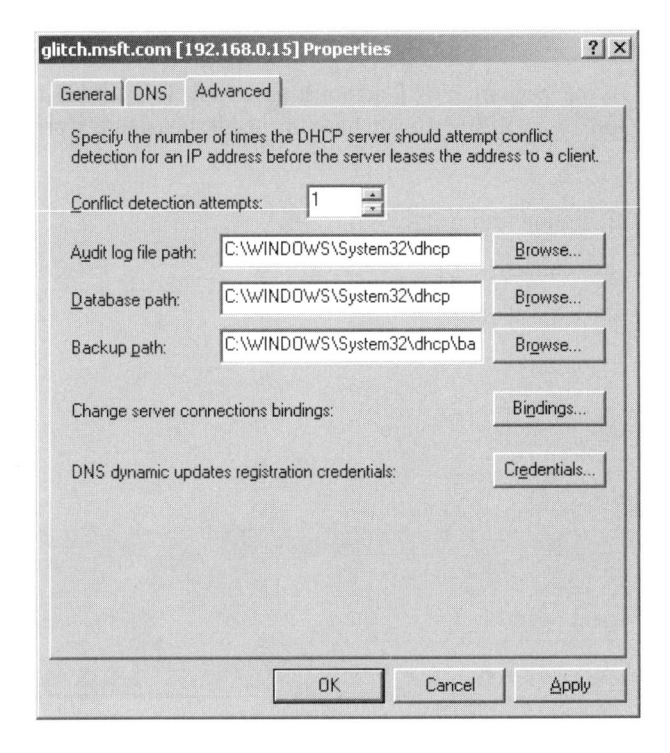

Figure 10-2. Setting DHCP conflict detection attempts to 1

DHCP Troubleshooting Tools

Three handy tools exist for troubleshooting and locating problems on DHCP servers:

- DHCP MMC
- Audit logging
- `dhcploc`

Primarily, the DHCP MMC snap-in is the most often used, since it allows you to quickly view configuration information. When you want to spot errors, audit logging provides a quick way to locate problems with a server. Each of these tools, along with the support tool `dhcploc`, is discussed next.

DHCP MMC

The DHCP MMC is the standard DHCP administrative tool. To open this tool, click Start > Administrative Tools > DHCP. Once you have opened it, you can perform the following tasks:

- Check configuration settings
- View lease assignments
- Configure scope options
- Enable audit logging

The DHCP MMC is shown in Figure 10-3.

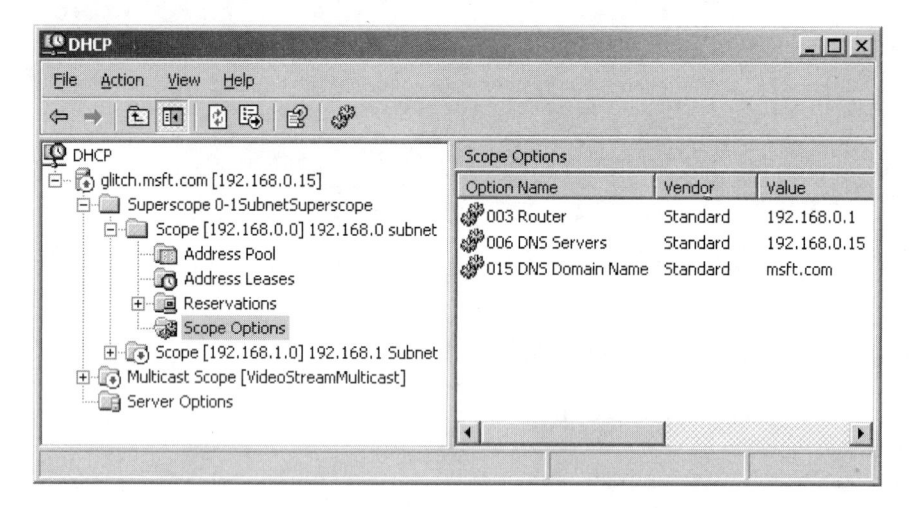

Figure 10-3. DHCP MMC snap-in

Audit Logging

When enabled, the audit logging feature provides the most detailed information available about failures relating to the DHCP service. Although it is enabled by default, to verify that audit logging is enabled, you would follow these steps.

1. Open the DHCP MMC snap-in.
2. Right-click the DHCP server object and select Properties.
3. Under the General tab, verify that the Enable DHCP Audit Logging checkbox is selected.

4. Click the Advanced tab and note the path to the audit log file.

5. Close the DHCP server Properties dialog box.

Once you have information on the location of the audit log file, you then check for error messages in the log file. Tables 10-1 through 10-3 list the possible event IDs you will see in the log file, along with their associated error messages and corrective action steps.

Table 10-1. General Audit Events

Event ID	Error Message	Probable Faults and Corrective Action
00	The log was started.	The audit log was enabled. No problem.
01	The log was stopped.	The audit log was disabled. This assumes that troubleshooting was completed. If you didn't disable the audit log, find out who did!
02	The log was temporarily paused due to low disk space.	The amount of physical disk space dropped below its default (20MB) or configured value. Free up disk space on the server by deleting unneeded files and folders.
10	A new IP address was leased to a client.	A new client requested and received a new IP address.
11	A lease was renewed by a client.	A client successfully renewed its lease. No problem.
12	A lease was released by a client.	A client successfully released its lease. No problem.
13	An IP address was found in use on the network.	Conflict detection detected that an IP address the server planned to lease was found on the network. Consequently, the address was not leased, and another address was used. If the message occurred after a recent DHCP database restore, this is normal behavior, since some leases may have been given to clients after the time of the last backup. If this is not the case, you need to locate the client system with the IP address, since it is likely a manually entered static IP address. Browse the dynamic registrations in the domain's DNS zone to match the IP address with a client computer name.
14	A lease request could not be satisfied because the address pool of the scope was exhausted.	You have run out of addresses in the scope. Either modify the range of addresses in the scope so that more addresses are available or shorten the scope's lease duration.

continues

Table 10-1. General Audit Events, continued

Event ID	Error Message	Probable Faults and Corrective Action
15	A lease was denied.	A client requesting to renew a lease was denied. This is likely because the IP address is already associated with another system's MAC address. This type of conflict is usually the result of a normal inconsistency that may result from having to restore a DHCP database to an earlier period in time.
20	A BOOTP address was leased to a client.	A client received an IP lease via a BOOTP forward from a router or a DHCP relay agent. This may indicate normal behavior or that the DHCP server on a subnet is down.

Table 10-2. Dynamic Update Audit Events

Event ID	Error Message	Probable Faults and Corrective Action
30	DNS dynamic update request	The DHCP server sent a request to dynamically update DNS zone data. No problem.
31	DNS dynamic update failed	Dynamic update failed. Verify that dynamic update is enabled for the failed registration's appropriate zone. Verify that the DHCP server computer account is a member of the DnsUpdateProxy global group.
32	DNS dynamic update successful	Dynamic update completed as expected. No problem.

Table 10-3. Authorization Failure Audit Events

Event ID	Error Message	Probable Faults and Corrective Action
50	Unreachable domain	The DHCP server could not find a domain controller in the domain of its Active Directory installation. Check for networking problems or the availability of domain controllers on the network.
51	Authorization succeeded	DHCP was authorized to start on the network. No problem.
52	Upgraded to Windows Server 2003	The server was upgraded to Windows Server 2003, and the unauthorized DHCP server detection feature has been disabled. No problem.

Table 10-3. Authorization Failure Audit Events, *continued*

Event ID	Error Message	Probable Faults and Corrective Action
53	Cached authorization	The DHCP server was authorized to start based on previously cached authorization information. Check for the availability of domain controllers or network connectivity to domain controllers.
54	Authorization failed	The DHCP server has not been authorized by a member of the Enterprise Administrators group.
55	Authorization (servicing)	The DHCP server was successfully authorized to start. No problem.
56	Authorization failure, stopped servicing	The DHCP service was not authorized to start and was shut down by the operating system. Have a member of the Enterprise Administrators group authorized the DHCP server.
57	Server found in domain	Another authorized DHCP server exists in the same domain. No problem.
58	Server could not find domain	The DHCP server could not find its domain. Check for network connectivity to a domain controller and the status of domain controllers in the domain.
59	Network failure	The DHCP server could not see if it is authorized, due to a network failure.
60	No DC is DS enabled	The DHCP server could find a domain controller (DC), such as a Windows NT BDC, but could not find one that has Active Directory installed. Check for connectivity to a Windows 2000 or W2K3 domain controller (the DHCP server needs this to see if it's authorized).
61	Server found that belongs to DS domain	Another server was found on the network that belongs to the same Active Directory domain. No problem.
62	Another DHCP server was found on the network	This could be a rogue server. Locate the server, and if needed, take it offline.
63	Restarting rogue detection	The DHCP server is attempting to contact a domain controller to see if it is authorized to start. No problem.
64	No DHCP enabled interfaces	Network devices are not present or are not connected to the network. Verify that the NICs appear in Device Manager, and check to see that they have TCP/IP installed and are configured with static IP addresses. Next, verify that connectivity to the hub or switch exists.

dhcploc (ST)

If you're looking for an easy way to identify DHCP servers on a network, then look no further—dhcploc is the tool you need. This support tool can be run on any non-DHCP server, and it reports on DHCP traffic and the servers involved. If you suspect that the dreaded "rogue" DHCP server is wreaking havoc on your DHCP infrastructure, you can locate it by IP address with this tool.

To run the command, you would run the following on a server that is not a DHCP server:

```
dhcploc <local IP address>
```

In the command syntax, you must specify the IP address of the system on which you are executing the command. This should not be the IP address of a DHCP server. Running the command on a DHCP server may produce erroneous results. Note that the command output displays DHCP messages such as offers and acknowledgments. This is shown in Figure 10-4. Pay close attention to the far right portion of the display, since it lists the IP address of the server involved in the DHCP communications. If the server listed has an IP address that is not one of your configured DHCP servers, you have found the rogue.

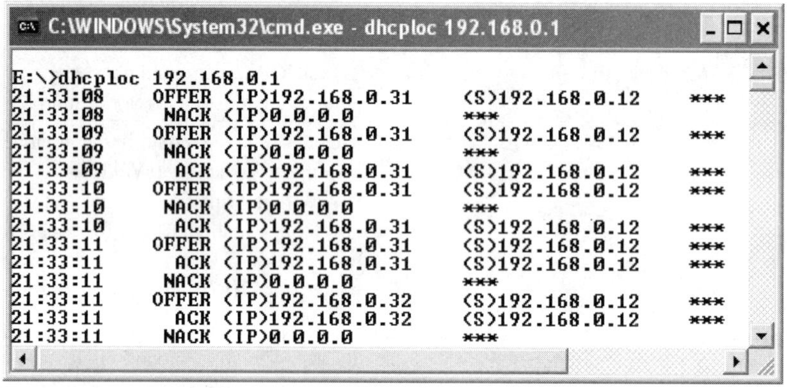

```
C:\WINDOWS\System32\cmd.exe - dhcploc 192.168.0.1

E:\>dhcploc 192.168.0.1
21:33:08        OFFER (IP)192.168.0.31    (S)192.168.0.12   ***
21:33:08        NACK  (IP)0.0.0.0          ***
21:33:09        OFFER (IP)192.168.0.31    (S)192.168.0.12   ***
21:33:09        NACK  (IP)0.0.0.0          ***
21:33:09        ACK   (IP)192.168.0.31    (S)192.168.0.12   ***
21:33:10        OFFER (IP)192.168.0.31    (S)192.168.0.12   ***
21:33:10        NACK  (IP)0.0.0.0          ***
21:33:10        ACK   (IP)192.168.0.31    (S)192.168.0.12   ***
21:33:11        OFFER (IP)192.168.0.31    (S)192.168.0.12   ***
21:33:11        ACK   (IP)192.168.0.31    (S)192.168.0.12   ***
21:33:11        NACK  (IP)0.0.0.0          ***
21:33:11        OFFER (IP)192.168.0.32    (S)192.168.0.12   ***
21:33:11        ACK   (IP)192.168.0.32    (S)192.168.0.12   ***
21:33:11        NACK  (IP)0.0.0.0          ***
```

Figure 10-4. dhcploc output

Troubleshooting DHCP Clients

DHCP client problems are usually the result of an improper static configuration or a network connection issue, or are related to the availability of a DHCP server. When a client computer is having trouble accessing network resources, perform the following general steps on the client to identify the problem.

1. Verify hardware connectivity (LED on NIC).
2. From the command prompt on the client, run `ipconfig /all`.
3. First check the IP address against the known address range for the client's subnet. If an address exists, then you know that the client is properly receiving an IP address from the DHCP server. If the address is in the 169.254.x.x range, is 0.0.0.0, or is a static address provided as an alternate IP configuration, then you can assume that the client does not have connectivity to the server.
4. If you have determined that connectivity to the server is the problem, then you should check the network elements between the client and the server, including cables, routers, switches, and a DHCP relay agent, if one exists.
5. If other TCP/IP configuration information (DNS server address, default gateway, and so on) is missing or is incorrect, then it can be assumed that the client is not receiving the proper DHCP options, which indicates an improper configuration on the server or may mean that the client is not configured to use a specific user class, if one exists.

With DHCP clients, the process to locate a problem is relatively simple, which normally means that you will find the source of the problem within a few minutes. The key points to remember when checking a client are to

- Verify physical network connectivity.
- Use `ipconfig /all` to examine TCP/IP configuration information on the client.

The most common DHCP client problems and their associated faults are listed in Table 10-4.

Table 10-4. Common DHCP Client Problems

Symptom	Probable Faults
The client cannot access other systems on the network.	• Check the client's network configuration. (Is the network interface set to Obtain an IP Address Automatically?)
	• There is no physical connection to the network.
	• An invalid NIC driver exists.
	• An invalid static IP address exists.

continues

Table 10-4. Common DHCP Client Problems, continued

Symptom	Probable Faults
The client cannot access other systems on the network. The client's IP address is on the 169.254.x.x subnet, is 0.0.0.0, or matches the client's designated alternate IP address.	The DHCP server could not be contacted. Check for the availability of • The DHCP server • A BOOTP forwarder • A DHCP relay agent
The client cannot resolve the names of other systems.	DNS options on the DHCP scope either are not configured or are configured incorrectly.
The client cannot contact systems beyond its local subnet. No default gateway is specified.	The router option on the DHCP scope either is not configured or is configured incorrectly.
The client has not received DHCP options for its defined user class.	The client is not configured to use the class. Run `ipconfig /setclassid <interface name> <class name>` on the client system.

When everything checks out on the client side, or if multiple clients are experiencing network problems, then odds are that you will find that the problem is associated with the DHCP server.

An often overlooked problem when you are troubleshooting a single DHCP client is the DHCP Client service. If a single client is not receiving a DHCP address, but all other clients on the network are not having any problems, verify that the client's DHCP Client service is configured as Automatic and is in a Started state.

Troubleshooting DHCP Servers

Most DHCP server problems are the result of improper configuration, the server not being authorized, or one of the following faults.

- The DHCP database (DHCP.mdb) is corrupted.
- There is a problem with DHCP relay agent access.
- A DHCP service is not running.
- A network interface is disabled or not connected to the network.
- The DHCP scope is out of leasable IP addresses.

Remember that when you encounter a problem with a DHCP server, audit logging can often quickly point you right to the source of the problem, so check it first, since it may provide all of the information you need. If the audit log does not provide any information in relation to the problem, you should then open the DHCP MMC snap-in on the DHCP server. From here, you can verify that the DHCP service is running and that there are available IP leases for the DHCP clients. Oftentimes, identifying the problem is the easy part when you are troubleshooting DHCP servers. When server connectivity is at issue, the problem may include the network, routers, or DHCP relay agents between the clients and servers, and all of this does not include the configuration problems that can be the result of the "savvy" user.

Let's start by quickly examining the common problems and solutions that you may run into when troubleshooting DHCP servers. These symptoms and related faults are shown in Table 10-5.

Table 10-5. Common DHCP Server Problems

Symptom	Probable Faults
The DHCP Server service will not start.	• The DHCP server is not authorized. Have a member of the Enterprise Admins group authorize the server. • The database is corrupted. Restore the database from backup and reconcile all scopes.
A multihomed server does not respond to some clients.	• Check the server bindings. Also verify that all NICs on the server have static IP addresses. • Check to see that the DHCP scopes are activated.
The server does not respond to client requests.	• The scope is out of addresses. • BOOTP forwarding is not enabled on the router of a remote subnet. • A DHCP relay agent is offline.
The server is handing out duplicate IP addresses.	The server was likely restored and is not aware of all previously issued leases. Set the server's conflict detection attempts value to 1 for a period of 50% of the longest lease duration (4 days by default).
Leases for a newly created scope are not being issued.	• The new scope is not activated. • Clients continue to renew leases from an existing old scope. You need to create a Superscope containing the old and new scopes, and then exclude all of the leases in the old scope. When clients attempt to renew, they will be forced to obtain a new address from the new scope.

For general server access problems, always remember the reliable TCP/IP utilities, such as ping to verify network connectivity. In the next four sections, we'll look at how to test and resolve specific DHCP server problems.

Troubleshooting DHCP Scope Migration

Sometimes it is necessary to migrate a range of DHCP lease addresses from one logical subnet to another. This may be necessary to implement a new addressing scheme on the network or to facilitate larger subnets allowing for more hosts per subnet. During the migration phase, a multinet containing at least two logical subnets is present. Normally, scope migration on a Windows Server 2003 DHCP server involves the use of a Superscope. The need for the Superscope stems from how a DHCP server responds to client requests. The server maps a one-to-one relationship between physical network interfaces and scopes. So the interface with a 172.16.12.10/24 IP address would lease addresses for the 172.16.12.0/24 network. A second interface could be used to lease addresses to a different network. With this relationship, a problem exists when trying to migrate leases to a new subnet range and subsequent DHCP scope. In this situation, there are two general ways to go about the migration.

- Create a new scope and change the IP address of the DHCP server's network adapter to an address on the same network as the new defined scope. All new DHCP leases will be assigned from the new scope.

- Create a Superscope that contains the old and new scopes. Activate both scopes and then exclude the entire address range in the original scope. Clients requesting to renew leases in the old scope will be refused (DHCP NACK), due to the exclusion, and will have to instead request a new lease by broadcasting a DHCP Discover message. The DHCP server will then allocate a new lease from the range of addresses present in the new scope.

Based on these two migration methodologies, there are only a couple of possible faults to check for when DHCP clients are not receiving addresses from the new scope. If you attempted to perform the migration without using a Superscope, you should check to see that you have configured the DHCP server's network adapter, so that its associated IP address resides on the network of the new scope.

If you are using a Superscope to facilitate the new migration, which is the Microsoft recommended methodology, then you should check for the following if clients are not receiving IP addresses in the new scope.

- The IP address of the DHCP server should reside on the new scope.
- All addresses contained in the old scope should be excluded.
- The Superscope must be activated (inactive scopes are represented by a red down arrow in the DHCP MMC).

To set up an exclusion in the original scope, you would perform the following steps.

1. In the DHCP MMC, expand the new Superscope and then expand the original scope that you are migrating clients from.

2. Right-click the Address Pool object under the original scope and select New Exclusion Range.

3. In the Add Exclusion dialog box, enter the first and last available IP address in the scope and click OK.

If the exclusions are correct, you should then verify that the new scope contained in the Superscope is active. If it is not, you can activate it by right-clicking the new scope and selecting Activate.

Once there are no leases for the original scope (see Figure 10-5), follow these steps to remove the Superscope from the DHCP server.

1. Right-click the original scope and select Delete. When prompted, click Yes to delete the scope.

2. You should now have a single scope in the Superscope. Now right-click the remaining scope and select Remove From Superscope. When prompted, click Yes to remove the scope. The Superscope is automatically deleted at this time as well.

Once the Superscope has been removed, you are left with only the new scope on the DHCP server, completing the migration process.

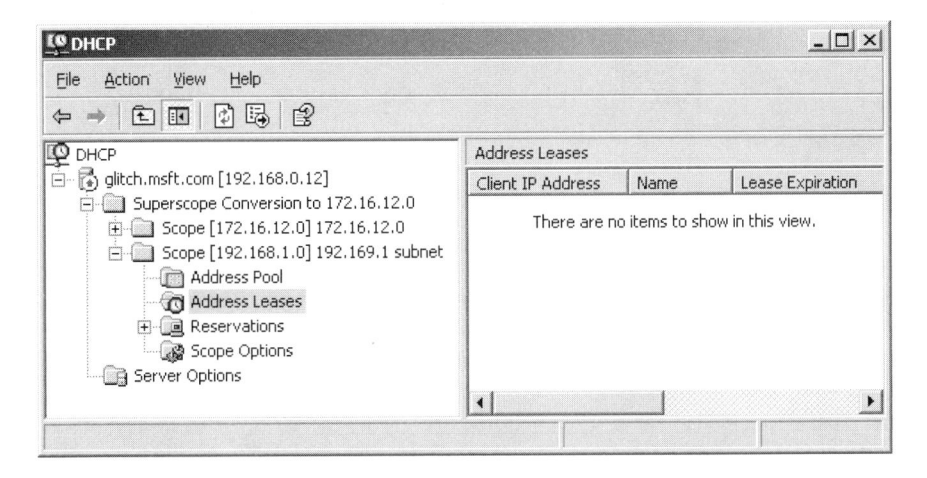

Figure 10-5. Verifying current leases in a DHCP scope

Troubleshooting DHCP-RAS Integration

To troubleshoot DHCP server issues when the DHCP server is responsible for servicing remote access clients connecting to a remote access server (RAS), you must first understand the roles of the DHCP server and the RAS server in the lease process. When remote clients connect to a RAS server, the server can be configured either to allocate dynamic IP addresses itself or to obtain IP addresses from a DHCP server. These configuration options are illustrated in Figure 10-6.

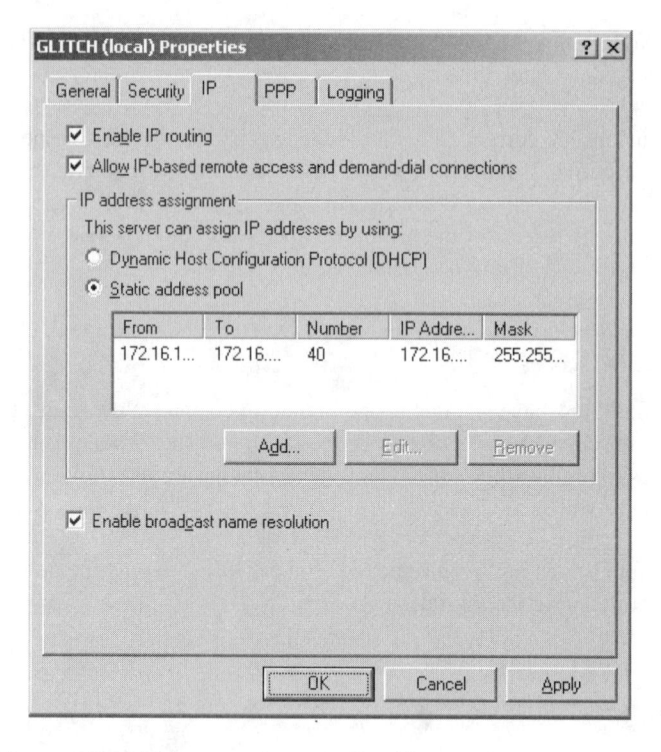

Figure 10-6. RAS server dynamic IP address assignment settings

When using a RAS server to offer its own dynamic IP addresses, you are limited in what can be dynamically allocated to clients. Since under the RAS server properties you can only indicate an IP address range, RAS clients assume the DNS server IP address and default gateway address that is configured on the RAS server. Even if you indicate that the RAS server obtains addresses automatically from a DHCP server, by default the RAS clients still receive the DNS server and default gateway options that are locally configured on the RAS server, regardless of what is actually configured in the DHCP lease.

The default behavior can be changed by configuring the RAS server to also act as a DHCP relay agent. When it does, the RAS clients receive all DHCP options from the DHCP server.

With an understanding of how DHCP and RAS work together, let's now move on to looking at the common problems that you may encounter.

Clients Unable to Access Resources Beyond RAS's Subnet

For starters, let's begin with clients not being able to access resources beyond the local subnet of the RAS server. This problem, like similar problems on LANs, is likely attributed to the clients having either no default gateway or the wrong default gateway specified in the TCP/IP configuration properties. The gateway configuration can be quickly checked on the client by running `ipconfig /all` on the client system. If the RAS server is configured to dynamically allocate from its own local address pool, then you should check the configuration settings of its local area network connection for the proper gateway. If the RAS server is configured to allocate addresses that were obtained from a DHCP server, then it must be configured as a DHCP relay agent in order to pass DHCP scope options to its clients.

To configure a RAS server as a DHCP relay agent, follow these steps.

1. From the Routing and Remote Access MMC Snap-in, expand the server object to IP Routing > DHCP Relay Agent.

2. Right-click DHCP Relay Agent and select Properties.

3. In the DHCP Relay Agent Properties dialog box, enter the IP address for the network's DHCP server and then click the Add button.

4. Click OK to close the DHCP Relay Agent Properties dialog box.

With the RAS server configured as a DHCP relay agent, its clients can now receive all client options from the DHCP server. However, even as a relay agent, the RAS server will still not act like other DHCP relay agents in that it will continue to secure DHCP leases in blocks of ten.

Clients Unable to Access Resources on RAS's Subnet

This problem can be looked at the same way as when a DHCP server is out of addresses. When a RAS server is configured to obtain IP addresses for its clients from a DHCP server, it takes addresses from the DHCP server in blocks of ten. With this in mind, do not just assume that the DHCP server allocates addresses for RAS clients only as needed. As with DHCP clients connected to a LAN, RAS clients using the IP address 169.254.x.x or 0.0.0.0 are screaming out to you that they cannot contact a DHCP server.

To solve this problem, check the leases in the DHCP MMC snap-in. If you notice that the server is out of leases, you could take one of the following actions to solve the problem.

- Shorten the lease duration under the scope's properties.

- Change the starting and ending IP range for the scope so that it has more available addresses.

- Shorten the scope's range of excluded addresses so that it only excludes necessary static addresses.

If having to give up 10 addresses at a time to the RAS server is a problem (11 RAS connections = 20 DHCP leases), then you could consider excluding a range of addresses on the DHCP server for use by the RAS server. This way, the RAS server and DHCP server would never get in each other's way. With this setup, your only other consideration would be to verify that the RAS server's local network connection has the proper gateway and DNS server specified, since it will provide those IP addresses to its RAS clients along with a leased IP address.

Troubleshooting DHCP Relay Agents

You have already seen the importance of configuring a RAS server as a DHCP relay agent to facilitate the integration of DHCP leasing between a RAS server and a DHCP server for the purpose of dynamically providing IP address leases to RAS clients. In addition to their use with RAS for remote clients, DHCP relay agents are also valuable tools in the distribution of dynamic IP addresses to local clients.

In a routed network, DHCP relay agents are needed if the routers do not support BOOTP forwarding, or if BOOTP forwarding is not enabled on the routers. Unlike WINS Proxies, DHCP relay agents can only be configured on Windows 2003 (or Windows 2000) servers. The steps to configuring a DHCP relay agent were already mentioned in a previous section and thus are not mentioned again here. However, to summarize, once the Routing and Remote Access Service (RRAS) is configured and enabled on a Windows server, you can set it up as a relay agent with just a few clicks.

Once you have set up a properly configured relay agent, it listens for DHCP Discover broadcasts on its local network, and then forwards the Discover request to a DHCP server on a remote subnet. The clues to a faulty DHCP relay agent are very similar to those of the DHCP server, since the relay agent is practically acting like a DHCP server to its local clients, although in just a proxy capacity.

With relay agents participating in your DHCP infrastructure, you do have more to think about when clients are having trouble communicating on the network. Again, the first sign of a DHCP-related problem is clients having trouble communicating with systems on the network, which in turn have IP addresses of 169.254.x.x or 0.0.0.0. If this problem is occurring on multiple subnets, then the DHCP server (single point of failure) is likely the source of the problem. If only clients on a single subnet are having trouble, then you should check the DHCP relay agent on their specific subnet.

The fastest way to query the state of a DHCP relay agent is to open up the Routing and Remote Access MMC snap-in on the relay agent machine. When you open the console, you should first look to see that the server object has green arrow pointing up adjacent to it. This means that the RRAS service is running. If you see a down red arrow next to the server object, then you will need to start the RRAS service. This can be done by right-clicking the server object, selecting All Tasks, and then clicking Start. Once the service starts, your problem is likely solved.

The only other problem that you may need to check in the console is to see that the DHCP Relay Agent object has the proper DHCP server IP address specified. If you are using fault-tolerant DHCP, you could configure each relay agent with the IP addresses of two DHCP servers. This way, if one server failed, the DHCP relay agent would forward requests to the second server. You can check the DHCP server IP addresses by right-clicking the DHCP Relay Agent object and selecting Properties.

Once you have resolved the relay agent problem, you need to force clients with invalid addresses to obtain a new lease from the DHCP server. To do this, you could run `ipconfig /release` and then `ipconfig /renew` on each client, or if you are working with dozens of faulty clients, you could consider telling each user to just reboot his or her system.

> The DHCP Relay Agent service cannot be configured to run on the same computer as a DHCP server. Both the DHCP server and the Relay Agent service listen and respond to DHCP Discover packets on UDP ports 67 and 68, and conflict with each other when running on the same physical system. Under nearly all circumstances, it is neither necessary nor practical to have a DHCP server also configured as a DHCP relay agent.

Recovering a Corrupted DHCP Database

Whenever inconsistencies arise in the DHCP database, causing the DHCP service to hang or fail to start, you need to take corrective action on the database. Errors caused by database corruption are usually easy to detect, since they are logged in the Event Viewer's system log. DHCP Jet database (corruption) errors are noted in the system log with event ID 1014, with the event source being the DHCP server and the event description beginning with "The Jet database returned the following error…" The message ends with an error code number, which will be one of the following: -510, -1022, or -1850.

Recovering from Backup

If the DHCP server cannot start due to a corrupted database, then you are left with two options: recover the DHCP database from a backup copy, or start over from scratch.

Let's start with recovering from scratch, since it is the easiest solution but certainly not the best. If all is lost and you do not have a good backup, or if you need to set up a new DHCP server without a backup of the old DHCP database, then you are faced with manually re-creating the DHCP scopes and scope options on the new server. Once you have reconfigured the scopes, you need to enable conflict detection on the DHCP server, which was discussed earlier in this chapter in the Conflict Detection section. Before activating any of the re-created scopes, set conflict detection attempts to 1, and leave that setting at 1 for at least half of the longest lease duration value. So for an eight-day lease, you need to leave conflict detection on for four days. When you are running conflict detection, the DHCP server runs significantly slower, since each lease takes slightly longer than one second to process, which is an eternity in computer time. Remember that the one-second delay is determined by conflict detection. With conflict detection set to 1, for every address to be leased by the DHCP server, it first pings the address and then waits one second for a reply. When no reply is received, the address is leased.

Database Backups
As you can see, starting from scratch should always be a last resort. The best option is to restore from backup. Online DHCP backups run automatically every 60 minutes by default and are known as *synchronous backups*. *Asynchronous backups*, which are user initiated, can be executed on demand anytime from the DHCP MMC snap-in.

To manually initiate a DHCP backup from the DHCP MMC, perform these steps.

1. Right-click the DHCP server object and select Backup.

2. When prompted to specify the backup path, click OK to use the default Backup folder, or enter a different backup path and click OK.

Chapter 10 DHCP

A backup of the DHCP server secures the following information:

- DHCP server configuration, including all server options
- DHCP scope configuration, including all scope options, leases, and reservations

Simple Recovery

Simple recovery is used when the DHCP database has become corrupted or deleted, but the server itself has not suffered a complete failure. This restore type is seamless and can be completed within minutes. Here are the steps to simple recovery.

1. From the DHCP MMC snap-in, right-click the DHCP server object and select Restore.
2. Browse to and select the "DHCP backup" folder (see Figure 10-7) and then click OK.
3. When prompted that the DHCP Server service must be stopped and restarted to perform the restore, click Yes.
4. If you are unsure if leases have been assigned since the last backup, then you need to set conflict detection attempts to 1 for at least half the time of the longest lease duration.

When an entire DHCP server fails, then your choices are to perform a full system restore of the DHCP server, which should fully recover the DHCP database, or to

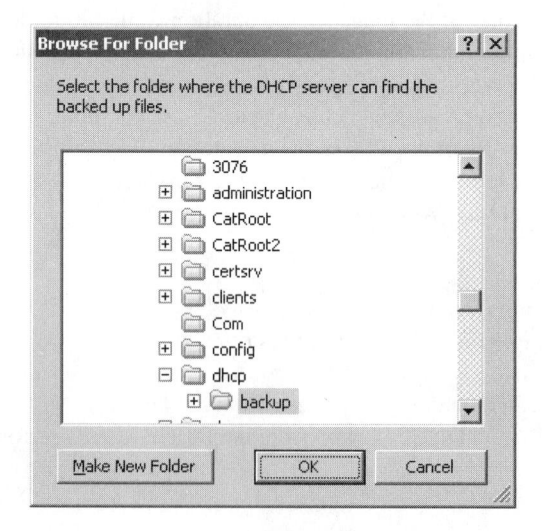

Figure 10-7. Selecting the "DHCP backup" folder

configure an alternate server as a DHCP server, using the configuration information from the previous DHCP server. This task involves performing advanced recovery, which is outlined next.

Advanced Recovery

To perform advanced recovery, you must start by installing the DHCP service on the new server. Once finished, you then need to copy the "DHCP backup" folder to the new server. The contents of this folder are used in the restore operation. To perform the restore, follow these steps.

1. From the DHCP MMC snap-in, right-click the DHCP server object and select Restore.

2. Browse to and select the "DHCP backup" folder and then click OK.

3. When prompted that the DHCP Server service must be stopped and restarted to perform the restore, click Yes.

4. On the new DHCP server, set conflict detection attempts to 1 for at least half the time of the longest lease duration.

After you have restored the DHCP database, inconsistencies may exist between the DHCP server configuration and the restored data. These inconsistencies are resolved by reconciling the DHCP scopes.

Reconciling Scopes

Reconciling scopes finds and repairs inconsistencies for client IP address leases in DHCP scopes. This task should always be performed immediately after a restore of the DHCP database. After a performing a heart transplant, doctors don't just throw you out of the hospital. At the very least, they take a moment to make sure you are relatively healthy before you leave the hospital. The same can be said for a DHCP database transplant. A quick sanity check performed by reconciling all scopes provides a simple means to verify and correct any problems caused by the restore operation.

To reconcile the DHCP scopes, follow these steps.

1. From the DHCP MMC snap-in, right-click the DHCP server object and select Reconcile All Scopes.

2. In the Reconcile All Scopes dialog box, click Verify.

3. Now click Reconcile.

4. Once the scopes have been reconciled, click Verify again in the Reconcile All Scopes dialog box.

5. You should now be prompted that the database is consistent. Click OK.

6. Click Cancel to close the Reconcile All Scopes dialog box.

Once all scopes have been reconciled, the DHCP server is fully operational. You have now seen all aspects of the necessary procedures for recovering a corrupted or lost DHCP database.

Summary

This chapter presented you with the tools and techniques for diagnosing and resolving DHCP server and client problems. One of the advantages to the DHCP service is that the types of problems that you may encounter are limited in scope (no pun intended). When troubleshooting suspected DHCP problems, always remember to consider the big picture. If the problem only affects a single client, then odds are that the client is the problem, not the DHCP server. For faults on an entire network subnet, you may need to consider checking one of the DHCP server network interfaces, a DHCP relay agent, or the router BOOTP configuration. Remember that APIPA is your best friend when you are troubleshooting server connectivity issues. Clients having a 169.254.x.x IP address are screaming at you, "Hey, I can't talk to the DHCP server, so I'm giving myself an address!" To confirm the existence of a DHCP server on a network subnet, remember that you can run the `dhcploc` support tool. Finally, don't forget about the reliable DHCP MMC snap-in. The tool lets you monitor lease and configuration status, check server authorization, back up and restore the DHCP database, and reconcile DHCP scopes. When you take the right approach, troubleshooting and resolving a DHCP problem should never equate to a late night at the office.

11

Network and Application Services

In the previous few chapters, we looked at individual core network services and ways to resolve their most common problems. While services such as DNS and DHCP are seen as necessities on many large networks, other network services are important to practically all networks. In this chapter, we examine the many network services that can still contribute to a sleepless night but whose problems are not so vast that they need an entire chapter dedicated to them. Services that commonly reside on many networks include

- Print services
- Terminal Services
- Distributed File System (DFS)
- Remote Installation Services (RIS)
- NetWare integration

While you are almost certainly managing at least a few network printers, you also may be managing other services, such as Terminal Services and DFS. When problems arise in this vast array of important services, you need to understand the underlying architecture of these services, the tools to use to pinpoint problems, and the steps needed to resolve those problems.

The Lay of the Land

Troubleshooting network and application services is much easier with an understanding of each service's core concepts. While this section does not replace all of the information found in a good Windows XP or Windows Server 2003 administration book—my favorite is *The Ultimate Windows Server 2003 System Administrator's Guide*, by Robert Williams and Mark Walla (Addison-Wesley, 2003)—it gives you the survival skills needed to recognize and resolve network service and application problems. With that in mind, let's get started with a quick look at printer survival.

Print Services

Sometimes, both users and administrators become confused about how Microsoft defines printers and their relationship to the operating system. If you are unsure of the difference between a *printer* and a *print device*, then this section is definitely for you. Here are some of the fundamental printer definitions.

- *Print device*—This is the piece of hardware that spits out the paper. A print device refers to the physical object that prints.

- *Printer*—A printer is a logical representation of a physical print device. It is important to know the difference between the terms *print device* and *printer* because it is possible to have several logical printers send documents to a single physical print device.

- *Print server*—A print server is a system that acts as a host to print devices. When clients want to print to a particular print device, they can send their documents to the print server over the network.

- *Print driver*—This is the software driver that allows an operating system to communicate with a print device. Oftentimes, when clients of several operating systems all print to the same printer, you need to ensure that the appropriate print drivers are available on the print server. This way, when the client tries to add the printer to his or her system, the appropriate driver is downloaded automatically. Otherwise, the user would have to manually install the driver.

- *Print queue*—This is the collection bucket for documents to be printed. When a document is sent to a printer, it is first stored in the queue and then sent to the print device.

- *Ports*—Ports define how a printer connects to a print device. For example, a line printer (LPT) port is frequently used for connections to parallel ports, and you can add Standard TCP/IP Ports to define connections to print devices located on an IP network.

- *Print pooling*—This concept allows you to configure several physical print devices as a single logical printer. This provides load balancing for user print jobs. However, for you to be able to pool printers, they must all use the same driver set and thus should be the same physical devices. Also, since there is no control over which physical print device gets which document, all print devices should be located in the same room.

Advanced Settings

Now with the basic terminology out of the way, let's examine some of the more advanced printer settings. Figure 11-1 shows the advanced settings for a printer. To access a printer's Properties dialog box (shown), you first click Start > Printers and Faxes. Then you right-click the desired printer and select Properties.

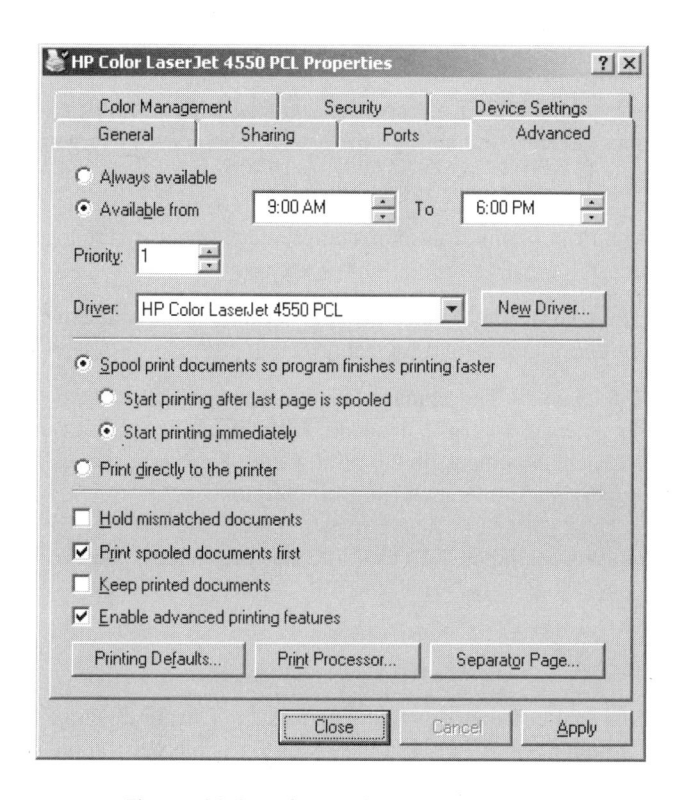

Figure 11-1. Advanced printer properties

Two important advanced properties to be aware of are priority and availability. With printer priority numbers, the higher value has the first priority. You can configure the priority numbers anywhere between 1 and 99. Suppose that a server has a single print device, and managers are complaining that they often have to wait for their documents to print. To allow managers' documents to always print before the staff documents, you could configure two logical printers. You would assign the staff print permissions to one printer and the managers' print permissions to the other. You could then instruct staff to print to the printer with a priority of 10, for example, and managers to print to the printer with a priority of 50. Whenever competition exists for a print device, the printer with the higher priority value always wins. However, this does not cause currently running print jobs to be interrupted. Once a printer starts printing a job, it finishes its work. After the job completes, then the printer with the highest priority that has a document waiting can take over the print device resources.

One other consideration in the advanced settings that may lead to confusion as to why a printer is not printing deals with setting printer availability. You can configure a printer to be always available to users, or you can set time restrictions on when a particular printer can print. Jobs sent to the printer remain in the print queue until its window of operations opens.

Printer Permissions
Under the Security tab of a printer's Properties window, you can configure permissions for users and groups to print to or manage the printer. These are the three basic permissions that can be granted.

- *Print*—With Print permissions, you can print documents to the logical printer but cannot manage operations on the printer

- *Manage Printers*—With Manage Printers permissions, a user can change the configuration settings of a logical printer

- *Manage Documents*—The Manage Documents permission allows a user to manage documents in a printer's queue. With this ability, a user can pause, resume, or delete documents in the print queue. This permission allows you to give a supervisor limited control over a printer.

With printer basics behind us, let's examine the core concepts behind Windows Terminal Services.

Terminal Services

The concept of Terminal Services was first mentioned in Chapter 5 with Remote Desktop. The idea of Terminal Services is to allow users to remotely run applications on or access the complete desktop of a remote server. Allowing users to connect to and run an application remotely on another server is advantageous in that you only have a few single points (depending on the number of terminal servers) where you need to install and maintain applications. This certainly aids in streamlining application maintenance. Also, in enabling you to access a complete desktop, Terminal Services makes it easy for administrators to remotely manage network servers right from their local systems. Both Windows XP and W2K3 systems can connect to a terminal server using the Remote Desktop client software. For a Windows server to act as a terminal server, it needs to have the Terminal Services service installed. If you plan to have several clients accessing terminal servers, you will need appropriate licensing for the client connections; however, for remote administration purposes, Windows Server 2003 does allow up to two remote connections from members of the Administrators group.

Distributed File System

Distributed File System provides a way for you to seamlessly and logically manage network shares. Instead of users having to know the physical location of shared network folders (by server name), they can simply connect to a DFS root. DFS roots act as logical distribution points for network shares. What this means is that users can simply navigate to a DFS root and view what appears to be a list of shared folders attached to that root. When they click on a folder, they see its contents. However, what users may not realize is that the contents of the share may be on another server. What this means is that DFS provides a layer of transparency for network resource access. Many refer to this concept as *storage virtualization*. With DFS, users never really have to know where data physically is. Instead, they just have to remember to start at the root.

By logically manipulating the location of network shares, you could move data between servers on the network without impacting users. As far as they are concerned, the data would still be at the DFS root. To do this, all you would have to do is copy the data to another location and then update the DFS pointer reference to the shared object to reflect the new location.

In addition to providing transparent storage access, you can also configure shares managed by DFS as replication partners. This allows you to provide a level of fault tolerance for shared network data and also provide a means to load balance data access (automatically done by DFS). The replication of this data is managed by the File Replication Service (FRS), which is the same service that manages SYSVOL replication of Active Directory group policy objects.

When you first set up DFS, you have to configure a starting point for the DFS tree. This is known as the DFS root, as was previously mentioned. There are two types of available DFS roots.

- *Standalone*—The DFS namespace configuration and architecture is stored locally on the root server. The access path (UNC path) to the root starts with the name of the server. With standalone roots, only one root can exist for each configured DFS namespace, meaning that the root is not fault tolerant and thus represents a single point of failure for data access.

- *Domain*—The DFS namespace is stored in the Active Directory. With domain DFS, you can have multiple fault-tolerant roots, and clients can access the DFS root by the domain name. With AD integration, clients are automatically directed to a root in their local Active Directory site, which is advantageous for large networks where the DFS infrastructure spans several sites.

One other significant DFS term to be aware of is a *DFS link*. Roots are the starting point for DFS. When you add links, you define network share names and locations for network data. When a user accesses the DFS root, the links appear as logical subfolders of the root.

Remote Installation Services

RIS provides a means for on-demand installations of Windows operating systems. Among the supported operating system installations are Windows 2000 Professional, Windows XP Professional, and Windows Server 2003. With RIS, a client can perform a network boot, connect to a RIS server, and install Windows. For clients that do not support a network boot, you can create a RIS boot floppy to provide them with network connectivity to connect to the RIS server and download an operating system installation.

RIS has yet to fully gain ground on other third-party operating system imaging applications, such as Symantec Ghost, mainly because RIS does not offer compression. With Ghost, you can deploy an operating system image to network clients via a multicast session in under five minutes. Using RIS, the same process would take 30 minutes to an hour. However, while Ghost images are designed for systems with identical hardware, since RIS is literally a clean installation, the system hardware on each RIS client does not have to be similar in order for the OS installation to be successful.

As an operating system technology, RIS does have several requirements.

- It needs Active Directory, DNS, and DHCP.
- Servers running the RIS service must be authorized.
- An installer must have the right to "create computer accounts."

Like DHCP servers, RIS servers must be authorized by an Enterprise Administrator in order to start responding to clients. RIS does not have its own administrative console, so to authorize a RIS server, you can open the DHCP MMC snap-in and select the option to Manage Authorized Servers. From there, you can authorize the RIS server for use.

A new feature with Windows Server 2003 that has all but eliminated many of the Windows 2000 RIS troubleshooting scenarios is the Remote Installation Services Setup Wizard, which can be accessed by clicking Start > Administrative Tools > Remote Installation Services Setup. This wizard walks you through the entire RIS deployment process, including authorizing the RIS server, so that the server should be ready to go at the time it is deployed. If you need to make further modifications to a RIS server after the initial setup, you can do so by opening Active Directory Users and Computers. From this tool, you need to locate a RIS server's computer object and view its properties. The RIS settings can be configured under the Remote Install tab, as shown in Figure 11-2.

One of the most common mistakes with RIS servers is that they refuse to respond to clients because their "Respond to clients" checkbox is not enabled. With this box cleared, you have effectively shut off the RIS server. While the Remote Install tab contains the RIS

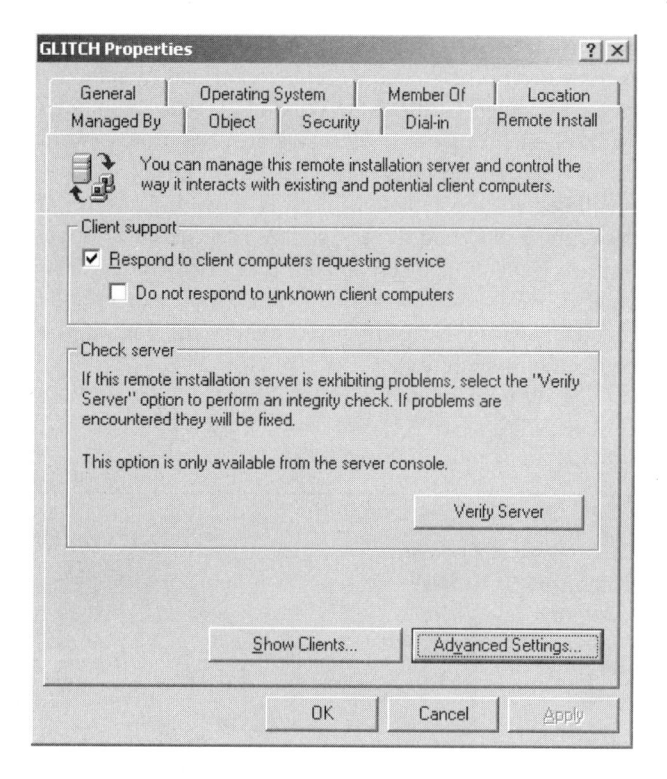

Figure 11-2. RIS server properties

"on-off switch," most of the configuration settings are found by clicking the Advanced Settings button. When you access the advanced settings, you can configure

- The RIS client computer-naming strategy
- The client account location in the Active Directory
- Client images

Now that you have the RIS basics down, we'll get to the details of overcoming RIS problems later. Next, we'll take a look at what is becoming a dying service: Client and Gateway Services for NetWare (CSNW/GSNW).

Client and Gateway Services for NetWare

CSNW and GSNW allow Windows systems to use the IPX/SPX (NWLink) protocol to communicate with NetWare servers. CSNW allows a Microsoft system to log on to a NetWare server, while GSNW allows a Microsoft server to act as a gateway to a NetWare server. Organizations use GSNW so that they do not have to install CSNW or NetWare client software on every one of their Windows clients. Instead, Windows clients can connect to a Windows server using TCP/IP. If the Windows server is running GSNW, Windows clients will see shares that actually reside on a NetWare server as appearing to be on the Windows server. Microsoft has long envisioned GSNW as a way to ease in the migration to what will become a complete Microsoft network. However, there are still many organizations running NetWare servers, so these services are not going anywhere for a while. This service is mentioned here in the event that Windows 2000 Servers are still on your network. GSNW support was dropped in Windows Server 2003, so if you haven't fully migrated away from NetWare, now might be the time (if you are looking for complete Windows interoperability).

The concept of GSNW is shown in Figure 11-3.

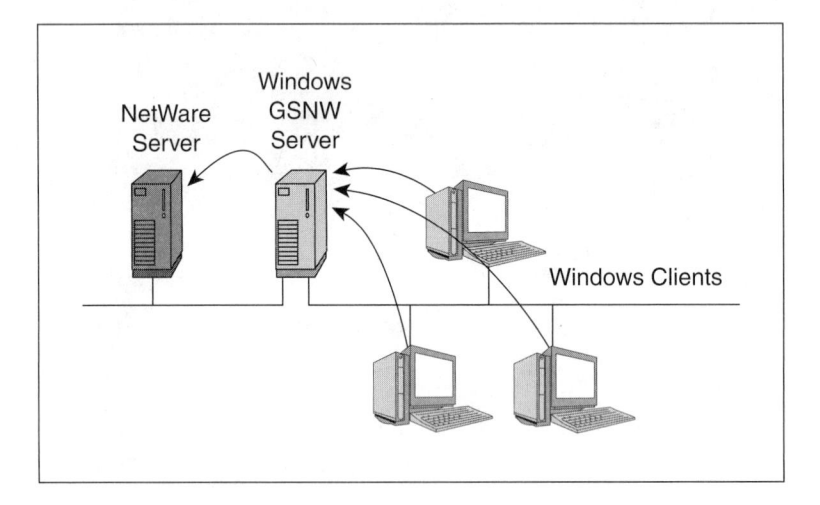

Figure 11-3. Using GSNW to provide NetWare file access

For GSNW to be used properly, several configuration requirements must be satisfied.

- A user group named NTGateway must exist in the NetWare environment and have appropriate permissions to access data on the target server.
- A NetWare user account (to be used by Windows GSNW) must belong to the NTGateway group.
- A Windows GSNW server to a NetWare server is a one-to-one relationship (you cannot have one GSNW server map to two NetWare servers).

Shortly, we'll look at specifically how to fix problems relating to GSNW. Next, we'll examine the tools used to troubleshoot these services.

Network Service Troubleshooting Tools

Now that you have the basics down, let's examine the tools of the trade. This section looks at the most common tools for locating problems with faulty network services and applications. As you will see, there are several GUI and command line tools that greatly simplify troubleshooting the services covered in this chapter.

DFS MMC

The DFS MMC snap-in is the most common DFS troubleshooting and management tool. When you open the snap-in, you can quickly examine the DFS hierarchy and make modifications if necessary. To access the DFS MMC, just click Start > Administrative Tools > Distributed File System. This tool is shown in Figure 11-4.

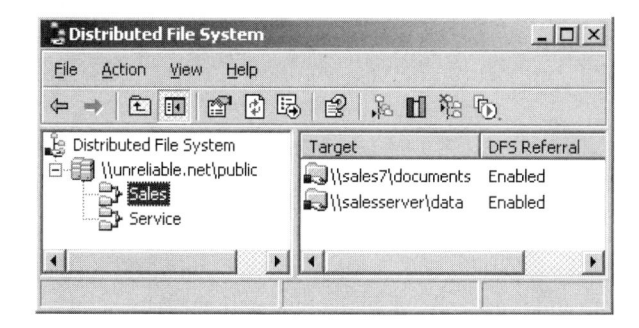

Figure 11-4. DFS MMC snap-in

With this tool, you can quickly check the status of your DFS roots and DFS links. If the root and link hosts are online, they are shown accompanied by a green check mark. For offline resources, you will see a red X. To check the status of a particular root or link, just right-click the object and select Check Status. This feature allows you to easily document the state of your DFS topology.

dfsutil (ST)

The DFS utility (`dfsutil`) is instrumental in both troubleshooting and repairing Distributed File System problems. With `dfsutil`, you can make DFS configuration changes in order to resolve user, server, or replication problems, and also clean up orphaned DFS metadata in the Active Directory. The general syntax for this utility is:

```
dfsutil [parameters]
```

This tool is very complex and provides a multitude of available switches. So as not to be too overwhelming, we'll look individually at each available command switch that is helpful for troubleshooting purposes, and then will look at some common uses for this command when you are troubleshooting and repairing DFS problems. Other versions of this command that strictly aid in DFS administration are not covered in this section.

General dfsutil Switches

There are several switches that can be used in conjunction with the other options that follow this section. The generic switches allow you to define the scope of the command, such as by defining target servers, DFS roots, or shares and by specifying verbose command output. The general command switches are described in Table 11-1.

Table 11-1. General dfsutil Switches

Option	Use
`/root:<RootName>`	Specifies the UNC path to the target DFS root on which to perform the command.
`/server:<Server>`	Specifies the target DFS namespace server for the command.
`/share:<Share>`	Specifies the DFS or server message block (SMB) target share for the command.
`/domain:<Domain>`	Specifies the target DFS domain for the command.
`/verbose`	Causes the output to display more detailed information.

The choice of general options that you select is dictated by the type of operations that you are performing on your network's DFS hierarchy. In the remaining sections, you will see examples of how to use the general switches in conjunction with the task-oriented switches in order to define the command's target.

/clean

This command is needed when users report intermittent availability to DFS resources in your DFS hierarchy. Oftentimes the reason that some DFS shares appear unavailable is that DFS is trying to reference a root that is no longer online. This may have been the result of a system failing or becoming decommissioned. When the `dfsutil` command is executed with the `/clean` option, references to nonexistent root references are deleted. The syntax for this command is:

```
dfsutil /clean /server:<Server> /share:<Share> [/verbose]
```

The target server for this command is the server hosting DFS that contains an obsolete root reference record. For the `/share` parameter, you specify the name of the obsolete root reference. For example to remove the \\Sales\public root from the server glitch.aw.com, you would run this command:

```
dfsutil /clean /server:glitch.aw.com /share:\\sales\public
```

/export

The /export command is very useful for securing backups of your DFS namespaces. Having a backup of the namespace configuration allows you to quickly import the configuration to another server in the event that a DFS root host server fails. Since you can run the /export command using a single line of code, this command can be easily scripted to work with your existing backup utility.

The syntax for dfsutil /export is:

```
dfsutil /root:<RootName> /export:<FileName>
```

When you run this command, you need to specify the full UNC path to the root context that you wish to export, along with a filename for the exported data. For example, if you wanted to secure a backup of the \\aw.com\public DFS root and copy the backup to the E:\Backups\awpublicroot.txt file, you would run this command:

```
dfsutil /root:\\aw.com\public /export:E:\Backups\awpublicroot.txt
```

/import

When you export a DFS configuration to a text file, you can in turn import the configuration to another server that you wish to act as a DFS root. On the target server, you need to re-create the root and then use this command to import the previous root configuration. The syntax for this command is:

```
dfsutil /root:<RootName> /import:<FileName> /<verify | set | merge> [/verbose]
```

As with the /export command, when you execute this command, you need to specify a target DFS root for the command as well as the name of the file containing the DFS configuration to import. The other required parameter for this command is either the /verify, /set, or /merge switch. These options are explained in Table 11-2.

Table 11-2. /import Required Parameters

Option	Use
/verify	Outputs changes that may happen during the import. Provides a method to view the changes that are made by the command prior to the changes being implemented with either the /set or /merge option. This option should be run first, to analyze the effect of the import operation prior to permanently making the changes.
/set	Causes the target namespace to be completely overwritten with the namespace configuration of the import file.
/merge	Allows you to import a namespace configuration to complement an existing namespace configuration. With this option, the current target namespace and the namespace defined in the import file are merged, with the import file's configuration settings taking precedence if any conflicting settings exist.

Since importing a root configuration to a new server requires that a root be established on the target server, you can either create a new root with the DFS MMC or use the `dfsutil` command with the `/addftroot` (domain-based DFS) or the `/addstdroot` (standalone DFS) switch to create the root on the target system. Here is an example of using the `/addftroot` and `/import` switches to import a DFS backup file to a new DFS root host server called DFS2.aw.com.

```
C:\>dfsutil /addftroot /server:dfs2.aw.com /share:public

Microsoft(R) Windows(TM) DFS Utility Version 4.0
Copyright (C) Microsoft Corporation 1991-2001. All Rights Reserved.

DfsUtil command completed successfully.

C:\>dfsutil /root:\\aw.com\public /import:D:\Backups\awpublicroot.txt
/set

Microsoft(R) Windows(TM) DFS Utility Version 4.0
Copyright (C) Microsoft Corporation 1991-2001. All Rights Reserved.

Backups of \\AW\public before modifications being written to
AW.public.dfsutil.backup.06.10.2003.11.10.534

Update Statistics: Number of Apis 2
Links: Added 38 Deleted 0 Modified 1
Targets: Added 50 Deleted 0 Modified 0

Done processing this command.

C:\>
```

Prior to importing data to an existing DFS root, `dfsutil` creates a backup of the target root configuration in the directory from where you are running the `dfsutil` command. The backup filename contains the name of the DFS root along with the date and time of the backup, so a sample backup filename is aw.public.dfsutil.backup.06.10.2003.11.10.534. You could use this file with the `/import` switch if you needed to undo the changes made by the previous import operation.

/importroot

The `/importroot` command option is similar to the `/import` option, with the exception that it works with another online DFS root server, as opposed to importing backup data from a text file. This allows you to quickly add fault tolerance to DFS roots across your enterprise, or to move a DFS root configuration to an alternate server in the event that you need to take a DFS server down for maintenance.

The syntax for this command is:

```
dfsutil /root:<TargetRoot> /importroot:<SourceRoot> [/mirror | compare]
```

The command options are described in Table 11-3.

Table 11-3. /importroot Command Options

Option	Use
`/root:<TargetRoot>`	Identifies the target root where data will be imported to.
`/importroot:<SourceRoot>`	Identifies the source root where data will be imported from.
`/mirror`	Creates a backup of the source DFS namespace.
`/compare`	Generates a comparison between the source and target DFS roots.

Suppose that you wanted to import the content from the sales.aw.com root to the aw.com root. To do this, you would run the following command:

```
dfsutil /root:\\aw.com\public /importroot:\\sales.aw.com\public
```

> Unlike with the `/import` switch, no backup is automatically created of the target DFS root prior to an import using the `/importroot` switch. You should use `dfsutil /export` to secure a backup copy of the target DFS root prior to performing an `/importroot` operation.

/pktflush

Suppose that a particular file share was moved to an alternate server and the original source server for the share was taken offline for maintenance. What you may find after that happens is that some clients may not be able to access the new share location and instead receive an error that the resource is unavailable. The problem occurs because clients can cache DFS server referrals similarly to how they cache IP addresses for host names. As with cached IP addresses, DFS referrals are also cached for a given Time to Live (TTL) period, which can be configured at the DFS root level. The default value is 300 seconds (5 minutes). This means that if the clients wait long enough, they will receive the correct referral. However, if you want a particular client to be able to immediately access moved resources (or if the TTL value was changed to a higher value), you need to flush the DFS Partition Knowledge Table (PKT) on a DFS client.

To flush the PKT on a DFS client, you would run this command on the client: `dfsutil /pktflush`. There is no additional syntax for this command.

/purgemupcache

This command's use is similar to that of `/pktflush`, with the exception that it is used to clear a client's multiple UNC provider (MUP) cache. The purpose of this local cache is to maintain information about both DFS shares and other shares, such as SMB shares, on the client system. Like other client caches, this aids in performance when network resources are accessed. If you have clients that had a particular SMB share mapped and then attempted to map a DFS share with the same name, they may not be able to access the DFS share due to the SMB share information still being in their cache. If the client waits a few minutes, the DFS share will become accessible. However, if you are looking to quickly fix the problem, you can do so by running `dfsutil /purgemupcache` on the client system.

/purgewin2kstaticsitetable

This command option is needed to resolve compatibility problems when DFS is running on a mixed mode network, where there are both Windows 2000 and Windows Server 2003 systems hosting domain-based DFS roots. This problem arises when an update is made to a Windows Server 2003 root host. By default, site information is not propagated to the Windows 2000 server due to an issue with the DFS blob, mainly because Windows 2000 site information is static. You can manually update the Windows 2000 DFS root by running `dfsutil /purgewin2kstaticsitetable` on the DFS root that was updated. The complete syntax for this command is:

```
dfsutil /root:<RootName> /purgewin2kstaticsitetable
```

When you run this command, for the `/root` parameter, you specify the UNC path to the updated root. For example, if the aw.com\public root was updated, you would run this command:

```
dfsutil /root:\\aw.com\public /purgewin2kstaticsitetable
```

This would update the Windows 2000 site table to match the Windows Server 2003 site table.

/showwin2kstaticsitetable

If you are unsure if a Windows 2000 DFS root has knowledge of all the sites associated with various DFS objects, you can run this command to display the Windows 2000 Static Site Table contents. If you notice a discrepancy, you can then run `dfsutil` with the `/purgewin2kstaticsitetable` switch to correct the problem. The syntax for this command is:

```
dfsutil /root:<RootName> /showwin2kstaticsitetable
```

As with the previous command, the root name specified must be a complete UNC path to the DFS root in question. When you execute this command, you will see the current DFS target-to-site mappings stored in the Windows 2000 server running DFS.

/spcflush

This command can be run on DFS clients to flush their cached knowledge of trusted domains and domain controllers. This in turn causes the clients to obtain the latest information on the trusted domains and domain controllers within the DFS hierarchy. This may be necessary if a client is having trouble accessing DFS shares. An alternative to running this command is to simply wait for the client's cached contents to expire, or you can simply reboot the client to clear out all cached DFS information.

To use this command to clear a client's software publishing certificate (SPC) cache, you would run `dfsutil /spcflush` on the client system.

/unmapftroot

This command is used to manually remove references to a domain-based DFS root target that no longer exists. This may be necessary if a DFS root server fails or is permanently decommissioned. If the root's metadata references are not removed from the DFS topology, other DFS hosts will continually fail in their attempts to replicate with the now nonexistent root. To eliminate these failures, you can run `dfsutil /unmapftroot`. The full syntax and parameters for this command are:

```
dfsutil /unmapftroot /server:<Server> /share:<Share>
```

The target server for this command is any server hosting the domain-based DFS root that references the nonexistent system. For the `/share` parameter, you specify the name of the DFS share that is replicated to the obsolete system. For example, to remove the \\aw.com\public root from the server bigserver.aw.com, you would run this command:

```
dfsutil /unmapftroot /server:bigserver.aw.com /share:\\aw.com\public
```

/updatewin2kstaticsitetable

This command option is needed to resolve compatibility problems when DFS is running on a mixed mode network, where there are both Windows 2000 and Windows Server 2003 systems hosting domain-based DFS roots. This problem arises when an update is made to a Windows Server 2003 root host. By default, site information is not propagated to the Windows 2000 server due to an issue with the DFS blob, mainly because Windows 2000 site information is static. You can manually update the Windows 2000 DFS root by running `dfsutil /updatewin2kstaticsitetable` on the DFS root that was updated. The alternative to using this command is to use the `/purgewin2kstaticsitetable` switch to cause a complete refresh of the Static Site Table on a Windows 2000 server. The complete syntax for this command is:

```
dfsutil /root:<RootName> /updatewin2kstaticsitetable
```

When you run this command, for the `/root` parameter, you specify the UNC path to the updated root. For example, if the aw.com\public root was updated, you would run `dfsutil /root:\\aw.com\public /updatewin2kstaticsitetable`. This would update the Windows 2000 site table to match the Windows Server 2003 site table.

health_chk (ST)

When you are troubleshooting File Replication Service problems, `health_chk` is likely to become your favorite tool. By executing a single command, you can use this tool to run tests that are normally performed by running each of the following commands:

- `connstat`
- `dcdiag`
- `eventquery.vbs`
- `iologsum`
- `netdiag`
- `ntfrsutil`
- `reg`
- `repadmin`
- `topchk`

Each of these commands is useful for troubleshooting and diagnosing FRS problems. However, it is extremely cumbersome to note the correct syntax and execute each command in order to collect data relating to FRS replication. Instead, when you execute the `health_chk` command, it generates 17 text files containing an abundance of information on potential causes of replication problems. Once you collect these files, it is very likely that one of them will provide the details on the particular error that is leading to a replication failure. The contents of each output file generated by running `health_chk` are described in Table 11-4.

Table 11-4. health_chk Output Files

Filename	Information Collected
Ds_showconn.txt	Provides information on the connection objects of the target system.
Ds_showreps.txt	Provides information on replication partnerships.
Evl_application.txt	Lists application event log content.
Evl_dns.txt	Lists DNS server event log content.
Evl_ds.txt	Lists Directory Service event log content.
Evl_ntfrs.txt	Lists File Replication Service event log content.
Evl_system.txt	Lists system event log content.
Ntfrs_config.txt	Lists all replica sets.
Ntfrs_ds.txt	Displays FRS replication topology from the perspective of the target machine.
Ntfrs_errscan.txt	Lists error messages found in the FRS debug logs.

Table 11-4. health_chk Output Files, continued

Filename	Information Collected
Ntfrs_inlog.txt	Lists inbound Change Orders (COs).
Ntfrs_machine.txt	Lists the available disk space on all hard disks in the target system.
Ntfrs_outlog.txt	Lists outbound COs.
Ntfrs_reg.txt	Lists FRS Registry information (found in HKLM\System\currentcontrolset\services\ntfrs subkey).
Ntfrs_sets.txt	Lists inbound and outbound FRS replication connections, as well as the status of each connection.
Ntfrs_sysvol.txt	Displays all directories and subdirectories in the SYSVOL share.
Ntfrs_version.txt	Provides FRS version information.

Once you collect this information, you can search the pertinent generated logs for errors. To run this command, you would use the following syntax:

```
health_chk <ResultsFolderPath> [RemoteSystem]
```

When you execute this command, you have to provide the path to a folder where the output text files will be stored. You have the option to specify a remote system name or IP address. If the `RemoteSystem` parameter is not used, the `health_chk` command runs on the local machine in which you initiate the command.

Suppose that you wanted to collect diagnostic information on the DFS root server DFSRoot1 and store the diagnostic data in the D:\FRSHealth folder on your local hard disk. The results of running this command follow.

```
C:\>health_chk d:\FRSHealth DFSRoot1
****** Creating output directory: d:\frshealth\dfsroot1
Please WAIT....
Netdiag /debug is running
 NTFRSUTIL checks are running ...
 Dumping FRS inbound and outbound logs ...
 Dumping FRS registry parameters ...
SYSVOL check is running
SMB/DFS check is running
Repadmin /showreps DFSRoot1 is running
Repadmin /showconn DFSRoot1 is running
Dcdiag /v /s:DFSRoot1 is running
 Scanning eventlogs ...
 Scanning FRS debug logs for error/warning info ...
 Done ...
C:\>
```

Since numerous commands must execute and complete, the `health_chk` command takes a few minutes to finish. Once execution completes, you should begin examining the output text files for errors. One method to do this is to open up each text file individually and use the Notepad Find feature to look for words indicating a failure, such as "error" or "fail." Using small versions of these words (i.e., "fail" instead of "failed") will return the most hits. As you find failures in logs, note the log file as well as the date and time that the failure is recorded. This will help to establish a pattern and provide a point of reference to look for similar events in other log files.

ipxroute

The `ipxroute` command is used to display information about routing tables used by the IPX protocol. This command can also be used to modify IPX routing information on a Windows client or server that is connected to an IPX network. The syntax for this command is:

```
ipxroute servers [/type=x]
ipxroute ripout <network>
ipxroute resolve guid <guid> | name <AdapterName>
ipxroute board=<adapter> [def] [gbr] [mbr] [remove=<xxxxxxxx>]
ipxroute config
```

As you can see, there are several variations of this command. Table 11-5 sheds light on each command variation and its associated options.

Table 11-5. ipxroute Command Options

Option	Use
servers [/type=x]	Shows the Service Access Point (SAP) table for the specified server type. If no type is specified, all servers are listed by server name.
ripout <network>	Sends a Routing Information Protocol (RIP) request to the destination network specified to determine if the network is reachable. You must specify the remote network's IPX network segment number by using the <network> parameter.
resolve guid <guid> | name <AdapterName>	Resolves a network adapter's name to its GUID, or vice versa.
board=<adapter>	Specifies the network adapter to query or configure.
def	Used with the `board` option. Causes a packet sent to a MAC address that is not in the source routing table to be sent to the ALL ROUTES broadcast. These packets are sent to the SINGLE ROUTES broadcast by default.
gbr	Used with the `board` option. Causes a packet sent to the broadcast address (FFFFFFFFFFFF) to be sent to the ALL ROUTES broadcast. These packets are sent to the SINGLE ROUTES broadcast by default.
mbr	Used with the `board` option. Causes a packet sent to a multicast address to be sent to the ALL ROUTES broadcast. These packets are sent to the SINGLE ROUTES broadcast by default.
remove=<xxxxxxxxxx>	Removes the specified node address from the source routing table.
config	Displays information about all network bindings that have IPX configured.

For an example of using this command, suppose that a Windows Server 2003 system running Gateway Services for NetWare is having trouble communicating with a NetWare server on an IPX network. To view the Windows server's attached IPX segments, node address, and IPX frame type in use, you would run `ipxroute config`. For more information on IPX troubleshooting, turn to the Troubleshooting NetWare Integration section later in this chapter.

lpq

Running this command allows you to check the status of the print queue on a print server running the line printer daemon (LPD) service, allowing you to determine a possible problem with a print server. The LPD service runs on UNIX print servers. Clients running the line printer remote (LPR) service can print to LPD print servers. Windows clients can run the LPR service. Also, you can configure a Windows server to emulate a UNIX print server by installing Print Services for UNIX on the server.

The syntax for `lpq` is:

```
lpq -s <Server> -p <PrinterName> [-l]
```

The `lpq` command's options are described in Table 11-6.

Table 11-6. lpq Command Options

Option	Use
`-s <Server>`	Required parameter. Specifies the target server that hosts the LPD printer.
`-p <PrinterName>`	Required parameter. Indicates the printer whose print queue you would like the command to display.
`-l`	Displays additional details about the print queue status.

If you wanted to check the status of the print queue on the print server bigbadserver, you would run this command:

```
lpq -s bigbadserver -p "Xerox Laser" -l
```

prndrvr.vbs

The `prndrvr.vbs` tool is a very powerful script that allows you to manage printer drivers on local and remote printers. This may be especially useful if you have a Windows NT 4.0 user that needs to print to a particular printer, but the print server's NT driver is not installed for the printer. With this command, you can remotely add the necessary print driver so that the user can properly print.

There are four ways that you can run this script, depending on the task you need to achieve. The four versions of this command are as follows:

- `prndrvr.vbs -a`—Adds a printer driver to a print server
- `prndrvr.vbs -d`—Removes a printer driver from a print server
- `prndrvr.vbs -l`—Lists printer drivers installed on a print server
- `prndrvr.vbs -x`—Removes all unused printer drivers from a print server

Each of these scripts is detailed in the next four sections.

> When running .vbs scripts, you must run the script from the directory in which the file resides. By default, the `prn...` VB script files are in the %systemroot%system32 folder. So with a default installation, you should ensure that you are at the C:\Windows\System32> prompt before running the command.

prndrvr.vbs -a (Add Driver)

Running this script allows you to install a printer driver on a print server. This is useful if you need to update a driver for a print server or add a driver to a print server to support users connecting to the print server using an OS that the server previously did not have an installed driver for.

The syntax for the `prndrvr.vbs -a` command is:

```
cscript prndrvr.vbs -a [-m <DriverName>] [-v <0|1|2|3>] [-e
<Environment>] [-s <RemoteComputer>] [-h <Path>] [-i <DriverFile>]
[-u <user> -w <password>]
```

The command options are described in Table 11-7.

Table 11-7. prndrvr.vbs -a Command Options

Option	Use
-m <DriverName>	Specifies the name of the driver you are installing. The driver is normally named after the printer that it supports.
-v <0 | 1 | 2 | 3>	Specifies the version of the driver to install: • 0 = Windows 95/98/ME • 1 = Windows NT 3.51 • 2 = Windows NT 4.0 • 3 = Windows Server 2003/XP/2000 If a version is not specified, the driver version that matches the OS of the print server is installed.

Table 11-7. prndrvr.vbs –a Command Options, continued

Option	Use
`-e <Environment>`	Specifies the environment for the installed driver. Valid environment options are shown in Table 11-8. When no environment is specified, the environment of the print server on which the driver is installed is assumed.
`-s <RemoteComputer>`	When the command is run remotely, this option specifies the name or IP address of the remote print server.
`-h <path>`	Specifies the path to the driver's information (.inf) file.
`-i <DriverFile>`	Specifies the name of the driver's information (.inf) file.
`-u <user>`	If your currently logged-on account does not have Manage Printers permission (Administrators and Power Users by default), you can use this parameter to run the command under the context of a different user.
`-w <password>`	When the –u parameter is included in the command, the –w parameter specifies the user's password.

Table 11-8 lists the valid environment settings. When you use the –e parameter, your input must match the quoted text in the table.

Table 11-8. Valid Environment Settings

Environment Setting	Compatible Version Setting(s)
"Windows NT 4.0"	0
"Windows NT PowerPC"	1
"Windows NT R4000"	1
"Windows IA64"	3
"Windows NT Alpha_AXP"	1, 2
"Windows NT x86"	1, 2, 3

Suppose that you wanted to remotely install an NT 4.0 printer driver for a print server (PS1) with an HP LaserJet 5 printer attached that currently supports Windows 2000 and XP clients. To achieve this, you would run this command:

```
cscript prndrvr.vbs -a -m "HP LaserJet 5" -v 2 -e "Windows NT x86"
```

prndrvr.vbs –d (Delete Driver)

If a driver is no longer needed on a particular print server, this command can be used to uninstall the driver.

The syntax for the `prndrvr.vbs -d` command is:

```
cscript prndrvr.vbs -d [-m <DriverName>] [-v <0|1|2|3>] [-e
<Environment>] [-s <RemoteComputer>] [-u <user> -w <password>]
```

The command options are described in Table 11-9.

Table 11-9. prndrvr.vbs –d Command Options

Option	Use
`-m <DriverName>`	Specifies the name of the driver you are removing.
`-v <0 | 1 | 2 | 3>`	Specifies the version of the driver to remove: • 0 = Windows 95/98/ME • 1 = Windows NT 3.51 • 2 = Windows NT 4.0 • 3 = Windows Server 2003/XP/2000 If a version is not specified, the driver version that matches the OS of the print server is installed.
`-e <Environment>`	Specifies the environment for the removed driver. Valid environment options are shown in Table 11-8. When no environment is specified, the environment of the print server on which the driver is installed is assumed.
`-s <RemoteComputer>`	When the command is run remotely, this option specifies the name or IP address of the remote print server.
`-u <user>`	If your currently logged-on account does not have Manage Printers permission (Administrators and Power Users by default), you can use this parameter to run the command under the context of a different user.
`-w <password>`	When the `-u` parameter is included in the command, the `-w` parameter specifies the user's password.

For an example of using this command, assume that you need to remove an old NT 3.51 driver from the print server PrintMaster2. To do this, run the following command:

```
cscript prndrvr.vbs -d -m "HP LaserJet 5" -v 1 -s printmaster2
```

prndrvr.vbs –l (List Drivers)

If you are unsure if a driver needs to be installed on a print server, or if you are looking for a list of installed drivers in order to uninstall unneeded drivers, you can run this command to display a list of installed printer drivers on a system. When run, this command displays the following driver information:

Network Service Troubleshooting Tools

- The driver name
- The driver version (0, 1, 2, or 3)
- The driver path
- Dependent files

The syntax for the `prndrvr.vbs -l` command is:

```
cscript prndrvr.vbs -l [-s <RemoteComputer>] [-u <user> -w <password>]
```

The command options are described in Table 11-10.

Table 11-10. prndrvr.vbs –l Command Options

Option	Use
`-s <RemoteComputer>`	When the command is run remotely, this option specifies the name or IP address of the remote print server.
`-u <user>`	If your currently logged-on account does not have Manage Printers permission (Administrators and Power Users by default), you can use this parameter to run the command under the context of a different user.
`-w <password>`	When the -u parameter is included in the command, the -w parameter specifies the user's password.

Suppose that you wanted to see a list of installed drivers on the server PS1. To query a list of installed drivers, you would run this command:

```
cscript prndrvr.vbs -l -s ps1
```

prndrvr.vbs –x (Remove All Unused Drivers)

The syntax for the `prndrvr.vbs -x` command is:

```
cscript prndrvr.vbs -x [-s <RemoteComputer>] [-u <user> -w <password>]
```

The options for this command are identical to those listed in Table 11-10. If you would like to clean up all unused drivers on the print server Cosmo, you would run this command:

```
cscript prndrvr.vbs -x -s cosmo
```

prnmngr.vbs

For troubleshooting purposes, the most useful part of this script is to obtain a list of printers on a server. Once you know the names of the printers on a server, you can use those names in other print management commands, such as `prnqctl.vbs`. The syntax for using this command to list printers and their configuration information on a server is:

```
cscript prnmngr.vbs -l [-s <RemoteComputer>] [-u <user> -w <password>]
```

The command options are described in Table 11-11.

Table 11-11. prnmngr.vbs Command Options

Option	Use
`-s <RemoteComputer>`	When you are not at the system that hosts the target printer, this option specifies the name or IP address of the remote print server.
`-u <user>`	If your currently logged-on account does not have Manage Printers permission (Administrators and Power Users by default), you can use this parameter to run the command under the context of a different user.
`-w <password>`	When the `-u` parameter is included in the command, the `-w` parameter specifies the user's password.

Suppose that you wanted to pause a printer on the print server PS1 but did not know the names of its printers. To obtain information on the printers on this server, you would run this command:

```
cscript prnmngr.vbs -l -s PS1
```

For other versions of this command, see Windows online Help.

prnqctl.vbs

When you are troubleshooting printer problems, this command can be used to print a test page, to pause or resume a printer, and to clear all documents in the printer queue. The syntax for `prnqctl.vbs` is:

```
cscript prnqctl.vbs <-z | -m | -e | -x> [-s <RemoteComputer>] -p <PrinterName> [-u <user> -w <password>]
```

When you run the command, you must specify one of the first listed options (z, m, e, or x) to indicate the type of action that the command is to perform. The other required parameter for this command is `-p`, which indicates the target printer for the command. The command options are described in Table 11-12.

Suppose that a user is complaining about a particular printer. To use this command to print a test page on the printer HpLaserJet located on the server PrntSvr1, you would run this command:

```
cscript prnqctl.vbs -e -s prntsvr1 -p hplaserjet
```

Table 11-12. prnqctl.vbs Command Options

Option	Use
`-z`	Pauses a printer.
`-m`	Resumes a paused printer.
`-e`	Prints a test page.
`-x`	Cancels all jobs spooled to the printer.
`-s <RemoteComputer>`	When you are not at the system that hosts the target printer, this option specifies the name or IP address of the remote print server.
`-p <PrinterName>`	Required parameter. Specifies the name of the target printer for the command.
`-u <user>`	If your currently logged-on account does not have Manage Printers permission (Administrators and Power Users by default), you can use this parameter to run the command under the context of a different user.
`-w <password>`	When the `-u` parameter is included in the command, the `-w` parameter specifies the user's password.

query

The `query` command is used to collect information about terminal server sessions. This command has these four versions:

- `query process`
- `query session`
- `query termserver`
- `query user`

Each of these commands is valuable when you are troubleshooting terminal server connection problems, and they are explained in the next four sections.

query process

This command displays all user processes running on the terminal server, as well as the user that is running each process. If a user is experiencing difficulties with a terminal session and you need to determine the programs that the user is actually executing, you can use this command to do so.

The syntax for `query process` is:

```
query process [* | <ProcessID> | <UserName> | <SessionName> |
/id:<SessionID> | <ProgramName>] [/server:<servername>]
```

Notice that you can perform only one type of process query. In other words, you cannot query by both user name and process ID in the same command. To do this, you would need to run the command twice. The command options are described in Table 11-13.

Table 11-13. query process Command Options

Option	Use
`*`	Lists the processes for all sessions (the default).
`ProcessID`	Specifies the PID of a process you wish to query. Command output displays users running the process with the PID specified.
`UserName`	Causes the command to output running processes for the user specified.
`SessionName`	Causes the command to output running processes for the session specified.
`/id:<SessionID>`	Causes the command to output running processes for the session ID specified.
`ProgramName`	Specifies the name of an executable to query. Only files with .exe extensions can be queried.
`/server:<servername>`	Specifies a remote terminal server to query. When the command is run without this parameter, the local terminal server is queried.

This command makes it easy to record all running processes on a terminal server. For example, to have the command return a list of all running user processes on the server TS1.aw.com, you would run this command:

```
query process * /server:TS1.aw.com.
```

query session

Running this command allows you to obtain a list of all sessions (active or inactive) that are running on a terminal server. The syntax for `query session` is:

```
query session [<SessionName> | <UserName> | <SessionID>]
[/server:<servername>] [/mode] [/flow] [/connect] [/counter]
```

The `query session` command options are described in Table 11-14.

This command is very useful for displaying all current terminal server sessions. For example, to retrieve a list of all terminal sessions on the server TS2.aw.com, you would run this command:

```
query session /server:ts2.aw.com
```

Network Service Troubleshooting Tools

Table 11-14. query session Command Options

Option	Use
SessionName	Specifies the name of the session to query. The command returns information on the state of the provided session.
UserName	Specifies the name of a user to query. The command returns information on the state of the user's session.
SessionID	Specifies the name of the session ID to query. The command returns information on the state of the provided session ID.
/server:<servername>	Specifies a remote terminal server to query. When the command is run without this parameter, the local terminal server is queried.
/mode	Displays terminal server line settings.
/flow	Displays terminal server flow-control settings.
/connect	Displays current terminal server connection settings.
/counter	Displays current terminal server counter information (sessions created, disconnected, reconnected).

query termserver

When you wish to acquire a list of all terminal servers running on a network or all terminal servers in a particular domain, this command is valuable. For example, you may have users complaining that they cannot access a particular terminal server. If other terminal servers in the domain host similar applications, you could query a list of available servers and give the user an alternate server to try. The syntax for this command is:

```
query termserver [ServerName] [/domain:<domain>] [/address]
[/continue]
```

The options for this command are explained in Table 11-15.

Table 11-15. query termserver Command Options

Option	Use
ServerName	Displays a particular terminal server's list of known terminal servers on the network.
/domain:<domain>	Allows you to retrieve a list of all terminal servers in a particular domain.
/address	Specifies the network and node addresses for each terminal server found in the command output.
/continue	Prevents the command from pausing after each screen of output data is displayed.

374 Chapter 11 Network and Application Services

As mentioned earlier, using this command is an excellent method of obtaining a list of terminal servers in a domain. For example, to query for a list of terminal servers in the aw.com domain, you would run `query termserver /domain:aw.com`.

query user

The `query user` command allows you to see information about a user's session on a terminal server. The command output displays the following session information:

- User name
- Session name
- Session ID
- Session state (Active, Disconnected)
- Idle time
- Logon time

To run this command to retrieve this information, you would use the following syntax:

```
query user [UserName] [SessionName] [SessionID] [/server:<servername>]
```

The options for this command are explained in Table 11-16.

Table 11-16. query user Command Options

Option	Use
`UserName`	Specifies the name of a user to query.
`SessionName`	Specifies the name of the session to query.
`SessionID`	Specifies the name of the session ID to query.
`/server:<servername>`	Specifies a remote terminal server to query. When the command is run without this parameter, the local terminal server is queried.

An example of using this command would be to query the terminal server for information on the status of the session for the user "dwells" on the server Brooklyn.aw.com. To retrieve this information, you would run this command:

```
query user dwells /server:Brooklyn.aw.com
```

reset session

Suppose that users are being denied access to a terminal server because the server is running at its maximum allowable number of connected sessions. Having too many concurrent sessions could be a result of users closing their session but not logging off. The result of this action would be that their session would remain open. In the Troubleshooting Terminal Services section later in this chapter, you will learn more about how to automatically end users' sessions. Before you run this command, it is best to run the `query session` command to obtain a list of all sessions on a terminal server. You can then use the session information in the `reset session` command. The syntax for `reset session` is:

```
reset session [<SessionName> | <SessionID>] [/server:<servername>] [/v]
```

The options for this command are explained in Table 11-17.

Table 11-17. reset session Command Options

Option	Use
SessionName	Specifies the name of the session to reset.
SessionID	Specifies the name of the session ID to reset.
/server:<servername>	Specifies a remote terminal server containing the session you wish to reset. When the command is run without this parameter, the command connects to the local system.
/v	Verbose output—the command displays information about the actions it is performing.

Suppose you wanted to use this command to reset the session of the user klow on the server hackme.unreliable.net. Here is the complete command syntax that you would use to achieve this (note that the `query session` command is also used).

```
C:\>query session /server:hackme.unreliable.net
 SESSIONNAME       USERNAME          ID    STATE        TYPE
>console           Administrator     0     Active       wdcon
 rdp-tcp           klow              1     Disc         rdpwd
 rdp-tcp           mdahlmeier        2     Active       rdpwd

C:\>   reset session 1 /server:hackme.unreliable.net /v
Resetting session ID 1
Session ID 1 has been reset

C:\>
```

Terminal Services Manager MMC

If you prefer GUI tools over command line tools, then you will probably prefer to use the Terminal Services Manager MMC snap-in, which is shown in Figure 11-5. To access this tool, click Start >Administrative Tools > Terminal Services Manager.

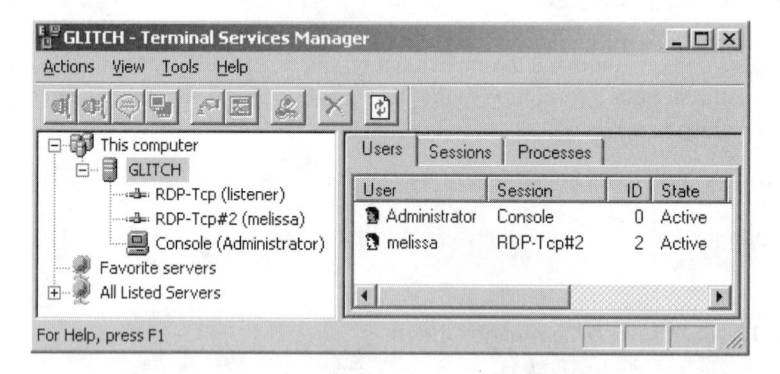

Figure 11-5. Terminal Services Manager MMC

This tool allows you to quickly check the status of Terminal Services sessions as well as take control of sessions and terminate sessions. If you log on to a terminal server using the Remote Desktop client, you can open the Terminal Services Manager MMC and remotely control another user's session. This feature is particularly valuable for allowing a user to watch you troubleshoot and resolve problems or for demonstrating a process to a particular user. The only caveat to remote control with Terminal Services is that it can only be done through a Terminal Services client session. In other words, you cannot directly log on locally to a terminal server and take over a user session. To remotely control a user session, all that you need to do is right-click the user connection and select Remote Control. It is very easy to identify user sessions in the Terminal Services Manager since they are listed by logon name.

Other tasks that can be performed with this tool include sending messages to remote client users as well as disconnecting their sessions and logging them off. When you disconnect a session, the user's applications remain open, so the next time she connects, her open programs will be running at the exact same point as when she was disconnected. When you log off a user, all running programs are closed. This is the same as if a user logged off of a system. Consider disconnecting to be equivalent to locking a local system.

Now that the tools of this trade are covered, let's put them to work!

Troubleshooting Printers

There are many components involved in the print process, which can often make print troubleshooting trickier than troubleshooting other applications or services. For example, when clients are printing to a print device attached to a print server, the following components are possible causes of a print failure:

- Print device (hardware failure)
- Printer driver
- Client application
- Client OS
- Network between client and server
- Printer permissions
- Print queue

With so many possible failures, it is best to try to eliminate as many of the possibilities as you can at once. For example, when a single client is experiencing trouble printing, you can try to print a document from another client on the same network. If the operation succeeds, then you have eliminated the network, print server, and print device as possible problems and can then concentrate your efforts on the problematic client. In this section, we will first look at general troubleshooting considerations that apply to both local and network print devices, and then will look at diagnosing problems when clients cannot print to a particular print server.

General Printing Concerns

General printing problems can result in failures of both local and network print devices. Some of the most common problems resulting in a failure to print are that the incorrect driver is installed, a user does not have Print permissions (or is a member of a group with Deny Print permission), or a connection problem with the printer has put it in an offline state.

Whenever you suspect a problem with a printer, your first course of action should be to print a test page on the printer's host system. To print a test page, follow these steps.

1. Click Start > Printers and Faxes.
2. Right-click the printer that you believe has a problem and select Properties.
3. Under the General tab of the Printer Properties dialog box, click the Print Test Page button.

If the page prints correctly, you have verified that the print server, logical printer, and print device are operating properly. If the page does not print correctly, then you should check the printer driver, print device, and cable connection to the print device.

Table 11-18 lists other possible printer problems that you may encounter.

Chapter 11   Network and Application Services

Table 11-18. Common Printer Problems

Symptom	Probable Faults
The local printer does not print.	• An incorrect printer driver is installed. • The print device is not physically connected to the computer or powered on. • The print device is not in a ready state. • Not enough free disk space exists to spool the print job.
Users of other operating systems cannot print.	Additional printer drivers needed to support down-level operating systems have not been installed.
Users receive the message "Access Denied" when attempting to print.	• The user is not a member of a group that has Print permissions on the printer. • The user is member of a group that has Deny Print permissions.
Printed documents are illegible.	An incorrect printer driver is installed. Download and reinstall the proper printer driver.

Table 11-18 listed numerous possible causes for print problems but stopped short of offering complete solutions. These solutions are described next, as we examine the complete network printing process.

Network Printers

When a document is sent to a network printer, the following processes always occur.

1. The logical printer is shared by an administrator so that it can be accessed over the network.
2. A client connects to the printer over the network.
3. An application on the client system generates a print job.
4. The client system sends the print job to the print server.
5. The print server receives and spools the print job and then places the job in its print queue.
6. The print server sends the job to the print device to be printed.
7. The print device generates the hard-copy output.

With seven different processes involved in the network print process, there are several possible problems that can cause the network print job to fail. To cover all possible failures, let's examine each part of the print process piece by piece.

Administrator Configures the Share

When the administrator first configures the shared printer, the appropriate print drivers are installed, the printer may be given a priority and hours of operation, and permissions are set. The default permissions grant the Everyone group Print permissions, so network printers can generally work with limited configuration.

Based on the initial configuration, you can anticipate the types of problems that you may encounter. If a user cannot print, is he in a group that is on the printer's DACL? Is the user in a group with Deny Print permissions? If permissions allow the user to print, then you could also check to see if time restrictions are preventing a user's job from printing. Since time restrictions still allow a printer to spool jobs and place them in its queue, the user will not receive any errors but will not see his document printed until the printer reaches its operating window.

Aside from permissions and time restrictions, you may find that users attempting to add the printer are being prompted to install the correct driver. If this happens, you should install additional drivers on the printer so that they can be automatically downloaded when users add the printer. Oftentimes, the only driver that is installed with a printer is the driver that is needed for its host operating system. So if you have a printer on a Windows Server 2003 system, you may find that Windows 98 clients cannot print. You can correct this problem by installing additional drivers for clients. To install additional print drivers, follow these steps.

1. Click Start > Printers and Faxes.
2. Now right-click the printer to add drivers to and select Properties.
3. In the Properties dialog box, click the Sharing tab.
4. Under the Sharing tab, click the Additional Drivers button.
5. You should now see a list of other drivers that can be installed for the printer and saved on the server (see Figure 11-6). You have choices for earlier OSes such as Windows NT 4.0 and Windows 95. By checking the appropriate boxes, you can install the additional drivers needed to support other operating systems.
6. Once you select the needed drivers, click OK.
7. When prompted, browse to the folder where the driver file is located and click OK.
8. Close the Printer Properties dialog box.

Client Connects to Network Printer

Now that we have covered the possible problems that can occur when the printer is initially configured, let's look at the problems that are possible when the client tries to connect to the shared printer. For the client to connect to the print server successfully, a valid

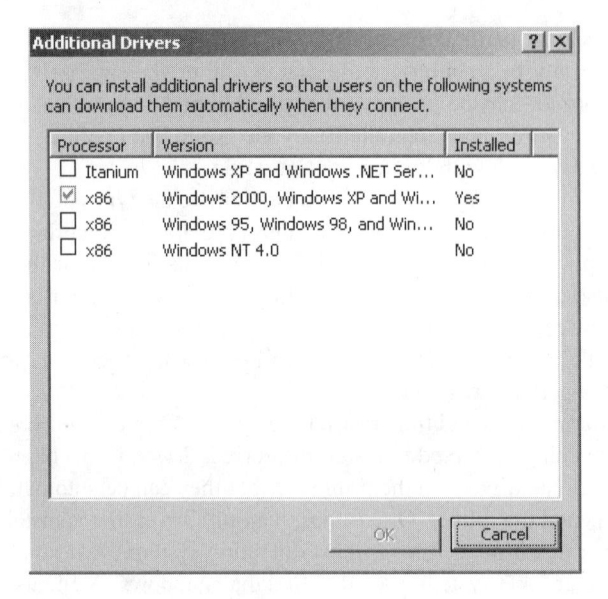

Figure 11-6. Installing additional printer drivers

network connection must exist between the two systems. If the client cannot connect to the print server, you can begin the troubleshooting process by attempting to first ping the print server by FQDN and if that fails, then ping the server by its IP address. If the IP address ping passed, then the fact that pinging by name failed indicates that there is a name resolution problem on the network. This could indicate a problem with the DNS or WINS server, or even a problem in the client's local Hosts file. If the ping even failed by IP address, then you need to verify the physical network components between the two systems and the TCP/IP settings of both systems.

Aside from network issues preventing the connection, you should again verify that the user attempting to make the connection has print permissions on the printer.

Client Application Generates Job

Most applications have little trouble reliably sending documents to printers. However, you cannot simply overlook an application as being the source of a printing problem. To determine if the application is the problem, try printing a document from another application. If the document can print from another application, then you have isolated the source of the printing problem.

For Microsoft Office applications, you can find information on how to repair each application in Chapter 6. For applications provided by other vendors, you should verify with the vendor that the application is compatible with the operating system. One other test to perform, if possible, is to try to print from the same application on another computer. If the application can print successfully on a different system, then that indicates that the application is corrupted on the system you are troubleshooting. The easiest way to resolve this type of problem is to uninstall and then reinstall the application.

Client Sends Job to Print Server

Once the application generates the print job, it is passed to the system on which the application is running. At this point the local system sends the print job either to a locally attached print device or to a network printer. From here, the client needs to get the data to the print server. For networking problems, take these actions.

- Verify the correct IP address, subnet mask, and default gateway on the client and the print server.
- Ping by FQDN to verify name resolution and connectivity.
- If the FQDN ping fails, ping by IP address. If that ping fails, then check the network connectivity components between the two systems (for a routed network, use `pathping` to locate the source of the failure).
- Check permissions. Verify that the client is joined to the domain and that the domain user printing the job has Print permissions.

If the client can get the data to the print server, the document has neared the end of its journey.

Server Spools and Queues Job

When the print server receives the document, it then spools the document (saves it to its hard disk) and sends it to the print queue. A common problem with printers that have too many documents in the queue is that they run out of hard disk space to spool print documents. Also, by default, documents are spooled to the boot partition. If this partition runs out of space, the print server cannot spool documents and thus clients cannot print to the print server. The spool folder is configured at the print server level, so all logical printers share the same spool folder. To check or modify the location of the spool folder, follow these steps.

1. On the print server, click Start > Printers and Faxes.
2. In the Printers and Faxes window, click the File menu and select Server Properties.
3. In the Print Server Properties dialog box, click the Advanced tab.
4. Now you will see the location of the spool folder. It is recommended that the spool folder be placed on another drive or partition (see Figure 11-7).
5. When you have changed the spool folder path, click OK.

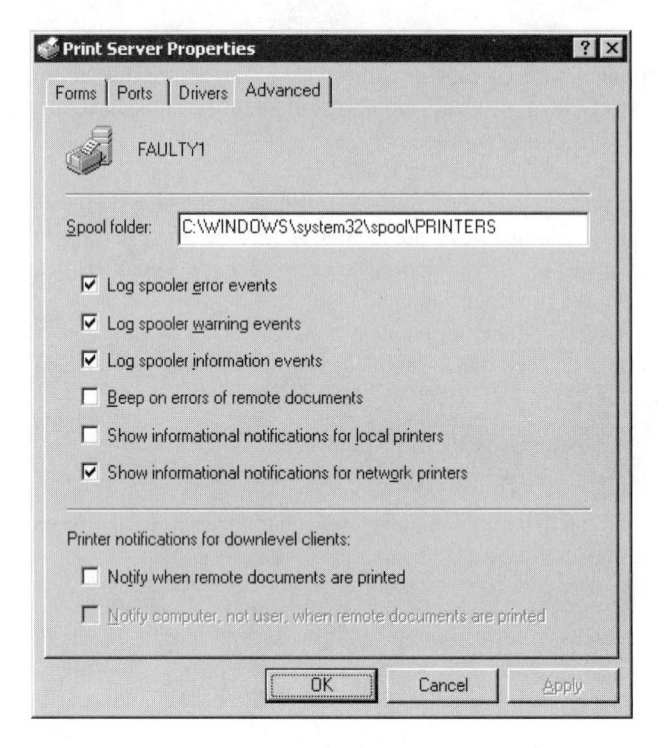

Figure 11-7. Print server properties

> Note that when you set print server properties, you can also enable logging of spooler events. When logging is enabled, spooler events are written to the print server's system log.

Server Sends Job to Print Device

After the job is spooled and queued, it is sent to the print device by the print server. From this stage, problems with the communication path to the printer are likely the cause of a failure. For locally attached printers, verify that they are detected by the system and that they are shown in a ready state. If the destination print device is a network printer (logically attached to the print server), then you need to verify the network connectivity between the two devices. A good test to run if you are unsure whether a problem exists with the print server or with the clients is to print a test page from the print server. If the test page prints from the server, then you have isolated the problem as being between the client and the server connection, and have ruled out the printer itself as a possible problem.

Print Device Prints Job

Once the job reaches the print device, there is little that can go wrong as far as the OS configuration is concerned. When a print device is not printing correctly, it could indicate that the printer is not online, you are using the wrong print driver (garbled characters are printed), or the print device is experiencing a hardware failure. Many print devices have their own internal diagnostics that you can run to test the printer hardware. For more information on how to perform these diagnostic tests, consult the print device manufacturer's Web site or the documentation that was provided when the print device was purchased.

Another popular network service that can cause troubleshooting headaches is Terminal Services, which we look at next.

Troubleshooting Terminal Services

Terminal Services has steadily improved with each Windows operating system release, making it a very reliable service at this stage of the Windows evolution. However, you will still run into some problems with this useful service. Terminal server problems can basically be divided into two categories:

- Server connection problems
- Session problems

In this section, we'll look at how to overcome problems that may occur in each of these two categories.

Remember that you can quickly collect information on terminal server availability, connections, and sessions using the `query` command.

Troubleshooting Server Connection Problems

When clients connect to a terminal server, you must ensure that TCP port 3389 is available. For terminal servers that reside behind a firewall, this port may not be accessible and thus can cause connection problems. If you are running the terminal server Remote Desktop Web Connection software, which allows users to connect to the terminal server with their Web browser, then you need to ensure that both ports 80 (HTTP) and 3389 are open.

Aside from networking issues, if a user cannot connect to a terminal server, you should ensure that the user has the appropriate rights in order to do so. Terminal server connection rights are set by modifying a user's properties in Active Directory Users and Computers. By default, all users are allowed to connect to a terminal server remotely.

However, if a single user is having a problem connecting to the server, you should perform the following steps to verify that the user is allowed to log on to a terminal server.

1. From a domain controller, click Start >Administrative Tools > Active Directory Users and Computers.

2. Locate the user's account object, right-click the object, and select Properties.

3. Now click the Terminal Services Profile tab.

4. Verify that the "Allow logon to terminal server" box is checked (see Figure 11-8) and click OK.

Another source of user connection problems that is also configurable in the user account properties of Active Directory Users and Computers is the user account's environment settings. This configuration is located under the Environment tab, as shown in Figure 11-9.

With user environment settings, you can enable or disable the user of clients to map their drives at logon, connect their printers to the terminal server, or default to print to the

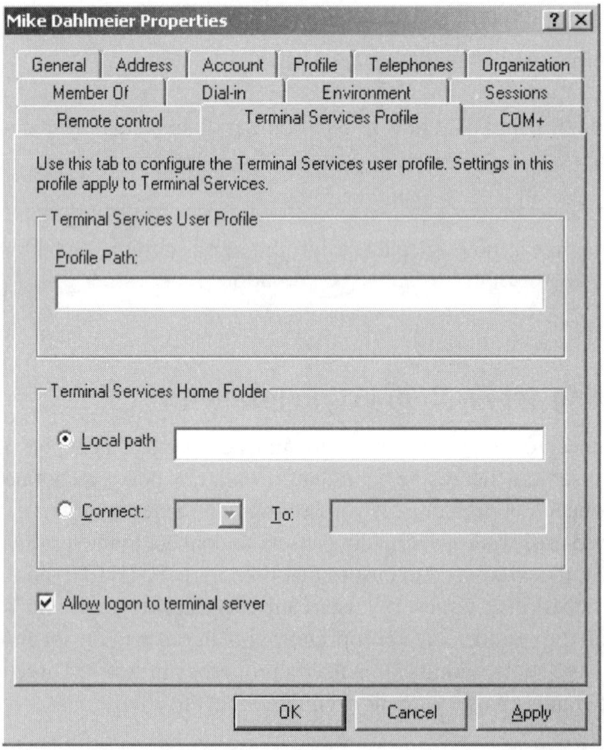

Figure 11-8. Verifying that the terminal server logon is enabled

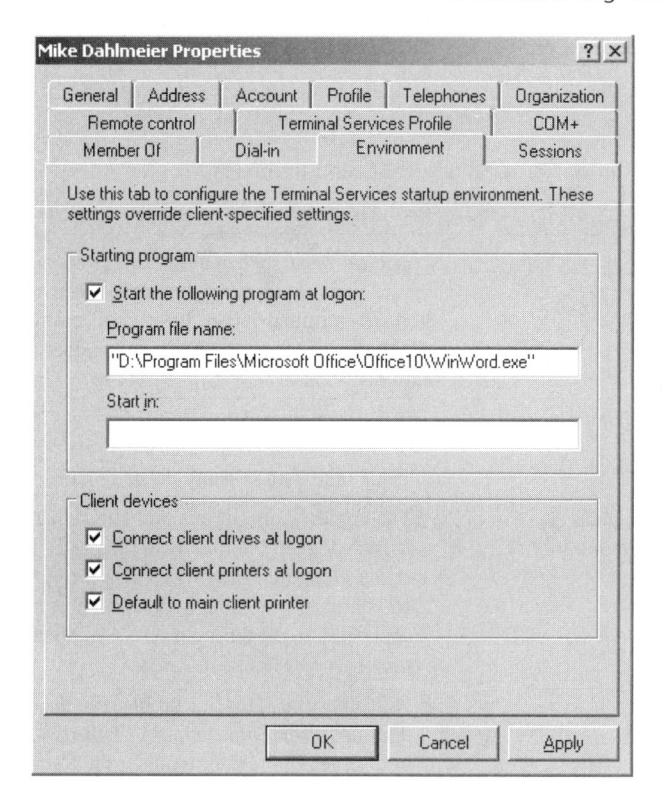

Figure 11-9. Checking user environment settings

terminal server's printer. If clients are experiencing problems with any of these types of connections, you should verify in Active Directory Users and Computers that each is enabled. If user accounts are configured to run a specific application at logon, you need to ensure that the path to the application is correct and that the proper executable to start the application is specified. If these parameters are not correct, the user will receive the error message "This initial program cannot be started" when attempting to connect to the server.

Remember to not overlook the obvious. If no users can connect to a terminal server, verify that its Terminal Services service is running.

Troubleshooting Session Problems

While connecting properly is half the battle, it is also important that a user's experience while she is connected to a terminal server is enjoyable. While users are logged on to a terminal server, other problems can arise when they attempt to install or run a particular application. Common application-related terminal server problems are described in Table 11-19.

Table 11-19. Common Terminal Server Session Problems

Symptom	Probable Faults
Users cannot install .msi applications.	This error occurs when a user that is not a member of the Administrators group attempts to run an MSI installation on a terminal server. If the application is needed for all users, it should be installed on the server by an administrator.
An installed application does not run properly.	The program was likely installed before Terminal Services was installed on the terminal server. To correct this, uninstall and then reinstall the application.
One user cannot remotely control another user's terminal session.	• The biggest cause of this problem is that one of the users is logged on directly to the physical terminal server computer. In order for a user to remotely control another user's session, both users must be remotely connected to the terminal server computer with the terminal server client software.
	• One other cause for this problem is that a user account does not have remote control enabled. You can enable or disable remote control under the Remote Control tab of a user account's Properties dialog box in Active Directory Users and Computers.

Since Terminal Services is a reliable service, most of the problems encountered with terminal servers are a result of configuration problems, including firewall, user account, and application settings. Next, we'll look at repairing another service that has steadily risen in reliability: DFS.

Troubleshooting DFS

As with Terminal Services, most DFS errors occur as a result of a configuration problem. However, while DFS was designed to provide a layer of virtualization to data access, it is only as reliable as the number of file share replicas that have been created on the network to provide fault tolerance. Remember that you can always obtain a quick glimpse of the availability of your DFS infrastructure by opening the DFS MMC, right-clicking an object, and selecting Check Status. For available objects, you will see a green check mark, while unavailable objects are represented by a red X. Also, don't forget about using the valuable `dfsutil` tool for collecting configuration information as well as managing DFS clients (for example, clearing the PKT cache on a client).

With DFS, you may encounter problems in one of these error categories.

- A DFS root is inaccessible.
- A DFS shared folder is inaccessible.
- A user does not have sufficient permissions to access a particular share.

In the remaining parts of this section, we'll examine how to overcome problems in these three specific areas.

Inaccessible Root

Once your highly available DFS root is set up, suppose that it is suddenly inaccessible. When proper fault tolerance is configured, this problem is unlikely, but it does occur. When you find that your DFS root cannot be accessed from the network, look for the following problems.

- The DFS service is not running on a root host.
- The DFS service is not running on domain controllers.
- The NetLogon service is not running on a root host.
- The DFS root is not present in the Active Directory DFS Configuration container.

For service problems, you can quickly query and check the status of the DFS service on each domain controller and DFS host by using a GUI tool such as Computer Management. To ensure that an Active Directory connection is present for domain-based DFS roots, you can open and view the root in the DFS MMC (which connects to AD when the domain-based root is first read by the MMC), or you can use Active Directory Users and Computers to check for the presence of a DFS root in a particular domain. This is shown in Figure 11-10. To locate DFS roots for a domain, you must set the Active Directory Users and Computers MMC to the Advanced view (click View menu and select Advanced Features) and then expand the System container to locate the DFS Configuration container.

If a root is not present in the appropriate Active Directory container, you should verify that Active Directory replication is properly running (see Chapter 13), or alternatively, you can delete and then re-create the root.

Inaccessible Share Folder

One of the nice features of DFS is that as a user attempting to access a DFS share, you can determine the physical location of your DFS redirected connection by examining the properties of a shared folder in Windows Explorer. Under the shared folder's properties, you will see a DFS tab, which displays the true UNC path to the actual shared folder.

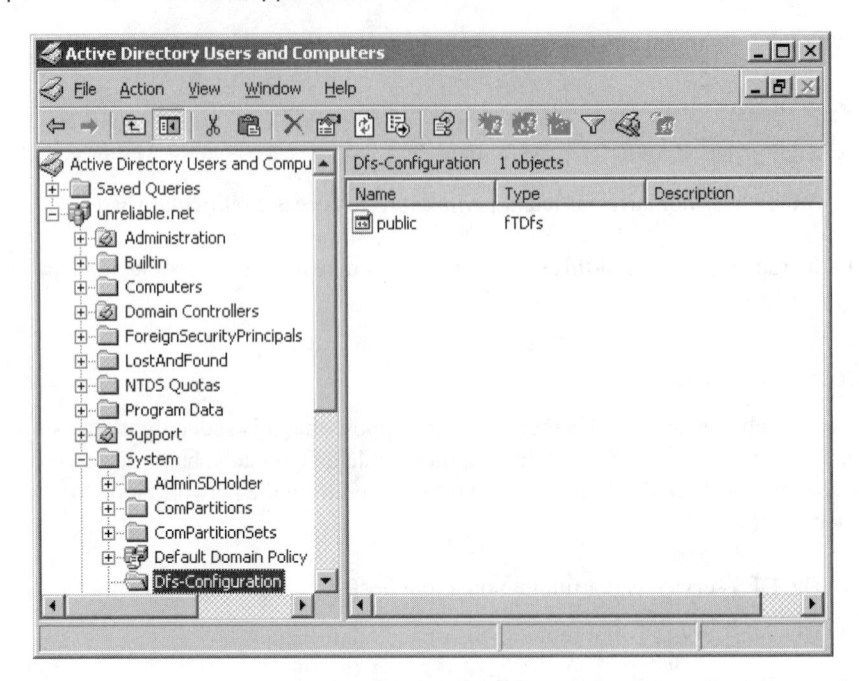

Figure 11-10. Checking the DFS Configuration container

Remember that when you are working with replicated links, for example, it is possible for an administrator to configure permissions for a folder on a particular server one way and configure them differently for the folder's replication partner on another server. This could result in a user sometimes being able to access data, while at other times having no access to the data. With replicated folders, both NTFS and share permissions should be identical for all shares that replicate within the same DFS link. As a policy and for preventative maintenance, you should get in the habit of checking your DFS tree structure before modifying share folder permissions in order to ensure that you are not forgetting to adjust the permissions of a single shared folder (while remembering all others).

If a particular share just becomes unavailable due to a server failure, for example, remember that a DFS client needs to wait a few minutes (up to five) in order to access one of the share's replication partners. If you want to clear the client's cache, you can run the `dfsutil /pktflush` command on the client. Following the execution of the command, the client will not have any DFS paths cached and then will need to return to the DFS root for information on accessing any share in the DFS hierarchy.

User Permissions

Remember that DFS is just a service that has the ability to transparently redirect users to file shares located on other servers throughout your enterprise. With this in mind, NTFS and share permissions are established at each server that is participating in the DFS hierarchy. If a user does not have permission to a particular share, you can verify that the user should have access and then add the user or user's group account to the DACL of the appropriate shared folder (remember to set both share and NTFS permissions accordingly).

Troubleshooting Remote Installation Services

The problems that were commonly encountered with RIS in Windows 2000 have been all but eliminated with Windows Server 2003. With the Remote Installation Services Setup Wizard, the entire RIS imaging and setup process is automated, and thus it is much more difficult to make a mistake when you are initially configuring a server to support RIS.

However, although the RIS setup wizard is a substantial improvement for this relatively new service, it still does have its problems. When a client cannot download a RIS image from a RIS server, you need to determine whether the problem lies with the client or the RIS server. In this section, we'll examine how to correct problems with both RIS servers and RIS clients.

RIS servers will do very little if they are not configured properly. Since RIS does not have a management console, you must manage RIS servers with Active Directory Users and Computers. When you access a RIS server's properties, you will see a Remote Install tab (see Figure 11-2, earlier) that displays the enable state of the RIS server (whether or not it will respond to client requests). Another important feature shown on the Remote Install tab is the Verify Server button. Using this feature is often a first step in RIS server troubleshooting, since it performs an integrity check of RIS server data and corrects any problems that are found.

For RIS clients to obtain an IP address automatically and then download a RIS image, they must be able to boot off their network interface cards. In order to boot from their NICs and to connect to a RIS server, clients must have a NIC that supports PXE Boot PROM 99c or higher. If the clients do not have an interface that supports network boot, you can create a RIS boot floppy for the clients by running the Remote Boot Floppy Generator (RBFG.exe) utility located in the RemoteInstall\Admin\i386 share on the RIS server. When you run this utility, you will see a list of supported client network interfaces. If your clients' interfaces are listed as supported by the utility, then you will be able to use the floppy disk to boot RIS clients and then allow them to download an image from a RIS server.

When a RIS client attempts to download an image from a RIS server, it goes through the following processes, each of which are displayed on the client's screen.

1. The client displays "DHCP".

2. The client displays "BINL".

3. The client displays "TFTP".

4. The client successfully downloads the image.

In the next three sections, we'll look at how to correct problems that would prevent a RIS client from getting past one of the first three RIS download messages.

Client Does Not Get Past "DHCP"

During this stage, a RIS client is attempting to acquire an IP address from a DHCP server and then connect to a RIS server. When the RIS client does not progress past its "DHCP" message during startup, check the following possible causes.

- The DHCP server is unavailable.
- The DHCP server is not authorized.
- The BOOTP forwarder/DHCP Relay Agent is unavailable.
- The DHCP scope is out of IP addresses.

Client Does Not Get Past "BINL"

If the RIS client completes the DHCP process but cannot get past the boot information negotiation layer (BINL) message, you can be certain that the client is not getting a response from the RIS server. These are some possible causes for this problem.

- The RIS server is not authorized.
- The RIS server property "Respond to client computers requesting service" is not enabled.
- The client computer does not have an account in the Active Directory, and the RIS server is configured to not respond to unknown clients.
- The client's PXE Boot PROM is not version 99c or higher.

Client Does Not Get Past "TFTP"

Use of Trivial File Transfer Protocol (TFTP) is the final stage in the RIS imaging process. In this phase, the client has successfully contacted the RIS server and is waiting for the image download from the server. If a problem is encountered during the download, the client will eventually time out, and you will see an error message that the RIS client did not receive a file from DHCP, BINL, or TFTP. This problem can almost always be solved by simply stopping and restarting the Remote Installation service on the RIS server. If this does not correct the problem, you should then check the RIS server for other errors, such as not being configured to respond to clients or being configured to not respond to unknown clients (computer accounts not found in AD).

Troubleshooting NetWare Integration

Since NetWare servers have steadily lost market share in the server market to Microsoft servers, Microsoft has done little to provide seamless integration between Microsoft and NetWare systems on a network. Instead, Microsoft hopes that you will just get rid of all NetWare systems in favor of Microsoft servers. This is why Microsoft operating systems still require use of the the NWLink (IPX/SPX) protocol to connect as a client to a NetWare server, even though TCP/IP has been the default NetWare server protocol since NetWare 5.0.

Unfortunately for you, if you want a Windows server or client to act as a client to a NetWare server, you need to install and configure the NWLink protocol (or you can install the NetWare client software, which for most is the best choice). If you decide to install CSNW, you do need to be aware of how Windows NWLink works with different IPX frame types. By default, the network interface autodetects and binds to the first IPX frame type found on the network. If you have older versions of NetWare and newer OS versions, you may find that the Windows system can communicate with only a few of the NetWare servers. To correct this problem, you need to manually specify the frame types to be used (when frame type detection is set to auto, only one type is ever used). The valid frame types that can be configured for NWLink are

- 802.2—Use with NetWare 3.3 or higher
- 802.3—Use with pre–NetWare 3.3 OSes
- 802.5—Use with token ring adapters

To change the IPX frame type detection from automatic to a manual configuration on a Windows Server 2003 system, follow these steps.

1. Right-click the network adapter and select Properties.
2. In the adapter Properties dialog box, click NWLink IPX/SPX Compatible Transport Protocol and then click the Properties button.
3. Now click the "Manual frame type detection" radio button.
4. To add each frame type on the network, click the Add button, select the frame type, and then enter the appropriate IPX network number for the frame type (see Figure 11-11).
5. When finished configuring frame types, click OK to close the NWLink IPX/SPX Properties dialog box.
6. Now in the network connection Properties window, click OK.

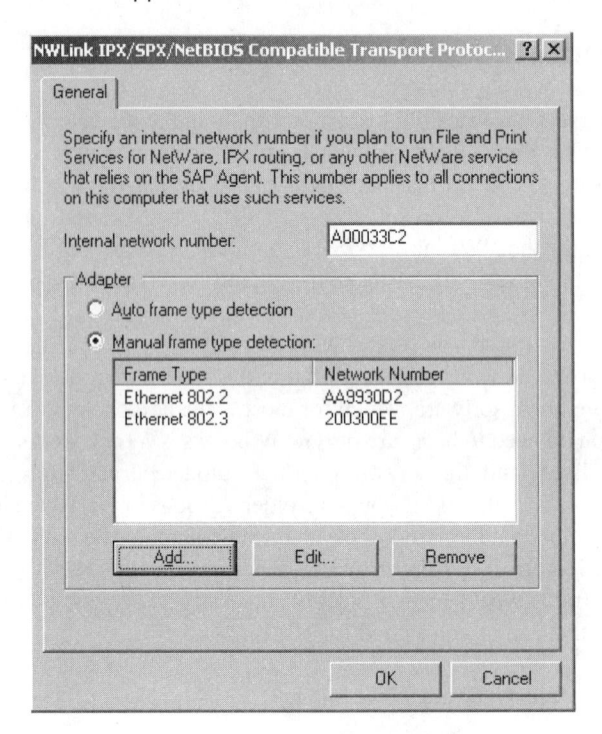

Figure 11-11. Manually adding IPX frame types

Summary

When you are troubleshooting network and application services, understanding the flow of the service processes is most important in resolving a particular problem. In this chapter, we methodically stepped through the network print process, eliminating the good components along the way, and took that same approach with Terminal Services and RIS. You should always have a map (physical or mental) in place when troubleshooting, so that you can easily cross off the good components of a service as they're found.

Next we'll look at troubleshooting another map of sorts: Routing and Remote Access.

12

Routing and Remote Access

Routing and Remote Access Service (RRAS) allows you to configure Windows servers to perform a host of networking tasks. A server can be configured as a remote access server (RAS), for example, allowing users to dial in to the company network using modems on their laptops. With RRAS, a server can be configured to provide Internet access using Network Address Translation (NAT), to act as a router, or to act as a virtual private network (VPN) server that can allow users to access company resources via an encrypted tunnel through the Internet.

RRAS is a very complex Microsoft service, with entire books dedicated to its management alone. Therefore, this chapter cannot possibly cover every conceivable RRAS administration scenario. This is significant because many RRAS problems stem from improper configuration.

While this chapter cannot be an RRAS "catch-all," it does provide you with a sound overview of the core RRAS concepts as well as techniques and commands for digging in and methodically troubleshooting and solving RRAS problems. As with previous chapters, let's begin with a look at the architecture.

RRAS Architecture

Windows Server 2003 Routing and Remote Access Service works with a variety of protocols, policies, and services. In this section, we'll define the components of RRAS and look at how they are used.

Remote Access Servers

For dial-up connections, Windows systems can connect with two different protocols.

- *Point-to-Point Protocol (PPP)*—This is the industry-standard dial-up protocol, providing multiprotocol communication. Dial-up clients connecting to Windows RAS servers must connect using PPP.

- *Serial Line Interface Protocol (SLIP)*—This protocol is primarily used to connect to older UNIX RAS servers. Windows systems can act as SLIP clients and thus use SLIP to connect to UNIX RAS servers, but a Windows RAS server cannot accept connections from SLIP clients.

Once a connection is made to a remote access server, the remote user's credentials must be authenticated. Here are the available authentication protocols.

- *Password Authentication Protocol (PAP)*—PAP authentication means that a user name and password are sent over the network in clear-text (unencrypted) to the RAS server. This is the least secure authentication protocol.

- *Shiva PAP (SPAP)*—SPAP is a version of PAP that is commonly used to support Shiva LANRover clients. This protocol does not provide encryption.

- *Challenge Handshake Authentication Protocol (CHAP)*—CHAP is an authentication protocol that does offer encryption but requires that user passwords be stored using reversible encryption. You can configure a user account to store its password using reversible encryption by editing a user object's properties in Active Directory Users and Computers. After making this change, a user must first change his password (to store it reversibly encrypted) before logging on using CHAP. Due to the requirement for reversible encryption, CHAP is not recommended.

- *Microsoft CHAP (MS-CHAP)*—MS-CHAP is a more secure version of CHAP and does not require that passwords be stored using reversible encryption.

- *MS-CHAP v2*—MS-CHAP v2 is the most secure Microsoft authentication protocol.

- *Extensible Authentication Protocol (EAP)*—EAP is an authentication protocol that is commonly used to support verifying user logon credentials using smart cards.

Once a connection is established, you can encrypt the transmitted data by using one of the following encryption methods, or you can use no encryption:

- Basic—Microsoft Point-to-Point Encryption (MPPE) 40-bit

- Strong—MPPE 56-bit

- Strongest—MPPE 128-bit

The encryption method that you choose determines the security of the data over a RAS connection. However, keep in mind that as you increase encryption, you increase CPU overhead on both the RAS server and RAS client systems.

Multilink

Remote access servers can be configured to allow connections that utilize two or more modems simultaneously in order to increase the bandwidth of a connection. This is known as *multilink*. For a RAS server to accept multilink connections, multilink must be enabled under the RAS server's properties. When multilink is enabled on a RAS server, you can also enable Bandwidth Allocation Protocol (BAP) and Bandwidth Allocation Control Protocol (BACP). These protocols allow the RAS server to drop multilink connections (reduce the modems used for connection from two to one, for example) when bandwidth utilization reaches a certain threshold.

LCP Extensions

With Link Control Protocol (LCP) extensions enabled, the capabilities of a RAS server are extended to track Time Remaining information and ID packets, and to allow the RAS server to call back a particular remote access client.

Remote Access Policies

Remote Access Policies are used to specify conditions under which users can connect to a RAS server. Policies allow you to restrict connections by many criteria, including the following:

- Time of day
- Group membership
- Caller ID
- VPN tunnel type
- Caller IP address

With Remote Access Policies, you can group different users by a set of policies for access to remote servers. For example, you may allow administrators to access a server automatically, any time of the day, but the clerical staff may have access only from 6:00 to 10:00 each night. One key consideration to remember with Remote Access Policies is that the first policy in which all criteria are met (user group, time of day) is applied to the user. Policies can be used to either allow or deny access, but you can also allow access without policies by enabling Dial-in permission under a user's properties in Active Directory Users and Computers. However, in a Native Mode domain, you have the ability to configure a user's properties to "Control access through Remote Access Policy," which means that the policy always determines whether or not a user has access. Without that setting, if a policy denied a user, but her account had "Dial-in" enabled, she would still be granted access. With standalone servers not joined to a domain, access to the RAS server would be strictly determined by the server's RAS policies.

Remote Access Profiles

Remote Access Profiles allow you to define exactly how connections are established to the RAS server. In allowing you to limit connection parameters, the profile allows you to define

- The permissible authentication protocols to use
- Encryption settings
- Idle timeout and session timeout values
- Caller ID parameters (source number doesn't match—call dropped)
- IP filters
- Multilink settings

With profiles, you can highly define and restrict user call settings. Each profile is associated with a particular policy, so this allows you to separate the Remote Access Profile that is used for managers from the profile used for staff, for example.

User Dial-in Properties

Additional remote access settings can be configured under the Dial-in tab under a user account's properties in the Active Directory. This is shown in Figure 12-1. As mentioned earlier, if a RAS policy disallows a user access, but a user's account is set to "Allow access" remote access permission, the user will be able to log on to the RAS server. To streamline remote access configurations, many organizations whose domains are configured as native mode Windows 2000 or higher can set the Dial-in permission to "Control access through Remote Access Policy." This means that whatever the policy says, goes. Other custom user properties that can be configured under this tab include

- Verify Caller ID
- Callback (number, set by caller at time of connection, or always call back to a specific number)
- Static IP assignment for RAS connections
- Assignment of static routes for RAS connections

Now that we have covered the basic aspects of remote access, let's quickly look at VPNs.

Virtual Private Networks

With VPNs, you can securely encapsulate and encrypt data between two points. This technology is especially useful for remote users wishing to access corporate servers, such as e-mail, through the Internet. When a VPN is set up, clients running VPN client

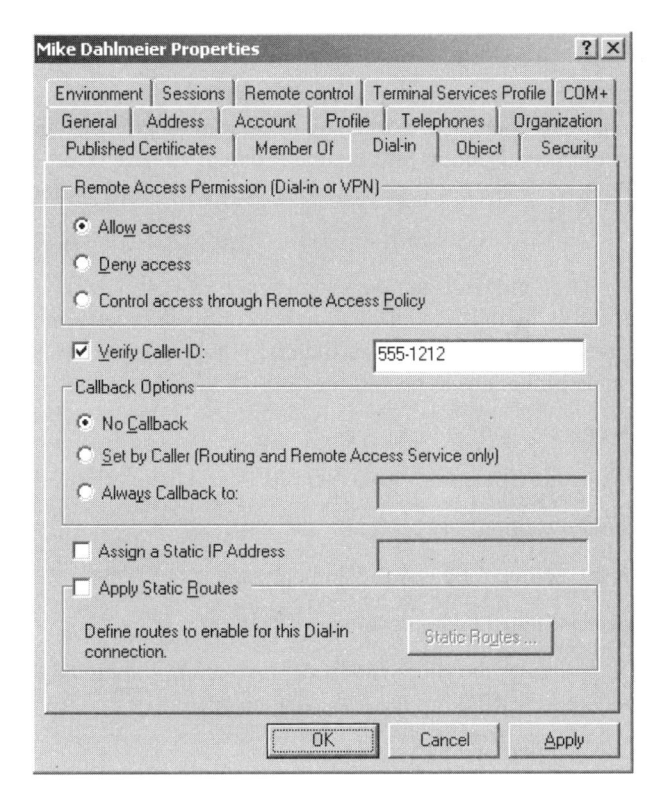

Figure 12-1. User account Dial-in properties

software can connect to a VPN server through the Internet. To facilitate the encryption, one of two possible VPN tunneling protocols may be used.

- *Point-to-Point Tunneling Protocol (PPTP)*—PPTP is an older tunneling protocol that is supported by down-level Microsoft clients, such as NT and Windows 95 for VPN access. PPTP packets are encrypted using Microsoft Point-to-Point Encryption.

- *Layer 2 Tunneling Protocol (L2TP)*—L2TP is a more secure VPN tunneling protocol that is only compatible with Windows 2000 or higher operating systems. L2TP packets can be encrypted using IPSec, which is more secure than MPPE.

Protocol support for down-level clients is an important consideration. When many organizations implement a VPN on a Windows RRAS server, they often want to go with the latest and greatest protocols, only to later realize that some client operating systems are unable to connect. Knowing the limits of L2TP can help you to plan and deploy your VPN server to meet the needs of its clients.

Routing Protocols

With Windows RRAS, you can configure a Windows server as a router and configure it to work with a static routing table or to use a dynamic routing protocol such as Routing Information Protocol (RIP), Routing Information Protocol v2 (RIP2), or Open Shortest Path First (OSPF). Here are the key differences between the routing protocols used by a Windows server router.

- *RIP*—RIP routing protocols are the simplest and easiest to deploy of all routing protocols. With RIP, you can quickly configure routers on your network to share route tables with other routers. When you use RIP, however, there are some limitations to be aware of.
    - RIP can only support up to 15 routers.
    - Routing announcements are made via broadcasts (network overhead).
    - Only classful routing is supported.
    - There is no method for password authentication.
    - Routes are weighted by hop count.
- *RIP2*—RIP2 provides the simplicity of deployment of traditional RIP, but with added features. RIP2 has the following characteristics.
    - It can only support up to 15 routers.
    - Routing announcements are made via multicasts (less network overhead than RIP).
    - Classful routing and classless inter-domain routing (CIDR) are supported.
    - It provides a means for password authentication between neighboring routers (routers will not accept just any route from any anonymous router).
    - Routes are weighted by hop count.
- *OSPF*—OSPF is the most complex of all routing protocols to implement, but it is also the most dynamic. Here are the key features of OSPF.
    - There is no maximum hop count.
    - It supports classful and CIDR routing.
    - It provides password authentication.
    - A cost, instead of a hop count, is assigned to routes, giving you more flexibility.

- It is not compatible with 64-bit Windows versions.
- Routing updates to other routers are incremental (only changes are replicated; RIP replicates the entire routing table).

> Plenty of additional information on routing protocols can be found by searching Microsoft TechNet at www.microsoft.com/technet.

Network Address Translation

If all you need a server at a small company to do is provide access to the Internet for other systems on the LAN, then NAT is probably just what you're looking for. NAT works like ICS, which was discussed in Chapter 5, but is much more configurable. For example, when you install and configure NAT on a Windows RRAS server, the server can act as a DNS proxy for clients connecting to the Internet through it, route outbound Internet traffic, provide DHCP services, and even provide simple firewall protection. Unlike ICS, NAT can work with any range of LAN IP addresses and is fully configurable. When you set up NAT, clients on the LAN will configure the default gateway and DNS server address to be the IP address of the NAT server. Beyond that, there is really nothing more to configure in order to get NAT to work right out of the box.

RAS Troubleshooting Tools

Most that have been working with and deploying Windows RRAS solutions are generally aware of the abilities of the Routing and Remote Access MMC snap-in but have little knowledge of the other available tools that can be used to troubleshoot and support RRAS. There are actually several diagnostic GUI and command line tools that streamline RRAS troubleshooting and even allow you to quickly report on and collect log information for specific problems. We'll look at all of these tools in this section.

atmadm

If your RAS server connects to an asynchronous transfer mode (ATM) network, you will find this command very useful when troubleshooting problems on the ATM network. The `atmadm` command allows you to check and monitor addresses registered by the ATM call manager on an ATM network. This command is useful for checking the status of an ATM adapter, when you suspect a problem with ATM connections. The command displays statistics for both incoming and outgoing calls on a system's ATM adapters.

The syntax for `atmadm` is:

```
atmadm [/c] [/a] [/s]
```

The command options are described in Table 12-1.

Table 12-1. atmadm Command Options

Option	Use
/c	Shows call information for all current connections on the system's ATM adapter(s). The elements of the command output when using the /c option are described in Table 12-2.
/a	Shows the registered ATM network service access point (NSAP) address for each ATM adapter on the system.
/s	Shows monitoring statistics for active ATM connections. The components of the statistical output that is displayed when this option is selected are described in Table 12-3.

Table 12-2. atmadm /c Output Data

Data Displayed	Description
Connection	Under the Connection heading in the command output, you will see abbreviations that detail the types of connections to the ATM adapter. Under this heading, you will see the following types of data. • In/Out—Specifies the type of connection. In = connection from another network to the ATM adapter. Out = connection from the ATM adapter to another network. • PMP—Signifies a point-to-multipoint call. • P-P—Signifies a point-to-point call. • SVC—Signifies that the connection is on a switched virtual circuit. • PVC—Signifies that the connection is on a permanent virtual circuit.
VPI/VCI	This heading displays the virtual path or virtual channel of the incoming or outgoing call.
Remote Address / Media Parameters	The first piece of information displayed under this heading is the NSAP address of the calling (In) or called (Out) ATM device. Two other elements of this heading are TX and RX. • TX—The TX portion of this heading identifies the connection's transmitting default or selected bit-rate type (ABR, CBR, UBR, or VBR), the default or selected line speed, and the service data unit (SDU) size. • RX—The RX portion of this heading provides information on the connection's receiving default or selected bit-rate type (ABR, CBR, UBR, or VBR), the default or selected line speed, and the SDU size.

Table 12-3. atmadm /s Output Data

Statistic	Description
Current Active Calls	Current open calls on the system's ATM adapter
Total Successful Incoming Calls	Total number of calls successfully received from other adapters on the ATM network
Total Successful Outgoing Calls	Calls successfully made to other devices on the ATM network
Unsuccessful Incoming Calls	Total number of incoming calls that failed to connect to the local system
Unsuccessful Outgoing Calls	Total number of outgoing calls that failed to connect to remote devices on the ATM network
Calls Closed by Remote	Total number of calls closed by remote devices on the ATM network
Calls Closed Locally	Total number of calls closed by the local system
Signaling and ILMI Packets Sent	Total number of integrated local management interface (ILMI) packets sent to the system's local ATM switch
Signaling and ILMI Packets Received	Total number of ILMI packets received from the system's local ATM switch

When you are attempting to document problems on the ATM network, the /s command option is the most valuable. However, the /c option is also useful for documenting specific performance information for connections to the ATM adapter on the RAS server, especially when identifying the speed of connections when you believe that performance problems may be related to the ATM network itself.

Here is a sample of the output that you can expect to receive when running atmadm /c.

```
C:\>atmadm /c

Windows ATM Call Manager Statistics

ATM Connections on Interface: [006] 3com ATM Link Network Interface Card

   Connection     VPI/VCI    Remote Address/
                             Media Parameters (rates in bytes/sec)
   In  P-P SVC    0/190      470000973FFE2111111F48B48C3200A995444110
                             TX:VBR,Peak 15503392,Avg 14898203,MaxSdu 8564
                             RX:VBR,Peak 15503392,Avg 14898203,MaxSdu 8564

   Out PMP SVC    0/187      470000973FFE2111111F48B48C3200A995444110
                             TX:VBR,Peak 16288420,Avg 16143297,MaxSdu 9165
                             RX:VBR,Peak 16288420,Avg 16143297,MaxSdu 9165

C:\>
```

Here is a sample of the output you may see from running `atmadm /s`.

```
C:\>atmadm /s

Windows ATM Call Manager Statistics

ATM Call Manager Statistics for Interface: [006] 3com ATM Link Network
Interface Card

          Current Active Calls                      = 7
          Total Successful Incoming Calls           = 853
          Total Successful Outgoing Calls           = 814
          Unsuccessful Incoming Calls               = 2
          Unsuccessful Outgoing Calls               = 1
          Calls Closed by Remote                    = 632
          Calls Closed Locally                      = 732
          Signaling and ILMI Packets Sent           = 29460
          Signaling and ILMI Packets Received       = 30186

C:\>
```

iasparse (ST)

The `iasparse` command line tool is useful for collecting information about a Windows server running Internet Authentication Service (IAS). If certain connections are failing and users are reporting that the failures are authentication related, you can use this tool to dump all IAS server log information into a single log file. From there, you can search the log file, using a text editor such as Notepad to locate failure events. The easiest way to find problems is to search the output log using the word "fail." Among the key information that you will find in the output log file is

- Server IP address
- Client IP address
- Client name
- User name
- Connection date
- Framed protocol type (PPP)
- Tunnel type (L2TP, PPTP)

When a particular user is having connection problems, collecting and searching the IAS logs helps you determine whether the problem is related to the IAS server, thus affecting all users, or to just a single user. Having this information earlier helps you determine where to concentrate your troubleshooting efforts.

Here is the syntax for `iasparse`:

```
iasparse [-f:<filename>] [-p] [-v]
```

The command options are described in Table 12-4.

Table 12-4. iasparse Command Options

Option	Use
`-f:<filename>`	Specifies the IAS log file to parse in order to collect logon, protocol, and accounting information. By default, the default IAS server log file (system32\logfiles\iaslog.log) is parsed.
`-p`	Sends the command output to the display.
`-v`	Verbose output. A description is also displayed for attributes collected in the log file.

One useful way of using the parser so that its output can be searched by a text editor is to redirect its output to a text file using the file redirector (>). For example, you could use this syntax to store the parsed iaslog.log file in the file D:\logs\iasparsed.log: `iasparse -v > d:\logs\iasparsed.log`.

Netsh RAS Diagnostics

There are many other versions of the RAS Netshell (`netsh`) commands that aid in administering RAS servers from the command line. In this section, instead we'll look at the myriad of commands available from within the Netsh RAS Diagnostics command shell, which is a specific command environment geared toward troubleshooting and acquiring diagnostic information on RAS servers. The commands that are available within the Netsh RAS Diagnostics environment are examined in the next several sections. To enter the Netsh RAS Diagnostics environment, perform these steps.

1. From the command prompt, type `netsh` and press Enter.
2. Now type `ras diagnostics` and press Enter.
3. You should now be at the `netsh ras diagnostics>` prompt. From here, you can run any of the commands listed in the remainder of this section. To exit from the `netsh` shell, type `quit` and press Enter.

dump

The `dump` command is used from within the RAS Diagnostics environment to display the current environment settings. In particular, this command allows you to see which diagnostic components have tracing enabled. When tracing is enabled, traced RAS events are written to log files stored in the %windir%\tracing folder. The `set` commands that appear later in this section allow you to enable or disable RAS tracing for particular RAS components. Tracing does place a heavier burden on CPU and disk resources, and thus should only be enabled when you are attempting to resolve a problem on your RAS server.

show all

The `show all` command queries all of the RAS tracing log files and outputs the log file data into an HTML file. This allows you to troubleshoot your RAS problems by looking in, and thus being able to search, a single file. The syntax for the `show all` command is:

```
show all type=<file|email> destination=<FileLocation|EmailAddress>
[compression=<enabled|disabled>] [hours=<hours>]
[verbose=<enabled|disabled>]
```

Table 12-5 describes the `show all` command's options.

Table 12-5. show all Command Options

Option	Use
`type=<file	email>`	Tells the command what to do with the output. Your choice is to either save it as a file or send it to an e-mail address.
`destination=<FileLocation	EmailAddress>`	Depending on the output type specified with the `type` parameter, this option allows you to specify the command's output file or the e-mail address for the e-mail recipient that will receive the report.
`compression=<enabled	disabled>`	Allows you to specify if the report should be compressed into a cabinet (.cab) file. By default, if the report is e-mailed, it is compressed, and if it is saved locally, it is not compressed.
`hours=<hours>`	Specifies the number of past hours' data to include in the report. The parameter must be an integer between 1 and 24.
`verbose=<enabled	disabled>`	Allows you to specify if you want highly detailed information in the output report. Verbose output is disabled by default.

For an example of this command at work, suppose that you want to use `show all` to save RAS tracing log information to the file RASDiagnostics.html. Since the RAS server has been uncharacteristically slow for the past three hours, you decide to look at the last four hours of RAS server activity in the report. To generate the report, you would run the following commands.

```
C:\>netsh
netsh>ras diagnostics
netsh ras diagnostics>show all type=file
destination=c:\reports\RASDiagnostics.html hours=4
Tracing Logs
Modem Logs
```

```
Connection Manager Logs
IP Security Log
Remote Access Event Logs
Security Event Logs
Information Files
Installation Check
Installed Networking Components
Registry Check
Installed Devices
Process Information
Command-Line Utilities
Phone Book Files

Successfully created the Diagnostic Report:

C:\reports\RASDiagnostics.html

Netsh ras diagnostics>
```

The output report generated by this command is shown in Figure 12-2.

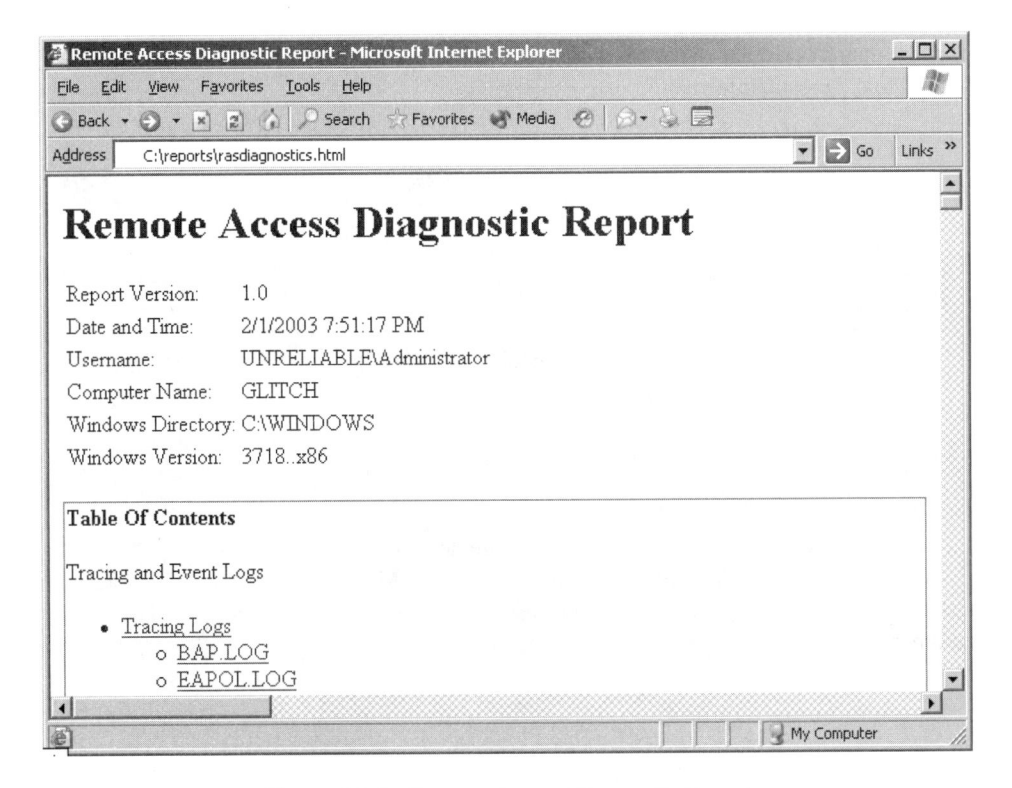

Remote Access Diagnostic Report

Report Version: 1.0
Date and Time: 2/1/2003 7:51:17 PM
Username: UNRELIABLE\Administrator
Computer Name: GLITCH
Windows Directory: C:\WINDOWS
Windows Version: 3718..x86

Table Of Contents

Tracing and Event Logs

- Tracing Logs
    - BAP.LOG
    - EAPOL.LOG

Figure 12-2. Remote Access Diagnostic Report

show cmtracing

This simple command is used to show the logging status of Connection Manager (CM) tracing. When run, this command returns a status of either enabled or disabled. If you run this command and realize that Connection Manager tracing (logging) is disabled, you can then run the `set cmtracing` command to enable logging. The syntax to display the CM tracing state is `show cmtracing`. Once the command is run, if CM logging is disabled, for example, the command will output the message "Connection Manager logging is disabled..."

set cmtracing

If you need to troubleshoot CM problems, or if you have completed the troubleshooting process, then you need to either enable or disable CM tracing. This is done with the `set cmtracing` command. The syntax for this command is:

```
set cmtracing <enabled|disabled>
```

If you were planning to troubleshoot Connection Manager problems, you would run `set cmtracing enabled`. When finished troubleshooting, you would then run `set cmtracing disabled`.

show configuration

This command is similar to the `show all` command with the exception that its output is limited to diagnostic information on

- Installed devices
- Process information
- Command line utilities
- Phone book files

The syntax for `show configuration` is:

```
show configuration type=<file|email>
destination=<FileLocation|EmailAddress>
[compression=<enabled|disabled>] [hours=<hours>]
[verbose=<enabled|disabled>]
```

The options for `show configuration` are described in Table 12-6.

So to dump the configuration diagnostics to the HTML file C:\Reports\RASConfiguration.html detailing information logged over the past two hours, you would run this command:

```
netsh ras diagnostics show configuration type=file
destination=c:\reports\rasconfiguration.html hours=2
```

Table 12-6. show configuration Command Options

Option	Use
type=<file | email>	Tells the command what to do with the output. Your choice is to either save it as a file or send it to an e-mail address.
destination=<FileLocation | EmailAddress>	Depending on the output type specified with the type parameter, this option allows you to specify the command's output file or the e-mail address for the e-mail recipient that will receive the report.
compression=<enabled | disabled>	Allows you to specify if the report should be compressed into a .cab file. By default, if the report is e-mailed, it is compressed, and if it is saved locally, it is not compressed.
hours=<hours>	Specifies the number of past hours' data to include in the report. The parameter must be an integer between 1 and 24.
verbose=<enabled | disabled>	Allows you to specify if you want highly detailed information in the output report. Verbose output is disabled by default.

Note that by including netsh ras diagnostics in the command, you can execute this directly from the command prompt without having to be in the netsh environment.

show installation

This show command generates a RAS Diagnostic Report that includes information on

- Information files
- An installation check
- Installed network components
- A Registry check

The syntax for show installation is:

```
show installation type=<file|email>
destination=<FileLocation|EmailAddress>
[compression=<enabled|disabled>] [hours=<hours>]
[verbose=<enabled|disabled>]
```

Table 12-7 describes the `show installation` command options.

Table 12-7. show installation Command Options

Option	Use
`type=<file | email>`	Tells the command what to do with the output. Your choice is to either save it as a file or send it to an e-mail address.
`destination=<FileLocation | EmailAddress>`	Depending on the output type specified with the `type` parameter, this option allows you to specify the command's output file or the e-mail address for the e-mail recipient that will receive the report.
`compression=<enabled | disabled>`	Allows you to specify if the report should be compressed into a .cab file. By default, if the report is e-mailed, it is compressed, and if it is saved locally, it is not compressed.
`hours=<hours>`	Specifies the number of past hours' data to include in the report. The parameter must be an integer between 1 and 24.
`verbose=<enabled | disabled>`	Allows you to specify if you want highly detailed information in the output report. Verbose output is disabled by default.

Since the previous examples of the `show` command provided information on dumping the output report to a file, let's look at sending the output to an e-mail address. To generate an installation report and e-mail it to the address questions@ChrisWolf.com, you would run the following command:

```
netsh ras diagnostics show installation type=email
destination=questions@chriswolf.com hours=6
```

Since the output will be sent to an e-mail address, it will automatically be compressed as a cab file.

show logs

The `show logs` command allows you to generate a Remote Access Diagnostic Report that includes information from the following log files:

- All tracing logs
- Connection Manager logs
- Modem logs
- IP Security log

RAS Troubleshooting Tools   409

- Remote Access event logs
- Security event logs

The syntax for `show logs` is:

```
show logs type=<file|email> destination=<FileLocation|EmailAddress>
[compression=<enabled|disabled>] [hours=<hours>]
[verbose=<enabled|disabled>]
```

Table 12-8 describes the `show logs` command options.

Table 12-8. show logs Command Options

Option	Use
`type=<file | email>`	Tells the command what to do with the output. Your choice is to either save it as a file or send it to an e-mail address.
`destination=<FileLocation | EmailAddress>`	Depending on the output type specified with the `type` parameter, this option allows you to specify the command's output file or the e-mail address for the e-mail recipient that will receive the report.
`compression=<enabled | disabled>`	Allows you to specify if the report should be compressed into a .cab file. By default, if the report is e-mailed, it is compressed, and if it is saved locally, it is not compressed.
`hours=<hours>`	Specifies the number of past hours' data to include in the report. The parameter must be an integer between 1 and 24.
`verbose=<enabled | disabled>`	Allows you to specify if you want highly detailed information in the output report. Verbose output is disabled by default.

Suppose that you are having trouble with your RAS server and want to e-mail your RAS logs to a friend whose address is phoneafriend@unreliable.net. To generate the report and e-mail it to your friend, you would run this command:

```
netsh ras diagnostics show logs type=email
destination=phoneafriend@unreliable.net hours=5 verbose=enabled
```

show modemtracing

Running this command allows you to see if RAS is logging all modem events. To check and see if modem tracing is enabled, you would run `show modemtracing`. The command outputs the status of modem tracing as either enabled or disabled.

set modemtracing

If you need to enable or disable modem tracing, you do so by running this command. The syntax for set modemtracing is:

```
set modemtracing=<enabled|disabled>
```

As with the other set commands, enabled turns on logging, and using the disabled value turns off logging.

show rastracing

The show rastracing command is used to display the tracing status of each RAS component as either enabled or disabled. There are no additional options for this command, so to view the status of each RAS tracing log, you would run this command:

```
netsh ras diagnostics show rastracing
```

You can modify the use of particular tracing logs by running the set rastracing command, which is explained next.

set rastracing

The set rastracing command allows you to turn on tracing either for specific RAS components or for all RAS components. If you are unsure of each component name, you can use the * wildcard to enable tracing for all components. The syntax for this command is:

```
set rastracing component=<component|*> state=<enabled|disabled>
```

Once you enable RAS tracing, you can check the status of tracing components by running show rastracing. This also allows you to note the name of individual components in the event that you want to individually disable certain components.

show securityeventlog

This command is used to determine if the RAS server is logging security events. There are no parameters for this command, so to see the status of RAS server security logging, you would run show securityeventlog.

set securityeventlog

If you want to enable or disable logging of RAS security events, you can run this command. The syntax for set securityeventlog is:

```
set securityeventlog=<enabled|disabled>
```

So, to enable security event logging on a RAS server, you would run this command:

```
netsh ras diagnostics set securityeventlog=enabled
```

show tracefacilities

This command is used to show the tracing status of all logging activities on the RAS server. The command lists each traceable component and its logging status. The syntax for this command is `show tracefacilities`.

set tracefacilities

If you want to modify the tracing activities of all traceable RAS components with a single command, then this is the command for you. The syntax for `set tracefacilities` is:

```
set tracefacilities state=<enabled|disabled|clear>
```

You can turn on all tracing for all components by specifying enabled as the state and turn off all tracing by specifying a state of disabled. If you use the clear parameter, you clear the content of all tracing logs.

netsh routing

Unlike the Netsh RAS Diagnostics commands, `netsh routing` does not offer a single group of commands dedicated exclusively to troubleshooting. In this section, we examine the commands that allow you to obtain diagnostic information about routing components. For each section, the aspects of the commands that relate exclusively to routing administration are not addressed. If after reading this section, your appetite for `netsh routing` commands has not been satisfied, take a look at Windows Online Help to find out additional information on the other available `netsh routing` commands. The eight subsections in this section address acquiring information exclusive to a particular routing component, such as NAT, RIP, and the DHCP Relay Agent.

netsh routing ip autodhcp

From this `netsh` command context, you can check the settings of the DHCP Allocator, which can be used by NAT to dynamically assign IP addresses to clients. The commands that can be used to check the `autodhcp` configuration are `show global` and `show interface`.

show global

The `show global` command allows you to see the general configuration settings of the DHCP Allocator, if the DHCP Allocator is enabled. This could allow you to determine if your NAT server is interfering with IP address assignments provided by another DHCP server on the network, for example. Here is a sample of this command's execution and output.

```
C:\>netsh
netsh>routing ip autodhcp
netsh routing ip autodhcp>show global
```

```
DHCP Allocator Configuration Information
───────────────────────────────────
Scope Network              : 192.168.0.0
Scope Mask                 : 255.255.255.0
Lease Time (minutes)       : 10080
Logging Level              : Errors Only

netsh routing ip autodhcp>
```

show interface

The `show interface` command is similar to the `show global` command, with the exception that DHCP Allocator information for a single interface is displayed. The syntax for this command is:

```
show interface interfacename=<InterfaceName>
```

You need to know the name of the interface to query in order to run this command. For the `interfacename` parameter, you specify the name of a network interface as it is listed in the Network Connections window (i.e., "Local Area Connection").

netsh routing ip relay

If an RRAS server is not properly relaying DHCP client requests to a DHCP server, you can use this command environment to collect information on the configuration of the DHCP Relay Agent service. In the `netsh routing` DHCP Relay Agent command environment, there are three commands that are helpful for troubleshooting:

- `show interface`
- `show global`
- `show ifstats`

Each of these commands is looked at next.

show interface

This command is used to display the DHCP Relay Agent configuration for a specific network interface. The syntax for this command is:

```
show interface interfacename=<InterfaceName>
```

When executed, this command displays the DHCP Relay Agent configuration information for the interface specified with the `interfacename` parameter. The name used to identify the interface must match the way that the interface is identified under Network Connections.

show global

The `show global` command is similar to `show interface` in purpose, with the exception that it displays configuration information for all network interfaces. The syntax for this command is:

```
show global [rr=<seconds>]
```

If you run this command with the `rr` parameter, you can specify a number of seconds for the command output to automatically refresh. If this parameter is used, you can end the command execution by pressing Ctrl-C.

show ifstats

The `show ifstats` command allows you to view DHCP Relay Agent statistics for a specified interface. The statistics that you can collect from this command include

- Interface state
- Send failures
- Receive failures
- Address Resolution Protocol (ARP) update failures
- Requests received
- Requests discarded
- Replies received
- Replies discarded

If you do not specify an interface with the command options, the command returns statistics for all interfaces on which the DHCP Relay Agent is enabled. Here is the syntax for `show ifstats`:

```
show ifstats [index=<integer>] [rr=<seconds>]
```

The `index` parameter can be used to specify the index value of a target interface. When no index value is specified, statistics are accumulated collectively for all interfaces. The `rr` parameter allows you to have the command run continually, with its refresh rate in seconds equaling the `rr` value that you enter. For example, if you wanted to monitor all DHCP Relay Agent interfaces on an RRAS server and have the output refresh every five seconds, you would run this command:

```
netsh routing ip relay show ifstats rr=5
```

netsh routing ip dnsproxy

When you install and enable NAT, you can have the NAT server act as a DNS proxy for clients. This allows all clients to potentially use the NAT server as their DNS server. The NAT server then will relay client requests to an alternate server (usually external), and the NAT server will in turn relay the DNS response back to the client. When you are troubleshooting DNS proxy configuration, there are two commands of concern: `show global` and `show interface`.

show global

This command allows you to see the DNS proxy global configuration, which contains the default DNS proxy configuration settings for all interfaces that act as DNS proxies. If you are looking to collect configuration information for a specific interface, you could run the `show interface` command.

show interface

The `show interface` command allows you to view the DNS proxy configuration of a specific interface. Here is this command's syntax:

```
show interface interfacename=<InterfaceName>
```

For the `interfacename` parameter, you need to specify the name of the network interface as it appears in the Network Connections window. For example, if the DNS proxy was on the interface labeled "Private," you would run this command:

```
netsh routing ip dnsproxy show interface interface="private"
```

netsh routing ip igmp

The `netsh routing ip igmp` command environment has several commands for monitoring and troubleshooting Internet Group Management Protocol (IGMP)–enabled interfaces. In this section, we'll examine seven commands that are useful when you are troubleshooting IGMP problems.

show interface

With `show interface`, you can view the IGMP configuration of a single routing interface. If you do not specify an interface name with this command, you will see the configuration information for all interfaces. The syntax for this command is:

```
show interface interfacename=<InterfaceName>
```

The `interfacename` parameter must equal the exact name of a network interface as it appears in Network Connections.

show global

The `show global` command allows you to see the global IGMP configuration settings that apply to all interfaces. There are no parameters for this command, so its syntax is simply `show global`.

show ifstats
This command allows you to see IGMP statistics for a routing interface. If you do not specify an interface, statistics are collected for all IGMP interfaces. The syntax for this command is:

```
show ifstats [index=<integer>] [rr=<seconds>]
```

With this command, the `index` parameter allows you to specify the index number of a specific network interface. If you would like the command to run continually and automatically update its output statistics, you can use the `rr` parameter and specify the command refresh rate in seconds.

show iftable
This command allows you to see the IGMP host groups that are assigned to a particular routing interface. If you do not specify an interface, all IGMP host groups are displayed. The syntax for this command is:

```
show iftable [index=<integer>] [rr=<seconds>]
```

As with previous commands, the `index` parameter allows you to select a specific interface, and the `rr` parameter allows you to have the command output continually refresh.

show grouptable
This command is used to display the IGMP Hosts Group Table for a multicast group. If you do not specify an interface, the command shows all IGMP Hosts Group Tables for all multicast groups on all interfaces. The syntax for this command is:

```
show grouptable [index=<integer>] [rr=<seconds>]
```

Again, with this command, the `index` parameter is used to target a specific interface, and the `rr` option allows you to set a refresh period for the command.

show rasgrouptable
This command outputs the Hosts Group Table for a specific RAS client interface. If a client interface is not specified, the command returns all Hosts Group Tables for all client interfaces. Here is the syntax for show rasgrouptable:

```
show rasgrouptable [index=<ClientIPAddress>] [rr=<seconds>]
```

Unlike the previous commands, for the `index` parameter, you need to specify the IP address of a remote RRAS client.

show proxygrouptable
With this command, you can examine the IGMP Hosts Group Table for an IGMP Proxy interface. Like previous commands, if no interface is specified, the command returns the IGMP Hosts Group Table for all interfaces. The syntax for this command is:

```
show proxygrouptable [interfacename=<InterfaceName>] [rr=<seconds>]
```

In this command, the `interfacename` parameter is used to define the network interface whose IGMP Hosts Group Table you would like to examine. As with earlier commands, the `rr` parameter allows you to select a refresh rate in seconds for the command output.

netsh routing ip nat

The `netsh routing ip nat` commands allow you to quickly view configuration information for the NAT service and for NAT-enabled interfaces. Two commands that are useful for troubleshooting NAT problems are `show global` and `show interface`.

show global
When you view the global NAT configuration information, you will see the TCP and UDP timeout parameters (in minutes) and the NAT logging level (errors only by default). The syntax for using this command to view global configuration settings is simply `show global`, with no available options.

show interface
The `show interface` command allows you to see the configuration of NAT-enabled interfaces. In particular, this command outputs the configuration type for the interface, which is one of the following:

- Address and port translation
- Address and port translation with firewall
- Firewall only
- Private interface

The syntax for this command is:

```
show interface [interfacename=<InterfaceName>]
```

If you do not specify an interface with the `interfacename` parameter, then the configuration of all NAT interfaces is displayed. This command is useful for verifying that you have at least one private interface and one address and port translation interface enabled for NAT, which are the minimum requirements for NAT to operate.

netsh routing ip ospf

There are several `netsh` diagnostic utilities that are helpful when you are troubleshooting OSPF router issues. This section examines each of these available commands.

show global
The `show global` command allows you to check the global state of an RRAS server's OSPF configuration. In particular, you can see the router state (enabled or disabled), router ID, and logging level (errors only by default). There are no optional parameters for

this command, so to view global settings, you would run `show global` from the `netsh routing ip ospf` command environment.

show virtif
This command allows you to see configuration information on OSPF virtual interfaces, if any are enabled. When virtual interfaces are in use, running this command allows you to check the following information on a virtual interface:

- Interface status (enabled, disabled)
- Transit area ID
- Virtual neighbor router ID
- Transit delay
- Retransmission interval
- Hello interval
- Dead interval

Again, there are no option parameters for this command, so to see virtual interface information, you would run `show virtif`.

show interface
The `show interface` command allows you to see the configuration of OSPF-enabled interfaces. In particular, this command allows you to check the following:

- Interface state (enabled or disabled)
- IP address and subnet mask
- Area ID
- Interface type—broadcast, point-to-point, or non-broadcast multiple access (NBMA)
- Router priority
- Retransmission interval
- Hello interval
- Dead interval
- Poll interval
- Metric
- MTU size

The syntax for this command is:

```
show interface [interfacename=<InterfaceName>]
```

If you do not specify an interface with the `interfacename` parameter, then the configuration of all OSPF interfaces is displayed.

show routefilter

This command allows you to see if the OSPF router drops specific routes that it receives from other OSPF routers. When filters are enabled, you can configure the filter either to accept a specific list of network IDs or to drop a specific list of network IDs. When you execute this command (`show routefilter`), you will see a filter action (accept or drop) displayed as well as a list of the filtered routes.

show protofilter

This command is similar to `show routefilter` in that its output format is identical. However, this command differs in that it displays the OSPF protocol filter settings. When the command is executed, you will see the general filter configuration (accept or drop) as well as a list of filtered protocols.

show area

When you run `show area`, you can see configuration information on each configured OSPF area. Among the data that you can check is the following:

- Area state (enabled, disabled)
- Authentication type (simple password, no authentication)
- Stub area (yes or no)
- Stub metric
- Import summary advertisement configuration (yes or no)

This command has no optional parameters, so to check the area configuration of an OSPF router, you would run `show area`.

netsh routing ip rip

The `netsh routing ip rip` command environment provides the following five commands that will help you in troubleshooting RIP routing:

- `show interface`
- `show flags`
- `show global`
- `show ifstats`
- `show ifbinding`

show interface

The `show interface` command allows you to see the RIP configuration for a single RIP interface or for all RIP routing interfaces. The syntax for this command is:

```
show interface [interfacename=<InterfaceName>]
```

The `interfacename` parameter must equal the exact name of a network interface as it appears in Network Connections.

show flags

This command is used to display the flags (Split Horizon, Poison Reverse, and so on) for a given RIP interface. If no interface name is specified, the flags for all interfaces are returned. The syntax for `show flags` is:

```
show flags [interfacename=<InterfaceName>]
```

The `interfacename` parameter must equal the exact name of a network interface as it appears in Network Connections.

show global

The `show global` command allows you to see the general RIP routing configuration settings. This command does not offer optional parameters, so its syntax is simply `show global`. Here is an example of the command execution as well as its output data.

```
netsh routing ip rip>show global

RIP Global Configuration Information
------------------------------------
Logging Level                 : Errors Only
Max Receive Queue Size        : 1048576
Max Send Queue Size           : 1048576
Min Triggered Update Interval : 5
Peer Filter Mode              : Disabled
Peer Filter Count             : 0

netsh routing ip rip>
```

show ifstats

The `show ifstats` command is the "MVP" of RIP troubleshooting commands. This command shows you the RIP statistics for a given RIP routing interface and includes the following information:

- Send failures
- Receive failures
- Requests sent
- Requests received

- Responses sent
- Responses received
- Bad response packets received
- Bad response entries received

This information makes it easy for you to determine if a problem exists with your Windows server RIP router. The syntax for `show ifstats` is:

```
show ifstats [index=<integer>] [rr=<seconds>]
```

With this command, the `index` parameter allows you to specify the index number of a specific network interface. If you would like the command to run continually and automatically update its output statistics, you can use the `rr` parameter and specify the command refresh rate in seconds.

show ifbinding

The `show ifbinding` command allows you to see information on a particular network interface bound to the RIP routing protocol. For any given interface, the command displays the interface name, its binding state, IP address, and subnet mask. The syntax for this command is:

```
show ifbinding [index=<integer>] [rr=<seconds>]
```

Suppose that you wanted to display the binding information for the second bound RIP interface. To do this, you would run this command:

```
netsh routing ip rip show ifbinding index=2
```

netsh routing ip routerdiscovery

The `netsh routing ip routerdiscovery` command environment offers one command that is of troubleshooting value: `show interface`. The `show interface` command allows you to see statistics for a single interface or for all interfaces. The syntax for this `netsh routing ip routerdiscovery show interface` command is:

```
show interface [interfacename=<InterfaceName>]
```

If the `interfacename` parameter is not included in the command syntax, then router discovery statistics are displayed for all routing interfaces.

portqry (ST)

The Port Query (`portqry`) command allows you to troubleshoot TCP/IP port connectivity issues. With this tool, you can test the connectivity and check the status of a single TCP or UDP port or of a range of ports. If you are unsure if a remote port is even accessible, due to a possible firewall setting or server service being down, this is a great tool to use to find the answer.

When you query a remote port, `portqry` returns a status for the remote port, which will be one of the statuses listed in Table 12-9.

Table 12-9. portqry Output Statuses

Status	Description
Listening	The target port is active and listening.
Not Listening	The target destination/port is not reachable.
Filtered	The port on the target system is listening but is being filtered by the target system or by a firewall. Port filtering is a way for a server or firewall to limit traffic that connects on a particular port, such as by only allowing port 80 connections from a single network source.

The status that is returned is valuable in troubleshooting port availability. For example, if you receive a Not Listening response, that tells you that no system can connect to the remote host on the queried port number. This may indicate that a service on the remote system that manages the port is down or that requests to connect on a particular port are being blocked by a firewall. If you receive a Listening response, then you can determine that the target system's queried port is active, and this may mean that a connectivity problem may be a failure residing on the client that is trying to connect, and not with the remote server.

Now that you've seen the reason to use this command, let's look at its syntax.

```
portqry /n <name> [/p <protocol>] [/e <port>] [/r <StartPort:EndPort>]
[/o <port,port,...>] [/l <logfile>] [/s] [/q] [/i]
```

Table 12-10 describes the `portqry` command's options.

Table 12-10. portqry Command Options

Option	Use
/n <name>	Used to specify the FQDN or IP address of the remote host that `portqry` will try to connect to.
/p <protocol>	Used to specify the type of port or protocol used to connect to the target port. The default is TCP. Valid protocol values are `tcp`, `udp`, or `both`.
/e <port>	Used to specify the port number to query. Valid numbers range from 1 to 65535. This option cannot be used in conjunction with /r or /o.

continues

Table 12-10. portqry Command Options, continued

Option	Use
/r <StartPort:EndPort>	Used to specify a range of ports to be queried in sequential order. This option cannot be used in conjunction with /e or /o.
/o <port,port, ...>	Used to specify a list of ports to query. You cannot have spaces between port numbers or commas. This option cannot be used in conjunction with /e or /r.
/l <logfile>	Used to copy the portqry output to a text file. In the logfile value, you should specify the complete path and filename to where you want the output written.
/s	Causes portqry to wait longer for UDP requests before replying with a Not Listening status.
/q	Suppresses screen output except for error messages. This command cannot be used with /0 or /r, or when both is specified as the protocol type in the /p switch.
/i	Causes portqry to bypass an IP–to–host name lookup if an IP address is provided for the target name. This allows the portqry command to complete faster.

Here is an example of using portqry to check for the availability of a remote terminal server named glitch.unreliable.net.

```
C:\>portqry /n glitch.unreliable.net /p 3389

Querying target system called:
 Glitch.unreliable.net
Attempting to resolve name to IP address...
Name resolved to 192.168.0.201

TCP port 3389 (unknown service): LISTENING

C:\>
```

route

The route command is very valuable when you are troubleshooting both client and server routing issues. For example, a client may have persistent static routes in its local routing table so that it can reach a test network that is accessible to the organization's public network. If the IP settings of the router that the client uses to access the network change, then you will have to modify the client's static routing table accordingly. In a perfect world, all static routes are stored on the company's router to centralize routing administration. One example of the use of static routes is for a Windows Server 2003 system running RRAS to connect the corporate network to satellite offices. The router may have several demand-dial interfaces that allow connection to remote networks. This information may be in the form of static routes that must be maintained. With the `route` command, you can view, modify, delete, or add static routes to a system's routing table.

Here is the syntax for `route`:

```
route [-f] [-p] <add | change | delete | print> [destination] [mask
<netmask>] [gateway] [metric <metric>] [if <interface>]
```

The command options are described in Table 12-11.

Table 12-11. route Command Options

Option	Use
`-f`	Clears from the routing table all routes that are not host routes. Host routes consist of the following routing entries: routes with the subnet mask 255.255.255.255, routes with a destination of 127.0.0.0 and a subnet mask of 255.0.0.0, and multicast routes (destination ranges from 224.0.0.0 to 240.0.0.0). If this option is used in conjunction with the `add`, `change`, or `delete` options, the routing table is cleared prior to the processing of the particular command option.
`-p`	Used to make a new or modified routing entry persistent. This means that the routing information is retained by the system even after a reboot. Without the `-p` parameter, any route that is added to the routing table is lost the next time the system reboots.
`add`	Adds a new route to the routing table.
`change`	Changes an existing route in the routing table.
`delete`	Deletes a route from the routing table.
`print`	Displays the contents of the routing table.
`destination`	When a route is added or modified, this parameter is used to specify the destination network ID.
`mask <netmask>`	When a route is added or modified, this parameter is used to specify the destination network's subnet mask.
`gateway`	When a new route is added or modified, this parameter is used to specify the gateway (router) to send the data to in order to reach the destination network.
`metric <metric>`	Used to specify an integer (from 1 to 9999) cost metric for the route. When multiple routes exist for the same destination, the route with the lowest cost metric is used.
`if <interface>`	Used to specify the interface index for the interface that connects to the destination network. You can view a list of available interfaces by running `route print`. The interface index can be specified in either decimal or hexadecimal. When hex is used, the interface value must be preceded with `0x`.

There are several troubleshooting uses for the `route` command. Here are a few examples of this command in action.

- Display a system's routing table:
  `route print`

- Display all routes to the 172.16.x.x network:
  `route print 172.16.*`

- Add a default route for all unknown networks to be sent to the gateway address 172.19.67.1:
  `route -p add 0.0.0.0 mask 0.0.0.0 172.19.67.1`

- Add a route for a system to reach the 10.2.84.0 network via the router address 10.2.75.1:
  `route -p add 10.2.84.0 mask 255.255.255.0 10.2.75.1`

- Delete a static route from a system:
  `route delete 172.16.12.0 mask 255.255.0.0`

RRAS MMC

Of all the tools discussed in this section, the RRAS MMC snap-in is the most frequently used. This tool allows you to monitor the status of your RRAS configurations (RAS, VPN, NAT, and so on) as well as make changes when necessary. To access this tool, click Start >Administrative Tools > Routing and Remote Access. Then you will see the RRAS MMC, as shown in Figure 12-3. The first time you open this tool, you are prompted to configure and enable Routing and Remote Access. The RRAS Configuration Wizard is actually very useful, since it allows you to quickly configure the RRAS server to meet your needs. For example, if you wanted to set up a NAT server, you would select the NAT option in the wizard, select your public (Internet connected) and private (LAN connected) network interfaces, answer a couple of more questions, and your network clients would be able to get to the Internet through your NAT server.

With the RRAS MMC, you can view information on connected clients' sessions and even disconnect clients. At the server properties level, you can configure the default security settings for the server and configure error logging. This is done under the Logging tab of the server Properties window. By default, the server logs all errors and warnings to the %windir%\tracing folder. Here is what you can see or configure at the other object levels in the RRAS MMC.

- *Network Interfaces*—View the connection status of each interface.

- *Remote Access Clients*—View statistics on each connected RAS client.

- *IP Routing*—Configure routing interfaces, view routing tables, check DHCP Relay Agent configuration, and check the NAT/Basic Firewall settings.

- *Remote Access Policies*—Configure Remote Access Policy settings (who can access the server at what times). For each policy, you can configure the policy's profile to indicate the allowable connection and authentication protocols.

While many of the other tools in this section will help you locate problems, you will most likely use the RRAS MMC to correct the problems that you find.

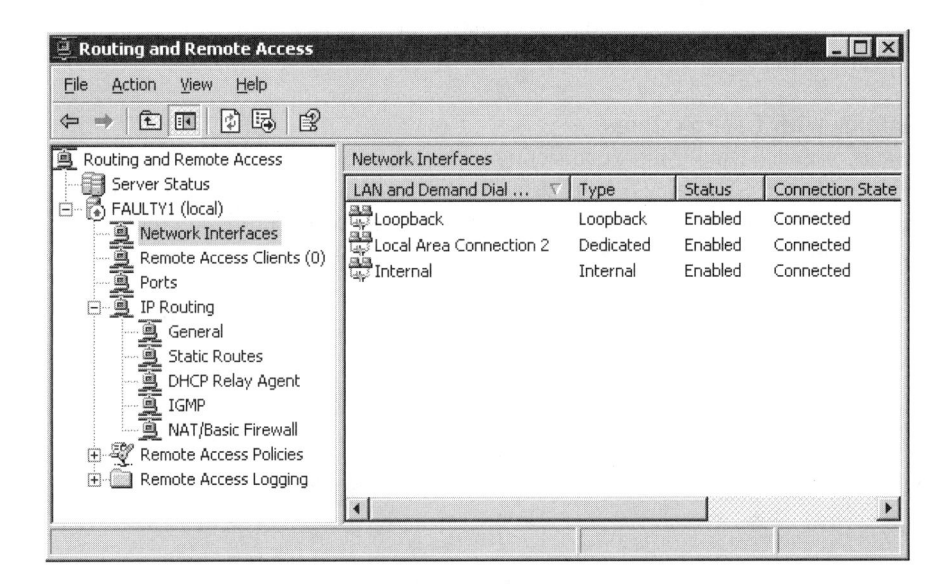

Figure 12-3. RRAS MMC snap-in

Troubleshooting RAS

RAS is one of the most popular features of the Routing and Remote Access Service, so it's a great way to kick off our look into RRAS troubleshooting. RAS server troubleshooting can be looked at as two different categories:

- Troubleshooting RAS client connections
- Troubleshooting the RAS server network

Common problems encountered with RAS servers normally fall into either of these two categories. You may find that users report that they are unable to connect to the RAS server, or you may learn that once connected to the RAS server, users cannot access any resources beyond the server itself. For example, users may dial up to the RAS server so that they can check their e-mail settings, and report that the mail server is unreachable.

Troubleshooting RAS Client Connections

When clients are unable to access the RAS server, it is best to determine whether the source of the connection problem is related to the server or to the individual client. If several users are complaining that the RAS server is unreachable, then it is best to start checking for problems with the RAS server. On the other hand, if only one user appears to have a problem, then you should direct your initial troubleshooting focus to the user's system and settings.

Problems with User Systems

If a single user is having trouble connecting to the RAS server, oftentimes the server may provide an error message that is helpful for troubleshooting. For example, if a RAS policy is preventing a user from connecting, and if Remote Access permission for the user account is set to Deny Access, the user will receive an error message similar to the message in Figure 12-4.

Figure 12-4. RAS connection failure

If the problem is not related to a policy or user account setting, then the problem could reside on the user's system. With that in mind, you should examine the connection device itself: the modem. In Chapter 5, the process for troubleshooting a modem was described. If the user's modem appears to be in a problem state in Device Manger, or if the modem cannot receive a dial tone, it is likely that you have located the problem. As always, never underestimate the lack of common sense a user may have. For example, both ends of the telephone cable may not be plugged in. Sure, one end is connected to the modem, but possibly the end connected to the oxygen the user is breathing is not working too well.

Now supposing that the phone line is connected properly, you should still have the user confirm that a dial tone is present by plugging a regular telephone into the phone line. If the phone line appears to be OK, you should check to see if the right driver is installed. If the user has used the modem before, then it is unlikely that the driver is incorrect, but it is still worth checking. Remember that you can also test the modem itself by performing modem diagnostics as was outlined in Chapter 5.

Problems with the RAS Server

When the user can connect to other networks but not to the RAS server, or if other users are reporting similar problems, then it is time to turn your attention to the RAS server. Numerous configuration, resource usage, or policy problems can prevent users from connecting to the server. When a user cannot connect, refer to Table 12-12, which lists the possible causes of the connection problem as well as processes to solve the problem.

Table 12-12. Common RAS Server Problems

Symptom	Probable Faults
RAS is not enabled on the RAS server.	In the RRAS MMC, right-click the RAS server object, select Properties, and then click the General tab. Verify that the Remote Access Server box is checked.
The RAS server is out of static IP addresses to lease to RAS clients.	• If a RAS server cannot give any more IP addresses to connecting clients, it will not accept any more connections. You can check a RAS server's address pool by right-clicking the server object in the RRAS MMC and selecting Properties. From there, click the IP tab to view the IP lease configuration settings. If you need to manually add additional addresses to the pool, you can do so under this tab as well. If the RAS server is getting its IP addresses from a DHCP server (default), then check the availability of the DHCP server. • The local Hosts file is improperly configured.
Routing and Remote Access Service is not started.	Open the Services MMC snap-in and check the status of the RRAS service. It if is stopped, start the service.
The RAS server's interfaces are not configured to allow inbound port connections.	In the RRAS MMC, right-click the Ports object and select Properties. Select the RAS inbound network connection and click Configure. Verify that the Remote Access Connections (Inbound Only) box is selected.
The profile settings conflict with the allowable RAS server settings.	Verify that at least one of the allowable authentication protocols for a RAS profile is the same as what is set at the RAS server level.
The RAS server is sharing a modem with the Windows Fax service, and the modem does not support adaptive answer.	When a RAS shares a modem with the Fax service, contention for the fax resource could arise for inbound calls. If the modem cannot support adaptive answer, you must disable the Fax service's fax-receive feature. This way, the Fax service will not compete with the RAS.
A client cannot contact the RAS server by its host or fully qualified domain name.	• A host (A) record has the wrong IP address. Modify the IP address for the host on the DNS server, clear the client's resolver cache, and have the client run the query again. • The client's requests are being resolved by a secondary DNS server whose zone is out of date. Decrease the refresh interval for the zone. Add the secondary server to the zone's Notify List.

continues

Table 12-12. Common RAS Server Problems, continued

Symptom	Probable Faults
The RAS server cannot contact the Active Directory.	• Verify that the "RAS and IAS Servers" domain local group exists. If not, create it.
	• Verify that the "RAS and IAS Servers" group has Read permission for the "RAS and IAS Servers Access Check" object in the Active Directory.
	• Verify that the computer account of the problematic RAS server is a member of the "RAS and IAS Servers" group. This can be done by running the `netsh ras show registeredserver` command. If the RAS server is not present, you can use the `netsh ras add registeredserver` command to add the RAS sever to the group, or add the server to the group using Active Directory Users and Computers.
RAS server is not calling back RAS clients.	• Check the callback configuration under the Dial-in tab of the remote user's user account. Is callback enabled?
	• LCP extensions are not enabled. Open the RAS server Properties dialog box and then click the PPP tab. Verify that the Multilink checkbox is selected.

Troubleshooting the RAS Server Network

If clients can connect to the RAS server but cannot access any network resources beyond the RAS server, the possible problems that you need to examine are minimal. The problems that can prevent a RAS client from accessing network resources beyond the RAS server are described in Table 12-13.

Table 12-13. Common RAS Server Network Problems

Symptom	Probable Faults
Hosts and routers on the intranet cannot route back to RAS clients.	If the RAS server is handing out a unique range of IP addresses, the routers on the LAN must have knowledge of the network ID clients use when connected to the RAS, and they should be configured to use the RAS server as a gateway for connecting to the remote clients.
Packet filters on the RRAS server are blocking RAS client traffic.	• Remove filters for the client network on the RRAS server.
	• The local Hosts file is improperly configured.

Table 12-13. Common RAS Server Network Problems, continued

Symptom	Probable Faults
IP Routing is disabled on the RAS server.	From the RAS server's Properties dialog box, click the IP tab. Verify that the Enable IP Routing box is selected.
RAS clients are not receiving any scope options (DNS server, gateway, and so on) from the RAS server.	Install the DHCP Relay Agent service on the internal network interface of the RAS server.
RAS clients are getting wrong or no DNS or gateway information from the RAS server using a static pool of addresses.	When a RAS server uses its own static pool of addresses to provide IP addresses for clients, it gives the clients its own DNS and gateway addresses to use as well. If these addresses are improperly configured on the RAS server, the RAS clients will have problems accessing network resources.

Unless you are very familiar with the RAS server configuration, RAS server troubleshooting entails a thorough process of elimination. When you narrow down a problem, consider the tables in this section to be checklists for eliminating what you have confirmed as working, until you arrive at the cause of the problem.

Troubleshooting Routing

Since Windows routers can be configured in a vast variety of ways, your troubleshooting approach and symptom checks must be specific to the particular router configuration. In this section, we'll look at the methods for diagnosing routing problems on Windows RRAS servers. In particular, we'll examine

- General routing problems
- Troubleshooting NAT
- Troubleshooting DHCP relay agents
- Troubleshooting demand-dial routing
- Troubleshooting RIP
- Troubleshooting OSPF

General routing problems are those that are applicable to all Windows router configurations, so let's begin there.

General Routing Problems

All configurations of Windows Server 2003 RRAS can fall victim to a common set of faults. These faults are described in Table 12-14.

Table 12-14. General Routing Problems

Symptom	Probable Faults
Routing and Remote Access Service is not running.	Open the Windows Services MMC and verify the state of the Routing and Remote Access Service. If the service is not running, start the service.
IP routing is not enabled on the server.	From the RAS server's Properties dialog box, click the IP tab. Verify that the Enable IP Routing box is selected.
LAN/WAN routing is not enabled.	From the RAS server's Properties dialog box, click the General tab. Now select the Router checkbox and the "Local area network (LAN) routing only" or "LAN and demand-dial routing" radio button. This is shown in Figure 12-5.
The default gateway address is incorrect.	Verify that the default gateway is correctly configured on the RRAS box.
Routing tables cannot be shared/updated with other routers.	Proper routing protocols are not enabled. Routing protocols are added by right-clicking the IP Routing\General object and selecting New Routing Protocol. To confirm routing updates from other routers, click the IP Routing\General object, and then right-click one of the listed routing interfaces and select Show IP Routing Table. When the table is displayed, you can confirm updates from other routers by viewing the Protocol column in the routing table. This column lists the routing protocol responsible for the route information (RIP, OSPF) or displays the word "Local."
The router is not receiving updates from router neighbors.	Proper routing protocols are not installed on the proper router interfaces. Under IP Routing, select the appropriate routing protocol (RIP, and so on), and you will see the protocol's enabled interfaces. To add a new interface for the protocol to use, right-click the protocol and select New Interface.

Troubleshooting NAT

As with other client-server troubleshooting scenarios, your first objective when troubleshooting NAT problems should be to determine whether the problem is related to an individual client or the NAT server. If a single user is having trouble, try connecting to a remote network (via the NAT server) from another computer on the LAN. If that computer does not experience any problems, then you can troubleshoot the single problematic client. Otherwise, you can start at the NAT server.

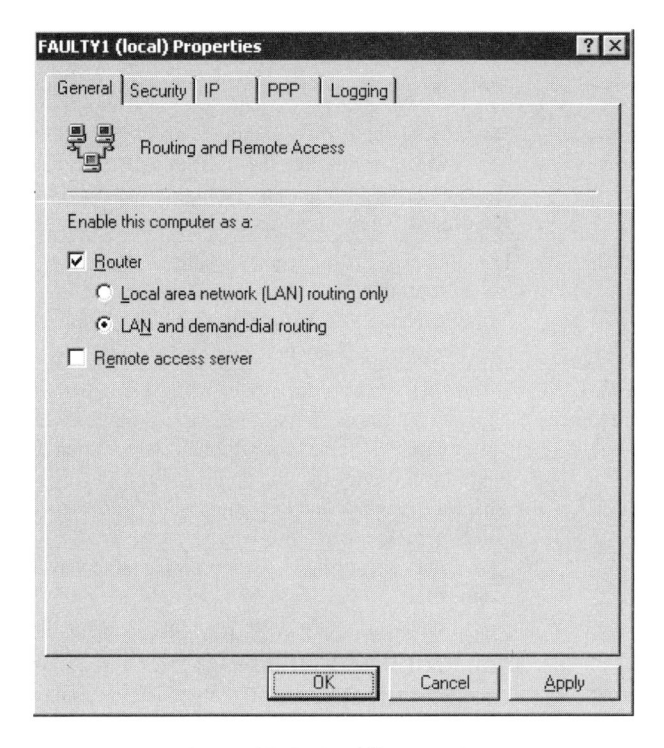

Figure 12-5. Enabling routing

Problems with NAT Clients

If a single NAT client cannot access a remote network via a NAT server, the likely problem is the client's network adapter or TCP/IP configuration. This type of fault can usually be pinpointed within minutes. If the NAT server is configured as a DHCP Allocator (acts like a DHCP server), verify that the client's TCP/IP settings are configured to obtain an IP address automatically. If static IP addresses are being used on the network, verify that the client is using the LAN IP address of the NAT server as its default gateway and DNS server. Finally, verify that the client can ping the private and public interfaces of the NAT server; if so, the problem is resolved.

Problems with the NAT Server

The NAT server has a tremendous responsibility. In addition to providing basic routing functions, the NAT server can be configured to act as a firewall, DHCP Allocator, or DNS proxy. If clients are configured to obtain their IP address automatically, then it is critical that these services be properly configured and enabled on the NAT server. And of course, one cannot forget about address translation problems with the NAT server itself. Each of the NAT server possible faults and related solutions is outlined in Table 12-15.

Table 12-15. NAT Server Problems

Symptom	Probable Faults
LAN clients are not receiving IP address assignments (have APIPA addresses).	The NAT server is not configured as a DHCP Allocator. In the RRAS MMC, right-click the IP Routing\NAT-Basic Firewall object and select Properties. From the Address Assignment tab, you can configure automatic address assignment for NAT clients.
LAN clients are unable to resolve remote FQDNs.	The DNS proxy is not enabled. In the RRAS MMC, right-click the IP Routing\NAT-Basic Firewall object and select Properties. From the Name Resolution tab, enable the "Resolve IP addresses for Clients using Domain Name System" checkbox.
Clients are unable to access resources beyond the NAT server.	• The NAT server is not properly translating packets. Public and private interfaces are not properly configured. Click the IP Routing\NAT-Basic Firewall object to see a list of NAT-enabled interfaces. Verify that the public interface is connected to the external network and that the private interface is connected to the internal network. Sometimes during the NAT setup, these interfaces are configured opposite from the way they should have been. • TCP/UDP port header translation is not enabled. In the RRAS MMC click the IP Routing\NAT-Basic Firewall object. Then right-click the public NAT-enabled interface and select Properties. Verify that the "Enable NAT on this Interface" checkbox is selected. • IP packet filtering is enabled, blocking interface traffic. In the RRAS console, click the General object. Now right-click one of the LAN interfaces listed and select Properties. Under the General tab, click the Inbound Filters or Outbound Filters buttons (if available) and confirm that no filtering is present on the network interface. If a filter is enabled, remove the filter for the port that is needed by the NAT client. Repeat this process for all NAT-enabled interfaces.

NAT is a very reliable service that normally requires little or no configuration right out of the box. Sometimes when you are having problems with a server that just provides NAT services, it might be easier to disable Remote Access and then reconfigure and enable the service.

Troubleshooting DHCP Relay Agents

DHCP relay agents are needed for relaying DHCP discover packets to other DHCP servers and for supporting RAS clients that require DHCP options. When a DHCP relay agent fails, it can quickly have a significant impact on network clients. This will be noticed pretty quickly, because clients will not be able to access network resources and will likely have an IP address in the 169.254.x.x range (unless alternate IP addressing is configured).

When trying to locate the source of a DHCP relay agent failure, note the problems and solutions listed in Table 12-16.

Table 12-16. DHCP Relay Agent Problems

Problem	Solution
IP packet filtering is preventing the sending or receiving of DHCP traffic.	DHCP requires UDP ports 67 and 68. In the RRAS console, click the General object. Now right-click one of the LAN interfaces listed and select Properties. Under the General tab, click the Inbound Filters or Outbound Filters buttons (if available) and confirm that no filtering is present on the network interface that is blocking ports 67 or 68.
The DHCP server is unreachable.	Right-click the DHCP Relay Agent object in the RRAS MMC and select Properties. Add or modify the correct DHCP server address. If the correct address is entered, then check for network connectivity to the DHCP server using commands such as ping. Also make sure that the DHCP server service is running and that its scope has not run out of valid IP addresses.
A network interface on the network segment of the DHCP clients is not enabled as a DHCP relay agent.	Click the DHCP Relay Agent object in the RRAS MMC. You should now see a list of network interfaces. Right-click each listed interface and verify that its Relay DHCP Packets checkbox is enabled. If the correct network interface is not listed, right-click the DHCP Relay Agent object and select New Interface to add the interface that is connected to the DHCP clients.

Troubleshooting Demand-Dial Routing

Demand-dial routing is a useful method for connecting a central office to a satellite office or for connecting other offices together via an inexpensive telephone connection. This solution is ideal for remote networks that only need to periodically connect with one another to access data. Testing demand-dial routing is a very easy task. From your local network, you should be able to ping an IP address on a remote network, and once the ping is initiated, the router should attempt to dial the remote network. When a failure occurs with demand-dial routing, it can usually be attributed to one of the following causes.

- The router is not dialing the modem on demand.
- Data cannot get beyond the calling or the answering router.

The solutions to overcoming each of these two problem sets are explained in the next two sections.

Router Not Dialing on Demand

Several problems can cause an on-demand router to sit idle while attempts are made to access networks through its remote dial-up interfaces. Since modems are involved in the connections between the two remote routers, never forget about the hardware aspects of modem troubleshooting, as was discussed in Chapter 5. As always, correct driver installation is crucial. Once you have ruled out the modem as a suspect in the troubleshooting mystery, turn to Table 12-17 for possible causes and solutions for resolving the routing problem.

Table 12-17. Demand-Dial Routing Problems

Problem	Solution
The RRAS service is not started.	Open the Windows services MMC and verify the state of the Routing and Remote Access Service. If the service is not running, start the service.
IP routing is disabled on the RAS server.	From the RAS server's Properties dialog box, click the IP tab. Verify that the Enable IP Routing box is selected.
IP packet filtering is preventing the sending or receiving of network traffic.	To check for the presence of packet filters, in the RRAS console, click the General object. Now right-click one of the LAN interfaces listed and select Properties. Under the General tab, click the Inbound Filters or Outbound Filters buttons (if available) and confirm that no filtering is present that is conflicting with the data transmission to the remote network.
LAN/WAN routing is not enabled.	From the RAS server's Properties dialog box, click the General tab. Now select the Router checkbox and the "Local area network (LAN) routing only" or "LAN and demand-dial routing" radio button.
A static route for the remote network is configured incorrectly.	In the RRAS console, click Static Routes. The configured static routes are listed in the right pane of the interface. To edit a static route, right-click the route and select Properties. To add a new route, right-click Static Routes and select New Static Route. In the Static Route dialog box, select the demand-dial interface, and enter the destination network ID and subnet mask.
The demand-dial interface is disabled.	From the Network Connections window, right-click the interface and select Enable.
Dial-out hours are restricting modem use.	In the RRAS console, click Network Interfaces. Now right-click the demand-dial interface and select Dial-out Hours. Adjust the allowable dial-out hours accordingly and click OK.

To configure a default route for a router to route data for all unknown networks to a specific gateway, use the parameters Destination 0.0.0.0, Network mask 0.0.0.0, and then specify the proper gateway in which to route the data.

Data Not Reaching Beyond Calling or Answering Router

When this problem occurs, you should check the previous demand-dial problems listed, and then verify that the static routes configured on each demand-dial router are correct. If a route of one router is wrong, clients at one site can send data to another site but will not receive a reply. You need to verify that routes exist on both routers so that clients at one site and their associated network IDs can see clients at the other, and vice versa.

Troubleshooting RIP

With RIP routers, some problems can arise from mixing RIP1 and RIP2 routers. While RIP2 routers have no trouble receiving routing table updates from RIP1 routers, RIP1 routers listen for broadcasts and thus cannot receive multicast routing tables from RIP2 routers. This causes RIP1 routers to not be in sync with RIP2 routers on the network. The best solution in this scenario is to employ W2K3 RIP2 routers.

While it would be nice if all RIP routers had to worry about was compatibility, that is not the case. Since RIP is a protocol for sharing routing information, when two or more routers are not fully sharing their routing information, it's time to troubleshoot. Table 12-18 lists other RIP router problems and solutions.

Table 12-18. RIP Router Problems

Problem	Solution
A password is not matched on all RIP interfaces.	This causes routers to not exchange information. If the passwords are not the same, the routers will not share information. To change the password for a RIP interface, click the RIP object in the RRAS console, then right-click each routing interface and select Properties. Under the General tab of the interface Properties dialog box, you can configure the RIP authentication password. This is shown in Figure 12-6.
RIP neighbors are incorrectly configured.	Neighbors allow RIP interfaces to unicast new route information to other neighbors. For this to work, you need to ensure that the correct neighbors are specified for a particular RIP router. This is done by right-clicking a RIP router interface and selecting Properties. From the Properties dialog box, click the Neighbors tab. Under the Neighbors tab, add the IP addresses of the RIP routing interface's appropriate neighbors.
Peer filtering is incorrectly configured.	To configure peer filters, right-click the RIP object in the RRAS MMC and select Properties. Under the Security tab, you can specify the IP addresses of other RIP routers that your RIP router will either accept or decline routes from.

Troubleshooting OSPF

Open Shortest Path First is the most efficient routing protocol but is also the most complex. Before implementing OSPF, you should take the time read about and learn this protocol. A great source on OSPF is *OSPF Complete Implementation*, by John T. Moy (Addison-Wesley, 2000). This book is loaded with over 400 pages of detailed information on how to properly plan and deploy routing using OSPF.

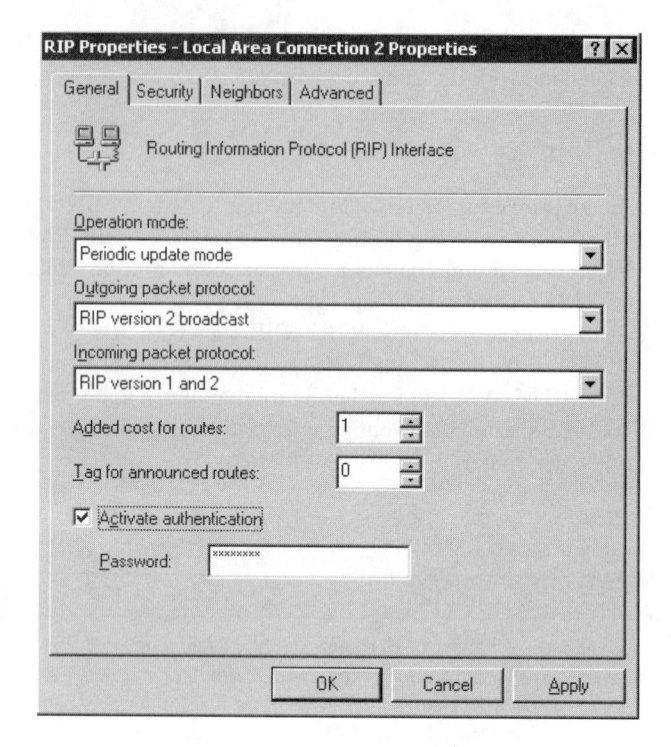

Figure 12-6. Configuring RIP authentication

For those that are already seasoned with OSPF, Table 12-19 provides guidance on common OSPF routing problems that are found on Windows Server 2003 Routing and Remote Access systems.

Table 12-19. OSPF Router Problems

Symptom	Problem/Solution
There is a lack of OSPF routes.	• Summarized routes are not being received. Check that the area border routers (ABRs) have the proper destination and subnet mask pairs that summarize the area's routes.
	• External routes are not being received from the autonomous system boundary router (ASBR). Check to see that there is not too restrictive route filtering implemented on the router. This is configured under the External Routing tab of the OSPF protocol properties.
	• All ABRs are not connected to the network backbone. All ABRs must be physically connected to the backbone or logically connected via a virtual link. No backdoor routers should exist.

Table 12-19. OSPF Router Problems, continued

Symptom	Problem/Solution
OSPF adjacency is not forming.	• OSPF is not enabled on the routing interface. • Neighboring routers have mismatched hello or dead intervals. • There is a lack of IP connectivity to a neighboring router. • There is a mismatched OSPF configuration. Try using OSPF logging to log errors and warnings. • There are mismatched authentication or password settings.
A virtual link is not forming.	• The retransmit interval is too short (this may be a problem in large networks that incur substantial round-trip delays). • There is an incorrect router ID of a virtual link neighbor. • Virtual link neighbors have incorrect transit area IDs. • Check for a mismatched password configuration, dead interval, or hello interval.

Troubleshooting VPN Access

In this section, we are going to wrap up Microsoft Routing and Remote Access troubleshooting with a look at virtual private network connection problems. Windows VPNs can be employed in two different ways.

- *Remote access VPNs*—Remote client computers connect to a single VPN server via the Internet.
- *Router-to-router VPNs*—Two VPN servers provide a secure tunnel through the Internet between two sites.

When most people think about a VPN, they consider the traditional VPN that allows users to securely access company resources from anywhere in the world. With the drop in the cost of broadband Internet connections, another VPN configuration has been gaining momentum. The "other" way to use a VPN is to create an encrypted tunnel between two remote routers. This way, data is secured through the public network but left unsecured over the corporate private network. This approach has advantages in that there is no overhead for the clients and servers on the networks in both remote sites. Instead, all of the encryption and decryption is performed by the two VPN routers. Since the configurations of the two VPN concepts are unique to themselves, the approach to troubleshooting each configuration is unique as well. In the next two sections, troubleshooting problems and solutions for each VPN configuration type are examined.

> Windows Server 2003 and Windows Server 2003 Enterprise Edition can accept up to 1,000 simultaneous VPN connections, while Windows Server 2003 Web Edition is only equipped to handle a single VPN connection at a time.

Troubleshooting Remote Access VPNs

Remote access VPNs are the most common VPN type. This VPN provides an easy method for mobile users and telecommuters to connect to corporate resources from anywhere in the world. With Windows operating systems, you can quickly set up a VPN connection to a Windows server running RRAS. From Network and Dial-up Connections, you just select the option to make a new connection, and then simply follow the prompts. All that is required for the connection is the name or IP address of the VPN server as well as a logon and password. In order to access corporate resources through a VPN, you first need to connect to and then get through a VPN server. Problems associated with these two aspects of a VPN connection are looked at next.

Server Connection Problems

The first part of the VPN connection process involves connecting to and logging on to a VPN server. Table 12-20 breaks down the common hurdles that may get in your way with VPN server connections.

Table 12-20. VPN Server Connection Problems

Problem	Solution
The RRAS service is not started.	Open the Windows services MMC and verify the state of the Routing and Remote Access Service. If the service is not running, start the service.
IP routing is disabled on the RAS server.	From the RAS server's Properties dialog box, click the IP tab. Verify that the Enable IP Routing box is selected.
IP packet filtering is preventing the sending or receiving of network traffic.	To check for the presence of packet filters, in the RRAS console, click the General object. Now right-click one of the LAN interfaces listed and select Properties. Under the General tab, click the Inbound Filters or Outbound Filters buttons (if available) and confirm that no filtering is present that is conflicting with the data transmission to the remote network.
There is an invalid user account or password for the remote access user.	Verify that the remote user is using an account that has Dial-in permission allowed either via a Remote Access Policy or in the user's account properties.
The VPN protocol being used by the client may not be enabled on the VPN server.	The VPN client may be configured to use PPTP, and the VPN server may be set to only allow L2TP connections.

Table 12-20. VPN Server Connection Problems, continued

Problem	Solution
RAS is not enabled on the RAS server.	In the RRAS MMC, right-click the RAS server object, select Properties, and then click the General tab. Verify that the Remote Access Server box is checked.
PPTP and/or L2TP ports are not enabled for inbound VPN connections, or there are no available ports.	Enable the required ports by right-clicking the Ports object and selecting Properties. Then select the appropriate VPN port type (PPTP or LT2P) and click the Configure button (see Figure 12-7) to enable and select a number of allowable ports for the VPN connection.
There are conflicting settings between the RRAS server and the Remote Access Policy profile.	If a client connects with an authentication protocol allowed by the profile but disallowed by the server, the connection will be dropped. Change the profile settings to ensure that it meets the minimum security parameters as the VPN server.

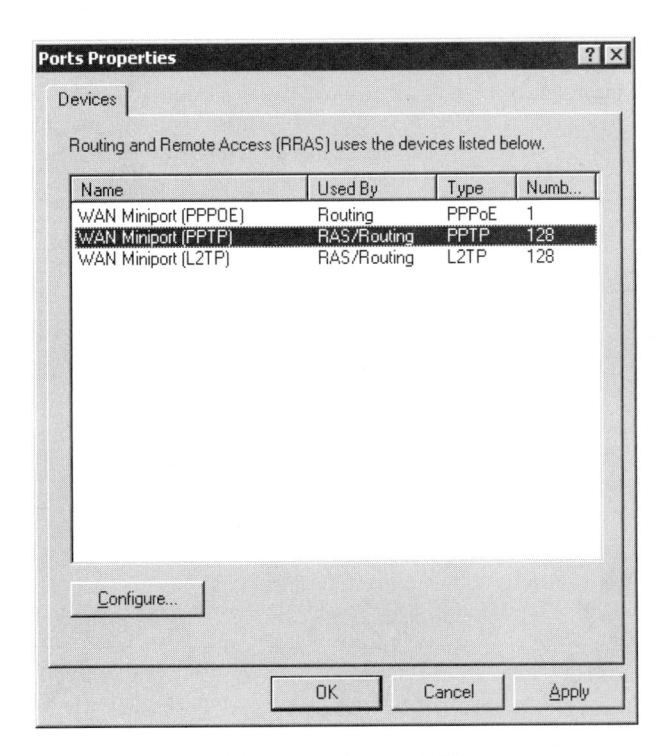

Figure 12-7. Configuring VPN ports

Resource Access Problems

Once connected to the VPN server, the VPN client should be able to access network resources. If not, check for one of the problems described in Table 12-21.

Table 12-21. VPN Resource Access Problems

Problem	Solution
Packet filters on the RRAS server are blocking RAS client traffic.	• Remove filters for the client network on the RRAS server. • The local Hosts file is improperly configured.
IP routing is disabled on the RAS server.	From the RAS server's Properties dialog box, click the IP tab. Verify that the Enable IP Routing box is selected.
RAS clients are not receiving any scope options (DNS server, gateway, and so on) from the RAS server.	Install the DHCP Relay Agent service on the internal network interface of the RAS server.
RAS clients are getting the wrong or no DNS or gateway information from the RAS server using a static pool of addresses.	When a RAS server uses its own static pool of addresses to provide IP addresses for clients, it gives the clients its own DNS and gateway addresses to use as well. If these addresses are improperly configured on the RAS server, the RAS clients will have problems accessing network resources.

Troubleshooting Router-to-Router VPNs

Router-to-router connections are often easier to set up and manage than remote access VPNs. This is mainly because the operating system and configurations for each server can easily be made identical. With remote clients, the VPN server has to be able to work with a variety of operating systems as well as possible tunneling and authentication protocols. Table 12-22 lists the most common problems with router-to-router VPN configurations.

Table 12-22. Router-to-Router VPN Connection Problems

Problem	Solution
The RRAS service is not started.	Open the Windows services MMC and verify the state of the Routing and Remote Access Service. If the service is not running, start the service.
IP routing is disabled on the RAS server.	From the RAS server's Properties dialog box, click the IP tab. Verify that the Enable IP Routing box is selected.

Table 12-22. Router-to-Router VPN Connection Problems, continued

Problem	Solution
IP packet filtering is preventing the sending or receiving of network traffic.	To check for the presence of packet filters, in the RRAS console, click the General object. Now right-click one of the LAN interfaces listed and select Properties. Under the General tab, click the Inbound Filters or Outbound Filters buttons (if available) and confirm that no filtering is present that is conflicting with the data transmission to the remote network.
There is an invalid user account or password for the remote access user.	Verify that the remote user is using an account that has Dial-in permission allowed either via a Remote Access Policy or in the user's account properties.
PPTP and/or L2TP ports are not enabled for inbound and outbound VPN connections, or there are no available ports.	Enable the required ports by right-clicking the Ports object and selecting Properties. Then select the appropriate VPN port type (PPTP or LT2P) and click the Configure button (see Figure 12-7) to enable and select a number of allowable ports for the VPN connection.

Summary

This chapter provided you with plenty of possible solutions for navigating through and solving Routing and Remote Access Service troubles. Most problems with this service occur when the RRAS server is initially configured. Otherwise, most problems that you will find are with client access or an RRAS server running out of free ports and thus not accepting any new connections. The configuration problems discussed in this chapter are designed to get you over the hump for new implementations of what many view as the toughest Windows service to master.

In this book's final chapter, we examine the problems that arise in the heart of a Windows infrastructure: Active Directory.

13

Active Directory

When Windows 2000 was first introduced, many administrators ran into problems with their Active Directory (AD) infrastructure. Some of these problems were related to configuration mistakes, while others were the result of system failures. Now with Windows Server 2003, Active Directory has aged and matured, and many administrators have been able to tune this service so that it provides reliable directory services for their enterprise.

Since the Active Directory represents the heart of your organization's security, any failures of the Active Directory often require an immediate response and a fast resolution. In this final chapter, we examine how to identify and repair problems with the Active Directory so that you can quickly repair any problems that may arise. Before looking at how to repair each of the specific components of the Active Directory, we begin with a brief overview of Active Directory essentials and then look at the new features of Active Directory. Following the introductory topics, we move toward examining the many troubleshooting tools available for finding Active Directory problems and wrap up with a look at troubleshooting specific problems with the directory service.

Since Active Directory has a hierarchical architecture, a large part of problem solving requires knowing where, or at what level of the architecture, to look. With this in mind, let's begin by reviewing the core components of the Active Directory architecture.

AD Architectural Overview

Before we discuss troubleshooting Active Directory problems, let's start with the basics. In this section, we will look at the core components of the Active Directory service, which include

- Forests
- Domains
- Organizational units

- Sites
- Domain controllers
- Group policy objects

With so many parts to the Active Directory puzzle, it is important to understand their interrelationships. Let's begin with forests and domains.

> For a more in-depth look at Active Directory architecture, pick up a copy of *Inside Active Directory*, by Sakari Kouti and Mika Seitsonen (Addison-Wesley, 2001).

Forests and Domains

An Active Directory forest defines a collection of one or more domains that share a common schema, configuration, and global catalog. All domains also share two-way transitive trust relationships. Before going any further, let's pause for a moment and look at the key terms in the previous explanation of forest.

- *Domain*—Domains provide a way to secure and organize objects, such as users and computers that are part of the same namespace. For example, Microsoft.com and Amazon.com are domains. Computers in each domain share the common configuration of that domain and may be subject to policies and restrictions set forth by the domain administrators. The use of domains allows you to streamline security throughout your enterprise.

- *Schema*—The Active Directory schema is common to all domains in a forest. The schema is the configuration information that governs the structure and content of the directory.

- *Configuration*—Configuration defines the logical structure of a forest, such as the number and configuration of sites in the forest.

- *Global catalog*—Think of the global catalog as the yellow pages for a forest. It contains information about all objects in the forest and, in particular, where to find them. Global catalogs also contain membership information for universal groups.

- *Trusts*—Trusts provide a way to allow different domains to work together. Without trusts, domains operate as completely separate entities, meaning that users in domain A would not have access to resources in domain B. If a trust relationship is established between the domains so that domain B trusts domain A, then domain A's users can access domain B's resources, provided that they have the proper permissions.

With trusts, there are three general types.

- *Transitive*—Transitive trusts are automatically created trusts between all domains in the same forest. They allow users in any domain to potentially have access to resources in any other domain in the forest, provided that the users have the appropriate permissions.
- *Shortcut*—Shortcut trusts are trust relationships between domains in the same forest that already have transitive trust relationships established. Shortcut trusts provide faster authentication and validation of resource access between nonadjacent domains in the same forest.
- *External*—External trusts allow domains in different forests to share resources. These trusts are not transitive, meaning that they only apply to the domains for which they were explicitly created.

With these basic terms out of the way, let's look at a sample forest. Figure 13-1 shows a single forest that contains two domain trees.

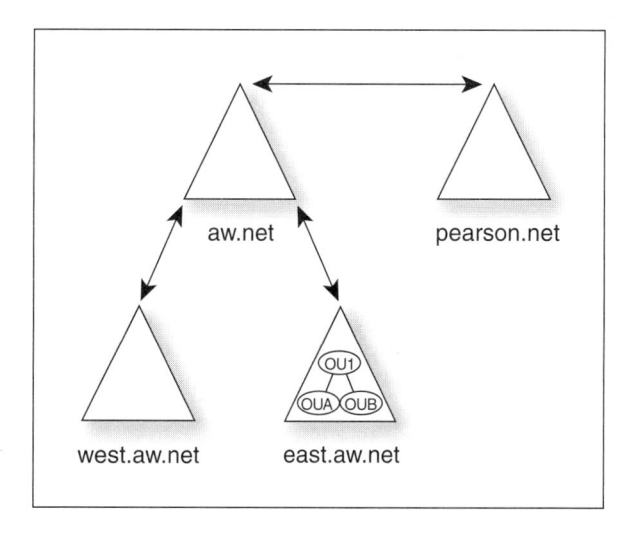

Figure 13-1. Active Directory forest

In the illustration, there are four domains: aw.net, west.aw.net, east.aw.net, and pearson.net. The domains aw.net, west.aw.net, and east.aw.net are all in the same domain tree because they share the same namespace (aw.net). The pearson.net domain is in a different domain tree, since it is not part of the aw.net namespace. Notice that in the east.aw.net domain, there are OUs displayed. OUs are organizational units, which we will get to shortly. The arrows in the illustrations represent the transitive trust relationships that are automatically created when the domains are initially set up in the forest. Note that the aw.net child domains (east and west) do not have arrows that directly connect to pearson.net. In spite of this, they still trust pearson.net. The reason for this trust is that each aw.net child domain trusts aw.net. Since aw.net trusts pearson.net, aw.net's children automatically trust pearson.net too. With this in mind, you can consider Active Directory domains to behave just like young children. They blindly trust everything that their parent says. If the parent says another domain is trustworthy, then so it is. The difference between child domains and children, however, is that child domains will never disagree with or question their parents.

Now that we have the core technologies under our belt, let's go a little further and look at some of the other specific components that make up an Active Directory forest.

Organizational Units

Organizational units (OUs) are logical containers that are commonly used to define departments or locations. Microsoft strongly recommends that Active Directory implementations use as few forests and domains as possible. When you need to define an administrative structure for a department or a company location, you can use OUs instead of domains. The only time to create additional domains should be if security requirements, such as password settings, differ from one region to another, or if administrators in a region insist on complete control of their resources.

With organizational units, you can quickly group users and computers together to streamline administration. You can even give particular users a level of control over the objects in the OU. For example, in the Support OU, you could give the Support Manager user account the right to create and delete user accounts and to reset user passwords. This is done with the Delegation of Control Wizard. By giving a user just the administrative duties that are needed, you can extend administrative duties throughout an enterprise while not compromising security.

As with domains, OUs can also have child OUs. However, OUs differ from domains in that OUs do not share a common namespace. For example, you could have a Marketing OU, with East and West as child OUs. Aside from providing delegation of administrative privileges and logical organization of objects by department or location, configuring OUs allows you to tailor the deployment of group policy objects to particular departments or groupings of users.

Sites

Sites are logical entities in the Active Directory that are often designed to model an organization's physical locations. Creating multiple sites allows you to define the times that replication between domain controllers (covered shortly) can run as well as narrow the list of domain controllers that will validate a user's logon. When a single domain spans multiple physical locations, any domain controller in the domain could validate a user's logon request. However, with sites, when a user logs on, the user's system connects to a domain controller that resides in its site to process the logon request. This provides better logon performance.

Since sites define replication boundaries, you can schedule times when replication can occur over WAN connections between two business locations, for example. Without the creation and organization of sites, replication between all domain controllers would be continual and could significantly impact WAN network performance. Domains in the same site have a maximum replication latency of 15 minutes, meaning that any change made on any domain controller will be propagated to all other domain controllers within the domain in the site within 15 minutes.

With sites, it was mentioned that computers would know which domain controller to contact in order to process a user's logon. The way that computers can determine which site they are in, and thus know which domain controller to contact, is with the use of subnets. Subnets are used to identify the particular network IDs that exist at each site. So if the East site had the subnets 10.0.0.0/16 and 10.1.0.0/16, a computer with an IP address of 10.0.87.201 (on the 10.0 network) would know that it is in the East site and would then attempt to contact a domain controller in the site. We will be looking at sites again later in this chapter when we examine the techniques for troubleshooting Active Directory replication.

Domain Controllers

Domain controllers are the servers that host the Active Directory. Every domain controller has its own writable copy of the Active Directory database. Domain controllers act as the central security component of a domain. All security and account validation is performed by a domain controller. Every domain must have at least one domain controller, and it is recommended that for fault tolerance every domain have at least two domain controllers. With Windows NT, only a single domain controller was writable, meaning that you could only create and manage users, for example, when you were connected to the domain controller that was designated as the primary domain controller (PDC). Beginning with Windows 2000, the architecture of domain controllers was changed so that you can perform updates on any domain controller, and those updates will replicate to all other domain controllers in the domain.

While all domain controllers are writable, they are not all the same. In Active Directory domains and forests, there are certain jobs that are only performed by specific domain controllers. Domain controllers that have these additional duties are known as operations masters. Some Microsoft references still refer to these systems as Flexible Single-Master Operations (FSMOs). Many believe that the FSMO designation has been able to last primarily due to the fact FSMO is just a fun acronym to pronounce.

Anyway, there are five operations master roles. By default all five roles are given to the first domain controller installed in an Active Directory forest. Three of the operations master roles are domain-wide and by default are assigned to the first domain controller installed in any new domain. Using the Active Directory tools, which are explained shortly, you can move an operations master role from one domain controller to another or have a domain controller seize a particular role.

These are the two forest-wide operations master roles.

- *Domain naming master*—This operations master must be contacted whenever changes are made involving domain hierarchy naming in a forest. The domain naming master's job is to ensure that all domain names are unique within the forest. This FSMO must be available during any new domain creation, removal of a domain, or renaming of a domain.

- *Schema master*—The schema master FSMO is the only domain controller in a forest through which schema changes can be made. Once the changes are made, those changes are replicated to all other domain controllers in the forest. One example of needing schema modifications is the installation of Microsoft Exchange server, which makes several alterations to the schema to allow administrators to manage user accounts and e-mail mailboxes together.

Each of the forest-wide roles can only exist on one domain controller in the forest. So you could have one domain controller that acts as the domain naming master and one that acts as the schema master, or you could have both roles reside on a single domain controller, which is the default.

Each domain in the forest has a domain controller that hosts each of the three domain-wide FSMOs.

- *RID master*—The RID master is responsible for managing Relative ID (RID) assignments. RIDS are the unique portion of a Security ID (SID), which is used to define a security principal (user, computer, group, and so on) in a domain. One of the RID master's biggest responsibilities is the removal of an object from one domain and placement in another domain when the object is being moved.

- *Infrastructure master*—The infrastructure master's job is to ensure the synchronization of group memberships. When changes occur to group memberships, the infrastructure master notifies all other domain controllers of the changes.

- *PDC emulator*—This FSMO emulates an NT 4 PDC to support replication to NT 4 backup domain controllers (BDCs) in a domain. The other job of the PDC emulator is to act as a central administration point for changes to user passwords and user lockout policies.

The word "policies" has been used quite frequently in this section in order to reference group policy objects (GPOs). GPOs are one of the strengths of Active Directory administration and are examined next.

Group Policy Objects

Group policy objects provide a means to configure standard settings for users and computers in a site, domain, or organizational unit. With a GPO, you can deploy software to users, restrict desktop settings, and even configure specific Internet Explorer parameters, for example. Once a policy is configured with the desired settings, you can then link the policy to a container in the Active Directory, such as a domain or an OU. Any user or computer objects that reside in the container in which a policy is applied have the potential of getting the group policy object's settings. In order to have a GPO's settings applied, an AD object must meet the following criteria.

- The object must reside within the container, or be in a child container of the container, in which the policy was applied.
- The user must have, or be a member of a group that has, both Allow Read and Allow Apply Group Policy permissions for the GPO.
- The user must not have, or not be a member of a group that has, Deny Read or Deny Apply Group Policy permissions for the GPO.

If all conditions are met, the user or computer will have the GPO applied. Every GPO has two portions: a user portion and a computer portion. The computer portion of a GPO is applied to a computer at startup, and the user portion of a GPO is applied to a user when he or she logs on. We will be getting into much more detail with GPOs and GPO troubleshooting later in this chapter in the Troubleshooting Group Policy Objects section.

Active Directory Functional Levels

Active Directory functional levels were originally introduced with Windows 2000 and have been expanded with Windows Server 2003. The types of domain controllers that exist in a particular domain determine the type of functional level that the domain controllers in the domain can operate at. With Windows 2000 Active Directory, there were only two types of functional levels: native mode and mixed mode. Native mode domains were those that contained only Windows 2000 domain controllers, while mixed mode domains could contain both Windows 2000 and Windows NT domain controllers. The reason that the two different modes existed was for domain controller compatibility. Windows NT domain controllers were not capable of supporting some of Windows 2000's advanced features, such as universal groups, and allocating callback numbers for specific remote access users. To take advantage of these features, a domain had to be in native mode and thus have only Windows 2000 domain controllers.

Windows Server 2003 is backward compatible all the way to Windows NT. Since this latest OS traverses additional operating system generations, it offers four functional levels. Windows Server 2003 functional levels operate similarly to Windows 2000, with the highest level allowing you to take advantage of the newest features. The four available Windows Server 2003 functional levels are as follows:

- *Windows 2000 mixed (default)*—Supports Windows NT/2000/2003 domain controllers
- *Windows 2000 native*—Supports Windows 2000/2003 domain controllers
- *Windows Server 2003 interim*—Supports Windows NT/2003 domain controllers
- *Windows Server 2003*—Supports Windows Server 2003 domain controllers only

You should only adjust the domain controller functional level to the lowest common denominator. Once you raise the functional level, unsupported domain controller types (Windows NT or Windows 2000) cannot be introduced into the domain. Functional levels can be set at the domain level and at the forest level, so you can have two domains at different functional levels residing in the same forest. The impact of the two functional level types on forest and domain configurations is discussed in the next two sections.

Domain Functional Levels

Domain functional levels affect the type of administrative tasks that you can perform at the domain level. The differences between Windows 2000 mixed, Windows 2000 native, and Windows Server 2003 functional levels are described in Table 13-1.

Table 13-1. Domain Functional Level Comparison

Active Directory Feature	Windows 2000 Mixed	Windows 2000 Native	Windows Server 2003
Converting group types	No	Yes	Yes
Nesting groups	Distribution groups only	Distribution and security groups	Distribution and security groups
Universal groups	Distribution groups only	Distribution and security groups	Distribution and security groups
SID history	No	Yes	Yes
Renaming domains	No	No	Yes
Updating logon timestamps	No	No	Yes
User password for InetOrgPerson object	No	No	Yes

In case you are unsure of any of the features listed in Table 13-1, here is a quick description:

- *Converting group types*—Allows you to convert one group type to another, such as convert a domain local group to a global group

- *Nesting groups*—Allows groups to have other groups as members

- *Universal groups*—A user group type whose membership can contain users and groups from any domain in the forest

- *SID history*—Allows you to migrate security principals (users, computers) from one domain to another

- *Renaming domains*—Allows you to change the name of a domain without having to demote all of its domain controllers

- *Updating logon timestamps*—Allows you to track the last logon time of a user or computer account for security auditing purposes

- *User password for InetOrgPerson object*—Provides an efficient means to migrate account information from one LDAP directory, such as Novell's NDS, to Windows Server 2003 Active Directory

As you can see, there are several advantages to configuring a domain's functional level to Windows Server 2003, such as the logon timestamp and the ability to rename a domain. Now let's look at the features of the forest functional levels.

Forest Functional Levels

Several forest-wide improvements were made to the Windows Server 2003 directory service that can substantially impact replication performance. The specific improvements and the differences between the Windows 2000 (the default functional level) and Windows Server 2003 forest functional levels are described in Table 13-2.

Table 13-2. Forest Functional Level Comparison

Active Directory Feature	Windows 2000	Windows Server 2003
Improved AD replication	No	Yes
Improved global catalog replication	Yes, if running on a Windows Server 2003 system. This is not supported on Windows 2000 systems.	Yes
Linked value replication	No	Yes
Forest trusts	No	Yes

Here is a quick description of the AD features that are affected by forest functional levels.

- *Improved AD replication*—Replication has been improved to operate much more efficiently.

- *Improved global catalog replication*—Replication of the global catalog is now faster (discussed in more detail in the next section).

- *Linked value replication*—Values added to a multivalue attribute can be replicated separately, improving replication efficiency.

- *Forest trusts*—Seamless user access to resources across forests has been provided (discussed in more detail in the next section).

Now that we have covered the fundamentals of Active Directory, let's look at the new features that have arrived with Windows Server 2003.

What's New?

As the second-generation Active Directory–based operating system, Windows Server 2003's Active Directory service capitalized on what Microsoft learned with Windows 2000. In Windows Server 2003, you will find that the directory service is much more manageable, efficient, and most of all troubleshooting friendly. Several Active Directory troubleshooting tools now come standard with the operating system, which makes finding and resolving AD problems significantly easier. Here are the major AD improvements with the Windows Server 2003 OS.

- *Domain rename*—You can now rename a domain without having to demote any domain controllers. Previously, to rename a domain you had to create a new domain from scratch and migrate accounts from the old domain to the new domain. Now, renaming a domain is a simple task that is performed using the `rendom.exe` command line tool.

- *Domain controller rename*—You can now rename domain controllers without having to demote them. This can be accomplished by using the `netdom` command line tool.

- *Drag-and-drop*—You can now use drag-and-drop to move Active Directory objects, such as users or computers, from one container to another.

- *Multiple object select*—You can now use the Shift or Ctrl keys to select multiple objects, such as users or groups, and simultaneously modify their properties.

- *Forest trusts*—You can quickly create two-way transitive trust relationships between two separate forests.

- *Forest restructuring*—You can move existing domains to other locations in the forest.

- *Better global catalog replication*—With Windows 2000, changes to the global catalog caused a full replication of it throughout all global catalog servers in the forest. With Windows Server 2003, only attributes that are added to a global catalog are replicated to other global catalog servers.

As you can see, there is quite a bit to get excited about. At the beginning of this section, it was mentioned that many Active Directory tools have been improved, and many new tools added. That's what we'll look at next.

AD Troubleshooting Tools

Because of Active Directory's logical architecture, troubleshooting it can be a relatively straightforward process. With the right tools, you will be able to identify problems in minutes, as opposed to hours. In this section, we will look at the command line and GUI tools that are available for Active Directory troubleshooting. Whether you are trying to troubleshoot group policies or replication, or just cannot figure out exactly what is the problem with a domain controller, this section has the tool for you.

acldiag (ST)

The `acldiag` tool allows you to check the access control list entries (ACEs) for objects in the Active Directory, and it can detect and repair problems encountered when inconsistent modifications are made to ACEs. For example, suppose that you use the Delegation of Control Wizard to allow specific users in departmental OUs to create users in their OUs and to reset user passwords. If another administrator makes modifications to the advanced permissions of an OU, or of a parent OU, the settings provided by the Delegation Template applied by the Delegation of Control Wizard may not match. This could cause users that once were able to create users, to no longer have that ability. Fortunately for you, Microsoft provides `acldiag` to quickly repair such problems.

The syntax for `acldiag` is:

```
acldiag <DN> [/schema] [/chkdeleg] [/geteffective:<user|group|*>
[/fixdeleg] [/skip] [/tdo]
```

The command options are described in Table 13-3.

Table 13-3. acldiag Command Options

Option	Use
DN	The Distinguished Name (DN) is a required parameter and identifies the command's target object. Here is an example of a DN: cn=jpeterman,ou=support,dc=sales,dc=aw,dc=com.
/schema	This parameter causes the schema to be checked to see if the target object's ACL includes the ACEs that are the schema defaults. The result of the check is displayed in the command output.
/chkdeleg	This switch causes the command to perform delegation diagnostics, which reports on whether the object includes ACEs that are in the Delegation Template (created by the Delegation of Control Wizard). If the command reports a status of Misconfigured, that means that at least one permission in the ACL does not match what is listed in the Delegation Template.
/geteffective:<user | group | *>	Displays effective permissions to the target object that are held by a specific user or group. If you use the * wildcard, the effective permissions of all users and groups are displayed.
/fixdeleg	Causes acldiag to reapply the Delegation Template to the object's ACT. This eliminates any special permissions assigned to the object and restores any incomplete delegations. Instead of automatically fixing misconfigured delegations, the command prompts you to decide if you want to repair each problem it detects.
/skip	Causes the command output to not display the ACEs that are contained in the object's ACL.
/tdo	Causes the output to be displayed in tab-delimited format, which is useful for exporting the output to a spreadsheet or database.

Here is a sample of using this command after an administrator accidentally modified the advanced permissions of an OU. The `acldiag` command is run to restore the advanced permissions to match what was originally granted by the Delegation Template.

```
C:\>acldiag OU=support,DC=unreliable,DC=net /skip /chkdeleg /fixdeleg

Security Diagnosis for OU=support,DC=unreliable,DC=net

Delegation Template Diagnosis:
 Create, delete, and manage user accounts allowed to
mkelly@unreliable.net

        Status: OK
        Applies on this object: YES
        Inherited from parent: NO
```

```
    Reset user passwords and force password change at next logon allowed
to mkelly@unreliable.net

            Status: OK
            Applies on this object: YES
            Inherited from parent: NO

    Read all user information
            Status: NOT PRESENT

    Create, delete and manage groups allowed to mkelly@unreliable.net
            Status: MISCONFIGURED
            Applies on this object: YES
            Inherited from parent: NO

            Do you want to fix this delegation? (y/n) y

    Modify the membership of a group

            Status: NOT PRESENT

    Manage Group Policy links

            Status: NOT PRESENT

    Generate Resultant Set of Policy (Planning)

            Status: NOT PRESENT

    Generate Resultant Set of Policy (Logging)

            Status: NOT PRESENT

    Create, delete, and manage inetOrgPerson accounts

            Status: NOT PRESENT

    Reset inetOrgPerson passwords and force password change at next logon

            Status: NOT PRESENT

    Read all inetOrgPerson information

            Status: NOT PRESENT

C:\>
```

When the command was executed, it found a misconfiguration in the "Create, delete, and manage user groups" delegation. Since the /fixdeleg switch was used with the command, the command prompted the user to decide if she wanted to repair the delegation. As you can see, this command is very useful when you are troubleshooting user access problems after users were previously delegated control by using the Delegation of Control Wizard.

Active Directory MMCs

With Windows Server 2003, you have four very useful GUI tools for troubleshooting and repairing Active Directory faults:

- Active Directory Users and Computers
- Active Directory Domains and Trusts
- Active Directory Sites and Services
- Active Directory Schema

Each tool has its own purpose for troubleshooting and AD management. When you need to repair the Active Directory, for example, it is helpful to understand which tool will do the trick.

Active Directory Users and Computers

The Active Directory Users and Computers MMC snap-in is the most commonly used of all Active Directory MMCs. The tool allows you to check and configure objects in the Active Directory. Among the objects that you can configure and manage are

- Users and groups
- Organizational units
- Group policy objects
- Published folders and printers
- The transfer of domain-wide FSMO roles (RID master, infrastructure master, PDC emulator)
- Raising the domain functional level

The Active Directory Users and Computers MMC snap-in is shown in Figure 13-2.

This tool can be loaded into a custom MMC console, or you can access it from the Administrative Tools menu. Some administrators prefer to make a single MMC console that contains each of the Active Directory management snap-ins. This way, they can perform all Active Directory maintenance operations from a single window.

Most of the changes that you can make with this tool will be to edit an object's settings, which can be done by right-clicking an object and then selecting Properties from the power menu. You can transfer domain FSMOs from the power menu at the domain level, and if you right-click the Active Directory Users and Computers object, you can select to connect to and manage a different domain.

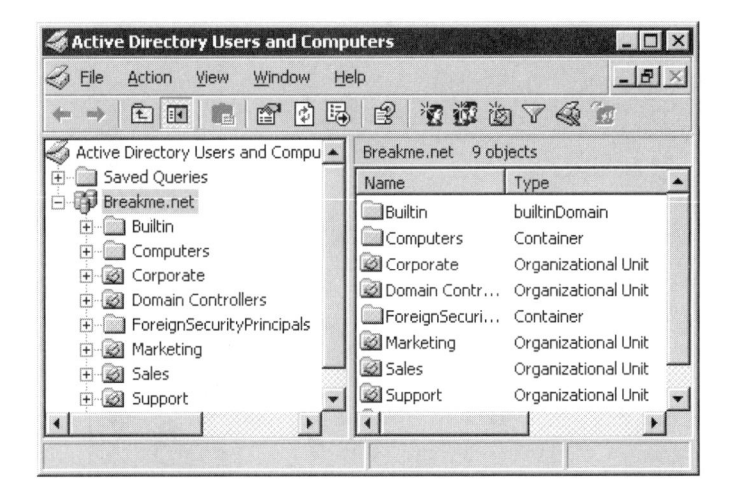

Figure 13-2. Active Users and Computers MMC

Many administrators use Active Directory Users and Computers to modify a particular object property, only to find that they cannot locate the property value, such as when a particular tab is missing from a user account's Properties dialog box. In order to see all available settings, change the Active Directory Users and Computers view to Advanced by clicking the View menu and selecting Advanced Features.

Active Directory Domains and Trusts

When users in one domain in a forest cannot access resources in another domain in a different forest, it may be because the trust relationships between the domains are not configured properly. You can configure and check the status of trust relationships by using the Active Directory Domains and Trusts MMC snap-in. This tool can also be accessed in the Administrative Tools folder. Most often when using this tool, administrators right-click a particular domain object shown and select Properties. As shown in Figure 13-3, from here you can verify the status of trust relationships.

In the example in Figure 13-3, a two-way trust exists between the breakme.net domain and the unreliable.net domain. For breakme.net to allow unreliable.net users access to its resources, you would first configure an outgoing trust at the top of the window for the unreliable.net domain. This means that breakme now trusts unreliable. An administrator in the unreliable domain can complete the trust relationship by then configuring an incoming trust for breakme.net. Once the trusts are verified, the trust process is complete, and administrators in each domain can assign access to resources for users in the trusted domain. Using this tool also allows you to transfer the domain naming master FSMO role and to change the forest functionality level.

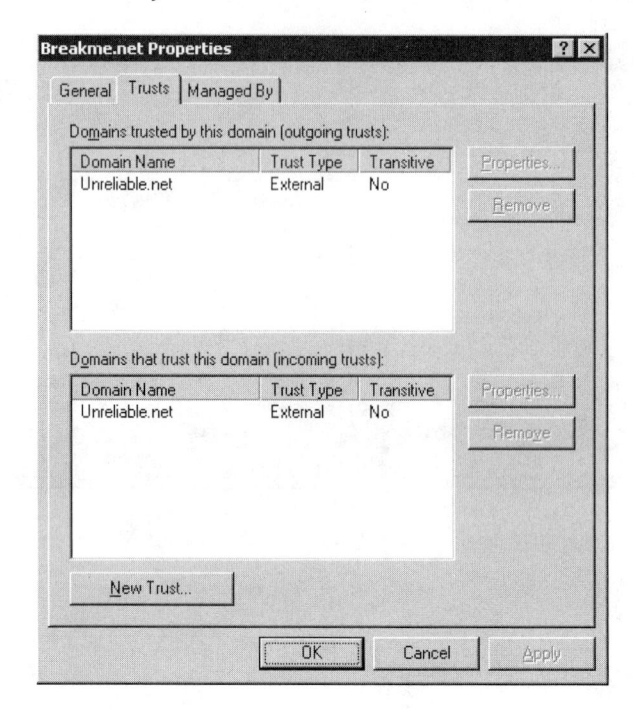

Figure 13-3. Verifying trusts by checking domain properties in the Active Directory Domains and Trusts MMC

Active Directory Sites and Services

The Active Directory Sites and Services MMC snap-in allows you to configure and manage the location of domain controllers and their relationship to Active Directory sites. You can also manage and check the configuration of site links, which can be used to limit the replication time between sites. Another object to check with this tool is subnets. When you configure subnets, Windows clients can try to connect to a domain controller on their same network and thus not attempt to contact remote domain controllers across a WAN link unless absolutely necessary. This tool is shown in Figure 13-4.

When you expand the Inter-Site Transports folder, you can check and configure site links. The sites that are listed in this diagram are NYC, LA, and Mexico. If you expand each site, you will see replication connection objects listed for the site. You can force replication to particular domain controllers within a site by right-clicking a connection object and selecting the Replicate Now option. This is very useful if you have just made a change on a particular domain controller and you want the change applied to other domain controllers immediately.

Active Directory Schema

The Active Directory Schema MMC snap-in is the least often used Active Directory management tool. In fact, use of this tool is disabled by default, and it is not listed in the Administrative Tools folder. The reason for not initially showing access to this tool is to

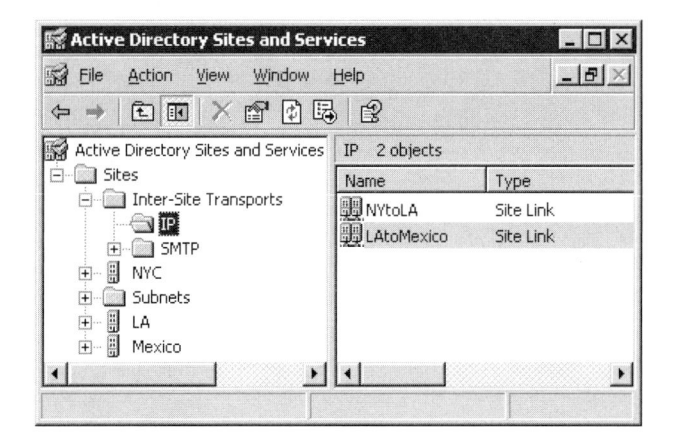

Figure 13-4. Active Directory Sites and Services MMC

prevent curious administrators from deciding to explore and in turn make changes to the schema. Since the schema is shared by all domain controllers in a forest, making an errant change that corrupts the schema could have devastating consequences that may force you to restore your domain from backup. This tool should only be used if absolutely necessary. For example, if you wish to allow restores of Active Directory objects older than 60 days, you can modify the Active Directory schema to change the value of the Active Directory Tombstone Lifetime. This tool is also used to transfer the schema master FSMO.

In order to use the Active Directory Schema MMC, you must first register it with the OS. To do this, follow these steps.

1. Click Start > Run, type `regsvr32 schmmgmt.dll`, and press Enter.

2. When prompted that the registration succeeded, click OK.

Once the tool has been registered, follow these steps to add the Active Directory Schema MMC snap-in to a MMC console:

1. Click Start > Run, type `mmc`, and press Enter.

2. Click the File menu and select Add/Remove Snap-in.

3. In the Add/Remove Snap-in dialog box, click the Add button.

4. Now select the Active Directory Schema snap-in and click Add.

5. Click Close to close the Add Standalone Snap-in dialog box.

6. Click OK to close the Add/Remove Snap-in dialog box.

7. You should now see the snap-in displayed in the console.

This tool is shown in Figure 13-5. Again, only use this tool when you have a specific problem to solve and you are given detailed instructions on how to perform a particular

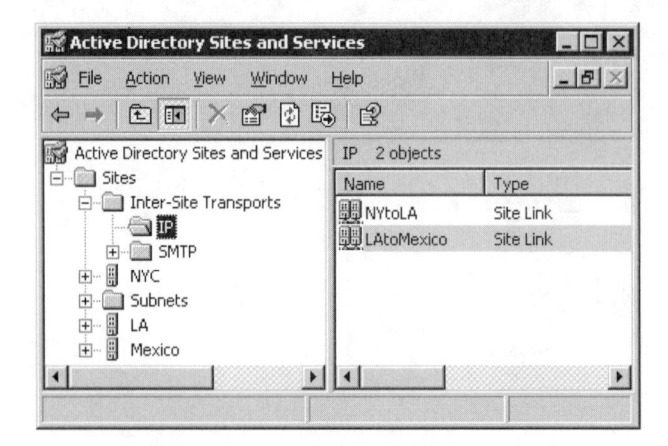

Figure 13-5. Active Directory Schema MMC

schema modification. Performing schema modifications can seriously disrupt or even corrupt the Active Directory service.

dcdiag (ST)

The `dcdiag` tool performs over 20 tests on your Active Directory infrastructure. Some tests provide diagnostic information on a particular domain controller, while others detail your forest-wide replication configuration. The specific tests performed by this tool are described in Table 13-4.

Table 13-4. dcdiag Tests

Test	Description
`Advertising`	Verifies that each domain controller is properly advertising itself and its operations master roles. This test will fail if the NetLogon service is not running.
`CheckSDRefDom`	Verifies that all application directory partitions possess the correct security descriptor reference domains.
`Connectivity`	Checks the DNS registration of each domain controller, pings each domain controller, and verifies the LDAP and RPC connectivity on each domain controller.
`CrossRefValidation`	Verifies that domain cross-references are valid.
`FRSSysvol`	Verifies that the FRS SYSVOL is in a ready state.
`FRSEvent`	Checks for FRS replication errors, which could indicate replication problems with the SYSVOL and thus with the consistency of GPO replicas.

Table 13-4. dcdiag Tests, continued

Test	Description
FSMOCheck	Does not check for server operations master roles, but instead queries to contact a global catalog server, PDC, preferred time server, time server, and a key distribution center (KDC).
Intersite	Checks for failures that could prevent or delay inter-site replication. Microsoft warns that the results output by this test are not always accurate.
KCCEvent	Checks to see that the knowledge consistency checker (KCC) is creating intrasite replication connection objects without errors.
KnowsOfRoleHolders	Verifies that the target domain controller can contact each of the five operations masters.
MachineAccount	Verifies that the target system's machine account is properly registered and its services are advertised. If a failure is encountered, it can be repaired by using the /fixmachineaccount or /recreatemachineaccount parameter with the dcdiag command.
NCSecDesc	Verifies that the security descriptors for the naming context heads contain the appropriate permissions for replication.
NetLogons	Verifies that appropriate logon privileges exist for each domain controller to allow replication.
ObjectsReplicated	Verifies that directory server agent (DSA) and machine account objects are replicating properly.
OutboundSecureChannels	Verifies that secure channels exist between all domain controllers in the target domain.
Replications	Verifies the ability to replicate between domain controllers, and reports any encountered replication errors.
RidManager	Verifies that the RID master operations master is online and functioning properly.
Services	Verifies that all domain controller–specific services are running on the target domain controller.
SystemLog	Checks to see that the system log is running without errors.
VerifyEnterpriseReferences	Verifies that FRS and replication system references are valid for all objects on all domain controllers in the forest.
VerifyReferences	Verifies that FRS and replication system references are valid for all objects on the target domain controller.
VerifyReplicas	Checks and verifies the validity of all application directory partitions on all replica servers.

Chapter 13 Active Directory

Here is the syntax for `dcdiag`:

```
dcdiag /s:<DomainController> [/n:<NamingContext>] [[/u:<domain\user>]
[/p:<password>]] [{/a|/e}{/q|/v}] [/i] [/f:<LogFile>]
[/ferr:<ErrorLog>] [/c [/skip:<test>]] [/test:<test>] [/fix]
```

The command options are described in Table 13-5.

Table 13-5. dcdiag Command Options

Option	Use
/s:<DomainController>	Used to specify the target domain controller for the command.
/n:<NamingContext>	Used to specify the naming context to test. You can specify the naming context in NetBIOS, DNS (FQDN), or DN format.
/u:<domain\user>	Allows you to run the command under the credentials of another user.
/p:<password>	Used with the /u parameter to specify a user password.
/a	Tests all servers in the target site.
/e	Tests all servers in the entire forest (overrides /a).
/q	Quiet output. Displays only error messages.
/v	Verbose output. Displays detailed information.
/i	Ignores nonessential error messages.
/f:<LogFile>	Redirects the command output to the log file specified.
/ferr:<ErrorLog>	Collects and redirects all output fatal errors to the log file specified.
/c	Performs a comprehensive test, performing all tests except DCPromo and RegisterInDNS.
/skip:<test>	When the /c parameter is used, allows you to skip a specified test.
/test:<test>	Runs only the test specified.
/fix	During the `MachineAccount` test, erroneous service principal names (SPNs) on the domain controller's machine account object are repaired.

One common way to run this command is to specify just a target server. This will perform a quick test of the Active Directory that should complete within a few seconds if no problems are encountered. Here is a sample of what you would see after executing this command.

```
C:\>dcdiag /s:glitch
Domain Controller Diagnostics
```

```
Performing initial setup:
  Done gathering initial info.

Doing initial required tests

  Testing server: EastSite\GLITCH
    Starting test: Connectivity
       .................... GLITCH passed test Connectivity

Doing primary tests

  Testing server: EastSite\GLITCH
    Starting test: Replications
       .................... GLITCH passed test Replications
    Starting test: NCSecDesc
       .................... GLITCH passed test NCSecDesc
    Starting test: NetLogons
       .................... GLITCH passed test NetLogons
```

Several more tests follow this line, but at this point you can see how easy it is to test domain controllers and the general state of the Active Directory in an entire forest using `dcdiag`. To make the output easier to read, you could consider using either the /f or /ferr switch to direct the command output to a log file.

gpresult

The `gpresult` command allows you to determine the Resultant Set of Policy (RSoP) for group policy settings applied to a user or computer object. For most of your GPO troubleshooting, you should consider the RSoP GUI tool, since it provides easy-to-read graphical analysis of policy settings. This tool is good for quickly gathering RSoP settings when a user is having problems. If, after running `gpresult`, you find that you need more or better-organized information, you can then run RSoP. Think of this tool as a way to get a quick glimpse of a user or computer's resultant policy settings. Here is the syntax for `gpresult`:

```
gpresult [/s:<computer>] [/user:<UserName>] [[/u:<domain\user>]
[/p:<password>]] [/scope <user|computer>] [/v] [/z]
```

The command options are described in Table 13-6.

Table 13-6. gpresult Command Options

Option	Use
/s <computer>	Used to specify the computer whose effective policy settings you wish to view.
/user <UserName>	Used to specify the user whose effective policy settings you wish to view.

continues

Table 13-6. gpresult Command Options, continued

Option	Use
/u:<domain\user>	Allows you to run the command under the credentials of another user.
/p:<password>	Used with the /u parameter to specify a user password.
/scope <user | computer>	Allows you to have just the computer or user portion of the resultant policy displayed.
/v	Verbose output. More detailed output information is displayed.
/z	Displays all available GPO information, providing more detail than the /v switch. You should consider redirecting the command output to a text file (use > *filename*) when running this command.

For an example of using this command, suppose that you wanted to view the resultant policy settings of the user mshanehsaz. To view the policy settings, you would run gpresult /user mshanehsaz.

gpupdate

The gpupdate command is the replacement for the secedit /refreshpolicy command that was used with Windows 2000 to manually initiate a refresh of GPOs on a system. While all policies do refresh automatically, using this command allows you to immediately refresh a policy. This is often important if you want to refresh policy settings immediately after making changes to a GPO. This way, you can verify that your GPO changes behaved, or made the corrections that you anticipated. Unlike secedit /refreshpolicy, gpupdate by default refreshes both computer and user policy settings. With secedit, you would have to run two commands to refresh both settings.

The syntax for gpupdate is:

```
gpupdate [/target:<computer|user>] [/force] [/wait:<seconds>]
[/logoff] [/boot] [/sync]
```

The gpupdate command options are described in Table 13-7.

Table 13-7. gpupdate Command Options

Option	Use
/target:<computer | user>	Causes the command to refresh only the computer or user GPO settings on the system. By default, both the computer and user portions of the applicable GPOs are refreshed.
/force	Ignores all GPO processing optimizations, such as slow link detection, and reapplies all settings.

Table 13-7. gpupdate Command Options, continued

Option	Use
/wait:<seconds>	Allows you to specify the number of seconds that policy processing can take to complete. The default value is 600 seconds (10 minutes). The values 0 = no wait and –1 = wait indefinitely.
/logoff	Logs off the user after the policy refresh completes. A user logoff is often required to refresh many policy settings, such as changes to the desktop, so this command simply automates the logoff process, which would likely be required anyway.
/boot	Reboots the system after the policy refresh completes. Some computer settings, such as software installation, are applied only when the system starts, so a reboot is required for those changes to be applied.
/sync	Causes group policy objects to be applied synchronously to computers at startup and to users at logon, which is the default with Windows 2000. This causes all policies to be applied during the logon process. With Windows XP and W2K3, by default policies are applied asynchronously, which can cause users to log on with cached credentials and policy settings, and thus not receive any newly implemented policy changes right away.

Suppose that you just updated a user's policy settings. To verify that the changes have occurred, you can run `gpupdate /target:user /logoff`. This command refreshes only the User portion of the GPO and automatically logs the user off once the refresh completes. Once the user logs back on, he should see the changes.

nltest (ST)

The versatile command line tool `nltest` allows you to perform the following tasks:

- Acquire a list of domain controllers
- Provide the status of secure channels, which provide trusts between domains
- Query the status of domain trusts
- Register domain controller SRV records with a dynamic DNS server

The syntax for this command is:

```
nltest [/server:<servername>] [test operation]
```

The `/server` parameter allows you to run the test on a remote domain controller. If no server is specified, the test runs on the local system. This command provides several operations that can be run. Each operation and its related switch are described in Table 13-8.

Table 13-8. nltest Command Operations

Operation	Description
`/query`	Displays the status of the secure channel, which is established by the NetLogon service, and provides information on the last time the channel was used.
`/sc_query:<domain>`	Displays information on the state of the secure channel to the target domain, and lists the name of the remote domain controller that was contacted.
`/sc_reset:<domain>`	Removes and then re-creates the secure channel of the target domain.
`/sc_verify:<domain>`	Reports on the status of the secure channel, and if a problem is detected, the secure channel is re-created.
`/sc_change_pwd:<domain>`	Changes the trust account password for the specified domain.
`/dclist:<domain>`	Displays the names of all domain controllers for the specified domain.
`/dcname:<domain>`	Displays the name of the PDC emulator for the specified domain.
`/dsgetfti:<domain>`	Displays information about any interforest trusts that exist for the target domain.
`/dsgetsite`	Displays the name of the Active Directory site where your system is located.
`/dsregdns`	Refreshes the registration of all domain controller–specific records on the DNS server. This allows you to refresh a domain controller's SRV records without having to stop and restart its NetLogon service.
`/dsderegdns:<dnsserver>`	Removes a domain controller's SRV records from the DNS server specified.

Suppose that you wished to quickly obtain a list of all domain controllers for the aw.com domain. To display this list, you would run `nltest /dclist:aw.com`. If you wanted to check the status of the secure channel for the domain aw.com, you would run `nltest /sc_query:aw.com`.

ntdsutil

The Active Directory management tool `ntdsutil` is very powerful. While this tool may not necessarily provide diagnostic information to determine a problem, it is frequently used to repair problems, especially in the following circumstances:

- Authoritatively restoring AD objects
- Seizing FSMO roles
- Removing references to decommissioned domain controllers
- Changing the location of the AD database and log files
- Performing an offline compaction of the AD database

There are several repair instances in which this command is required.

- The AD database must be moved to another disk that has more available space.
- AD objects must be restored authoritatively to undo a mistaken operation by another administrator.
- AD log files must be moved to different physical disks to improve domain controller performance.
- Offline database compaction must be performed to repair a corrupted AD database.
- In order to rebuild a domain controller through reinstallation, references to a previous domain controller with the same host name must be removed from the AD database; otherwise, the promotion of the new domain controller will fail, since Active Directory will think that it already has a domain controller with the system's name.

Any maintenance operations involving the movement, compaction, or restoration of the Active Directory database require that the domain controller be started in Directory Services Restore Mode. The steps for starting a domain controller in this diagnostic mode can be found in Chapter 5. Other tasks, such as seizing a FSMO role from a decommissioned domain controller to a new domain controller, can be performed without starting a domain controller in Directory Services Restore Mode. Like other command line tools such as `nslookup` or `netsh`, `ntdsutil` is normally run in interactive mode. To enter this mode of operation and to run other `ntdsutil` commands, at the command prompt type `ntdsutil`. Each of the available `ntdsutil` interactive modes that are useful for troubleshooting and repairing Active Directory is described in the next five subsections.

> For a quick reference of all available commands at any level within the `ntdsutil` interactive mode, type ? and hit Enter.

authoritative restore

Following a restore of System State data to a domain controller that has been booted into Directory Services Restore Mode, you can use this utility to mark the entire Active Directory database or a select object as authoritative for replication throughout the domain. More information on Active Directory recovery strategies can be found later in this chapter in the AD Backup and Recovery section.

To enter this `ntdsutil` command mode, type `authoritative restore` from the `ntdsutil` prompt. From the `authoritative restore` prompt, you can restore the Active Directory database or portions of it by using the following syntax:

```
restore database
restore database verinc <increment>
restore subtree <subtree>
restore subtree <subtree> verinc <increment>
```

This command can be run in any of the four formats listed. The differences between the methods for running this command are described in Table 13-9.

Table 13-9. authoritative restore Command Operations

Option	Description
`restore database`	Marks the entire Active Directory database (Ntds.dit file) as authoritative for replication, causing it to overwrite like AD database content on other domain controllers in the domain.
`restore subtree <subtree>`	Marks a portion of the AD database—such as a user, group, or OU—as authoritative for replication. Only the subtree marked as authoritative overwrites like information on other domain controllers.
`verinc <increment>`	Allows you to define the version number, or update sequence number (USN), of the restored data. By default, authoritatively restored data has its USN incremented by 100,000. The `verinc` option is useful when you need to authoritatively restore data over previously authoritative data and thus need to increase the restored data's USN to a value higher than 100,000.

Here is an example of using this command to authoritatively restore the Sales OU in the aw.net domain, following the restore of a domain controller's System State.

```
C:\>ntdsutil
ntdsutil:authoritative restore
authoritative restore:restore subtree ou=sales,dc=aw,dc=net

Opening DIT database... Done.
The current time is 5-20-03 10:34.30.
The most recent database update occurred at 5-20-03 07:15.68.
Increasing attribute version numbers by 100000.
```

```
Counting records that need updating...
Records found: 0000000012.
Done.

Found 12 records to update.

Updating records...
Records remaining: 0000000000
Done.

Successfully updated 12 records.

Authoritative Restore completed successfully.

authoritative restore:quit
ntdsutil:quit
C:\>
```

When this command is executed, all of the objects in the Sales OU would overwrite any object settings in the Sales OU on all other domain controllers in the domain.

files

The `files` command is useful for managing the Active Directory database and log files. For example, if the Active Directory service will not start on a domain controller due to low disk space, you can use the `files` command to move the database to a different disk. In addition to moving the Ntds.dit (AD database) file, you can perform several other recovery tasks from the `files` subcommand. Each of the available commands from the `files` level is described in Table 13-10.

Table 13-10. files Commands

Command	Description
compact to <path>	Compacts the Active Directory database and stores the database in the location specified. If you want the compacted database to replace the original database, you need to manually do so.
header	Displays AD database file configuration information, including the date and time of the last database consistency check, and the Active Directory database transaction log backup status.
info	Displays information on the system's local hard disks as well as information on the storage locations for the Active Directory database and log files.
integrity	Performs an integrity check of the Active Directory database and may identify low-level corruption problems in the database. Before performing this command, you should first run the recover command.

continues

Table 13-10. files Commands, continued

Command	Description
`move db to <path>`	Moves the Active Directory database file to the location specified.
`move logs to <path>`	Moves the Active Directory database log files to the location specified.
`recover`	Initiates a database recovery. During recovery, the transaction log files are checked to ensure that all transactions marked as committed to the AD database actually exist in the database. If not, uncommitted transactions are entered into the database.
`set path backup <path>`	Sets a disk-to-disk backup path for the Active Directory database, which allows you to perform periodic online backups of the Active Directory database.
`set path db <path>`	Updates the Registry to identify the path to the Active Directory database file.
`set path logs <path>`	Updates the Registry to identify the path to the Active Directory database transaction log files.
`set path working dir <path>`	Updates the Registry to identify the Active Directory database's working directory.

There are several important recovery tasks that can be performed with this tool. Let's look at a few examples.

First, assume that the Active Directory database has become corrupted, and before attempting to recover from backup, you first decide to perform an offline compaction. To do this, you would start the domain controller in Directory Services Restore Mode and then perform the following command sequence.

```
C:\>ntdsutil
ntdsutil:files
file maintenance:compact to f:\temp
Opening database [current]
Creating dir: f:\temp
Executing command c:\windows\system32\esentutl.exe
/d"C:\windows\ntds\ntds.dit" /t"f:\temp\ntds.dit" /p /o

Initiating DEFRAGMENTATION mode...
        Database: C:\Windows\NTDS\ntds.dit
  Temp. Database: f:\temp\ntds.dit

                Defragmentation Status (% complete)
         0    10   20   30   40   50   60   70   80   90  100
         |----|----|----|----|----|----|----|----|----|----|
         ....................................................

Note:
  It is recommended that you immediately perform a full backup of this
  database. If you restore a backup made before the defragmentation, the
```

```
        database will be rolled back to the state it was in at the time of
        that backup.

Operation completed successfully in 39.2 seconds.

Spawned Process Exit code 0x0(0)

If compaction was successful you need to:
    Copy "f:\temp\ntds.dit" "C:\Windows\NTDS\ntds.dit"
And delete the old log files:
    Del C:\Windows\NTDS\*.log

File maintenance:quit
ntdsutil:quit
C:\>
```

Notice that as the command completes, you are prompted with additional commands to run. In fact, the `compact` command is so smart that it gives you the exact syntax of the next commands that you need to run. Following any successful compaction, you need to copy the compacted database over the original database using the `copy` command and then delete the old transaction log files using the `del` command. Now let's look at one more example of a command at the `file maintenance` menu. Suppose that you wish to move the AD database to a new location, but first want to check to see the available disk space on a domain controller. Here are the commands that you would run.

```
        C:\>ntdsutil
        ntdsutil:files
        file maintenance:info

        Drive Information:
                C:\ NTFS (Fixed Drive ) free(120.7 Mb) total(3.1 Gb)
                F:\ NTFS (Fixed Drive ) free(319.1 Mb) total(10.7 Gb)
                G:\ NTFS (Fixed Drive ) free(20.7 Gb) total(25.0 Gb)

        DS Path Information:

                Database    : C:\Windows\NTDS\ntds.dit - 700.42 Mb
                Backup dir  : C:\Windows\NTDS\dsadata.bak
                Working dir: C:\Windows\NTDS
                Log dir     : C:\Windows\NTDS
                              Res2.log 10.0Mb
                              Res1.log 10.0Mb
                              Ntds.INTEG.RAW - 10.4 Kb
                              Edb00001.log - 10.0 Mb
                              Edb.log - 10.0 Mb
file maintenance:move db to g:\ntds
Opening database [Current].
If move database was successful, please make a backup immediately
 Else restore will not retain the new file location.

File maintenance:quit
ntdsutil:quit
C:\>
```

In this command sequence, it was discovered that there was over 20GB of free disk space on the G drive, so the Active Directory database was moved to that drive. When you need to repair or relocate the Ntds.dit file, the `files` commands allow you to quickly repair the database and get on with life.

metadata cleanup

Normally domain and domain controller metadata in the Active Directory database is created and removed during the DCPromo process. However if a domain controller fails outright without being demoted, then its metadata references remain in the Active Directory database. As was mentioned earlier, in order to re-create a failed domain controller from scratch, you first need to have another domain controller seize the failed domain controller's FSMOs, if necessary, and then delete the failed domain controller's metadata. Following the delete, you could then promote a new domain controller with the same name as the old domain controller as its replacement. The `metadata cleanup` subcommands are described in Table 13-11.

Table 13-11. metadata cleanup Commands

Command	Description
`connections`	Used to go to the `server connections` window in order to connect to a domain controller or a domain in order to remove metadata.
`remove selected domain`	Removes the metadata for the domain selected by the `select operation target` command.
`remove selected naming context`	Removes the metadata for the naming context selected by the `select operation target` command.
`remove selected server`	Removes the metadata for the domain controller selected by the `select operation target` command.
`select operation target`	Used to go to the `select operation target` window, which is used to select the domain controller whose metadata references you wish to remove.

When you first start `metadata cleanup`, you need to connect to either a domain or a domain controller by using the `connections` menu. Once connected, you then need to select the target for the cleanup operation. In other words, you need to select the object to be removed. To select a target, you need to navigate to the `select operation target` menu. Finally, once the target has been selected, you can then remove the selected target from the Active Directory by using one of the `remove` commands. The available `connections` and `select operation target` commands are described in Tables 13-12 and 13-13.

Table 13-12. server connections Commands

Command	Description
connect to domain <domain>	Specifies the domain to connect to. The target domain's Active Directory database must be online.
connect to server <server>	Specifies the domain controller to connect to. The target domain controller must be online.
info	Displays current connection information.

Table 13-13. select operation target Commands

Command	Description
list current selections	Displays the current site/domain/server/naming context choices.
list domains	Displays all domains.
list domains in site	Displays domains in the selected site.
list naming contexts	Displays all known naming contexts.
list roles for connected server	Displays FSMO roles for the connected server.
list servers for domain in site	Lists servers for the selected domain and site.
list servers in site	Lists domain controllers in the selected site.
list sites	Lists sites in the enterprise.
select domain <domain>	Makes the domain specified the operation target.
select server <server>	Makes the server specified the operation target.
select site <site>	Makes the site specified the operation target.

Since this command is quite lengthy and often confusing, let's look at an example of using it. Here is the syntax that would be required to remove the metatdata for the server Faulty1 in the domain Unreliable.net.

```
C:\>ntdsutil
ntdsutil:metadata cleanup
metadata cleanup:connections
server connections:connect to domain unreliable.net
Binding to \\glitch.unreliable.net...
Connected to \\glitch.unreliable.net using credentials of locally
logged on user
```

```
Server connections:quit
Metadata cleanup:select operation target
Select operation target:list sites
Found 2 site(s)
0 - CN=NYC,CN=Sites,CN=Configuration,DC=unreliable,DC=net
1 - CN=LA,CN=Sites,CN=Configuration,DC=unreliable,DC=net
select operation target:select site 0
Site - CN=NYC,CN=Sites,CN=Configuration,DC=unreliable,DC=net

No current domain
No current server
No current Naming Context
Select operation target:list servers in site
Found 2 server(s)
0 - CN=Glitch,CN=servers,CN=NYC,CN=Sites,CN=Configuration,
DC=unreliable,DC=net
1 - CN=Faulty1,CN=servers,CN=NYC,CN=Sites,CN=Configuration,
DC=unreliable,DC=net

select operation target:select server 1

select operation target:quit

metadata cleanup:remove selected server

metadata cleanup:quit
ntdsutil:quit
C:\>
```

Following the selection of the target object for the command, you can remove it. Many find this command confusing since you have to jump between menus to reach an end result. Unfortunately, since `metadata cleanup` provides the only method to remove metadata, there are no other choices.

> Be very careful when using this command, since it is possible to delete the metadata references for valid domains and domain controllers.

roles

The `roles` menu allows you to transfer and seize FSMO roles from other domain controllers. Roles are transferred when the current operations master and new operations master are online. You should only seize a role when a FSMO's operations master has completely failed and will not be returning to an online state. The available commands for the `roles` menu are listed in Table 13-14.

AD Troubleshooting Tools

Table 13-14. FSMO Maintenance Commands

Command	Description
connections	Used to go to the `server connections` window in order to connect to a domain controller or a domain in order to move or seize FSMO roles (see Table 13-12).
seize domain naming master	Grants the domain naming master FSMO role to the target domain controller.
seize infrastructure master	Grants the infrastructure master FSMO role to the target domain controller.
seize pdc	Grants the PDC emulator FSMO role to the target domain controller.
seize rid master	Grants the RID master FSMO role to the target domain controller.
seize schema master	Grants the schema master FSMO role to the target domain controller.
select operation target	Used to go to the `select operation target` window, which is used to select the domain controller that will become the new owner for a transferred or seized FSMO (see Table 13-13).
transfer domain naming master	Transfers the domain naming master FSMO role to the target domain controller.
transfer infrastructure master	Transfers the infrastructure master FSMO role to the target domain controller.
transfer pdc	Transfers the PDC emulator FSMO role to the target domain controller.
transfer rid master	Transfers the RID master FSMO role to the target domain controller.
transfer schema master	Transfers the schema master FSMO role to the target domain controller.

This command is executed in the same sequence as the `metadata cleanup` commands. First, you connect to a domain, then you select a target domain controller, and finally you run a `seize` or `transfer` command to enable a FSMO on the target.

Normally, this command is used to seize FSMO roles from servers that have failed and that you have no intention of returning to an online state. Remember that each FSMO is important for specific domain-wide or forest-wide functions, so sometimes you may have to have a particular FSMO online and cannot wait for the failed FSMO domain controller to be repaired. In these instances, seizing roles is the best option.

semantic database analysis

This tool is used to analyze and query current Active Directory database semantics. It is similar to the `files` command in that it checks and verifies database integrity. However, with this tool, integrity is verified against Active Directory semantics and not ESENT database semantics, as is the case with the `files integrity` command. The semantic database analysis often performs a more thorough check of database integrity. To use this command to check database integrity, you first enter `semantic database analysis` from the `ntdsutil` menu and then type `go`. This starts the integrity check of the database.

Replmon (ST)

Replmon is a versatile GUI-based support tool that allows you to check the low-level status of Active Directory replication as well as check the replication topology, force a synchronization between domain controllers, and monitor the status and performance of domain controller replication.

When troubleshooting Active Directory replication, most administrators usually reach for this tool first. This is because you can do all of the following with Replmon:

- Locate replication failures
- View the history of successful and failed replication changes
- Display the replication topology
- Initiate replication
- View the properties of replication partners
- Generate a status report for replication partners
- Poll replication partners
- Trigger the knowledge consistency checker to recalculate the replication topology
- Display the trust relationships of a domain controller being monitored

To open this tool, just click Start > Run, enter `replmon` in the Run dialog box, and then click OK.

Resultant Set of Policy

The RSoP tool was first introduced as a resource kit add-on (in a light version) to Windows 2000 servers. This tool was added to address the complex task of troubleshooting and analyzing group policy objects. To troubleshoot site-, domain-, and organizational unit–level policies, you would have to manually calculate the end result of the policy deployment. The most accurate way of determining the resultant policy settings for a particular user would be to:

1. Print a screenshot of the local computer policy settings for a particular machine.
2. Print a screenshot of the site group policy settings for the computer.
3. Print a screenshot of the domain group policy settings for the user and the computer.
4. Print a screenshot of the OU group policy settings for the user and the computer.
5. Compare the screenshots from each policy to arrive at a final determination of the resultant policy.

This is no easy task. To determine a resultant policy, you need to remember L-S-D-OU (local, site, domain, OU), which is the order that policies are applied in, and then compare screen captures of each set of policies to determine the end result of the policy deployment. Unfortunately, this approach doesn't even account for the possibility of the Block Policy Inheritance or No Override group policy property settings. When dealing with site, OU, and child OU policies, policy management basically boiled down to making an educated guess as to the end result. This problem was solved with RSoP, which allows you to quickly analyze GPOs and display their resultant policy settings.

RSoP can be run in two different modes: logging mode and planning mode. Logging mode is used when you need to determine the actual resultant GPO settings for a user or computer object. Planning mode is the more flexible operating mode, letting you simulate "what if" scenarios based on AD data. For example, with logging mode, you can view the resultant policy settings for a single user or computer object in the forest. With planning mode, you can create an OU and child OUs, set up default policies for each OU, and then use RSoP to determine the resultant policy for one of the child OUs. Put another way, logging mode gives you policy settings that you have, while planning mode allows you to see the policy settings that you would have based on the conditions you specify.

Since RSoP is built into the Windows Server 2003 operating system, you can find hooks to run it nearly anywhere. For example, you can right-click an OU in the AD Users and Computers MMC, select All Tasks, and then execute RSoP (Planning), or right-click a user object, select All Tasks, and then choose RSoP (Planning) or RSoP (Logging). You'll also see shortcuts to launch RSoP in AD Sites and Services and in AD Domains and Trusts.

The easiest way to analyze policy settings by using RSoP in logging mode is to launch RSoP.msc from the Run dialog box. For planning mode, it is best to create an empty MMC and add the RSoP snap-in. This is done by launching the MMC from the Run dialog box by typing `mmc` and hitting Enter. From the MMC, snap-ins can be added by pressing Ctrl-M, clicking Add, and then selecting the appropriate snap-ins.

Since planning mode is the most powerful and offers more configuration options, that's where we'll focus our attention. With the RSoP snap-in loaded into the console, you begin by right-clicking the snap-in and selecting Generate RSoP Data. This action launches the Resultant Set of Policy Wizard, which lets you specify exactly what you'd like to analyze. This wizard is shown in Figure 13-6.

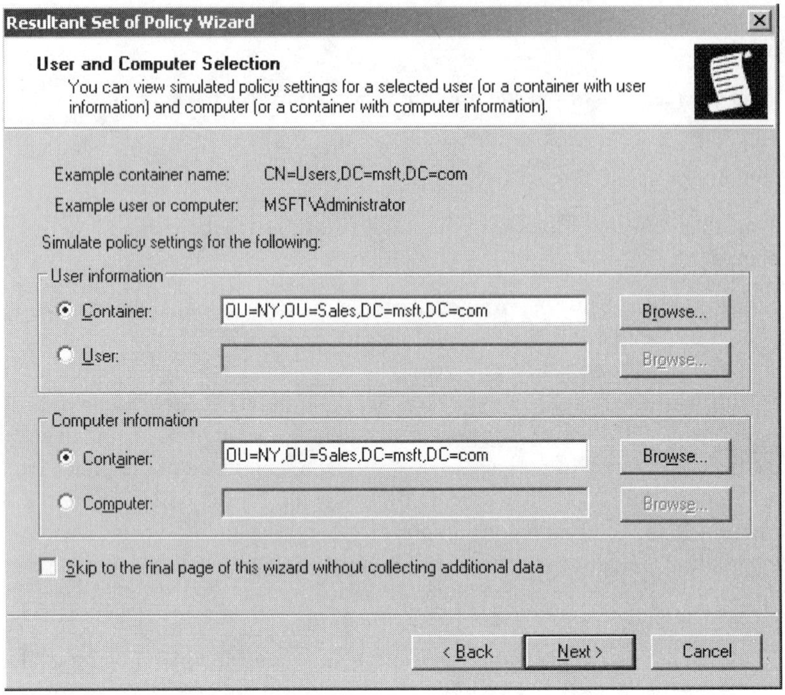

Figure 13-6. Using the RSoP Wizard to select objects to analyze

After selecting the objects to analyze, you are tasked with selecting advanced options. This is where the simulation comes into play. As shown in Figure 13-7, the wizard lets you select simulation options, including slow bandwidth conditions, a loopback processing mode, and a site.

Sometimes you may not want to push all group policy settings over a network connection, especially if a user is connecting via a dial-up modem. For example, you wouldn't want to use a policy to force the installation of Office XP to all users over the network, including dial-up users. With slow link detection enabled (User or Computer Configuration\Administrative Templates\System\Group Policy\Group Policy Slow Link Detection), only the Administrative Template (Registry settings) and Security settings portions of the GPO are applied. The remaining policy settings, including software distribution and folder redirection, are not applied. The default value of "slow" is listed as 500Kbps but can be changed when you enable slow link detection.

Once you've set the advanced options for the policy analysis, the last steps in configuring the RSoP analysis are to select the user and computer objects that the simulation should apply to, and select which Windows management instrumentation (WMI) filters—which allow you to filter the effective settings of a group policy object—to apply to user and computer objects. You can simulate the inclusion of all WMI filters or only the ones you select for the analysis.

After successfully navigating the wizard, you can finally enjoy the fruits of your labor: the resultant policy. Figure 13-8 shows a sample analysis.

AD Troubleshooting Tools 479

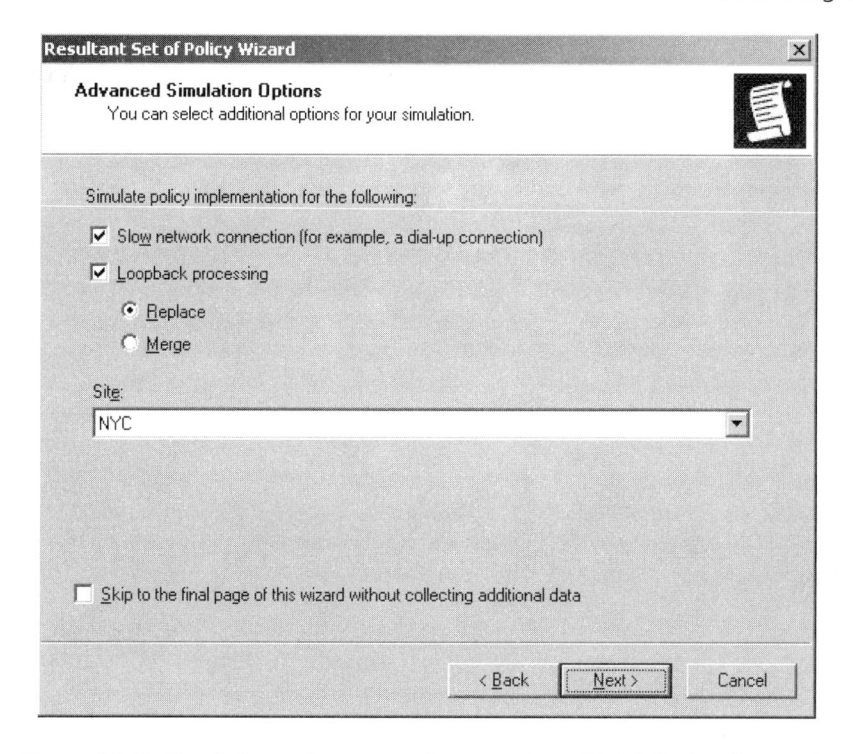

Figure 13-7. Simulating a slow network connection with RSoP planning mode

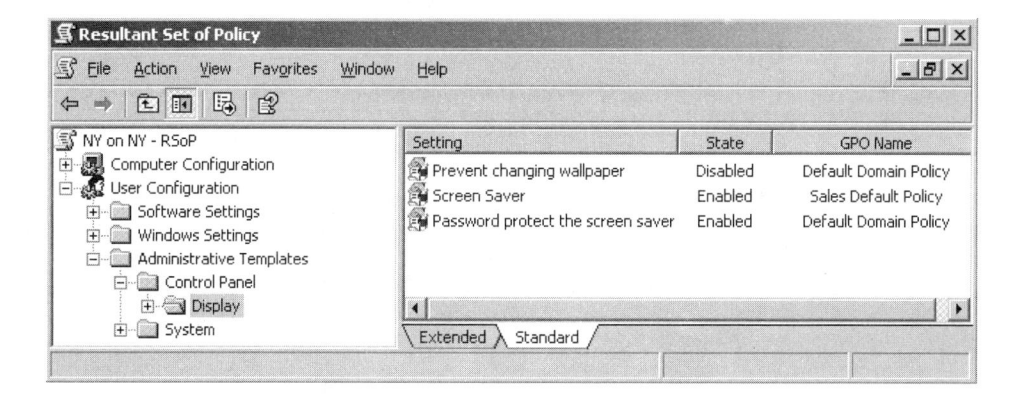

Figure 13-8. RSoP analysis display

A nice feature of RSoP is that for each applied setting, the analysis displays the policy that caused the setting. What it doesn't show, however, is whether resultant policy settings are due to one policy overriding another. To view all the policies involved in a particular resultant setting, you need to double-click a single setting, such as "Prevent changing wallpaper properties," and then click the Precedence tab.

Figure 13-9 shows the "Prevent changing wallpaper properties" resultant policy setting and the two policies that had the setting defined. As you can see, the Default Domain Policy is listed at the top and thus is the applied setting.

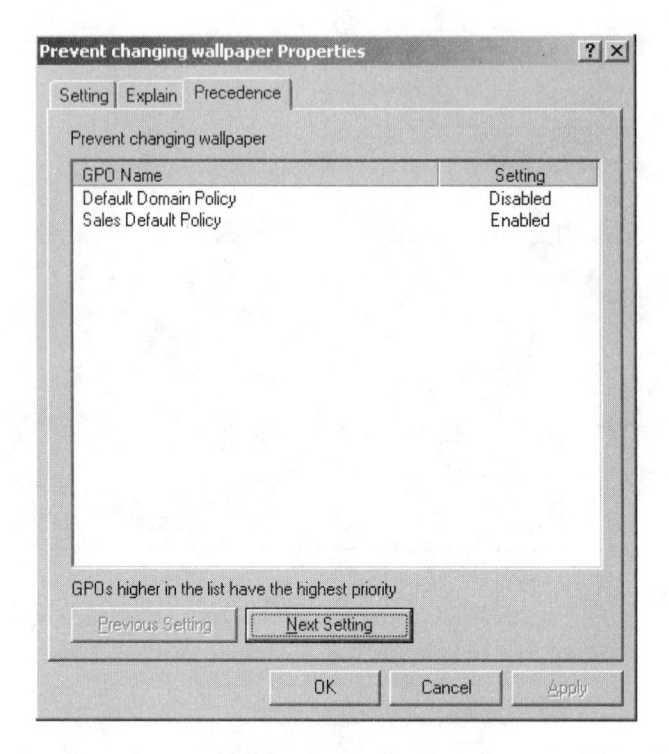

Figure 13-9. GPO Precedence tab displaying the policy that wins out

The remainder of this chapter focuses on troubleshooting specific portions of the Active Directory. With the many troubleshooting tools at your disposal that have been discussed in this chapter, you will find that diagnosing and repairing Active Directory problems is likely much easier than you initially imagined.

Troubleshooting Domain Controllers

Several things can go wrong with individual domain controllers. However, you also cannot discount the possibility that a problem that appears to be on a local domain controller may actually be caused by the unavailability of a remote domain controller hosting a needed FSMO. When you are unsure of a local domain controller problem, running `dcdiag` is a good way to start troubleshooting, since this command performs a full battery of tests on the domain controller.

If the domain controller is exhibiting a specific symptom, try referencing the many domain controller failures and solutions described in this section and throughout the remainder of this chapter.

Cannot Connect to a Windows 2000 Domain Controller

If you are having trouble connecting to a Windows 2000 domain controller from a Windows Server 2003 system, the likely cause of the problem is that the Windows 2000 domain controller does not have at least Service Pack 3 installed. To solve this problem, install the most recent service pack on the Windows 2000 domain controller. If the most recent service pack is installed, you should then verify that the Windows 2000 domain controller is properly registering its SRV records with a DNS server that is common to both the Windows 2000 and Windows Server 2003 systems. For more information on troubleshooting DNS problems, see Chapter 8.

DCPromo Fails to Promote a New Server to Be a Domain Controller

When you are having trouble promoting a new system to become a domain controller in an existing Active Directory forest, the failure usually stems from one of the following conditions.

- An unauthorized user is attempting the promotion process.
- A DNS server is unavailable or does not have proper SRV records for the domain.
- The domain naming master FSMO is offline.

Normally problems in the promotion process are related to the domain naming master FSMO being unavailable or a DNS problem that is preventing other domain controllers from being identified properly. Oftentimes when a DNS problem is encountered, you will receive one of the error messages that are described in the next section, so you can refer to that section to take appropriate measures to resolve the problem.

If the domain naming master FSMO is offline, you can use Active Directory Domains and Trusts to determine which system hosts the FSMO role. Once you identify the system, you can troubleshoot network connectivity problems using `ping`, and you should also verify that the domain controller's NetLogon service is running.

Receive "Domain Not Found," "Server Not Available," or "RPF Server Is Unavailable" Error Message

When you receive one of these error messages, you should jump up and down for joy. That is because this error type points directly to a single problem, which is DNS. Remember, DNS problems could mean inaccurate DNS server records, an invalid entry in a client's local Hosts file, or a negative entry in a client's DNS resolver cache. For this error, you should start by running `netdiag /debug` on the problematic server. This command checks the Active Directory registration of its services in DNS. You should verify that DNS is set up to allow dynamic update or to allow secure dynamic update, and if dynamic update had to be corrected, you can run `nltest /dsregdns` to refresh a domain controller's DNS registration information. Also, remember that after updating DNS, you need to clear the DNS resolver cache of the DNS client by running `ipconfig /flushdns`. Finally, remember to verify that an invalid static entry in the DNS client's Hosts file is not present. Once the DNS issue has been resolved, you should see this problem disappear.

Unable to Log On Locally

A common problem that users sometimes run into with domain controllers is that when attempting to log on, they are refused and receive a message that they do not have the right to log on locally. For domain controllers, by default only the following user groups have the right to log on locally:

- Account operators
- Administrators
- Backup operators
- Print operators
- Server operators

If the user is not a member of the appropriate group, she will be denied local logon access to the domain controller. This is also true for attempting to access the domain controller through a Terminal Server session. To correct the problem, you can add the user to a group that has the right to log on locally, or you can grant the right to the individual user. To do this, you can either modify the Domain Controller Security Policy for single domain controller access, or you can edit the Default Domain Controllers GPO. To do this, follow these steps:

1. From Active Directory Users and Computers, right-click the Domain Controllers OU and select Properties.
2. From the OU Properties dialog box, click the Group Policy tab.
3. Now click the Default Domain Controllers GPO and click Edit.
4. In the GPO Editor, expand the Computer Configuration > Windows Settings > Security Settings > Local Policies object, and click User Rights Assignment.
5. Now right-click the Allow Log On Locally user right, and select Properties.
6. In the Allow Log On Locally dialog box, click the Add User or Group button.
7. Enter the name or Browse for the user or group to add, and click OK.

8. Click OK to close the Allow Log On Locally dialog box.

9. Close the GPO Editor.

10. On the domain controller, run `gpupdate` to refresh its GPO settings.

Once you have finished, the user can log on to the domain controller. Remember to ensure that the user account or group that the user has membership in does not have the Deny Log On Locally user right for the domain controller as well.

Unable to Uninstall Active Directory

If you are decommissioning a domain controller, and the DCPromo process repeatedly fails to remove the domain controller from the domain, your best option is to use `ntdsutil` to manually remove the domain controller's metadata from the Active Directory database. At that point, you can then reinstall Windows on the failed domain controller and reconfigure it as a server or workstation.

Another possibility that exists for failed uninstallations is that a DNS problem is preventing a domain controller from contacting other domain controllers in its domain. You should verify that DNS is set up to allow dynamic update or to allow secure dynamic update, and if dynamic update had to be corrected, you can run `nltest /dsregdns` to refresh a domain controller's DNS registration information.

Group Membership Changes Fail

When attempting to add or remove users from a group, you may find that the operation fails, even though you may be sitting at the domain controller in which you are making these changes. This problem is usually the result of the infrastructure master FSMO being offline, or the target domain controller not being able to reach the infrastructure master FSMO due to a network problem, such as a down WAN link. You can use Active Directory Users and Computers to determine the name of the domain's infrastructure master FSMO. Once you have the name of the system, you can then use the `ping` command to test for network connectivity. If the domain controller responds to a ping request, you should then verify that its NetLogon service is running. If you can connect to the domain controller from the network, then you can always use Active Directory Users and Computers to connect to the remote DC and try the modification again. If the modification is still failing, perhaps the account being used to attempt the changes is not a domain administrator or has not been delegated proper authority to an OU, for example.

Finally, the problem could be that the infrastructure master has failed and will not be coming back online. In this situation, you need to run `ntdsutil` and use the `roles` command menu to seize the role of infrastructure master.

Security Principals Cannot Be Created

When you cannot create a new security principal, such as a user, group, or computer, the likely cause of the problem is that the RID master FSMO is unavailable. Since the RID master is a domain-wide FSMO, you can determine the system acting as the RID master

FSMO by opening Active Directory Users and Computers. Once you determine the name of the system that is acting as the RID master, you can take appropriate action. If the system is supposed to be online, you can ping the system to verify network connectivity. If the ping responds, you should then verify that the system's NetLogon service is running. As with troubleshooting group membership changes, if the FSMO is decommissioned, then you should use `ntdsutil` to seize the RID master role so that it can be assumed by another domain controller.

Troubleshooting Replication

When replication problems are encountered, you should begin by looking at the network connections between the replicating domain controllers. You can use commands such as `ping` and `pathping` to verify routing and network connectivity. Next, you should verify that the File Replication Service is running on all domain controllers involved in the replication. You can check status of the FRS remotely either by running the `sc` command or by using the Computer Management MMC snap-in. When you are using site links to restrict replication time between sites, remember that each site link can have a replication schedule (see Figure 13-10) and a replication frequency, which is every 180 minutes by default.

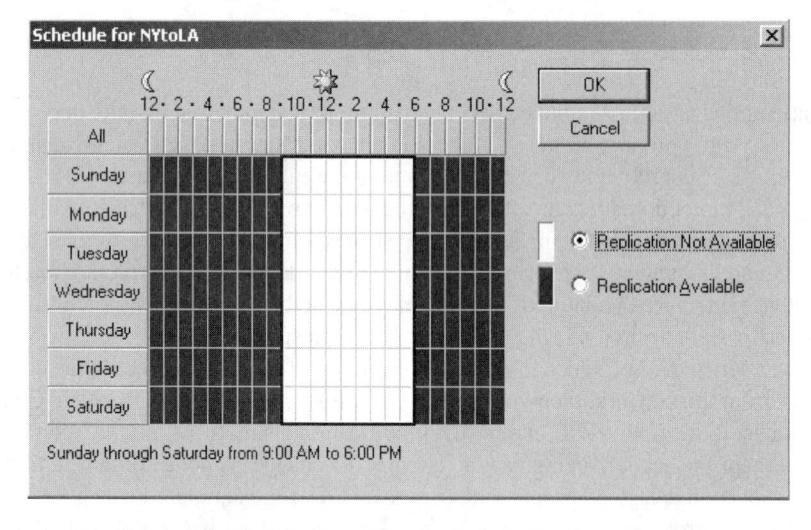

Figure 13-10. Checking the site link replication schedule

In the replication schedule, the shaded areas allow replication during the specified days and times, while the clear areas do not. Remember that to troubleshoot replication, seeing the replication topology is usually very helpful. You can use the Replmon utility to provide a picture of the logical replication topology between domain controllers, and you can use that topology to determine where a problem occurs. Whenever you want to reproduce a replication failure, the easiest approach to take is to expand AD Sites and Services to a site, then a server, and finally a server's NTDS Settings object. To force replication, right-click a connection object under NTDS settings and then select Replicate Now.

The remaining subsections in this portion of the chapter provide guidance on how to resolve specific replication problems that you may encounter.

Access Denied Error Occurs When Attempting Manual Replication

In order to force replication between replication partners, you must have the Replication Synchronization permission. By default Domain Admins and Enterprise Admins have this permission. If you can access the Replmon tool, then you can use it as an alternative to force replication, which is just as effective.

Event ID 1265 in the Directory Service Log

This error occurs when a domain controller fails to authenticate with its replication partner either when attempting to replicate or when trying to create a replication link. During replication, replication partners identify each other's computer account passwords as a means of validation. If a domain controller has been disconnected from the network for a few weeks or longer, its computer account password may become out of sync with its password stored in the Active Directory database of its replication partner. To correct this problem, follow these steps.

1. From the command prompt, type `net stop kdc` to stop the KDC service.

2. Now purge the ticket cache on the local domain controller. This can be done by running `klist purge`. Note that the `klist` tool is located in the resource kit.

3. Reset the domain controller's computer account password on the PDC emulator FSMO by running `netdom /resetpwd`.

4. Synchronize the failed domain controller with the PDC emulator by running the `net time` command.

5. Use Active Directory Sites and Services to force replication between the domain controllers.

6. From the command prompt, type `net start kdc` to start the KDC service.

With the computer account password reset, the problem should be resolved, and replication should now be able to continue normally.

If problems are still occurring, then a DNS lookup failure may be present. You should verify that DNS is set up to allow dynamic update or to allow secure dynamic update, and if dynamic update had to be corrected, you can run `nltest /dsregdns` to refresh a domain controller's DNS registration information. Also, remember that after updating DNS, you need to clear the DNS resolver cache of the DNS client by running `ipconfig /flushdns`. Finally, remember to verify that an invalid static entry in the DNS client's Hosts file is not present. Once the DNS issue has been resolved, you should see this problem disappear. For more information on DNS troubleshooting concepts, turn to Chapter 8, DNS.

Event ID 1311 Appears in Event Log

When you encounter this error while investigating a replication failure, it normally points to a physical network availability or configuration problem. When sites are created to enhance Active Directory performance, they are often modeled after a physical WAN topology. If the WAN topology changes, you need to reconfigure site links and possibly bridgehead servers so that they match the new site physical topology. When you see this problem, here are some specific problem areas to check.

- One or more domain controllers are offline.
- One or more sites are not contained within site links.
- Preferred bridgehead servers are configured improperly.
- Preferred bridgehead servers are offline.

To resolve this problem, you should first verify that your Active Directory sites, site links, and subnets are configured to meet Microsoft guidelines. If so, you can use the TCP/IP utilities `ping` and `pathping` to identify a problem on the network or with a router. If preferred bridgehead servers are configured, you should ensure that they are online. If your network is not fully routed, you should make sure that the "Bridge all site links" checkbox is cleared (this can be found in the site link type Properties dialog box). For example, Figure 13-11 shows "Bridge all site links" configured for IP site links.

With created site links, you need to ensure that the site links line up with your enterprise's physical network WAN topology so that domains in different sites do have a means by which to replicate with each other. All sites should belong to at least one site link, and all nonadjacent sites should have a site link in common. For example, if your organization has three locations—New York, Chicago, and Los Angeles—you could configure two site links: NYtoCHI and CHItoLA. As long as both site links were open (not blocked by a schedule) long enough for New York's data to reach Los Angeles, you should have no problems with the site link configuration.

Slow Replication between Sites

Slow replication between sites could be the result of limited bandwidth on the physical network topology or possibly the result of a configuration problem. You can monitor replication using Replmon to check for problems with replication, but primarily you should check the configuration of your site topology. For example, you may have one big site that traverses three physical locations, or you could have too many sites for a single location that is restricting the times that changes replicate. For each physical location or well-connected metropolitan campus, you should have one Active Directory site. Additional

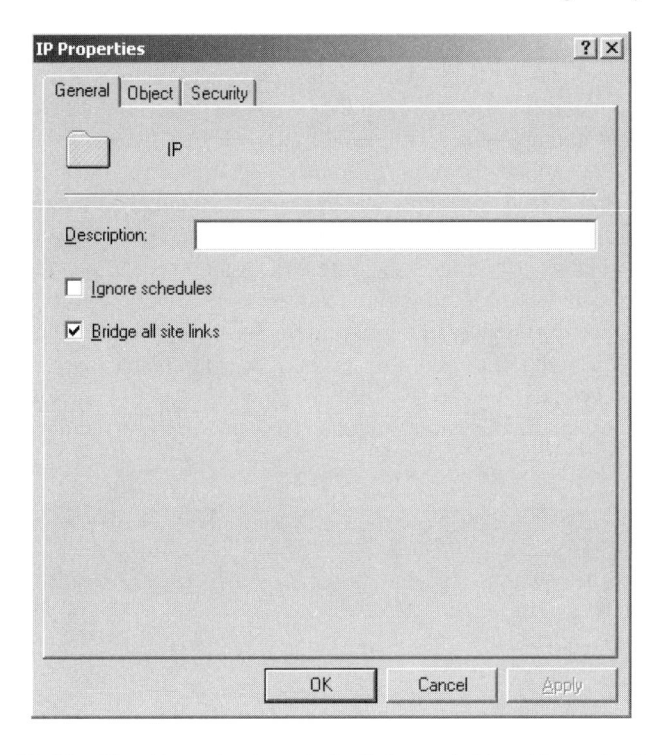

Figure 13-11. Checking whether all site links are bridged for a site link type

sites will just induce latency into the replication topology. Also, increasing the forest functional level to Windows Server 2003 will greatly enhance replication efficiency and thus improve performance.

> If you are looking to document replication performance, you can also run `dcdiag /test:replications` to test the replication topology.

Troubleshooting Group Policy Objects

In order to troubleshoot the application of group policy objects, you must understand the order in which they are applied. Group policies are always applied in the following order:

1. Local
2. Site
3. Domain
4. Organizational unit

A common trick to commit the GPO application order to memory is to remember L-S-D-OU. Local policies are applied first, followed by site policies. Any settings at the site policy level that conflict with a local policy override the local policy. After site policies, domain GPOs are applied next, followed by OU GPOs. In order for any user or group to have a GPO applied, the user's account object must be in the hierarchy path of the GPO and also have Read and Apply GPO permissions on the GPO. If the user is in any group that has Deny Apply GPO permissions, then the GPO will not be applied to the user. An important aspect of understanding GPO assignment is to realize that GPOs apply to users and computers, not to groups. For example, if your user account was in the West OU, but you were a member of a group in the East OU, you would not get any policies linked to the East OU, since your user account does not reside there. However, understanding GPO processing can be a little tricky when a user in one OU or site is logging on to a computer in a different OU or site. That's when understanding loopback processing is important.

> Password policies break the traditional L-S-D-OU rule in that they are configured at the domain level. In other words, if a password policy exists at the domain level, you cannot configure different password policies at the OU level.

Loopback Processing

Now to loopback processing, which is configured in the computer portion of any GPO under Computer Configuration\Administrative Templates\System\Group Policy\User Group Policy Loopback Processing Mode. Suppose you have a user in one OU logging on to a computer in another OU. Whose GPOs get applied to the system? To begin, remember that each GPO has a computer and a user portion. Computer policies are applied once the computer boots up, and user policies are applied at logon. With the default policy settings, you get the site policy from where you log on, and the user portion of your GPOs apply to where your user object is located in the Active Directory. By default, the user gets the user settings in her GPO and not the computer object's GPO. This can be changed by enabling loopback settings in the computer portion of the computer's GPO. With loopback, you can configure loopback merge or loopback replace. In a nutshell, when loopback replace is used, the user settings in the computer's GPO override the user settings in the user's GPO. With loopback merge, the user settings in both the user's GPO and computer's GPO are merged, with like settings in the computer's GPO overriding those in the user's GPO. Still confused? Consider the example shown in Figure 13-12.

The illustration shows a domain dispersed over two sites, with OUs located in each site. There are six GPOs deployed (CA site, NY site, AW.com domain, OU1, OU1B, OU2). Now consider that your user object is in OU1B, and you logged on to a computer in OU2A. At logon, the user portion of the following policies would be applied: local computer policy, NY site, AW.com domain, OU1, and OU1B. Site policies are always physical, whereas domain and OU policies are logical. That is why you will get the NY site policy instead of the CA policy.

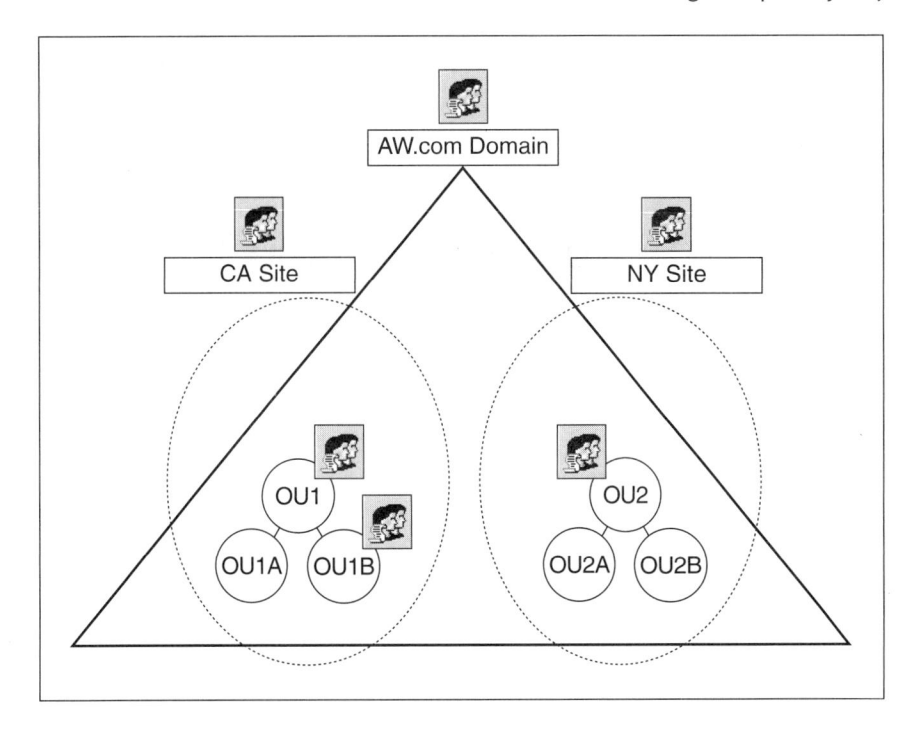

Figure 13-12. Single domain containing two sites and six OUs

Now let's assume that loopback merge is configured in the same scenario. That means that at logon, the user portion of the following GPOs would be applied in the order listed: local computer policy, NY site, AW.com domain, OU1, OU1B, and OU2. Since the OU2 policy is applied last, its settings have the potential to override earlier configurations in OU1 and OU1B policies.

Finally, let's consider the scenario when loopback replace is configured instead. At logon, the user would have these policies applied: local computer policy, NY site, AW.com domain, and OU2. With loopback replace, only the user GPOs in the computer's logical AD hierarchy are applied. This configuration is ideal in areas such as a public computer lab or kiosks, where you want all users to have identical configurations.

Remember that you can simulate loopback processing settings using RSoP.

Block Inheritance versus No Override

Remember that you can configure any GPO to block the inheritance of settings of higher policies. So an OU could, for instance, block the settings of domain and site policies. To block inheritance, you navigate to the object's (GPO, domain, and so on) properties and click the Block Policy Inheritance checkbox, as shown in Figure 13-13.

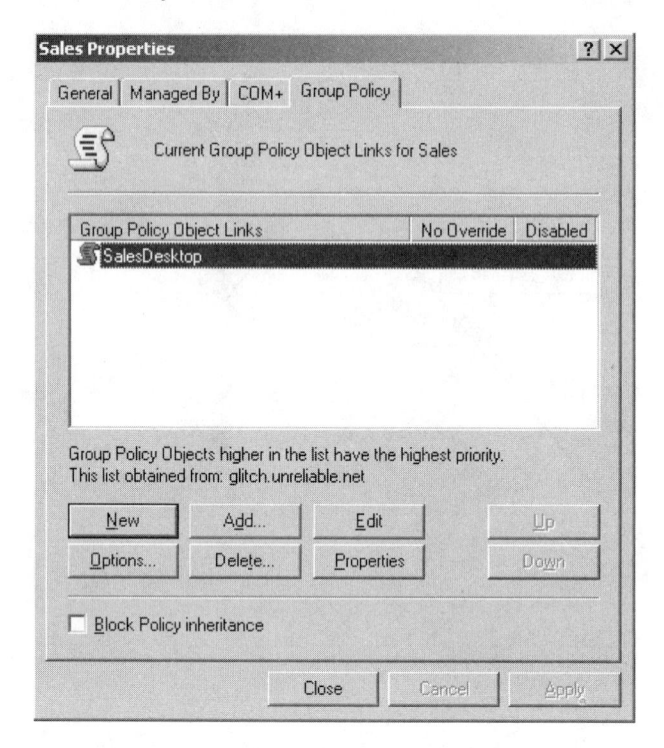

Figure 13-13. Blocking policy inheritance

Since a domain administrator may not want a wily OU administrator to block his policies, he could enable No Override for his policies. No Override forces higher policies on lower objects, such as a domain policy down to all child OUs, or a site policy down to all domains and OUs in the site. Each of these considerations is important, since you may be stumped as to why your policy settings are not be applied to a particular OU, but everyone else is getting the policies without any problem. In these events, make sure that Block Policy Inheritance is not enabled for the OU, or just configure the No Override option for the domain GPO. Also, when users in an OU are not getting the proper settings, check the GPO's DACL to verify that the Authenticated Users group (or any other user group that requires the policy) has Read and Apply GPO permissions on the policy.

Troubleshooting Considerations

When you are troubleshooting GPO application problems, it is often best to start with the RSoP tool to analyze a particular user's or computer's GPO settings. RSoP allows you to see exactly what policies are being applied to a particular user, as well as the resultant GPO settings received by the user. If you are not having much success isolating a problem with RSoP, refer to Table 13-15, which lists other common GPO problems and solutions.

Table 13-15. Common GPO Problems and Solutions

Symptom	Probable Faults
GPO application to a user is intermittent.	• SYSVOL is not replicating between domain controllers. Verify that FRS is running on all domain controllers. The contents of the Windows\sysvol\sysvol folder should be consistent across all domain controllers.
	• Network problems are preventing a reliable connection to a domain controller. Use tools such as `ping`, `pathping`, and Netperf to diagnose the network.
A user is not getting the correct GPO settings.	• The user is located in the wrong OU.
	• Another GPO is overriding the settings.
	• The user does not have Read and Apply GPO permissions for the GPO.
A user is not receiving any GPO settings.	• The user is located in the wrong OU.
	• The user does not have Read and Apply GPO permissions for the GPO.
	• Block Policy Inheritance has been selected for the user's OU.
	• GPO settings are being overridden by a higher GPO (S-D-OU).
Software deployment—an application cannot be installed.	• The user does not have appropriate permissions for the application's software distribution point (network share).
	• The software distribution point is not online.
	• Validate the network settings (TCP/IP, DNS, and so on) between the client and the distribution point.
Software deployment—an application is not installed as expected.	• Verify permissions for GPO (Read, Apply, no Denies).
	• Verify that no conflicts exist with other software installation packages.
Software deployment—application shortcuts are not available on the user's desktop.	• Verify that the application has been assigned to users and not published.

For even more granular GPO troubleshooting, take a look at FAZAM 2000 on the companion CD, and read its related documentation in Appendix C.

Troubleshooting the AD Schema

One of the biggest problems with troubleshooting the schema is that administrators cannot find the Active Directory Schema MMC snap-in. Remember that you must first register the snap-in in order to see it and use it. Another problem that administrators commonly run into with the Active Directory schema is that an application attempting to make schema modifications fails. In order to make schema modifications, you must be a member of the Schema Admins group.

It should be rare that a schema modification needs to be made. Normally, this is done by applications that extend the schema, such as an Exchange Server installation. In the event that you do run into trouble with the Active Directory schema, the next three sections provide guidance on how to get out of the jam.

Cannot Modify or Extend Schema

When this error occurs, it usually caused by one of two faults.

- The schema master FSMO is not online or is unreachable.
- You are not a member of the Schema Admins group.

Remember that there is only one schema master in a forest, so for you to be able to make schema modifications from any domain in the forest, that domain must be able to resolve the name of the schema master domain controller via DNS and also be able to connect to it over the network. When Exchange Server installations fail during the Forest Prep phase, for example, it is often due to the schema master being unreachable. Also with Windows 2000 schema masters, you had to enable schema changes by accessing the properties of the Active Directory Schema object in the Active Directory Schema MMC. This is not required with Windows Server 2003 but should be a consideration if Windows Server 2003 domain controllers have been added to a Windows 2000 domain.

Cannot Add Attributes to a Class

When attributes cannot be associated with an Active Directory schema class, it is often because the schema cache has not been updated. To update the schema cache, right-click the Active Directory Schema object in the Active Directory Schema MMC snap-in and select Reload the Schema. Also if you are attempting to perform schema updates on a system that is not the schema master FSMO, if proper connectivity is not present to the schema master FSMO (TCP/IP, DNS, and so on) or if the schema master FSMO is offline, this operation will also fail. Whenever possible, it is always best to perform any schema updates on the actual schema master FSMO. This way, you rule out any network or name resolution issues from causing a failure.

Cannot Connect to a Windows 2000 Domain Controller

If you are having trouble connecting to a Windows 2000 domain controller from a Windows Server 2003 system, the likely cause of the problem is that the Windows 2000 domain controller does not have at least Service Pack 3 installed. To solve this problem, install the most recent service pack on the Windows 2000 domain controller. As mentioned previously, you should also verify that DNS is configured properly.

Troubleshooting Trusts

When systems in one domain are having trouble accessing resources in another domain—most likely outside of the forest—you need to examine the root of interforest relationships, which begins with trusts. After all, what is a relationship if there is no trust?

In this section, we'll examine the most common trust-specific problems that you may encounter when you run into cross-domain resource access problems.

Clients Cannot Access Resources in Trusted Domain

When this error occurs, you should first verify that the trust relationship exists, which can be verified by using the Active Directory Domains and Trusts MMC snap-in. When you open the snap-in, you should check the Trusts tab under your domain object's properties. An external trust should be present (remember that within a forest, all trusts are transitive and automatic). Also, in order to verify trusts between domains, each domain's PDC emulator FSMO must be online and accessible. You can verify the server that is the PDC emulator for each domain by using Active Directory Users and Computers.

When you are dealing with separate domains, you also must remember that DNS servers in each domain should have knowledge of the trusted domain's systems. This could be configured by adding secondary DNS zones or by enabling forwarders.

Errors Occur After Upgrade from Windows NT

When Windows NT domains are upgraded to Windows Server 2003, the original NT trusts remain intact. This creates a problem because these trust types are not compatible with IPSec. To correct this problem, you should simply delete the trusts and then manually re-create any needed trusts.

With Windows Server 2003 and the transitive nature of trusts, you should rarely run into a trust-related problem. You can create shortcut trusts between domains within the same forest as a means to improve trust validation efficiency. And for complete interforest resource sharing, you can now create forest trusts if the forest functional level is set to Windows Server 2003. With such ease in the trust creation process, you should find that once trusts are set up, they stay up. If any problems arise, just remember to validate network connectivity and to ensure that the PDC emulator in each domain is online.

AD Backup and Recovery

One important concern with Active Directory is recovering the directory service in the event of failure. To protect against failure, you should always ensure that you have a reliable backup of the System State. Backing up the System State ensures that all critical system files are backed up, including the Active Directory, the Registry, and the contents of the SYSVOL folder, which contains logon scripts and group policy templates. When a domain controller fails, often the best way to recover it is to not restore anything at all. Whenever possible, if bandwidth permits and a second domain controller exists on the network, you could simply reinstall Windows (or recover from an ASR boot floppy and ASR backup) and then rerun DCPromo to repromote the domain controller. You will be left with a clean system.

Since the Active Directory can only be backed up and restored as part of the System State, when you are restoring the Active Directory, you need to restore the entire System State as well. If a server completely fails, you may run into problems if you are restoring data to a server with completely different hardware. Following the restore, if problems are encountered, you can perform a repair of the operating system to repair any configuration errors.

So if all else has failed, you have a good System State backup, and you need to restore the Active Directory database, you are faced with three restore types.

- *Primary*—Select this option when you are restoring the first domain controller and no other domain controllers are online in the domain. When this option is selected, restores to all other domain controllers should be nonauthoritative.

- *Authoritative*—Use only when you need to roll the Active Directory database back to the time of the backup used in the restore. This should only be performed if major errors have occurred, such as the deletion of entire OUs, or if you need to roll back everything. This option requires that you run the `ntdsutil` command following the restore to select the objects that you wish to mark as authoritative for replication.

- *Nonauthoritative*—This restore option is used 99% of the time for Active Directory restores. This option causes the restored data to be brought back, and the domain controller then receives updates from other domain controllers in the forest in order to resynchronize.

When initiating an Active Directory restore, you can select the Active Directory restore type in the Advanced Restore Options in Backup. Again, you should only look at performing a restore as a very last resort.

> If your domain controller is your only DNS server and you use Active Directory integrated zones, your DNS zone data will not be available when your domain controller is booted to Directory Services Restore Mode. If you are restoring the System State over the network with a third-party backup utility, you may need to configure Hosts files to provide name resolution for all computers involved in the restore operation.

Summary

This chapter took you though the joys of troubleshooting Active Directory. What had been a major challenge with Windows 2000 and often required the help of third-party vendors and products is often no longer the case with Windows Server 2003 Active Directory. When problems arise, you need to pinpoint the source quickly. Since Active Directory is logical and hierarchical in nature, this is often easy to accomplish.

While this is it for the individual troubleshooting sections of this book, you may want to go ahead and turn to the appendices. Appendix A serves as a complete reference to the troubleshooting command line tools, with all tools listed alphabetically so that it is easy to locate the syntax for a tool you plan to use. Appendix B has all the common stop messages that you may encounter, along with all possible Device Manager error codes. The last appendix, Appendix C, describes each of the third-party tools that are included on the companion CD.

I hope you have enjoyed the ride. Remember that troubleshooting is mostly about understanding the processes and eliminating all potential problems involved in a failure. No book or reference can possibly document every possible failure, since all of us find new and creative ways to break computers every day. However, with an understanding of the core architecture of any technology and the tools that you can use to identify problems, you will find troubleshooting to be a source of both enjoyment and pride, with maybe just a pinch of pain mixed in.

A

Troubleshooting Command Line Reference

This appendix provides an alphabetical index and syntax for the available Windows command line troubleshooting tools. For each tool listed, you will see a brief description of the tool as well as its syntax and command options.

acldiag (ST)

The `acldiag` tool allows you to check the access control list entries (ACEs) for objects in the Active Directory, and it can detect and repair problems encountered when inconsistent modifications are made to ACEs. For example, suppose that you use the Delegation of Control Wizard to allow specific users in departmental OUs to create users in their OUs and to reset user passwords. If another administrator makes modifications to the advanced permissions of an OU or of a parent OU, the settings provided by the Delegation Template applied by the Delegation of Control Wizard may not match. This could cause users that once were able to create users, to no longer have that ability. Fortunately for you, Microsoft provides `acldiag` to quickly repair such problems.

The syntax for `acldiag` is:

```
acldiag <DN> [/schema] [/chkdeleg] [/geteffective:<user|group|*>]
[/fixdeleg] [/skip] [/tdo]
```

The command options are described in Table A-1.

Table A-1. acldiag Command Options

Option	Use
DN	The Distinguished Name (DN) is a required parameter and identifies the command's target object. Here is an example of a DN: cn=jpeterman,ou=support,dc=sales,dc=aw,dc=com.
/schema	This parameter causes the schema to be checked to see if the target object's ACL includes the ACEs that are the schema defaults. The result of the check is displayed in the command output.
/chkdeleg	This switch causes the command to perform delegation diagnostics, which reports on whether the object includes ACEs that are in the Delegation Template (created by the Delegation of Control Wizard). If the command reports a status of Misconfigured, that means that at least one permission in the ACL does not match what is listed in the Delegation Template.
/geteffective:<user | group | *>	Displays effective permissions to the target object that are held by a specific user or group. If you use the * wildcard, the effective permissions of all users and groups are displayed.
/fixdeleg	Causes `acldiag` to reapply the Delegation Template to the object's ACT. This eliminates any special permissions assigned to the object and restores any incomplete delegations. Instead of automatically fixing misconfigured delegations, the command prompts you to decide if you want to repair each problem it detects.
/skip	Causes the command output to not display the ACEs that are contained in the object's ACL.
/tdo	Causes the output to be displayed in tab-delimited format, which is useful for exporting the output to a spreadsheet or database.

arp

The `arp` command can be handy for troubleshooting when one system cannot contact another system on the same subnet. An example of when you would run into an improper ARP cache entry could be when two systems on the same subnet were accidentally assigned the same IP address. When this happens, a computer could have the wrong MAC address cached for a particular IP address. This is where the `arp` command is useful. Here's its syntax:

```
arp -a [IP address] [-N <Interface_address>]
arp -d <IP address> [Interface address]
arp -s <IP address> <MAC address> [Interface address]
```

The `arp` command options are explained in Table A-2.

Table A-2. arp Command Options

Option	Use
`-a`	Displays IP address–to–MAC address mappings stored in a system's ARP cache.
`-d`	Deletes the ARP cache entry for the IP address specified.
`-s`	Adds a static (permanent) IP address–to–MAC address mapping to the ARP cache.
`<IP address>`	Causes information to be displayed only for the IP address entered.
`<Interface address>`	For systems with multiple NICs, this is used to specify the MAC address of the local NIC that you wish to run the `arp` command on; otherwise, the command is always run on the first bound NIC in the network binding order.
`<MAC address>`	Used to specify a MAC address on which to create a static ARP cache entry.

atmadm

If your RAS server connects to an asynchronous transfer mode (ATM) network, you will find this command very useful when troubleshooting problems on the ATM network. The `atmadm` command allows you to check and monitor addresses registered by ATM call manager on an ATM network. This command is useful for checking the status of an ATM adapter, when you suspect a problem with ATM connections. The command displays statistics for both incoming and outgoing calls on a system's ATM adapters.

The syntax for `atmadm` is:

```
atmadm [/c] [/a] [/s]
```

The command options are described in Table A-3.

Table A-3. atmadm Command Options

Option	Use
`/c`	Shows call information for all current connections on the system's ATM adapter(s). The elements of the command output when using the `/c` option are described in Table A-4.
`/a`	Shows the registered ATM network service access point (NSAP) address for each ATM adapter on the system.
`/s`	Shows monitoring statistics for active ATM connections. The components of the statistical output that is displayed when this option is selected are described in Table A-5.

Appendix A   Troubleshooting Command Line Reference

Table A-4. atmadm /c Output Data

Data Displayed	Description
Connection	Under the Connection heading in the command output, you will see abbreviations that detail the types of connections to the ATM adapter. Under this heading, you will see the following types of data. • In/Out—Specifies the type of connection. In = connection from another network to the ATM adapter. Out = connection from the ATM adapter to another network. • PMP—Signifies a point-to-multipoint call. • P-P—Signifies a point-to-point call. • SVC—Signifies that the connection is on a switched virtual circuit. • PVC—Signifies that the connection is on a permanent virtual circuit.
VPI/VCI	This heading displays the virtual path or virtual channel of the incoming or outgoing call.
Remote Address / Media Parameters	The first piece of information displayed under this heading is the NSAP address of the calling (In) or called (Out) ATM device. Two other elements of this heading are TX and RX. • TX—The TX portion of this heading identifies the connection's transmitting default or selected bit-rate type (ABR, CBR, UBR, or VBR), the default or selected line speed, and the service data unit (SDU) size. • RX—The RX portion of this heading provides information on the connection's receiving default or selected bit-rate type (ABR, CBR, UBR, or VBR), the default or selected line speed, and the SDU size.

Table A-5. atmadm /s Output Data

Statistic	Description
Current Active Calls	Current open calls on the system's ATM adapter
Total Successful Incoming Calls	Total number of calls successfully received from other adapters on the ATM network
Total Successful Outgoing Calls	Calls successfully made to other devices on the ATM network
Unsuccessful Incoming Calls	Total number of incoming calls that failed to connect to the local system
Unsuccessful Outgoing Calls	Total number of outgoing calls that failed to connect to remote devices on the ATM network
Calls Closed by Remote	Total number of calls closed by remote devices on the ATM network

Table A-5. atmadm /s Output Data, continued

Statistic	Description
Calls Closed Locally	Total number of calls closed by the local system
Signaling and ILMI Packets Sent	Total number of integrated local management interface (ILMI) packets sent to the system's local ATM switch
Signaling and ILMI Packets Received	Total number of ILMI packets received from the system's local ATM switch

bootcfg

The `bootcfg` tool automates editing the boot.ini file, eliminating much of the guesswork that is normally associated with editing the file. There are 11 different ways to run `bootcfg`, each of which will be addressed shortly. Before we get to each command version, first note the switches that each command option has in common. The common command switches are for executing the command to manage a remote system and are shown in Table A-6.

Table A-6. bootcfg Common Command Options

Option	Use
/s <system>	Used to specify the name or IP address of the remote system you wish to manage.
/u <user>	Specifies the name of the domain user under which the command should run.
/p <password>	When /u is used, specifies the password for the domain user.

bootcfg /addsw

The `bootcfg /addsw` command allows you to configure loading options, such as maximum allowable RAM for a specific operating system entry in the boot.ini file. The syntax for `bootcfg /addsw` is:

```
bootcfg /addsw /id <OSNumber> [/s <system>] [/u <domain\user>] [/p
<password>] [/mm <MaxRAM>] [/bv] [/so] [/ng]
```

The `bootcfg /addsw` options are described in Table A-7.

Table A-7. bootcfg /addsw Command Options

Option	Use
/id <OSNumber>	This switch is required to tell the command which OS reference in the boot.ini file to apply to. Numbering for this switch begins at 1, so to apply the command to the second OS listed in the [operating systems] portion of the boot.ini file, you would enter /id 2. You can determine the OS–line number relationship by running bootcfg /query.
/mm <MaxRAM>	Adds the /maxmem switch along with the amount of memory specified (in megabytes) to the OS line number specified with the /id switch.
/bv	Adds the /basevideo switch to the OS line number specified with the /id switch. Adding /basevideo to an OS entry in the boot.ini file causes the operating system to boot using a standard VGA video driver.
/so	Adds the /sos switch to the OS line number specified with the /id switch. Adding this switch causes the OS to display device driver names as they are loaded when the system boots.
/ng	Adds the /noguiboot switch to the OS line number specified with the /id switch. This switch hides the Windows progress bar that appears while the system boots.

bootcfg /copy

The `bootcfg /copy` command is used to duplicate an operating system reference line in the boot.ini file. For example, if only one OS was referenced, you could use `bootcfg /copy` to duplicate the reference and cause the boot.ini file to list two operating systems. Once the line is duplicated, you can then use other `bootcfg` commands to edit the OS entry; otherwise, the new entry will point to the same operating system as the original entry, leaving you with two entries that reference the same operating system.

Here is the syntax for `bootcfg /copy`:

```
bootcfg /copy /id <OSNumber> [/s <system>] [/u <domain\user>] [/p <password>] [/d <description>]
```

Table A-8 describes the command options for `bootcfg /copy`.

Table A-8. bootcfg /copy Command Options

Option	Use
/id <OSNumber>	This switch is required to tell the command which OS reference in the boot.ini file to apply to. Numbering for this switch begins at 1, so to apply the command to the second OS listed in the [operating systems] portion of the boot.ini file, you would enter /id 2. You can determine the OS–line number relationship by running bootcfg /query.
/d <description>	Provides a description for the new operating system entry in the boot.ini file.

bootcfg /dbg1394

This option is primarily a concern of developers and not for systems administrators and help desk staff. With `boofcfg /dbg1394`, 1394 port debugging is configured for the operating system specified. The primary advantage of 1394 port debugging is that it offers a substantial performance advantage of using debugging tools through a standard serial port.

The syntax for `boofcfg /dbg1394` is:

```
bootcfg /dbg1394 <on|off|edit> /id <OSNumber> [/s <system>] [/u
<domain\user>] [/p <password>] [/ch <channel>]
```

The `boofcfg /dbg1394` options are explained in Table A-9.

Table A-9. bootcfg /dbg1394 Command Options

Option	Use
on	Adds the `/dbg1394` switch to the OS line number specified with the `/id` switch. Adding `/dbg1394` to an OS entry in the boot.ini file enables 1394 remote debugging support for that OS.
off	Removes the `/dbg1394` switch from the OS line number specified with the `/id` switch, thus disabling 1394 remote debugging support.
edit	Allows you to change the port and baud rate settings for the specified OS entry based on the values provided in the `/ch` switch.
/id <OSNumber>	This switch is required to tell the command which OS reference in the boot.ini file to apply to. Numbering for this switch begins at 1, so to apply the command to the second OS listed in the [operating systems] portion of the boot.ini file, you would enter `/id 2`. You can determine the OS–line number relationship by running `bootcfg /query`.
/ch <channel>	Allows you to specify the channel to use for debugging. Allowable values are any integer between 1 and 64. This switch cannot be used in conjunction with the `off` option.

bootcfg /debug

This command is used to configure standard debugging (via serial port) to an OS entry in the boot.ini file. With serial communications, unlike with IEEE 1394, you need to specify a baud rate and a COM port for the system to use for communication. This syntax for `bootcfg /debug` is:

```
bootcfg /debug <on|off|edit> /id <OSNumber> [/s <system>] [/u
<domain\user>] [/p <password>] [/port <COM Port>] [/baud <baud rate>]
```

The command options are described in Table A-10.

Table A-10. bootcfg /debug Command Options

Option	Use
on	Adds the /debug switch to the OS line number specified with the /id switch. Adding /debug to an OS entry in the boot.ini file enables standard remote debugging support for that OS.
off	Removes the /debug switch from the OS line number specified with the /id switch, thus disabling standard remote debugging support.
edit	Allows you to change the port and baud rate settings for the specified OS entry based on the values provided in the /port and /baud switches.
/id <OSNumber>	This switch is required to tell the command which OS reference in the boot.ini file to apply to. Numbering for this switch begins at 1, so to apply the command to the second OS listed in the [operating systems] portion of the boot.ini file, you would enter /id 2. You can determine the OS–line number relationship by running bootcfg /query.
/port <COM Port>	Adds the /port switch to the OS line number specified with the /id switch. This is used to indicate which COM port should be used for remote debugging. Valid COM Port values are COM1, COM2, COM3, or COM4.
/baud <baud rate>	Adds the /baud switch to the OS line number specified in the /id switch. This is used to indicate the baud rate to be used for debugging. Valid baud rate values are 9600, 19200, 38400, 57600, or 115200.

bootcfg /default

The `bootcfg /default` command is used to specify an operating system listed in the boot.ini file as the default OS. The syntax for this command is:

```
bootcfg /default /id <OSNumber> [/s <system>] [/u <domain\user>]
[/p <password>]
```

As with other `bootcfg` command versions, the `/id` switch is used to specify the operating system line in the boot.ini file to designate as the default.

bootcfg /delete

This command is used to delete an operating system reference in the boot.ini file by removing its associated entry in the [operating systems] portion of the file. The syntax for `bootcfg /delete` is:

```
bootcfg /delete /id <OSNumber> [/s <system>] [/u <domain\user>]
[/p <password>]
```

When you run the command, you use the `/id` switch to indicate the OS reference line to delete, so to delete the second OS reference, you would run `bootcfg /delete /id 2`.

bootcfg /ems

This command allows you to change the redirection configuration of the Emergency Management Services (EMS) console (Windows Server 2003 systems only) to a remote computer. When you run this command, a `redirect-Port#` entry is added to the [boot loader] section of the boot.ini file, and a `/redirect` switch to the specified operating system in the [operating systems] portion of the file.

Here is the syntax for `bootcfg /ems`:

```
bootcfg /ems <on|off|edit> /id <OSNumber> [/s <system>] [/u
<domain\user>] [/p <password>] [/port <COM Port>] [/baud <baud rate>]
```

The command options are described in Table A-11.

Table A-11. bootcfg /ems Command Options

Option	Use
`on`	Enables remote output for the OS line number specified with the `/id` switch. When this parameter is used, the `/redirect` switch is added to the OS number specified, and redirect settings are added to the [boot loader] file section based on the value you specify with the `/port` switch.
`off`	Disables EMS remote output on the OS specified.
`edit`	Allows you to change current EMS port settings (set with the `/port` switch) for an OS you specify.
`/id <OSNumber>`	This switch is required to tell the command which OS reference in the boot.ini file to apply to. Numbering for this switch begins at 1, so to apply the command to the second OS listed in the [operating systems] portion of the boot.ini file, you would enter `/id 2`. You can determine the OS–line number relationship by running `bootcfg /query`.
`/port <COM Port>`	Indicates which COM port should be used for redirection. Valid `COM Port` values are `COM1`, `COM2`, `COM3`, `COM4`, or `BIOSSET`. When `BIOSSET` is used as the `COM Port` value, EMS gets the valid COM port to use from the system BIOS.
`/baud <baud rate>`	Indicates the baud rate to be used for redirection. Valid `baud rate` values are 9600, 19200, 38400, 57600, or 115200.

bootcfg /query

The `bootcfg /query` command allows you to see the [boot loader] and [operating systems] configuration settings in the boot.ini file of a local or remote system. The syntax for this command is:

```
bootcfg /query [/s <system>] [/u <domain\user>] [/p <password>]
```

bootcfg /raw

This command is used to add text to the end of an operating system entry in the boot.ini file and replaces any text that had previously existed at the end of the entry. The syntax for `bootcfg /raw` is:

```
bootcfg /raw "<OptionString>" /id <OSNumber> [/s <system>] [/u
<domain\user>] [/p <password>]
```

The command options are described in Table A-12.

Table A-12. bootcfg /raw Command Options

Option	Use
`OptionString`	Specifies a string of options, in quotes, to list at the end of the operating system reference line.
`/id <OSNumber>`	This switch is required to tell the command which OS reference in the boot.ini file to apply to. Numbering for this switch begins at 1, so to apply the command to the second OS listed in the [operating systems] portion of the boot.ini file, you would enter `/id 2`. You can determine the OS–line number relationship by running `bootcfg /query`.

bootcfg /rmsw

The `bootcfg /rmsw` command allows you to remove options associated with operating system entries in the boot.ini file. Here is the syntax for `bootcfg /rmsw`:

```
bootcfg /rmsw /id <OSNumber> [/s <system>] [/u <domain\user>]
[/p <password>] [/mm] [/bv] [/ng]
```

The `bootcfg /rmsw` options are described in Table A-13.

Table A-13. bootcfg /rmsw Command Options

Option	Use
/id <OSNumber>	This switch is required to tell the command which OS reference in the boot.ini file to apply to. Numbering for this switch begins at 1, so to apply the command to the second OS listed in the [operating systems] portion of the boot.ini file, you would enter /id 2. You can determine the OS–line number relationship by running bootcfg /query.
/mm	Removes the /maxmem switch from the specified OS reference.
/bv	Removes the /basevideo switch from the specified OS reference.
/so	Removes the /sos switch from the specified OS reference.
/ng	Removes the /noguiboot switch from the specified OS reference.

bootcfg /timeout

When a system is dual booted, the user has a configured amount of seconds to choose an OS before the default OS is loaded. The waiting period is known as the timeout value, which can be modified with bootcfg /timeout.

The syntax for bootcfg /timeout is:

```
bootcfg /timeout <time> [/s <system>] [/u <domain\user>]
[/p <password>]
```

In the command syntax, time is the number of seconds that you would like the boot menu to appear before the default OS is loaded. The default time value is 30 seconds.

cacls

The cacls command allows you to display or modify the discretionary access control list (DACL) for a file or files. If you suspect that failure of a user to access a particular file is related to permissions, you can use cacls to confirm your suspicions. If you notice a problem with the access control list for a folder or file after running cacls, you can also use the command to modify the access control list.

Here is the syntax for cacls:

```
cacls <filename> [/t] [/e] [/c] [/g <user|group:permission>]
[/r <user|group>] [/p <user|group:permission>] [/d <user|group>]
```

The cacls command options are shown in Table A-14.

Table A-14. cacls Command Options

Option	Use
`<filename>`	Specifies the folder or file whose DACL you wish to manage. The * and ? wildcards can be used to specify multiple files.
`/t`	Causes the command to apply to the specified folders and files in the current directory and all subdirectories.
`/e`	Edits the DACL for the file or folder specified.
`/c`	Causes the command to continue changing DACLs, even if errors are encountered.
`/g <user|group:permission>`	Grants permission to the user or group specified. Valid permissions are shown in Table A-15.
`/r <user|group>`	Revokes access rights for the specified user.
`/p <user|group:permission>`	Replaces the access rights for the user or group specified. Valid permission choices are shown in Table A-15.
`/d <user|group>`	Denies access for the user or group specified.

Table A-15. Valid cacls Permission Values

Permission Value	Description
F	Full Control
C	Change (write)
W	Write
R	Read
N	None

When the DACL is displayed in the command output, in addition to permissions displayed for specific users and user groups, you will see whether the permissions apply to the current folder, subfolders, and/or files for each access control entry listed. The output codes for the "where" portion of the output are displayed in Table A-16.

Table A-16. cacls Output Codes

Output Code	User/Group Permissions Apply To
No code displayed	Target folder only
CI	Target folder and subfolders
IO	ACE does not apply to the current file or folder.
OI	Target folder and files

Table A-16. cacls Output Codes, continued

Output Code	User/Group Permissions Apply To
(CI)(IO)	Subfolders of target folder only
(OI)(CI)	Target folder, subfolders, and files
(OI)(IO)	Target's files only
(OI)(CI)(IO)	Target's subfolders and files only

chkdsk

Suspect that a faulty hard disk is at the root of a problem? Then running `chkdsk` may allow you to verify your suspicions. When run, `chkdsk`, short for *check disk*, performs a check of a hard disk and alerts you of any problems with the disk. You can also use the command to fix any errors that it finds on the specified disk. The syntax for the command is:

```
chkdsk [volume | [[path] filename]]] [/c] [/f] [/i] [/l:[size]] [/r]
[/v] [/x]
```

The command parameters are explained in Table A-17.

Table A-17. chkdsk Command Options

Option	Use
volume	Indicates the drive letter (followed by a :), mount point, or volume name on which the `chkdsk` command should be run.
filename	Only for FAT or FAT32 volumes; lists the file(s) to check for fragmentation.
/c	On NTFS volumes only; causes the command to skip checking cycles within the folder structure, thus reducing the amount of time needed for the command to complete.
/f	Causes the command to fix any errors it finds on the disk.
/i	On NTFS volumes only; causes a less detailed check of the volume's indexes to be performed, thus shortening the amount of time required for the command to complete.
/l:size	On NTFS volumes only; when used, can either display the log file or change its size. The log file is used if the system crashes while `chkdsk` is running, allowing the `chkdsk` command to complete from where it left off once the computer restarts.
/r	Recovers readable information found on bad disk sectors (implies /f).
/v	Verbose mode—for NTFS, cleanup messages are displayed; for FAT or FAT32 file systems, the full path and name of every file on the disk that is checked is displayed.
/x	Forces the volume to dismount before `chkdsk` is run, invalidating all open handles on the volume.

chkntfs

By default, when Windows restarts after an improper shutdown, `chkdsk` runs automatically. For large gigabyte or even terabyte file systems, `chkdsk` could take hours to complete. Since it is run during startup after a system crash, you may decide that it is better to have the system restart automatically, without running `chkdsk` on certain volumes. This is where `chkntfs` comes into the picture. With `chkntfs`, you can disable `chkdsk` from automatically running on certain volumes, thus preventing a slow system restart after a failure.

Here is the syntax for `chkntfs`:

```
chkntfs [/C] [/X] volume
chkntfs /D
chkntfs /T:time
```

The command options are described in Table A-18.

Table A-18. chkntfs Command Options

Option	Use
`volume`	Indicates the drive letter (followed by a `:`), mount point, or volume name on which the `chkntfs` command should be run.
`/C`	Schedules `chkntfs` to run on the drive at the next reboot.
`/X`	Causes the command to skip checking cycles within the folder structure, thus reducing the amount of time needed for the command to complete.
`chkntfs /D`	Resets the `autochk` (`chkdsk`) settings to the system defaults.
`chkntfs /T:<time>`	Used to show or set the `autochk` initiation countdown time, which is the time the system pauses before running `chkdsk` when a "dirty" volume is detected at startup.

dcdiag (ST)

The `dcdiag` tool performs over 20 tests on your Active Directory infrastructure. Some tests provide diagnostic information on a particular domain controller, while others detail your forest-wide replication configuration. The specific tests performed by this tool are described in Table A-19.

Table A-19. dcdiag Tests

Test	Description
`Advertising`	Verifies that each domain controller is properly advertising itself and its operations master roles. This test will fail if the NetLogon service is not running.
`CheckSDRefDom`	Verifies that all application directory partitions possess the correct security descriptor reference domains.
`Connectivity`	Checks the DNS registration of each domain controller, pings each domain controller, and verifies the LDAP and RPC connectivity on each domain controller.
`CrossRefValidation`	Verifies that domain cross-references are valid.
`FRSSysvol`	Verifies that the FRS SYSVOL is in a ready state.
`FRSEvent`	Checks for FRS replication errors, which could indicate replication problems with the SYSVOL and thus with the consistency of GPO replicas.
`FSMOCheck`	Does not check for server operations master roles, but instead queries to contact a global catalog server, PDC, preferred time server, time server, and a key distribution center (KDC).
`Intersite`	Checks for failures that could prevent or delay intersite replication. Microsoft warns that the results output by this test are not always accurate.
`KCCEvent`	Checks to see that the knowledge consistency checker (KCC) is creating intrasite replication connection objects without errors.
`KnowsOfRoleHolders`	Verifies that the target domain controller can contact each of the five operations masters.
`MachineAccount`	Verifies that the target system's machine account is properly registered and its services are advertised. If a failure is encountered, it can be repaired by using the `/fixmachineaccount` or `/recreatemachineaccount` parameter with the `dcdiag` command.
`NCSecDesc`	Verifies that the security descriptors for the naming context heads contain the appropriate permissions for replication.
`NetLogons`	Verifies that appropriate logon privileges exist for each domain controller to allow replication.

continues

Table A-19. dcdiag Tests, continued

Test	Description
`ObjectsReplicated`	Verifies that directory server agent (DSA) and machine account objects are replicating properly.
`OutboundSecureChannels`	Verifies that secure channels exist between all domain controllers in the target domain.
`Replications`	Verifies the ability to replicate between domain controllers, and reports any encountered replication errors.
`RidManager`	Verifies that the RID master operations master is online and functioning properly.
`Services`	Verifies that all domain controller–specific services are running on the target domain controller.
`SystemLog`	Checks to see that the system log is running without errors.
`VerifyEnterpriseReferences`	Verifies that FRS and replication system references are valid for all objects on all domain controllers in the forest.
`VerifyReferences`	Verifies that FRS and replication system references are valid for all objects on the target domain controller.
`VerifyReplicas`	Checks and verifies the validity of all application directory partitions on all replica servers.

Here is the syntax for `dcdiag`:

```
dcdiag /s:<DomainController> [/n:<NamingContext>] [[/u:<domain\user>]
[/p:<password>]] [{/a|/e}{/q|/v}] [/i] [/f:<LogFile>]
[/ferr:<ErrorLog>] [/c [/skip:<test>]] [/test:<test>] [/fix]
```

The command options are described in Table A-20.

Table A-20. dcdiag Command Options

Option	Use
`/s:<DomainController>`	Used to specify the target domain controller for the command.
`/n:<NamingContext>`	Used to specify the naming context to test. You can specify the naming context in NetBIOS, DNS (FQDN), or DN format.
`/u:<domain\user>`	Allows you to run the command under the credentials of another user.

Table A-20. dcdiag Command Options, continued

Option	Use
`/p:<password>`	Used with the `/u` parameter to specify a user password.
`/a`	Tests all servers in the target site.
`/e`	Tests all servers in the entire forest (overrides `/a`).
`/q`	Quiet output. Displays only error messages.
`/v`	Verbose output. Displays detailed information.
`/i`	Ignores nonessential error messages.
`/f:<LogFile>`	Redirects the command output to the log file specified.
`/ferr:<ErrorLog>`	Collects and redirects all output fatal errors to the log file specified.
`/c`	Performs a comprehensive test, performing all tests except DCPromo and RegisterInDNS.
`/skip:<test>`	When the `/c` parameter is used, allows you to skip a specified test.
`/test:<test>`	Runs only the test specified.
`/fix`	During the `MachineAccount` test, erroneous service principal names (SPNs) on the domain controller's Machine Account object are repaired.

defrag

The `defrag` command allows you to initiate a defragmentation of a disk from the command line. This allows you to quickly solve disk performance problems.

Here is the syntax for `defrag`:

```
defrag <volume> [-a] [-f] [-v]
```

Table A-21 describes the command options.

Table A-21. defrag Command Options

Option	Use
`volume`	Indicates the drive letter (followed by a **:**), mount point, or volume name on which the `defrag` command should be run.
`-a`	Analyze only—displays a report on disk fragmentation status.
`-f`	Forces defragmentation to run even if defragmentation is not necessary.
`-v`	Verbose mode—causes detailed information about the defragmentation analysis to be displayed.

dfsutil (ST)

The DFS utility (dfsutil) is instrumental in both troubleshooting and repairing Distributed File System (DFS) problems. With dfsutil, you can make DFS configuration changes in order to resolve user, server, or replication problems, and also clean up orphaned DFS metadata in the Active Directory. The general syntax for this utility is:

```
dfsutil [parameters]
```

This tool is very complex and provides a multitude of available switches. So as not to be too overwhelming, we'll look individually at each available command switch that is helpful for troubleshooting purposes, and then will look at some common uses for this command when you are troubleshooting and repairing DFS problems. Other versions of this command that strictly aid in DFS administration are covered in this section.

General dfsutil Switches

There are several switches that can be used in conjunction with the other options that follow this section. The generic switches allow you to define the scope of the command, such as by defining target servers, DFS roots, or shares and by specifying verbose command output. The general command switches are described in Table A-22.

Table A-22. General dfsutil Switches

Option	Use
/root:<RootName>	Specifies the UNC path to the target DFS root on which to perform the command.
/server:<Server>	Specifies the target DFS namespace server for the command.
/share:<Share>	Specifies the DFS or server message block (SMB) target share for the command.
/domain:<Domain>	Specifies the target DFS domain for the command.
/verbose	Causes the output to display more detailed information.

The choice of general options that you select is dictated by the type of operations that you are performing on your network's DFS hierarchy. In the remaining sections, you will see examples of how to use the general switches in conjunction with the task-oriented switches in order to define the command's target.

/clean

This command is needed when users report intermittent availability to DFS resources in your DFS hierarchy. Oftentimes the reason that some DFS shares appear unavailable is because DFS is trying to reference a root that is no longer online. This may have been the result of a system failing or becoming decommissioned. When the dfsutil command is executed with the /clean option, references to nonexistent root references are deleted. The syntax for this command is:

    dfsutil /clean /server:<Server> /share:<Share> [/verbose]

The target server for this command is the server hosting DFS that contains an obsolete root reference record. For the /share parameter, you specify the name of the obsolete root reference.

/export

The /export command is very useful for securing backups of your DFS namespaces. Having a backup of the namespace configuration allows you to quickly import the configuration to another server in the event that a DFS root host server fails. Since you can run the /export command using a single line of code, this command can be easily scripted to work with your existing backup utility.

The syntax for dfsutil /export is:

    dfsutil /root:<RootName> /export:<FileName>

When you run this command, you need to specify the full UNC path to the root context that you wish to export, along with a filename for the exported data.

/import

When you export a DFS configuration to a text file, you can in turn import the configuration to another server that you wish to act as a DFS root. On the target server, you need to re-create the root and then use this command to import the previous root configuration. The syntax for this command is:

    dfsutil /root:<RootName> /import:<FileName> /<verify | set | merge>
    [/verbose]

As with the /export command, when you execute this command, you need to specify a target DFS root for the command as well as the name of the file containing the DFS configuration to import. The other required parameter for this command is either the /verify, /set, or /merge switch. These options are explained in Table A-23.

Table A-23. /import Required Parameters

Option	Use
/verify	Outputs changes that may happen during the import. Provides a method to view the changes that will be made by the command prior to the changes being implemented with either the /set or /merge option. This option should be run first, to analyze the effect of the import operation prior to permanently making the changes.
/set	Causes the target namespace to be completely overwritten with the namespace configuration of the import file.
/merge	Allows you to import a namespace configuration to complement an existing namespace configuration. With this option, the current target namespace and the namespace defined in the import file are merged, with the import file's configuration settings taking precedence if any conflicting settings exist.

Since importing a root configuration to a new server requires that a root be established on the target server, you can either create a new root with the DFS MMC or use the dfsutil command with the /addftroot (domain-based DFS) or the /addstdroot (standalone DFS) switches to create the root on the target system.

/importroot

The /importroot command option is similar to the /import option, with the exception that it works with another online DFS root server, as opposed to importing backup data from a text file. This allows you to quickly add fault tolerance to DFS roots across your enterprise, or to move a DFS root configuration to an alternate server in the event that you need to take a DFS server down for maintenance.

The syntax for this command is:

```
dfsutil /root:<TargetRoot> /importroot:<SourceRoot> [/mirror |
compare]
```

The command options are described in Table A-24.

Table A-24. /importroot Required Parameters

Option	Use
/root:<TargetRoot>	Identifies the target root where data will be imported to.
/importroot:<SourceRoot>	Identifies the source root where data will be imported from.
/mirror	Creates a backup of the source DFS namespace.
/compare	Generates a comparison between the source and target DFS roots.

/pktflush

Suppose that a particular file share was moved to an alternate server, and the original source server for the share was taken offline for maintenance. What you may find after that happens is that some clients may not be able to access the new share location and instead receive an error that the resource is unavailable. The problem occurs because clients can cache DFS server referrals similarly to how they cache IP addresses for host names. As with cached IP addresses, DFS referrals are also cached for a give Time to Live (TTL) period, which can be configured at the DFS root level. The default value is 300 seconds (5 minutes). This means that if the clients wait long enough, they will receive the correct referral. However, if you want a particular client to be able to immediately access moved resources (or if the TTL value was changed to a higher value), you can do so by flushing the DFS Partition Knowledge Table (PKT) on a DFS client.

To flush the PKT on a DFS client, you would run this command on the client: `dfsutil /pktflush`. There is no additional syntax for this command.

/purgemupcache

This command's use is similar to that of `/pktflush`, with the exception that it is used to clear a client's multiple UNC provider (MUP) cache. The purpose of this local cache is to maintain information about both DFS shares and other shares, such as SMB shares, on the client system. Like other client caches, this aids in performance when accessing network resources. If you have clients that had a particular SMB share mapped and then attempted to map a DFS share with the same name, they may not be able to access the DFS share due to the SMB share information still being in their cache. If the client waits a few minutes, the DFS share will become accessible. However, if you are looking to quickly fix the problem, you can do so by running `dfsutil /purgemupcache` on the client system.

/purgewin2kstaticsitetable

This command option is needed to resolve compatibility problems when DFS is running on a mixed mode network, where there are both Windows 2000 and Windows Server 2003 systems hosting domain-based DFS roots. This problem arises when an update is made to a Windows Server 2003 root host. By default, site information is not propagated to the Windows 2000 server due to an issue with the DFS blob, mainly because Windows 2000 site information is static. You can manually update the Windows 2000 DFS root by running `dfsutil /purgewin2kstaticsitetable` on the DFS root that was updated. The complete syntax for this command is:

```
dfsutil /root:<RootName> /purgewin2kstaticsitetable
```

When you run this command, for the `/root` parameter, you specify the UNC path to the updated root. This updates the Windows 2000 site table to match the Windows Server 2003 site table.

/showwin2kstaticsitetable

If you are unsure if a Windows 2000 DFS root has knowledge of all the sites associated with various DFS objects, you can run this command to display the Windows 2000 Static Site Table contents. If you notice a discrepancy, you can then run `dfsutil` with the `/purgewin2kstaticsitetable` switch to correct the problem. The syntax for this command is:

```
dfsutil /root:<RootName> /showwin2kstaticsitetable
```

As with the previous command, the root name specified must be a complete UNC path to the DFS root in question. When you execute this command, you will see the current DFS target-to-site mappings stored in the Windows 2000 server running DFS.

/spcflush

This command can be run on DFS clients to flush their cached knowledge of trusted domains and domain controllers. This in turn causes the clients to obtain the latest information on the trusted domains and domain controllers within the DFS hierarchy. This may be necessary if a client is having trouble accessing DFS shares. An alternative to running this command is to simply wait for its cached contents to expire, or you can simply reboot the client to clear out all cached DFS information.

To use this command to clear a client's software publishing certificate (SPC) cache, you would run `dfsutil /spcflush` on the client system.

/unmapftroot

This command is used to manually remove references to a domain-based DFS root target that no longer exists. This may be necessary if a DFS root server fails or is permanently decommissioned. If the root's metadata references are not removed from the DFS topology, other DFS hosts will continually fail in their attempts to replicate with the now nonexistent root. To eliminate these failures, you can run `dfsutil /unmapftroot`. The full syntax and parameters for this command are:

```
dfsutil /unmapftroot /server:<Server> /share:<Share>
```

The target server for this command is any server hosting the domain-based DFS root that references the nonexistent system. For the `/share` parameter, you specify the name of the DFS share that is replicated to the obsolete system.

/updatewin2kstaticsitetable

This command option is needed to resolve compatibility problems when DFS is running on a mixed mode network, where there are both Windows 2000 and Windows Server 2003 systems hosting domain-based DFS roots. This problem arises when an update is made to a Windows Server 2003 root host. By default, site information is not propagated to the Windows 2000 server due to an issue with the DFS blob, mainly because Windows

2000 site information is static. You can manually update the Windows 2000 DFS root by running `dfsutil /updatewin2kstaticsitetable` on the DFS root that was updated. The alternative to using this command is to use the `/purgewin2kstaticsitetable` switch to cause a complete refresh of the Static Site Table on a Windows 2000 Server. The complete syntax for this command is:

```
dfsutil /root:<RootName> /updatewin2kstaticsitetable
```

When you run this command, for the `/root` parameter, you specify the UNC path to the updated root. This would update the Windows 2000 site table to match the Windows Server 2003 site table.

dhcploc (ST)

If you're looking for an easy way to identify DHCP servers on a network, then look no further—`dhcploc` is the tool you need. This support tool can be run on any non-DHCP server, and it reports on DHCP traffic and the servers involved. If you suspect that the dreaded "rogue" DHCP server is wreaking havoc on your DHCP infrastructure, you can locate it by IP address with this tool.

To run the command, you would run the following on a server that is not a DHCP server:

```
dhcploc <local IP address>
```

In the command syntax, you must specify the IP address of the system on which you are executing the command. This should not be the IP address of a DHCP server. Running the command on a DHCP server may produce erroneous results. Note that the command output displays DHCP messages such as offers and acknowledgments.

dmdiag (ST)

The `dmdiag` command is used to quickly retrieve configuration information on a system's hard disks. You can run the command and have its output dumped to a file or displayed on the screen. One of the most useful features of this command is that it displays all the configured mount points on a system, as well as any symbolic links on the system. If a computer's storage configuration is unknown to you, running `dmdiag` is a quick way to get brought up to speed.

Here is the complete list of what you will learn after running `dmdiag`:

- Drive letter usage
- A kernel list
- Logical Disk Manager (LDM) file versions
- The LDM size

- A listing of all physical disks and their disk type (basic or dynamic)
- The mount points on the system
- Partition configuration information
- Symbolic links
- The system name and OS version

Here is the syntax for dmdiag:

`dmdiag [/v] [/f <filename>]`

The dmdiag command options are described in Table A-25.

Table A-25. dmdiag Command Options

Option	Use
/v	Used to provide verbose output, which displays all of the configuration data mentioned earlier in this section. Without this switch, very little information is displayed in the output.
/f	Causes command output to be dumped to a text file named by the filename parameter. If no filename is specified, the file will be called dmdiag.txt and will be placed in the folder from where the command was run.
filename	Used with the /f switch to provide a path and a filename for the dmdiag output file.

dnscmd (ST)

The dnscmd support tool is one of two very popular DNS troubleshooting command line tools. The nslookup command, which is covered later, generally is used for performing queries and testing DNS server responses, while dnscmd allows you to diagnose and resolve configuration issues as well as perform an abundance of administrative tasks on a DNS server.

The general syntax for dnscmd is:

`dnscmd [server] <operation> [Parameters] [Arguments]`

In the syntax, you need to specify the name of the DNS server to administer, or the command executes on the local system. There are countless different operation values that can be used with dnscmd. The operations that are relevant to DNS troubleshooting are discussed in the next two sections.

clearcache

The `clearcache` operation allows you to remove all cached resource records in a DNS server's cache. This is useful, for example, when a DNS server forwards a query to another DNS server that responds with the wrong answer. Even if you correct the address on the DNS server hosting the queried zone, other DNS servers may have the address cached. To correct the problem, you can run `clearcache` on each DNS server in your enterprise that may have cached the entry. Any new queries to the DNS server will cause it to forward the request to the server with the proper record and then will cache the correct record.

Now that you have seen why to use it, this is how to use it.

```
dnscmd [server] /clearcache
```

So, to clear the cache of the name server ns1.aw.com, you would run `dnscmd ns1.aw.com /clearcache`.

statistics

The `statistics` operation allows you to see an abundance of information about a DNS server, including

- Queries received and sent
- Query types received (A, NS, MX, PTR)
- Zone transfer attempts and the success rate
- WINS referrals
- Dynamic update statistics (secure updates, record types)
- Write performance statistics

The command syntax for the `statistics` operation is:

```
dnscmd [server] /statistics [id] [/clear]
```

The options for the `statistics` operation are described in Table A-26.

Table A-26. dnscmd /statistics Command Options

Option	Use
server	Used to specify the name or IP address of the remote DNS server on which to report statistics.
id	When you do not want to report on all DNS server statistical categories, this option allows you to specify the categories to return in the command output. Valid id values are listed in Table A-27.
/clear	Resets the target DNS server's statistics counter to 0. Counters automatically clear and start once the DNS server is started or resumed.

Table A-27. dnscmd /statistics id Parameter Values

Value	Associated Statistics
1	Time
2	Query
4	Query2
8	Recurse
10	Master
20	Secondary
40	WINS
100	Update
200	SkwanSec
400	DS
10000	Memory
40000	Database
80000	Records
100000	Packet Memory
200000	NBTStat Memory

dnslint (ST)

The `dnslint` command is a tool that lets you check and verify DNS records for a particular domain. The most common use for `dnslint` is troubleshooting problems in a multidomain enterprise DNS infrastructure utilizing stub zones and delegation. This tool is very quick, traversing a network and reporting in under a minute, and generates its output as an HTML page. The command does the following:

- Verifies all A, NS, MX, and glue records associated with delegation
- Checks that all authoritative DNS servers are responding to queries
- Verifies that data on all DNS servers is synchronized

In addition to testing name servers, you can also use `dnslint` to test mail servers on the network. The `dnslint` command identifies mail servers by locating MX records on DNS servers, and then tests the following e-mail-related ports on each mail server:

- Internet Mail Access Protocol (IMAP) version 4 (TCP port 143)
- Post Office Protocol (POP) version 3 (TCP port 110)
- Simple Mail Transfer Protocol (SMTP) (TCP port 25)

The `dnslint` syntax is:

```
dnslint /d <domain> [/r <report name>] [/s <alternate DNS server>]
[/y] [/v]
```

The command options are described in Table A-28.

Table A-28. dnslint Command Options

Option	Use
`/d <domain>`	Required parameter; specifies the domain to test.
`/r <report name>`	Used to specify a custom name for the report file. By default, the file is named Dnslint.htm and is stored in the folder from which the command was executed.
`/s <alternate DNS server>`	Used to specify an alternate DNS server address, bypassing the InterNIC servers, which is ideal for testing nonregistered domains.
`/y`	Causes the existing report file to be overwritten without prompting the user.
`/v`	Verbose output—highly detailed output data is returned.

driverquery

If you suspect that the cause of a problem may be related to the wrong device driver being installed, you can confirm your suspicion by running `driverquery`. When executed, `driverquery` lists all installed device drivers and information on their properties. For example, you can run `driverquery` to retrieve a list of all device drivers installed on the system that are not digitally signed.

Here is the syntax for `driverquery`:

```
driverquery [/s <remote system>] [/u <domain\user>] [/p <password>]
[/fo <table|list|csv>] [/nh] [/v] [/si]
```

The options for `driverquery` are described in Table A-29.

Table A-29. driverquery Command Options

Option	Use
/s <remote system>	Specifies the name or IP address of the remote system on which to query drivers.
/u <domain\user>	Allows you to run the command under the context of a different account.
/p <password>	When the /u switch is used, this options allows you to specify the password associated with the user account.
/fo <table|list|csv>	Used to specify the format for the command's output (the default is table).
/nh	When the output is set to table or csv, this option suppresses the table header information from the command output.
/v	Verbose output—highly detailed driver information is displayed in the output.
/si	Displays digital signature and manufacturer information for each installed driver.

efsinfo (ST)

Encrypting File System (EFS) information (efsinfo) provides an easy way to list files and folders encrypted with Encrypting File System on NTFS partitions. Users sometimes may not understand why they cannot access a file or folder created by another user that is stored locally or on a network share, when the reason may be that the file or target folder was encrypted by its creator. In this situation, users not having the proper key or certificate cannot open the file.

When you suspect encrypted files may be the cause of access problems to files or shared folders, efsinfo will provide you with everything you need, not only telling you if a folder has the encrypted attribute, for example, but also telling you who can decrypt the folder or its contents.

Here is the syntax for efsinfo:

```
efsinfo [/u] [/r] [/c] [/i] [/y] [/s:<directory>] [path]
```

The command options are described in Table A-30.

Table A-30. efsinfo Command Options

Option	Use
/u	Displays encryption information about files and folders in the current folder from where the command is executed (the default).
/r	Displays EFS recovery agent information.
/c	Displays certificate thumbprint information.
/i	Continues execution of the command, even if errors are encountered.
/y	Displays the digest (thumbprint) of the certificate data.
/s:<directory>	Used to specify a path in which to check the target directories and all subdirectories for encrypted files.
path	Used to provide a path (local or Universal Naming Convention, UNC) in which to check for encrypted files. If no path is specified, efsinfo checks for encrypted files in the current directory.

eventquery

The eventquery command allows you to retrieve event information from the event logs on local or remote systems. With this tool, you can search events based on their

- Date and time
- Event ID
- Type
- User
- Computer

If you are not running any event monitoring tools, you could, for example, configure a batch file that runs eventquery at regular intervals to report any critical system events on remote systems. If you redirect the command output to a text or log file, you could check the files every week or every other week to look for early signs of trouble.

Now that you have seen where eventquery can be used, let's look at its syntax.

```
eventquery.vbs [/s <remote system>] [/u <domain\user>] [/p <password>]
[/fi <filter>] [/fo <table|list|csv>] [/r <range>] [/l <log name>]
```

The many options for eventquery are described in Table A-31.

Appendix A Troubleshooting Command Line Reference

Table A-31. eventquery Command Options

Option	Use
`/s <remote system>`	Specifies the name or IP address of the remote system to query.
`/u <domain\user>`	Specifies the user account under which to execute the script.
`/p <password>`	When a user account is specified with the `/u` switch, this option is used to provide a password.
`/fi <filter>`	Allows you to use one of the filters listed in Table A-32 in the query to find specific event types.
`/fo <table|list|csv>`	Used to specify the format for the script's output (the default is `table`).
`/r <range>`	Allows you to set the number of events to display. Use a positive integer to signify the most recent and a negative integer to show the oldest. For example, a `range` value of 15 would return the 15 most recent events, whereas a `range` value of –8 would return the 8 oldest events.
`/l <log name>`	Allows you to specify the name of the log to query (application, security, system, and so on). The * wildcard can be used to indicate multiple logs.

Table A-32. Valid eventquery Filters and Operators

Filter	Operator	Allowable Values
`Category`	`eq, ne`	Any string of characters
`Computer`	`eq, ne`	Any string of characters
`Datetime`	`eq, ne, ge, le, gt, lt`	`mm/dd/yyyy, hh:mm:ss (AM|PM)`
`ID`	`eq, ne, gt, lt, ge, le, or`	Any positive integer
`Source`	`eq, ne`	Any string of characters
`Type`	`eq, ne`	`Error | Information | Warning | SuccessAudit | FailureAudit`
`User`	`eq, ne`	Any string of characters

eventtriggers /create

One of the easiest ways to arrive at optimum system uptime is to have systems tell you when they have something wrong, instead of you continually polling and monitoring network servers. With `eventtriggers`, you can have systems send alerts or execute a program (.bat, .exe, .vbs, and so on) when a particular type of event is encountered.

Here is the syntax for `eventtriggers /create`:

```
eventtriggers /create [/s <system>] [/u <domain\user>] [/p <password>]
[/tr <trigger>] [/l <log name>] {[/eid <ID>] | [/t <type>] | [/so
<source>]} [/d <description>] [/tk <task>] [/ru <domain\user>] [/rp
<password>]
```

The command parameters are described in Table A-33.

Table A-33. eventtriggers /create Command Options

Option	Use
/s <system>	Specifies the name or IP address of the remote system to set up an event trigger for.
/u <domain\user>	Specifies the user account under which to execute the command.
/p <password>	When a user account is specified with the /u switch, this option is used to provide a password.
/tr <trigger>	Allows you to specify a friendly name to associate with the event trigger.
/l <log name>	Allows you to specify the name of the log to monitor (application, security, system, and so on). The * wildcard can be used to indicate multiple logs. All logs are monitored by default.
/eid <ID>	Specifies the event ID number type that `eventtriggers` should monitor.
/t <type>	Used to have `eventtriggers` monitor a specific event type. Valid type values are error, warning, information, successaudit, or failureaudit. This parameter cannot be used in conjunction with either /eid or /so.
/so <source>	Used to specify an event source for the trigger to monitor. The source value can be represented by any string. This parameter cannot be used in conjunction with either /eid or /t.
/d <description>	Allows you to specify a description for the trigger.
/tk <task>	Allows you to specify a command to execute when the trigger conditions are satisfied.
/ru <domain\user | system>	When a task is run, this parameter allows you to specify the account that the task will run under. You can specify a user name or enter system to have the task run under the local system account.
/rp <password>	When user information is entered with /ru, /rp is used to specify a password for the user account. When the system account is specified with /ru, no password is required.

eventtriggers /delete

To delete a trigger, you need its trigger ID, which is displayed in the output of `eventtriggers /query`. Once you have the trigger ID, you are ready to delete the event trigger. Here is the syntax to do so:

```
eventtriggers /delete [/s <system>] [/u <domain\user>] [/p <password>]
[/tid <trigger ID>]
```

The `eventtriggers /delete` options are explained in Table A-34.

Table A-34. eventtriggers /delete Command Options

Option	Use
/s <system>	Specifies the name or IP address of the remote system in which to delete event triggers.
/u <domain\user>	Specifies the user account under which to execute the command.
/p <password>	When a user account is specified with the /u switch, this parameter is used to provide a password.
/tid <trigger ID>	Used to specify the trigger ID of the event trigger to be deleted. The * wildcard can be used in place of the `trigger ID` value to delete all event triggers.

eventtriggers /query

The `eventtriggers /query` command allows you to identify all of the event triggers configured on a system. To run the command, you would use the following syntax:

```
eventtriggers /query [/s <system>] [/u <domain\user>] [/p <password>]
[/fo <table|list|csv>] [/nh] [/v]
```

The options for this `eventtriggers` command version are described in Table A-35.

Table A-35. eventtriggers /query Command Options

Option	Use
/s <system>	Specifies the name or IP address of the remote system to check for a list of event triggers.
/u <domain\user>	Specifies the user account under which to execute the command.

Table A-35. eventtriggers /query Command Options, *continued*

Option	Use
`/p <password>`	When a user account is specified with the `/u` switch, this parameter is used to provide a password.
`/fo <table|list|csv>`	Used to specify the format for the command's output (the default is `table`).
`/nh`	When the output is set to `table` or `csv`, this parameter suppresses the table header information from the command output.
`/v`	Verbose mode—output displays specific information about each event trigger, including the parameters of the event associated with the trigger. Normally, only the trigger name, trigger ID, and trigger task are displayed.

fsutil behavior

The `fsutil behavior` command allows you to check several FAT and NTFS volume configuration characteristics as well as modify them. Among the configuration settings that you can modify with `fsutil behavior` are

- Support of 8.3 filename conversion
- The last access timestamp for a volume
- Disk quota notification
- Paged pool memory
- The Master File Table (MFT) size

The syntax for `fsutil behavior` is:

```
fsutil behavior query <disable8dot3 | allowextchar | disablelastaccess
| quotanotify | memoryusage | mftzone>
fsutil behavior set {disable8dot3 <1 | 0> | allowextchar <1 | 0> |
disablelastaccess <1 | 0> | quotanotify <frequency> | memoryusage
<memvalue> | mftzone <zonevalue>}
```

The `query` command option allows you to check the setting of one of the available parameters, while you can use the `set` option to modify an existing setting. With the `set` command option, a value of 1 turns on the option, while a value of 0 turns it off. All other available command parameters and options are described in Table A-36.

Table A-36. fsutil behavior Command Options

Option	Use
`disable8dot3`	Disables (1) or enables (0) creation of 8.3 character length filenames on FAT and NTFS volumes.
`allowextchar`	Enables (1) or disables (0) the use of characters from the extended character set in short file names on NTFS volumes.
`disablelastaccess`	Disables (1) or enables (0) the use of the last access timestamp for NTFS folders.
`quotanotify`	Allows you to set the frequency in which disk quota violations are written to the system event log.
`<frequency>`	Used with the `quotanotify` parameter to set the time period in seconds (values of 0 to 4294967295 are valid) in which Quota-notify events are written to the system event log. The default is 3600 (one hour).
`memoryusage`	Used to modify the internal cache settings for NTFS paged pool and non–paged pool memory, which may improve disk performance by changing the `memvalue` parameter to 2.
`<memvalue>`	This parameter has two allowable values: 1 (the default) and 2. When the parameter is set to 2, the size of NTFS memory thresholds and lookaside lists is expanded, and additional memory cache is available for file system read operations, thus improving disk performance at the expense of storage space.
`mftzone`	Used to change the volume's MFT Zone setting, which may prevent Master File Table fragmentation that would diminish disk performance. This parameter requires that a `zonevalue` be specified.
`<zonevalue>`	Used with the `mftzone` parameter to specify a new MFT Zone configuration settings. Allowable values are 1 (the default) to 4. Each value increment represents one-eighth of the volume's allocated space, so by default, 12.5% of the volume is automatically allocated to the MFT Zone. Changing the `zonevalue` to 4 would offer the best read performance, but at the cost of 50% of the available storage space.

fsutil dirty

With `fsutil dirty`, you can query or set a volume's dirty bit. In Chapter 4 in the section on `chkdsk`, it was mentioned that when a volume's dirty bit is set, `chkdsk` automatically runs the next time the system is restarted.

With `fsutil dirty`, you can query the status of or set the dirty bit for a volume. Here is its syntax:

```
fsutil dirty <query | set> <volumepath>
```

fsutil file

The `fsutil file` command is a very versatile tool that allows you to

- List files by user name (if disk quotas are enabled).
- Create new files of any size for testing purposes (ideal for testing backup performance).
- Set a file's short name.
- Check allocated ranges for a file.

The command syntax for `fsutil file` is:

```
fsutil file createnew <filepath> <size>
fsutil file findbysid <username> <filepath>
fsutil file queryallocranges offset=<offset> length=<length> <filepath>
fsutil file setshortname <filepath> <shortname>
fsutil file setvaliddata <filepath> <datalength>
fsutil file setzerodata offset=<offset> length=<length> <filepath>
```

As you can see, this command comes in several different versions. The options for each version are described in Table A-37.

Table A-37. fsutil file Command Options

Option	Use
createnew	Creates a new file (the contents consist of all 0s) with the name and size specified.
filepath	Used to specify the complete path to a file, folder, or volume.
size	Specifies the size of a file in kilobytes.
findbysid	Used to locate files owned by a specific user (only works on volumes with disk quotas enabled).
username	Used with the `findbysid` option to specify a user name.
queryallocranges	Reports the allocated ranges a file consumes on a volume. This is ideal for determining if a file has sparse regions.
offset	Used to indicate the start of the range to set to 0s.
length	Specifies the length of the range (in bytes).
setshortname	Used to set the short name (8.3) for a file.
shortname	Used to specify a file's short name for the `setshortname` parameter. It must follow the 8.3 standard.
setvaliddata	Used to configure the valid data length for a file on an NTFS volume.
datalength	Specifies the length of data (in bytes) for use with the `setvaliddata` parameter.
setzerodata	Used to fill a portion of a file with 0s.

fsutil fsinfo

The `fsutil fsinfo` command allows you to quickly retrieve information on a system's drives. In particular, you can find out the following information by executing this command:

- A list of drives on the system
- The type of drives on a system (fixed disk, CD-ROM, and so on)
- Disk configuration information (sectors, clusters, MFT Zone parameters)
- Statistical data for a drive (metadata, MFT reads/writes)
- Volume-related information (file system type, disk quotas, Unicode support, case-sensitive filename support)

As with other `fsutil` commands, the `fsinfo` option allows you to quickly retrieve very specific information on a particular volume. The `fsutil fsinfo` syntax is:

```
fsutil fsinfo drives
fsutil fsinfo drivetype <volumepath>
fsutil fsinfo ntfsinfo <rootpath>
fsutil fsinfo statistics <volumepath>
fsutil fsinfo volumeinfo <rootpath>
```

The command parameters are described in Table A-38.

Table A-38. fsutil fsinfo Command Options

Option	Use
`drives`	Displays all drives on the system by their access path (drive letter or mount path).
`drivetype`	Displays the type of the drive for the drive specified (CD-ROM, fixed disk, and so on).
`ntfsinfo`	Displays NTFS configuration information (total sectors, total clusters, bytes per sector, bytes per cluster, and MFT Zone configuration).
`statistics`	Lists statistics on read and write data for the specified volume.
`volumeinfo`	Displays configuration information for the specified volume.
`volumepath`	Used with the `drivetype` and `statistics` parameters to specify the path to a logical volume (drive letter, mount path, volume name).
`rootpath`	Used to specify the drive letter (followed by a colon) of a root drive.

fsutil hardlink

Suppose that after you have moved files from one volume to another, an application that is hard-coded to find a file in a single location no longer works properly. This is where fsutil hardlink is handy. With this tool, you can create multiple logical files in different locations that all reference the same physical file. With hard links, users and applications accessing a particular file in one location can be transparently redirected to another location, where the actual file data is stored.

To create a hard link using fsutil hardlink, you would use the following syntax:

```
fsutil hardlink create <newpath> <existingpath>
```

When you run this command, you must specify the path and a name for the new file that will link to the original file, along with the complete path and name of the original file.

fsutil objectid

The fsutil objectid command allows you to manage Object Identifiers (OIDs) associated with files, folders, and links. Both the Distributed Link Tracking (DLT) Client service and File Replication Service (FRS) track objects (files, folders, and links) by their associated OIDs, which are 16-byte (32-character) hexadecimal codes that uniquely identify an object on a volume. With fsutil objectid, you can create, delete, query, and set OID parameters. Since there is rarely ever an instance where you would need to modify an OID (Microsoft even recommends only doing so at your own risk!), simply keep the usage of this tool in the back of your mind.

Here is the command syntax:

```
fsutil objectid <create | delete | query> <volumepath>
fsutil objectid set <ObjectID> <BirthVolumeID> <BirthObjectID>
<DomainID> <volumepath>
```

These command options are fully described in Table A-39.

Table A-39. fsutil objectid Command Options

Option	Use
create	Creates an OID for the file or folder specified. If one already exists, then this command acts like the query command.
delete	Deletes a file or folder's OID.
query	Displays a file or folder's OID.
set	Modifies a file or folder's OID.

continues

Table A-39. fsutil objectid Command Options, continued

Option	Use
`volumepath`	Specifies the complete path to a file, folder, or link.
`ObjectID`	Used with the `set` parameter to provide a specific 32-hex-character OID.
`BirthVolumeID`	Used with the `set` parameter to provide the OID for the volume where the object originally resided.
`BirthObjectID`	Used with the `set` parameter to provide the original OID for the object.
`DomainID`	Used with the `set` parameter to provide the domain OID for the object. This should be 32 0s.

fsutil quota

The `fsutil quota` command allows you to manage disk quota configuration from the command line, as opposed to using Windows Explorer. Suppose that a user is unable to save documents to his home folder, which gets backed up nightly on a network server. You suspect that the user's problem may be the result of his exceeding his quota limit. You can quickly verify your suspicions by running `fsutil quota`.

The syntax for `fsutil quota` is:

```
fsutil quota disable <volume>
fsutil quota enforce <volume>
fsutil quota modify <volume> <threshold> <limit> <domain\user>
fsutil quota query <volume>
fsutil quota track <volume>
fsutil quota violations
```

The options and usage for each `fsutil quota` command version are described in Table A-40.

Table A-40. fsutil quota Command Options

Option	Use
`disable`	Disables disk quotas on the specified volume.
`enforce`	Enforces disk quota limits on the specified volume.
`modify`	Changes an existing disk quota or creates a new quota for the specified volume.
`query`	Displays disk quota information for the specified volume.
`track`	Tracks disk usage on the specified volume.
`violations`	Checks the local system and application logs, and displays a list of users that have exceeded quota limits or have reached their quota threshold.

Table A-40. fsutil quota Command Options, continued

Option	Use
`volume`	Used to indicate the volume to manage.
`threshold`	Used with the `modify` parameter to set a limit (in bytes) at which a user is warned that he or she is approaching the quota limit.
`limit`	Used with the `modify` parameter to set a maximum amount of disk space (in bytes) that can be used by the user.
`domain\user`	Used with the `modify` parameter to specify a user account to which the quota entry applies.

fsutil reparsepoint

This tool allows you to query reparse points, letting you determine what true object they reference, and also allows you to cleanly delete reparse points.

The syntax for `fsutil reparsepoint` is:

```
fsutil reparsepoint <query | delete> <filepath>
```

The three options for this command are described in Table A-41.

Table A-41. fsutil reparsepoint Command Options

Option	Use
`query`	If a reparse point exists for the file or folder in the specified path, information on its data length, tag value, and globally unique identifier (GUID) is displayed.
`delete`	Deletes a reparse point associated with the file or folder in the specified path.
`filepath`	Used to specify the path to a file or folder containing a reparse point.

fsutil sparse

With `fsutil sparse`, you can

- Identify sparse files.
- Mark a file as a sparse file.
- Scan a file, looking for its ranges of nonzero data.
- Fill a portion of a file with 0s.

Appendix A   Troubleshooting Command Line Reference

The `fsutil sparse` syntax is:

```
fsutil sparse <queryflag | queryrange | setflag | setrange> <path>
[offset] [length]
```

The `fsutil sparse` options are explained in Table A-42.

Table A-42. fsutil sparse Command Options

Option	Use
queryflag	Determines if a file is set as a sparse file.
queryrange	Displays ranges in the sparse file that contain nonzero data.
setflag	Sets a file to be a sparse file.
setrange	Fills the designated sparse file with a range (specified with the `offset` and `length` parameters) with 0s.
path	Specifies the complete path to the sparse file. If the path contains spaces, include the path in quotes.
offset	Specifies the point within the file to mark as sparse (beginning of continuous string of 0s).
length	Specifies the length (in bytes) of the region to be marked as sparse.

fsutil USN

The `fsutil USN` command allows you to perform the following administrative tasks on a volume's Change Journal:

- Create a new Change Journal
- Modify an existing Change Journal
- List Change Journal entries between a low and high update sequence number (USN) value
- Query general Change Journal information (capacity, record information)
- Display USN data for a given file

These tasks can be performed using the following syntax:

```
fsutil USN createjournal <MaxSize> <AllocationDelta> <VolumePath>
fsutil USN deletejournal <flags> <VolumePath>
fsutil USN enumdata <FileRef> <LowUSN> <HighUSN> <VolumePath>
fsutil USN queryjournal <VolumePath>
fsutil USN readdata <FilePath>
```

As you can see, there are several variations of this command. The options for each command version are explained in Table A-43.

Table A-43. fsutil USN Command Options

Option	Use
`createjournal`	Creates a new Change Journal on the volume specified. If one already exists, the Change Journal is modified with the parameters specified in the command.
`Maxsize`	Used to indicate the maximum size (in bytes) to allocate on the volume for the Change Journal.
`AllocationDelta`	Used to specify the amount of data (in bytes) to be removed from the beginning and added to the end of the Change Journal. In other words, once the Change Journal reaches its maximum size, how much of the oldest data should be purged to make room for new data.
`VolumePath`	Used to specify the drive letter or mount path to a particular volume.
`deletejournal`	Used to disable an active Change Journal.
`flags`	Two flag options are available for the `fsutil USN deletejournal` command. • `/d`—Disables the active Change Journal, with I/O control returned to the system before the operation completes. • `/n`—Disables the active Change Journal, with I/O control returned to the system after the operation completes.
`enumdata`	Itemizes and lists Change Journal data between two specified points.
`FileRef`	Specifies the ordinal file position at which itemization is to begin.
`LowUSN`	Specifies the lower boundary of USN records in the Change Journal that are returned in the command output.
`HighUSN`	Specifies the upper boundary of USN records in the Change Journal that are returned in the command output. Files with USNs equal to or between the `LowUSN` and `HighUSN` values are returned by the command.
`queryjournal`	Used to display Change Journal configuration information, including the first USN, the maximum journal size, and the allocation delta.
`readdata`	Used to display the USN data for a single file.
`Filepath`	Used to specify the complete path to a file to be checked with the `fsutil USN readdata` command.

fsutil volume

The `fsutil volume` command allows you to dismount a volume or to check the amount of free space on the volume. The syntax for `fsutil volume` is:

```
fsutil volume <diskfree | dismount> <drivename | volumepath>
```

The command syntax requires that either `diskfree` or `diskmount` be specified, along with a drive name or a volume path. These options are further explained in Table A-44.

Table A-44. fsutil volume Command Options

Option	Use
`diskfree`	Used to query the amount of free space on the drive or volume specified.
`dismount`	Used to dismount the drive or volume specified.
`drivename`	Used to specify the logical drive on which to run the command.
`volumepath`	Used to specify the logical path to a mount point or volume name representing a logical volume.

ftonline (ST)

With `ftonline`, you can temporarily mount and bring failed fault-tolerant basic disks online so that you can copy or back up their data. Once you reboot the system, the fault-tolerant basic disks will again show a failed status and should be deleted and reconfigured.

Here is `ftonline`'s syntax:

```
ftonline <Driveletter>
```

getmac

With `getmac`, you can determine the MAC address of a remote system without having to leave your desk. Here is the syntax for `getmac`:

```
getmac [/s <system> [/u <username> [/p <password>]]] [/fo <format>]
[/nh] [/v]
```

The `getmac` parameters are explained in Table A-45.

Table A-45. getmac Command Options

Option	Use
/s <system>	Used to specify the name or IP address of the remote system for which you need the MAC address(es).
/u <username>	Specifies the name of the domain user under which the command should run.
/p <password>	When /u is used, specifies the password for the domain user.
/fo <format>	Specifies the format for the output data; valid choices are table (default), list, or csv.
/nh	For table and csv output formats, causes the column header not to be displayed.
/v	Verbose mode—causes more detailed information to be displayed.

gpresult

The gpresult command allows you to determine the Resultant Set of Policy (RSoP) for group policy settings applied to a user or computer object. For most of your GPO troubleshooting, you should consider the RSoP GUI tool, since it provides easy-to-read graphical analysis of policy settings. This tool is good for quickly gathering RSoP settings when a user is having problems. If, after running gpresult, you find that you need more or better-organized information, you can then run RSoP. Think of this tool as a way to get a quick glimpse of a user or computer's resultant policy settings. Here is the syntax for gpresult:

```
gpresult [/s:<computer>] [/user:<UserName>] [[/u:<domain\user>]
[/p:<password>]] [/scope <user|computer>] [/v] [/z]
```

The command options are described in Table A-46.

Table A-46. gpresult Command Options

Option	Use
/s <computer>	Used to specify the computer whose effective policy settings you wish to view.
/user <UserName>	Used to specify the user whose effective policy settings you wish to view.
/u:<domain\user>	Allows you to run the command under the credentials of another user.

continues

Table A-46. gpresult Command Options, continued

Option	Use
/p:<password>	Used with the /u parameter to specify a user password.
/scope <user | computer>	Allows you to have just the computer or user portion of the resultant policy displayed.
/v	Verbose output. More detailed output information is displayed.
/z	Displays all available GPO information, providing more detail than the /v switch. You should consider redirecting the command output to a text file (use > *filename*) when running this command.

gpupdate

The gpupdate command is the replacement for the secedit /refreshpolicy command that was used with Windows 2000 to manually initiate a refresh of GPOs on a system. While all policies do refresh automatically, using this command allows you to immediately refresh a policy. This is often important if you want to refresh policy settings immediately after making changes to a GPO. This way, you can verify that your GPO changes behaved or made the corrections that you anticipated. Unlike secedit /refreshpolicy, gpupdate by default refreshes both computer and user policy settings. With secedit, you would have to run two commands to refresh both settings.

The syntax for gpupdate is:

```
gpupdate [/target:<computer|user>] [/force] [/wait:<seconds>]
[/logoff] [/boot] [/sync]
```

The gpupdate command options are described in Table A-47.

Table A-47. gpupdate Command Options

Option	Use
/target:<computer | user>	Causes the command to refresh only the computer or user GPO settings on the system. By default, both the computer and user portions of the applicable GPOs are refreshed.
/force	Ignores all GPO processing optimizations, such as slow link detection, and reapplies all settings.
/wait:<seconds>	Allows you to specify the number of seconds that policy processing can take to complete. The default value is 600 seconds (10 minutes). The values 0 = no wait and –1 = wait indefinitely.

Table A-47. *gpupdate Command Options, continued*

Option	Use
/logoff	Logs off the user after the policy refresh completes. A user logoff is often required to refresh many policy settings, such as changes to the desktop, so this command simply automates the logoff process, which would likely be required anyway.
/boot	Reboots the system after the policy refresh completes. Some computer settings, such as software installation, are applied only when the system starts, so a reboot is required for those changes to be applied.
/sync	Causes group policy objects to be applied synchronously to computers at startup and to users at logon, which is the default with Windows 2000. This causes all policies to be applied during the logon process. With Windows XP and W2K3, by default policies are applied asynchronously, which can cause users to log on with cached credentials and policy settings, and thus not receive any newly implemented policy changes right away.

health_chk (ST)

When you are troubleshooting File Replication Service problems, `health_chk` is likely to become your favorite tool. By executing a single command, you can use this tool to run tests that are normally performed by running each of the following commands:

- connstat
- dcdiag
- eventquery.vbs
- iologsum
- netdiag
- ntfrsutil
- reg
- repadmin
- topchk

Each of these commands is useful for troubleshooting and diagnosing FRS problems. However, it is extremely cumbersome to note the correct syntax and execute each command in order to collect data relating to FRS replication. Instead, when you execute the `health_chk` command, it generates 17 text files containing an abundance of information on potential causes of replication problems. Once you collect these files, it is very likely that one of them will provide the details on the particular error that is leading to a replication failure. The contents of each output file generated by running `health_chk` are described in Table A-48.

Table A-48. health_chk Output Files

Filename	Information Collected
Ds_showconn.txt	Provides information on the connection objects of the target system.
Ds_showreps.txt	Provides information on replication partnerships.
Evl_application.txt	Lists application event log content.
Evl_dns.txt	Lists DNS server event log content.
Evl_ds.txt	Lists Directory Service event log content.
Evl_ntfrs.txt	Lists File Replication Service event log content.
Evl_system.txt	Lists system event log content.
Ntfrs_config.txt	Lists all replica sets.
Ntfrs_ds.txt	Displays FRS replication topology from the perspective of the target machine.
Ntfrs_errscan.txt	Lists error messages found in the FRS debug logs.
Ntfrs_inlog.txt	Lists inbound Change Orders (COs).
Ntfrs_machine.txt	Lists the available disk space on all hard disks in the target system.
Ntfrs_outlog.txt	Lists outbound COs.
Ntfrs_reg.txt	Lists FRS Registry information (found in HKLM\System\currentcontrolset\services\ntfrs subkey).
Ntfrs_sets.txt	Lists inbound and outbound FRS replication connections, as well as the status of each connection.
Ntfrs_sysvol.txt	Displays all directories and subdirectories in the SYSVOL share.
Ntfrs_version.txt	Provides FRS version information.

Once you collect this information, you can search the pertinent generated logs for errors. To run this command, you would use the following syntax:

```
health_chk <ResultsFolderPath> [RemoteSystem]
```

When you execute this command, you have to provide the path to a folder where the output text files will be stored. You have the option to specify a remote system name or IP address. If the `RemoteSystem` parameter is not used, the `health_chk` command runs on the local machine in which you initiate the command.

hostname

The `hostname` command provides a quick way to determine the host name of a local system. This command cannot be run remotely. The command syntax is `hostname`. Once the command is executed, the host name of the system is displayed.

iasparse (ST)

The `iasparse` command line tool is useful for collecting information about a Windows server running Internet Authentication Service (IAS). If certain connections are failing and users are reporting that the failures are authentication related, you can use this tool to dump all IAS server log information into a single log file. From there, you can search the log file, using a text editor such as Notepad to locate failure events. The easiest way to find problems is to search the output log using the word "fail." Among the key information that you will find in the output log file is

- Server IP address
- Client IP address
- Client name
- User name
- Connection date
- Framed protocol type (PPP)
- Tunnel type (L2TP, PPTP)

When a particular user is having connection problems, collecting and searching the IAS logs helps you determine whether the problem is related to the IAS server, thus affecting all users, or to just a single user. Having this information earlier helps you determine where to concentrate your troubleshooting efforts.

Here is the syntax for `iasparse`:

```
iasparse [-f:<filename>] [-p] [-v]
```

The command options are described in Table A-49.

Table A-49. iasparse Command Options

Option	Use
-f:<filename>	Specifies the IAS log file to parse in order to collect logon, protocol, and accounting information. By default, the default IAS server log file (system32\logfiles\iaslog.log) is parsed.
-p	Sends the command output to the display.
-v	Verbose output. A description is also displayed for attributes collected in the log file.

ipxroute

The `ipxroute` command is used to display information about routing tables used by the IPX protocol. This command can also be used to modify IPX routing information on a Windows client or server that is connected to an IPX network. The syntax for this command is:

```
ipxroute servers [/type=x]
ipxroute ripout <network>
ipxroute resolve guid <guid> | name <AdapterName>
ipxroute board=<adapter> [def] [gbr] [mbr] [remove=<xxxxxxxx>]
ipxroute config
```

As you can see, there are several variations of this command. Table A-50 sheds light on each command variation and its associated options.

Table A-50. ipxroute Command Options

Option	Use
`servers [/type=x]`	Shows the Service Access Point (SAP) table for the specified server type. If no type is specified, all servers are listed by server name.
`ripout <network>`	Sends a Routing Information Protocol (RIP) request to the destination network specified to determine if the network is reachable. You must specify the remote network's IPX network segment number by using the `<network>` parameter.
`resolve guid <guid>	name <AdapterName>`	Resolves a network adapter's name to its GUID, or vice versa.
`board=<adapter>`	Specifies the network adapter to query or configure.
`def`	Used with the `board` option. Causes a packet sent to a MAC address that is not in the source routing table to be sent to the ALL ROUTES broadcast. These packets are sent to the SINGLE ROUTES broadcast by default.
`gbr`	Used with the `board` option. Causes a packet sent to the broadcast address (FFFFFFFFFFFF) to be sent to the ALL ROUTES broadcast. These packets are sent to the SINGLE ROUTES broadcast by default.
`mbr`	Used with the `board` option. Causes a packet sent to a multicast address to be sent to the ALL ROUTES broadcast. These packets are sent to the SINGLE ROUTES broadcast by default.
`remove=<xxxxxxxxxx>`	Removes the specified node address from the source routing table.
`config`	Displays information about all network bindings that have IPX configured.

lpq

Running this command allows you to check the status of the print queue on a print server running the line printer daemon (LPD) service, allowing you to determine a possible problem with a print server. The LPD service runs on UNIX print servers. Clients running the line printer remote (LPR) service can print to LPD print servers. Windows clients can run the LPR service. Also, you can configure a Windows server to emulate a UNIX print server by installing Print Services for UNIX on the server.

The syntax for `lpq` is:

```
lpq -s <Server> -p <PrinterName> [-l]
```

The `lpq` command's options are described in Table A-51.

Table A-51. lpq Command Options

Option	Use
`-s <Server>`	Required parameter. Specifies the target server that hosts the LPD printer.
`-p <PrinterName>`	Required parameter. Indicates the printer whose print queue you would like the command to display.
`-l`	Displays additional details about the print queue status.

memsnap (ST)

If you need documentation of memory consumption on a particular server or would like to prove the existence of a memory leak, you can do so by using the support tool `memsnap`. It takes a snapshot of all running processes and their associated resource consumption and dumps the snapshot to a log file. The default name for the file is Memsnap.log, but the name can be specified in the command syntax, which is shown next.

```
memsnap [/t] [/g] [file name]
```

Table A-52 details the options for the `memsnap` command.

Table A-52. memsnap Command Options

Option	Use
`/t`	Tagging information—causes the time (GMT), date, and computer name to be included in the output log file.
`/g`	Adds user and graphical device interface (GDI) information to the command output log file.
`file name`	Used to specify the name of the output log file. If this option is not used, the output file will be named Memsnap.log.

nbtstat

The `nbtstat` command is useful for displaying NetBIOS over TCP/IP (NetBT) information and is primarily useful when you are troubleshooting older systems (pre–Windows 2000) on your network. Beginning with Windows 2000, NetBT is no longer a Windows TCP/IP requirement, so you will find this tool helpful mainly when you are working with Windows NT workstations.

Here is the syntax for `nbtstat`:

```
nbtstat [-a <computer name>] [-A <IP address>] [-c] [-n] [-r] [-R]
[-RR] [-s] [-S][Refresh interval]
```

The `nbtstat` parameters are explained in Table A-53.

Table A-53. nbtstat Command Options

Option	Use
`-a <computer name>`	Used to display the NetBIOS name table of the remote computer specified.
`-A <IP address>`	Used to display the NetBIOS name table for the remote computer with the IP address specified.
`-c`	Displays the NetBIOS cache table.
`-n`	Displays the NetBIOS name table of the local computer.
`-r`	Used to display NetBIOS name resolution statistics, including name resolution performed by broadcast and by a WINS server.
`-R`	Purges the contents of the NetBIOS cache. Any static NetBIOS name–to–IP address mappings with the "#PRE" designation in the LMHosts file are then added to the NetBIOS cache.
`-RR`	Used to release the client's NetBIOS names from its associated WINS server(s) and then refresh the client's NetBIOS names with its WINS server(s). This command is useful for updating a WINS server after a client's IP address has changed.
`-s`	Used to display the NetBIOS session table, listing remote hosts by NetBIOS names.
`-S`	Used to display the NetBIOS session table, listing remote hosts by IP addresses.
`Refresh interval`	If a refresh interval is specified (number of seconds), the command will continually loop and refresh its output until it is manually terminated by pressing Ctrl-C.

netdiag (ST)

The `netdiag` command is a great tool for troubleshooting networking-related issues on workstations. When run from the command prompt, this tool performs a series of tests on the client's TCP/IP network configuration and reports any errors that it finds. When it is run without parameters, all possible tests are run; otherwise, you can run one or more tests. The tests that the command performs are

- `Autonet`—Automatic Private IP Addressing (APIPA)
- `Bindings`—Network bindings
- `Browser`—Browser and Redirector
- `DCList`—Domain controller list
- `DefGW`—Default gateway
- `DNS`—DNS recursive query
- `DsGetDC`—Domain controller discovery
- `IPConfig`—IP address configuration
- `IPLoopBk`—IP address loopback ping
- `IPX`—IPX networking
- `Kerberos`—Kerberos security
- `Ldap`—Lightweight Directory Access Protocol (LDAP)
- `Member`—Domain membership
- `Modem`—Modem diagnostics
- `NbtNm`—NetBT name
- `Ndis`—Netcard queries
- `NetBTTransports`—NetBT transports
- `Netstat`—Network statistical information
- `NetWare`—NetWare server
- `Route`—Routing table
- `Trust`—Trust relationships
- `WAN`—WAN configuration
- `WINS`—WINS service
- `Winsock`—Winsock test

The `netdiag` syntax is:

```
netdiag [/q] [/v] [/l] [/debug] [/d:<domain name>] [/fix]
[/dcaccountenum] [/test:<test name>] [/skip:<test name>]
```

The `netdiag` options are described in Table A-54.

Table A-54. netdiag Command Options

Option	Use
/q	Quiet output—only reports errors (normally the results of all tests are displayed).
/v	Verbose output—detailed information is shown.
/l	Log output—output data is sent to the Netdiag.log file stored in the same directory where the command was run.
/debug	Even more verbose output than with the /v switch (the command takes longer to complete).
/d:<domain name>	Locates a domain controller in the specified domain.
/fix	Repairs minor problems.
/dcaccountenum	Enumerates domain controller computer accounts.
/test:<test name>	Performs only the test listed (except for basic tests that cannot be skipped).
/skip:<test name>	Used to release the client's NetBIOS names from its associated WINS server(s) and then refresh the client's NetBIOS names with its WINS server(s). This command is useful for updating a WINS server after a client's IP address has changed.

net start | stop | pause | continue

The `net start`, `stop`, `pause`, and `continue` commands are used to administer services from the command line. The syntax for these commands is:

```
net <start | stop | pause | continue> <service name>
```

net statistics

The `net statistics` command is useful for identifying operational networking statistics for both the Server and Workstation services. This command is useful for identifying TCP/IP networking problems such as

- Network errors
- Hung sessions
- Failed sessions
- Failed operations

While the command only reports on errors, it does allow you to confirm or deny your suspicions about a suspected problem. Here is the syntax for the `net statistics` command:

```
net statistics [server | workstation]
```

net session

The `net session` command, which only works on servers, allows you to view active sessions and to disconnect sessions. The syntax for `net session` is:

```
net session [\\computer name] [/delete]
```

The command options are explained in Table A-55.

Table A-55. net session Command Options

Option	Use
\\computer name	Displays session information for the named computer.
/delete	When this option is used by itself, all sessions with the server are terminated and all open files are closed. When a computer name is specified, only the sessions with the selected computer are terminated.

net view

With NetBIOS over TCP/IP enabled, many use Windows Explorer as a means to browse resources on the network. The `net view` command provides the same functionality from the command line. If you want to see a list of shared resources on a particular server, `net view` provides a quick way to view the system's shared folders and printers. The syntax for `net view` is:

```
net view [\\computer name] [/domain:<name>]
net view /Network:NW [\\computer name]
```

Table A-56 describes the command options.

Table A-56. net view Command Options

Option	Use
`\\computer name`	The name of the computer whose shared resources you want to view.
`/domain:<name>`	Used to view a list of computers in the specified domain.
`/Network:NW`	Used to display all available servers in a NetWare network.

Netsh RAS Diagnostics

There are many versions of the RAS Netshell (`netsh`) commands that aid in administering RAS servers from the command line. In this section, we'll look at the myriad of commands available from within the Netsh RAS Diagnostics command shell, which is a specific command environment geared toward troubleshooting and acquiring diagnostic information on RAS servers. The commands that are available within the Netsh RAS Diagnostics environment are examined in the next several sections. To enter the Netsh RAS Diagnostics environment, perform these steps.

1. From the command prompt, type `netsh` and press Enter.
2. Now type `ras diagnostics` and press Enter.
3. You should now be at the `netsh ras diagnostics>` prompt. From here, you can run any of the commands listed in the remainder of this section. To exit from the `netsh` shell, type `quit` and press Enter.

dump

The `dump` command is used from within the RAS Diagnostics environment to display the current environment settings. In particular, this command allows you to see which diagnostic components have tracing enabled. When tracing is enabled, traced RAS events are written to log files stored in the %windir%\tracing folder. The `set` commands that appear later in this section allow you to enable or disable RAS tracing for particular RAS components. Tracing does place a heavier burden on CPU and disk resources, and thus should only be enabled when you are attempting to resolve a problem on your RAS server.

show all

The `show all` command queries all of the RAS tracing log files and outputs the log file data into an HTML file. This allows you to troubleshoot your RAS problems by looking in, and thus being able to search, a single file. The syntax for the `show all` command is:

```
show all type=<file|email> destination=<FileLocation|EmailAddress>
[compression=<enabled|disabled>] [hours=<hours>]
[verbose=<enabled|disabled>]
```

Table A-57 describes the `show all` command's options.

Table A-57. show all Command Options

Option	Use
`type=<file | email>`	Tells the command what to do with the output. Your choice is to either save it as a file or send it to an e-mail address.
`destination=<FileLocation | EmailAddress>`	Depending on the output type specified with the `type` parameter, this option allows you to specify the command's output file or the e-mail address for the e-mail recipient that will receive the report.
`compression=<enabled | disabled>`	Allows you to specify if the report should be compressed into a cabinet (.cab) file. By default, if the report is e-mailed, it is compressed, and if it is saved locally, it is not compressed.
`hours=<hours>`	Specifies the number of past hours' data to include in the report. The parameter must be an integer between 1 and 24.
`verbose=<enabled | disabled>`	Allows you to specify if you want highly detailed information in the output report. Verbose output is disabled by default.

show cmtracing

This simple command is used to show the logging status of Connection Manager (CM) tracing. When run, this command returns a status of either enabled or disabled. If you run this command and realize that Connection Manager tracing (logging) is disabled, you can then run the `set cmtracing` command to enable logging. The syntax to display the CM tracing state is `show cmtracing`.

set cmtracing

If you need to troubleshoot CM problems, or if you have completed the troubleshooting process, then you need to either enable or disable CM tracing. This is done with the `set cmtracing` command. The syntax for this command is:

```
set cmtracing <enabled|disabled>
```

show configuration

This command is similar to the `show all` command, with the exception that its output is limited to diagnostic information on

- Installed devices
- Process information
- Command line utilities
- Phone book files

The syntax for `show configuration` is:

```
show configuration type=<file|email>
destination=<FileLocation|EmailAddress>
[compression=<enabled|disabled>] [hours=<hours>]
[verbose=<enabled|disabled>]
```

The options for `show configuration` are described in Table A-58.

Table A-58. show configuration Command Options

Option	Use
`type=<file | email>`	Tells the command what to do with the output. Your choice is to either save it as a file or send it to an e-mail address.
`destination=<FileLocation | EmailAddress>`	Depending on the output type specified with the `type` parameter, this option allows you to specify the command's output file or the e-mail address for the e-mail recipient that will receive the report.
`compression=<enabled | disabled>`	Allows you to specify if the report should be compressed into a .cab file. By default, if the report is e-mailed, it is compressed, and if it is saved locally, it is not compressed.
`hours=<hours>`	Specifies the number of past hours' data to include in the report. The parameter must be an integer between 1 and 24.
`verbose=<enabled | disabled>`	Allows you to specify if you want highly detailed information in the output report. Verbose output is disabled by default.

show installation

This `show` command generates a RAS Diagnostic Report that includes information on

- Information files
- An installation check
- Installed network components
- A Registry check

The syntax for `show installation` is:

```
show installation type=<file|email>
destination=<FileLocation|EmailAddress>
[compression=<enabled|disabled>] [hours=<hours>]
[verbose=<enabled|disabled>]
```

Table A-59 describes the `show installation` command options.

Table A-59. show installation Command Options

Option	Use
`type=<file | email>`	Tells the command what to do with the output. Your choice is to either save it as a file or send it to an e-mail address.
`destination=<FileLocation | EmailAddress>`	Depending on the output type specified with the `type` parameter, this option allows you to specify the command's output file or the e-mail address for the e-mail recipient that will receive the report.
`compression=<enabled | disabled>`	Allows you to specify if the report should be compressed into a .cab file. By default, if the report is e-mailed, it is compressed, and if it is saved locally, it is not compressed.
`hours=<hours>`	Specifies the number of past hours' data to include in the report. The parameter must be an integer between 1 and 24.
`verbose=<enabled | disabled>`	Allows you to specify if you want highly detailed information in the output report. Verbose output is disabled by default.

show logs

The `show logs` command allows you to generate a Remote Access Diagnostic Report that includes information from the following log files:

- All tracing logs
- Connection Manager logs
- Modem logs
- IP Security log
- Remote Access event logs
- Security event logs

The syntax for `show logs` is:

```
show logs type=<file|email> destination=<FileLocation|EmailAddress>
[compression=<enabled|disabled>] [hours=<hours>]
[verbose=<enabled|disabled>]
```

Table A-60 describes the `show logs` command options.

Table A-60. show logs Command Options

Option	Use
`type=<file | email>`	Tells the command what to do with the output. Your choice is to either save it as a file or send it to an e-mail address.
`destination=<FileLocation | EmailAddress>`	Depending on the output type specified with the `type` parameter, this option allows you to specify the command's output file or the e-mail address for the e-mail recipient that will receive the report.
`compression=<enabled | disabled>`	Allows you to specify if the report should be compressed into a .cab file. By default, if the report is e-mailed, it is compressed, and if it is saved locally, it is not compressed.
`hours=<hours>`	Specifies the number of past hours' data to include in the report. The parameter must be an integer between 1 and 24.
`verbose=<enabled | disabled>`	Allows you to specify if you want highly detailed information in the output report. Verbose output is disabled by default.

show modemtracing

Running this command allows you to see if RAS is logging all modem events. To check and see if modem tracing is enabled, you would run `show modemtracing`. The command outputs the status of modem tracing as either enabled or disabled.

set modemtracing

If you need to enable or disable modem tracing, you do so by running this command. The syntax for `set modemtracing` is:

```
set modemtracing=<enabled|disabled>
```

As with the other `set` commands, `enabled` turns on logging and using the `disabled` value turns off logging.

show rastracing

The `show rastracing` command is used to display the tracing status of each RAS component as either enabled or disabled. There are no additional options for this command, so to view the status of each RAS tracing log, you would run this command:

```
netsh ras diagnostics show rastracing
```

You can modify the use of particular tracing logs by running the `set rastracing` command, which is explained next.

set rastracing

The `set rastracing` command allows you to turn on tracing either for specific RAS components or for all RAS components. If you are unsure of each component name, you can use the * wildcard to enable tracing for all components. The syntax for this command is:

```
set rastracing component=<component|*> state=<enabled|disabled>
```

Once you enable RAS tracing, you can check the status of tracing components by running `show rastracing`. This also allows you to note the name of individual components in the event that you want to individually disable certain components.

show securityeventlog

This command is used to determine if the RAS server is logging security events. There are no parameters for this command, so to see the status of RAS server security logging, you would run `show securityeventlog`.

set securityeventlog

If you want to enable or disable security event logging of RAS security events, you can run this command. The syntax for `set securityeventlog` is:

    set securityeventlog=<enabled|disabled>

So, to enable security event logging on a RAS server, you would run this command:

    netsh ras diagnostics set securityeventlog=enabled

show tracefacilities

This command is used to show the tracing status of all logging activities on the RAS server. The command lists each traceable component and its logging status. The syntax for this command is `show tracefacilities`.

set tracefacilities

If you want to modify the tracing activities of all traceable RAS components with a single command, then this is the command for you. The syntax for `set tracefacilities` is:

    set tracefacilities state=<enabled|disabled|clear>

You can turn on all tracing for all components by specifying enabled as the state and turn off all tracing by specifying a state of disabled. If you use the clear parameter, you clear the content of all tracing logs.

netsh routing

Unlike the Netsh RAS Diagnostics commands, `netsh routing` does not offer a single group of commands dedicated exclusively to troubleshooting. In this section, we examine the commands that allow you to obtain diagnostic information about routing components. For each section, the aspects of the commands that relate exclusively to routing administration are not addressed. If after reading this section, your appetite for `netsh routing` commands has not been satisfied, take a look at Windows online Help to find out additional information on the other available `netsh routing` commands. The eight subsections in this section address acquiring information exclusive to a particular routing component, such as NAT, RIP, and the DHCP Relay Agent.

netsh routing ip autodhcp

From this `netsh` command context, you can check the settings of the DHCP Allocator, which can be used by NAT to dynamically assign IP addresses to clients. The commands that can be used to check the `autodhcp` configuration are `show global` and `show interface`.

show global

The `show global` command allows you to see the general configuration settings of the DHCP Allocator, if the DHCP Allocator is enabled. This could allow you to determine if your NAT server is interfering with IP address assignments provided by another DHCP server on the network, for example.

show interface

The `show interface` command is similar to the `show global` command, with the exception that DHCP Allocator information for a single interface is displayed. The syntax for this command is:

```
show interface interfacename=<InterfaceName>
```

You need to know the name of the interface to query in order to run this command. For the `interfacename` parameter, you specify the name of a network interface as it is listed in the Network Connections window (i.e., "Local Area Connection").

netsh routing ip relay

If an RRAS server is not properly relaying DHCP client requests to a DHCP server, you can use this command environment to collect information on the configuration of the DHCP Relay Agent service. In the `netsh routing` DHCP Relay Agent command environment, there are three commands that are helpful for troubleshooting:

- `show interface`
- `show global`
- `show ifstats`

Each of these commands is looked at next.

show interface

This command is used to display the DHCP Relay Agent configuration for a specific network interface. The syntax for this command is:

```
show interface interfacename=<InterfaceName>
```

When executed, this command displays the DHCP Relay Agent configuration information for the interface specified with the `interfacename` parameter. The name used to identify the interface must match the way that the interface is identified under Network Connections.

show global

The `show global` command is similar to `show interface` in purpose, with the exception that it displays configuration information for all network interfaces. The syntax for this command is:

```
show global [rr=<seconds>]
```

If you run this command with the `rr` parameter, you can specify a number of seconds for the command output to automatically refresh. If this parameter is used, you can end the command execution by pressing Ctrl-C.

show ifstats

The `show ifstats` command allows you to view DHCP Relay Agent statistics for a specified interface. The statistics that you can collect from this command include

- Interface state
- Send failures
- Receive failures
- Address Resolution Protocol (ARP) update failures
- Requests received
- Requests discarded
- Replies received
- Replies discarded

If you do not specify an interface with the command options, the command returns statistics for all interfaces on which the DHCP Relay Agent is enabled. Here is the syntax for `show ifstats`:

```
show ifstats [index=<integer>] [rr=<seconds>]
```

The `index` parameter can be used to specify the index value of a target interface. When no index value is specified, statistics are accumulated collectively for all interfaces. The `rr` parameter allows you to have the command run continually, with its refresh rate in seconds equaling the `rr` value that you enter. For example, if you wanted to monitor all DHCP Relay Agent interfaces on an RRAS server and have the output refresh every five seconds, you would run this command:

```
netsh routing ip relay show ifstats rr=5
```

netsh routing ip dnsproxy

When you install and enable NAT, you can have the NAT server act as a DNS proxy for clients. This allows all clients to potentially use the NAT server as their DNS server. The NAT server in turn will relay client requests to an alternate server (usually external), and the NAT server will in turn relay the DNS response back to the client. When you are troubleshooting DNS proxy configuration, there are two commands of concern: `show global` and `show interface`.

show global

This command allows you to see the DNS proxy global configuration, which contains the default DNS proxy configuration settings for all interfaces that act as DNS proxies. If you are looking to collect configuration information for a specific interface, you could run the `show interface` command.

show interface

The `show interface` command allows you to view the DNS proxy configuration of a specific interface. Here is this command's syntax:

```
show interface interfacename=<InterfaceName>
```

For the `interfacename` parameter, you need to specify the name of the network interface as it appears in the Network Connections window. For example, if the DNS proxy was on the interface labeled "Private," you would run this command:

```
netsh routing ip dnsproxy show interface interface="private"
```

netsh routing ip igmp

The `netsh routing ip igmp` command environment has several commands for monitoring and troubleshooting Internet Group Management Protocol (IGMP)–enabled interfaces. In this section, we'll examine seven commands that are useful when you are troubleshooting IGMP problems.

show interface

With `show interface`, you can view the IGMP configuration of a single routing interface. If you do not specify an interface name with this command, you will see the configuration information for all interfaces. The syntax for this command is:

```
show interface interfacename=<InterfaceName>
```

The `interfacename` parameter must equal the exact name of a network interface as it appears in Network Connections.

show global

The `show global` command allows you to see the global IGMP configuration settings that apply to all interfaces. There are no parameters for this command, so its syntax is simply `show global`.

show ifstats

This command allows you to see IGMP statistics for a routing interface. If you do not specify an interface, statistics are collected for all IGMP interfaces. The syntax for this command is:

```
show ifstats [index=<integer>] [rr=<seconds>]
```

With this command, the `index` parameter allows you to specify the index number of a specific network interface. If you would like the command to run continually and automatically update its output statistics, you can use the `rr` parameter and specify the command refresh rate in seconds.

show iftable

This command allows you to see the IGMP host groups that are assigned to a particular routing interface. If you do not specify an interface, all IGMP host groups are displayed. The syntax for this command is:

```
show iftable [index=<integer>] [rr=<seconds>]
```

As with previous commands, the `index` parameter allows you to select a specific interface, and the `rr` parameter allows you to have the command output continually refresh.

show grouptable

This command is used to display the IGMP Hosts Group Table for a multicast group. If you do not specify an interface, the command shows all IGMP Hosts Group Tables for all multicast groups on all interfaces. The syntax for this command is:

```
show grouptable [index=<integer>] [rr=<seconds>]
```

Again with this command, the `index` parameter is used to target a specific interface, and the `rr` option allows you to set a refresh period for the command.

show rasgrouptable

This command outputs the Hosts Group Table for a specific RAS client interface. If a client interface is not specified, the command returns all Hosts Group Tables for all client interfaces. Here is the syntax for `show rasgrouptable`:

```
show rasgrouptable [index=<ClientIPAddress>] [rr=<seconds>]
```

Unlike the previous commands, for the `index` parameter, you need to specify the IP address of a remote RRAS client.

show proxygrouptable

With this command, you can examine the IGMP Hosts Group Table for an IGMP Proxy interface. Like previous commands, if no interface is specified, the command returns the IGMP Hosts Group Table for all interfaces. The syntax for this command is:

```
show proxygrouptable [interfacename=<InterfaceName>] [rr=<seconds>]
```

In this command, the `interfacename` parameter is used to define the network interface whose IGMP Hosts Group Table you would like to examine. As with earlier commands, the `rr` parameter allows you to select a refresh rate in seconds for the command output.

netsh routing ip nat

The `netsh routing ip nat` commands allow you to quickly view configuration information for the NAT service and for NAT-enabled interfaces. Two commands that are useful for troubleshooting NAT problems are `show global` and `show interface`.

show global

When you view the global NAT configuration information, you will see the TCP and UDP timeout parameters (in minutes) and the NAT logging level (errors only by default). The syntax for using this command to view global configuration settings is simply `show global`, with no available options.

show interface

The `show interface` command allows you to see the configuration of NAT-enabled interfaces. In particular, this command outputs the configuration type for the interface, which is one of the following:

- Address and port translation
- Address and port translation with firewall
- Firewall only
- Private interface

The syntax for this command is:

```
show interface [interfacename=<InterfaceName>]
```

If you do not specify an interface with the `interfacename` parameter, then the configuration of all NAT interfaces is displayed. This command is useful for verifying that you have at least one private interface and one address and port translation interface enabled for NAT, which are the minimum requirements for NAT to operate.

netsh routing ip ospf

There are several `netsh` diagnostic utilities that are helpful when you are troubleshooting OSPF router issues. This section examines each of these available commands.

show global

The `show global` command allows you to check the global state of an RRAS server's OSPF configuration. In particular, you can see the router state (enabled or disabled), router ID, and logging level (errors only by default). There are no optional parameters for this command, so to view global settings, you would run `show global` from the `netsh routing ip ospf` command environment.

show virtif

This command allows you to see configuration information on OSPF virtual interfaces, if any are enabled. With virtual interfaces in use, running this command allows you to check the following information on a virtual interface:

- Interface status (enabled, disabled)
- Transit area ID
- Virtual neighbor router ID
- Transit delay
- Retransmission interval
- Hello interval
- Dead interval

Again, there are no option parameters for this command, so to see virtual interface information, you would run `show virtif`.

show interface

The `show interface` command allows you to see the configuration of OSPF-enabled interfaces. In particular, this command allows you to check

- Interface state (enabled or disabled)
- IP address and subnet mask
- Area ID
- Interface type—broadcast, point-to-point, or non-broadcast multiple access (NBMA)
- Router priority

- Retransmission interval
- Hello interval
- Dead interval
- Poll interval
- Metric
- MTU size

The syntax for this command is:

```
show interface [interfacename=<InterfaceName>]
```

If you do not specify an interface with the `interfacename` parameter, then the configuration of all OSPF interfaces is displayed.

show routefilter

This command allows you to see if the OSPF router drops specific routes that it receives from other OSPF routers. When filters are enabled, you can configure the filter either to accept a specific list of network IDs or to drop a specific list of network IDs. When you execute this command (`show routefilter`), you will see a filter action (accept or drop) displayed, as well as a list of the filtered routes.

show protofilter

This command is similar to `show routefilter` in that its output format is identical. However, this command differs in that it displays the OSPF protocol filter settings. When the command is executed, you will see the general filter configuration (accept or drop), as well as a list of filtered protocols.

show area

When you run `show area`, you can see configuration information on each configured OSPF area. Among the data that you can check is the following:

- Area state (enabled, disabled)
- Authentication type (simple password, no authentication)
- Stub area (yes or no)
- Stub metric
- Import summary advertisement configuration (yes or no)

This command has no optional parameters, so to check the area configuration of an OSPF router, you would run `show area`.

netsh routing ip rip

The `netsh routing ip rip` command environment provides the following five commands that will help you in troubleshooting RIP routing:

- `show interface`
- `show flags`
- `show global`
- `show ifstats`
- `show ifbinding`

show interface

The `show interface` command allows you to see the RIP configuration for a single RIP interface or for all RIP routing interfaces. The syntax for this command is:

```
show interface [interfacename =<InterfaceName>]
```

The `interfacename` parameter must equal the exact name of a network interface as it appears in Network Connections.

show flags

This command is used to display the flags (Split Horizon, Poison Reverse, and so on) for a given RIP interface. If no interface name is specified, the flags for all interfaces are returned. The syntax for `show flags` is:

```
show flags [interfacename=<InterfaceName>]
```

The `interfacename` parameter must equal the exact name of a network interface as it appears in Network Connections.

show global

The `show global` command allows you to see the general RIP routing configuration settings. This command does not offer optional parameters, so its syntax is simply `show global`.

show ifstats

The `show ifstats` command is the "MVP" of RIP troubleshooting commands. This command shows you the RIP statistics for a given RIP routing interface and includes the following information:

- Send failures
- Receive failures

- Requests sent
- Requests received
- Responses sent
- Responses received
- Bad response packets received
- Bad response entries received

This information makes it easy for you to determine if a problem exists with your Windows server RIP router. The syntax for show ifstats is:

```
show ifstats [index=<integer>] [rr=<seconds>]
```

With this command, the index parameter allows you to specify the index number of a specific network interface. If you would like the command to run continually and automatically update its output statistics, you can use the rr parameter and specify the command refresh rate in seconds.

show ifbinding

The show ifbinding command allows you to see information on a particular network interface bound to the RIP routing protocol. For any given interface, the command displays the interface name, its binding state, IP address, and subnet mask. The syntax for this command is:

```
show ifbinding [index=<integer>] [rr=<seconds>]
```

Suppose that you wanted to display the binding information for the second bound RIP interface. To do this, you would run this command:

```
netsh routing ip rip show ifbinding index=2
```

netsh routing ip routerdiscovery

The netsh routing ip routerdiscovery command environment offers one command that is of troubleshooting value: show interface. The show interface command allows you to see statistics for a single interface or for all interfaces. The syntax for this netsh routing ip routerdiscovery show interface command is:

```
show interface [interfacename=<InterfaceName>]
```

If the interfacename parameter is not included in the command syntax, then router discovery statistics are displayed for all routing interfaces.

netsh wins

With `netsh wins`, you can both troubleshoot and administer local and remote WINS servers. Some of the `netsh wins` commands are useful in troubleshooting, while others are provided exclusively to allow you to perform the same administrative tasks from the command line that you could in the WINS MMC. Since there are over 50 versions of this command, this section documents only the versions of the command that are valuable when you are troubleshooting a suspected WINS problem. If you would like information on all WINS `netsh` commands, open Windows Help and perform a search using the keywords "netsh wins."

The first version of the command that you need to understand is `netsh wins server`. All other commands presented in this section are run under the `netsh wins server` command. The easiest way to run this command is to first access the `netsh wins` shell. To do this, follow these steps.

1. From the command prompt, type `netsh` and press Enter.
2. Type `wins` and press Enter. You should now be in the `netsh wins` shell, as indicated by the `netsh wins>` prompt.

The `netsh wins server` command is used to specify a local or remote WINS server to manage. The syntax for this command is:

```
server [\\servername | ipaddress]
```

When run without parameters, the command connects you to the local system, assuming that WINS is installed. To manage a remote system, provide either the server's name or IP address as a command parameter.

Once you connect to a WINS server, the command outputs the access rights that you have to the server. As an administrator, you should see that you have read and write access to the server you connected to. Once connected to a server, you can type `help` to see a list of available management commands, or you can run one of the two diagnostic commands discussed in this section. The four most popular Netshell WINS server troubleshooting tools are `dump`, `check`, `init`, and `show`. Each of these commands is described in more detail in the following subsections.

dump

This command allows you to quickly review basic configuration information for a WINS server. This command's output includes information about

- The WINS database backup path
- Name record renewal, extinction, extinction timeout, and verification intervals
- Push and pull replication parameters

- Replication partners
- Burst handling parameters

To view this information, from the `netsh wins server>` menu, type `dump` and press Enter. While `dump` is relatively simple in scope, you will find the next two commands much more powerful.

check

The following two versions of the `check` command are useful for troubleshooting:

- `check database`—Checks and reports on WINS database consistency
- `check version`—Checks for consistency of version ID numbers for WINS record owners in the WINS database

check database

The `check database` command triggers a database consistency check to run on a WINS server. When the command is run, you can execute a single consistency check on the local WINS database or have the command check consistency on all replicas of the database. If you elect to check consistency on all database replicas, a significant load will be placed on all WINS servers and on the network. By default, the command is not executed immediately on any WINS server that is currently overloaded. In these situations, the command is queued until some of the WINS server's resources are free, and then it is executed.

Once the command completes, you need to check the system event log on each WINS server to verify that the consistency check was successful. The syntax for `check database` is:

```
check database [all=<1|0>] [force=<1|0>]
```

The command's optional parameters are described in Table A-61.

Table A-61. check database Command Options

Option	Use
`all=<1|0>`	When this option is used with a value of 1, a consistency check is performed on the database of the target WINS server and all of its replication partners. With a value of 0 specified, the consistency check runs on the WINS server and its partners only if their consistency check verification interval has expired. This interval is disabled by default. When the interval is enabled, the default verification interval is 24 hours.
`force=<1|0>`	When used with a value of 1, this option overrides the WINS overload condition check, forcing a database consistency check to run regardless of how busy the system is. Using this option with a value of 0 is the same as not using it at all, meaning that when an overload condition is detected, the consistency check operation is delayed.

check version

This command allows you to verify the version number consistency of a WINS server's records with those of its replication partners. If version number inconsistency is found, you should use the WINS MMC to force replication between the WINS servers. The replication and subsequent record updates should correct any inconsistencies between WINS records. When executed, the command checks for and reports on any version inconsistencies found and also displays a mapping table of WINS records found in the server's database. For the table to display properly, you should widen the size of the command window so that it is much larger than its default size. If the output does not display properly, it is also written to a text file, so you can read it from there as well. By default, the text output file is named wins.rec and is stored in the directory from where the `netsh` command was run.

Here is the syntax for `check version`:

```
check version server=<ipaddress> [file=<filename>]
```

The `check version` command options are described in Table A-62.

Table A-62. check version Command Options

Option	Use
`server=<ipaddress>`	This required parameter specifies the IP address of the WINS server where version checking should begin.
`file=<filename>`	If you would like the command output stored as a different filename in a different location, you can use this parameter to do so.

init

The `netsh wins server init` command is primarily used for database maintenance operations, including backups, restores, database compaction, and initiating replication. In previous versions of Windows, the Jetpack utility was used to perform compaction of the WINS database. With Windows Server 2003, this utility is no longer available, and thus the `netsh wins server init` command is the only method for performing database compaction. Compaction is often the best method for recovering from database corruption and often salvages the WINS database so that you do not have to restore the database from backup. The six versions of this powerful command are invaluable for troubleshooting WINS server problems. Each version is explained next.

init backup

Once you specify a database backup path for the WINS database in the WINS MMC, online backups of the WINS database will run every three hours. If you would like to manually perform a backup or perform the backup as part of a script, you can do so by running `netsh wins init backup`.

The syntax for this command is:

```
init backup [dir=<backupdir>] [type=<0|1>]
```

The options for this command are described in Table A-63.

Table A-63. init backup Command Options

Option	Use
`dir=<backupdir>`	Used to specify the directory in which the backup should be stored. If this option is not used, the database will be backed up to the default directory that is specified in the WINS MMC.
`type=<0|1>`	Used to specify the type of backup: 0 = full and 1 = incremental. If no type is specified, a full backup will run.

This command is useful for securing a full backup of the database as a part of a backup script or for backing up the database prior to compacting it.

init compact

The `init compact` command is used to compact the WINS database. Database compaction is normally the first resolution step taken to repair a corrupted WINS database. There are no options for this command, so to compact a WINS database, you would run `init compact` from the `netsh wins server>` command prompt.

init pull

Suppose that you are aware that a remote WINS server was just updated, and you want to manually initiate a pull replication so that your local WINS server will be updated by the new data on the remote WINS server. This may be needed to prevent name resolution problems. To perform this task, you can use the `init pull` command. The syntax for this command is:

```
init pull server=<remoteserver>
```

When you run this command from the `netsh wins server>` command prompt, you need to specify the name or IP address of the remote server that you wish to pull the data to your server from.

init push

This command allows you to initiate a push replication of data from a local WINS server to its remote replication partners. A good time to run this command is after updating a WINS record on a WINS server. This ensures that the WINS server's replication partner(s) receive the new updates. Here is the syntax to use this command to initiate push replication:

```
init push server=<remoteserver> [propreq=<0|1>]
```

As with `init pull`, you use the `remoteserver` parameter to specify the name or IP address of your WINS server's remote replication partner. If you want to initiate a push replication to all replication partners, you could use the `propreq` parameter. When this parameter is set to 0, the push only propagates to the specified server in the command syntax. When `propreq` is set to 0, the push propagates data to all replication partners.

init replicate

The `init replicate` command is the most popular method for forcing WINS replication, because it initiates both push and pull replication with all of the WINS server's replication partners. The syntax for this command is `init replicate`, so to initiate replication on your local WINS server, you would enter `init replicate` from the `netsh wins server>` prompt.

init restore

When you need to recover a WINS database from an earlier backup, you use the `init restore` command. The backup you use for the restore could be located in the default WINS backup directory, which is specified under the WINS server properties in the WINS MMC. You could also restore data from an alternate backup path that may have been created when using the `init backup` command to manually perform a backup.

The syntax for `init restore` is:

```
init restore [dir=<backupdir>]
```

If the `dir` parameter is not specified, the restore data will come from the default backup directory. Otherwise, you can specify a particular backup directory by entering a path to directory with the `dir` parameter.

show

As with `init`, there are several versions of `show` that are useful for troubleshooting purposes. As was the case with the section on `init`, this section details the versions of the `show` command that are most relevant to troubleshooting and resolving WINS-related problems. Many of the `show` commands are most useful for resolving replication-related problems, where improper configuration is the overriding source of the problem.

show info

The output for `show info` is very similar to that of `dump`, but the output is presented in a format that is much easier to read and interpret. The `show info` command provides the following information about a WINS server:

- The database backup path
- Name record settings (refresh interval, extinction interval, extinction timeout, and verification interval)

- Database consistency check parameters
- WINS logging parameters
- Burst handling configuration

When you are trying to quickly get a glimpse of a WINS server's configuration, this command is ideal. The syntax for the command is:

```
show info
```

There are no optional parameters. To get information on a WINS server, you would run `show info` from the `netsh wins server>` prompt.

show partner

The `show partner` command allows you to quickly acquire a list of a WINS server's replication partners. The syntax for this command is:

```
show partner [type=<0|1|2|3>]
```

When you run the command without the `type` parameter, all replication partnerships are shown. If you were looking for a particular list of partners, such as only push partners, then you would use the `type` parameter. These are the valid values that can be entered with the `type` parameter:

- 0—All (the same as not using the `type` parameter)
- 1—Pull
- 2—Push
- 3—Push/pull

If you were looking specifically for the remote pull partners of a WINS server, you would run the command `show partner type=1` from the `netsh wins server>` prompt. Now that you have seen how to get a list of servers by replication type, next you'll see how to list the properties for each of those servers.

show partnerproperties

Once you have identified all of a WINS server's replication partners, you can use `show partnerproperties` to view their configurations. The syntax for the command is `show partnerproperties`. There are no parameters for this command. If you are just looking to list the configuration for a single replication partner, you can use either the `show pullpartnerconfig` or `show pushpartnerconfig` commands, which are described next.

show pullpartnerconfig

The `show pullpartnerconfig` command is used to display the configuration information of a single pull partner of a WINS server. The syntax for this command is:

```
show pullpartnerconfig server=<servername|ipaddress>
```

The required parameter for this command is the name or IP address of the remote server whose configuration you wish to view.

show pushpartnerconfig

The `show pushpartnerconfig` command works just like `show pullpartnerconfig`, except that it is for checking the configuration of a WINS server's push replication partners. The syntax for this command is:

```
show pushpartnerconfig server=<servername|ipaddress>
```

As you can see, the syntax and options are virtually the same.

show server

If you forget which server you are currently administering in the `netsh wins server>` context, you can use this command to remind you. The syntax is simply `show server`, and when the command is executed, you will see the name and IP address of the WINS server that you are currently connected to.

Once you are finished running commands from within the `netsh wins` shell, type `quit` to exit the shell.

netstat

A useful command called `netstat` allows you to view information on the TCP and UDP port connections to a system. The command can be executed so that it runs every *n* number of seconds and allows you to see the following in a table format:

- The protocol (TCP or UDP)
- The local IP address and port number used by the socket connection
- The foreign (destination) IP address and port number used by the socket connection
- The status of the connection (Listening, Established, and so on)

Here is the syntax for `netstat`:

```
netstat [-a] [-e] [-n] [-o] [-p <protocol>] [-r] [-s] [interval]
```

The `netstat` options are listed in Table A-64.

Table A-64. netstat Command Options

Option	Use
`-a`	Displays all connections and listening ports.
`-e`	Shows Ethernet statistics.
`-n`	Shows addresses and ports in numerical format (IP address instead of interface name).
`-o`	Displays the owning process ID for each connection.
`-p <protocol>`	Shows connections for the protocol specified. Protocol choices are TCP, TCPv6, UDP, and UDPv6. When used in conjunction with `-s`, this may also include IP, IPv6, ICMP, and ICMPv6.
`-r`	Displays the system's routing table.
`-s`	Displays statistics on a per-protocol basis; by default, statistics are shown for TCP, TCPv6, UDP, UDPv6, IP, IPv6, ICMP, and ICMPv6. A small subset of protocols can be specified using the `-p` switch.
`interval`	The interval in seconds in which the command output data refreshes. When an interval is specified, press Ctrl-C to terminate the command.

nltest (ST)

The versatile command line tool `nltest` allows you to perform the following tasks:

- Acquire a list of domain controllers
- Provide the status of secure channels, which provide trusts between domains
- Query the status of domain trusts
- Register domain controller SRV records with a dynamic DNS server

The syntax for this command is:

```
nltest [/server:<servername>] [test operation]
```

The `/server` parameter allows you to run the test on a remote domain controller. If no server is specified, the test runs on the local system. This command provides several operations that can be run. Each operation and its related switch are described in Table A-65.

Table A-65. nltest Command Operations

Operation	Description
`/query`	Displays the status of the secure channel, which is established by the NetLogon service, and provides information on the last time the channel was used.
`/sc_query:<domain>`	Displays information on the state of the secure channel to the target domain, and lists the name of the remote domain controller that was contacted.
`/sc_reset:<domain>`	Removes and then re-creates the secure channel of the target domain.
`/sc_verify:<domain>`	Reports on the status of the secure channel, and if a problem is detected, the secure channel is re-created.
`/sc_change_pwd:<domain>`	Changes the trust account password for the specified domain.
`/dclist:<domain>`	Displays the names of all domain controllers for the specified domain.
`/dcname:<domain>`	Displays the name of the PDC emulator for the specified domain.
`/dsgetfti:<domain>`	Displays information about any interforest trusts that exist for the target domain.
`/dsgetsite`	Displays the name of the Active Directory site where your system is located.
`/dsregdns`	Refreshes the registration of all domain controller–specific records on the DNS server. This allows you to refresh a domain controller's SRV records without having to stop and restart its NetLogon service.
`/dsderegdns:<dnsserver>`	Removes a domain controller's SRV records from the DNS server specified.

nslookup

The `nslookup` command is the most powerful of all the available DNS troubleshooting tools. With a little practice, use of this tool to locate the source of any DNS problem will become instinctive. With `nslookup`, you can directly make name queries to a DNS server, thus simulating the actions taken by a DNS client computer. To use this command to query DNS servers, you can simply run `nslookup`, or you can extend the command's capabilities by including any one of its several subcommands. The syntax for the core `nslookup` command is:

```
nslookup [-<subcommand>] [host] [-<nameserver>]
```

Much of `nslookup`'s functionality is derived from its multitude of subcommands. The easiest way to reach any subcommand menu is to first type `nslookup` and press Enter. This brings you to interactive mode, from where you can directly enter any of the `nslookup` subcommands, which are covered in the next several sections.

exit

The `exit` command is used to return you to the command prompt when you are running `nslookup` in interactive mode. You know when you are in interactive mode because the prompt appears as just > with a flashing cursor.

ls

The `ls` subcommand is used to display the contents of a particular zone on the DNS server. If the zone is not configured to allow zone transfers to the system where you are running the `nslookup` command, you will get a Refused error. Since zone data can be very large, you also have the option with the `ls` subcommand to redirect the command output to a file.

The syntax for `ls` is:

```
ls [option] <domain> [> <filename>]
```

The `domain` parameter in the `ls` syntax is used to specify the zone whose contents you would like to view. If the > redirector is used, you can specify the filename where you would like the command output directed to. The `option` parameter has five possible values, which are listed in Table A-66.

Table A-66. ls Command Options

Option	Use
-a	Returns the aliases (CNAME records) of computers in the specified domain.
-d	Returns all records in the specified domain.
-h	Returns CPU and operating system information for the specified domain, if HINFO (host information) records are present in the zone.
-t <querytype>	Returns all records of the type specified with the `querytype` parameter. Valid `querytype` values are listed in Table A-67.
-s	Returns well-known services of systems in the specified domain.

Table A-67 lists the valid query types that can be performed with the -t option. Some queries may return no data if no records of the query type exist in the target domain.

Table A-67. Valid querytype Values

Value	Records Returned
a	Host records (names and IP addresses)
any	All records
cname	Aliases
gid	Group identifier number (used by NFS in UNIX applications)
hinfo	Host information records (specify the CPU and OS type for systems)
mb	Mailbox domain names
mg	Master group members
minfo	Mailbox information
mr	Mail rename domain names
mx	Mail exchangers
ns	Name servers
ptr	All pointer records
soa	Start of authority records
txt	Text information records
uid	User ID (used by NFS in UNIX applications)
uinfo	User information records
wks	Well-known service records

lserver

When you run `nslookup` in interactive mode, you are connected to either your local system's default name server or a server that you specified at the time you executed the command. If you want to change the server you're connected to, that's what `lserver` is for.

The syntax for `lserver` is:

```
lserver <server | domain>
```

When a server name is specified, `nslookup` connects directly to the server. When you specify a domain, `nslookup` connects to the first name server listed in the domain's associated DNS zone.

server

The `server` subcommand works exactly like `lserver`, with the exception that the system's current default DNS server is used to resolve the name of the new name server to connect to, as opposed to resolving the name through the context of the current `nslookup` connection.

Take away the L from the `lserver` syntax, and you have the syntax for this command, which is:

```
server <server | domain>
```

set

The `set` subcommand is used to configure how the currently running `nslookup` command shell queries and retrieves records. There are several versions of `set`, and each is described in the next several sections.

set all

This command displays the current configuration settings for the name server that you're connected to with `nslookup`. The syntax for `set all` is:

```
set all
```

Once the command has executed, configuration information about the DNS server in context is displayed.

set class

This is a setting that you will likely never have to change, since practically every name server today is using the Internet class of resource records. However, before the growth of the Internet class well over a decade ago, there were two other popular classes for DNS records: Chaos and MIT Athena Hesiod. The Chaos class supported Chaosnet networks and is likely of value to you only if you appear on computer "Jeopardy" one day. The same can probably be said for the Hesiod class, since you are unlikely to run into it as well. Rather than bore you with any more history, let's just get to the `set class` syntax.

```
set cl[ass]=<class>
```

For this command, you do not need to enter the three letters that follow `cl`, but feel free to if you feel your fingers need the exercise. The default class for `nslookup` is Internet, but this can be modified by specifying one of the classes listed in Table A-68.

Table A-68. Valid class Values

Class	Description
`in`	Internet class
`chaos`	Chaos class
`hesiod`	MIT Athena Hesiod class

set d2

This subcommand allows you to turn on exhaustive debugging (debugging[2]). When exhaustive debugging is enabled, not only does your computer get pretty tired, but also you will see all fields of every `nslookup` packet displayed in the command output. When this feature is enabled, each `nslookup` query result displays the information that was sent, the answer that was received, and the system that provided the answer. For difficult-to-solve problems where you are looking for every bit of information that you can collect to analyze, you may want to turn on exhaustive debugging; otherwise, you can leave it off.

The syntax for this command is:

```
set [no]d2
```

set debug

The `set debug` subcommand allows you turn debugging on and off for `nslookup` queries. With debugging mode enabled, you will see detailed information about the question-and-answer packets involved in `nslookup` queries, but not to the detail of the information provided when exhaustive debugging is enabled.

The `set debug` syntax is:

```
set [no]deb[ug]
```

set defname

This command is used to append the local system's default domain name to `nslookup` queries (which is the system default).

The syntax for `set defname` is:

```
set [no]def[name]
```

To configure `nslookup` to automatically append the local system's default domain name, you would enter `set def`. When you are performing multiple queries for the same local domain, using this subcommand can save you quite a bit of time.

set domain

The `set domain` subcommand allows you to append a domain name other than the default domain name to lookup requests. This syntax for this command is:

```
set do[main]=<domain>
```

set ignore

This subcommand allows you to configure `nslookup` to ignore packet truncation errors, which result from name servers truncating host record names longer than 28 characters, as may be the case with Windows 9x clients. By default, `nslookup` does not ignore these errors, so if you wanted them to be ignored, you would run the `set ignore` command.

The syntax for this command is:

```
set [no]ig[nore]
```

To configure `nslookup` to ignore packet truncation errors, you would run `set ig`. To return `nslookup` back to its default and have it no longer ignore truncation errors, you would then run `set noig`.

set port

By default, DNS servers use TCP/UDP port 53. If you are using `nslookup` to connect to a DNS server not using port 53, this command allows you to change the port number used by `nslookup` for communications with the DNS server. Here's `set port`'s syntax:

```
set po[rt]=<port>
```

set querytype

The `set querytype` subcommand is used to configure `nslookup` to look up a particular type of resource record. The syntax for this command is:

```
set q[uerytype]=<record type>
```

set recurse

Recursion is set by default with `nslookup`. This means that if the target name server does not have knowledge of the record you are requesting, it automatically queries other name servers. The `set recurse` command allows you to change this default behavior by turning off recursion or by turning it back on. The command syntax is:

```
set [no]rec[urse]
```

To disable recursion, you would run `set norec`. If you then wanted to enable recursion, you could run `set rec`.

set retry

When a request is made with `nslookup`, the command waits a predetermined amount of time for a response before timing out. Two factors that determine the amount of elapsed time before a timeout are the Retry Interval and the timeout period. The default value for retries is 4, and the default timeout is 5 seconds. The `set retry` command, as you might have guessed, allows you to change the Retry Interval. The syntax for `set retry` is:

```
set ret[ry]=<value>
```

In the command syntax, the `value` parameter represents an integer value for the new Retry Interval.

set root

This command allows you to specify a root name server other than the default (ns.nic.ddn.mil) to be used by `nslookup`. You may decide to use this option when running `nslookup` to find names on an internal network that has a root name server configured. The syntax for set root is:

```
set ro[ot]=<rootserver>
```

set search

By default, when a name is queried with `nslookup`, any DNS suffixes listed to be appended in the local system's advanced TCP/IP properties are appended to the name until a match is found. If you want to turn off this default behavior and have no DNS suffixes appended to the name, you can use set search to turn off automatic DNS suffix appending in `nslookup`. The syntax for this command is:

```
set [no]sea[rch]
```

set srchlist

If you want to specify a custom domain suffix search list to be used by `nslookup`, you can run set srchlist. The syntax for this command is:

```
set srchl[ist]=<domain>[/<domain2>...]
```

If you want to specify multiple domains to be searched, each domain must be separated by a /.

set timeout

Aside from the Retry Interval, the timeout period is the other parameter in an `nslookup` timeout. The default timeout value is 5 seconds. To change the timeout value, you would use the following command syntax:

```
set ti[meout]=<seconds>
```

Remember that the timeout period is multiplied by the Retry Interval to give you the total query timeout value. So if you used set timeout to change the timeout period to 10 seconds, assuming that the Retry Interval was still set to its default value of 4, queries would wait up to 40 seconds for a response.

set vc

The set vc command is used to tell `nslookup` whether or not to use a virtual circuit when querying a DNS server. The syntax for set vc is:

```
set [no]v[c]
```

By default, `nslookup` does not use virtual circuits. To allow `nslookup` to use a virtual circuit when querying a name server, you would run set v.

You have seen an abundance of parameters that can be set to customize how `nslookup` responds. Some of the most frequently used versions of the `set` command are:

- `all`
- `debug`
- `domain`
- `querytype`
- `recurse`
- `srchlist`

view

When the output of the `nslookup ls` command is redirected to a text file, you can use the `nslookup view` subcommand to see the file's contents. The syntax for this command is:

```
view <filename>
```

pagefileconfig /change

The `/change` version of the `pagefileconfig` command allows you to modify the configuration of the pagefile on a system. Its syntax is:

```
cscript pagefileconfig.vbs /change [/s <computer> [/u <domain\user>
[/p <password>]]] [/i <initial size>] [/m <maximum size>] [vo <volume
letter | *>]
```

The `pagefileconfig /change` options are described in Table A-69.

Table A-69. pagefileconfig /change Command Options

Option	Use
/s <computer>	Used to specify the IP address or FQDN of the remote computer on which to run the command.
/u <domain\user>	Executes the command using the domain and user account specified. By default, the credentials for the user issuing the command are used.
/p <password>	When a domain and user are specified, this switch allows you to include a password for the user account.

continues

Table A-69. pagefileconfig /change Command Options, continued

Option	Use
/i <initial size>	Used to specify a new initial size (in megabytes) for the pagefile on the system.
/m <max size>	Used to specify a new maximum size (in megabytes) for the pagefile on the system.
/vo <volume letter | *>	If the pagefile is distributed across multiple logical volumes, this option allows you to select the volume you would like the change in configuration specified in the command to apply to. When used with the * parameter, the command modifies all volumes.

pagefileconfig /create

The /create option allows you to add an additional paging file to a system. Here is its syntax:

```
cscript pagefileconfig.vbs /create [/s <computer> [/u <domain\user>
[/p <password>]]] [/i <initial pagefile size>] [/m <maximum pagefile
size>] [vo <volume letter>]
```

The command options are explained in Table A-70.

Table A-70. pagefileconfig /create Command Options

Option	Use
/s <computer>	Used to specify the IP address or FQDN of the remote computer on which to run the command.
/u <domain\user>	Executes the command using the domain and user account specified. By default, the credentials for the user issuing the command are used.
/p <password>	When a domain and user are specified, this switch allows you to include a password for the user account.
/i <initial size>	Used to specify the initial size (in megabytes) for the new pagefile on the system.
/m <max size>	Used to specify the maximum size (in megabytes) for the new pagefile on the system.
/vo <volume letter>	Used to specify the volume on which to create the new pagefile.

pagefileconfig /delete

This command is used to delete a paging file for a particular drive. Its syntax is:

```
cscript pagefileconfig.vbs /delete [/s <computer> [/u <domain\user>
[/p <password>]]] [vo <volume letter>]
```

The command options are described in Table A-71.

Table A-71. pagefileconfig /delete Command Options

Option	Use
/s <computer>	Used to specify the IP address or FQDN of the remote computer on which to run the command.
/u <domain\user>	Executes the command using the domain and user account specified. By default, the credentials for the user issuing the command are used.
/p <password>	When a domain and user are specified, this switch allows you to include a password for the user account.
/vo <volume letter>	Used to specify the volume from which to delete the pagefile.

pagefileconfig /query

If you are unsure of the pagefile configuration on a remote system, the /query option can be quite handy. If you are an administrator tasked with remotely troubleshooting a user's system on the LAN, running this command from your desktop is much easier than stepping the user through the process of determining his or her pagefile configuration.

Here is the syntax for pagefileconfig /query:

```
cscript pagefileconfig.vbs /query [/s <computer> [/u <domain\user> [/p
<password>]]] [/fo <table|list|csv>]
```

The options for pagefileconfig /query are detailed in Table A-72.

Table A-72. pagefileconfig /query Command Options

Option	Use
/s <computer>	Used to specify the IP address or FQDN of the remote computer on which to run the command.
/u <domain\user>	Executes the command using the domain and user account specified. By default, the credentials for the user issuing the command are used.

continues

Table A-72. pagefileconfig /query Command Options, continued

Option	Use
`/p <password>`	When a domain and user are specified, this switch allows you to include a password for the user account.
`/fo <table|list|csv>`	Used to specify the format for the script's output (the default is `list`).

pathping

The `pathping` command allows you to isolate the location of a problem a packet is having when traveling between two routed networks. To test the routers between two communication points, `pathping` sends multiple Echo Request messages to each router and displays the percentage of packets that were lost when sent to each router in the path. A high value of lost packets may indicate a faulty router or a saturated network segment and thus the source of your WAN connectivity problems.

The syntax for `pathping` is:

```
pathping <destination name or IP> [-n] [-h <max hops>] [-g <host list>] [-p <period>] [-q <number of queries>] [-w <timeout>] [-T] [-R]
```

Table A-73 describes the `pathping` command options.

Table A-73. pathping Command Options

Option	Use
`<destination name or IP>`	Specifies the destination FQDN or IP address.
`-n`	Speeds up the command execution by preventing `pathping` from trying to resolve the IP addresses of intermediate routers.
`-h <max hops>`	Specifies the maximum hops to travel to search for the destination (default maximum = 30).
`-g <host list>`	Causes the Echo Request messages to use the Loose Source Router option in the IP header.
`-p <period>`	Lets you specify the time in milliseconds (ms) that the command will wait between consecutive pings (default = 250ms). Too frequent consecutive pings may inaccurately result in network congestion being reported.
`-q <number of queries>`	Lets you set the number of Echo Requests to be sent to each router in the path (default = 100).
`-w <timeout>`	Lets you set the time (in milliseconds) to wait for a reply from each router (default = 3000ms, or 3 seconds).

Table A-73. pathping Command Options, continued

Option	Use
-T	Used to test for Quality of Service (QoS) connectivity by checking for devices that do not have layer 2 priority capability.
-R	Also used for QoS; determines if each network device along the route supports Resource Reservation Protocol (RSVP).

pfmon (ST)

When you suspect that a disk bottleneck resulting from hard page faults is occurring, you can verify your suspicions by running `pfmon`, which allows you to

- Identify the number of page faults for a process
- Identify the source of page faults in a process

When run, `pfmon` attaches itself to a process and displays any page faults resulting from the process until the command is manually terminated when Ctrl-C is pressed. Instead of having the output displayed on the screen, you can have the command's output dumped to a file for later analysis.

Here is the syntax for `pfmon`:

```
pfmon <[/p <PID>] | [Application Command]> [/n] [/c] [/h] [/k]
[/K] [/d]
```

The `pfmon` command options are described in Table A-74.

Table A-74. pfmon Command Options

Option	Use
/p <PID>	Specifies the process ID (PID) to monitor (the currently running process). You can find a process's PID by accessing a list of the currently running processes under the Processes tab in Task Manager. When you terminate `pfmon`, the process that you have the command attach to also terminates.
Application Command	Used to list the full path of the process to invoke and monitor (for example: D:\Program Files\Doom\Doom.exe). If you specify an application command to run, you cannot use the /p switch to specify a process ID.

continues

Table A-74. pfmon Command Options, continues

Option	Use
/n	Faults are written to the pfmon.log file (written in the directory where `pfmon` is executed) and are not displayed in the command window.
/l	Faults are written to the pfmon.log file and are displayed in the command window as well.
/c	Displays soft page faults and summary information. Hard page faults are not displayed.
/h	Displays hard page faults and summary information. Soft page faults are not displayed.
/k	Displays both kernel mode and user mode page faults.
/K	Displays only kernel mode page faults.
/d	Causes the following tab-delineated information to be displayed in the command output: • Page fault number • Fault type (hard or soft) • Program counter's module, symbol, and decimal value • Decimal value for the program counter of the virtual address accessed • Virtual address's symbol and value

ping

With `ping`, you can quickly verify

- Network connectivity between two systems
- Name resolution

The `ping` command also allows you to perform additional tests on the network between two systems, as you will see in its syntax.

```
ping <destination name or IP> [-a] [-f] [-i <TTL>] [-j <host list>]
[-k <host list>] [-l <size>] [-n <count>] [-r <count>] [-s <count>]
[-t] [-v <TOS>]
```

The options for the `ping` command are described in Table A-75.

Table A-75. ping Command Options

Option	Use
`<destination name or IP>`	Specifies the destination FQDN or IP address.
`-a`	Performs reverse name resolution on the destination IP address, causing the destination's FQDN to be displayed in the command output.
`-f`	Helpful when troubleshooting Maximum Transmission Unit (MTU) problems; `ping` Echo Request messages are sent with the "Don't Fragment" flag in the IP header set to 1, preventing the Echo Request message from being fragmented by routers on its path to its destination.
`-i <TTL>`	Specifies a Time to Live (TTL) value for the Echo Request messages; the default value is 128; with this option, you can change the value to as high as 255, meaning that the Echo Request message sent by the `ping` command will travel a maximum of 255 hops before being discarded by the 256th router.
`-j <host list>`	Allows you to list intermediate destinations by IP addresses separated by spaces (the `host list` portion of the switch). This option specifies Loose Source Routing, meaning that the intermediate destinations specified can be separated by one or more routers. With this command, you can list up to nine hosts.
`-k <host list>`	Allows you to list intermediate destinations by IP addresses separated by spaces (the `host list` portion of the switch). This option specifies Strict Source Routing, meaning that the intermediate destinations specified cannot be separated by one or more routers (they must be adjacent). With this command, you can list up to nine hosts.
`-l <size>`	Allows you to specify the size of the payload in bytes of the Data field in the Echo Request messages sent by `ping`. The default size is 32, but you can specify a maximum payload up to 65,527 bytes. This is a good way to test whether limited bandwidth or congestion is the source of networking problems.
`-n <count>`	Used to specify the number of Echo Requests sent by `ping`. The default value is 4.
`-r <count>`	Allows you to specify a count (1–9) of hops recorded in the Echo Request and Echo Reply messages. The count specified must be greater than or equal to the number of routers in the path.
`-s <count>`	Allows you to specify a hop count (1–4), where the time of arrival for each Echo Request and Echo Reply message is recorded. This is possible when the routers in the path support the Internet Timestamp option in the IP header.
`-t`	Forces `ping` to continually send Echo Request messages until the command is interrupted when Ctrl-C is pressed.
`-v <TOS>`	Lets you specify the Type of Service (TOS) value in the IP header for the `ping` Echo Request message. The default value is 0. You can specify any value between 1 and 255.

pmon (ST)

The `pmon` command closely simulates the output you see under the Processes tab in the Task Manager. The primary difference, however, is that it is run from the command line, and its output is displayed in tabular format in the command window, periodically refreshing every few seconds. Since it is a command line utility, this is something you could consider running when remotely troubleshooting through a Telnet session.

There is no syntax for `pmon`, so to execute it, you just type `pmon` from the command prompt.

portqry (ST)

The Port Query (`portqry`) command allows you to troubleshoot TCP/IP port connectivity issues. With this tool, you can test the connectivity and check the status of a single TCP or UDP port or a range of ports. If you are unsure if a remote port is even accessible, due to a possible firewall setting or server service being down, this is a great tool to use to find the answer.

When you query a remote port, `portqry` returns a status for the remote port, which is one of the statuses listed in Table A-76.

Table A-76. portqry Output Statuses

Status	Description
Listening	The target port is active and listening.
Not Listening	The target destination/port is not reachable.
Filtered	The port on the target system is listening but is being filtered by the target system or by a firewall. Port filtering is a way for a server or firewall to limit traffic that connects on a particular port, such as by only allowing port 80 connections from a single network source.

The status that is returned is valuable in troubleshooting port availability. For example, if you receive a Not Listening response, that tells you that no system can connect to the remote host on the queried port number. This may indicate that a service on the remote system that manages the port is down, or that requests to connect on a particular port are being blocked by a firewall. If you receive a Listening response, then you can determine that the target system's queried port is active, and this may mean that a connectivity problem may be a failure residing on the client that is trying to connect, and not with the remote server.

Now that you've seen the reason to use this command, let's look at its syntax.

```
portqry /n <name> [/p <protocol>] [/e <port>] [/r <StartPort:EndPort>]
[/o <port,port,...>] [/l <logfile>] [/s] [/q] [/i]
```

Table A-77 describes the `portqry` command's options.

Table A-77. portqry Command Options

Option	Use
`/n <name>`	Used to specify the FQDN or IP address of the remote host that `portqry` will try to connect to.
`/p <protocol>`	Used to specify the type of port or protocol used to connect to the target port. The default is TCP. Valid protocol values are `tcp`, `udp`, or `both`.
`/e <port>`	Used to specify the port number to query. Valid numbers range from 1 to 65535. This option cannot be used in conjunction with `/r` or `/o`.
`/r <StartPort:EndPort>`	Used to specify a range of ports to be queried in sequential order. This option cannot be used in conjunction with `/e` or `/o`.
`/o <port,port, ...>`	Used to specify a list of ports to query. You cannot have spaces between port numbers or commas. This option cannot be used in conjunction with `/e` or `/r`.
`/l <logfile>`	Used to copy the `portqry` output to a text file. In the `logfile` value, you should specify the complete path and filename to where you want the output written.
`/s`	Causes `portqry` to wait longer for UDP requests before replying with a Not Listening status.
`/q`	Suppresses screen output except for error messages. This command cannot be used with `/o` or `/r`, or when `both` is specified as the protocol type in the `/p` switch.
`/i`	Causes `portqry` to bypass an IP-to-host name lookup if an IP address is provided for the target name. This allows the `portqry` command to complete faster.

prndrvr.vbs

The `prndrvr.vbs` tool is a very powerful script that allows you to manage printer drivers on local and remote printers. This may be especially useful if you have a Windows NT 4.0 user that needs to print to a particular printer, but the print server's NT driver is

590 Appendix A Troubleshooting Command Line Reference

not installed for the printer. With this command, you can remotely add the necessary print driver so that the user can properly print.

There are four ways that you can run this script, depending on the task you need to achieve. The four versions of this command are as follows:

- `prndrvr.vbs -a`—Adds a printer driver to a print server
- `prndrvr.vbs -d`—Removes a printer driver from a print server
- `prndrvr.vbs -l`—Lists printer drivers installed on a print server
- `prndrvr.vbs -x`—Removes all unused printer drivers from a print server

Each of these scripts is detailed in the next four sections.

prndrvr.vbs –a (Add Driver)

Running this script allows you to install a printer driver on a print server. This is useful if you need to update a driver for a print server or add a driver to a print server to support users connecting to the print server using an OS that the server previously did not have an installed driver for.

The syntax for the `prndrvr.vbs -a` command is:

```
cscript prndrvr.vbs -a [-m <DriverName>] [-v <0|1|2|3>] [-e
<Environment>] [-s <RemoteComputer>] [-h <Path>] [-i <DriverFile>][-u
<user> -w <password>]
```

The command options are described in Table A-78.

Table A-78. prndrvr.vbs –a Command Options

Option	Use
`-m <DriverName>`	Specifies the name of the driver you are installing. The driver is normally named after the printer that it supports.
`-v <0 | 1 | 2 | 3>`	Specifies the version of the driver to install. • 0 = Windows 95/98/ME • 1 = Windows NT 3.51 • 2 = Windows NT 4.0 • 3 = Windows Server 2003/XP/2000 • If a version is not specified, the driver version that matches the OS of the print server is installed.
`-e <Environment>`	Specifies the environment for the installed driver. Valid environment options are shown in Table A-79. When no environment is specified, the environment of the print server on which the driver is installed is assumed.

Table A-78. prndrvr.vbs –a Command Options, continued

Option	Use
-s <RemoteComputer>	When the command is run remotely, this option specifies the name or IP address of the remote print server.
-h <path>	Specifies the path to the driver's information (.inf) file.
-i <DriverFile>	Specifies the name of the driver's information (.inf) file.
-u <user>	If your currently logged-on account does not have Manage Printers permission (Administrators and Power Users by default), you can use this parameter to run the command under the context of a different user.
-w <password>	When the -u parameter is included in the command, the -w parameter specifies the user's password.

Table A-79 lists the valid environment settings. When you use the –e parameter, your input must match the quoted text in the table.

Table A-79. Valid Environment Settings

Environment Setting	Compatible Version Setting(s)
"Windows NT 4.0"	0
"Windows NT PowerPC"	1
"Windows NT R4000"	1
"Windows IA64"	3
"Windows NT Alpha_AXP"	1, 2
"Windows NT x86"	1, 2, 3

prndrvr.vbs –d (Delete Driver)

If a driver is no longer needed on a particular print server, this command can be used to uninstall the driver.

The syntax for the `prndrvr.vbs -d` command is:

```
cscript prndrvr.vbs -d [-m <DriverName>] [-v <0|1|2|3>] [-e
<Environment>] [-s <RemoteComputer>] [-u <user> -w <password>]
```

The command options are described in Table A-80.

592 Appendix A Troubleshooting Command Line Reference

Table A-80. prndrvr.vbs –d Command Options

Option	Use
-m <DriverName>	Specifies the name of the driver you are removing.
-v <0 | 1 | 2 | 3>	Specifies the version of the driver to remove. • 0 = Windows 95/98/ME • 1 = Windows NT 3.51 • 2 = Windows NT 4.0 • 3 = Windows Server 2003/XP/2000 • If a version is not specified, the driver version that matches the OS of the print server is installed.
-e <Environment>	Specifies the environment for the removed driver. Valid environment options are shown in Table A-79. When no environment is specified, the environment of the print server on which the driver is installed is assumed.
-s <RemoteComputer>	When the command is run remotely, this option specifies the name or IP address of the remote print server.
-u <user>	If your currently logged-on account does not have Manage Printers permission (Administrators and Power Users by default), you can use this parameter to run the command under the context of a different user.
-w <password>	When the -u parameter is included in the command, the -w parameter specifies the user's password.

prndrvr.vbs –l (List Drivers)

If you are unsure if a driver needs to be installed on a print server, or if you are looking for a list of installed drivers in order to uninstall unneeded drivers, you can run this command to display a list of installed printer drivers on a system. When run, this command displays the following driver information:

- The driver name
- The driver version (0, 1, 2, or 3)
- The driver path
- Dependent files

The syntax for the `prndrvr.vbs -l` command is:

`cscript prndrvr.vbs -l [-s <RemoteComputer>] [-u <user> -w <password>]`

The command options are described in Table A-81.

Table A-81. prndrvr.vbs –l Command Options

Option	Use
`-s <RemoteComputer>`	When the command is run remotely, this option specifies the name or IP address of the remote print server.
`-u <user>`	If your currently logged-on account does not have Manage Printers permission (Administrators and Power Users by default), you can use this parameter to run the command under the context of a different user.
`-w <password>`	When the `-u` parameter is included in the command, the `-w` parameter specifies the user's password.

prndrvr.vbs –x (Remove All Unused Drivers)

The syntax for the `prndrvr.vbs -x` command is:

```
cscript prndrvr.vbs -x [-s <RemoteComputer>] [-u <user> -w <password>]
```

The options for this command are identical to those listed in Table A-81.

prnmngr.vbs

For troubleshooting purposes, the most useful part of this script is to obtain a list of printers on a server. Once you know the names of the printers on a server, you can use those names in other print management commands, such as `prnqctl.vbs`. This syntax for using this command to list printers and their configuration information on a server is:

```
cscript prnmngr.vbs -l [-s <RemoteComputer>] [-u <user> -w <password>]
```

The command options are described in Table A-82.

Table A-82. prnmngr.vbs Command Options

Option	Use
`-s <RemoteComputer>`	When you are not at the system that hosts the target printer, this option specifies the name or IP address of the remote print server.
`-u <user>`	If your currently logged-on account does not have Manage Printers permission (Administrators and Power Users by default), you can use this parameter to run the command under the context of a different user.
`-w <password>`	When the `-u` parameter is included in the command, the `-w` parameter specifies the user's password.

For other versions of this command, see Windows online Help.

prnqctl.vbs

When you are troubleshooting printer problems, this command can be used to print a test page, to pause or resume a printer, and to clear all documents in the printer queue. Since this is a .vbs command, you must run this command from the directory in which the file resides. By default, the Prnqctl.vbs file is in the %systemroot%system32 folder, so with a default installation, you should ensure that you are at the C:\Windows\System32> prompt before running the command.

The syntax for `prnqctl.vbs` is:

```
cscript prnqctl.vbs <-z | -m | -e | -x> [-s <RemoteComputer>] -p
<PrinterName> [-u <user> -w <password>]
```

When you run the command, you must specify one of the first listed options (z, m, e, or x) to indicate the type of action that the command is to perform. The other required parameter for this command is -p, which indicates the target printer for the command. The command options are described in Table A-83.

Table A-83. prnqctl.vbs Command Options

Option	Use
-z	Pauses a printer.
-m	Resumes a paused printer.
-e	Prints a test page.
-x	Cancels all jobs spooled to the printer.
-s <RemoteComputer>	When you are not at the system that hosts the target printer, this option specifies the name or IP address of the remote print server.
-p <PrinterName>	Required parameter. Specifies the name of the target printer for the command.
-u <user>	If your currently logged-on account does not have Manage Printers permission (Administrators and Power Users by default), you can use this parameter to run the command under the context of a different user.
-w <password>	When the -u parameter is included in the command, the -w parameter specifies the user's password.

query

The `query` command is used to collect information about terminal server sessions. This command has these four versions:

- query process
- query session
- query termserver
- query user

Each of these commands is valuable when you are troubleshooting terminal server connection problems, and they are explained in the next four sections.

query process

This command displays all user processes running on the terminal server, as well as the user that is running each process. If a user is experiencing difficulties with a terminal session and you need to determine the programs that the user is actually executing, you can use this command to do so.

The syntax for `query process` is:

```
query process [* | <ProcessID> | <UserName> | <SessionName> |
/id:<SessionID> | <ProgramName>] [/server:<servername>]
```

Notice that you can perform only one type of process query. In other words, you cannot query by both user name and process ID in the same command. To do this, you would need to run the command twice. The command options are described in Table A-84.

Table A-84. query process Command Options

Option	Use
*	Lists the processes for all sessions (the default).
ProcessID	Specifies the PID of a process you wish to query. Command output displays users running the process with the PID specified.
UserName	Causes the command to output running processes for the user specified.
SessionName	Causes the command to output running processes for the session specified.
/id:<SessionID>	Causes the command to output running processes for the session ID specified.
ProgramName	Specifies the name of an executable to query. Only files with .exe extensions can be queried.
/server:<servername>	Specifies a remote terminal server to query. When the command is run without this parameter, the local terminal server is queried.

query session

Running this command allows you to obtain a list of all sessions (active or inactive) that are running on a terminal server. The syntax for `query session` is:

```
query session [<SessionName> | <UserName> | <SessionID>]
[/server:<servername>] [/mode] [/flow] [/connect] [/counter]
```

The `query session` command options are described in Table A-85.

Table A-85. query session Command Options

Option	Use
SessionName	Specifies the name of the session to query. The command returns information on the state of the provided session.
UserName	Specifies the name of a user to query. The command returns information on the state of the user's session.
SessionID	Specifies the name of the session ID to query. The command returns information on the state of the provided session ID.
/server: <servername>	Specifies a remote terminal server to query. When the command is run without this parameter, the local terminal server is queried.
/mode	Displays terminal server line settings.
/flow	Displays terminal server flow-control settings.
/connect	Displays current terminal server connection settings.
/counter	Displays current terminal server counter information (sessions created, disconnected, reconnected).

query termserver

When you wish to acquire a list of all terminal servers running on a network or all terminal servers in a particular domain, this command is valuable. For example, you may have users complaining that they cannot access a particular terminal server. If other terminal servers in the domain host similar applications, you could query a list of available servers and give the user an alternate server to try. The syntax for this command is:

```
query termserver [ServerName] [/domain:<domain>] [/address]
[/continue]
```

The options for this command are explained in Table A-86.

Table A-86. query termserver Command Options

Option	Use
ServerName	Displays a particular terminal server's list of known terminal servers on the network.
/domain:<domain>	Allows you to retrieve a list of all terminal servers in a particular domain.
/address	Specifies the network and node addresses for each terminal server found in the command output.
/continue	Prevents the command from pausing after each screen of output data is displayed.

query user

The `query user` command allows you to see information about a user's session on a terminal server. The command output displays the following session information:

- User name
- Session name
- Session ID
- Session state (Active, Disconnected)
- Idle time
- Logon time

To run this command to retrieve this information, you would use the following syntax:

```
query user [UserName] [SessionName] [SessionID] [/server:<servername>]
```

The options for this command are explained in Table A-87.

Table A-87. query user Command Options

Option	Use
UserName	Specifies the name of a user to query.
SessionName	Specifies the name of the session to query.
SessionID	Specifies the name of the session ID to query.
/server:<servername>	Specifies a remote terminal server to query. When the command is run without this parameter, the local terminal server is queried.

recover

The `recover` command allows you to get back the portions of a file that remain on the good sectors of a disk when portions of a disk have become corrupted. If the file is an important document and no good backup exists, this command provides you with an alternative with which you can save at least a portion of the lost data.

The `recover` command only works at the filename level and does not support the use of wildcards, so this command can only be executed on a single file at a time. The syntax for `recover` is:

```
recover [drive:] [path] filename
```

When the command is run in the directory in which the corrupted file resides, only the filename needs to be included in the command syntax. Otherwise, you can list the complete path to the filename in the command syntax.

reset session

This command allows you to terminate user sessions on a terminal server. Before you run this command, it is best to run the `query session` command to obtain a list of all sessions on a terminal server. You can then use the session information in the `reset session` command syntax. The syntax for `reset session` is:

```
reset session [<SessionName> | <SessionID>] [/server:<servername>] [/v]
```

The options for this command are explained in Table A-88.

Table A-88. reset session Command Options

Option	Use
`SessionName`	Specifies the name of the session to reset.
`SessionID`	Specifies the name of the session ID to reset.
`/server: <servername>`	Specifies a remote terminal server containing the session you wish to reset. When the command is run without this parameter, the command connects to the local system.
`/v`	Verbose output—the command displays information about the actions it is performing.

route

The `route` command is very valuable when you are troubleshooting both client and server routing issues. For example, a client may have persistent static routes in its local routing table so that it can reach a test network that is accessible to the organization's public network. If the IP settings of the router that the client uses to access the network change, then you will have to modify the client's static routing table accordingly. In a perfect world, all static routes are stored on the company's router to centralize routing administration. One example of the use of static routes is for a Windows Server 2003 system running RRAS to connect the corporate network to satellite offices. The router may have several demand-dial interfaces that allow connection to remote networks. This information may be in the form of static routes that must be maintained. With the `route` command, you can view, modify, delete, or add static routes to a system's routing table.

Here is the syntax for `route`:

```
route [-f] [-p] <add | change | delete | print> [destination] [mask
<netmask>] [gateway] [metric <metric>] [if <interface>]
```

The command options are described in Table A-89.

Table A-89. route Command Options

Option	Use
`-f`	Clears from the routing table all routes that are not host routes. Host routes consist of the following routing entries: routes with the subnet mask 255.255.255.255, routes with a destination of 127.0.0.0 and a subnet mask of 255.0.0.0, and multicast routes (destination ranges from 224.0.0.0 to 240.0.0.0). If this option is used in conjunction with the `add`, `change`, or `delete` options, the routing table is cleared prior to the processing of the particular command option.
`-p`	Used to make a new or modified routing entry persistent. This means that the routing information is retained by the system even after a reboot. Without the `-p` parameter, any route that is added to the routing table is lost the next time the system reboots.
`add`	Adds a new route to the routing table.
`change`	Changes an existing route in the routing table.
`delete`	Deletes a route from the routing table.
`print`	Displays the contents of the routing table.
`destination`	When a route is added or modified, this parameter is used to specify the destination network ID.
`mask <netmask>`	When a route is added or modified, this parameter is used to specify the destination network's subnet mask.

continues

Table A-89. route Command Options, continued

Option	Use
`gateway`	When a new route is added or modified, this parameter is used to specify the gateway (router) to send the data to in order to reach the destination network.
`metric <metric>`	Used to specify an integer (from 1 to 9999) cost metric for the route. When multiple routes exist for the same destination, the route with the lowest cost metric is used.
`if <interface>`	Used to specify the interface index for the interface that connects to the destination network. You can view a list of available interfaces by running `route print`. The interface index can be specified in either decimal or hexadecimal. When hex is used, the interface value must be preceded with `0x`.

sfc

The name `sfc` is short for System File Checker, and the command is primarily used to scan your system and verify the authenticity of all protected files. If a user is complaining about system instability, there is a chance that the problem is the result of a protected file that has been altered. To eliminate this as a possible problem, you could run `sfc` on the system.

Here is the syntax for `sfc`:

```
sfc [/scannow] [/scanonce] [/scanboot] [/revert] [/purgecache]
[/cachsize=<size>]
```

The `sfc` command options are explained in Table A-90.

Table A-90. sfc Command Options

Option	Use
`/scannow`	System protected files are scanned immediately.
`/scanonce`	System protected files are scanned once at the next reboot.
`/scanboot`	System protected files are scanned each time the system boots.
`/revert`	Reverts the System File Checker to its default setting (does not scan at startup).
`/purgecache`	Purges the contents of the dllcache folder and runs an immediate scan of protected files. Files in the dllcache folder are replaced by their original versions on the installation CD.
`/cachesize=<size>`	Sets a maximum size (in megabytes) for the dllcache folder.

systeminfo

The `systeminfo` command can almost be thought of as a trimmed-down command line version of the GUI tool MSinfo32 which is described in the next section. The `systeminfo` command provides general system information on either a local or remote system, and from a troubleshooting perspective provides the following useful information:

- The operating system version and service pack level
- The product ID (if you need to call support)
- Processor type(s)
- The BIOS version
- Windows and system directory locations
- Physical and virtual memory
- A list of each installed hotfix

To run `systeminfo`, you would use the following syntax:

```
systeminfo [/s <system>] [/u <domain\user>] [/p <password>] [/fo
<table|list|csv>] [/nh]
```

Table A-91 describes the available command options.

Table A-91. systeminfo Command Options

Option	Use
/s <system>	Specifies the name or IP address of the remote system in which to acquire system information.
/u <domain\user>	Specifies the user account under which to execute the command.
/p <password>	When a user account is specified with the /u switch, this parameter is used to provide a password.
/fo <table|list|csv>	Used to specify the format for the command's output (the default is `table`).
/nh	When the output is set to `table` or `csv`, this parameter suppresses the table header information from the command output.

takeown

Suppose that you have a renegade user that, before leaving the company, decides to make your life more difficult by denying everyone in the organization access to his files. The solution for this type of problem is for you, as an administrator, to take ownership of the affected files and then modify their DACL. One easy way to perform this task is to use the `takeown` command line utility.

The `takeown` syntax is:

```
takeown /f <file> [/s <system>] [/u <domain\user>] [/p <password>]
```

The `takeown` command options are described in Table A-92.

Table A-92. takeown Command Options

Option	Use
/f <file>	Used to indicate the file of which to take ownership. The * wildcard can be used to indicate multiple files.
/s <system>	Used to provide the name or IP address of a remote computer on which to run the command. By default, the command will run on the local system where it is executed.
/u <domain\user>	Used to execute the command with the credentials of another user. This may be needed if you need to take ownership of files on a standalone system using its local administrator account.
/p <password>	Used to specify a password for the user account specified with the /u switch.

taskkill

The `taskkill` command allows you to terminate processes on a local or remote system from the command line. Its syntax is:

```
taskkill [/s <computer>] [/u <domain\user>] [/p <password>] [/fi <filter name>] [ /pid <Process ID>] [/im <image name>] [/f] [/t]
```

The `taskkill` command options are described in Table A-93.

Table A-93. taskkill Command Options

Option	Use
/s <computer>	Specifies the name or IP address of the remote computer.
/u <domain\user>	Specifies the name of user under which to execute the command.

Table A-93. taskkill Command Options, continued

Option	Use
/p <password>	Used with the /u switch to specify user's password.
/fi <filter name>	Allows you to filter processes to include in or exclude from termination. Valid filter names and operators are shown in Table A-94.
/pid <Process ID>	Specifies the process ID of the process to be terminated.
/im <image name>	Used to specify an image name of the process(es) to terminate. It can be used with the * wildcard for multiple processes.
/f	Forcefully terminates the process. This is done automatically when the command is run on a remote system.
/t	Terminates the entire process tree, terminating all child processes for the process specified.

Table A-94. Valid taskkill Filters and Operators

Filter	Operator	Allowable Values
CPUTime	eq, ne, gt, lt, ge, le	Valid time expressed in hh:mm:ss
Hostname	eq, ne	Any string of characters
Imagename	eq, ne	Any string of characters
Memusage	eq, ne, gt, lt, ge, le	Any positive integer
PID	eq, ne, gt, lt, ge, le	Any positive integer
Services	eq, ne	Any string of characters
Session	eq, ne, gt, lt, ge, le	Any active session number
Status	eq, ne	Running | Not Responding
Username	eq, ne	Any user name
Windowtitle	eq, ne	Any string of characters

The meanings of the operators shown in Table A-94 are listed in Table A-95.

Table A-95. Common Command Operators

Operator	Meaning
eq	Filter processes equal to the specified value
ne	Filter processes not equal to the specified value
gt	Greater than the specified number
lt	Less than the specified number
ge	Greater than or equal to the specified number
le	Less than or equal to the specified number

tasklist

The `tasklist` command displays information on each running task, including the task's process ID, which is useful if you need a PID in order to run `taskkill`. The syntax for `tasklist` is:

```
tasklist [/s <computer name> [/u <domain\user>] [/p <password>] [/fo
<table | list | csv>] [/nh] [/fi <filter name>] [/m [module name] |
/svc | /v]
```

Each of the command options is explained in Table A-96.

Table A-96. tasklist Command Options

Option	Use
/s <computer name>	Specifies the name or IP address of the remote computer.
/u <domain\user>	Specifies the name of the user under which to execute the command.
/p <password>	Used with the /u switch to specify the user's password.
/fo <table | list | csv>	Allows you to specify how the command output is displayed. When the switch is not used, the output is in `table` format.
/nh	When the /fo switch is used to set the output to tabular or `csv` format, this switch causes the column headers to not be displayed in the output.
/fi <filter name>	Allows you to filter processes to include in or exclude from the list. Valid filter names and operators are shown in Table A-97.
/m [module name]	Displays the modules associated with each process, which allows you to see all the .dlls associated with the processes on a system. If a module name is included with the switch, all processes associated with the module are displayed. This switch cannot be used in conjunction with /svc or /v.
/svc	When the /fo switch is set to `table`, it allows you to see service information for each process. This switch cannot be used with /m or /v.
/v	Verbose output—highly detailed output information is displayed. This switch cannot be used with /m or /svc.

Table A-97. Valid tasklist Filters and Operators

Filter	Operator	Allowable Values
CPUTime	eq, ne, gt, lt, ge, le	Valid time expressed in hh:mm:ss
Imagename	eq, ne	Any string of characters
Memusage	eq, ne, gt, lt, ge, le	Any positive integer
Modules	eq, ne	Any string of characters
PID	eq, ne, gt, lt, ge, le	Any positive integer
Services	eq, ne	Any string of characters
Session	eq, ne, gt, lt, ge, le	Any active session number
SessionName	eq, ne	Any string of characters
Status	eq, ne	Running | Not Responding
Username	eq, ne	Any user name
Windowtitle	eq, ne	Any string of characters

telnet

Telnet has long roamed the UNIX world as a means to remotely administer servers, and beginning with Windows 2000 Server, the OS had its own Telnet Server service. With `telnet`, you can quickly access the command line interface of a remote system and perform tasks such as

- Starting and stopping services
- Managing files and directories
- Running scripts

While there are variations of how to Telnet to another system, the following basic syntax allows you to connect to and manage a remote system.

```
telnet <remote host> [port:<port number>]
```

The two options for the `telnet` command are described in Table A-98.

Table A-98. telnet Command Options

Option	Use
remote host	The host name or IP address of the remote server running the Telnet Server service.
port: <port number>	The port to use for the Telnet session. The default port is 23. Specifying a port number allows you to test connectivity over a range of ports, such as seeing if you can negotiate a session over a particular port for a service you are having trouble with between two WAN sites.

tracert

The `tracert` command is somewhat similar to `pathping` in usage, allowing you to check the path between two routed networks, but it does not check each router in the path as thoroughly as `pathping`. Like `pathping` and `ping`, `tracert` uses ICMP Echo Requests to check for network connectivity. Like `pathping`, `tracert` displays each hop (or router) between the source where the command is run from and the destination entered, but it does not display the statistical information, such as the percentage of lost packets, that you see with `pathping`.

Here's the syntax for `tracert`:

```
tracert <destination name or IP> [-d] [-h <maximum hops>] [-j <host list>] [-w <timeout>]
```

The `tracert` command options are explained in Table A-99.

Table A-99. tracert Command Options

Option	Use
`destination name or IP`	Specifies the destination FQDN or IP address.
`-d`	Speeds up the execution of `tracert` by preventing the command from attempting to resolve the IP addresses of intermediate routers to their respective host names.
`-h <maximum hops>`	Used to specify the maximum number of hops in the path to the destination. The default value is 30.
`-j <host list>`	Allows you to list intermediate destinations by IP addresses separated by spaces (the `host list` portion of the switch). This option specifies Loose Source Routing, meaning that the intermediate destinations specified can be separated by one or more routers. With this command, you can list up to nine hosts.
`-w <timeout>`	Used to specify the time (in milliseconds) to wait for an ICMP Time Exceeded or Echo Reply message from an Echo Request. If a reply is not received within the time represented by the `timeout` parameter value, an asterisk (*) is displayed. The default value is 4000 (4 seconds).

B

Common Error Codes and Messages

This appendix acts as a quick index to common error messages that you may encounter on your systems. In this appendix, you will find two sections: Device Errors and Stop Errors. The first section addresses Device Manager error codes and provides guidance for how to resolve the problems that generate each error code type. The second part of this appendix indexes each of the most common stop errors, which are the generators of the notorious blue screen of death. When your system freezes and displays a blue screen with a small message and error code, you should write down the error and message, and then turn to the Stop Errors section for steps on how to identify and resolve the cause of the stop error.

Device Errors

When troubleshooting problems with system hardware, you can often find specific clues to the hardware problem in Device Manager. When you open Device Manager, you can clearly see the difference between normally operating devices, disabled devices, and failed devices. Normal devices are simply listed, while disabled devices have a red X adjacent to them. Failed devices are accompanied by a black exclamation point inside a yellow circle. When you open Device Manager, the application automatically expands hardware object trees to display any failed devices on the system. This means that there is no need to expand each hardware component in a blind search for failed devices.

When a device is listed as disabled, you can bring it back online by right-clicking the device and selecting Enable. Failed devices require a little more investigation. For each failed device, you will see an error code. To locate the error code, right-click the failed device and select Properties. You will see the error code listed in the Device Status field of the device's Properties window (see Figure B-1). The remainder of this section provides guidance on how to resolve the cause of each particular device error code that you may encounter.

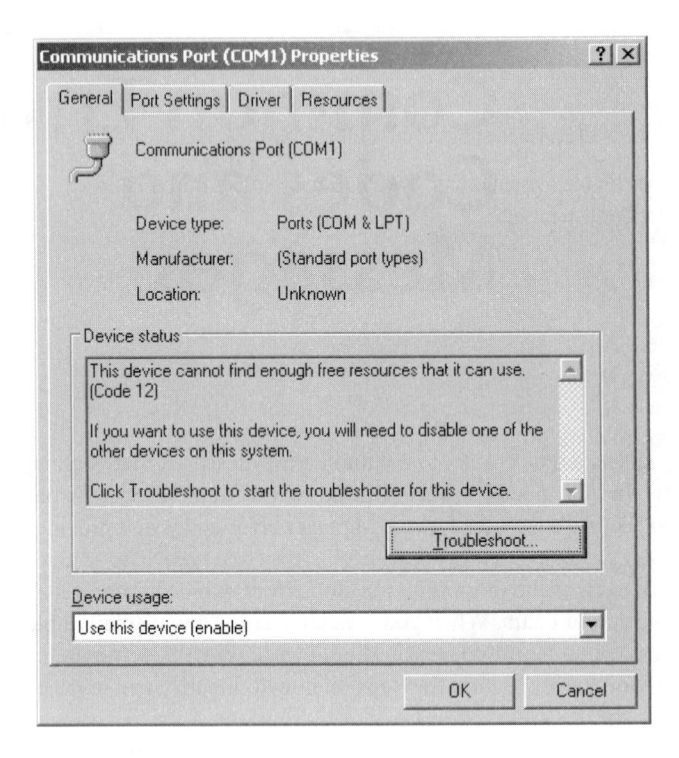

Figure B-1. Viewing a device error code

Code 1—The device is not configured correctly

The error code tells you that the device either has no driver installed or has the incorrect driver installed. To solve this problem, you simply need to update the driver. To do this, right-click the device and select Update Driver. If Windows cannot find an appropriate driver, you should navigate to the device manufacturer's Web site to download the driver for the device.

Code 3—The driver for this device might be corrupted...

The complete error message for this error code reads, "The driver for this device might be corrupted, or your system may be running low on memory or other resources." When you receive this error, you should first assume that the device driver is corrupted. To resolve this problem, you need to uninstall the device driver and reinstall the appropriate driver by following these steps.

1. Right-click the device and select Uninstall.
2. When prompted to confirm the device removal, click OK.
3. Once the device has been uninstalled and is no longer listed in Device Manager, you then need to reinstall the device. To do this, right-click the computer icon in Device Manager and select Scan for Hardware Changes.
4. When the device is redetected, you can then select and install the appropriate driver for the device.

If the driver problem persists, you should contact the device manufacturer for an updated driver.

If no problem exists with the driver itself, this error may be a result of your system not having enough free memory to support the device. You can check for available memory using the Task Manager. If there is little available memory, consider adding or upgrading the system's RAM to provide more free physical memory.

Code 10—This device cannot start

When a device fails to start, the cause of the failure is almost always an incorrect driver. To ensure that you have the correct driver, you power off the system and read the part number off of the hardware device. With the proper part number in hand, you should check the device manufacturer's Web site for the most recent driver for your operating system. If the problem persists, you should then contact the hardware device manufacturer's technical support team for further assistance.

Code 12—This device cannot find enough free resources that it can use...

The complete error message for error code 12 is "This device cannot find enough free resources that it can use. If you want to use this device, you will need to disable one of the other devices on this system." When a device has this error, that means that it is configured to use the same hardware resource as another device on the system. The hardware resource conflict is the result of two or more devices trying to use the same

- Interrupt request (IRQ)
- Direct Memory Access (DMA) Channel
- Input/output (I/O) port

Appendix B Common Error Codes and Messages

Resource allocation for the conflicting devices could have come from the BIOS or the operating system. To locate the conflicting device, follow these steps.

1. Right-click the device and select Properties.
2. Click the Resources tab and then click the Set Configuration Manually button.
3. You will see the conflict and conflicting device listed in the Conflicting Device List field at the bottom of the window (see Figure B-2).

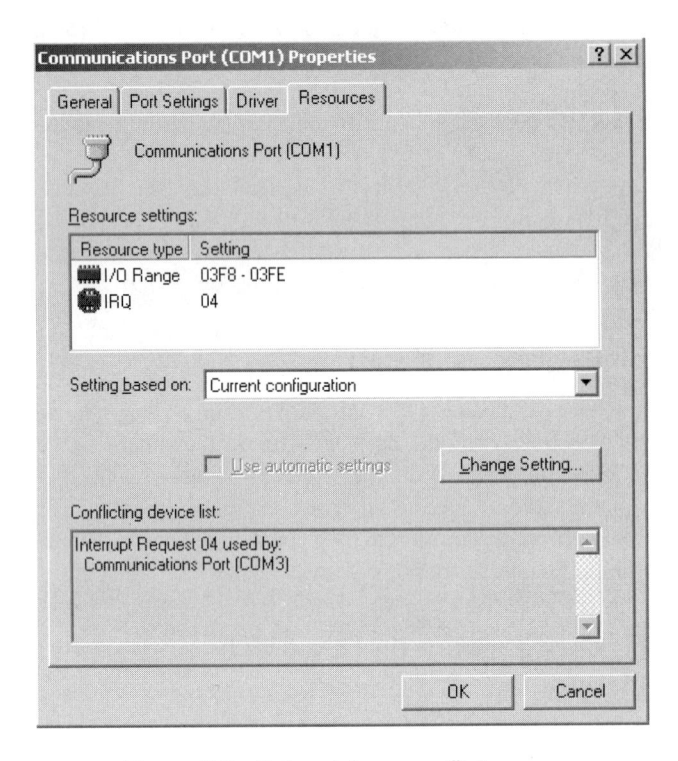

Figure B-2. Determining a conflict source

To have the current device work properly, you can disable the conflicting device. Otherwise, you can check for manual hardware settings in the BIOS for the associated devices and change the BIOS hardware configuration to automatic. In Device Manager, if you see that either of the devices has a manual resource configuration, you should change its configuration settings to automatic. Normally, allowing the operating system to dynamically assign hardware resources prevents resource conflicts from occurring.

Code 14—This device cannot work properly until you restart your computer

This error code provides specific guidance on the corrective action. To correct the problem, simply do what the message is telling you to do, and reboot the computer. This error type is usually caused by a new driver installation that requires a reboot. If the reboot request following the driver installation was ignored, you may see this error.

Code 16—Windows cannot identify all the resources this device uses

This error results when a user attempted to manually configure a device but only partially completed the needed configuration information. To correct this problem, perform these steps.

1. Right-click the device and select Properties.
2. Click the Resources tab.
3. If the Use Automatic Settings checkbox is cleared, check the box and then click OK. This should resolve the problem. If this does not resolve the problem, proceed to step 4.
4. Note the resources listed in the Resource Settings portion of the window. If a question mark appears next to one of the listed resources, select the resource and assign it to the device.
5. If the resource cannot be changed, click the Change Setting button to select the appropriate resource.
6. If the Change Setting button is grayed out, then clear the Use Automatic Settings checkbox and then click the Change Setting button.
7. To input the correct manual configuration information, check the device's related documentation for valid assignable hardware resources.

Code 18—Reinstall the drivers for this device

This error indicates that there is a problem with the current device driver in use, and the original driver must be reinstalled or you need to install a newer, updated driver for the device. When you see this error under the General tab of the device's Properties dialog box, you can update the driver by clicking the Driver tab and then clicking the Update Driver button.

Code 19—Windows cannot start this hardware device because its configuration...

The complete error message for this code states, "Windows cannot start this hardware device because its configuration information (in the Registry) is incomplete or damaged.

To fix this problem you can first try running a troubleshooting wizard. If that does not work, you should uninstall and then reinstall the hardware device." The very lengthy error message for this error code is certainly valuable in providing guidance for this problem.

This error is caused by a Registry problem that is the result of more than one service being defined for a single device. The error is generated when the operating system detects a problem with a Registry subkey or when the driver name cannot be found under the Service subkey.

You can first try to resolve this problem by launching the Troubleshooting Wizard from the General tab of the device's Properties window. If the Troubleshooting Wizard is unsuccessful, you should next uninstall the driver, scan for hardware changes, and reinstall the driver. If a new driver was recently installed, you can click the Driver tab in the device's Properties window and click the Roll Back Driver button. This returns the driver to its previous version.

Code 22—This device is disabled

This error indicates that the device was manually disabled by a user. To correct the problem, right-click the device and select Enable.

Code 24—This device is not present, is not working properly...

The full error message for code 24 reads, "This device is not present, is not working properly, or does not have all its drivers installed." This error is caused by one of the following circumstances.

- A hardware failure occurred.
- The device was prepared to be removed on a mobile system but has not been removed.
- An incorrect device driver exists.

You should always assume hardware failure last, so if the device is not on a laptop and thus no attempt has been made to disable it for removal, when you see this error you should first update the device driver. If the problem is not resolved, you should then look to the hardware itself as the problem. You could attempt to first update the device's firmware. If the update fails or if the device still does not respond, you should then replace it with a known good device to see if the problem is solved. If so, you have identified the problem and need to replace the hardware.

Code 28—The drivers for this device are not installed

This error indicates that the device was detected, but no user attempted to install the driver for the device. After reading this message, click the Driver tab and then click the

Update Driver button. The Hardware Update Wizard will guide you through the process of updating the driver.

Code 29—This device is disabled because the firmware of the device...

The complete error message for this error code reads, "This device is disabled because the firmware of the device did not give it the required resources." This error code indicates that the operating system was able to detect the device but the device has been disabled by its own firmware BIOS. To correct this problem, you need to enable the device using its own BIOS program. You can usually access a device's BIOS when a system first boots up. At bootup, you will see a message such as "Press F2 to enter the BIOS." Once you enter the BIOS program, you can reenable the device. For specific instructions on working with the device's BIOS program, consult the device's documentation or contact the device manufacturer.

Code 31—This device is not working properly because Windows cannot load the driver...

The full message for this error is "This device is not working properly because Windows cannot load the driver required for this device." This error indicates that there is a problem with the current device driver in use, and the original driver must be reinstalled, or you need to install a newer, updated driver for the device. When you see this error under the General tab of the device's Properties dialog box, you can update the driver by clicking the Driver tab and then clicking the Update Driver button.

Code 32—A driver (service) for this device has been disabled. An alternate driver...

The entire error message associated with this error code reads, "A driver (service) for this device has been disabled. An alternate driver may be providing this functionality." This error indicates that the current driver is either disabled or corrupted. For this problem type, there are three possible courses of action.

- Enable the device in Device Manager (right-click the device and select Enable).
- Roll back the device driver to an earlier version.
- Uninstall and then reinstall the driver.

To roll back the driver, click the Driver tab of the device's Properties dialog box and then click the Roll Back Driver button. If there is no previous version to roll the driver back to, or if the problem persists, then you should click the Uninstall button under the Driver tab to remove the device. Once the device disappears from Device Manager, right-click the computer object in Device Manager and select Scan for Hardware Changes. This will detect the new device and allow you to install the proper driver.

Code 33—Windows cannot determine which resources are required for this device

This error indicates that the operating system translator was unable to conclude the types of resources required by the device. This problem indicates an internal failure within the hardware. To resolve the problem, you can first try to contact the hardware vendor to see if an internal hardware problem can be corrected; otherwise, you need to replace the device.

Code 34—Windows cannot determine the settings for this device...

The complete error message for code 34 states, "Windows cannot determine the settings for this device. Consult the documentation that came with this device and use the Resources tab to set the configuration." This error indicates that the device cannot work with the operating system's plug-and-play service and that you must manually configure the device's needed hardware resource settings. You need to configure the resources on the device by moving jumpers on the device, manipulating dip switches, or running a utility supplied by the device manufacturer. Once you have set the hardware resource settings for the device, you can then click the Resources tab under the device's Properties window in Device Manager and set the resource configuration to match the hardware settings that you configured for the device.

Code 35—Your computer's system firmware does not include enough information...

The full error message for this problem reads, "You computer's system firmware does not include enough information to properly configure and use this device. To use this device, contact your computer manufacturer to obtain a firmware or BIOS update." This error is very specific in providing instructions on how to resolve the problem. To correct this error, you need to visit the device manufacturer's Web site and download a BIOS update for the device or call the manufacturer to acquire a BIOS update. Once you update the device's BIOS, the problem will be resolved.

Code 36—This device is requesting a PCI interrupt but is configured for an ISA...

Code 36 states, "This device is requesting a PCI interrupt but is configured for an ISA interrupt (or vice versa). Please use the computer's system setup program to reconfigure the interrupt for this device." This error indicates that the interrupt request translation between the operating system and the computer hardware has failed.

This problem can usually be resolved by accessing the system's BIOS on startup. The BIOS allows you to create IRQ reservations for specific hardware ISA or PCI devices. Normally, the default settings are to autodetect devices, and IRQs are usually assigned properly. One course of action to resolve this problem is to reset the BIOS to its default, which should restore the automatic configuration settings. If this does not solve the problem, you should consult the computer manufacturer's documentation for specific instructions on how to change the IRQ reservations in the BIOS.

Code 37—Windows cannot initialize the device driver for this hardware

This error indicates that there is a problem with the current device driver in use, and the original driver must be reinstalled, or you need to install a newer, updated driver for the device. When you see this error under the General tab of the device's Properties dialog box, you should remove and then install the correct driver by following these steps.

1. Click the Driver tab under the device's Properties window.
2. Click the Uninstall button.
3. Click OK to confirm the removal of the device.
4. Now right-click the computer object in Device Manager and select Scan for Hardware Changes.
5. When the device is redetected, you can select the correct driver for the device to be installed.

Code 38—Windows cannot load the device driver for this hardware...

The complete message associated with this error is "Windows cannot load the device driver for this hardware because a previous instance of the device driver is still in memory." This error occurs when Windows attempts to load a device driver, but a previous instance of the driver still resides in memory. You can resolve this problem by rebooting the system. Upon reboot, the correct driver will be loaded into memory.

Code 39—Windows cannot load the device driver for this hardware...

Error 39's full message states, "Windows cannot load the device driver for this hardware. The driver may be corrupted or missing." This error is caused by the occurrence of one of the following problems.

- The driver cannot be found.
- A file I/O problem occurs when retrieving the driver.
- A corrupt driver binary file exists.

To correct this problem, you need to uninstall and then reinstall the device driver. To do this, follow these steps.

1. Click the Driver tab under the device's Properties window.

2. Click the Uninstall button.

3. Click OK to confirm the removal of the device.

4. Now right-click the computer object in Device Manager and select Scan for Hardware Changes.

5. When the device is redetected, you can select the correct driver for the device to be installed.

Code 40—Windows cannot access this hardware because its service key...

The complete description of this error is "Windows cannot access this hardware because its service key information in the registry is missing or recorded incorrectly." This error indicates a problem with the information in the Registry relating to this device. To correct the problem, you need to uninstall the device and then reinstall it using its most recent driver. The steps to perform this task are listed with error code 39, shown earlier in this chapter.

Code 41—Windows successfully loaded the device driver for this hardware...

The full error message for code 41 states, "Windows successfully loaded the device driver for this hardware but cannot find the hardware device." This means that the operating system loaded a device driver for a particular device but could not find the device itself. This is usually the result of using non-plug-and-play hardware in a system.

If the non-plug-and-play device was removed from the system, you can correct the problem by uninstalling the driver. To do this, right-click the device in Device Manager and select Uninstall. If the device is in the system, then this error indicates that the driver is incorrect. To correct this, you should go to the device manufacturer's Web site and download the latest driver for the device. When you have downloaded the new driver, right-click the device in Device Manager and select Update Driver to install the new driver.

Code 42—Windows cannot load the driver for this hardware...

The full error message associated with this code is "Windows cannot load the driver for this hardware because there is a duplicate device already running in the system." This error can be caused by two different problems.

- A bus driver error—the driver errantly creates two identically named children.
- A device with a serial number is discovered by the OS in a new location before the OS has logically removed it from its previous location.

To remedy this problem, restart the computer.

Code 43—Windows has stopped this device because it has reported problems

You will see this error in Device Manager when the device's driver reports to the operating system that it has encountered problems with the device. Normally, this indicated a failure within the hardware device itself. However, prior to replacing the device, you should attempt the following two remedies.

- Upgrade the firmware for the device.
- Upgrade the driver for the device.

The easiest way to correct firmware issues is to download a firmware update from the device manufacturer's Web site. Sometimes new device drivers are made available that require a particular firmware revision in order to work properly. If the driver for a device is upgraded, and its firmware is not, this incompatibility is likely the cause of the device error.

For device driver problems, you should consult the device manufacturer to obtain the latest driver for your operating system. Another consideration with the driver is to see if the driver is digitally signed by Microsoft. Installing an unsigned driver means that it has not been certified by Microsoft to be compatible with the operating system.

Code 44—An application or service has shut down this hardware device

When a device is unavailable due to this error, your course of action is to restart the computer. If the device again stops, you should determine whether any recently installed application is causing the problem or the device has a faulty driver. You can search for and obtain an updated driver from the device manufacturer's Web site.

Code 45—Currently this hardware device is not connected to the computer

This error tells you that a device listed in Device Manager is not connected to the system. You only see unconnected devices displayed in Device Manager when the Show Hidden Devices view option is selected. More information on setting this option can be found in the section for code 49 later in this appendix.

If you no longer need the device that displays this error, you can resolve the error by uninstalling the device. To do this, right-click the device in Device Manager and select Uninstall.

Code 47—Windows cannot use this hardware device...

The full error message associated with error code 47 reads, "Windows cannot use this hardware device because it has been prepared for 'safe removal,' but it has not been removed from the computer." This error in Device Manager results from a user selecting to remove a device with the Safe Removal application (normally on a laptop), but not removing it. You can correct this error by removing and then reinserting the device. If this is a task that you do not want the user to do—for example, if the laptop is connected to a docking station—you can have the user reboot the system to resolve the problem.

Code 48—The software for this device has been blocked from starting...

This error tells you that the driver a device is attempting to use is not compatible with the Windows version of the operating system. This problem can be resolved by obtaining an updated driver. You can find a more recent driver for the device by running Windows Update or by checking the device manufacturer's Web site.

Code 49—Windows cannot start new hardware devices because the system hive is too large

This error indicates that the size of the system hive has exceeded the Registry size limit. When this error occurs, there are two ways to resolve the problem.

- Remove unneeded devices from Device Manager (clearing the Registry to make room for the new device).
- Reinstall Windows.

When this error occurs, your best option is to remove unneeded hardware devices from Device Manager. It is possible that there are many devices stored in the Registry that are no longer used. The Registry maintains information about previously connected devices so that if they are reconnected to the system, you will not need to reconfigure the device. By default, disconnected devices do not appear in Device Manager. In order to see these devices, from the Device Manager MMC, click the View menu and select the Show Hidden Devices option. You can then see the hidden hardware components.

When you locate devices that are no longer needed, you can remove them by right-clicking a device and selecting Uninstall. Removing several devices should free up the room you need in the Registry to install the new hardware device.

If removing devices from the Registry does not correct the problem, then your next logical step should be to repair the Windows installation using the Setup CD, but this should only be done as a last resort.

Stop Errors

This section provides guidance on how to resolve the most frequent problems that generate stop error messages. Although the notorious blue screen of death (BSOD) certainly makes far fewer appearances on XP and Windows Server 2003 systems, it does not disappear altogether. Actually, from a troubleshooting perspective, a BSOD can be your best friend. That is because the stop error that appears on the screen may lead you directly to the problem. The remainder of this section lists the most common stop messages, organized in ascending order, and provides guidance on how to resolve their related problems.

Stop 0x0000000A (IRQL Not Less or Equal)

This stop message usually indicates a hardware or software incompatibility problem. In particular, this message is generated when a kernel mode process or driver attempts to access a memory location at an interrupt request level (IRQL) that is too high or tries to access a memory location for which it does not have permission.

If you closely examine the screen that generates this stop message, you should see the name of the driver that had the problem near the end of the message. The driver name is preceded by the text "... has base at *<address>* - *<driver name>*". The name of the driver should help you to determine the problem's source. Also, you should consider recent work that was performed on the system generating the error.

Once you note the driver name at the source of the problem, you should begin by examining the driver itself. If a new driver was recently installed, you can use Device Manager to roll back the driver to a previous version. To do this, follow these steps.

1. In Device Manager, right-click the device you suspect as generating the problem and select Properties.

2. Now click the Driver tab and then click the Rollback Driver button.

If a previous version of the driver exists, Windows returns the device to its previous driver version. If no previous version exists, you need to acquire a new driver from the device manufacturer and use it to update the driver for the problematic device. If no recent maintenance has been performed on the device in question, this error could mean that the device itself is failing. If you have a known good version of the device in another system, trying replacing the suspected faulty hardware with a known good device. If the problem disappears, you need to order a replacement device.

Stop 0x0000001E (KMode Exception Not Handled)

This error tells you that the operating system kernel detected an illegal or unknown processor instruction. There are several possible causes for this problem, with the most common being the following:

- Firmware incompatibilities
- A faulty driver or service
- An application memory leak
- Insufficient disk space
- A third-party remote control program

The easiest way to correct firmware issues is to download a firmware update from the device manufacturer's Web site. Sometimes new device drivers are made available that require a particular firmware revision in order to work properly. If the driver for a device is upgraded, and its firmware is not, this incompatibility is likely the cause of the stop message.

For device driver problems, you should consult the device manufacturer to obtain the latest driver for your operating system. Another consideration with the driver is to see if the driver is digitally signed by Microsoft. Installing an unsigned driver means that it has not been certified by Microsoft to be compatible with the operating system.

If an application is improperly allocating large amounts of memory, it could mean that the application is not compatible with the operating system. If the error resulted after the installation of a faulty service, you should uninstall the service to correct the problem. Common software that can cause this problem if it is not compatible with the OS (which may result from an upgrade) is antivirus programs, backup agents, and multimedia programs.

If you recently installed a new application and suspect that the problem may be a result of a memory leak, you can use Task Manager or `pmon` (both discussed in Chapter 4) to verify your suspicions. If the amount of memory consumption by the application steadily increases, you should check with the application vendor for a patch to its software.

If the problem is caused by insufficient disk space, which may have triggered the error during an application installation, you can correct the problem by installing the application to a different disk or by deleting unneeded files. The Disk Cleanup utility can be run to detect and delete unnecessary files, such as .tmp files and Internet cache files.

Normally, you will likely know whether the problem was caused by a third-party remote control application if the problem occurs immediately after the application is installed. When you receive this stop message, if you see the file Win32k.sys mentioned in the message body, this is your indication that the problem was caused by the remote control application. To correct this problem, you can start the system in Safe Mode and then uninstall the application.

Stop 0x00000024 (NTFS File System) or Stop 0x00000023 (FAT File System)

This error tells you that a problem was encountered with the Ntfs.sys file for NTFS file systems or with the File Allocation Table on a FAT file system. This normally indicates that some type of corruption has occurred on the disk. At this point, you should first run `chkdsk <driveletter:> /f` on the system volume. If you are unable to start Windows in order to access the command prompt, then boot into the Recovery Console by booting the system on the Windows installation CD and run `chkdsk` from there. If physical corruption was found on the disk and resolved by `chkdsk`, your troubles may be over. However, if this is not the first time that the system has experienced this problem, you need to dig a little deeper.

If the problem is repetitive, failing or malfunctioning hardware should be the next components to check. The most common hardware issues related to this type of error are

- A malfunctioning IDE controller
- A bad IDE cable
- A malfunctioning SCSI controller
- A bad SCSI cable
- An improper SCSI termination

Also, don't automatically rule out software as possibly causing the corruption. If software was recently installed on the system, that should be the first place you look. If the following application types are not compatible with the Windows OS version, disk corruption may result:

- Disk defragmenters
- Virus scanners
- Backup utilities

Stop 0x0000002E (Data Bus Error)

This particular error usually indicates a system hardware failure. Among the failed devices that can cause this error are

- RAM
- Onboard memory (L2 cache)
- Video RAM
- The motherboard
- Mismatched hardware
- Hard disk

In addition to the possible hardware failures, this error may be caused by a faulty device driver. The most common cause of this problem is failed RAM. If you recently installed RAM into the system that is encountering this problem, you should remove the RAM. The RAM may be bad or may be incompatible with the system bus. If no RAM has recently been added to the system, you should systematically power down the system and remove RAM chips (with power-ups in between) to see if the absence of a particular chip resolves the problem.

Common motherboard problems may also cause this error. Common hardware failures on motherboards are cracks in the board or defective electronic components. Sometimes this is caused by mishandling of a laptop, such as by holding the laptop chassis on only one side so that the board arcs or flexes in a way that causes the system board to crack.

If disk corruption is indicated, first attempt to fix the problem by running `chkdsk /f` on the bad volume. If disk corruption is excessive, you then need to replace the defective disk.

Stop 0x0000003F (No More System PTES)

This error indicates that the system has run out of Page Table Entries (PTEs). This error can be caused by one of the following problems.

- A faulty device driver is mismanaging memory.
- The system is performing an excessive amount of I/O transfer.
- An application is improperly allocating large amounts of kernel memory.

The first step in resolving this problem is to consult the device manufacturer to obtain the latest driver for your operating system. Another consideration with the driver is to see if the driver is digitally signed by Microsoft. Installing an unsigned driver means that it has not been certified by Microsoft to be compatible with the operating system. If the driver was recently updated, you should use Device Manager to roll the driver back to an earlier version.

When this problem is being caused by a high amount of I/O traffic, you can correct the problem by increasing the number of PTEs allocated. To make this adjustment, you must edit the SystemPages value in the Registry. To do this, perform these steps.

1. Click Start > Run, type `regedit` in the Run dialog box, and press Enter.

2. In the Registry Editor, navigate to the following Registry subkey:
   HKEY_LOCAL_MACHINE\SYSTEM|CurrentControlSet\Control\Session Manager\Memory Management.

3. Double-click the PagedPoolSize value. If it is not set to 0, change the value to 0 and click OK.

4. Double-click the SystemPages value. For systems with 128MB of RAM or less, assign SystemPages a value of 40000. For systems with more than 128MB of RAM, set the SystemPages value to 110000 and click OK.

5. Close the Registry Editor.

6. Restart the computer.

If increasing these values does not help, you can contact Microsoft support for additional acceptable values.

If an application is improperly allocating large amounts of memory, it could mean that the application is not compatible with the operating system. If the error resulted after the installation of a faulty service, you should uninstall the service to correct the problem. Common software that can cause this problem if it is not compatible with the OS (which may result from an upgrade) is antivirus programs, backup agents, and multimedia programs.

Stop 0x00000050 (Page Fault in Nonpaged Area)

The stop error occurs when requested data cannot be found in memory. This type of page fault is caused by a problem with system memory and is not directly related to a hard disk fault. If RAM was recently added, then that is the likely problem. If this is not the case, then you need to isolate the physical memory that is the cause of the problem. Don't limit the possible faults for this problem to only system RAM. This paging error can also be caused by any of the following being bad:

- Main memory
- L2 cache
- Video RAM

The easiest way to isolate the problem is to replace what is suspected of being bad with a known good component. To eliminate bad video RAM as the cause, replace the video card with a known good card and see if the error no longer occurs. A problem with onboard cache can be isolated by disabling the cache in the system BIOS. After you do this, the system will run noticeably slower, which is normal for a system operating without the use of onboard cache. If the stop error disappears, you most likely need to replace the motherboard to resolve the problem. Since most organizations have plenty of RAM on hand, whether stored or in other systems, you can quickly replace RAM chips to see if the problem is corrected. If several sticks of RAM are in the system, replace one stick at a time and then reboot the system to see if the problem disappears. With a little patience, you can easily pinpoint the failed hardware that caused this problem.

As with other memory problems, you should not give software a free pass on this problem either. If the hardware checks out OK, or if a new application was recently installed, you should first look at the software. Besides applications, also check system services and drivers. This stop error has also been known to appear as a result of the wrong driver being used. For example, an incorrect video driver may cause a video RAM–related paging error. The driver can be updated by running Windows Update, or you can check with the hardware manufacturer for the latest driver.

Stop 0x00000077 (Kernel Stack Inpage Error)

This error message alerts you that a page of kernel data requested from virtual memory could not be found. Since virtual memory is stored on the hard disk, the disks that store virtual memory are where you should focus your troubleshooting efforts. These are the main culprits for this failure.

- Disk corruption—Fix it by running `chkdsk /f`.
- Disk hardware failure—Check all of the disk hardware that was mentioned in the section on stop 0x00000024.
- Virus infection—Download the latest virus signatures and run a virus scan on the volume.

Oftentimes, the status code that is listed in the stop error message will point you directly to the problem. Table B-1 lists the most common status codes for this stop error along with their related problem.

Table B-1. Stop 0x00000077 Status Codes

Code	Related Problem
0xC000009A (Status Insufficient Resources)	Depleted nonpaged pool resources (very rare)
0xC000009C (Status Device Data Error)	Bad sectors on hard disk
0xC000009D (Status Device Not Connected)	Loose or disconnected power or data cables, a controller or disk configuration problem, or a SCSI termination problem
0xC000016A (Status Disk Operation Failed)	Bad sectors on hard disk
0xC00000185 (Status IO Device Error)	Loose or disconnected power or data cables, a controller or disk configuration problem, SCSI termination, or multiple devices attempting to access the same resources

For hardware-related problems, you again need to test and replace the defective component. If disk corruption is indicated, first attempt to fix the problem by running `chkdsk /f` on the bad volume. If disk corruption is excessive, you then need to replace the defective disk.

Stop 0x00000079 (Mismatched HAL)

This error occurs when the hardware abstraction layer (HAL) and the computer's kernel type don't match. This error is typically caused by a System State restore from a System State backup on a system with different hardware. Sometimes this may be unavoidable if the reason for a restore is hardware failure on the original server. This error can also be caused by a change in the advanced configuration and power interface (ACPI) firmware settings of a system. The easiest way to repair this problem is to perform a repair of the operating system by booting the system from the Windows Setup CD.

More advanced users can recover the system faster through the Recovery Console. From the Recovery Console, you can copy the appropriate system files from the Windows Setup CD to the Windows\System32 folder on the boot partition. For example, this error could be caused by a single CPU kernel being copied to a multiprocessor system. To correct this, you can copy the appropriate hall.dll file and kernel file (ntoskrnl.exe or ntoskrnlmp.exe) to the Windows\system32 folder while in the Recovery Console.

Stop 0x0000007A (Kernel Data Inpage Error)

This error code indicates that a page of kernel data could not be located in virtual memory (the pagefile). The problems that cause this error are very similar to the ones associated with the previous stop error (0x00000077). With this stop error, you will see the same status codes that were previously listed in Table B-1. These status codes give you the information you need to quickly isolate the problem.

The primary culprits behind this error are

- Bad sectors on disk
- Memory hardware (RAM, L2 cache, video RAM)
- Disk cables
- SCSI termination
- A disk controller
- A virus infection

As was mentioned earlier, the easiest way to isolate memory hardware problems is to replace what is suspected to be bad with a known good card or chip from another system. With onboard cache, simply disable it in the BIOS and see if the problem returns.

Stop 0x0000007B (Inaccessible Boot Device)

This error indicates that the operating system has lost access to either the system or boot partition during system startup. This stop error is generally the result of an incorrect storage device driver being installed. For example, after you upgrade the driver for a system's SCSI host bus adapter (HBA) card, this error may appear when the system restarts. If you added new storage devices, such as additional SCSI hard disks to a SCSI bus, it is possible that the SCSI IDs assigned to the new disks may conflict with existing

626 Appendix B Common Error Codes and Messages

settings in the boot.ini file. For example, assume that a system's boot partition was located on a SCSI disk with SCSI ID 3, with no other disks attached to the SCSI adapter with BIOS enabled. The operating system's entry in the boot.ini file would look similar to `multi(0)disk(0)rdisk(0)partition(1)`. If the new SCSI disk's SCSI ID was lower than 3, then you would get an Inaccessible Boot Device error. To correct the problem, you could take these actions.

- Edit the operating system entry in the boot.ini file to read `multi(0)disk(0)rdisk(1)partition(1)` (the `rdisk` value is incremented to signify the second logical SCSI disk in the chain).

- Change the SCSI ID of the new disk to a value higher than that of the original disk (ideally 4 to 6 in this situation, since 7 is normally reserved for the SCSI adapter).

When a boot device is inaccessible, don't rule out taking the error literally. Perhaps a cable is loose or disconnected, the disk's controller is bad, or the disk is corrupted. As always, a virus may be lurking and causing the problem as well. For hardware connection–related troubleshooting, a quick check to see if a physical connection exists is to use the BIOS menu. Use the system BIOS to autodetect IDE drives and access the SCSI adapter's BIOS to detect the presence of SCSI drives.

Stop 0x0000007F (Unexpected Kernel Mode Trap)

This error is usually caused by a failure on the system board or its related hardware, such as RAM memory. When you see this stop message, you will also see a *process exception code* displayed. This code is very important, because it pinpoints the cause of the stop message. Table B-2 lists each stop exception code for the stop 0x0000007F error, along with the code's associated problem.

Table B-2. Common Stop 0x0000007F Exception Codes

Code	Related Problem
0x00000000 (Divide by Zero Error)	Caused by system board failures, memory corruption, or software problems.
0x00000004 (Overflow)	Indicates a processor problem.
0x00000005 (Bounds Check Fault)	Caused by system board failures, memory corruption, software, or CPU problems.
0x00000006 (Invalid Opcode)	The processor attempts an invalid instruction, which is usually caused by bad memory.
0x00000008 (Double Fault)	Caused by system board failures, bad memory, or a bad CPU.

The most common cause of this problem is failed RAM. If you recently installed RAM into the system that is encountering this problem, you should remove the RAM. The RAM may be bad or may be incompatible with the system bus. If no RAM has recently been added to the system, you should systematically power down the system and remove RAM chips (with power-ups in between) to see if the absence of a particular chip resolves the problem.

Common motherboard problems may also cause this error. Common hardware failures on motherboards are cracks in the board or defective electronic components. Sometimes this is caused by mishandling of a laptop, such as by holding the laptop chassis on only one side so that the board arcs or flexes in a way that causes the system board to crack.

Another cause for this problem relates to users that overclock CPUs in an effort to increase system performance. Due to sufficient heat build-up in the CPU, the CPU can start to fail and, as a result, generate this error message.

Finally, one other cause for this error can be related to defective software. If the error resulted from the installation of a faulty service, you should uninstall the service to correct the problem. Common software that can cause this problem if it is not compatible with the OS (which may result from an upgrade) is antivirus programs, backup agents, and multimedia programs.

Stop 0x0000009F (Driver Power State Failure)

This problem is the result of a device driver that is in an inconsistent power state or in a power state that is not expected (on instead of off, or vice versa). These problems are normally encountered during one of the following power state transitions:

- Going to or returning from standby mode
- Going to or returning from hibernate mode
- Shutting down the system

This error has been common with many non-Windows-certified wireless NIC drivers. When a laptop returns from standby mode, the wireless NIC driver does not restart. To resolve this problem, consult the device manufacturer to obtain the latest driver for your operating system. Another consideration with the driver is to see if the driver is digitally signed by Microsoft. Installing an unsigned driver means that it has not been certified by Microsoft to be compatible with the operating system. If the driver was recently updated, you should use Device Manager to roll the driver back to an earlier version.

Stop 0xBE (Attempted Write to Read Only Memory)

The message associated with this error clearly states the problem encountered. An attempt was made to write to memory that was read-only. This error can be caused by a fault in one of the following areas:

- A hardware device
- A hardware device driver
- Device firmware

For device driver problems, you should consult the device manufacturer to obtain the latest driver for your operating system. Another consideration with the driver is to see if the driver is digitally signed by Microsoft. Installing an unsigned driver means that it has not been certified by Microsoft to be compatible with the operating system.

Hardware failures could be the result of an internal hardware problem on the device itself or the fact that the hardware is not compatible with the operating system. To check for compatibility, point your Web browser to www.microsoft.com/hcl and verify that the driver is listed on the Microsoft Hardware Compatibility List (HCL). If the device is listed on the HCL and you are certain that the proper driver is installed, then you should check to see if the device itself has failed. The device vendor may have some diagnostic utilities that you can run to verify proper operation, or you can replace the suspected faulty device with a known good version from another system.

The easiest way to correct firmware issues is to download a firmware update from the device manufacturer's Web site. Sometimes new device drivers are made available that require a particular firmware revision in order to work properly. If the driver for a device is upgraded and its firmware is not, this incompatibility is likely the cause of the stop message.

Stop 0xC2 (Bad Pool Caller)

This error indicates that a kernel-mode driver or process attempted to perform memory operations on memory that was either nonexistent, at too high an IRQL, or at a level of 0 bytes, or attempted to free memory that was already free. Like many other stop errors, this problem is the result of a faulty driver or software.

As with previous stop messages, you should consider any recent maintenance performed on the system as the likely cause of the problem. The easiest problem to resolve is a bad driver, so it is best to consider driver issues first. If an updated device driver was recently installed, you can roll back to the previous driver by performing these steps.

1. In Device Manager, right-click the device you suspect as generating the problem and select Properties.
2. Now click the Driver tab and then click the Rollback Driver button.

If a previous version of the driver exists, Windows returns the device to its previous driver version. If no previous version exists, you need to acquire a new driver from the device manufacturer and use it to update the driver for the problematic device.

Hardware failures could be the result of an internal hardware problem on the device itself or the fact that the hardware is not compatible with the operating system. To check for compatibility, point your Web browser to www.microsoft.com/hcl and verify that the driver is listed on the Microsoft Hardware Compatibility List. If the device is listed on the HCL and you are certain that the proper driver is installed, then you should check to see if the device itself has failed. The device vendor may have some diagnostic utilities that you can run to verify proper operation, or you can replace the suspected faulty device with a known good version from another system.

Stop 0x000000CE (Driver Unloaded without Canceling Pending Operations)

This error results from installing a lazy driver on your system. A lazy driver is a driver that does not clean up after itself before exiting. This error is caused by installing an improper driver for a particular device. To correct this problem, you should consult the device manufacturer to obtain the latest driver for your operating system. Another consideration with the driver is to see if the driver is digitally signed by Microsoft. Installing an unsigned driver means that it has not been certified by Microsoft to be compatible with the operating system. If the driver was recently upgraded, you can roll back the driver by accessing the driver's associated device's properties in Device Manager.

Stop 0x000000D1 (Driver IRQL Not Less or Equal)

This error is normally caused by drivers that attempt to use improper memory addresses and thus use an interrupt request level that is too high. The cause of this error thus relates to using an improper device driver or installing a service that is not compatible with the operating system. If the error resulted from the installation of a faulty service, you should uninstall the service to correct the problem. Common software that can cause this problem if it is not compatible with the OS (which may result from an upgrade) is antivirus programs, backup agents, and multimedia programs.

For device driver problems, you should consult the device manufacturer to obtain the latest driver for your operating system. Another consideration with the driver is to see if the driver is digitally signed by Microsoft. Installing an unsigned driver means that it has not been certified by Microsoft to be compatible with the operating system. If the driver was recently upgraded, you can roll back the driver by accessing the driver's associated device's properties in Device Manager.

Stop 0x000000D8 (Driver Used Excessive PTES)

This error indicates that the system has run out of Page Table Entries. This error can be caused by one of the following problems.

- A faulty device driver is mismanaging memory.
- The system is performing an excessive amount of I/O transfer.
- An application is improperly allocating large amounts of kernel memory.

The first step in resolving this problem is to consult the device manufacturer to obtain the latest driver for your operating system. Another consideration with the driver is to see if the driver is digitally signed by Microsoft. Installing an unsigned driver means that it has not been certified by Microsoft to be compatible with the operating system. If the driver was recently updated, you should use Device Manager to roll the driver back to an earlier version.

When this problem is being caused by a high amount of I/O traffic, you can correct the problem by increasing the number of PTEs allocated. To make this adjustment, you must edit the SystemPages value in the Registry. To do this, perform these steps.

1. Click Start > Run, type `regedit` in the Run dialog box, and press Enter.
2. In the Registry Editor, navigate to the following Registry subkey: HKEY_LOCAL_MACHINE\SYSTEM|CurrentControlSet\Control\Session Manager\Memory Management.
3. Double-click the PagedPoolSize value. If it is not set to 0, change the value to 0 and click OK.
4. Double-click the SystemPages value. For systems with 128MB of RAM or less, assign SystemPages a value of 40000. For systems with more than 128MB of RAM, set the SystemPages value to 110000 and click OK.
5. Close the Registry Editor.
6. Restart the computer.

If increasing these values does not help, you can contact Microsoft support for additional acceptable values.

If an application is improperly allocating large amounts of memory, it could mean that the application is not compatible with the operating system. If the error resulted after the installation of a faulty service, you should uninstall the service to correct the problem. Common software that can cause this problem if it is not compatible with the OS (which may result from an upgrade) is antivirus programs, backup agents, and multimedia programs.

Stop 0x000000EA (Thread Stuck in Device Driver)

This problem is commonly generated by a video driver that hangs while waiting for the video display adapter to enter an idle state. The result of this problem is that the system hangs. To resolve this problem, you should obtain the most recent video driver from the device manufacturer. If the driver was recently updated, you can roll back the driver to a previous version to correct the problem.

If it is determined that the display driver is not the problem (it works fine with other systems running the same OS), then you should look at the video display adapter itself as the cause of the problem. If you can replace the display adapter with a known good adapter and the problem subsides, you need to replace the video card.

Stop 0x000000ED (Unmountable Boot Volume)

The error associated with this stop error code clearly explains the cause of the problem. The system is unable to access the boot volume in order to start. The exact cause of this error relates to a hardware problem in accessing the physical disk. In particular, these are the most common causes of this problem.

- A hard disk is damaged.
- A hard disk lacks power.
- Improper disk cabling is used that does not support the disk throughput.

A common problem that results in this error involves using older 40-pin IDE cables with newer 80-pin cables. If the disk or controller is capable of 33.3MBps throughput, 40-pin IDE cables are incompatible and result in this error being generated. To isolate a damaged volume, you can try to boot the same system from a known good volume by replacing the damaged volume with the good volume. Another hardware check is to ensure that the disk's power plug is firmly connected and that the power supply output is at or near its rated voltage values.

Stop 0x000000F2 (Hardware Interrupt Storm)

Interrupt storms can be caused by several different problems and thus are about as predictable as the weather. When an interrupt storm is triggered, it is because a particular device failed to release an interrupt request. This release failure can be caused by one of the following problems:

- A poorly written device driver
- A device failure
- A device firmware problem

For device driver problems, you should consult the device manufacturer to obtain the latest driver for your operating system. Another consideration with the driver is to see if the driver is digitally signed by Microsoft. Installing an unsigned driver means that it has not been certified by Microsoft to be compatible with the operating system.

Hardware failures could be the result of an internal hardware problem on the device itself or the fact that the hardware is not compatible with the operating system. To check for compatibility, point your Web browser to www.microsoft.com/hcl and verify that the driver is listed on the Microsoft Hardware Compatibility List. If the device is listed on the HCL and you are certain that the proper driver is installed, then you should check to see if the device itself has failed. The device vendor may have some diagnostic utilities that you can run to verify proper operation, or you can replace the suspected faulty device with a known good version from another system.

The easiest way to correct firmware issues is to download a firmware update from the device manufacturer's Web site. Sometimes new device drivers are made available that require a particular firmware revision in order to work properly. If the driver for a device is upgraded, and its firmware is not, this incompatibility is likely the cause of the stop message.

Finally, if you are still having trouble isolating the source of the stop message, you can use Device Manger and select the view option to display resources by connection. This displays each IRQ and its associated devices. To isolate the problem, you could first make a note of the devices that share an IRQ. Next power down the system and remove each of the devices that share the IRQ one at a time, while booting the system in between, until the problem is found. Once the system stabilizes without another stop error, you can be assured that you have found the problem.

Stop 0x0000021A (Status System Process Terminated)

This particular error can be caused by a myriad of unique problems. Among the possible problems that can generate this message are

- A third-party application or device driver error
- Improper security settings being applied to system files
- A system file mismatch

The first possible cause of this problem is a faulty driver or application that is not compatible with the operating system. If you updated a driver, you should roll back the driver to an earlier version using Device Manager. If there are no earlier driver versions to roll back to, you should consult that device manufacturer's Web site for a recent device driver that is compatible with the system's OS. If the problem occurred after the recent installation of an application, you should boot the system into Safe Mode and then use Add/Remove Programs to remove the software. If the software cannot be successfully uninstalled with Add/Remove Programs, on XP systems you can use System Restore to return the system to an earlier state in time.

Stop Errors   **633**

If a wily administrator decided to strip the essential permissions from the C drive, for example, by removing the System account from the C drive's access control list, you may also encounter this error. The System account requires access to operating system files in order for the OS to run properly. To ensure that this is not a problem, you should verify that the System account has access to data on the boot and system volumes. To check volume permissions, follow these steps.

1. In Windows Explorer, right-click the volume and select Properties.

2. In the volume's Properties dialog box, click the Security tab.

3. As shown in Figure B-3, the System account should be listed and have Full Control permission. If so, you are finished verifying system access and can move to the next step of checking for system file mismatches. If the account is not listed, it needs to be added, so proceed to step 4.

4. If the System account is not listed, click the Add button under the Security tab of the volume's Properties dialog box.

5. In the Select Users, Computers, or Groups dialog box, enter System in the Object Names field and click OK.

6. The System account will now be listed in the access control list. Click the System account and then click the checkbox to grant it Full Control permission.

7. Now click OK to close the volume's Properties dialog box.

One final cause of this problem is mismatched permissions with system files. This problem is caused by partially restoring core System State files from backup. If the System State is not restored as a complete set of files, inconsistencies can occur between the files that make up the System State. If you are using a Windows-certified backup application, such as Windows Backup, you should not encounter this problem. However, if the problem exists, it can be resolved by repairing the operating system installation from the Windows Setup CD.

Stop 0x00000221 (Status Image Checksum Mismatch)

This stop message can be caused by one of the following problems:

- Faulty RAM
- A corrupted pagefile
- Disk corruption
- A faulty or corrupt driver

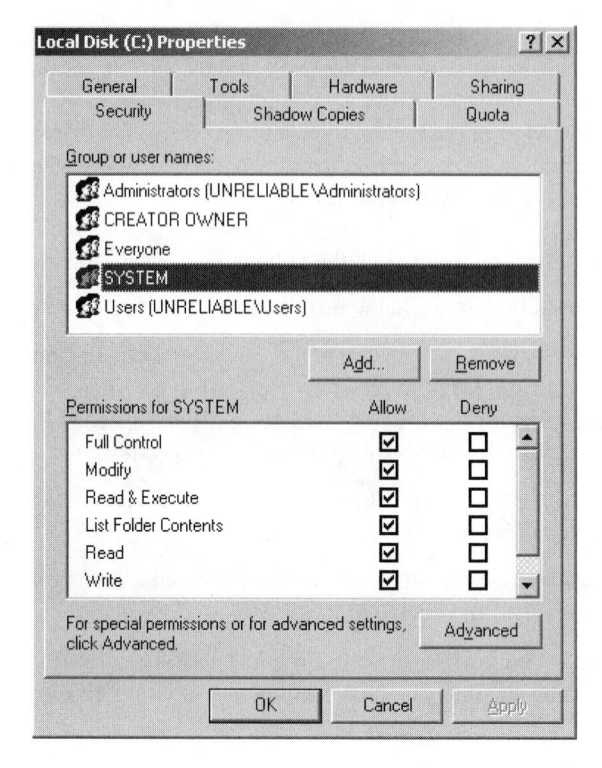

Figure B-3. Verifying System account access to a volume

As with previous stop messages, you should consider any recent maintenance performed on the system as the likely cause of the problem. The easiest problem to resolve is a bad driver, so it is best to consider driver issues first. If an updated device driver was recently installed, you can roll back to the previous driver by performing these steps.

1. In Device Manager, right-click the device you suspect as generating the problem and select Properties.

2. Now click the Driver tab and then click the Rollback Driver button.

If a previous version of the driver exists, Windows returns the device to its previous driver version. If no previous version exists, you need to acquire a new driver from the device manufacturer and use it to update the driver for the problematic device.

If no recent driver maintenance was performed, you should then look toward disk corruption as the likely source of the problem. If a pagefile is being written to a faulty hard disk containing bad disk sectors, information written to the paging file may not be able to be retrieved. You can check for and repair disk corruption by running the `chkdsk` command, specifying the driver letter for the drive that contains the paging file, and including the /f switch, which tells the command to repair any errors that it encounters. For example, to check for and repair bad disk sectors on the D drive, you would run `chkdsk d: /f`.

Finally, if no problems with drivers or the hard disk are encountered, you should then check the physical RAM in the system. The easiest way to isolate a RAM fault is to remove a single stick of RAM at a time while booting the system in between. If you find that the system stabilizes when a particular stick of RAM is removed, you have found the faulty hardware device.

C

Third-Party Tools

While you can go into battle with Microsoft tools alone, the fight is much easier with the support of other vendors. This chapter shows you how to install and use the many third-party tools that are located on the companion CD. The vendors that have allowed their products to be included with this book are

- Executive Software
- FullArmor Corporation
- SmartLine, Inc.
- TechTracker, Inc.
- Tsarfin Computing
- Wildpackets, Inc.

The remaining sections in this appendix are organized by software vendor, allowing you to quickly locate documentation on this book's included troubleshooting utilities.

Executive Software

The companion CD contains three valuable products from Executive Software. Each product is described in the next three sections.

Diskeeper

In designing Diskeeper for Windows, Executive Software established the following goals.

- It must be completely safe to use.
- It must improve Windows system performance.

- It should process live disks without interfering with user access to files.
- It should run without operator intervention.
- It must defragment all possible files and consolidate free space into the smallest possible number of large spaces.

Diskeeper for Windows comes in two "flavors." The Server version of Diskeeper permits defragmentation over a network, while the Workstation version of Diskeeper defragments only local disk volumes on the system where it is installed.

Measuring Fragmentation

Fragmentation can be measured with Diskeeper by running an analysis of the selected disk volume. After the analysis, Diskeeper reports information on the fragmentation state of the volume, such as the total number of file fragments. Another useful value is the average fragments per file. This figure is a good index of how fragmented the files on the selected disk volume are.

Fitting the Pieces Together

Defragmentation consists of taking the pieces of a fragmented file and reassembling them in a free space that is large enough to accommodate the entire file. To ensure safety on Windows NT/2000/XP systems, Diskeeper works closely with the file system and APIs. First, it locates the fragments of each file, copies them contiguously to a new location, verifies that the copy is an exact duplicate of the original, updates the Master File Table (MFT) so the new file location is set, and then deallocates the old location, reclassifying it as free space. However, it is the file system itself, not Diskeeper, that takes care of all data movement.

During the developmental stages of Windows NT, APIs were codeveloped by Microsoft and Executive Software to facilitate online defragmentation. These APIs were built into Windows NT/2000/XP to allow files to be moved safely while the operating system is running. The APIs have been enhanced, tested, and certified by Microsoft to ensure that no data loss, system crash, or corruption occurs when a file is moved. As a result, files can be defragmented online without risk.

Analysis versus Defragmentation

Before defragmenting a disk volume, you should determine how badly fragmented that volume is. This allows you to determine the effectiveness of Diskeeper. Performing an analysis is done by selecting a disk volume and then clicking the Analyze button.

When the analysis is complete, a window is displayed, reporting the number of fragmented files, the total number of fragments, the average fragments per file, and the percentage of free space. In addition, it presents an evaluation of the condition of the volume and advice on how to minimize fragmentation levels. A more detailed report can be viewed by clicking the View Report button.

After the analysis has been performed, the volume can be defragmented. As the defragmentation progresses, periodic updates are made to the Graphic Analysis Display.

Graphic Analysis Display

The Graphic Analysis Display consists of a number of colored bands on the screen, with different colored sections, depending on the state of the disk volume that is being analyzed or defragmented. Fragmented files are shown in red, contiguous files in blue, directory files in light blue, system files in green, and free space in white. Reserved system space is shown as striped green sections, and paging files are shown in yellow. A graphic display with a lot of red indicates that the volume is badly fragmented. Although the graphic display is very helpful, it is only an approximation of the real condition of the disk volume, since the screen resolution is insufficient to display all the details.

Analysis Report

The Analysis Report is produced after an analysis or defragmentation has taken place. It contains detailed information about the volume that has been analyzed or defragmented, such as the name and size of the volume, its amount of free space, and how fragmented it is. Further information is broken down into categories for volume fragmentation, file fragmentation, paging file fragmentation, directory fragmentation, and MFT fragmentation. In addition, a listing shows the most fragmented files, with the file size and the number of fragments for each file. For later reference, this report may be saved to disk as a text file.

Different Defragmentation Modes

Diskeeper is designed to operate in three different ways. The Manual Defragmentation and "Set It and Forget It" modes run while the disk volumes are online and available to users. The Boot-Time Defragmentation mode can run only when the Windows NT/2000/XP computer is being restarted.

Manual Defragmentation

Manual Defragmentation provides direct control over which disk volumes are defragmented, when defragmentation is started and stopped, and the priority at which defragmentation jobs run.

Highlighting the appropriate disk volume in the Diskeeper main window and clicking the Defragment button starts a manual defragmentation. After starting a defragmentation run, you can control it further with the Pause, Resume, and Stop buttons.

Set It and Forget It

Set It and Forget It allows Diskeeper to run automatically in the background, either after hours or while users and other processes are active on the system, according to an adjustable predetermined schedule. Set It and Forget It applies to two components of Diskeeper.

- The Disk Volume Scheduler allows you to set the times and days of the week that Diskeeper will (or will not) be allowed to run on the computer.

- The Network Scheduler is available only in the Server version of Diskeeper. It allows you to easily set the same Set It and Forget It schedule for all the disk volumes on one or more computers at a time.

In addition, there is Smart Scheduling, a feature that is available with both the Disk Volume Scheduler and the Network Scheduler. Smart Scheduling allows Diskeeper to automatically determine the optimum defragmentation schedule for individual disk volumes.

The concept of Smart Scheduling is simple. It schedules a disk volume to be defragmented at certain intervals—say, every three hours. If the level of fragmentation tends to increase with this schedule, then the defragmentation schedule is adjusted to take place more often. On the other hand, if the fragmentation level decreases, then defragmentation is scheduled to run less frequently.

Smart Scheduling optimizes the defragmentation schedule, and when it is activated, system managers can be confident that their disks are defragmented as often as needed, but not more often than necessary.

Boot-Time Defragmentation

Certain files cannot safely be defragmented online, because they are held open for exclusive use by the operating system. This includes the paging file, the Master File Table, and on Windows NT, directory files. It also includes directory files on FAT volumes on Windows 2000/XP systems. The Windows API will not move these types of files online. The Diskeeper Boot-Time Defragmentation feature addresses that problem by running at boot-time—when the computer is started up and before the operating system takes over control of the computer. This is the only safe time to process these files, since they are not being accessed at the time.

The Boot-Time Defragmentation feature is only available on the Windows NT/2000/XP versions of Diskeeper. Boot-Time Defragmentation has three parts.

- *Directory Consolidation*—In Windows NT (and on FAT volumes in Windows 2000/XP), a directory is actually a file, which cannot be moved safely while the operating system is active. These directory files are usually scattered over the disk volume, presenting a barrier to effective defragmentation. Directory Consolidation, done at boot-time, before the operating system starts up, moves directories to a single location on the disk, which frees up larger portions of the disk for defragmenting. Note that in Windows 2000/XP, NTFS directories *can* safely be moved online, but FAT file system directories must be defragmented at boot-time.

- *Paging File Defragmentation*—The paging file is a file that the Windows NT/2000/XP operating systems use that cannot be defragmented safely while the operating system is active, but it can be defragmented at boot-time, using the Boot-Time Paging File Defragmentation feature

- *MFT Defragmentation*—The Master file Table is another file that cannot be defragmented safely while Windows NT/2000/XP is active, but it can be defragmented at boot-time, using the Boot-Time MFT Defragmentation feature.

Frag Guard

Frag Guard is not a defragmentation method but a mechanism to protect the MFT and/or paging file from becoming fragmented. Frag Guard and the Diskeeper Boot-Time Defragmentation feature combine to defragment two critical areas of Windows NT/2000/XP disk volumes—the Master File Table and the paging file—and to keep them defragmented automatically.

Frag Guard has an online mechanism that inhibits MFT and paging file fragmentation, greatly reducing the need for boot-time defragmentation runs. This mechanism also monitors the fragmentation levels of the MFT and paging file, and may be set to perform a boot-time defragmentation automatically when either of these levels exceeds a certain adjustable threshold. For convenience, these automatic operations can be scheduled to take place only at certain preferred times.

Getting the Most from Diskeeper

Diskeeper provides a variety of features, all of which are designed to enhance system performance. While there are no "hard and fast" rules governing the use of Diskeeper, here are some general guidelines for getting the most from Diskeeper.

- Immediately after installing Diskeeper, you should analyze all disk volumes on the system to provide information about the initial extent of disk fragmentation. It is recommended that you save the Analysis Report for each volume analyzed.

- When the analysis is complete, the next step is to do a manual defragmentation of all disk volumes on the system. The manual method is the fastest, highest-priority method for defragmenting the files and free space on the system. It is recommended that you save the initial Defragmentation Reports and compare them to the earlier Analysis Reports, to get a good "before and after" impression of the effectiveness of Diskeeper.

- Systems running Windows NT/2000/XP should next be prepared for using the Boot-Time Defragmentation feature to consolidate the disk directories that are scattered all over the disk volumes and to defragment MFT and paging files. Since directories (on Windows NT), the MFT, or paging files cannot safely be moved while the operating system is in control of the computer, the Boot-Time Defragmentation feature performs these actions at boot-time, while the computer is being restarted.

- To keep the system defragmented on a continuing basis, Diskeeper should be scheduled to run in the background in Set It and Forget It mode. The schedule may be set for defragmentation to occur during low-usage periods. Alternatively, Smart Scheduling may be used, to automatically optimize the defragmentation schedule.

- Finally, on a Windows NT/2000/XP computer, setting up Frag Guard will help to keep the MFT(s) and paging file(s) defragmented.

Undelete

The Undelete Server and Workstation versions are exceptional file recovery solutions for Windows. The Server version of Undelete can be installed on any Windows 2000/XP or Windows NT 4.0 operating system, while the Workstation version of Undelete can be installed only on a Windows 2000/XP Professional or Windows NT 4.0 Workstation system. With the Workstation version you can recover and undelete files on your local computer. With the Server version you can recover and undelete files on your local machine as well as on remote computers on your network, provided they are running a compatible version of Undelete.

Undelete is made up of three major components: Recovery Bin, Undelete From Disk, and Emergency Undelete.

Recovery Bin

The Recovery Bin feature is similar to the Windows Recycle Bin. Deleted files aren't really deleted—they are simply moved to the bin and held there until the bin is "emptied" or purged. This allows you to recover files easily after they have been deleted. However, the Recovery Bin differs from the standard Windows Recycle Bin in several important ways.

- It allows you to recover files "deleted" by any method, including the Windows File Manager and other applications—even files deleted from the Windows command prompt! Note, however, that long filenames may be shortened to the DOS 8.3 file-naming convention when files are deleted from the command prompt.

- With the Server version of Undelete, you can see the contents of the Recovery Bins on remote computers, allowing you to recover "deleted" files across your network.

Undelete From Disk

The Undelete From Disk feature, as its name implies, allows you to recover files that have really been deleted, such as files purged from the Recovery Bin or files that were deleted when the Recovery Bin was not enabled. The Undelete From Disk feature can also be used to recover files from volumes or directory folders that have been excluded from Recovery Bin processing.

Emergency Undelete

The CD-ROM versions of both the Workstation and Server versions of Undelete include Emergency Undelete, a unique feature used to recover accidentally deleted files before you've installed the full Undelete product.

Using Undelete

With Undelete, deleted files aren't really deleted—the deletion request is intercepted by Undelete, and the deleted files are actually stored in another location, called the Recovery

Bin—so recovering these "deleted" files is only a few mouse clicks away. Note: You must have adequate permissions and ownership of a file in order to recover it from the Recovery Bin.

To view the contents of the Recovery Bin, double-click the Recovery Bin icon on your desktop. The files shown in the Recovery Bin display are files that have been deleted by any of a variety of methods, including the Windows Explorer, File Manager, or any other application capable of deleting files. It also includes files deleted via the Windows command prompt. (Note, however, that long filenames may be shortened to the DOS 8.3 file naming convention when files are deleted from the command prompt.)

You can have more than one Recovery Bin on your computer. By using the Recovery Bin Properties option, you can specify individual Recovery Bins for each disk volume or choose a single location to where "deleted" files are moved (known as a Common Recovery Bin).

> Using a Common Recovery Bin on a network server causes the deleted files on the server to be copied into a single location. If a large number of deletions take place on the network, this can add considerable I/O overhead. This overhead is apparent not only on the disk where the Common Recovery Bin is located, but also on the disk from where the files are being copied. For this reason, a Common Recovery Bin is not recommended on a busy server. Instead, enable the Recovery Bin individually on each drive.

Using Undelete From Disk

Use the Undelete From Disk option to recover files that have really been deleted.

When you delete a file under Windows NT/2000/XP, the system does not remove it from the disk but instead marks the space the file occupies as free space. When you recover a file with Undelete From Disk, a new file is created and the old file data is then copied into the new file. We recommend that you recover the file to a volume other than the one from which the file was deleted. This prevents the old file data from being overwritten by the new file, which would render it unrecoverable.

The Undelete From Disk feature allows you to recover files that have really been deleted, such as files purged from the Recovery Bin or files that were deleted when the Recovery Bin was not enabled. Undelete From Disk can also be used to recover files from volumes or directory folders that have been excluded from Recovery Bin processing. Note that this operation can only succeed if the space occupied by the file that is to be undeleted has not been overwritten during the time it was marked as free space.

Sitekeeper

Two major headaches for IT personnel are making sure your organization is in license compliance and installing new software, updates, and patches on workstations across the network. Sitekeeper is designed to automate and simplify both of these processes.

Sitekeeper's tracking system automatically logs and monitors installed programs on networked machines across your entire site. Additionally, you can use Sitekeeper to monitor the hardware devices installed on the machines on your network.

Sitekeeper has an easy-to-use remote installation feature to "push" software over your network. You can install or uninstall software, updates, upgrades, and patches that are logo-compliant for Windows 2000 and XP or Microsoft-Installer-compliant, on machines throughout your site from a central location.

You can create Sitekeeper software inventory reports by product or machine and hardware inventory reports by device or machine.

Microsoft SQL database software is required for Sitekeeper to store information it gathers about your machines. If you do not have SQL installed, Sitekeeper includes a copy of the Microsoft Data Engine (MSDE) database.

Using Sitekeeper

All major processes in Sitekeeper are performed through wizards. To set the initial configuration for Sitekeeper, follow these steps.

1. On the Configure Sitekeeper tab, click the Configure Database task link. The Configure Database Wizard launches. This wizard helps you specify the database server and build and configure the database. After this wizard is completed, the Manage Machines tab is available to establish other settings.

2. On the Manage Machines tab, click the Add or Remove Machines task link. The Add or Remove Machines Wizard launches. This wizard helps you select the machines you want Sitekeeper to manage.

3. Click the Schedule Scan task link. The Schedule Scan Wizard launches. This wizard helps you specify how often Sitekeeper scans your managed machines to gather inventory and licensing information. You can also scan selected machines at any time.

4. Click the Specify Permissions task link. The Specify Permissions Wizard launches. This wizard helps you specify network authentication data such as your user name and password. Sitekeeper uses this information to scan machines when you are not logged in to the network. Your information is encrypted and cannot be accessed by any other users of the network.

After you establish these settings, you are ready to use Sitekeeper.

Using PushInstaller

Use this feature to install or uninstall software on multiple machines from one location. For example, you may need to install Office XP Professional on 50 workstations. To achieve this, you would follow these steps.

1. First, create a share on the directory on the machine where Office XP Professional is located.

2. Open Sitekeeper and select the Manage Machines tab. Expand the tree view to display the machines you selected for Sitekeeper to manage (see Figure C-1).

3. In the Managed Machines frame, select the checkboxes by the workstations on which you want to install Office XP Professional.

4. Click the Add or Remove Programs task link to access the Add or Remove Programs Wizard.

5. The wizard guides you through the process of using PushInstaller. You must select the program to install. Command lines are included to run the install for many programs, including Office XP Professional. If you were installing a program not included in the list provided in the wizard, you would need to create a command line for it.

6. You must specify the path to the share you created that contains the program to be installed, and specify any domain permission information Sitekeeper needs to access that share.

7. Specify when you want the install to begin. For example, you may want to set it to run after most workers have left for the day.

8. If you set the installation to run at night, when you come in the next day you can run the Add or Remove Programs Report to see if the installation was successful on all workstations. If the installation failed on any workstations, details are provided. You can also run a Program Locations Report to view all machines on which Office XP Professional is now installed. If you need to send or show this report to another systems analyst, you can print a hard copy or export it as an HTML file.

As you can see, it is easy to quickly deploy software using this application.

Checking License Compliance

Now that the installation is complete, you may want to check your license compliance for Office XP Professional. To do this, follow these steps.

1. You must first enter license information into Sitekeeper. From the Manage Machines tab, click the Add or Remove Program Licenses task link to access the Add or Remove Program Licenses Wizard.

2. This wizard guides you through the process of entering or removing program license information. It shows the programs you currently have installed, including the version number and number of installations. You must enter licensing information. For example, you would enter the license key number and the number of seats included with that license. You can also enter the date the license was purchased and the licensee.

3. After you enter license information, you can check your compliance status using the License Report. Click Select All at the bottom of the Manage Machines tab so all managed machines appear in the report.

Appendix C Third-Party Tools

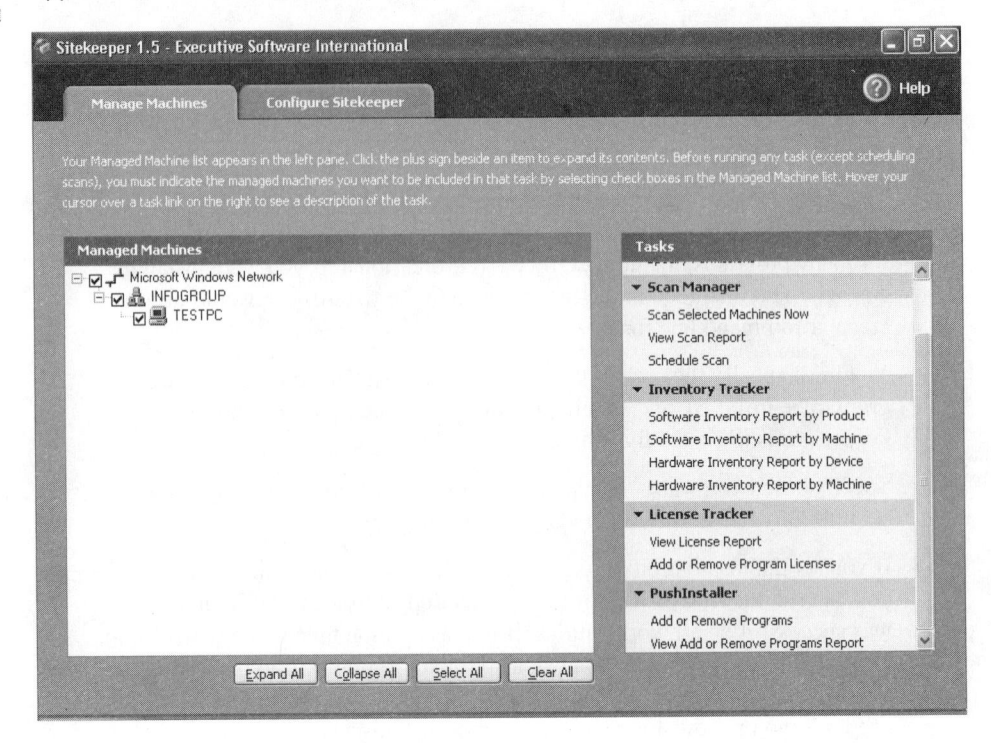

Figure C-1. Selecting systems to manage

If software has been installed or uninstalled on managed machines since your last scheduled scan, you may want to click the Scan Selected Machines task link to make sure Sitekeeper has the most recent information for all machines. This can be done by taking these actions.

1. Click the View License Report task link, and the License Report will be generated, as shown in Figure C-2.

2. It lists all software by publisher (if available), program name, and version. The report shows the number of instances the program is installed, the number of licenses you own (based on information entered in the Add or Remove Program Licenses Wizard), and any difference between the two. You can use this information to determine whether you need to purchase additional licenses or possibly uninstall copies of products to ensure compliance.

You can also use the report results to find incidents of users installing and running programs locally without your approval. All licensing information is reported only to

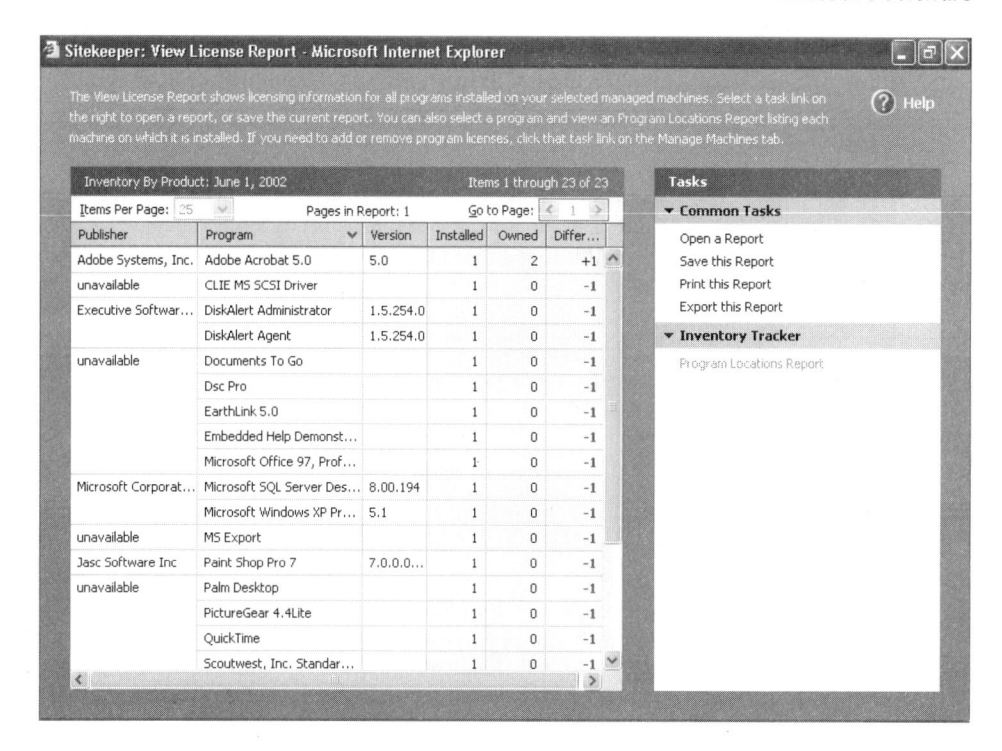

Figure C-2. License Report

you. It is not transmitted outside your organization. You can also run software inventory reports by product and by machine.

Checking Hardware Inventory

You can use Sitekeeper to monitor hardware devices installed on machines across your network. For example, you may want to update the BIOS on some of your machines. You can use the Hardware Inventory by Device Report to see exactly which BIOS versions are in use on machines on your network. Then you can select a specific version you want to update and run a Device Locations Report to pinpoint only the machines on which it is installed. To check hardware inventory, follow these steps.

1. From the Manage Machines tab, click Select All at the bottom of the tab so all machines you selected to be managed by Sitekeeper will appear in the report.

2. If hardware devices have been installed or uninstalled on managed machines since your last scheduled scan, you may want to click the Scan Selected Machines task link to make sure Sitekeeper has the most recent information for all machines.

3. Click the Hardware Inventory by Device task link. The report is generated. It lists the device, the manufacturer, a description, and the number of each device in use on your managed machines.

4. Select the BIOS version you want to update, and click the Device Locations Report task link. This report lists each machine on which the selected device is installed. You can print a hard copy of the report as a reference, or export it as HTML and e-mail it to another IT staff member.

> For more information on Executive Software products, read the product documentation on this book's companion CD, or point your Web browser to www.executive.com.

FullArmor—FAZAM 2000

FAZAM 2000 is a group policy management tool that is much more powerful than Windows Server 2003's RSoP. As with RSoP, you can use this tool to analyze and diagnose GPO settings when troubleshooting problems related to GPO deployment. However, RSoP is actually based on FAZAM 2000 technology and is simply a light version of FAZAM.

Here are some of the policy troubleshooting and management tasks that you can perform with FAZAM 2000.

- Analyze and report on GPO settings.
- Generate reports outlining the differences between GPOs.
- Determine effective GPO settings for a user or OU.
- Track changes to GPOs.
- Store and test GPOs before they are placed into production.
- Back up and restore GPOs without having to back up the entire System State.
- Query GPO health status, including replication and corruption problems.
- View a consolidated log of all GPO-related events on all domain controllers.

All of these troubleshooting and administrative tasks are achieved by using the four FAZAM 2000 MMC snap-ins, which are

- FAZAM 2000 GP Repository
- FAZAM 2000 Administrator

- FAZAM 2000 Policy and Planning
- FAZAM 2000 Auditing and Diagnostics

Each of these management tools is discussed in the next four sections.

FAZAM 2000 GP Repository

The FAZAM 2000 Group Policy Repository offers a new approach toward designing and managing GPOs. In current Windows environments, if you have the proper permissions, nothing prevents you from modifying a GPO whenever you want. While this is normally not a problem, it could be if another administrator is also making changes to the same GPO at the same time. A big problem with GPO management is that there is little or no tracking or accountability for changes. If changes are made, it is not easy to determine exactly what was changed. This could make troubleshooting policy changes extremely difficult.

These problems all disappear with the use of the GP Repository. FAZAM's GP Repository behaves similarly to many document management tools, allowing a user to check out a GPO (preventing concurrent modifications to the same GPO), make modifications, and then check the GPO back in. When satisfied with the GPO performance, you can then place the GPO into production.

Here are some of the benefits of using the GP Repository.

- Access to GPOs is more secure.
- All GPO modifications occur offline (they are not immediately applied to the production environment).
- Simultaneous editing of the same GPO is not possible.
- It tracks the who, what, when, and why of GPO changes.
- It provides the ability to roll back to a previous GPO version.

If you're thinking, "How is that even possible with Active Directory?" the answer is that it's not. To facilitate the check-out and check-in process, FAZAM stores group policy objects in an SQL database, while providing a method to migrate policies from the SQL database to a production domain controller. When you are convinced that a new GPO is ready for production, you can export the GPO from the GP Repository to the Active Directory database.

FAZAM 2000 Administrator

FAZAM 2000 Administrator takes GPO administration to a new level. With this tool, you can

- Back up and recover individual GPOs (with Windows, you must back up the entire System State)
- Manage policy filters

- Report on policy configuration
- Initiate policy replication

With backup and recovery ability for individual GPOs, FAZAM 2000 gives you new troubleshooting alternatives. If correcting the flaws in a particular policy will take up to hours to complete, just recover an earlier version of the policy from backup. Another nice feature of FAZAM 2000 Administrator is that it allows you to select a policy and just view the portions of the policy that have been configured. This saves you a great deal of time and eliminates errors, when compared with manually checking each portion of a GPO for configuration information.

FAZAM 2000 Policy and Planning

Similar to Windows Server 2003's RSoP tool, FAZAM 2000 Policy and Planning allows you to simulate "what if" scenarios for group policy objects. This includes the ability to simulate the effect of configurations such as loopback processing when a portion of a GPO is processed in a particular OU. This tool also allows you to generate GPO Summary Reports, which detail the configuration of all GPOs in a forest or domain. After generating a report, you can print the report, or you can save it as an HTML file or an Access file.

FAZAM 2000 Auditing and Diagnostics

Policy-related problems applying to specific users or computers are often difficult to pinpoint and resolve. With FAZAM 2000 Auditing and Diagnostics, you have a tool at your side that can aid you in determining the source of user or computer problems.

With this tool, you can view

- A list of the policies that were successfully applied to the user or system
- GPO-specific events for a selected computer

If you are looking to confirm the application or nonapplication of policy settings when troubleshooting GPO problems, this tool can be invaluable.

Installing FAZAM 2000

While the FAZAM 2000 software is included on the companion CD, you need a user license in order to install it. You can request a demo license from the FullArmor Web site at www.fullarmor.com. Once you have secured a license, you are ready to install the software.

To install FAZAM 2000, follow these steps.

1. Using Windows Explorer, navigate to the FullArmor\FAZAM 2000 Setup folder on the companion CD.

2. Double-click the FAZAM2000.msi file.

3. When the installation wizard opens, click Next.

4. Click the Browse button, then locate and select the FAZAM 2000 license file that you downloaded to your system, and click Open.

5. The license summary should now be displayed in the Setup window. Click Next.

6. Read the license agreement, then click the "I accept the license agreement" radio button, and click Next.

7. Verify that your user name and organization are correct and click Next.

8. Select the destination file in which to install the FAZAM 2000 program files and click Next.

9. Select the FAZAM 2000 installation components (Repository Server or Management Consoles) and click Next.

10. Select the installation type (Typical, Complete, or Custom) and click Next.

11. Click Next to copy the installation files.

12. When prompted to reboot, click OK.

If you would like to run remote diagnostics and analysis of individual machines in your forest, they will need the FAZAM client software installed. You can install this software by using the FAZAM2000client.msi file on the companion CD.

Opening the FAZAM 2000 Tools

You can load the FAZAM 2000 tools into an empty MMC console or an existing MMC console, or you can open them collectively by clicking Start > All Programs > FAZAM 2000 > FAZAM 2000. The FAZAM 2000 Console is shown in Figure C-3.

To learn more about using this product, read the FAZAM 2000 user guide by clicking Start > All Programs > FAZAM 2000 > FAZAM 2000 v3.0 User Guide, or point your Web browser to www.fullarmor.com.

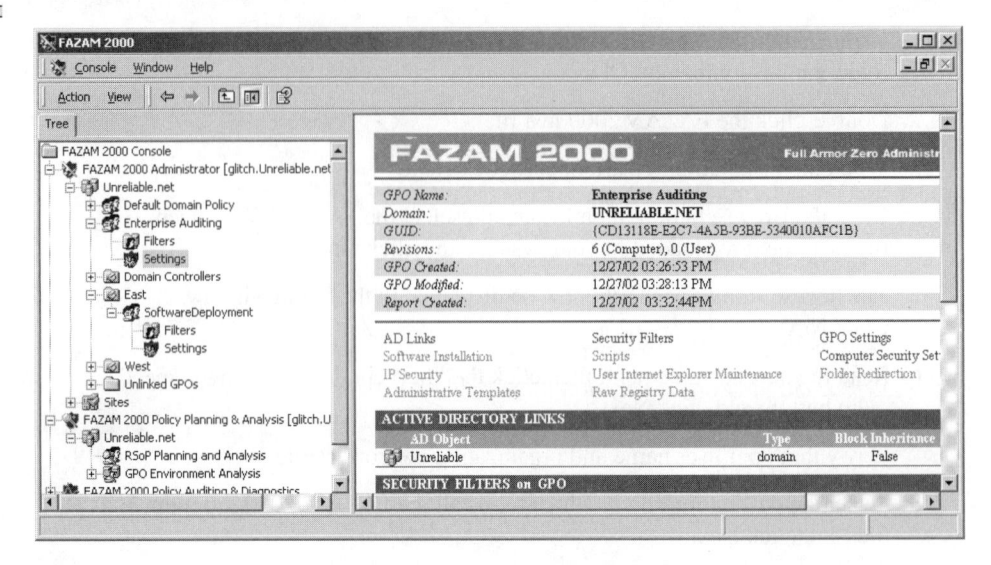

Figure C-3. FAZAM 2000 Console

SmartLine

SmartLine, Inc. (www.ntutility.com) offers an excellent suite of tools that are extremely valuable when you are remotely collecting diagnostic information on computers. This section shows you how to get started with these four SmartLine tools:

- Active Network Monitor
- Active Ports
- Active Server Watcher
- Remote Task Manager

Active Ports and Active Server Watcher are freeware utilities, while Active Network Monitor and Remote Task Manager offer 30-day trials.

Active Network Monitor

Active Network Monitor is an application that allows you to remotely monitor computers on your network without having to install a monitoring agent on any of them. This product is very versatile, allowing you to monitor Windows NT, Windows 2000, Windows XP, Windows Server 2003, Windows 98, and Windows ME systems. If you are wondering exactly what you can monitor, here are some of the product's best monitoring features.

- Scan computers by OS (Windows 2000, XP, and so on) or by installed services (SQL, Terminal Server, Cluster).
- Acquire a system's hotfix and service pack level.
- List installed applications.
- List the status of all services.
- Query computer information (processor type, processor speed, physical memory).
- Manage device drivers.
- View configuration information for each hard disk (label, size, free space, drive letter).
- Show video display settings (screen resolution, refresh rate, video memory).

Sometimes it can be very difficult to query configuration information from individual users. With Active Network Monitor, you can collect the needed information yourself. This should help you to troubleshoot and resolve problems on a system faster than normal.

Installing Active Network Monitor

To install Active Network Monitor, follow these steps.

1. Using Windows Explorer, navigate to the SmartLine\Active Network Monitor folder on the companion CD.
2. Double-click Setup.exe.
3. When the Setup Wizard welcome window appears, click Next.
4. Read the program description and click Next.
5. Enter the installation destination folder and click Next.
6. Select a program folder for the application, or leave the default folder of Active Network Monitor as is, and click Next.
7. Confirm that the setup information is correct and click Next.
8. When prompted to select the directory with the Active Network Monitor registration file, click Cancel. You can use the product for 30 days without registration.
9. Once the installation completes, you will be prompted to decide if you want an Active Network Monitor shortcut on your desktop. Click Yes or No.
10. When the installation completes, click Close.

With Active Network Monitor installed, you can launch the application by clicking Start > All Programs > Active Network Monitor > Active Network Monitor.

Collecting Diagnostic Information

Once you have installed the application, you can perform these steps to collect information on remote computers on your network.

1. Open Active Network Monitor.

2. In the left pane of the Scan Network window, select the types of systems that you would like to scan.

3. Next, in the right pane of the window, select the desired plug-ins to check. The selected plug-ins (devices, disks, computer information, and so on) provide detailed information about the systems being scanned.

4. With the desired plug-ins selected, click the Scan button to initiate the scan of all systems on your network.

5. After collecting the information determined by the selected plug-ins, Active Network Monitor then displays the results from each plug-in's analysis in a separate window. In these windows, computers are organized in a tree format. So under the Disks plug-in, you can select any computer that was scanned on your network and view its disk configuration information.

6. If desired, you can save the results for later reference by clicking the Save button. This is very useful if you are planning to upgrade systems on your network and need to inventory the configuration of each system.

For more information on Active Network Monitor, open the Active Network Monitor Manual (ActiveNetworkMonitorManual.pdf) located in the SmartLine\Active Network Monitor folder on the companion CD.

Active Ports

Active Ports is a very appropriately named application, since it displays the TCP and UDP ports that are active on your system. This utility is especially useful when you are trying to determine the port number(s) used by an application. Also, perhaps a user is complaining about slow Internet performance, and you suspect that some type of spyware may be running on the user's system. With Active Ports, you can quickly make that determination.

Installing Active Ports

To install Active Ports, follow these steps.

1. Using Windows Explorer, navigate to the SmartLine\Active Ports folder on the companion CD.

SmartLine

2. Double-click Setup.exe.
3. When the Setup Wizard welcome window appears, click Next.
4. Read the program description and click Next.
5. Read the Active Ports license agreement and click Yes to accept its terms.
6. Enter the installation destination folder and click Next.
7. Select a program folder for the application, or leave the default folder of Active Ports as is, and click Next.
8. Confirm that the setup information is correct and click Next.
9. Once the installation completes, you will be prompted to decide if you want an Active Ports shortcut on your desktop. Click Yes or No.
10. When the installation completes, click Close.

With Active Ports installed, you can launch the application by clicking Start > All Programs > Active Ports > Active Ports.

Using Active Ports

When you open Active Ports, you can see the following information for each TCP or UDP connection to your system:

- *Local IP address*—The IP address of your network connection
- *Local port*—The port number used by your network connection
- *Process ID*—The process ID for the process maintaining the connection
- *Remote IP address*—The IP address of the remote system connected to your computer
- *Remote port*—The TCP or UDP port number used by the remote connection
- *Connection state*—The connection status (Listening, Established)
- *Protocol*—The protocol used by the connection (TCP or UDP)
- *Path*—The path to the executable that initiated the connection

In addition to viewing this information for each connection, you can check the name of the remote IP address involved in a connection by clicking the Query Names button. Also, you can disconnect any connection by selecting the appropriate connection and then clicking the Terminate Process button. As you can see, this tool is very valuable for determining exactly what network services are being used on or are connecting to a particular system. An example of Active Ports in action is shown in Figure C-4.

656 Appendix C Third-Party Tools

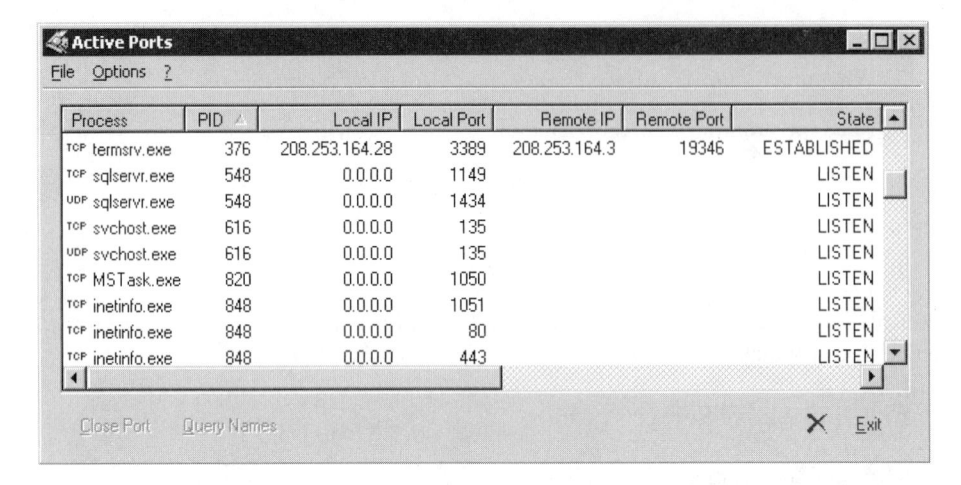

Figure C-4. Monitoring IP connections with Active Ports

Active Server Watcher

If you are responsible for monitoring the availability of Web sites, then you will certainly appreciate Active Server Watcher. This tool can monitor Web pages and scripts (.asp, .cgi, .psp, and so on) and alert you when a particular Web resource is no longer available. To configure Active Server Watcher, you need to enter the URL for the Web resource you wish to monitor, and by default you will receive an alert on your desktop when a monitored resource fails. This utility also allows you to configure individual scripts to run if any particular resource fails. This way, there is no limit to the corrective action that can be taken by Active Server Watcher.

Installing Active Server Watcher
To install Active Server Watcher, follow these steps.

1. Using Windows Explorer, navigate to the SmartLine\Active Server Watcher folder on the companion CD.

2. Double-click Setup.exe.

3. When Setup starts, you will first see information about the installation packager. Click Next.

4. You should now see the Setup Wizard welcome window. Click Next.

5. Read the program description and click Next.

6. Read the license agreement and click Yes to accept its terms.

7. Enter the installation destination folder and click Next.

8. Select a program folder for the application, or leave the default folder of Active Server Watcher as is, and click Next.

9. Confirm that the setup information is correct and click Next.

10. When the installation completes, click Close.

11. Following the installation, Active Server Watcher will start and you will be prompted to identify your Internet connection (LAN or dial-up). Select the appropriate connection and click OK.

With Active Server Watcher installed and started, you can access the application by double-clicking the globe icon that will appear in your system tray. If you close the application, you can access it by clicking Start > All Programs > Active Server Watcher > Active Server Watcher.

Configuring Active Server Watcher

When you start Active Server Watcher, you will see its associated icon on your system tray. To configure the application, double-click the Active Server Watcher icon. Once the application opens, you will see the Active Server Watcher window (see Figure C-5). You can add URLs to monitor by clicking the Add button. For each URL, you can select the action to be taken if the resource is no longer available, as well as configure the frequency in which the URL is checked for availability.

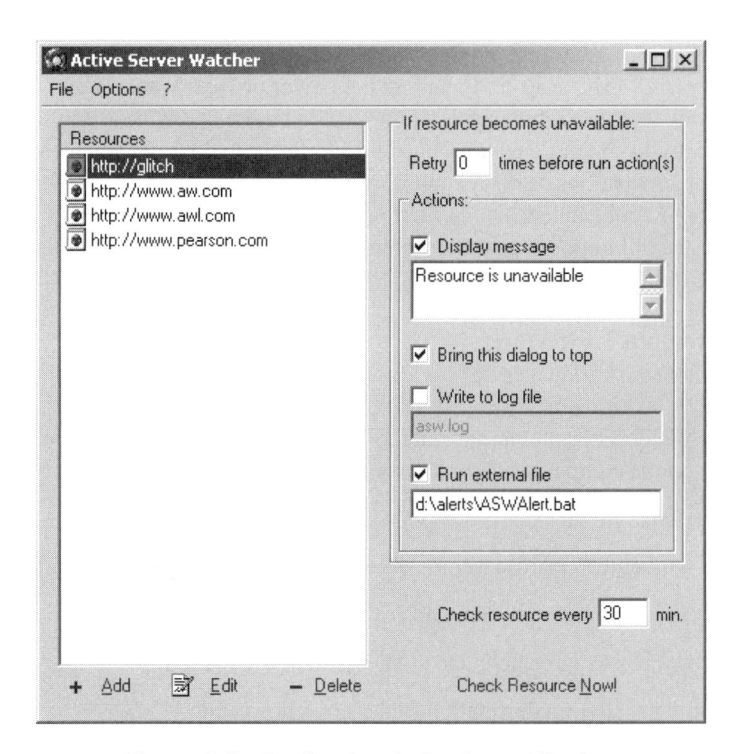

Figure C-5. Configuring Active Server Watcher

Remote Task Manager

Remote Task Manager (RTM) allows you to remotely view the Windows Task Manger on any system on your network. Since it is actually a standalone application, RTM is much more powerful than the traditional Windows Task Manager, allowing you to view the following information on either a local or remote system:

- CPU performance
- Physical memory usage
- Open applications
- Running processes
- Network connection performance
- Event logs
- Network shares and the number of connected users
- System services
- Hardware devices and driver status

RTM allows you to perform any task remotely that you would perform locally using the Task Manger and also offers many of the remote management options of the Computer Management MMC snap-in. In having the power of Task Manager and Computer Management together in a single application, you can quickly diagnose and solve user problems directly from your desktop. Since this application does not behave like other remote control applications, users are not aware that you are connected to their system. While you would not be able to see Solitaire open on the user's desktop, you would still be able to see the Solitaire.exe process running! In order to use this extraordinary tool, you must first install it.

Installing Remote Task Manager
To install Remote Task Manager, follow these steps.

1. Using Windows Explorer, navigate to the SmartLine\Remote Task Manager folder on the companion CD.
2. Double-click Setup.exe.
3. When the Setup Wizard welcome window appears, click Next.
4. Read the program description and click Next.
5. Read the license agreement and click Yes to accept its terms.
6. Enter the installation destination folder and click Next.
7. When prompted to select the setup type, select Custom and click Next.

SmartLine **659**

8. Select each checkbox so that you will install all RTM components, and click Next.

9. Select a program folder for the application, or leave the default folder of Remote Task Manager as is, and click Next.

10. Confirm that the setup information is correct and click Next.

11. When prompted to select the directory that contains the registration file, click Cancel to install the RTM trial version.

12. When prompted to decide if you want a Remote Task Manager shortcut added to your desktop, click Yes or No.

13. When the installation completes, click Close.

To start Remote Task Manger, click Start > All Programs > Remote Task Manager > Remote Task Manager.

Remotely Installing the RTM Service on Other Systems

By installing the RTM service on other systems on your network, you can take full advantage of the power of RTM and monitor performance, application usage, network usage, and the event logs on any system on your network. This allows you to quickly acquire system diagnostic information without having a user provide this information to you or having to walk over to the user's system to collect the information yourself.

In order to remotely install RTM on another system, you need to run the installation under an account that has administrative privileges on the remote system. If all systems are in the same domain, you can do this as a Domain Administrator. If you are in a workgroup, you need to ensure that your account exists on each remote system and is a member of each system's Administrators group.

To remotely install the RTM service on another computer, follow these steps from the RTM console.

1. Click the File menu and Select Connect.

2. In the Select Computer dialog box, enter the name of the remote computer that you wish to install the RTM service on and click Connect.

3. When prompted that the RTM service does not exist on the remote system, click Yes to install the service.

4. Next you will be prompted to select the rtmservice executable file. This file is located in the application installation folder. Browse to the Program Files\Remote Task Manager folder, select the rtmservice.exe file, and click Open.

5. In a few moments, the remote service installation will complete, and you will be connected to the remote system.

Subsequent connections to the remote system will not require any service installation. If you prefer to preinstall the service on each system that you need to manage, this can be done by running the Remote Task Manager setup program and selecting a custom installation. In the custom installation setup, you only need to check the RTM Service checkbox.

Another way to remotely install the service is to use RTM's Setup.exe command in a script. You can perform a silent install of the application by running `setup /s`. To perform the setup without user intervention, you need to create a file called setup.ini and store it in the same folder as the setup.exe file. To configure setup to just install the service, you would need the following lines in the setup.ini file:

```
[install]
Service = 1
Manager = 0
Documents = 0
```

For more information on installing the RTM service, see the Remote Task Manager User Manual located in the SmartLine\Remote Task Manager folder on the companion CD.

Querying the State of a Remote System

To connect to and query the state of a remote system, perform these steps.

1. Open the RTM console.

2. Click the File menu and select Connect.

3. In the Select Computer dialog box, enter the name of the remote system to connect to and click Connect.

Once connected, you can query information on the target system by clicking the appropriate tab. For example, viewing the system log of the remote system 2boxers is shown in Figure C-6.

TechTracker

This section provides you with instructions on how to get up and running with TechTracker ITX, which is an excellent enterprise workstation management tool. TechTracker is ideal for both monitoring and troubleshooting, giving you the ability to

- Centrally monitor crash and error messages for all systems across your enterprise.

- Track which applications are causing the most problems.

- Manage and monitor patch deployment and status.

- Prevent installation of unauthorized software.

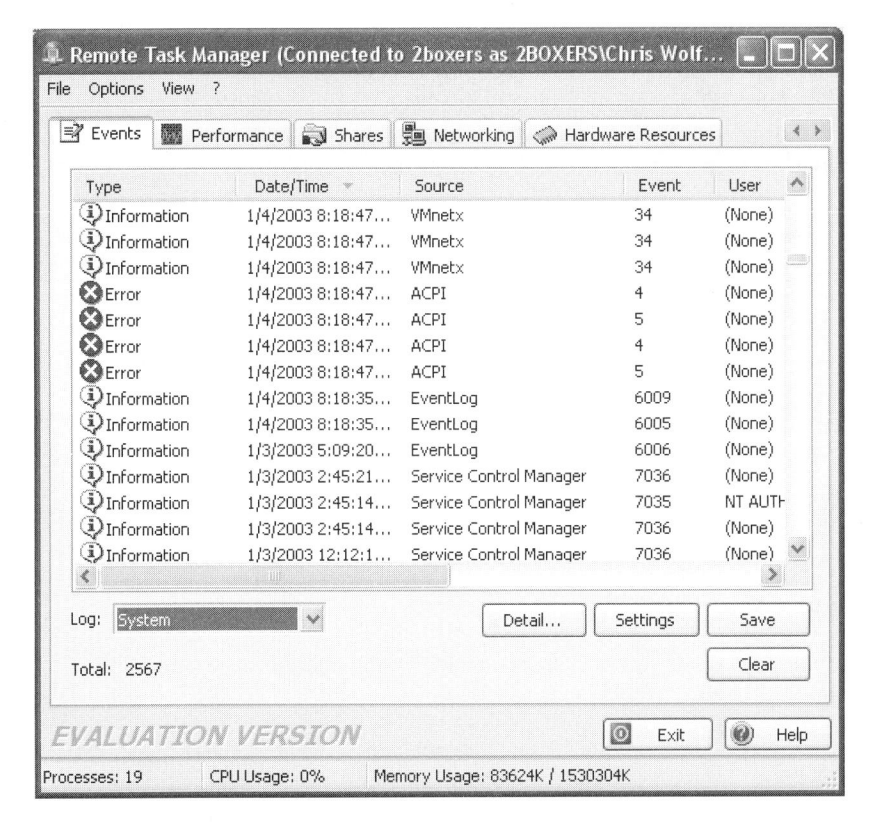

Figure C-6. Querying the system log of a remote computer

With TechTracker, you can install an agent on each workstation in your enterprise to periodically report on its health status. A central system can thus run the TechTracker administrator interface to monitor the status of all systems. The central monitoring approach allows you to discover problems before users possibly even report them. Also, unlike other applications, TechTracker is Web-based, with all client reporting sent to the TechTracker Web site. If you are a consultant and are responsible for monitoring the systems from several different businesses, the fact that all reporting is hosted by TechTracker allows you to easily check on any system from anywhere.

The remainder of this section addresses the details of how to install and initially configure TechTracker, as well as perform common administrative tasks.

Installing the TechTracker ITX Demo

Whether you're installing to one workstation or to hundreds of workstations, the TechTracker ITX Agent has been designed to be extremely easy to set up and install. When you are installing on a small number of workstations, the easiest method is to just install from the CD. When installing the ITX Agent to a large number of workstations, follow either the rapid or custom deployment options in the ITX User Guide on your installation CD or available for download at http://www.techtracker.com/downloads/itx_user_guide.pdf.

To sign up for a TechTracker ITX demo account, follow these steps.

1. Open a browser and go to http://www.techtracker.com/products/itx.

2. Enter your contact information in the fields on this page.

3. An ITX account manager will contact you and give you your Group Account Number for you to use in your trial.

4. Locate the TechTracker ITX.msi file on the CD-ROM and run it.

5. When prompted, enter your Group Account Number into the installer.

6. When installation is complete, the ITX Agent will scan your workstation and report your system and software data to the Administrator Console.

7. To view your data, log in to the Administrator Console at https://itx.techtracker.com.

8. Enter the e-mail address used to create the trial and the password given to you by the ITX account manager to log in.

> The TechTracker ITX Agent Installer requires a current version of the Windows Installer. Workstations running Microsoft Windows 95, 98 and NT 4.0 may need to be updated before installation can begin.

One TechTracker has been installed, you are ready to monitor workstations in your enterprise.

Monitoring Systems with TechTracker ITX

Once TechTracker has been installed on the systems you wish to monitor, you can begin to check on your systems. To do this, follow these steps.

1. Open your Web browser and navigate to https://itx.techtracker.com.

2. Enter your e-mail address and password, and then click the Login button.

3. Check on your systems using the Administrator Console.

From the console, you will see an abundance of data organized in a spreadsheet format, with tabs available to organize the data. The information provided under each tab is explained in the next several sections.

Workstations Tab

This tab allows you to monitor workstations that have the TechTracker ITX Agent installed. Each workstation is listed sequentially and can be sorted. Also, you can double-click any workstation to see additional information on it. Besides showing a list of monitored workstations, this tab provides the following information:

- *Crashes*—The number of fatal error occurrences on the system
- *Improper shutdowns*—The number of times the system was improperly shut down, including manual shutdowns, power failures, or system crashes
- *Application run time*—The combined total operational time of all applications on the system
- *System run time*—The total time, in minutes, of system uptime

Software Tab

Under the Software tab, you can view more granular information about a system's installed software. This tab lists the software installed on all systems in your enterprise and provides the following statistical information about the software:

- *Software name*—The name of the installed application or device driver
- *Latest version*—The most current available version of the software
- *Workstations with older versions*—The number of systems running earlier versions of the software
- *Launches*—The total number of times the application or service was launched by all workstations
- *Crashes*—The total number of fatal crashes on all systems resulting from the application

For a more granular look at any application, you can double-click it to see a list of workstations on which it is installed.

Configurations Tab

Under this tab, you can see configuration information for all monitored systems. The specific information that you can view is

- Computer name
- Operating system
- RAM
- Processor

Installed Software Tab

You access the Installed Software tab by clicking an individual system. Under this tab, you can see an inventory and the status of all installed software for a single system. In particular, this tab allows you to identify the following:

- *Software name*—The name of each installed application or driver
- *Latest version*—The most current available version of the software
- *Workstations with older versions*—The number of systems running earlier versions of the software
- *Launches*—The total number of times the application or service was launched by all workstations
- *Crashes*—The total number of fatal crashes on all systems resulting from the application

Stability Tab

This tab, which you also access by clicking on a single system, allows you to view information relating to the system's stability. For each system crash, you will see the date and time of the crash as well as the cause of the crash.

Crash Log Tab

You can access this tab by clicking one of a system's listed installed applications. This tab allows you to see and track an application's or service's failure history. A history of repeated failures on a single application installed on many systems may be an indication of a bug in the application.

Application Failure Rating

The Application Failure Rating (AFR) allows you to see the failure rate of all monitored systems. The higher the number, the more recent and more frequent the failures have been. This information is useful in identifying the order in which you should attempt to repair failed systems. Consider the systems with the highest AFR values to be the least stable.

Tsarfin

Two handy troubleshooting products from Tsarfin Computing (www.tsarfin.com) can be found on the companion CD. Both of these products are shareware and can be used for up to 30 days. The next two sections provide an overview and usage instructions for these products.

IPMonitor

IPMonitor allows you to receive instant notification when a particular network service on a system fails. This way, when a failure occurs, you will not first hear of it from a customer or even your supervisor. This may allow you to quickly resolve a problem before it is even discovered by a user. Here are some other key features with IPMonitor:

- Monitors up to 500 network devices or services
- Supports TCP, UDP, and ICMP
- Allows custom alerts to be created for each monitored resource
- Allows e-mail notification via SMTP
- Offers real-time and historical reporting capabilities

With IPMonitor running on your system, you can immediately be alerted when another system on the network fails. A very nice feature about this utility is that it works with standard TCP/IP protocols and thus does not require any agent software to be installed on the systems you wish to monitor.

Installing IPMonitor

To install IPMonitor, follow these steps.

1. Using Windows Explorer, navigate to the Tsarfin\IPMonitor folder on the companion CD.
2. Double-click Setup.exe.
3. When the Setup Wizard welcome window appears, click Next.
4. Read the software license agreement and click Yes to accept its terms.
5. Enter your name and your company name and click Next.
6. Browse to and select an installation destination folder, or select the default folder and click Next.
7. Select the installation program folder, or select the default folder IPMonitor and click Next.
8. Confirm that your setup choices are correct and click Next. Setup will now copy the required files to your system.
9. When setup completes, click Finish.

Once IPMonitor has been installed, you are ready to begin using this tool.

Using IPMonitor

In order to configure IPMonitor to check network services, you need to know the TCP or UDP port number used by the service. IANA's Web site offers a complete list of all known service ports http://www.iana.org/assignments/port-numbers. Once you have collected a list of hosts and their associated ports you wish to monitor, follow these steps to add a service to monitor.

1. Click Start > All Programs > IPMonitor > IPMonitor.

2. Double-click the IPMonitor icon on your system tray to open the IPMonitor console.

3. To add a host and service to monitor, click the Add button.

4. In the Add dialog box, enter the host name, port number, and description of the service to be monitored (see Figure C-7).

5. Select the alert type for the application to use if a failure is detected. You can select having an audible alarm (beep) sound if a failure is found or having the application send an SMTP mail message to a particular user. You can customize the mail message for each failure type.

6. Once you have configured the service-monitoring criteria, click OK.

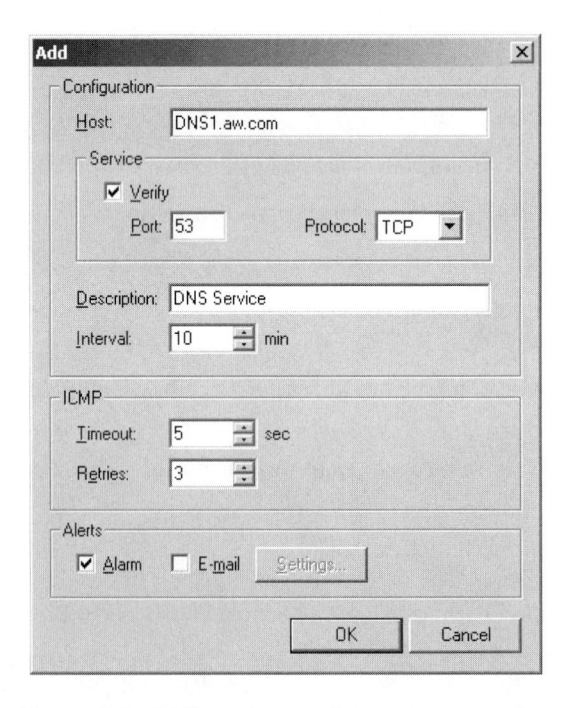

Figure C-7. Adding a host and a service to monitor

Figure C-8 shows a typical monitoring session, displaying checks for the DNS service and for an Internet server.

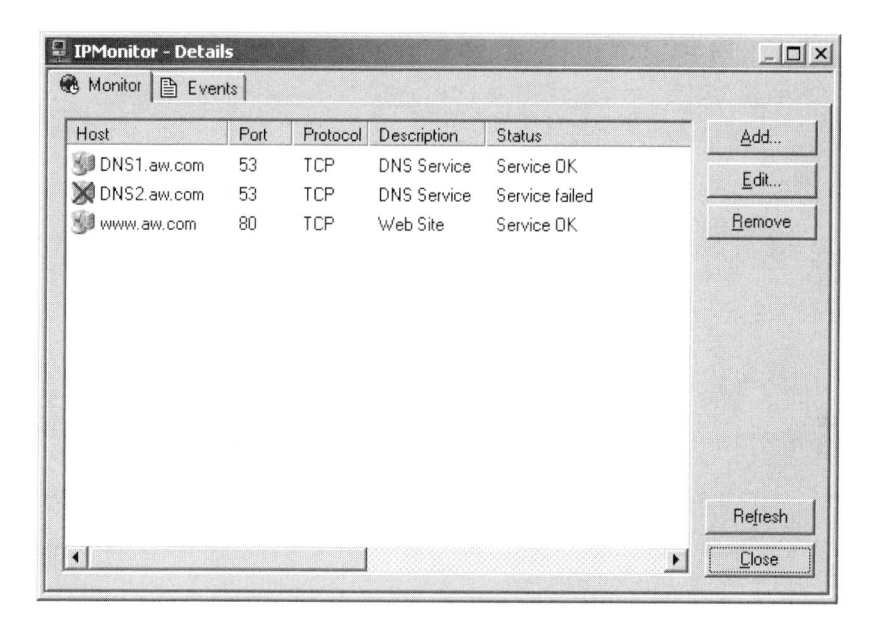

Figure C-8. Monitoring IP services

For more information on IPMonitor, point your Web browser to IPMonitor.tsarfin.com.

NetInfo

NetInfo provides a GUI interface that allows you to perform tasks that are common in many command line tools. When this application is run, its window is divided into 15 tabs, which allow you to perform the following tasks:

- *Local Info*—Displays system IP addresses and MAC addresses
- *Connections*—Displays all local TCP/IP connections and their foreign connection IP address
- *Ping*—Allows you to quickly verify network connectivity to another IP address on the network
- *Trace*—Displays a list of routers between your system and the destination system
- *Lookup*—Allows you to perform DNS forward and reverse lookup queries

- *Finger*—Displays information about users currently logged on to a specified server (the target server must be running the Finger service in order for this option to work)

- *Whois*—Allows you to query contact information for domains registered with a Whois server, such as InterNIC's server (whois.internic.net)

- *Daytime*—Displays the local time of day for any remote host specified

- *Time*—Allows you to query the time value from a remote time server and synchronize the time value with your local system clock

- *Quote*—Allows you to view quotations from a remote Quote server

- *HTML*—Displays the HTML header code for any Web page address specified

- *Scanner*—Scans for host names for a particular range of IP addresses and displays the state of each IP address in the range (offline, online)

- *Services*—Lists the available network services (HTTP, Telnet, DNS, SMTP, and so on) for a particular host

- *E-mail*—Allows you to verify any e-mail address by simply entering a full user principal name (user@domain.com), and displays the name of the mail server hosting the mail account

- *Web Center*—Displays available online tools, how-tos, tips, and news (requires product registration)

As you can see, there are countless tasks that you can perform with this tool. The next two sections cover installing the tool and performing simple tasks.

Installing NetInfo

To install NetInfo, follow these steps.

1. Using Windows Explorer, navigate to the Tsarfin\NetInfo folder on the companion CD.

2. Double-click Setup.exe.

3. When the Setup Wizard welcome window appears, click Next.

4. Read the software license agreement and click Yes to accept its terms.

5. Enter your name and your company name, and click Next.

6. Browse to and select an installation destination folder, or select the default folder and click Next.

7. Select the installation program folder, or select the default folder NetInfo and click Next.

8. Confirm that your setup choices are correct and click Next. Setup will now copy the required files to your system.

9. When setup completes, click Finish.

10. If prompted, reboot your system.

Once NetInfo has been installed, you are ready to begin using this tool.

Using NetInfo

In this section, we'll look at using NetInfo to query the available services for a single server. Keep in mind that there are many other tasks that can be performed in a similar fashion.

To use NetInfo to query available server services, follow these steps.

1. Click Start > All Programs > NetInfo > NetInfo.

2. Once the NetInfo application opens, click the Services tab.

3. Enter the name or IP address of the remote host to query, and click the Verify button.

4. Note the results displayed in the lower portion of the window. A sample output is displayed in Figure C-9.

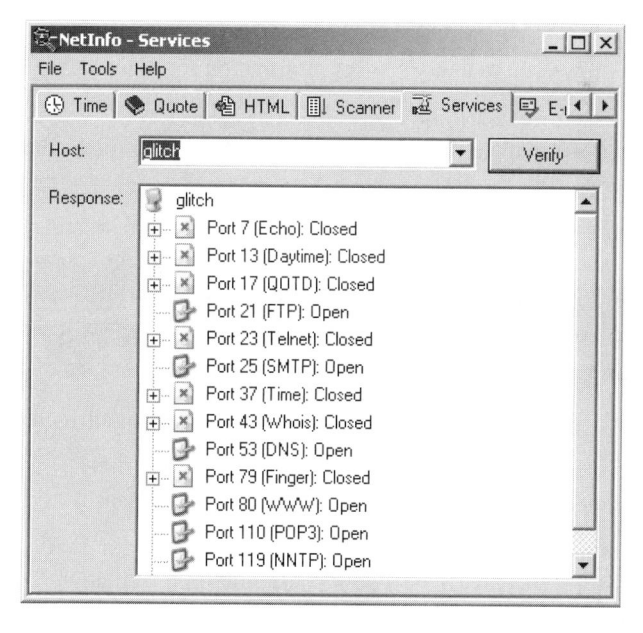

Figure C-9. Checking remote server services with NetInfo

Querying services is a valuable method for checking for port vulnerabilities on your network servers. You may find that ports are open that should not be. This tool is also ideal for checking the state of particular services when you are troubleshooting. For example, if a user is having trouble connecting to your intranet FTP server, you can use NetInfo to check the status of port 21 on the server.

For more information on NetInfo, point your Web browser to NetInfo.tsarfin.com.

Wildpackets—iNetTools

iNetTools has some similarities to Tsarfin's NetInfo, with the primary exception that the iNetTools applications all run as independent tools. iNetTools is a collection of GUI-based network diagnostic applications and includes the following 11 utilities.

- *Ping*—Tests network connectivity to a remote host by sending a specified number of ping packets.

- *Trace Route*—Displays a list of routers between your system and the destination system.

- *Name Lookup*—Allows you to perform forward and reverse DNS lookup queries.

- *Finger*—Displays information about users currently logged on to a specified server (the target server must be running the Finger service in order for this option to work).

- *Whois*—Allows you to query contact information for domains registered with a Whois server, such as InterNIC's server (whois.internic.net).

- *Throughput*—Calculates and displays throughput during the loading of a specified Web page.

- *Name Scan*—Allows you to enter a start and end IP address, and returns all host names associated with the valid addresses in the specified range. This allows you to see the names of all systems on a particular network.

- *Port Scan*—Scans the ports on a target system and returns a list of its available network services (Telnet, FTP, HTTP, and so on).

- *Ping Scan*—Pings the range of IP addresses that you provide and reports on which addresses in the range are in use.

- *Service Scan*—Allows you to check a range of IP addresses for systems offering a specified service, such as FTP.

- *Network Info*—Displays the network configuration information (IP addresses and MAC addresses) for your system.

As you can see, you can perform several administrative and diagnostic tasks with these tools.

Installing iNetTools
To install iNetTools, follow these steps.

1. Using Windows Explorer, navigate to the Wildpackets\iNetTools folder on the companion CD.
2. Double-click Intwdemo.exe.
3. The WinZip Self-Extractor window should now open. Click Setup.
4. When the Setup Wizard welcome window appears, click Next.
5. Read the software license agreement and click Yes to accept its terms.
6. Browse to and select and installation destination folder, or select the default folder and click Next.
7. When setup completes, click Finish.

The installation should complete very quickly. Following the installation, you are ready to put these tools to use.

Using iNetTools
To start using iNetTools, follow these steps.

1. Click Start > All Programs – Wildpackets iNetTools to launch the application.
2. When the application starts, you will first be prompted to either evaluate or register the software. To preview the product, click Evaluate.
3. iNetTools should now open with the default Ping utility selected. To open another tool, click the Tool menu and select the tool that you would like to use.

One common tool that is often used is Ping Scan. Suppose that you need to assign a user a static IP address but do not have access to the addresses already in use on the network. To check for used addresses on a given network, you decide to use Ping Scan. Here are the steps that you would need to take to complete this task.

1. Click Start > All Programs > Wildpackets iNetTools.
2. Click the Tool menu and select Ping Scan.
3. In the Ping Scan dialog box, enter the starting and ending IP address ranges for the network, enter the appropriate timeout values, and then click the Start button (see Figure C-10).
4. Each IP address that responds to the ping will be listed.

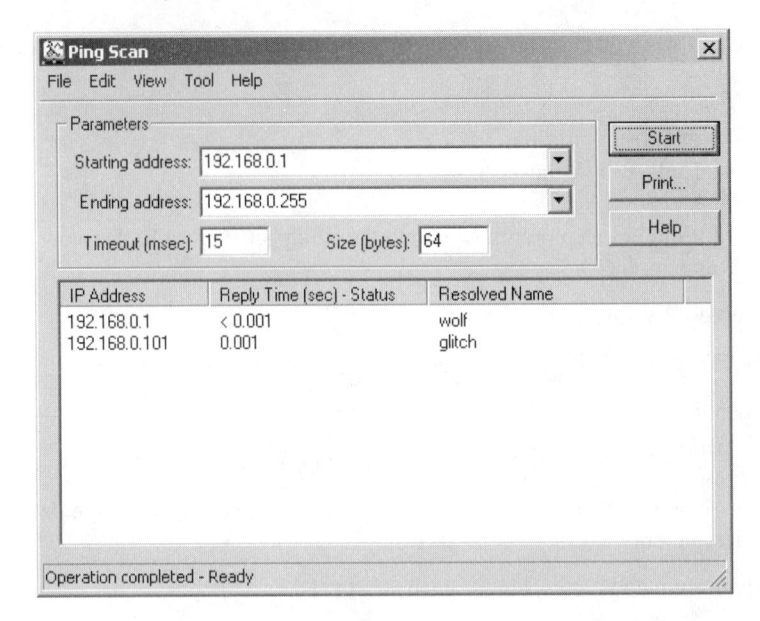

Figure C-10. Scanning for active IP addresses on a network with Ping Scan

For more information on the array of network tools available from Wildpackets, visit www.wildpackets.com.

The iNetTools trial version allows you to use the tool for only five minutes at a time. For continuous use, you should register the software.

Index

Symbols and Numbers

#DIV?0!, Excel error codes, 191
#N/A, Excel error codes, 191
#NAME, Excel error codes, 191
#NULL!, Excel error codes, 191
#NUM!, Excel error codes, 191
#REF!, Excel error codes, 191
#VALUE!, Excel error codes, 191
[ ] (optional parameter), 51
| (pipe symbol), 51
< > (required parameter), 51
1394 port, 219–220, 503
"4-5 Rule", 214

A

ABRs (area border routers), 436
Access control lists (ACLs), 453, 497–498
Access errors, 183–188
   Compact and Repair tool, 184–185
   database tables, 187–188
   macros or modules, 187
   manual repairs, 185–187
   overview of, 183–184
   reports, 186–187
ACK (acknowledgement), 68
ACLs (access control lists), 453, 497–498
acldiag tool, 453–455, 497–498
ACPI (advanced configuration and power interface), 625
Active Directory, 453–480
   alcdiag command, 453–455
   backup and recovery, 494
   dcdiag tool, 460–463
   Directory Services Restore Mode, 152
   Domain and Trusts snap-in, 457–458
   domain controllers, 480–484
   GPOs, 487–491
   gpresult command, 463–464
   gpupdate command, 464–465
   nltest command, 465–466
   ntdsutil tool. *see* ntdsutil tool
   RAS servers, 428
   replication, 484–487
   Replmon, 476
   Resultant Set of Policy, 476–480
   Schema snap-in, 458–460, 492–493
   Sites and Services snap-in, 458
   trusts, 493
   Users and Computers snap-in, 456–457
   Windows Server 2003 enhancements, 452–453
Active Directory, architecture, 443–453
   domain controllers, 447–448
   domains, 444–446
   forests, 444–446
   functional levels, 449–452
   GPOs, 449
   organizational units, 446
   sites, 446–447
Active Directory Domains and Trusts, 457–458, 493

673

Index

Active Directory Schema, 458–460, 492–493
Active Directory Sites and Services, 458
Active Directory Users and Computers
   overview of, 456–457
   RIS server management, 389
   troubleshooting DFS roots, 387
   troubleshooting Terminal Services, 383–386
Active Network Monitor
   collecting diagnostic information, 654
   installing, 653–654
   overview of, 652–653
Active Ports, SmartLine, 654–655
Active Registrations folder, WINS snap-in, 303
Active Server Watcher, SmartLine, 656–657
Add Driver (prndrvr.vbs-a) command, 366–367, 590–591
Add or Remove Program Licenses Wizard, 645–647
Address Resolution Protocol (ARP), 59–60, 498–499
addsw command, bootcfg, 218–219, 501–502
Administrators
   application compatibility and, 169
   device model numbers, 163
   Network Monitor and, 75–78
   printer configuration, 379
   RIS server authorization, 352
   takeown (taking file ownership), 98–99, 602
   terminal server session problems, 386
   uptime command, 90
Advanced configuration and power interface (ACPI), 625
Advanced RISC Computing (ARC), 213–216
Advanced tab, DNS server properties, 260–262
Advanced TCP/IP Settings, WINS, 313–315
AFR (Application Failure Rating), TechTracker ITX, 663
Alerts, 104–107, 526–529

Analysis, defragmentation vs., 638
Analysis Report, Diskeeper, 639, 641
Antivirus software, 35–36
APIPA (Automatic Private IP Addressing)
   NAT servers, 432
   overview, 26–27
   Windows 2000 DHCP, 324
Application Failure Rating (AFR), TechTracker ITX, 663
Application Recovery tool, 173–174
Applications. *see also* Network services
   analyzing current environment, 36–37
   compatibility, 169–171
   disabling during startup, 132–133
   logs, 111
   overview, 5–6
   printing, 380–381
   process-oriented corrective action for, 43
   shutdown, 158
   terminal server sessions, 386
   uninstalling with msicuu, 133–134
   uninstalling with System Restore, 145–149
ARC (Advanced RISC Computing), 213–216
Architecture
   Active Directory. *see* Active Directory, architecture
   DHCP. *see* DHCP (Dynamic Host Configuration Protocol), architecture
   disk subsystems. *see* Disk Subsystems, architecture
   DNS. *see* DNS (Domain Name Service), architecture
   RRAS. *see* RRAS (Routing and Remote Access Service), architecture
   WINS, 297–302
Area border routers (ABRs), 436
ARP (Address Resolution Protocol), 59–60, 498–499
arp command, 59–60, 498–499
ASBR (autonomous system boundary router), 436
ASR (Automated System Recovery), 127–129
Asynchronous backups, 343

Index

ATM (asynchronous transfer mode), 399–402, 499–501
atmadm command, 399–402, 499–501
Audit logging, 330–337
authoritative restore command, 468–469, 494
Authorization failure, 332–333, 337
AutoCorrect Backup utility, 204–208
Automated System Recovery (ASR), 127–129
Automatic Private IP Addressing. *see* APIPA (Automatic Private IP Addressing)
Automatic Recovery, 174–175
Autonomous system boundary router (ASBR), 436

B

B-node (Broadcast node), 23
Backups
    Active Directory, 494
    Automated System Recovery, 128
    DHCP, 324
    recovering Access database from, 183
    recovering DHCP database from, 343–346
    recovering WINS database from, 319–322
    shadow copies vs., 143
    WINS, 309
BACP (Bandwidth Allocation Control Protocol), 395
BAP (Bandwidth Allocation Protocol), 395
Bare metal restores, 128
Basic disks, 212, 239–240, 538
Basic Input Output System. *see* BIOS (Basic Input Output System)
behavior command, fsutil, 216, 226–229, 529–530
Best compression, TightVNC Viewer, 123
Binary conversion, 13–14
BIND servers, 262, 292–293
BINL (boot information negotiation layer), 390
BIOS (Basic Input Output System)
    analyzing settings, 32

firmware problems, 37–38
shutdown failures, 158
viewing version with MSinfo32, 112
viewing version with systeminfo, 107
Block inheritance, 489–490
blue-screen of death. *see* Stop errors (blue screens)
Boot devices
    inaccessible, 625–626
    Stop 0x0000007B error, 249–250
    Unmountable Boot Volume (Stop 0x000000ED), 631
boot information negotiation layer (BINL), 390
Boot logging
    enabling, 151
    Recovery Console and, 155–156
    shutdown failure and, 158–159
Boot sector, 213, 241–242
Boot-Time Defragmentation, Diskeeper, 640–641
bootcfg commands, 217–225
    addsw, 218–219, 501–502
    copy, 219, 502
    dbg1394, 219–220, 503
    debug, 220–221, 503–504
    default, 221, 504
    delete, 222, 504–505
    editing boot.ini after failure with, 216
    ems, 222–223, 505
    overview of, 217–218
    query, 223, 506
    raw, 223–224, 506
    reference guide, 501
    rmsw, 224–225, 506–507
    timeout, 225, 507
boot.ini file, 213–217
BOOTP forwarding
    DHCP discover packets and, 26
    DHCP relay agents vs., 342
    DHCP server not responding, 337
BOOTP.Microsoft user class, 328
Broadcast node (B-node), 23
Broadcasts
    DHCP, 26, 342
    DNS, 19, 22
Browse function, WINS, 313

BSOD (blue-screen of death). *see* Stop errors (blue screens)

C

Caching
    caching-only servers, 254
    clearcache DNS command, 268–269
cacls command, 95–97, 507–509
Canonical Name (CNAME) records, 254
Capture Buffer, Network Monitor, 77–78
Capture Filter, Network Monitor, 78
Capture, Network Monitor, 77
Capture Trigger, Network Monitor, 78
Case sensitivity, command switches, 62
Cell error codes, Excel, 191
Challenge Handshake Authentication Protocol (CHAP), 394
change command, pagefileconfig, 80–81, 581–582
Change Journal, 236–239, 536–537
Chaos class, DNS records, 277
CHAP (Challenge Handshake Authentication Protocol), 394
check command, netsh wins server, 307–308, 567–568
check database command, 307–308, 567
check version command, 308, 567
chkdsk command
    chkntfs disabling, 52, 510
    Data Bus Error (Stop 0x0000002E), 622
    overview of, 51–53
    reference guide, 509
    Stop 0x00000023/Stop 0x00000024 errors, 246, 621
chkntfs command
    overview of, 52–53
    reference guide, 510
Circular troubleshooting, 41
Classes, AD schema, 492
Classes, DHCP
    features of, 324
    user, 328
    vendor, 327
Classful addressing, 15
clean command, dfsutil, 356–357, 515
clearcache command, 268–269

Client and Gateway Services for NetWare, 353–356
Client-servers, 127–149
    application compatibility, 169–171
    Automated System Recovery, 127–129
    devices, 159–164
    displays, 166–167
    driverquery command, 129–131
    faxes, 164–166
    Internet Connection Sharing, 167–169
    msconfig command, 131–133
    msicuu command, 133–134
    Online Crash Analysis, 134–135
    OS installation, 156–157
    Recovery Console, 152–156
    Remote Assistance, 139–140
    Remote Desktop, 135–139
    Shadow Copy, 141–145
    System Restore, 145–149
    system shutdown, 157–159
    system startup, 149–152
    WINS, 299
Client Services for NetWare. *see* CSNW (Client Services for NetWare)
Clients
    DNS, 252, 262, 287–288
    NAT, 431
    RIS, 352–353
    WINS, 313–315
Clients, DHCP
    alternate configuration feature, 324
    leases, 337
    overview of, 334–336
    RAS server and, 340–341
Clients, RAS
    connections, 426
    RAS server, 428
    RAS server network, 429
    route command, 422–424
    RRAS snap-in, 424
CM (Connection Manager) tracing
    enabling/disabling, 406
    generating RAS Diagnostic Report, 408–409
    showing status of, 406
CNAME (Canonical Name) records, 254

Codes, error. *see* Device Manager, error codes
COM add-ins, 203
Command Prompt, Safe Mode with, 151
compact command, init, 309, 319, 321, 569
Compaction
    Compact and Repair tool, 184–185
    recovering WINS databases, 309, 319–322
Compression
    Ghost vs. RIS, 352
    TightVNC Viewer, 123
Computer Management snap-in
    Disk Management access, 56–57
    File Replication Service status, 484
    overview of, 110
Computers, comparing settings on, 38
Configurations tab, TechTracker ITX, 663
Configure Database Wizard, Sitekeeper, 644
Conflict detection, 328–329, 343
Connection Manager. *see* CM (Connection Manager) tracing
Connection monitoring
    netstat, 68
    ping, 71–72, 586–587
    TCP/IP ports with portqry, 420–422, 588–589
Connections
    DHCP clients, 335
    network printers, 379–380
    Outlook configuration, 194
    WINS clients, 313
Consistency checks, 307–308
Convert to Values command, 190
copy command, bootcfg, 219, 502
copy command, Recovery Console, 155
Corrupt files, 181
Counters, System Monitor, 92–93
CPUs, stop error message, 627
Crash Log tag, TechTracker ITX, 663
create command, pagefileconfig, 81–82, 582
CSNW (Client Services for NetWare)
    NWLink (IPX/SPX) protocol, 11–13
    overview of, 353–354
    troubleshooting integration, 391–392

ctrl key, 452
Custom.dic files, 207

D

DACL (discretionary access control), 95–97, 507–509
Data Registry key, 201
dbg1394 command, bootcfg, 219–220, 503
dcdiag tool
    overview of, 460–463
    reference guide, 510–513
    troubleshooting domain controllers, 480
DCPromo, 481
debug command, bootcfg, 220–221, 481–482, 503–504
Debugging
    dbg1394 command, 219–220, 503
    debug command, 220–221, 481–482, 503–504
    debug logging, 263, 264–265
    nslookup set d2 subcommand, 278
    nslookup set debug subcommand, 278
default command, bootcfg, 221, 504
Default gateways, 17
Defragmentation
    defrag command, 54–56, 228–229, 513
    Disk Defragmenter, 57–58
    Diskeeper, 638–641
Delegation, DNS zones
    overview of, 260
    troubleshooting with dnslint, 270–272
    verifying with nslookup, 284–285
Delegation, subdomains, 289–290
delete command
    bootcfg, 222, 504–505
    pagefileconfig, 82–83, 583
    Recovery Console, 155
Delete Driver (prndrvr.vbs-d), 367–368, 591–592
Delete Volume command, Disk Management, 244
Demand-dial routing, 433–435
Desktops, remote access, 350–351
Detect and Repair, 209
    fonts, 208
    overview of, 175–176

678   Index

Word applications, 206
Device drivers. *see also* Device Manager
   Attempted Write to Read Only Memory (Stop 0xBE), 628
   demand-dial routing, 433–434
   disabling with Recovery Console, 152–156
   displays, 167
   Driver IRQL... (Stop 0x000000D1), 629
   Driver Power State Failure (Stop 0x0000009F), 627
   Driver Unloaded... (Stop 0x000000CE), 629
   error messages. *see* Device errors
   faxes, 165
   Hardware Interrupt Storm (Stop 0x000000F2), 631–632
   Inaccessible Boot Device (Stop 0x0000007B), 625–626
   IRQL Not Less or Equal (Stop 0x0000000A), 619
   KMode Exception Not Handled (Stop 0x0000001E), 620
   No More System PTES (Stop 0x0000003F), 622–623
   printers. *see* Printer drivers
   recovery checkpoints, 146
   recovery from startup failure, 150
   shutdown failure problems, 158
   Status Image Checksum Mismatch (Stop 0x00000221), 633–635
   Status System Process Terminated (Stop 0x0000021A), 632–633
   troubleshooting with driverquery, 101–102, 523–524
   viewing with MSinfo32, 112
Device errors, 607–619
   about, 607–608
   Code 1 (wrong configuration), 608
   Code 3 (corrupted driver), 608–609
   Code 10 (device unable to start), 609
   Code 12 (conflicting devices), 609–610
   Code 14 (reboot instruction), 611
   Code 16 (incomplete configuration), 611
   Code 18 (reinstall different driver), 611
   Code 19 (wrong configuration), 611–612
   Code 22 (disabled device), 612
   Code 24 (device not working properly), 612
   Code 28 (drivers not installed), 612–613
   Code 29 (device disabled by firmware), 613
   Code 31 (driver cannot be loaded), 613
   Code 32 (current driver disabled), 613–614
   Code 33 (unable to determine resources), 614
   Code 34 (unable to determine settings), 614
   Code 35 (insufficient information on firmware), 614
   Code 36 (PCI interrupt error), 614–615
   Code 37 (initialization problem), 615
   Code 38 (unable to load driver), 615
   Code 39 (unable to load driver), 615–616
   Code 40 (service key problem), 616
   Code 41 (cannot find hardware device), 616
   Code 42 (unable to load driver), 616–617
   Code 43 (service stopped due to reported problems), 617
   Code 44 (application/service has shut down device), 617
   Code 45 (device not connected), 617–618
   Code 47 (unable to use device), 618
   Code 48 (device blocked from starting), 618
   Code 49 (system hive too large), 618
Device Manager, 159–164
   accessing, 159
   device status, 161–162
   disabling devices, 164
   error codes. *see* Device errors
   fax problems and, 165
   overview of, 159–161
   rolling back drivers, 150, 162
   uninstalling devices, 163–164
   updating drivers, 162–163

DFS (Distributed File System)
   deleting reparse point references, 235
   overview of, 351–352
   troubleshooting, 386–389
DFS links, 352
DFS roots
   inaccessible, 387
   overview of, 351–352
   troubleshooting. *see* dfsutil utility
DFS snap-in, 355, 386
dfsutil utility, 355–361, 514–519
   clean command, 356, 515
   export command, 357, 515
   import command, 357–358, 515–516
   importroot command, 358–359, 516
   pktflush command, 359, 517
   purgemupcache command, 360, 517
   purgewin2kstaticsitetable command, 360, 517
   showwin2kstaticsitetable command, 360, 518
   spcflush command, 361, 518
   switches, 356, 514
   troubleshooting with, 386
   unmapftroot command, 361, 518
   updatewin2kstaticsitetable command, 361, 518–519
DHCP Allocator
   NAT clients, 431
   NAT servers, 432
   netsh routing commands, 411–412, 556–557
DHCP broadcasts, 26, 342
DHCP Client Service, 336
DHCP Discover, 24–25, 342–343
DHCP (Dynamic Host Configuration Protocol), architecture, 323–329
   classes, 327–328
   conflict detection, 328–329
   enhancements to, 324
   overview of, 323–324
   scopes, 325–327
   terminology, 24–27
DHCP (Dynamic Host Configuration Protocol), troubleshooting
   clients, 334–336
   DNS integration, 291–292

DNS server, 289
   RIS clients, 390
   tools, 330–334
   WINS integration, 317–319
DHCP leases
   overview, 24–25
   RAS integration, 339–340
   renewing, 337
   scope migration, 338–339
   verifying, 338–339
DHCP Offer, 25
DHCP options, 26
DHCP relay agents
   DHCP-RAS integration, 341
   netsh routing ip relay, 412–413, 557–558
   overview, 26
   RAS server network, 429
   RRAS servers, 412–413, 432–433
   troubleshooting, 342–343
DHCP reservations, 25
DHCP scopes
   common problems, 337
   defined, 25
   migration, 338–339
   multicast, 326–327
   reconciling after restoring database, 345–346
   standard, 325
   superscopes, 325–326
   verifying current leases in, 338–339
   VPN resource access problems, 440
DHCP servers, 336–346
   accessing RAS resources, 340–341
   audit logging, 330–333, 336–337
   DHCP relay agents, 342–343
   dhcploc command, 334, 519
   dynamic updates, 252
   overview of, 336–337
   Properties dialog box, 328–329
   RAS integration, 339–340
   recovering corrupted database, 343
   recovering from backup, 343–346
   scope migration, 338–339
DHCP snap-in
   audit logging, 330–333
   database recovery, 344–345

680 Index

initiating DHCP backup from, 343–344
overview of, 330
reconciling scopes after restoring database, 345–346
troubleshooting DCHP servers, 337
dhcploc command, 334, 519
Diagnostic tools. *see* monitoring/diagnostic tools
Dial-in properties, 396
Dial-Out Hours, 434
Dictionaries, 207
Digital signatures, 627
Digital Video Disks (DVDs)
    Troubleshooting Wizard, 115
dir command, Recovery Console, 155
Directories
    Directory Consolidation, 640
    Directory Services Restore Mode, 152
    systeminfo providing location of, 107
Dirty bits
    chkdsk, 53
    fsutil dirty command, 229
    querying with fsutil dirty, 530
dirty command, fsutil, 229, 530
disable command, 154–155, 164
discretionary access control (DACL), 95–97, 507–509
Disk Cleanup Utility, 620
Disk Defragmenter, 57–58
Disk Management, 242–246
    dynamic disks with RAID errors, 244
    failed mirrored volumes, 245
    failed RAID 5 volumes, 246
    failed spanned or striped volumes, 244–245
    overview of, 56–57
    status indications, 243
Disk management tools, 51–58
    chkdsk command, 51–52
    chkntfs command, 52–53
    defrag command, 54–56
    Disk Defragmenter, 57–58
    Disk Management, 56–57, 242–246
Disk quotas, 233–234
Disk subsystems, 211–250
    boot sector/MBR problems, 241–242
    bootcfg/ addsw command, 218–219

bootcfg/ copy command, 219
bootcfg/ dbg1394 command, 219–220
bootcfg/ debug command, 220–221
bootcfg/ default command, 221
bootcfg/ delete command, 222
bootcfg/ ems command, 222–223
bootcfg/ query command, 223
bootcfg/ raw command, 223–224
bootcfg/ rmsw command, 224–225
bootcfg/ timeout command, 225
bootcfg tool, 217–218
common stop messages, 246–250
dmdiag command, 225–226
fsutil behavior command, 226–229
fsutil command, 226
fsutil dirty command, 229
fsutil file command, 229–230
fsutil fsinfo command, 230–231
fsutil hardlink command, 231–232
fsutil objectid command, 232–233
fsutil quota command, 233–234
fsutil reparsepoint command, 234–235
fsutil sparse command, 235–236
fsutil USN command, 236–239
fsutil volume command, 239
ftonline command, 239–240
recover command, 240–241
using Disk Management, 242–246
Disk subsystems, architecture, 211–217
    basic and dynamic disks, 212
    boot sector, 213
    boot.ini file, 213–216
    GPT disks, 217
    Master Boot Record, 212–213
    Master File Table, 216
Disk Volume Scheduler, Diskeeper, 639
diskfree option, fsutil volume command, 239
dismount option, fsutil volume command, 239
Display Filter, Network Monitor, 78
Display tab, Remote Desktop Connection, 138
Displays
    Display Troubleshooting Wizard, 115
    Program Compatibility Wizard test, 170
    troubleshooting, 166–167

Index **681**

Distributed File System. *see* DFS (Distributed File System)
#DIV?0!, Excel error codes, 191
dmdiag command, 225–226, 519–520
DNS (Domain Name Service)
 AD uninstallation, 483
 clearcache command, 268–269
 clients, 287–288
 debug logging, 264–265
 DHCP integration, 324
 DNS snap-in, 263–264
 dnscmd command, 267–268, 520–522
 dnslint command, 270–272, 522–523
 domain controllers, 481–482
 event logging, 265–266
 exit command, 274
 hierarchy, 255–256
 ls command, 274–276
 lserver command, 276–277
 monitoring, 267
 nslookup command, 272-274, 283–287, 574–581
 Outlook configuration, 194
 proxy configuration, 413
 query types, 22
 RAS server, 427
 RAS server network, 429
 replication, 485–486
 server subcommand, 277
 servers, 289–294
 set subcommand, 277–282
 statistics operation, 269–270
 view command, 282
 VPN resource access, 440
 WINS clients, 313–315
DNS (Domain Name Service), architecture, 251–263
 advanced features, 260–262
 BIND secondaries, 262
 caching-only server, 254
 client considerations, 262
 DNS hierarchy, 255–256
 DNS zones, 258–260
 dynamic updates, 252
 forwarders, 253
 name resolution process, 256–258
 netmask ordering, 262
 recursion and iteration, 252–253
 resource records, 254–255
 round robin, 261–262
 terminology, 19–22
 Windows Server 2003 enhancements, 263
 zone delegation, 260
DNS proxy
 netsh routing ip dnsproxy, 414, 559
 troubleshooting NAT server, 432
DNS Security Extensions (DNSSEC), 263
DNS snap-in
 debug logging, 264–265
 event logging, 265–266
 monitoring, 267–268
 overview of, 263–264
 updating DNS zone data, 289
DNS suffix, 281, 294
DNS zones
 common error events, 294
 configurations, 258–259
 delegation, 260, 270–272, 284–285
 displaying with ls command, 274–275
 overview of, 258–260
 resource records, 254–255
 transfers, 259–260, 292–293
 troubleshooting DNS clients, 288
 types of, 258
 updating data, 289
dnscmd command
 clearcache command, 268–269
 overview of, 267–268
 reference guide, 520–522
 statistics operation, 269–270
dnslint command, 270–272, 522–523
Document Recovery, 174, 176
Documentation, 31–34, 38–39
Domain controllers
 Active Directory Sites and Services snap-in and, 458–459
 metadata cleanup, 472–474
 nltest, 465–466, 573–574
 overview of, 447–448
 renaming, 452
 troubleshooting, 480–484
Domain DFS root, 351

Index

Domain Name Service. *see* DNS (Domain Name Service)
Domain naming master FSMO, 448
Domains
    Active Directory Domains and Trusts snap-in, 457–458
    functional levels, 450–451
    metadata cleanup, 472–474
    overview of, 444–446
    renaming, 452
Drag-and-drop, AD, 452
Driver Rollback, Device Manager, 162
Driverquery command
    options, 129
    overview of, 101–102
    reference guide, 523–524
    sample output, 130–131
Drivers. *see* Device drivers
Drives
    Drives and Network Adapters Troubleshooting Wizard, 115
    retrieving info with fsutil fsinfo, 230–231, 532
Duct tape mentality, 42–43
dump command, Netsh RAS Diagnostics, 403, 550
dump command, netsh wins command, 306, 317, 566–567
DVDs (Digital Video Disks)Troubleshooting Wizard, 115
Dynamic disks, 212, 244
Dynamic Host Configuration Protocol. *see* DHCP (Dynamic Host Configuration Protocol)
Dynamic updates
    DHCP audit events, 332
    DHCP options for, 291–292
    DNS clients, 288
    overview of, 252
    replication, 485–486

E

E-mail
    Outlook configuration, 192–195
    Remote Assistance, 139
    screenshots of error messages, 33
    testing mail servers with dnslint, 255
E-mail Accounts dialog box, Outlook, 194
/e switch, 96
EAP (Extensible Authentication Protocol), 394
Echo Request messages
    pathping command, 69
    ping command, 71–72
    tracert command, 73
EFI (Extensible Firmware Interface), 38
EFS (Encrypting File System), 97–98, 524–525
efsinfo command, 97–98, 524–525
Emergency Management Services (EMS), 222–223, 505
Emergency Repair Disks (ERDs), 128–129
Emergency Undelete, Executive Software, 642
ems command, bootcfg, 222–223, 505
EMS (Emergency Management Services), 222–223, 505
Enable Boot Logging option, 158–159
enable command, Recovery Console, 153
Encrypting File System (EFS), 97–98, 524–525
Encryption
    RAS methods, 394–395
    repairing OS installation and, 156–157
    VPNs for, 396–397
Enterprise Admins group, 337, 352
Environment
    analyzing, 34–38
    displaying with dump command, 403
    Environment tab, AD Users and Computers, 384–385
ERDs (Emergency Repair Disks), 128–129
Error messages. *see also* Device errors; Stop errors (blue screens)
    Access databases, 183, 184
    AD replication, 485–486
    audit logging, 331–333
    boot sector, 241
    disk-related stop messages, 246–250
    DNS, 293–294
    DNS clients, 288
    domain controllers, 481–482
    MBR, 241

Index

nslookup, 273–274
PowerPoint, 195
printing, 378
RAS client connections, 425
reading, 31
screenshot of, 33
WINS clients, 313–314
Word, 206
Error Reporting, 134–135
Evaluate Formula, Excel, 192
Event logging
    eventquery, 102–104, 525–526
    overview of, 265–266
    troubleshooting with, 32–33
    WINS, 304–305
Event Viewer
    overview of, 110–111
    recovering DHCP database, 343
    troubleshooting with, 32
eventquery command, 102–104, 525–526
Events
    DNS error, 293–294
    eventquery, 102
eventtriggers command, 104–107, 526–529
Excel, 188–192
    cell error codes, 191
    corrupted spreadsheets, 188–190
    invalid formulas, 191–192
    Open and Repair, 176–178
Executive Software, Diskeeper, 637–642
    Analysis Report, 639
    analysis vs. defragmentation, 638
    defragmentation modes, 639–640
    fitting pieces together, 638
    Frag Guard, 641
    getting the most from, 641
    Graphic Analysis Display, 639
    measuring fragmentation, 638
Executive Software, Sitekeeper, 643–648
    hardware inventory, 647–648
    license compliance, 645–647
    PushInstaller, 644–645
Executive Software, Undelete, 642
exit command, nslookup, 274, 575
Experience tab, Remote Desktop Connection, 139
export command, dfsutil, 357, 515

Extensible Authentication Protocol (EAP), 394
Extensible Firmware Interface (EFI), 38
External network numbers, NWLink, 13
External trusts, 445

F

Fast compression, TightVNC Viewer, 123
Fast User Switching, 169
FAT file systems
    checking with fsutil behavior, 226–227, 529–530
    FAT File System (Stop 0x00000023), 621
    Stop 0x00000023 error, 246–247
Fault tolerance
    ftonline command, 239–240, 538
    WINS enhancements, 298
Fax Console, 165–166
Faxes, 164–166, 427
FAZAM 2000, 648–652
    GP Administrator, 649–650
    GP Auditing and Diagnostics, 650
    GP Policy and Planning, 650
    GP Repository, 649
    installing, 650–651
    overview of, 648–649
    tool access, 651–652
File and Print Sharing Troubleshooting Wizard, 115
file command, fsutil, 229–230, 531
File Replication Service. *see* FRS (File Replication Service)
File System Utility. *see* fsutil command
Files
    fsutil file command, 229–230, 531
    fsutil sparse, 235–236, 535–536
    ownership of, 98–99, 602
    recovering with recover command, 598
    recovering with Undelete, 642
    Status System Process Terminated (Stop 0x0000021A), 632–633
    system protected, 600
    viewing, 282, 581
files command, ntdsutil tool, 469–472
Filtered status, portqry output, 421

Filters
  eventquery, 103, 526
  RIP, 435
  taskkill, 87, 603, 605
  tasklist, 89
  WINS enhancements to, 298
FIN messages, 68
Finger service scans, 670
Firmware
  analyzing currently installed, 37–38
  Attempted Write to Read Only Memory (Stop 0xBE), 628
  Code 29 error, 613
  Code 35 error, 614
  Code 43 error, 617
  Hardware Interrupt Storm (Stop 0x000000F2), 631–632
  KMode Exception Not Handled (Stop 0x0000001E), 620
  shutdown failures and, 158
fixboot command, 241–242
fixmbr command, 241–242
Flexible Single-Master Operations. *see* FSMOs (Flexible Single-Master Operations)
Floppy disks, 242
Follow up, 44
Fonts, 208
Forests
  functional levels, 451–452
  operations master roles, 448
  overview of, 444–446
  Windows Server 2003 enhancements, 453
Formulas
  isolating and resolving errors, 191–192
  recovering Excel spreadsheet data, 190
Forward lookup zones
  configuring, 258–259
  defined, 258
  verifying with nslookup, 283
Forwarders, DNS
  name resolution process, 256, 258
  overview of, 253
  Windows Server 2003 enhancements, 263
FQDNs (fully-qualified domain names)

DNS clients, 287
DNS mapping IP addresses to, 19–22
NAT servers, 432
NetBIOS names vs., 18
print servers, 381
printer connection problems, 380
RAS servers, 427
Frag Guard, Diskeeper, 641
Fragmentation, 638–639, 641
Frame types, NWLink (IPX/SPX), 12
Freeware, 117–124
FRS (File Replication Service)
  overview of, 351
  status of, 484
  troubleshooting with health_chk, 362–364, 541–542
fsinfo command, fsutil, 230–231, 532
FSMOs (Flexible Single-Master Operations)
  defined, 447
  transferring and seizing roles, 474–475
  troubleshooting domain controllers, 481, 483
fsutil commands, 528–529
  behavior, 216, 226–229, 529–530
  dirty, 229, 530
  file, 229–230, 531
  fsinfo, 230–231, 532
  hardlink, 231–232, 533
  objectid, 232–233, 533–534
  quota, 233–234, 534
  reparsepoint, 234–235, 535
  sparse, 235–236, 535–536
  USN, 236–239, 536–537
  volume, 239, 538
ftonline command, 239–240, 538
FullArmor. *see* FAZAM 2000
fully-qualified domain names. *see* FQDNs (fully-qualified domain names)
Functional levels, AD, 449–452

G

Gateway Services for NetWare. *see* GSNW (Gateway Services for NetWare)
getmac command, 60, 538–539
Ghost

compression features of, 352
reimaging with, 42
Global catalogs, AD
    defined, 444
    forest functional levels, 451–452
    Windows Server 2003 enhancements, 453
Globally Unique Identifier Partition Table (GPT) disks, 217
GPOs (Group Policy Objects)
    block inheritance vs. No Override, 489–490
    common problems and solutions, 490
    FAZAM 2000 management of, 648–651
    gpupdate, 464–465, 540–541
    loopback processing, 488–489
    overview of, 449
    RSoP, 463–464, 476–480, 539–540
    troubleshooting, 482–483, 487–491
gpresult command, 463–464, 539–540
GPT (Globally Unique Identifier Partition Table) disks, 217
gpupdate command, 464–465, 540–541
Grammar files, Detect and Repair, 209
Graphic Analysis Display, Diskeeper, 638, 639
Groups
    domain functional level comparisons, 450–451
    failure to change membership, 483
    Support Tools installation MSI file, 48
GSNW (Gateway Services for NetWare)
    NWLink (IPX/SPX) protocol, 11–13
    overview of, 353–354
    troubleshooting integration, 391–392

H

H-node (Hybrid node), 23
Hackers, 113
HAL (hardware abstraction layer) error message, 625
Hard disks. *see also* chkdsk command
    configuration info, 225–226, 519–520
    Data Bus Error (Stop 0x0000002E), 621–622
    defragmenting, 54–56, 513
    shutdown failures, 158–159
Hard links, 231–232, 533
Hard page faults
    monitoring with pfmon, 83–85, 585–586
    monitoring with System Monitor, 85
hardlink command, fsutil, 231–232, 533
Hardware
    Attempted Write to Read Only Memory (Stop 0xBE), 628
    Bad Pool Caller (Stop 0xC2), 629
    Data Bus Error (Stop 0x0000002E), 621–622
    Device Manager and, 159–164
    disk-related stop messages, 246–250
    display problems, 167
    Executive Software's Diskeeper, 647–648
    fax problems, 165
    firmware problems, 37–38
    Hardware Interrupt Storm (Stop 0x000000F2), 631–632
    inventorying with Sitekeeper, 647–648
    Kernel Data Inpage Error (Stop 0x0000007A), 625
    MSinfo32 and, 112
    shutdown failures, 158
hardware abstraction layer (HAL) error message, 625
Hardware Compatibility List (HCL), 165
Hardware Troubleshooting Wizard, 115
Hardware Update Wizard, 163
HCL (Hardware Compatibility List), 165
health_chk commands, 362–364, 541–542
Heartbeat, 90
Help and Support Center, 49–50, 75
History, documenting, 31–34
Home Networking Troubleshooting Wizard, 115
Host (A) records
    defined, 254
    DNS clients, 287–288
    forward lookup zones containing, 258
    RAS server networks, 428
    RAS servers, 427
    round robin and, 261–262
Host ID, 14–16

Index

hostname command, 60, 543
Hosts file
    defined, 19
    LMHosts file vs., 22
    overview of, 21
Hotfixes, 35, 107
Hotmail, 35
Hub-and-spoke replication topology, 301
Hung sessions, 65–67
Hybrid node (H-node), 23

I

I/O transfer error, 622–623
IAS (Internet Authentication Services), 402–403, 543
iasparse command, 402–403, 543
ICS (Internet Connection Sharing), 116, 167–169
ICS Troubleshooting Wizard, 167–169
/ id switch, 221, 222
IGMP (Internet Group Management Protocol), 413–416, 559–561
IMAP (Internet Mail Access Protocol), version 4, 255
import command, dfsutil, 357–358, 515–516
Import Objects dialog box, 186
importroot command, dfsutil, 358–359, 516
Inaccessible Boot Device error, 249–250
Incremental Zone Transfer (IXFR), 260
InetOrgPerson object, 450–451
iNetTools, 670–672
Infrastructure master FSMO, 448, 483
init backup command, 309, 568–569
init commands, netsh wins server, 309–311, 568–570
    compact, 309, 319, 321, 569
    pull, 310, 569
    push, 310, 569–570
    replicate, 310, 570
    restore, 310, 570
Input Devices Troubleshooting Wizard, 116
Inside Active Directory (Kouti and Seitsonen), 444
Installed Software tab, TechTracker ITX, 663

Inter-Site Transports folder, 458–459
Interfaces. *see also* show interface command
    DHCP relay agents, 433
    NAT server, 432
    RAS server, 427
    routing, 420
    RRAS snap-in, 424
Internal network numbers, 12–13
Internet Authentication Services (IAS), 402–403, 543
Internet Connection Sharing (ICS), 116, 167–169
Internet Explorer, 112, 116
Internet Group Management Protocol (IGMP), 413–416, 559–561
Internet Mail Access Protocol (IMAP), version 4, 255
Internet Packet Exchange/Sequenced Packed Exchange (IPX/SPX) protocol, 11–13
interrupt request level (IRQL), 619, 629
Interrupt storm errors, 631–632
IP addresses
    APIPA and, 26–27
    arp command, 59
    conflict detection, 328–329
    DHCP clients, 335
    DHCP leases, 24–25
    DHCP-RAS integration, 339–341
    DHCP relay agents, 26, 342–343
    DHCP reservations, 25
    DHCP scopes, 25, 338–339
    DHCP server problems, 337
    DNS clients, 287–288
    DNS error events, 293–294
    DNS name resolution, 19–22
    exclusions, 25
    Outlook configuration, 194
    RAS server, 427
    round robin, 261
    structure of, 13–16
    TCP/IP routing, 17–18
    WINS clients, 313
    WINS resolving NetBIOS names to, 23–24
    WINS servers, 316

Index

IP routing
   demand-dial routing, 434
   NAT server, 432
   overview of, 430
   RAS server network, 428–429
   RRAS snap-in, 424
   VPN connections, 438, 440
IP Security logs, 408–409
IP Subnet Calculator, 118–119
ipconfig command
   analyzing network configuration, 36
   APIPA and, 27
   DHCP clients, 335
   DHCP-RAS integration, 340–341
   DHCP relay agents, 342
   domain controllers, 482
   resolver cache, viewing, 20
IPMonitor, Tsarfin, 665–667
IPX frame types, 391–392
ipxroute command, 364–365, 544
IRQL (interrupt request level), 619, 629
Iterative queries, 22, 252–253, 256–257
IXFR (Incremental Zone Transfer), 260

K

Keep It Simple Stupid (KISS) rule, 41
Kernel data, 248, 249, 624
KISS (Keep It Simple Stupid) rule, 41

L

L-S-D-OU rule, 488
L2TP (Layer 2 Tunneling Protocol), 397, 438–439, 441
LAN routing, 430, 432, 434
Last Known Good Configuration (LKGC), 150, 167
LCP (Link Control Protocol) extensions, 395
.ldb files, 184–185
Leases. *see* DHCP leases
Licensing, 645–647, 650–651
line printer daemon (LPD) service, 365, 545
line printer remote (LPR) service, 365

Link Control Protocol (LCP) extensions, 395
Linked value replication, Active Directory, 451–452
List Drivers (prndrvr.vbs-l), 368–369, 592–593
Listen mode, TightVNC Viewer, 123
Listening status, portqry output, 421
listsvc command, 153
LKGC (Last Known Good Configuration), 150, 167
LMHosts file, 19, 22
Load balancing, 261
Local Resources tab, Remote Desktop Connection, 138
Log files
   AD, 469–472
   Event Viewer, 111
   RAS Diagnostic Report on, 408–409
   RAS tracing, 404–405
   recovering Excel spreadsheet data, 190
   Setup, 182–183
   Sitekeeper, 643–644
Log on
   domain controllers and, 482–483
   recovery from startup failure, 150
   updating timestamps, 450–451
Logging
   audit, 330–333
   boot, 151, 158–159
   status of Connection Manager, 406
Loopback processing, 488–489
LPD (line printer daemon) service, 365, 545
lpq command, 365, 545
LPR (line printer remote) service, 365
ls command, nslookup, 274–276, 575–576
lserver command, nslookup, 276–277, 576

M

M-node (Mixed node), 23
MAC (Media Access Control) address
   arp, 59–60
   DHCP leases, 24–25
   DHCP reservations, 25
   getmac, 60–61, 538–539

Index

Macros, 187
Mail Exchange (MX) records, 255
Mail servers, 194–195, 272
Manage Documents permission, 350
Manage Printers permissions, 350
Manual Defragmentation, Diskeeper, 639
Mapping, dependency diagrams, 38–39
MBR (Master Boot Record), 212–213, 241–242
Media Access Control. *see* MAC (Media Access Control) address
Memory, errors
    Bad Pool Caller (Stop 0xC2), 628–629
    Data Bus Error (Stop 0x0000002E), 621–622
    Driver Used Excessive PTES (Stop 0x000000D8), 630
    Kernel Data Inpage Error (Stop 0x0000007A), 625
    KMode Exception Not Handled (Stop 0x0000001E), 620
    No More System PTES (Stop 0x0000003F), 622–623
    Stop 0x00000050, 247–248
    Stop 0x00000077, 248–249
Memory, monitoring
    memsnap, 79, 545
    System Monitor, 92–93
    systeminfo, 107
memsnap command, 79, 545
metadata cleanup commands, ntdsutil, 472–474
MFT Defragmentation, Diskeeper's Boot-Time Defragmentation, 640, 641
MFT (Master File Table), 216, 227–229
MFT Zone, 216, 227–229
Microsoft
    CHAP (MS-CHAP), 394
    CHAP v2 (MS-CHAP v2), 394
    Client Services for NetWare, 11
    Gateway Services for NetWare, 11
    Hardware Compatibility List, 629
    Management Consoles. *see* MMCs (Microsoft Management Consoles)
    MSN Messenger, 139
    newsgroups, 40
    Remote Installation Service, 42
    Software Installation (MSI) files, 174
    Systems Management Server (SMS), 76
    Windows 2000. *see* Windows 2000
    Windows Advanced Option menu, 149
    Windows Backup program, 128
    Windows Installer, 182–183
    Windows Licensing Agreement, 157
    Windows NT, 449
    Windows Server 2003. *see* Windows Server 2003
    Windows servers, 10
    Word. *see* Word
Migrate-on, 316
Migration, 338–339
Mirrored volumes (RAID 1), 212, 245
MIT Athena Hesiod class, DNS records, 277
Mixed mode domains, AD, 449–450
Mixed node (M-node), 23
MMCs (Microsoft Management Consoles)
    Active Directory Domains and Trusts, 457–458
    Active Directory Sites and Services, 458–459
    Active Directory Users and Computers, 456–457
    configuring, 49
    DHCP snap-in, 330
    DNS snap-in, 263–264
    RRAS snap-in, 342, 424–425
    Terminal Services Manager snap-in, 376
    WINS snap-in, 303
Modem Troubleshooting Wizard, 116
Modems
    demand-dial routing, 433–434
    enabling/disabling tracing, 410
    event logging, 409
    fax problems and, 165
    RAS client connections, 426
    RAS Diagnostic Reports, 408–409
    RAS servers, 427
Modules, 187
Monitoring/diagnostic tools
    disk management. *see* disk management tools
    freeware, 117–124

Index **689**

network monitoring. *see* Network monitoring/troubleshooting tools
operating system, 47–51
performance monitoring. *see* Performance monitoring
security management. *see* Security
system management. *see* System management tools
troubleshooting wizards, 115–117
more command, Recovery Console, 155
Motherboards, 621–622, 627
Mouse problems, 206
MS-CHAP (Microsoft CHAP), 394
msconfig command, 131–133
msicuu command, 133–134, 158
MSinfo32, 38, 111–113
MSN Messenger, 139
MSO####.acl files, 207–208
multi, disk management, 214
Multicast addresses, 326–327
Multicast scopes, 326–327
Multilink, 395
Multimedia and Games Troubleshooting Wizard, 116
Multinet, 325
MUP (multiple UNC provider) cache, 360
MX (Mail Exchange) record type, 255

N

#N/A, Excel error codes, 191
#NAME, Excel error codes, 191
Name resolution
  broadcasts, 19, 22
  DNS, 19–22, 256–258
  DNS clients, 262, 287–288
  failures, 290
  hosts file, 19, 21
  LMHosts file, 19, 22
  NetBIOS, 18, 23–24
  nslookup, 272–273
  Outlook configuration, 194
  overview of, 18–19
  ping verification of, 71–72, 586–587
  WINS, 23–24
Name Server (NS) record type, 255
NAT (network address translation)
  configuration, 416, 561
  DHCP Allocator settings, 411–412, 556–557
  DNS proxy configuration, 414, 559
  overview of, 399
  routing on RRAS servers, 430–432
Native mode domains, Active Directory, 449–450
nbstat command, 61–62, 546
Neighbors tab, RIP, 435
Nesting groups, 450–451
net continue command, 64, 548
net pause command, 64, 548
Net Services commands, 64–67
  net session, 66–67
  net start | stop | pause | continue, 64
  net statistics, 65–66
  net view, 67
net session command, 66–67, 549
net start command, 64, 548
net statistics command, 65–66, 548–549
net stop command, 64, 548
net view command, 67, 549–550
NetBIOS cache, 22
NetBIOS Enhanced User Interface (NetBEUI), 10
NetBIOS name resolution
  FQDNs vs., 18
  nbstat, 62
  WINS, 23–24
  WINS servers, 315–316
NetBT (NetBIOS over TCP/IP), 61–62, 546
Netclient program, 119–121
netdiag command
  domain controllers, 481–482
  overview of, 62–64
  reference guide, 547–548
NetInfo, Tsarfin, 665–667
Netmask ordering, 252, 262
Netperf, 119–121
Netserver program, 119–121
netsh diag gui command, 75
netsh (Netshell) commands, 298
Netsh RAS Diagnostics, 402–411
  dump command, 403, 550
  overview of, 549–550

Index

set cmtracing command, 406, 551
set modemtracing command, 410, 555
set rastracing command, 410, 555
set securityeventlog command, 410, 556
set tracefacilities command, 411, 556
show all command, 404–405, 550–551
show cmtracing command, 406, 551
show configuration command, 406–407, 552
show installation command, 407–408, 553
show logs command, 408–409, 554
show modemtracing command, 409, 555
show rastracing command, 410, 555
show securityeventlog command, 410, 555
show tracefacilities command, 411, 556
netsh routing commands, 411–420, 556–565
  netsh routing ip autodhcp, 411–412, 556–557
  netsh routing ip dnsproxy, 414, 559
  netsh routing ip igmp, 414–416, 559–561
  netsh routing ip nat, 416, 561
  netsh routing ip ospf, 416–418, 562–563
  netsh routing ip relay, 412–413, 557–558
  netsh routing ip rip, 418–420, 564–565
  netsh routing ip routerdiscovery, 420, 565
  overview of, 411, 556
netsh wins command, 305–306, 566–567
netsh wins server commands, 306–313
  check, 307–308, 567–568
  dump, 306, 566–567
  init, 309–311, 568–570
  overview of, 566
  show, 311–313, 570–572
netstat command, 67–69, 572–573
NetWare Client Services. *see* CSNW (Client Services for NetWare)
NetWare Gateway Services. *see* GSNW (Gateway Services for NetWare)
Network
  configuration, 36
  Office setup, 180–181

Network address translation. *see* NAT (network address translation)
Network Associates Sniffer Pro, 75
Network Diagnostics, 75
Network ID, 14–16
Network interface cards (NICs)
  internal network numbers and, 12
  troubleshooting RIS, 389
Network Load Balanced (NLB) clusters, 261
Network Monitor
  Active Network Monitor vs., 652–654
  overview of, 75–78
Network Monitor Driver, 76–77
Network monitoring/troubleshooting tools, 58–75
  arp command, 59–60
  getmac command, 60
  hostname command, 60
  nbtstat command, 61–62
  Net Services commands, 64–67
  netdiag command, 62–64
  netstat command, 67–69
  Network Diagnostics, 75
  Network Monitor, 75–78
  pathping command, 69–70
  ping command, 71–72
  telnet command, 72–73
  tracert command, 73–74
Network protocols, 9–19
  accessing network configuration settings, 9–10
  DHCP overview, 24–27
  DNS, 19–22
  NetBEUI, 10
  NWLink (IPX/SPX), 11–13
  TCP/IP basics, 13–19
  WINS, 23–24
Network Scheduler, Diskeeper, 639–640
Network services, 347–392
  advanced settings, 349–350
  Client and Gateway Services for NetWare, 353–356
  DFS, 351–352, 386–389
  DFS snap-in, 355
  dfsutil utility, 355–361
  health_chk commands, 362–364

Index **691**

ipxroute command, 364–365
NetWare integration, 391–392
overview of, 5–6, 347
print services, 348–349
printer permissions, 350
prndrvr.vbs commands, 365–370
query commands, 371–374
Remote Installation Services, 352–353, 389–390
reset session command, 375
Terminal Services, 350–351, 383–386
Terminal Services Manager snap-in, 376
Network throughput, 119–121
Networking, 9–28. *see also* network protocols
 DHCP, 24–27
 DNS name resolution, 19–24
 network resources, 27–28
 Safe Mode, 151
Newsgroups, Microsoft, 40
NICs (network interface cards), 12, 389
NLB (Network Load Balanced) clusters, 261
nltest command
 domain controllers, 482
 overview of, 465–466
 reference guide, 573–574
 uninstalling Active Directory, 483
No Override, 490
Nonauthoritative restore, Active Directory, 494
Normal.dot Global Template, 202–203
Not Listening status, portqry output, 421
NS (Name Server) record type, 255
nslookup
 error messages, 273–274
 exit command, 274, 575
 forward lookup zones, 283
 ls command, 274–276, 575–576
 lserver command, 276–277, 576
 name resolution, 272–273
 overview of, 272–274, 574–575
 recursive queries, 280
 resource records, 280
 reverse lookup zones, 283
 server command, 277, 576–577
 troubleshooting with, 283–287

view command, 282, 581
zone delegation, 284–285
nslookup set commands
 set all command, 277, 577
 set class command, 277–278, 577
 set cmtracing command, 406, 551
 set d2 command, 278, 578
 set debug command, 278, 578
 set defname command, 279, 578
 set domain command, 279, 578
 set ignore command, 279, 578–579
 set port command, 279, 579
 set querytype, 280, 579
 set recurse, 280, 579
 set retry, 280–281, 579
 set root, 281, 580
 set search, 281, 580
 set srchlist, 281, 580
 set timeout, 282, 580
 set vc, 282, 580–581
Ntbtlog.txt file, 151
ntdsutil tool, 467–476
 authoritative restore, 468–469
 files command, 469–472
 group membership changes, 483
 metadata cleanup, 472–474
 overview of, 467
 roles menu, 474–475
 semantic database analysis, 476
 uninstalling Active Directory, 483
NTFS Change Journal, 236–239
NTFS file systems
 fsutil behavior, 227, 529–530
 NTFS File System (Stop 0x00000024), 621
 process-oriented corrective action, 43
 Stop 0x00000024 error, 246–247
#NULL!, Excel error codes, 191
#NUM!, Excel error codes, 191
NWLink (IPX/SPX) protocol, 11–13
 external network number, 13
 frame type, 12
 internal network number, 12–13
 overview of, 11
 troubleshooting NetWare integration, 391–392

O

Object Identifiers (OIDs), 232–233, 533–534
objectid command, fsutil, 232–233, 533–534
Octets, 13
Office XP, 173–210
    Access databases and, 183–188
    Application Recovery, 173–174
    Automatic Recovery, 174–175
    Detect and Repair, 175–176
    Document Recovery, 176
    Excel, 188–192
    installing/uninstalling with PushInstaller, 644
    license compliance, 645–646
    Open and Repair, 176–178
    Outlook, 192–195
    PowerPoint, 195–199
    Setup, 178–183
    Word. *see* Word
OIDs (Object Identifiers), 232–233, 533–534
Online Crash Analysis, 134–135
Online Help, 49–50, 556
Open and Repair
    Excel spreadsheets, 189–190
    overview of, 176–178
    Word applications, 206
Open Shortest Path First. *see* OSPF (Open Shortest Path First)
Operating systems. *see also* Client-servers
    analyzing current environment, 35
    boot.ini file, 221, 504
    default, 222, 504–505
    documenting, 31–34
    fax compatibility, 164–165
    installation repair, 156–157
    monitoring and diagnostic tools, 47–51
    Program Compatibility Wizard test, 170
    Remote Installation Services, 352–353
    versions, viewing with MSinfo32, 112
    versions, viewing with systeminfo, 107
Operations master, Active Directory
    defined, 447
    forests, 448
    types of, 448

Operations, net statistics command, 65–66
Operators
    eventquery, 103, 526
    taskkill, 87, 603
    tasklist, 89, 605
Optimism, 29–30
optional parameter ([ ]), 51
Options Registry key, 203–204
OSPF Complete Implementation (Moy), 435
OSPF (Open Shortest Path First)
    diagnosing routing, 435–437
    key features of, 398
    troubleshooting routers, 416–418, 562–563
OUs (organizational units), 446
Outlook, 192–195
Outlook Express (Messaging) Troubleshooting Wizard, 116
Ownership, 98–99, 602

P

P-node (Peer node), 23
-p switch, 120
Packet filtering
    demand-dial routing, 434
    DHCP relay agents, 433
    NAT servers, 432
    RAS server network, 428
    router-to-router VPN connections, 441
    VPN resource access, 440
    VPN server connection, 438
Packets
    monitoring networks with pathping, 69–71, 584–585
    monitoring with Network Monitor, 75–78
    truncation errors, 279
Page faults
    monitoring with pfmon, 83–85
    monitoring with System Monitor, 85
    Page Fault in Nonpaged Area (Stop 0x00000050), 623–624
    Stop 0x00000050 error, 247–248
Page Table Entries (PTEs), 622–623, 630
pagefileconfig commands

change, 80–81, 581–582
create, 81–82, 582
delete, 82–83, 583
query, 83, 583–584
Pagefiles
    configuring and managing, 80
    Status Image Checksum Mismatch
        (Stop 0x00000221), 633–635
Paging File Defragmentation, Diskeeper's
    Boot-Time Defragmentation, 640, 641
PAP (Password Authentication Protocol),
    394
Partition Knowledge Table (PKT), DFS,
    359
Password Authentication Protocol (PAP),
    394
Passwords
    configuring at domain level, 488
    InetOrgPerson objects and, 450–451
    RIP, 435
    router-to-router VPN connections, 441
    VPN server connections, 438
pathping command
    Active Directory replication, 484
    overview of, 69–70
    reference guide, 584–585
    tracert command vs., 73–74, 606
    WINS replication, 317
PCI interrupts, 614–615
PDC emulator FSMO
    overview of, 448
    replication, 485–486
    trusts, 493
PDC (primary domain controller), 447
Peer node (P-node), 23
Perfmon (System Monitor), 92–93
Performance monitoring, 79–94
    DHCP, 324
    memsnap command, 79
    pagefileconfig command, 80–83
    pfmon command, 83–85
    pmon command, 86
    System Monitor, 92–93
    Task Manager, 94
    taskkill command, 86–88
    tasklist command, 88–89
    uptime command, 90–91

Performance, WINS-DHCP integration,
    318
Permissions. *see also* Print permissions
    DACL and, 96
    DFS, 388–389
    Office Setup, 181
    process-oriented corrective action, 43
    Replication Synchronization, 485
Pessimism, 29–30
pfmon command, 83–85, 585–586
PIDs, 88–89
ping command
    Active Directory replication, 484
    DNS clients, 287
    network printer connections, 380
    Outlook configuration, 194
    overview of, 71–72
    print servers, 381
    reference guide, 586–587
    WINS replication, 317
Ping Scan, iNetTools, 671–672
pipe symbol (|), 51
PKT (Partition Knowledge Table), 359
pktflush command, dfsutil, 359, 517
pmon command
    KMode Exception Not Handled (Stop
        0x0000001E), 620
    overview of, 86
    reference guide, 588
Point-to-Point Protocol (PPP), 394
Point-to-Point Tunneling Protocol. *see*
    PPTP (Point-to-Point Tunneling
    Protocol)
Pointer (PTR) records, 254, 258
Policies, Remote Access, 395
POP (Post Office Protocol), version 3, 255
portqry command, 420–422, 588–589
Ports
    Active Ports, 654–655
    debugging with bootcfg /dbg1394,
        219–220, 503
    DNS errors, 294
    iNetTools, 670
    Netserver, 120
    netstat monitoring, 67–70, 572–573
    portqry, 420–422, 588–589
    printer, 348

694   Index

Remote Assistance connections, 139
set port command, 279
Telnet sessions, 73
Terminal Services server connections, 383
VPN, 439
zone transfers, 292–293
Post Office Protocol (POP), version 3, 255
PowerPoint, 195–199
PPP (Point-to-Point Protocol), 394
PPTP (Point-to-Point Tunneling Protocol)
  router-to-router VPN connections, 441
  VPN and, 397
  VPN server connections, 438–439
Presentations, PowerPoint, 195–199
primary domain controller (PDC), 447
Primary restore, Active Directory, 494
Primary zones, DNS, 258
Print devices
  common problems, 378
  defined, 348
  printing jobs, 383
  servers, 382
Print permissions
  common problems, 378
  defined, 350
  print servers, 381
  shared printers, 379
Print pooling, 348
Print queues
  defined, 348
  prnqctl.vbs, 370–371
  spool folder location, 381–382
  status checks, 365, 545
Print servers
  defined, 348
  network printer connections, 379–380
  networking problems with, 381
  problems sending job to print device, 382
Printer drivers
  common problems, 378
  errors when printing in Word, 206
  installing additional, 379
  managing with prndrvr.vbs, 365–369, 589–593
  print devices and, 348

shared printers, 379
Printers, 376–383
  advanced settings, 349–350
  all-in-one, 164–166
  common problems, 377–378
  defined, 348–349
  driver management, 365–369
  errors when printing in Word, 206
  listing, 369–370, 593
  pausing and resuming, 370–371
  permissions, 350
  Printing Troubleshooting Wizard, 116
  prnqctl.vbs, 370–371, 594
  problems with network, 378–383
  terminology, 348–349
  test pages, 370–371, 377
prndrvr.vbs commands, 365–369, 589–593
  overview of, 365–366, 589–590
  prndrvr.vbs-a (Add Driver), 366–367, 590–591
  prndrvr.vbs-d (Delete Driver), 367–368, 591–592
  prndrvr.vbs-l (List Drivers), 368–369, 592–593
  prndrvr.vbs-x (Remove All Unused Drivers), 369, 593
prnmngr.vbs command, 369–370, 593
prnqctl.vbs command, 370–371, 594
Process activity, 86–88
process command, query commands, 371–372, 595
Process exception code, 626
Process-oriented corrective action, 43–44
Processes, troubleshooting, 30–31
Processor type, 107
Product IDs, 107
Program Compatibility wizard, 170–171
Program name installation, 146
Programs tab, Remote Desktop Connection, 139
Protected files, 108–109
Proxy, WINS, 302
PTEs (Page Table Entries), 622–623, 630
PTR (Pointer) record type, 254, 258
pull command, init, 310, 569
Pull replication
  manually initiating, 310

Index **695**

overview of, 299
show pullpartnerconfig command, 312, 572
showing list/properties of partners, 311–312
troubleshooting, 317
purgemupcache command, dfsutil, 360, 517
purgewin2kstaticsitetable command, dfsutil, 360, 517
push command, init, 310, 569–570
Push replication
    manually initiating, 310
    overview of, 299
    show pushpartnerconfig command, 312, 572
    showing list/properties of partners, 311–312
    troubleshooting, 317
PushInstaller, Executive Software, 644–645

Q

Queries, DNS, 22, 289–290
query commands, 371–374, 594–597
    bootcfg commands, 223, 506
    pagefileconfig commands, 83, 583–584
    process, 371–372, 595
    session, 372–373, 596
    termserver, 373–374, 596–597
    user, 374, 597
quota command, fsutil, 233–234, 534

R

RAID, 212, 244–246
RAM
    Data Bus Error (Stop 0x0000002E), 621–622
    MSinfo32, 112
    Page Fault in Nonpaged Area (Stop 0x00000050), 623–624
    pfmon, 83–85
    Status Image Checksum Mismatch (Stop 0x00000221), 633–635
    Stop 0x00000050 error, 247–248
    System Monitor, 92–93

Unexpected Kernel Mode Trap (Stop 0x0000007F), 626–627
RAS (Remote Access Server)
    accessing resources on/beyond, 340–341
    integration with DHCP, 339–340
    troubleshooting, 427–429
    VPN server connection problems, 439
raw command, bootcfg, 223–224, 506
rdisk utility, 129, 214
Readme files, 40
Reconcile All Scopes dialog box, 345
records, WINS, 298
recover command, 178, 240–241, 598
Recover Formulas command, 190
Recovery
    Active Directory, 494
    client-initiated, 145
    recover command, 178, 240–241, 598
    server-initiated, 143–144
    Undelete command, 642
Recovery Bin, Executive Software, 642, 643
Recovery Console, 152–156
    accessing, 155–156
    boot sector/MBR errors, 241–242
    disable command, 154–155
    disabling services/drivers, 152–156
    display problems, 167
    enable command, 153
    listsvc command, 153
    Mismatched HAL (Stop 0x00000079), 625
    other commands, 155
    overview of, 152
    shutdown failure and, 159
Recursive queries
    defined, 22
    name resolution process, 256–257
    nslookup for, 280
    overview of, 252–253
#REF!, Excel error codes, 191
Refresh Interval, DNS zones, 289
Registry
    Code 19 device error, 611–612
    options tool, 204–205
    RAS Diagnostic Report, 407–408
    rebooting system after using fsutil, 226

system hive errors, 618–619
Reimaging, 42
Relationships, WINS, 299–301
Relay Agents. *see* DHCP relay agents
Remote Access Policies
   overview of, 395
   RRAS snap-in, 425
   VPN server connection problems, 439
Remote Access Profiles, 396
Remote Access Server. *see* RAS (Remote Access Server)
Remote access VPNs, 437, 438–440
Remote Assistance
   defined, 135
   overview of, 139–140
   remotely configuring pagefiles, 80
Remote Desktop
   connecting to remote system, 137–139
   connections, 136–137
   defined, 135
   Terminal Services and, 350–351, 376
   TightVNC compared with, 124
Remote Desktop Connection dialog box, 138
Remote Install tab, Remote Installation Services, 389
Remote Installation Services. *see* RIS (Remote Installation Services)
Remote Installation Services Setup Wizard, 352, 389
Remote Storage Service (RSS), 235
Remote Task Manager. *see* RTM (Remote Task Manager)
Remove All Unused Drivers (prndrvr.vbs-x), 369, 593
reparsepoint command, fsutil, 234–235, 535
replicate command, init, 310, 570
Replication, Active Directory
   forest functional levels, 451–452
   Replmon, 476
   sites boundaries, 447
   troubleshooting, 484–487
   Windows Server 2003 enhancements, 453
Replication Partners dialog box, WINS, 316

Replication Partners folder, WINS snap-in, 303
Replication Synchronization permission, 485
Replication, WINS
   configuring, 299–301
   enhancements, 298
   netsh wins server commands, 570–572
   push/pull, 310–312, 317
Replmon, 476, 484–487
Reports, Access, 186–187
required parameter (< >), 51
Reservations, DHCP, 25
Reset session command, 375
Resolver cache, 20–21
resource kit tools. *see* RK (resource kit) tools
Resource records
   nslookup, 280
   queries, 274–276
   types, 254–255
   verifying presence of SRV, 283–284
Resources
   IP subnetting tutorial, 16
   Microsoft newsgroups, 40
   networking fundamentals, 27–28
Restarts, 90–91
restore command, init, 310, 570
Restores
   conflict detection following, 328–329
   System Restore, 146–149
   Windows 2003 DHCP enhancements, 324
Resultant Set of Policy. *see* RSoP (Resultant Set of Policy)
Reverse lookup zones
   configuring, 258–259
   defined, 258
   nslookup, 283
   WINS, 287
RID master FSMO, 448, 483–484
RIP routing protocols
   key features, 398
   routing on RRAS servers, 435
   troubleshooting, 418–419, 564–565
   version 2, 398
RIS (Remote Installation Services)

overview of, 352–353
reimaging with, 42
troubleshooting, 389–390
RK (resource kit) tools
  installing, 48–49
  Support Tools compared to, 48
  tools included in, 47
  tracking with uptime, 90–91
rmsw, bootcfg commands, 224–225, 506–507
roles menu, ntdsutil tool, 474–475, 483
Root names, 281
Root zone, DNS, 256–258, 290, 294
Round robin, 261–262, 263
route command, 422–424, 599–600
Router-to-router VPNs, 437, 440–441
Routing
  Internet Connection Sharing, 167
  NetBEUI limitations, 10
  netsch routing. *see* netsh routing commands
  pathping command, 69–70, 584–585
  protocols, 398–399
  route command, 599–600
  RRAS. *see* RRAS (Routing and Remote Access Service)
  TCP/IP, 17–18
  tracert command, 73–74, 606
Routing and Remote Access Service. *see* RRAS (Routing and Remote Access Service)
Routing tables
  ipxroute, 364–365, 544
  TCP/IP routing, 17
  troubleshooting, 430
RRAS (Routing and Remote Access Service), 429–437
  atmadm command, 399–402
  demand-dial routing, 433–435
  DHCP relay agents, 432–433
  DHCP user class for, 328
  general problems, 429–430
  iasparse command, 402–403
  NAT, 430–432
  Netsh RAS Diagnostics, 402–411
  netsh routing commands, 411–420
  OSPF, 435–437

portqry command, 420–422
RAS, 425–429
RIP, 435
route command, 422–424
RRAS snap-in, 424–425
VPN access, 437–441
WINS enhancements, 298
RRAS (Routing and Remote Access Service), architecture, 393–399
  LCP extensions, 395
  multilink, 395
  NAT, 399
  Remote Access Policies, 395
  Remote Access Profiles, 396
  Remote Access Server, 394–395
  routing protocols, 398–399
  User Dial-in properties, 396
  VPNs, 396–397
RRAS snap-in
  DHCP relay agents, 342, 433
  overview of, 424–425
  RAS servers, 427
RSoP (Resultant Set of Policy)
  FAZAM 2000 vs., 648
  GPO troubleshooting with, 490
  gpresult, 463–464, 539–540
  loopback processing with, 489
  overview of, 476–480
RSoP Wizard, 477–479
RSS (Remote Storage Service), 235
RTM (Remote Task Manager)
  installing, 658–659
  overview of, 658
  querying state of remote systems, 660
  remotely installing, 659–660

S

Safe Mode
  with Command Prompt, 151
  display problems and, 167
  with networking, 151
  opening Support.dot template in, 200
  overview of, 150–151
  testing Office Setup in, 181
sc command, 484
Schedule Scan Wizard, Sitekeeper, 644

Index

Schema, Active Directory, 444, 459–460
Schema cache, updating, 492
Schema master FSMO, 448, 492
schtasks command, 55
Scopes. *see* DHCP scopes
Screenshots, 33
Scripts, 80
scsi, disk management, 214
SCSI stop errors, 625, 625–626
Secondary zones, DNS, 258
Security
    cacls command, 95–97
    domain controllers and, 447
    efsinfo command, 97–98
    Event Viewer, 111
    logging, 410
    management tools, 95–101
    principals, 483–484
    RAS Diagnostic Report, 408–409
    RAS server logging, 410
    Security Configuration and Analysis tool, 99–101
    Security Templates, 101
    Status System Process Terminated (Stop 0x0000021A), 632–633
    takeown command, 98–99
    Telnet service and, 73
Security Configuration and Analysis tool, 99–101
Semantic database analysis tool, ntdsutil, 476
Serial Line Interface Protocol (SLIP), 394
Server-initiated recovery, Shadow Copy, 143–144
Server Status, WINS snap-in, 303
Servers. *see also* Domain controllers
    Active Server Watcher, 656–657
    DHCP. *see* DHCP servers
    DNS, 289–294
    NAT, 431–432
    net statistics, 65–66, 548–549
    route command, 422–424
    session management, 66–67, 549
    WINS. *see* WINS servers
    zone transfers, 260
Service key error, 616
Service packs

    domain controllers, 481
    OS state, 35
    uptime, 90–91
Service (SRV) record type, 255
Services. *see also* Applications
    disabling, 132, 152–156
    enabling, 132
    shutdown failures and, 158
    viewing configuration with MSinfo32, 112
SEs (system engineers), 111–112
session command, query commands, 372–373, 596
Sessions
    net session command, 66–67, 549
    net statistics command, 65–66, 548–549
set all command, nslookup, 277, 577
set class command, nslookup, 277–278, 577
set cmtracing command, nslookup, 406, 551
set d2 command, nslookup, 278, 578
set debug command, nslookup, 278, 578
set defname command, nslookup, 279, 578
set domain command, nslookup, 279, 578
set ignore command, nslookup, 279, 578–579
Set It and Forget It, Diskeeper, 639, 641
set modemtracing command, 410, 555
set port command, nslookup, 279, 579
set querytype command, nslookup, 280, 579
set rastracing command, 410, 555
set recurse command, nslookup, 280, 579
Set Registry Option dialog box, 204–205
set retry command, nslookup, 280–281, 579
set root command, nslookup, 281, 580
set search command, nslookup, 281, 580
set securityeventlog command, 410, 556
set srchlist command, nslookup, 281, 580
set subcommand, 277–282
set timeout command, nslookup, 282, 580
set tracefacilities command, 411, 556
set type command, 280
set vc command, nslookup, 282, 580–581
Setup, 178–183

setup command, 180–181
Setup.exe log, 182–183
sfc command, 108–109, 600
Shadow Copy, 141–145
   client-initiated recovery, 145
   overview of, 141–143
   server-initiated recovery, 143–144
Share-level permissions, 43
Shared resources
   managing with DFS, 351–352
   net view command for, 67, 549–550
   Shadow Copy, 141–145
   troubleshooting with DFS, 387–388
Shift key, 452
Shiva PAP (SPAP), 394
Shortcut trusts, 445, 493
Shortcuts, restoring, 175
show all command, Netsh RAS Diagnostics, 404–405, 550–551
show area command, netsh routing ip ospf, 418, 563
show cmtracing command, Netsh RAS Diagnostics, 406, 551
show command, netsh wins server, 311–313, 317, 570–572
show configuration command, Netsh RAS Diagnostics, 406–407, 552
show flags command, netsh routing ip rip, 419, 564
show global command
   netsh routing ip autodhcp, 557
   netsh routing ip dnsproxy, 414, 559
   netsh routing ip igmp, 560
   netsh routing ip nat, 416, 561
   netsh routing ip ospf, 416–417, 562
   netsh routing ip relay, 413, 558
   netsh routing ip rip, 419, 564
show grouptable command, 560
   netsh routing ip igmp, 415
show ifbinding command, 565
   netsh routing ip rip, 420
show ifstats command
   netsh routing ip igmp, 415, 560
   netsh routing ip relay, 413, 558
   netsh routing ip rip, 419–420, 564–565
show iftable command, netsh routing ip igmp, 415, 560
show info command, netsh wins server, 311, 570–571
show installation command, Netsh RAS Diagnostics, 407–408, 553
show interface command
   netsh routing ip autodhcp, 412, 557
   netsh routing ip dnsproxy, 414, 559
   netsh routing ip igmp, 559
   netsh routing ip nat, 416, 561
   netsh routing ip ospf, 417–418, 562–563
   netsh routing ip relay, 412, 557
   netsh routing ip rip, 419, 564
   netsh routing ip routerdiscovery, 420, 565
show logs command, Netsh RAS Diagnostics, 408–409, 554
show modemtracing command, Netsh RAS Diagnostics, 409, 555
show partner command, netsh wins server, 311, 571
show partnerproperties command, netsh wins server, 312, 571
show protofilter command, netsh routing ip ospf, 418, 563
show proxygrouptable command, netsh routing ip igmp, 415–416, 561
show pullpartnerconfig command, netsh wins server, 312, 572
show pushpartnerconfig command, netsh wins server, 312, 572
show rasgrouptable command, netsh routing ip igmp, 415, 560
show rastracing command, Netsh RAS Diagnostics, 410, 555
show routefilter command, netsh routing ip ospf, 418, 563
show securityeventlog command, Netsh RAS Diagnostics, 410, 555
show server command, netsh wins server, 312, 572
show tracefacilities command, Netsh RAS Diagnostics, 411, 556
show virtif command, netsh routing ip ospf, 417, 562
showwin2kstaticsitetable command, dfsutil, 360, 518
Shutdowns. *see* system shutdown

Index

SID history, 450–451
Simple Mail Transfer Protocol (SMTP), 255
Simple recovery, DHCP, 344–345
Site links, replication, 486
Sitekeeper, Executive Software, 643–644
Sites, Active Directory
    Active Directory Sites and Services snap-in, 458–459
    overview of, 446–447
    slow replication, 486–487
Slide Design window, 198
Slide Finder dialog box, 197–198
Slides. *see* PowerPoint
SLIP (Serial Line Interface Protocol), 394
small office/home offices. *see* SOHO (small office/home office)
Smart Scheduling, Diskeeper, 640, 641
SmartLine, 652–660
    Active Network Monitor, 652–654
    Active Ports, 654–655
    Active Server Watcher, 656–657
    Remote Task Manager, 658–660
SMS (Systems Management Server), 76
SMTP (Simple Mail Transfer Protocol), 255
Snap-ins. *see* MMCs (Microsoft Management Consoles)
Snapshots, Shadow Copy, 141
SOA (Start of Authority) records, 255, 259–260
Soft page faults, 84
Software
    antivirus, 35–36
    comparing settings on two computers, 38
    firmware problems, 37–38
    GPO problems and solutions, 490
    hot lines/vendor's sites, 40, 41–42
    installing/uninstalling with PushInstaller, 644
    MSinfo32, viewing with, 112
    Stop 0x00000050 error, 247
    Unexpected Kernel Mode Trap (Stop 0x0000007F), 627
Software tab, TechTracker ITX, 663
SOHO (small office/home office)

ICS, 167–169
    NetBIOS used in, 10
    TCP/IP routing and, 17–18
Sound Troubleshooting Wizard, 116
Spanned volumes, 212, 244–245
SPAP (Shiva PAP), 394
sparse command, fsutil, 235–236, 535–536
Sparse files, 235–236, 535–536
spcflush command, dfsutil, 361, 518
Specify Permissions Wizard, Sitekeeper, 644
Spelling files, Detect and Repair, 209
Spool folders, 378, 381–382
Spreadsheets, Excel, 188–190
SRV resource records, 255, 283–284
ST (Support Tools)
    acldiag tool, 497–498
    dcdiag tool, 460–463
    defined, 47
    dfsutil utility, 355–361, 514–519
    dhcploc command, 334, 519
    dmdiag command, 519–520
    dnscmd command, 267–268, 520–522
    dnslint command, 270–272, 522–523
    efsinfo command, 86, 524–525
    ftonline command, 239–240, 538
    health_chk commands, 362–364, 541–542
    iasparse command, 543
    memsnap command, 79, 545
    MSI file installation, 47–48
    msicuu command, 133–134
    netdiag command, 62–64
    nltest command, 573–574
    pfmon command, 83–85, 585–586
    pmon command, 86, 588
    portqry command, 588–589
    Replmon, 476
    resource kit tools compared to, 48
Stability tab, TechTracker ITX, 663
Standalone DFS root, 351
Standard scopes, 325, 325–326
Start of Authority (SOA) records, 255, 259–260
StartType, enable command, 153
Startup, system. *see* system startup
Startup, Word, 200–204

Index

Static load balancing, 261
Static mapping, 302, 313, 316
Static routes, 434
Statistics
   net statistics command, 65–66
   Network Monitor, 75–78
Statistics operation, 269–270
Stop errors (blue screens), 619–636
   Attempted Write to Read Only Memory (Stop 0xBE), 628
   Bad Pool Caller (Stop 0xC2), 628–629
   Data Bus Error (Stop 0x0000002E), 621–622
   disk-related, 246–250
   Driver IRQL... (Stop 0x000000D1), 629
   Driver Power State Failure (Stop 0x0000009F), 627
   Driver Unloaded... (Stop 0x000000CE), 629
   Driver Used Excessive PTES (Stop 0x000000D8), 630
   FAT File System (Stop 0x00000023), 621
   Hardware Interrupt Storm (Stop 0x000000F2), 631–632
   Inaccessible Boot Device (Stop 0x0000007B), 249–250, 625–626
   IRQL Not Less or Equal (Stop 0x0000000A), 619
   Kernel Data Inpage Error (Stop 0x0000007A), 625
   Kernel Stack Inpage Error (Stop 0x00000077), 248, 249, 624
   KMode Exception Not Handled (Stop 0x0000001E), 620
   Mismatched HAL (Stop 0x00000079), 625
   No More System PTES (Stop 0x0000003F), 622–623
   NTFS and FAT file systems, 246–247
   NTFS File System (Stop 0x00000024), 621
   Online Crash Analysis, 134–135
   Page Fault in Nonpaged Area (Stop 0x00000050), 247–248, 623–624
   Status Image Checksum Mismatch (Stop 0x00000221), 633–635
   Status System Process Terminated (Stop 0x0000021A), 632–633
   Thread Stuck in Device Driver (Stop 0x000000EA), 631
   tracking with uptime, 90–91
   Unexpected Kernel Mode Trap (Stop 0x0000007F), 626–627
   Unmountable Boot Volume (Stop 0x000000ED), 631
Storage virtualization, 351
Striped volumes, 212, 244–245
Stub zones
   dnslint command, 270–272
   overview of, 260
   Windows Server 2003, 263
Subnet masks
   DHCP scopes and, 25
   IP address structure and, 15–16
   IP Subnet Calculator and, 118–119
   TCP/IP routing and, 17–18
Superscopes, 325–326, 338–339
Support
   Microsoft, 40
   tools. *see* ST (Support Tools)
   using hot lines/ vendor sites, 41–42
Support.dot template, 199–206
   AutoCorrect Backup, 204–206
   installing, 200
   Registry options, 204
   Troubleshoot Utility, 200–204
   using, 200
SUPTOOLS.msi file, 48
Switches
   ARC operating system, 215–216
   bootcfg command, 217–218
   dfsutil, 356, 514
Symantec Ghost. *see* Ghost
SYN messages, 68
Synchronous backups, 343
Syntax, 51
System checkpoints, 146
System engineers (SEs), 111–112
System File Checker. *see* sfc command
System Files Update log, Windows Installer, 182–183
System hive error, 618–619
System kernel, 620

Index

System log, 111
System management tools, 101–115
　Computer Management, 110
　driverquery command, 101–102
　Event Viewer, 110–111
　eventquery command, 102–104
　eventtriggers command, 104–107
　MSinfo32, 111–113
　sfc command, 108–109
　systeminfo command, 107–108
　Windows Update, 113–115
System Monitor (Perfmon), 92–93
System Restore, 145–149
System services. *see* Services
System Setup Troubleshooting Wizard, 116
System shutdown
　chkdsk, 52–53
　Startup/Shutdown Troubleshooting Wizard, 116
　troubleshooting, 157–159
　uptime, 90–91
System startup
　floppy disks and, 242
　msconfig, 132
　Recovery Console and, 152–156
　repairing OS installation, 156–157
　Startup/Shutdown Troubleshooting Wizard, 116–117
　Stop 0x0000007B error, 249–250
　troubleshooting, 149–152
System State, AD, 494
System Tools folder, 57–58
systeminfo command, 107–108, 601
System.ini file, 132
Systems Management Server (SMS), 76

T

Tables, Access, 187–189
takeown command, 98–99, 602
Task Manager
　KMode Exception Not Handled (Stop 0x0000001E), 620
　Remote, 658–660
　troubleshooting with, 94
Task Scheduler, 55–56
taskkill command, 86–88, 602–603

tasklist command, 88–89, 604–605
TCP/IP Illustrated, Volume I (Stevens), 19
TCP/IP (Transmission Control Protocol/Internet Protocol), 13–19
　address structure, 13
　binary conversion, 13–14
　connection handshake, 68
　DHCP clients, 335
　DNS name resolution, 19–22
　IP address structure, 14–16
　name resolution methods, 18–19
　NAT clients, 431
　net statistics command, 65–66, 548–549
　NetBIOS names vs. FQDNs, 18
　network printer connections, 380
　Outlook configuration, 194
　ports with portqry, 420–422, 588–589
　routed environments and, 17–18
　WINS clients, 313–315
TCP ports, 67–70
TechTracker ITX, 660–664
telnet
　managing with, 72–73, 605
　pmon and, 86, 588
Temp folder, 196–197
Templates. *see also* Support.dot template
　corrupted presentations and, 197–198
　Security Templates, 101
Terminal Services
　overview of, 350–351
　ports, enabling, 140
　Remote Desktop and, 136
　reset session command, 371–374, 598
　troubleshooting, 371–374, 383–386
Terminal Services Manager snap-in, 376
termserver command, query commands, 373–374, 596–597
Test Account Settings dialog box, Outlook, 192–193
Tests
　Active Directory infrastructure, 460–463, 510–513
　corrective action, 44
　demand-dial routing, 433
　faxes, 165–166
　netdiag command, 62–64, 547–548
　Outlook configuration, 192–195

Program Compatibility wizard, 170–171
Text, typing in Word, 207–208
TFTP (Trivial File Transfer Protocol), 390
Third-party tools, 637–672
    Executive Software. *see* Executive Software
    FullArmor - FAZAM 2000, 648–651
    SmartLine. *see* SmartLine
    TechTracker, 660–664
    Tsarfin. *see* Tsarfin
    Wildpackets - iNetTools, 670–672
TightVNC
    installing, 122
    overview of, 121–122
    server configuration, 123
    Viewer, 123–124
Time restrictions, 379
Time To Live (TTL), 20–21, 327
timeout command, bootcfg, 225, 507
Timeout values
    set retry command, 280–281
    set timeout command, 282
    timeout command, 225, 507
Trace Dependents, Excel, 191
Trace Error, Excel, 192
Trace Precedents, Excel, 191
tracert command, 73–74, 606
Tracing
    Connection Manager, 406, 408–409
    modems, 409–410
    RAS components, 410
    RAS Diagnostic Reports and, 408–409
    RAS server logging, 410, 411
Transfers, DNS zones, 259–260
Transitive trusts, 445, 453
Triggers, 104–107
Trivial File Transfer Protocol (TFTP), 390
Troubleshoot Utility, 200–204
Troubleshooting techniques, 29–46
    analyzing current environment, 34–38
    correcting problems, 42–44
    documenting problems, 31–34
    documenting solutions, 38–39
    eliminating what is right, 40–42
    following up, 44
    identifying problem, 31
    optimism vs. pessimism, 29–30

    process overview, 30–31
    testing corrective action, 44
    wizards, 115–117
Trusts
    Active Directory Domains and Trusts, 457–458
    defined, 444
    examples of, 445–446
    forest functional levels, 451–452
    nltest, 465–466, 573–574
    troubleshooting, 493
    types of, 445
Tsarfin, 664–670
    IPMonitor, 665–667
    NetInfo, 667–670
TTL (Time to Live), 20–21, 327
type command, Recovery Console, 155

U

UDP ports, 67–70
The Ultimate Windows Server 2003 System Administrator's Guide (Williams and Walla), 348
Undelete, Executive Software, 642
Undelete From Disk feature, Executive Software, 642, 643
Unicast addresses, 326
Uninstall command, 164
Universal groups, 450–451
UNIX DNS server, 262
unmapftroot command, dfsutil, 361, 518
Updates. *see also* Dynamic updates
    analyzing state of OS, 35
    application compatibility, 169
    device drivers, 162
    domain controllers, 447
    gpupdate, 464–465
    logon timestamps, 450–451
    Windows Update, 113–115
updatewin2kstaticsitetable command, dfsutil, 361, 518–519
uptime command, 90–91
USB Troubleshooting Wizard, 116
User classes, DHCP, 328
user command, query commands, 374, 597
Users

accounts, 156
Office Setup, 181
RAS dial-in properties, 396
USN command, fsutil, 236–239, 536–537

V

#VALUE!, Excel error codes, 191
Vendor classes, DHCP, 327
Vendors. *see* Third-party tools
VGA Mode, 151
Video Troubleshooter, 167
Video
    Data Bus Error (Stop 0x0000002E), 621–622
    display problems, 151, 166–167
    DVDs Troubleshooting Wizard, 115
    Thread Stuck in Device Driver (Stop 0x000000EA), 631
    VGA Mode, 151
Views
    Active Directory Users and Computers settings, 457
    hidden devices in Device Manager, 160
    net view command, 67, 549–550
    view command, 282, 581
Virtual circuits, 282
Virtual links, OSPF, 437
Virtual Network Computing (VNC) Viewer, 80. *see also* TightVNC
Virtual Private Networks. *see* VPNs (Virtual Private Networks)
Viruses
    analyzing current environment, 35–36
    Kernel Data Inpage Error (Stop 0x0000007A), 625
    Kernel Stack Inpage Error (Stop 0x00000077), 248, 624
    troubleshooting Office Setup, 181
    Windows Update protection, 113
VNC (Virtual Network Computing) Viewer, 80. *see also* TightVNC
volume command, fsutil, 239, 538
Volumes. *see also* Dirty bits
    administering Change Journal, 236–239, 536–537
    mirrored volume (RAID 1), 212, 245

striped volume (RAID 0), 212
striped volume with parity (RAID 5), 212, 246
using fsutil volume, 239, 538
VPNs (Virtual Private Networks), 437–441
    overview of, 396–397
    resource access problems, 440
    router-to-router connection problems, 440–441
    server connection problems, 438–439

W

WAN routing, 430, 434
Wildpackets - iNetTools, 16, 670–672
Windows 2000
    Active Directory functional levels, 449–452
    DHCP enhancements, 324
    domain controllers, 481, 493
    WINS enhancements, 298
Windows Advanced Option menu, 149
Windows Backup program, 128
Windows Installer, 182–183
Windows Licensing Agreement, 157
Windows Naming Service. *see* WINS (Windows Naming Service)
Windows NT, 449
Windows Server 2003
    Active Directory enhancements, 452–453
    Active Directory functional levels, 449–452
    DHCP enhancements, 324
    DNS enhancements, 263
    msconfig command, 131–133
    Shadow Copy tool, 141–145
    VPN connections in, 438
    WINS enhancements, 298–299
Windows Update
    analyzing state of OS, 35
    overview of, 113–115
    recovery checkpoints, 146
Windows XP
    Remote Desktop connections, 139
    System Restore tool, 141–145
WinMSD. *see* MSinfo32

Index   705

WINS servers
   configuring replication, 299–301
   Server Status, WINS snap-in, 303
   showing, 312
   troubleshooting, 315–317
WINS snap-in, 303, 319–322
WINS (Windows Naming Service), 297–322
   architecture, 297–302
   check command, 307–308
   client problems, 313–315
   defined, 19
   DHCP integration with, 317–319
   dump command, 306
   enhancements to, 298–299
   event logging, 304–305
   init command, 309–311
   lookup verification, 285–287
   name resolution, 22
   netsh wins command, 305–306
   overview of, 23–24
   Proxy agent, 302
   record types, 255
   recovering corrupted WINS database, 319–322
   relationships, 299–301
   replication, 299–301, 317
   server problems, 315–317
   show commands, 311–313
   static mapping, 302
WINSR records, 255, 258, 287
Wizards, troubleshooting
   client-server problems using, 127
   overview of, 115–117
   Sitekeeper, 644
Word, 199–209
   Document Recovery, 176–177
   file repair with Open and Repair, 176–178
   overview of, 199
   Support.dot template and, 199–206
   troubleshooting, 206–209
Word Startup Folder Add-ins, 203
Workstations
   net statistics, 65–66, 548–549
   netdiag, 62–64, 547–548
   TechTracker ITX Agent, 663
Workstations tab, TechTracker ITX, 663

Z

Zones. *see* DNS zones

CD-ROM Warranty

Addison-Wesley warrants the enclosed disc to be free of defects in materials and faulty workmanship under normal use for a period of ninety days after purchase. If a defect is discovered in the disc during this warranty period, a replacement disc can be obtained at no charge by sending the defective disc, postage prepaid, with proof of purchase to:

Editorial Department

Addison-Wesley Professional
Pearson Technology Group
75 Arlington Street, Suite 300
Boston, MA 02116
Email: AWPro@awl.com

Addison-Wesley makes no warranty or representation, either expressed or implied, with respect to this software, its quality, performance, merchantability, or fitness for a particular purpose. In no event will Addison-Wesley, its distributors, or dealers be liable for direct, indirect, special, incidental, or consequential damages arising out of the use or inability to use the software. The exclusion of implied warranties is not permitted in some states. Therefore, the above exclusion may not apply to you. This warranty provides you with specific legal rights. There may be other rights that you may have that vary from state to state. The contents of this CD-ROM are intended for personal use only.

More information and updates are available at:
http://www.awprofessional.com/